SPORT AND PE

a complete guide to

Advanced Level Study

SPORT AND PE

a complete guide to

Advanced Level Study

KEVIN WESSON • NESTA WIGGINS

GRAHAM THOMPSON • SUE HARTIGAN

Hodder & Stoughton

A MEMBER OF THE HODDER HEADLINE GROUP

A catalogue record for this title is available from The British Library

ISBN 0 340 683821

First published 1998
Impression number   10   9   8   7   6   5   4   3   2   1
Year   2002   2001   2000   1999   1998

Cover photography by Tony Stone

Typeset by Wearset, Boldon, Tyne & Wear
Printed in Great Britain for Hodder & Stoughton Educational, a division of Hodder Headline Plc, 338 Euston Road, London NW1 3BH by Scotprint, Musselburgh, Scotland.

Contents

Part 1: Anatomy and physiology   1

Introduction   1

Chapter 1   Skeletal considerations   5

Chapter 2   Muscular considerations   19

Chapter 3   Cardiovascular considerations   33

Chapter 4   Respiratory considerations   53

Chapter 5   Energy for movement   65

Chapter 6   Fatigue and recovery   77

Chapter 7   Physical fitness   83

Chapter 8   Training implications   97

Chapter 9   Nutritional implications   119

Chapter 10   Health-related implications   126

Chapter 11   Fundamental biomechanics   134

Part 2: Historical, cultural and social aspects   157

Chapter 12   The organisation of sport in the United Kingdom   157

Chapter 13   Concepts of physical activity   180

Chapter 14   Levels of sport participation   209

Chapter 15   Sport, politics and culture   226

Chapter 16   Issues and concerns in the modern day sports world   242

Chapter 17   The history of sport   261

Chapter 18   Physical activities   283

Chapter 19   Comparative studies   300

Conclusion   335

Part 3: Psychological aspects of sport and PE   339

Chapter 20   The nature of skilled performance   339

Chapter 21   The principles of learning   353

Chapter 22   Theories of learning   364

Chapter 23   Turning theory into practice   391

Chapter 24   Individual differences   410

Chapter 25   Motivation in physical education and sport   436

Chapter 26   Social influences and performance   461

Chapter 27   Optimising performance   487

Part 4: PE and sport studies project   509

Chapter 28   Requirements and assessment of the individual project   509

Chapter 29   Planning   514

Chapter 30   Developing the research problem and using relevant literature   519

Chapter 31   Reporting of method   527

Chapter 32   The results   532

Chapter 33   The final stages   540

Appendix 1   Project examples   543

Appendix 2   Suggested project titles   555

Appendix 3   Test ratings   557

Index   561

Acknowledgements

The authors would like to thank their families for all their support during the writing of this book. Nesta Wiggins would also like to thank Gwyneth Goodchild, Librarian of the Sixth Form College Colchester, for her assistance in compiling references for this book.

The publishers would like to thank the following picture libraries and photographers for permission to reproduce their images:

Action Plus

Steve Bardens:	figures 9.1, 13.9, 19.7, 22.7
Chris Barry:	figures 5.5, 15.4, 19.13, 27.5
Anne Bolton:	figure 25.9
Karen Burke:	figure 14.2
Richard Francis:	figures 5.7, 7.1, 16.5, 23.5, 25.12
Tony Henshaw:	figure 23.2
Glyn Kirk:	figures 7.2, 7.4, 8.2, 11.1, 11.4, 11.21, 11.27, 13.4, 14.3, 19.5, 19.16, 20.2, 21.3, 22.2, 23.9, 24.6, 24.7, 25.4, 25.6, 27.7, 27.9
Peter Tarry:	figures 26.1, 26.4
Neil Tingle:	figures 6.7, 11.14, 16.2, 20.1, 26.7

Action Images:

Figures 22.11 and 26.6

Mary Evans Picture Library:

Figures 7.5, 17.9, 18.3, 18.7

Jan Traylen:

Figure 21.2

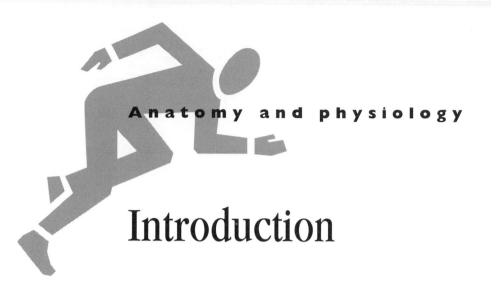

Introduction

When examining the performer in action, an understanding of anatomical and physiological concepts within a sporting context is required. For example, a distance run involves the interaction and coordination of many of the body's systems to enable successful performance; the cardiovascular and respiratory systems work together as a delivery service, delivering oxygen and nutrients to fuel the working muscles, while simultaneously ridding the body of any undesired waste products of metabolism such as carbon dioxide. Meanwhile the skeletal and muscular systems are interacting; the bones acting as levers to provide movement, while the muscles (the engines of movement) provide the power to drive the levers. The nervous and hormonal systems direct and control the body's actions to enhance performance. The body is therefore a complex machine with the components or systems working together to enable effective participation in sport.

What is exercise physiology?

Exercise or sports physiology (to ease confusion these terms have been used interchangeably in this book) is a branch of the much broader area of anatomy and physiology:

- Anatomy is the study of the body's **structure:**
- Physiology seeks to discover how the body works and **functions.**

Sports physiology then puts these findings into a sporting context and specifically examines how the body adapts and develops in response to exercise.
Training has a significant part to play in the body's development and as such is vital to the study of sports physiology. Training implications have therefore been highlighted throughout this section – do look out for them!
The terminology used when studying anatomy and physiology can sometimes be a little complex, particularly if you are new to the subject. The following section may ease your understanding, by explaining some of the terms that are regularly featured throughout the text.

Terms of direction

When describing regions of the body, positions relative to the 'anatomical position' are used. The anatomical position refers to a person standing upright, facing forwards, with arms positioned downwards and the palms of the hand facing forwards.

The table below provides a list of common terms of direction central to the study of anatomy and physiology. Relate these to the position of parts of your body.

superior	a structure higher or closer to the head than another
inferior	a structure lower or closer to the foot than another
medial	toward the midline of the body
lateral	away from the midline of the body
anterior/ventral	toward the front of the body
posterior/dorsal	toward the back of the body
superficial	toward the surface of the body
deep	internal or below the surface of the body
proximal	a structure or body part closer to the point of attachment than another
distal	a structure or body part further away from the point of attachment than another
left	toward the left side of the body
right	toward the right side of the body

 **ACTIVITY 1**

Using sticky labels place the following labels on the appropriate region of a partner's body:

The *lateral* aspect of the knee joint.
The *medial* aspect of the ankle joint.
The *proximal* region of the index finger.
The *distal* region of the big toe.
The *posterior* aspect of the upper leg.
The *anterior* aspect of the lower leg.
The most *superior* point of the body.
The most *inferior* point of the body.

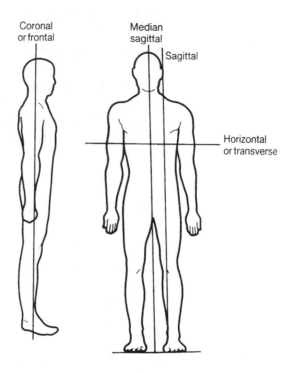

Body planes

Planes of the body

In order to explain the body's movements, it is often useful to view the body as having a series of imaginary lines running through it. These are known as the **planes of movement** or the planes section. The imaginary lines divide the body up in three ways (see fig A). Firstly, the sagittal plane splits the body vertically into the left and right sides, the transverse plane divides the body into superior and inferior sections and runs horizontally, while the frontal plane runs vertically and divides the body into anterior and posterior sections.

The body can move or rotate about these planes and a knowledge of them will certainly be of benefit to the coach and athlete. In gymnastics, for example, rotation about all planes may occur in the performance of full twisting somersaults. What other sporting situations can you think of where a knowledge of planes of movement may be of use? For further investigation into this, and other factors concerning the body's movement, refer to Chapter 11.

Sometimes it is possible to work out an anatomical term through basic understanding of more general terms. Words are often prefixed or suffixed to give greater meaning. For example, any word suffixed by **'itis'** means inflammation; any word prefixed by **'arthr'** relates to a joint. Therefore the condition **'arthritis'** is an inflammation of the joints. The table on p 4 gives common prefixes and suffixes together with their meanings.

PREFIX/SUFFIX	DEFINITION	PREFIX/SUFFIX	DEFINITION
a-	without	-itis	inflammation
ab-	away from	lip-	fat
ad-	towards	-lysis	breaking up
-algia	pain	macro-	large
an-	without	mono-	one
arthr-	joint	-morph	shape/form
brady-	slow	myo-	muscle
cardio-	heart	neuro-	nerve
cerebro-	brain	osteo-	bone
chondr-	cartilage	peri-	surrounding
-cyte	cell	pneumo-	air/gas/lungs
derm-	skin	poly-	many
ergo-	work	somato-	body
glyco-	sugar	syn-	together
hem-	blood	tachy-	fast
hepato-	liver	therm-	heat
hypo-	deficient	-trophy	nourishment
hyper-	excessive	-vascular	blood vessel

Using this table, define the following terms:

- **bradycardia**
- **osteocyte**
- **pericardium**
- **glycolysis**
- **hepatitis**
- **cardiac hypertrophy**
- **periosteum**
- **myofilament**
- **somatotype**
- **cardiovascular**

Skeletal Considerations

This chapter examines the structure and function of the skeletal system. The principal focus is on the functional aspects of the system, with particular reference to human movement during physical activity.

The chapter will take the student through an examination of the labelling and classification of **bones** and the structure of skeletal tissues, including the identification of bony landmarks.

Central to the study of movement is **arthrology** – the study of **joints**. This stage of the chapter will classify joints, giving practical examples from sporting action. A discussion of the types of movement occurring at the articulations follows, which forges specific links with the kinesiology unit of the muscular system (Chapter 2).

Finally, there is a discussion of the beneficial effects of exercise and training on the skeletal system, with reference made to other chapters of the book.

The skeletal system

The 206 bones that make up the human skeleton are specifically designed to provide several basic functions, which are essential for participation in physical activity. In conjunction with other components of the skeletal system (including the periosteum, ligaments and joints), the skeleton can perform the following functions.

Functions

Support
The skeleton provides a rigid framework to the body, giving it shape and providing suitable sites for attachment of skeletal muscle.

Protection
The skeleton provides protection for the internal organs. For example: the vertebral column protects the spinal cord; the cranium protects the brain; and the rib cage principally protects the heart and lungs.

Movement
The bones of the skeleton provide a large surface area for the attachment of muscles – the engines of movement. The long bones in particular provide a system of levers against which the muscles can pull.

Blood production
Within the bones, bone marrow produces both red and white blood cells. Red blood cells are generally produced at the ends of long bones such as the humerus (arm) and the femur (thigh), and in some flat bones such as the pelvis and sternum (breastbone). White blood cells are usually produced in the shafts of long bones.

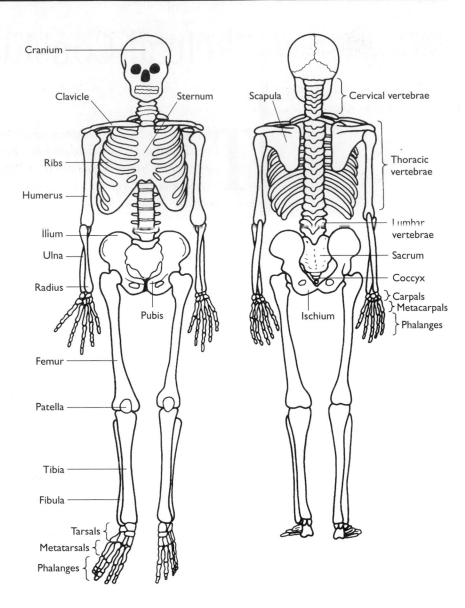

Fig. 1.1 THE HUMAN SKELETON

Mineral storage

The bones of the skeleton have storage capabilities for vital minerals such as calcium and phosphorus, which can be distributed to other parts of the body when required.

 **Using sticky labels, label the bones on a partner's body.**

The structure of the skeleton

The bones of the skeleton can be divided into two distinct categories; the axial and the appendicular skeleton:

- the **axial** skeleton provides the main area of support for the body, and includes the cranium (skull), the vertebral column (spine) and the rib cage.
- the **appendicular** skeleton consists of the appendages or the bones of the limbs, together with the girdles that join onto the axial skeleton.

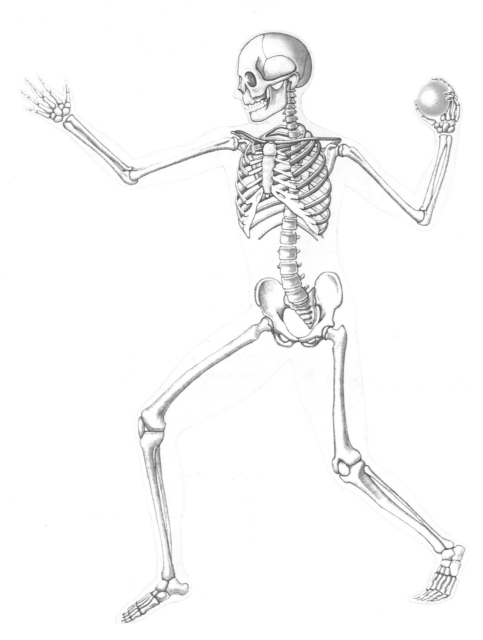

Fig. 1.2 BONES OF THE AXIAL AND
APPENDICULAR SKELTON
Source: Davis, Kimmet and Auty (1986)

 **List the bones in the axial and appendicular skeletons in fig 1.2.**

The structure of the vertebral column

The vertebral column consists of 33 bones; 24 bones are individual and unfused, while the remaining nine are fused together. There are five principle areas of the vertebral column.

The cervical vertebrae (7 unfused bones)

The cervical vertebrae support the weight of the head by enabling muscle attachment through the transverse and spinous processes. The top two vertebrae, the atlas and the axis (fig. 1.3(c)), enable the head to move up and down and side to side respectively.

The thoracic vertebrae (12 unfused bones)

The 12 thoracic vertebrae allow the attachment of the ribs via the transverse processes. These bones, together with the ribs, form the rib cage which protect the heart and lungs.

The lumbar vertebrae (5 unfused bones)

The 5 lumbar vertebrae are the largest of all the individual vertebrae. Their large centrum or body offer a great deal of weight-bearing capacity, while their large processes secure the attachment of the muscles. This muscle attachment, together with the intervertebral discs of cartilage, form cartilaginous joints, which enable flexion and extension (forward and backward movement) and lateral flexion (side to side movement) of the trunk.

The sacral vertebrae (5 fused bones)

The 5 fused sacral vertebrae form the sacrum which fuses to the pelvis at the sacroiliac joint. The sacrum and the pelvis bear and distribute the weight of the upper body.

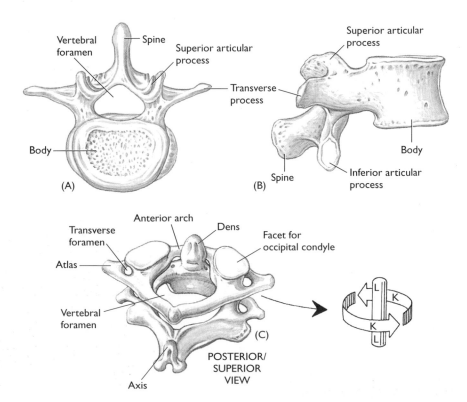

Fig. 1.3 STRUCTURE OF A TYPICAL VERTEBRA (A) THIRD LUMBAR VERTEBRA VIEWED FROM ABOVE (B) THIRD LUMBAR VERTEBRA VIEWED FROM THE SIDE (C) THE AXIS AND ATLAS

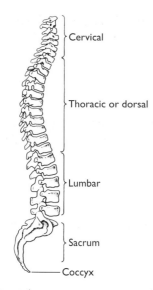

Fig. 1.4 STRUCTURE OF THE VERTEBRAL COLUMN

The coccyx (4 fused bones)

The coccyx forms the very base of the vertebral column, and acts as a process for muscle attachment.

Each vertebra consists of two parts:

1 a vertebral body (centrum)
2 a neural arch.

The size of each vertebral body increases from the cervical vertebrae to the lumbar vertebrae, in order to support the weight of the body. The neural arch enables muscles to attach via the transverse and the spinous processes, while the articular process link to adjacent vertebrae.

In between each vertebra exists a disc of fibro-cartilage – a tough, resilient tissue which helps to absorb shock and allow a small amount of movement between the vertebral bodies. The vertebral column also exhibits four curves as shown in fig 1.4. The cervical and lumbar curves are **convex** in shape; the thoracic and sacral curves are **concave**. These curves of the vertebral column increase the strength of the structure as well as absorbing shock from jumping or walking, and thus reducing the risk of injury.

ACTIVITY 3

State how the structure of each region of the vertebral column is suited to its function.

Structure of the rib cage

The rib cage is composed of 12 pairs of ribs which form the walls of the thoracic cavity:

- The first seven pairs of ribs attach directly onto the front of the sternum via costal cartilage.
- The next three pairs are attached to the seventh rib, also via costal cartilages. These are known as 'false' ribs.
- The remaining two pairs of ribs do not attach to anything other than the thoracic vertebrae, and are called 'floating' ribs.

The rib cage offers protection to vital organs such as the heart and lungs, and also enables the lungs to inflate by moving upwards and outwards during inspiration. The ribs are also attached to each other via intercostal muscles which help the rib cage carry out its respiratory function.

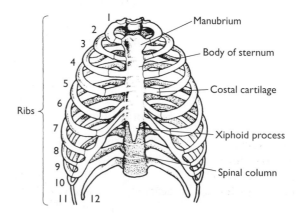

Fig. 1.5 STRUCTURE OF THE RIB CAGE

Bones

Types of bones

Bones are designed to carry out a variety of specific functions, and fall into one of five categories, largely according to their shape:

Long bones

Long bones are cylindrical in shape and are found in the limbs of the body. Examples of long bones:

- femur
- tibia
- humerus
- phalanges (although not great in length, these possess the cylindrical shape and so also fall into this category).

The primary function of long bones is to act as levers, and they are therefore essential in movement. Their other vital function is the production of blood cells which occurs deep inside the bone.

Short bones

Short bones are small and compact in nature, often equal in length and width. They are designed for strength and weightbearing and include:

- the bones of the wrist (carpals)
- the ankle (tarsals) and calcaneum.

Flat bones

Flat bones offer protection to the internal organs of the body. Examples include:

- the sternum
- the bones of the cranium
- the bones of the pelvis
- upon close inspection, it can be seen that the ribs are also flat.

Flat bones also provide suitable sites for muscle attachment, with the origins of muscles often attaching to them. The pelvis, sternum and cranium also produce blood cells.

Irregular bones

Irregular bones are so named due to their complex, individual shapes and the difficulty in classifying them. They have a variety of functions which include protection. Examples include:

- the vertebrae (protect the spinal cord)
- the face.

Sesamoid bones

Sesamoid bones have a specialised function: they ease joint movements and resist friction and compression. They are usually developed in tendons and are covered with a layer of articular cartilage as they exist where bones articulate. Although generally small in appearance, sesamoid bones do vary in size, the largest and most obvious being the patella which is situated in the quadriceps femoris tendon.

Bone landmarks and bony features

Upon close inspection of bones it can be seen that they are not smooth as depicted in many diagrams, but in fact possess an enormous landscape of their own. The surface of bones contain bumps and protrusions and indentations or depressions, each having a specific role and function.

Table 1.1   FEATURES AND ANATOMIC LANDMARKS OF BONES

ANATOMIC STRUCTURE	DEFINITION	EXAMPLE
condyle	a rounded projection of bone – forming part of a joint	tibial condyle
crest/ridge	a ridge on the surface of a bone	tibial crest
epicondyle	a bony bulge adjacent to a condyle	epicondyle of the humerus
fissure	clef/groove on the surface of a bone	bicipital groove
fossa	a depression in the bone	olecranon fossa
process	a bony projection	
spine	sharp pointed process	iliac spine
tubercle	a small surface nodule of a bone	iliac crest
tuberosity	a large surface nodule of a bone	tibial tuberosity
trochanter	large knob at the top of the femur	great trochanter

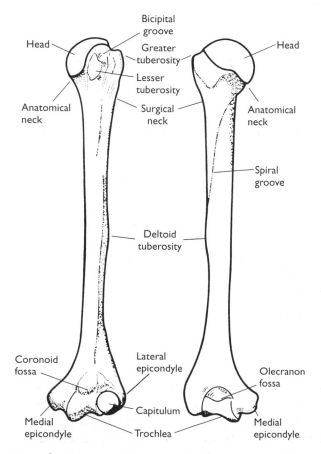

Fig. 1.6 THE HUMERUS (BONE OF THE UPPER ARM)

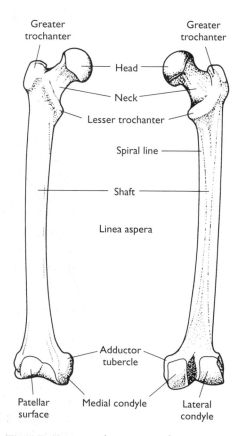

Fig. 1.7 THE FEMUR (UPPER LEG BONE)

Using a selection of bones, inspect and identify some of the structures and landmarks outlined in table 1.1.

The structure and development of skeletal tissues

The tissues making up the skeletal system consist of cartilage and bone.

Cartilage

Cartilage is a soft, slightly elastic tissue, consisting of cells (chondrocytes) which exist in small spaces called lacunae. Cartilage is avascular, meaning that it does not possess a blood supply and receives nutrition via diffusion from the capillary network outside the tissue.

All bones start out as cartilage in the developing foetus, until it is gradually replaced by bone.

There are three basic types of cartilage found in the body:

1 **Hyaline or articular cartilage** is a fairly resilient tissue and is found on the articulating surfaces of bones that form joints. It is bluish in colour and is composed of a fine network of collagen fibres. The cartilage protects the bone tissue from wear and reduces friction between articulating bones. Joint movement improves the nutrition supplied to this tissue and can encourage growth. Hyaline cartilage therefore often thickens as a result of exercise.

2 **White fibro-cartilage** is a much denser tissue. It is tough, and its shock absorption properties means that it is often found in areas of the body where high amounts of stress is imposed. For example, the semi-lunar cartilages of the knee joint resists the huge amount of stress often incurred as a result of performing activities such as the triple jump. Other examples are the intervertebral discs and in the socket of the hip.

3 **Yellow elastic cartilage** is a much more pliant and flexible tissue giving support and also flexibility. The external ear and the epiglottis are examples.

Bone

Bone differs from cartilage in that it is a rigid, non-elastic tissue and is composed approximately of 65% mineral components (including calcium phosphate and magnesium salts) and 35% organic tissue such as collagen, a protein which gives the bone some resilience and prevents the bones from breaking on the slightest of impacts. Viewed under a microscope, it can be seen that mature bone consists of cells called **osteocytes** which exist in spaces known as **lacunae**. These bone cells are supported by thick collagen fibres which exist in a matrix composed of minerals.

Bone tissue can be categorised into either compact or cancellous, and is best illustrated by viewing a longitudinal cross section of a long bone.

Compact bone or hard bone forms the surface layers of all bones and the whole of the cylindrical shaft of long bones. It goes some way in protecting bones from external forces or impacts and has great weight-bearing properties. Surrounding the compact bone is the **periosteum**, which is a fibrous and extremely vascular tissue. In addition to its vital role in bone development, the periosteum enables tendons to attach to bones, which transmit the muscular 'pull' and therefore allows movement to take place.

ANTERIOR VIEW
(left femur)

Coronal section through proximal epiphysis and dissection of medullary cavity

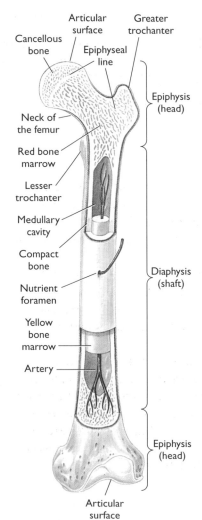

Fig. 1.8 STRUCTURE OF A LONG BONE VIEWED IN CROSS SECTION

Source: Kapit & Elson (1993)

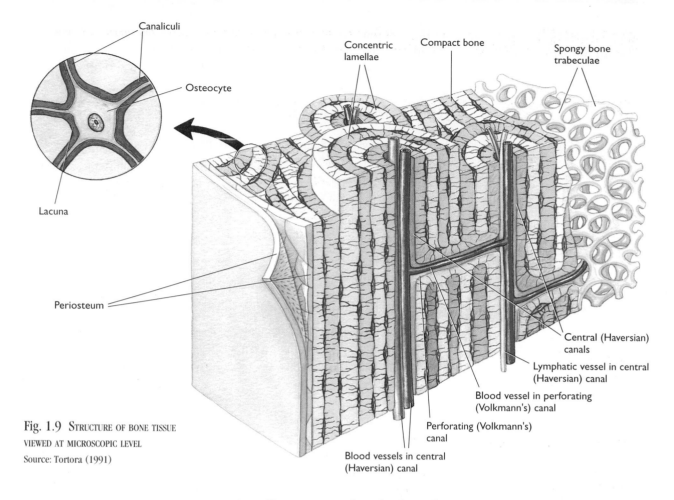

Fig. 1.9 STRUCTURE OF BONE TISSUE VIEWED AT MICROSCOPIC LEVEL
Source: Tortora (1991)

Cancellous or spongy bone lies beneath and inside to compact bone, and has a honeycomb or trabecular appearance. This criss-cross matrix of bony plates is developed along lines of stress on the bones and is constantly reorganised in response to the altering orientation of stress. For example: the stress alters when an infant starts to walk as opposed to crawl.

The Trabecular matrix has proved to be the most effective way of combining strength with the minimum of weight, so that bones can take much stress, yet are light and easily moved. In addition to this function, the spaces of the cancellate bone are filled with red bone marrow, since the bony plates offer some protection to the manufacture of red blood cells here.

With the important function of blood production, the bony tissue is extremely vascularised, enabling nutrients to reach the bone and blood produced within the bone to enter the body's circulatory system. **Vascularisation** is aided by Haversian and Volkmanns canals which conduct blood vessels to and from the bone. The nourishment by Haversian canals lead to the bone cells lying circuitously around the canal. This concentric pattern of bone cells is known as the Haversian system and occurs as a result of the vascularity of the bony tissue.

The growth and development of bones

Bone is formed via the process of **ossification**.

1 Some bones, such as the flat bones of the skull, form directly in membranes. This development is known as **direct** or **intramembranous ossification**.

2 The short and long bones are formed by the gradual replacement of hyaline cartilage, from the foetal stage of development until full maturation in our late teenage years. This is known as **indirect and endochondral ossification**.

Joints and articulations

So far we have seen that some bones of the skeleton act as levers, which move when muscles contract and pull on them. Where two or more bones meet, an articulation or joint exists. However, movement does not always occur at these sites, and joints are typically classified according to the degree of movement permitted.

Types of joint

Fixed or fibrous joints

These are very stable and allow no observable movement. Bones are often joined by strong fibres called sutures; eg, the sutures of the cranium.

Cartilaginous or slightly movable joints

These are joined by a tough, fibrous cartilage which provides stability and possess shock absorption properties. However, a small amount of movement usually exists: for example, the articulations between the lumbar bones due to the intervertebral discs of cartilage.

Synovial or freely movable joints

These are the most common type of joint in the body, and the most important in terms of physical activity, since they allow a wide range of movement.

The joint is enclosed in a fibrous joint capsule which is lined with a synovial membrane. Lubrication is provided by synovial fluid which is secreted into the joint by the synovial membrane. In addition, where the bones come into contact with each other, they are lined with smooth yet hard wearing hyaline or articular cartilage.

Synovial joint stability is provided by the strength of the muscles crossing the

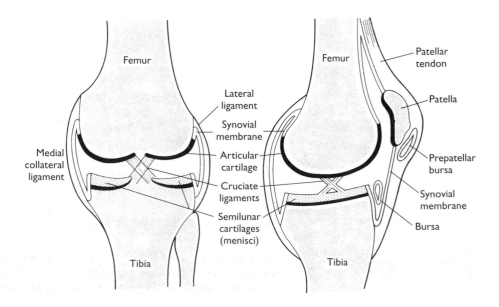

Fig. 1.10 THE KNEE JOINT

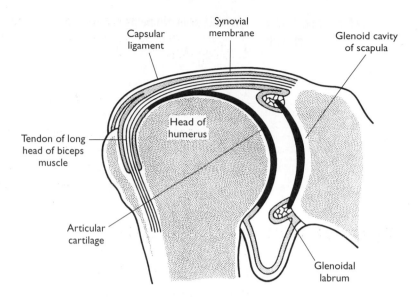

Fig. 1.11 THE SHOULDER JOINT

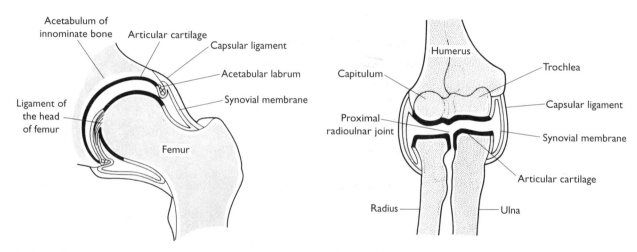

Fig. 1.12 THE HIP JOINT

Fig. 1.13 THE ELBOW JOINT

joint, which are supported by ligaments which may be inside or outside the capsule. Ligaments are very elastic and lose effectiveness to some degree when torn or stretched.

Some synovial joints possess sacs of synovial fluid known as bursae which are sited in areas of increased pressure or stress and help reduce friction as tissues and structures move past each other. Pads of fat help to absorb shock and improve the 'fit' of the articulating bones. This is particularly true in the knee joint to help the articulation of the femur and tibia.

 **ACTIVITY 5**

Explain how the knee joint is structured and how this suits its function. List as many examples from sporting activity as possible, and use diagrams to support your answer.

Types of synovial joint

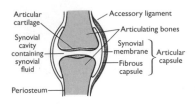

Articular cartilage
Synovial cavity containing synovial fluid
Periosteum
Accessory ligament
Articulating bones
Synovial membrane
Fibrous capsule
Articular capsule

Fig. 1.14 A SYNOVIAL JOINT

Synovial joints can be further subdivided into six basic types.

1 A **hinge joint** is a uniaxial joint which only allows movement in one plane. For example: the knee joint only allows movement back and forth. Strong ligaments exist in order to prevent any sideways movement.

2 A **pivot joint** is also uniaxial, which allows rotation only. For example: the cervical vertebrae where the axis rotates on the atlas.

3 An **ellipsoid** joint is biaxial, allowing movement in two planes. For example: the radio-carpal joint of the wrist allows back and forth as well as side to side movement.

4 A **gliding joint** is formed where flat surfaces glide past one another. Although mainly biaxial they may permit movement in all directions. For example: in the wrist, where the small carpal bones move against each other.

5 A **saddle** joint is biaxial and generally occurs where concave and convex surfaces meet. For example: the carpo-metacarpal joint of the thumb.

6 The **ball and socket joint** allows the widest range of movement and occurs where a rounded head of a bone fits into a cup-shaped cavity. For example: in the hip and shoulder.

Movement patterns occurring at synovial joints

The movements that occur at joints can be classified according to the action that is occurring between the articulating bones. These are called movement patterns.

Flexion

Flexion occurs when the angle between the articulating bones is decreased. For example: by raising the lower arm up to touch the shoulder, the angle between the radius and the humerus at the elbow has decreased. Flexion of the elbow has thus occurred.

Extension

Extension of a joint occurs when the angle of the articulating bones is increased. For example: when standing up from a seated position, the angle between the femur and tibia increases, thus causing extension at the knee joint. Extreme extension, usually at an angle of greater than 180° is known as **hyper extension**.

Abduction

This is movement of a body part away from the midline of the body or other body part. For example:

• if arms are placed by the sides of the body and then raised laterally, abduction has occurred at the shoulder joint

• if fingers are spread out, movement has occurred away from the midline of the hand, and abduction has occurred.

Adduction

Adduction is the opposite of abduction and concerns movement towards the midline of the body or body part. For example, by lowering the arm back to the sides of the body, movement towards the midline has occurred and is termed adduction.

Circumduction

Circumduction occurs where a circle can be described by the body part and is simply a combination of flexion, extension, abduction and adduction. True circumduction can only really occur at ball and socket joints of the shoulder and hip.

Rotation

Rotation of a joint occurs where the bone turns about its axis within the joint. Rotation towards the body is termed **internal** or **medial** rotation, while rotation away from the body is called **external** or **lateral** rotation.

To explain this further attempt the following exercise.

1 Grip a ruler at the bottom with your right hand.
2 Now raise your arm up in front of your body and move the ruler anticlockwise movement. Medial rotation has occurred at the shoulder joint.
3 Now move the ruler clockwise so that it ends up pointing to the side. This is lateral rotation and has once again occurred at the shoulder.

Pronation

Pronation occurs at the elbow and involves internal rotation between the radius and humerus. It typically occurs where the palm of the hand is moved from facing upwards to facing downwards.

Supination

Supination is the opposite of pronation and again takes place at the elbow. This time the movement is external rotation between the radius and humerus and generally occurs when the palm of the hand is turned so that it faces upwards.

Plantarflexion

Plantarflexion occurs at the ankle joint and is typified by the pointing of the toes.

Dorsiflexion

This also occurs at the ankle and occurs when the foot is raised upwards towards the tibia.

Inversion

This occurs when the sole of the foot is turned inwards towards the midline of the body.

Eversion

Eversion occurs when the sole of the foot is turned laterally outwards.

Using an articulated skeleton, examine the joints listed below. Describe the type of joint and the movements possible:

- **knee joint**
- **elbow joint**
- **hip joint**
- **shoulder joint**
- **skull and cervical vertebrae**
- **ribs and thoracic vertebrae**
- **lumbar region.**

What movement patterns occur at:

- **the shoulder and elbow during the performance of a tennis serve?**
- **the hip and knee during a squat thrust?**

Exercise and the skeletal system

Exercise has many beneficial effects for the skeletal system:

1 Skeletal tissues become stronger since exercise imposes stress upon the bones, which encourages the laying down of bony plates and the deposition of calcium salts along the lines of stress. This reinforces the criss cross matrix and improves the tensile stress of the bone.
2 Hyaline cartilage thickens which aids the cushioning of the joint.
3 Tendons thicken and can withstand greater muscle force.
4 Ligaments stretch slightly to enable a greater range of movement at the joint.

Participate in a circuit training session. For each activity, state what movement patterns are occurring at the various joints.

Summary

- The skeleton has five basic functions: support, protection, movement, blood production, mineral storage.
- The axial skeleton consists of those bones that provide the greatest support and include the skull, vertebral column and the rib cage.
- The appendicular skeleton consists of the bones of the limbs and their respective girdles.
- The vertebral column is divided into five areas: cervical vertebrae, thoracic vertebrae, lumbar vertebrae, sacral vertebrae and coccygeal vertebrae.
- The rib cage is composed of twelve pairs of ribs which together provide protection for the vital organs and enables the process of inspiration.
- Bones can be categorised as either long, short, flat, irregular or sesamoid.
- There are three types of cartilage in the body: hyaline or articular cartilage, white fibrocartilage, and yellow elastic cartilage.
- Bone is a rigid non-elastic tissue composed of mineral and organic tissue. There are two types of bone: compact or hard bone and cancellous or spongy bone.
- Ossification is the process of bone formation. It can occur within the membranes (intramembranous) or through replacement of cartilage (endochondral).
- Joints are classified according to the degree of movement allowed. There are three basic types of joint; fixed or fibrous joints, and cartilaginous joints.
- Movement at synovial joints can be classified as flexion, extension, abduction, adduction, rotation, pronation, supination, plantar flexion, dorsiflexion, inversion and eversion.
- The whole of the skeletal system can be strengthened through performing exercise.

chapter 2

Muscular Considerations

No study of human movement or exercise is complete without a study of the **muscular** system. The muscles interact with the skeleton to provide movement. This chapter will examine in detail how this happens.

The chapter highlights the structural and functional characteristics of **muscle tissue**, including types of muscle, properties of skeletal muscle (skeletal muscle is particularly relevant to the study of movement, so it will be examined in the greatest detail), the structure of skeletal muscle at molecular level, and the process and types of muscular contraction.

To emphasise the importance of muscle action in sporting situations, a unit on **kinesiology** has been included, which will encourage the reader to examine the muscle actions required in different sporting situations. Links to the skeletal system will be made specifically at this stage, and a discussion concerning the benefits of exercise and training will take place towards the end of the chapter.

What is a muscle?

Muscles comprise approximately 45% of the total body weight, and total in excess of 600.

There are three types of muscle tissue:

1 **Skeletal** muscle, which is external and used primarily for movement of the skeleton.
2 **Cardiac** muscle which is found only in the heart and used to force blood into the circulatory vessels.
3 **Smooth** muscle which lies internally and has several functions including forcing food through the digestive system (peristalsis) and squeezing blood throughout the circulatory system.

As skeletal muscle is responsible for the body's mechanical movement, its properties and functions are now examined. See p 28 for further information on skeletal muscle structure.

Table 2.1   COMPARING MUSCLE TYPES

SKELETAL	CARDIAC
• voluntary • contract by impulse from the brain • parallel fibres • less/smaller mitochondria • motor unit organisation	• involuntary • auto rhythmic contractions (myogenic) • interwoven, intercalating fibres • more/larger mitochondria • auto-ventricular network of fibres

Properties of skeletal muscle

Skeletal muscle possesses three essential properties:

1 **Extensibility:** this is the ability of muscle tissue to lengthen when contracting.
2 **Elasticity:** this is the ability of muscle tissue to return to its normal resting length once it has been stretched. This can be compared to an elastic band that will always resume its resting shape even after stretching.
3 **Contractility:** this refers to the capacity of a muscle to contract or shorten forcibly when stimulated by nerves and hormones (excitability).

All these properties are essential for all body actions including locomotion, posture and facial expressions.

Functions of skeletal muscle

Skeletal muscle has several important functions within the body.

1 **Movement:** Skeletal muscles attach to bones, against which they pull to enable movement.
2 **Support and posture:** The muscles are seldom fully relaxed and are often in a constant state of slight contraction. This is known as **muscle tone** and explains how the body can adopt and keep an upright position.
3 **Heat production:** The contraction of skeletal muscle involves the production of energy. In breaking down glycogen to provide this energy, heat is released. This accounts for why the body becomes hot when exercising. When the body is cold, the muscle often goes through a series of involuntary muscle contractions (commonly known as shivering) in order to heat up the body.

The muscular system

The following set of figures show the major muscles of the body:

- the arm
- the leg
- the torso.

1 **Using sticky labels, label the muscles on a partner's body. Try to label as many as you can without looking at your textbook.**
2 **Collect as many pictures of bodybuilders as you can and label/identify the defined muscles.**

Muscle characteristics

Muscle shapes

As can be observed from fig 2.5 on p 23, muscles come in a variety of shapes and sizes. The shape of a particular muscle will determine the degree of muscle contraction, and hence the amount of force that can be generated within.

Muscle shapes can be classified according to the position of the muscle fibres, in relation to the tendon which attach the muscle to the skeleton and transmits the muscular 'pull' to the bones.

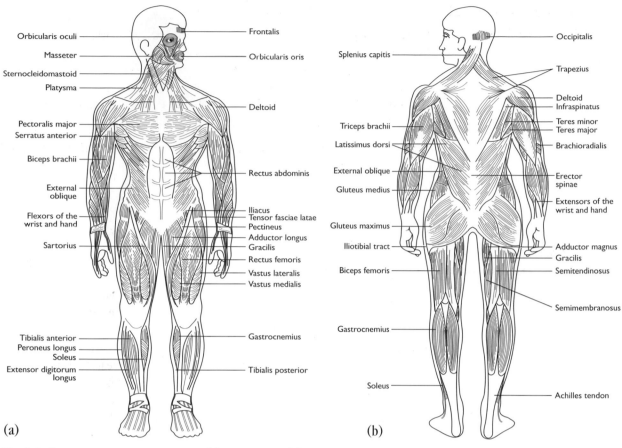

Fig. 2.1 Skeletal muscles of the human body (a) anterior view (b) posterior view

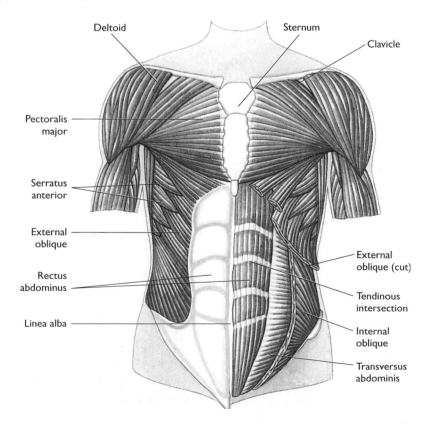

Fig. 2.2 Muscles of the torso

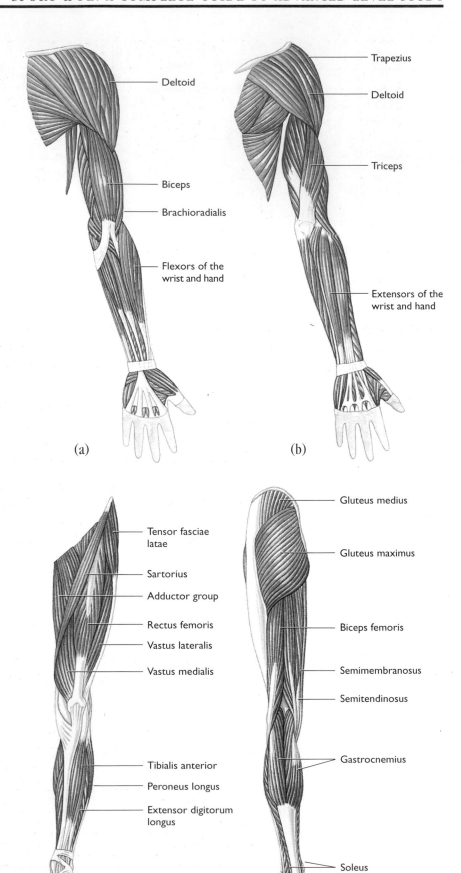

Fig. 2.3 MUSCLES OF THE ARMS
(A) ANTERIOR (B) POSTERIOR

Deltoid
Biceps
Brachioradialis
Flexors of the wrist and hand

Trapezius
Deltoid
Triceps
Extensors of the wrist and hand

(a)

(b)

Fig. 2.4 MUSCLES OF THE LEGS
(A) ANTERIOR (B) POSTERIOR

Tensor fasciae latae
Sartorius
Adductor group
Rectus femoris
Vastus lateralis
Vastus medialis
Tibialis anterior
Peroneus longus
Extensor digitorum longus

Gluteus medius
Gluteus maximus
Biceps femoris
Semimembranosus
Semitendinosus
Gastrocnemius
Soleus

(a)

(b)

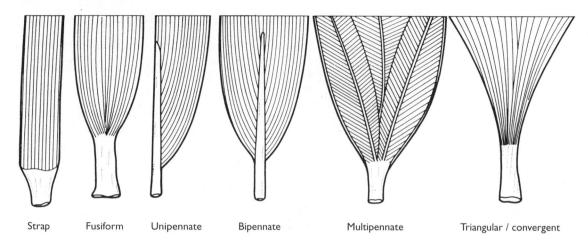

Strap   Fusiform   Unipennate   Bipennate   Multipennate   Triangular / convergent

Fig. 2.5 MUSCLE SHAPES

Characteristics of muscle shapes

Pennate muscle shapes (feather like) occur where muscle fibres are arranged around a single central tendon. The many short fibres enable a high degree of force to be developed within the muscle, and therefore occur where much power and strength is required (see fig 2.5).

- **Unipennate:** muscle fibres occur on one side of the tendon only.
- **Bipennate:** muscle fibres occur on both sides of the tendon.
- **Multipennate:** muscle fibres are placed around the central tendon.
- **Circumpennate:** muscle fibres are arranged in a circular pattern.

Fusiform muscles (straplike) occur where muscle fibres lie parallel to each other and a tendon occurs at either end of the muscle belly. They cannot achieve as great force as pennate muscle shapes.

Convergent muscles such as the deltoid muscle, occur where the base is much wider than the insertion, giving the muscle a triangular shape and enabling the muscle to contract with great force.

Muscle fibres

Skeletal muscle has two main fibre types: **slow twitch** and **fast twitch**; see table 2.2 for their characteristics.

Fast twitch and slow twitch fibres vary in different muscles and in different individuals; these proportions tend to be *inherited*.

Table 2.2   CHARACTERISTICS OF FAST TWITCH AND SLOW TWITCH

SLOW TWITCH (TYPE 1)	FAST TWITCH (TYPE 2)
red	white
contract slowly	contract rapidly
aerobic	anaerobic
endurance based	speed/strength based
can contract repeatedly	easily exhausted
exert less force	exert great forces

Fast twitch muscle fibres have recently been subdivided into type 2a and type 2b:

- **Type 2a**, also referred to as fast oxidative glycolytic fibres (F.O.G.) pick up certain type one characteristics through endurance training. They therefore tend to have a greater resistance to fatigue.
- **Type 2b**, pure fast twitch fibres called fast twitch glycolytic (F.T.G.), have a much stronger force of contraction for several reasons: the motor neuron that carries the impulse is much larger; there are generally more fibres within a fast twitch motor unit; and the muscle fibres themselves are larger and thicker.

Under the headings of slow twitch, fast oxidative glycolytic and fast twitch glycolytic, list as many sporting activities as you can which use that fibre type.

Table 2.3   Slow twitch muscle fibre composition of various athletes

ATHLETIC GROUP	SHOULDER (DELTOID)	CALF (GASTROCNEMIUS)	THIGH (VASTUS LATERALIS)
long distance runners		79% (m) 69% (f)	
canoeists	71% (m)		
triathletes	60% (m)	59% (m)	63% (m)
swimmers	67% (m) 69% (f)		
sprint runners		24% (m) 27% (f)	
cyclists			57% (m) 51% (f)
weight lifters	53% (m)	44% (m)	
shot putters		38% (m)	
non-athletes			47% (m) 46% (f)

Table 2.4   Structural characteristics of muscle fibres
(from Sharkey 'Physiology of Fitness', Human Kinetics 1990)

CHARACTERISTICS	SLOW TWITCH	FAST OXIDATIVE GLYCOLYTIC F.O.G.	FAST TWITCH GLYCOLYTIC F.T.G.
speed of contraction	slow	fast	fast
force of contraction	low	high	high
size	smaller	large	large
mitochondrial density	high	lower	low
myoglobin content	high	lower	low
fatigability	fatigue resistant	less resistant	easily fatigued
aerobic capacity	high	medium	low
capillary density	high	high	low
anaerobic capacity	low	medium	high

Connective tissues

Muscles are attached to bones via tendons, which transmit the 'pull' of the muscle to the bones, to cause movement and harness the power of muscle contractions. Tendons vary in length and are composed of parallel fibres of collagen. They attach directly to the periosteum of the bone via a tough tissue known as **Sharpey's fibres**.

The point of attachment for each muscle are termed the **origin** and the **insertion**:

- The origin is the end of the muscle attached to a stable bone; which is usually the nearest flat bone.
- The insertion is the muscle attachment on the bone that the muscle puts into action.

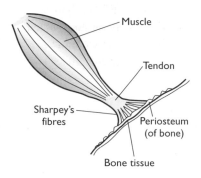

Fig. 2.6 SHARPEY'S FIBRES

For example: the bicep has its origin on the scapula. This gives a firm base against which the bicep can pull in order to raise the lower arm. (The bicep is a flexor muscle, and its job is to allow flexion at the elbow.) Since the bicep raises the lower arm, it must be attached to that body part via the insertion. In fact the bicep has its insertion on the radius.

The muscle belly is the thick portion of muscle tissue sited between the origin and insertion. It is not unusual for a muscle to have two or more origins, while maintaining a common insertion: the term 'bicep' can be broken down to mean two ('bi') heads ('ceps'). The bicep has two origins or heads which pull upon one insertion in the radius, and puts the lower arm into action.

Antagonistic muscle action

Muscles never work alone. In order for a coordinated movement to be produced, the muscles must work as a group or team, with several muscles working at any one time. Taking the simple movement of flexion of the arm at the elbow, the muscle responsible for flexion (bending of the arm) is the biceps brachii, and the muscle which produces the desired joint movement is called the **agonist** or **prime mover**. However, in order for the bicep muscle to shorten when contracting, the tricep muscle must lengthen. The tricep in this instance is known as the **antagonist**, since its action is opposite to that of the agonist. The two muscles however must work together to produce the required movement.

Fixator muscles also work in this movement. Their role is to stabilise the origin so that the agonist can achieve maximum and effective contraction. In this case the trapezius contracts to stabilise the scapula to create a rigid platform. **Neutralisers** or **synergist** muscles in this movement prevent any undesired movements which may occur, particularly at the shoulder where the bicep works over two joints.

It can thus be seen that for this apparently simple movement of elbow flexion, integrated and synergistic (harmonious) muscle actions are required to enable the necessary smooth movement.

Furthermore, the roles of each muscle are constantly changed for changing actions. For example, in the action of elbow extension, the roles of the bicep and tricep are reversed so that the tricep becomes the prime mover or agonist (since the tricep is an extensor and thus produces this movement pattern), while the bicep becomes the antagonist, to enable the smooth and effective contraction of the tricep.

Table 2.5   MUSCLE FUNCTIONS, ORIGINS AND INSERTIONS

MUSCLE	FUNCTION	INSERTION	ORIGIN
pectoralis major	flexes upper arm adducts upper arm	humerus	sternum clavicle rib cartilage
latissimus dorsi	extends and adducts upper arm	humerus	vertebrae (T6–L5) iliac crest
deltoid	abducts, flexes and extends upper arm	humerus	clavicle scapula acromion
biceps brachii	flexes lower arm	radius	scapula
triceps	extends lower arm	olecranon process	humerus scapula
iliopsoas	flexes trunk flexes thigh	ilium vertebrae femur	ilium vertebrae femur
gluteus maximus	extends thigh	femur	ilium sacrum coccyx
gluteus medius gluteus minimus	abducts thigh	femur	ilium
hamstring group biceps femoris semimembranosus semitendinosus	flexes lower leg extends thigh	tibia fibula	ischium femur
quadricep group rectus femoris vastus medialis vastus lateralis vastus intermedius	extends lower leg extends thigh	tibia (via patella tendon)	ilium femur
sartorius	flexes hip and knee	anterior superior iliac spine	tibia
adductors longus magnus brevis	adducts thigh	femur (linea aspera)	pubic bone
gastrocnemius	plantar flexion flexes knee	calcaneus	femur
soleus	plantar flexion	calcaneus	fibula tibia

As a rule of thumb, the origin of a muscle *is the nearest flat bone*, the insertion is the bone that the muscle *puts into action*

Types of muscular contraction

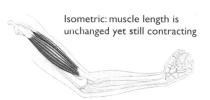

Concentric: muscle shortens whilst contracting

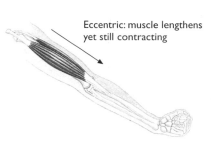

Isometric: muscle length is unchanged yet still contracting

Eccentric: muscle lengthens yet still contracting

Fig. 2.7 TYPES OF MUSCLE CONTRACTION IN THE BICEP BRACHII

In order to produce the vast range of movements of which it is capable, the body's muscles either shorten, lengthen or remain the same length whilst contracting. Indeed, muscle contractions are classified depending upon the muscle action which predominates:

- **Isotonic** contractions refer to those instances when the muscle is moving while contracting. This can further be divided into concentric and eccentric muscle actions.
- **Concentric** contractions involve the muscle shortening while contracting as happens in the bicep during the upward phase of a bicep curl performance or in the tricep during the upward phase of a push up.
- **Eccentric** contractions on the other hand involve the muscle lengthening whilst contracting (remember that a muscle is not always relaxing while lengthening!). This can be seen in the bicep during the downward phase of the bicep curl or in the tricep during the downward phase of the press up.

Plyometrics is a type of strength training which is based on a muscle contracting eccentrically (for further discussion refer to p 107). Sometimes, however, a muscle can contract without actively lengthening or shortening; in this instance the muscle is going through **isometric** contraction – the muscle remains the same length while contracting. In fact the majority of muscles will contract isometrically in order for us to maintain posture. **Static** contractions occur while holding a weight in a stationary position or when performing a handstand.

Table 2.6   TYPES OF MUSCLE CONTRACTION

	ISOTONIC		ISOMETRIC
	concentric	eccentric	static
muscle action	muscle shortens	muscle lengthens whilst contracting	muscle remains the same length whilst contracting
example	bicep: when raising a weight	bicep: when lowering a weight	bicep: holding a weight in a static position

Kinesiology

Kinesiology is the study of body movement, and thus includes muscle action. When studying this unit it is helpful to consider the following:

- the function of the muscles contracting
- how the muscle is contracting (eg, concentric or eccentric)
- the movement patterns occurring at joints as a result of the movement.

ACTIVITY 3

Table 2.7 shows joint movement used in basketball. Think of other sporting situations and complete the table accordingly.

Table 2.7   VARIETY OF JOINT MOVEMENTS

SPORT	ACTION	MOVEMENT PATTERN	MUSCLES WORKING	TYPE OF CONTRACTION
basketball	jump shot	extension at knee	quadricep group: rectus femoris vasti muscles	concentric

For each of the following joints, state which muscles are used for the movement patterns shown in brackets:

- **Knee (flexion and extension)**
- **Hip (flexion, extension, abduction, adduction)**
- **Shoulder (flexion, extension, abduction, adduction)**
- **Ankle (plantar flexion, dorsi flexion, inversion, eversion).**

Skeletal muscle

Structure

When viewed under the microscope, skeletal muscle can be seen at molecular level.

The muscle belly is surrounded by a layer of **epimysium**, a thick connective tissue surrounding the entire surface of the muscle. This is continuous and eventually forms tendons which join the muscle onto bones. The muscle belly is composed of many bundles of fibres known as **fasiculi**. Each fibre within a single fasiculus contains many smaller fibres called **myofibrils** which provide the contractile unit of the muscle. These myofibrils have characteristic dark and light bands (striations) which represent a **sarcomere**. This pattern is repeated along the length of the myofibril.

Sarcomeres have a highly organised structure, and at the most fundamental level the sarcomere is composed of two protein-based myofilaments:

- a thick myosin filament, and
- a thinner actin filament.

The interaction and overlapping of these two myofilaments enables muscles to contract through the **sliding filament theory**; see below.

Each actin filament is composed of two components:

1 **Fibrous actin** (F. Actin) which provide active sites to which myosin molecules can bind during muscle contraction.
2 **Tropomyosin** molecules and **troponin** molecules which aid in the attachment of the myosin cross bridge. Calcium ions are released during innervation (nervous stimulation of the muscle tissue) from the sarcoplasmic reticulum surrounding the myofibrils.

Myosin filaments are composed of many myosin molecules, which are made up of two parts: a rod, and a head, which together form a golf-club shaped molecule. The heads of each molecule contain ATPase, an enzyme used to break down adenosine triphosphate, which, in doing so, releases energy for muscular contraction (see page 67). This energy is used to bind the myosin cross bridge onto the actin filament, thereby allowing muscular contraction.

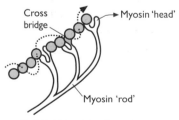

Detailed structure of an actin filament

Detailed structure of a myosin filament

Fig. 2.8 THE STRUCTURE OF ACTIN AND MYOSIN

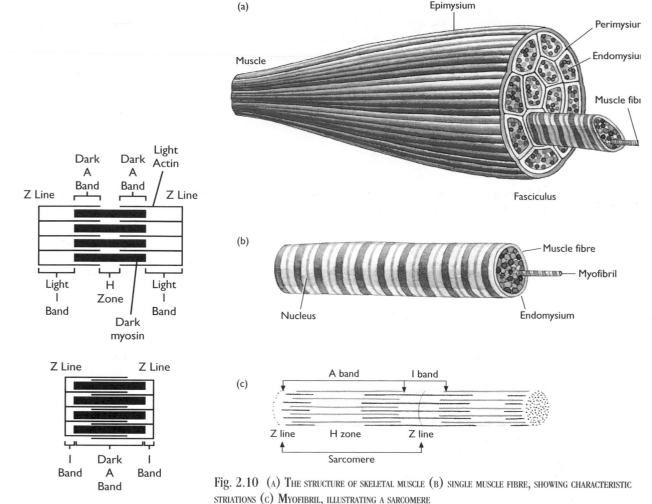

(a) Epimysium, Perimysium, Endomysium, Muscle fibre, Muscle, Fasciculus

(b) Muscle fibre, Myofibril, Nucleus, Endomysium

(c) A band, I band, Z line, H zone, Z line, Sarcomere

Fig. 2.10 (A) The structure of skeletal muscle (B) single muscle fibre, showing characteristic striations (C) Myofibril, illustrating a sarcomere

Dark A Band, Dark A Band, Light Actin, Z Line, Light I Band, H Zone, Light I Band, Dark myosin

Z Line, Z Line, I Band, Dark A Band, I Band

Z Line = Marks the boundary of one sarcomene
I Band = Actin Only
A Band = Actin and Myosin
H Zone = Mysosin Only

Fig. 2.9 The sliding filament theory (A) relaxed (B) contracted – notice that the H zone has disappeared

The sliding filament theory

The sliding of the filaments past each other takes the form of a ratchet mechanism, whereby the cross bridges continually attach, detach, reattach etc.; causing the actin filaments to be pulled towards the centre and slide past the myosin filaments.

The action of the sliding filaments during contraction causes shortening of all sarcomeres, and therefore all muscle fibres.

Muscle relaxation

The relaxation of muscle is a passive process: the cross bridges uncouple, causing the sarcomere to lengthen and return to its pre-contracted length.

Muscle contraction

To understand how skeletal muscle contracts, a basic understanding of the nervous system is needed, as muscle contraction involves the interaction of the muscular system with the nervous system (neuromuscular interaction).

When a muscle is required to contract, an electrical impulse is emitted from the **central nervous system**. The electrical impulse begins at the brain and is transmitted to a muscle via the spinal cord and by nerve cells called **motor neurones**.

One motor neurone (nerve) cannot stimulate the whole muscle, but is only capable of stimulating a number of fibres within it. The motor neurone and the fibres it stimulates, are called a **motor unit**, which is the functional unit of skeletal muscle.

The number of fibres innervated by a single motor unit varies, depending upon the precision of movement required. For example the eye, which requires a great deal of control and precision in order to focus, will possess between one and five fibres per motor neurone, while the rectus femoris muscle of the quadricep group requires greater power to enable a basketballer to perform a jump shot, and therefore possess up to 2,000 fibres per motor neurone.

Note: the fibres within a particular motor unit will usually be of the same type, either *fast* twitch or *slow* twitch. Motor units are therefore recruited depending upon the activity being undertaken, and the recruitment is based on twitch response time or speed of contraction.

Muscle fibre innervation

A muscle fibre is innervated when an impulse is of suitable strength. The point at which the motor nerve meets the muscle fibre is known as the **motor end plate**, and forms the **neuromuscular junction**.

When a nerve impulse arrives at the motor end plate, a transmitter substance called **acetylcholine** is released; this aids the spread of the impulse to the muscle fibre across a small gap called the synaptic cleft. If sufficient acetylcholine is released, the muscle fibre is said to have '**action potential**' – which is the capability to contract.

An incoming response may be either excitatory or inhibitory. An excitatory response which causes muscle contraction will produce an excitatory post-synaptic action potential (EPSP), which will cause a contraction of muscle fibres if a given threshold or intensity is reached or exceeded. If this threshold is not attained, then the sum of the individual effects of several impulses can be used until the threshold is exceeded. Once this point is reached, a depolarisation or decrease in the electrical potential across a membrane occurs, which triggers the release of calcium ions from the sarcoplasmic reticulum; this in turn enables the myosin cross bridge to attach to the actin filament to cause muscle fibre contraction.

Following excitation, a chemical called **cholinesterase** is released which blocks the effect of acetylcholine and prepares the muscle fibre for the arrival of subsequent stimuli, so that the muscle fibres in a given motor unit can once again contract.

The all or none law

Each fibre within a motor unit contracts according to the all or none law. This principle states that when a motor unit receives a stimulus of sufficient intensity to elicit a response, all the muscle fibres within the unit will contract at the same time and to the maximum possible extent. If, however, the stimulus is not of significant intensity, the muscle fibres will not respond and contraction will not take place.

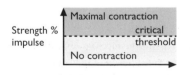

Fig. 2.11 The All or None law

The degree to which a muscle contracts is dependent upon several factors, including the number of motor units recruited by the brain. This will determine the force that can be generated within the muscle. The greater the strength required, the greater the number of motor units (and therefore the number of muscle fibres) that contract. For example, more motor units will be recruited in the biceps brachii when the body weight is being lifted in a chin up, than when performing a bicep curl with a very light weight.

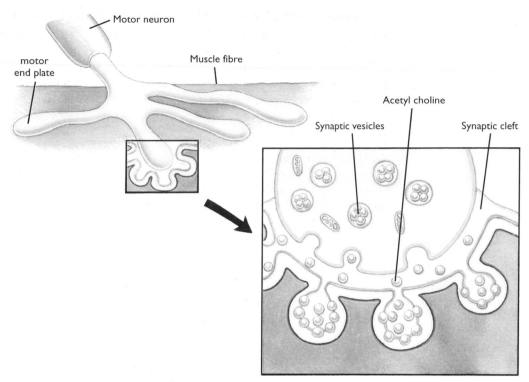

Fig. 2.12 THE NEUROMUSCULAR JUNCTION, SHOWING SYNAPTIC STIMULATION OF A MUSCLE FIBRE

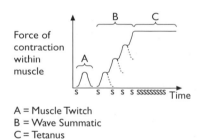

A = Muscle Twitch
B = Wave Summatic
C = Tetanus

Fig. 2.13 MUSCLE TWITCH AND CONTRACTION

A second consideration is the frequency with which impulses arrive at the muscle fibres. The motor unit will respond to a stimulus by giving a 'twitch' – a brief period of contraction followed by relaxation. When a second impulse is applied to the motor unit before it completely relaxes from the previous stimulus, the sum of both stimuli occurs, increasing the total contraction. This process is known as **multiple wave summation**. Furthermore, when rapid firing of stimuli occurs, giving muscles little or no time for relaxation, **tetanus or tetanic contraction** takes place, increasing the total contraction still further. This increase in total contraction can be explained by the augmented release of calcium ions which causes greater cross-bridge attachment of myosin onto actin.

Control of muscular contraction

In order for effective movement to be performed, muscle action should be controlled. The body possesses several internal regulatory mechanisms to ensure that smooth and safe movement prevails:

1 **Proprioceptors:** these are sense organs which provide kinaesthetic feedback concerning the body's movement. This informs the body of the extent of movement that has taken place.
2 **Muscle spindle apparatus:** this relays information via motor and sensory neurones concerning the state of muscle contraction and the length or extension of muscle. If a muscle is stretched too far, the muscle spindle apparatus will detect altering tension within the muscle and cause a stretch reflex, whereby the muscle is automatically shortened.
3 **Golgi tendon organs:** these receptors exist where muscle fibre and tendon meet, and serve the same purpose as muscle spindle apparatus by triggering a reflex action when very high tensions are developed within the muscle, causing it to shorten.

Further reading

Arnould-Taylor, *A text book of Anatomy and Physiology*, (Stanley Thornes Publishers Ltd, 1988)

Clegg, *Exercise Physiology* (Feltham Press, 1996)

Davis, Bull, Roscoe and Roscoe, *Physical Education and the Study of Sport* (Wolfe Medical Publishers, 1991)

Kapit and Elson, *The Anatomy Colouring Book* (Harpers Collins College Publishers, 1993)

Hay and Reid, *Anatomy, Mechanics and Human Motion* (Prentice Hall, 1988)

Seeley, Stephens and Tate, *Anatomy and Physiology* (Mosby Year Book Inc., 1992)

Sharkey, *Physiology of Fitness* (Human Kinetics, 1990)

Wilmore and Costill, *Physiology of Sport and Exercise* (Human Kinetics, 1994)

Wirhead, *Athletic Ability and the Anatomy of Motion* (Wolfe Medical Publishers, 1989)

Summary

- There are three types of muscle tissue: Skeletal, Smooth and Cardiac.
- Skeletal muscle properties include extensibility, elasticity and contractility.
- Functions include movement, support and posture, and heat production.
- Muscles can be classified according to shape, either fusiform or pennate.
- There are two basic types of muscle fibre; Slow twitch or type 1 and fast twitch or type 2 fibres. Fast twitch fibre can be further subdivided into Fast Oxidative Glycolytic or type 2a and Fast twitch glycolytic or type 2b.
- Muscle are attached to bones via tendons. The origin of a muscle is that attachment onto a stable bone, usually the nearest flat bone. The insertion is the muscle attachment onto the bone that the muscle puts into action.
- Muscles often work together in order to produce co-ordinated movements: antagonistic muscle action. A muscle directly responsible for the joint movement is the agonist. An antagonist often lengthens in order for the agonist to shorten.
- Muscles can contract in several ways. Isotonic (shortening or lengthening), concentric (the muscle shortens), eccentric (the muscle lengthens). A muscle can also contract without any visible movement (isometric).
- Skeletal muscle fibres are composed of many smaller myofibrils. Each myofibril is characterised by dark and light bands which represent sarcomeres. Sarcomeres are composed of two proteins – actin and myosin. Interaction of the actin and myosin causes muscular contraction (the Sliding filament theory).
- Muscular contraction: interaction of the muscular system and nervous system.
- A motor unit is the functional component of skeletal muscle and consists of a motor neurone and a number of muscle fibres that that motor neurone controls. A single muscle can possess thousands of motor units.
- Each fibre within a motor unit will contract maximally or not at all and depends upon the intensity of the stimulus. This is known as the all or none law.
- Strength of contraction can be determined by the number of motor units recruited by the brain to perform a specific task, or considering the frequency that impulses arrive at muscle fibres.
- Muscle action is controlled by internal regulatory mechanisms which include proprioceptors, muscle spindle apparatus, and Golgi tendon organs.
- The analysis of muscle contraction and joint action is called kinesiology.

chapter 3

Cardiovascular Considerations

This chapter will examine the structure and function of the cardiovascular system, including the heart, the vascular system, and the blood.

The second part of the chapter will focus upon the response of the cardiovascular system to exercise, looking at particular factors such as cardiac dynamics (including changes in heart rate, stroke volume and blood pressure).

We will learn how the heart, blood vessels and blood adapt in response to the demands of exercise; links are made to Chapters 8 and 10, on training and health-related implications.

The cardiovascular system

The human body is an amazing machine, and at the centre of its operation is the heart. The heart is a muscular pump that beats continuously, which together with the blood vessels and the blood provides the tissues and cells with the essentials for life itself – oxygen and nutrients.

The structure and function of the heart

The heart lies behind the sternum (breastbone) and ribs, which offer protection. In adults, it is about the size of a clenched fist – although trained athletes often experience **cardiac hypertrophy**, which is an enlargement of the heart.

In terms of structure, the heart is composed of four chambers:

- The two chambers at the top or superior part of the heart are called the **atria**.
- The two lower or inferior chambers are termed **ventricles**.

The ventricles are much more muscular than the atria since it is here that the pumping action of the heart which circulates the blood all over the body, occurs.

As well as being divided transversely (into upper and lower portions), the heart can also be divided into left and right halves (sagitally). This separation into left and right is essential for the heart to carry out its function effectively, since each side has slightly different roles:

- The left side of the heart is responsible for circulating blood throughout the entire body.
- The right side is responsible for ensuring oxygen-poor blood is pumped to the lungs where it can be reoxygenated.

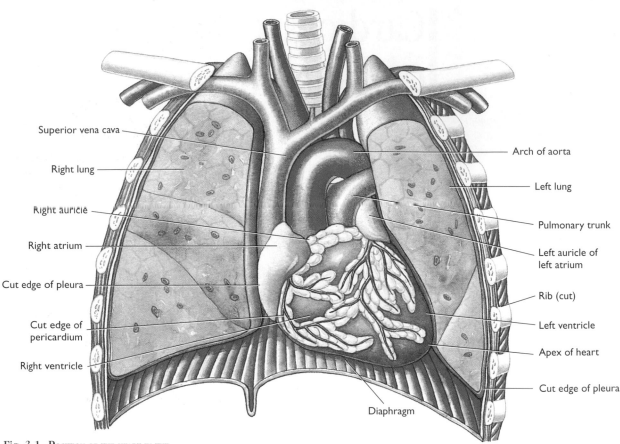

Fig. 3.1 POSITION OF THE HEART IN THE THORACIC CAVITY

The major vessels act as entry and exit points for the blood to enter or leave the heart, and are all situated towards the top of the heart. To ensure a smooth passage of blood through the heart, a number of **valves** exist. These valves make sure that the blood only flows in one direction and are also responsible for the 'lub-dup' sounds of the heart. The 'lub' results from the closure of the atrio-ventricular valves (also known as the bicuspid and tricuspid valves), and the much sharper 'dup' sound occurs when the semi-lunar valves (pulmonary and aortic valves) snap shut.

The muscular wall of the heart is called the **myocardium** and is situated between the **endocardium** on the inside (which lines the chambers), and the **pericardium** on the outside (a visceral membrane forming the pericardial sac in which the heart sits).

Covering the exterior of the heart are coronary **arteries** which feed the heart muscle with blood; being a muscle, it still requires the fuel to keep the pump working continually.

1 **Place the following terms in the correct sequential order to explain the flow of blood returning to the heart from the body and its path through the heart:**

- **aorta**
- **lungs**
- **bicuspid valve**
- **left ventricle**
- **pulmonary vein**
- **triscuspid valve**
- **venae cavae**
- **right atrium**
- **pulmonary valve**
- **left atrium**
- **right ventricle**
- **aortic valve**
- **pulmonary artery**

2 **Describe the location of the heart.**

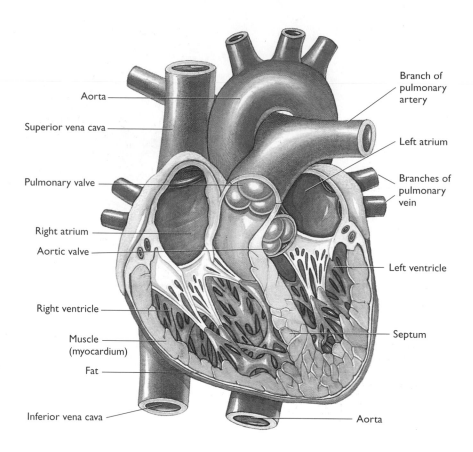

Aorta

Superior vena cava

Pulmonary valve

Right atrium

Aortic valve

Right ventricle

Muscle
(myocardium)

Fat

Inferior vena cava

Branch of
pulmonary
artery

Left atrium

Branches of
pulmonary
vein

Left ventricle

Septum

Aorta

Fig. 3.2 STRUCTURE OF THE HEART

The cardiac cycle

The cardiac cycle refers to the process of cardiac contraction and blood transportation through the heart. As mentioned above, the heart can be viewed as two separate pumps to serve its dual purpose, and the cardiac cycle explains the sequence of events that take place during one complete heartbeat. This includes the filling of the heart with blood and the emptying of the blood into the arterial system.

Each cycle takes approximately 0.8 seconds and occurs on average 72 times per minute. There are four stages to each heartbeat:

1 atrial diastole
2 ventricular diastole
3 atrial systole
4 ventricular systole.

Each stage depends upon whether the chambers of the heart are *filling* with blood while the heart is relaxing (**diastole**) or whether they are *emptying*, which occurs when the heart contracts (**systole**) and forces blood from one part of the heart to another or into the arterial system, and subsequently to the lungs and the body.

The first stage of the cardiac cycle is **atrial diastole**. The upper chambers of the heart are filled with blood returning from:

• the body via the venae cavae to the right atrium; and
• the lungs via the pulmonary artery to the left atrium.

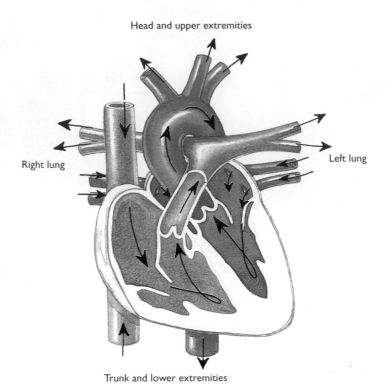

Head and upper extremities

Right lung

Left lung

Trunk and lower extremities

Fig. 3.3 The path of blood through the heart
Source: Tortora (1991)

At this time the atrioventricular valves are shut but as the atria fill with blood, atrial pressure overcomes ventricular pressure. Since blood always moves from areas of high pressure to areas of low pressure, the atrioventricular valves are forced open, and **ventricular diastole** now takes place. During this stage the ventricles fill with blood and the semi lunar valves remain closed. The atria now contract, causing **atrial systole** which ensures that all the blood is ejected into the ventricles. As the ventricles continue going through diastole, the pressure increases, which causes the atrioventricular valves to close. Ultimately, the ventricular pressure overcomes that in the aorta and the pulmonary artery. The semi lunar valves open and the ventricles contract, forcing all the blood from the right ventricle into the pulmonary artery and the blood in the left ventricle into the aorta. This is **ventricular systole**, and once completed, the semi-lunar valves snap shut. The cycle is now complete and ready to be repeated.

How the heart works

The heart works by producing impulses which spread and innervate the specialised muscle fibres. Unlike skeletal muscle, the heart produces its own impulses (ie, it is **myogenic**), and it is the conduction system of the heart which spreads the impulses and enables the heart to contract.

The electrical impulse begins at the pacemaker: a mass of cardiac muscle cells known as the **sino-atrial node (S.A. node)**. It is the rate at which the pacemaker emits impulses, that determines heart rate. As the impulse is emitted, it spreads to the adjacent inter-connecting fibres of the atrium, which causes the atria to contract. It then passes to another specialised mass of cells called the **atrioventricular node (A.V. node)**. The A.V. node acts as a distributor and

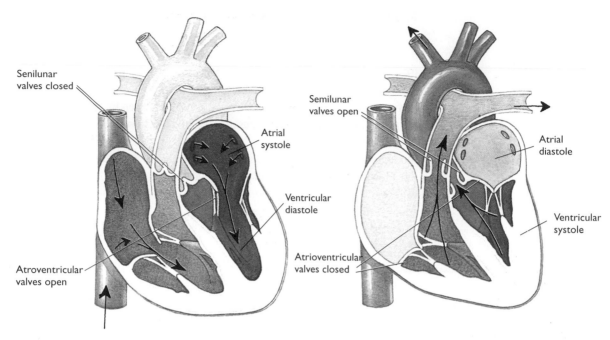

Fig. 3.4 STAGES OF THE CARDIAC CYCLE
Source: Tortora (1991)

passes the action potential to the Bundle of His, which, together with the branching Purkinje fibres, spread the excitation throughout the ventricles.

There is a delay of about 0.1 second from the time when the A.V. node receives stimulation, to when it distributes action potential throughout the ventricles. This is crucial to allow completion of atrial contraction, before ventricular systole begins. The relationship between the electrical activity of the heart and the cardiac cycle can be shown through an electrocardiogram trace (ECG).

Heart regulation

The heart is governed by the **autonomic** nervous system which determines the rate at which the pacemaker (S.A. node) send out impulses. The sympathetic and parasympathetic nervous systems are fundamental to the regulation of the heart and work antagonistically as follows:

1 The **sympathetic nervous system** increases heart rate by releasing adrenaline and noradrenaline from the adrenal medulla. Adrenaline increases the strength of ventricular contraction, and therefore stroke volume, while noradrenaline (a transmitter substance) aids the spread of the impulse throughout the heart, and therefore increases heart rate.

2 The **parasympathetic nervous system**, on the other hand, releases acetylcholine, which slows the spread of impulses and therefore reduces heart rate.

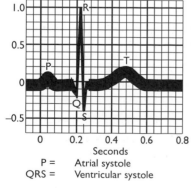

P = Atrial systole
QRS = Ventricular systole

Fig. 3.5 AN ELECTROCARDIOGRAM TRACE

Regulation during exercise

At rest, the parasympathetic system overrides the sympathetic system, and keeps heart rate down. However, once exercise begins, the sympathetic system increases its activity, the parasympathetic system decreases in activity, and so heart rate is allowed to rise. Increased metabolic activity causes an increased concentration of carbon dioxide and lactic acid content in the blood, which increases acidity and decreases blood pH. These changes are detected by **chemoreceptors** sited in the aortic arch and carotid arteries. They inform the sympathetic centre in the upper thoracic area of the spinal cord, to increase heart rate and transport the carbon dioxide to the lungs where it can be expelled. Messages from the sympathetic centre are sent to the S.A. node via **accelerator nerves** which release adrenaline (epinephrine) and noradrenaline (norepinephrine) upon stimulation.

Other factors which increase heart rate during exercise include:

*   increased body temperature (and therefore decreased blood viscosity)
*   increased venous return (a result of the increased action of the muscle pump).

Both of these factors will result in a greater cardiac output.

Once exercise ceases, sympathetic stimulation decreases and the parasympathetic system once again takes over. The parasympathetic system responds to information from **baroreceptors** – the body's in-built blood pressure recorders. When blood pressure is too high, messages are sent from the cardiac inhibitory centre to the S.A. node via the **vagus nerve**. The parasympathetic nerve then releases acetylcholine, which decreases the heart rate.

This continuous interaction of the sympathetic and parasympathetic system ensures that the heart works as efficiently as possible, and enables sufficient nutrients to reach the tissue cells to ensure effective muscle action.

Adrenaline and noradrenaline released from the adrenal medulla (situated at the top of the kidneys) generally have the same effect – increasing heart rate and increasing the strength of contraction. The release of such hormones, controlled by the sympathetic system, results from many factors including exercise, emotions, excitement and stress.

 **ACTIVITY 2**

I   **Fill in the missing gaps:**
    The _____ is a bundle of specialised cardiac muscle cells which generate action potentials and govern the heart rate. Impulses are spread across the atria and reach the _____ which delays the action potentials from spreading through the ventricles via the _____ and branching _____ .

2   **Discuss the difference between cardiac and skeletal muscle in terms of structure and function.**

3   **Describe the structure and function of the heart's conducting system.**

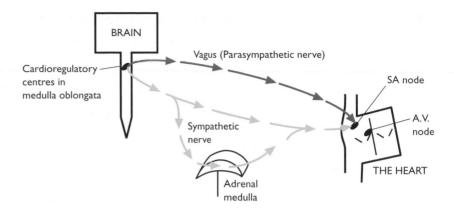

Fig. 3.6 THE REGULATION OF HEART RATE

Cardiac dynamics

Cardiac output

Cardiac output is the amount of blood that is pumped out of the heart from one ventricle per minute. Cardiac output is generally measured from the left ventricle, and is equal to the product of stroke volume and heart rate.

$$\text{Cardiac Output} = \text{Stroke Volume} \times \text{Heart Rate}$$
$$Q = \text{S.V.} \times \text{H.R.}$$

- The stroke volume is the amount of blood ejected into the aorta in one beat.
- The heart rate reflects the number of times the heart beats per minute.

On average, the resting stroke volume is 75 cm^3 per beat, and the resting heart rate for a person is 72 beats per minute. Therefore, cardiac output at rest is:

$$Q = \text{S.V.} \times \text{H.R.}$$
$$= 75 \text{ cm}^3 \times 72 \text{ bpm}$$
$$= 5,400 \text{ cm}^3 \ (5.4 \text{ Dm}^3)$$

However, during exercise the cardiac output may rise to 30 Dm^3 per minute – a six fold increase!

Training signals an improvement in cardiac output *during exercise*, brought about by an increase in stroke volume due to the larger volume of the left ventricle, and the hypertrophy (enlargement) of the heart (sometimes referred to as 'athletes' heart'). At rest, cardiac hypertrophy plays an important role, since increased stroke volume (which accompanies hypertrophy) allows the resting heart rate to decrease. This is known as **bradycardia**. The increased size of the ventricular cavity in trained athletes allows a longer diastolic phase during which time the heart can fill up with more blood. This stretches cardiac fibres and increases the strength of contraction, with the resultant effect of increasing stroke volume. Consequently, cardiac output does not change at rest following training.

Bradycardia occurs as a result of an increase in parasympathetic activity and a decrease in cardiac sympathetic activity, often to the extent that resting heart rate decreases to 60 bpm and below. During exercise, the hormones have a great influence on stroke volume and cardiac output. Adrenaline and noradrenaline increase the force of cardiac contraction, by increasing the contractility of cardiac muscle fibres. Muscle fibres are elastic and can stretch during the diastolic phase of the cardiac cycle which allows a more complete filling of the heart and thus increases cardiac output. This relationship is known as **Starling's Law** and there appears to be a linear relationship between cardiac output and exercise intensity.

ACTIVITY 3

What is cardiac output, and how is it measured?

The trained heart

We have examined how the heart responds and adjusts to exercise in the short time of an exercise session. Let us now turn our attention to the effects of long term training on the heart.

As mentioned above, the heart of an athlete is larger than that of a non-athlete. Cardiac hypertrophy is characterised by a larger ventricular wall and a thicker myocardium. Endurance athletes tend to display larger ventricular cavities, while those following high resistance or strength training regimes display thicker ventricular walls.

Cardiac hypertrophy is accompanied by a decreased resting heart rate. This can easily be demonstrated by comparing the resting heart rates of trained and untrained people. When the heart rate falls below 60 bpm, bradycardia is said to have occurred, and is due to a slowing in the intrinsic rate of the atrial pacemaker (S.A. node) and an increase in the predominance of the parasympathetic system acting upon the pacemaker. Since the resting cardiac output for an athlete is approximately the same as that of a non-athlete, the athlete compensates for the lower resting heart rate by increasing stroke volume. This increased resting stroke volume is greatest among endurance athletes, due to the increased ventricular cavity. The increase can also be as a result of improved contractility of the myocardium.

The vascular system

Having examined how the heart works to pump the blood into the network of blood vessels, we will now take a closer look at how the blood supports the functioning of the body and how the blood vessels ensure that sufficient blood reaches the body's tissues.

The blood

Blood consists of cells and cell fragments surrounded by a liquid matrix known as **plasma**. The average male has a total blood volume of 5–6 litres, and the average female blood volume is approximately 4–5 litres.

Functions of blood

The blood's functions are fundamental to life itself and include:

- transportation of nutrients
- protection
- the maintenance of homeostasis.

The blood is responsible for transporting oxygen to the body's cells and removing metabolites such as carbon dioxide from the muscle to the lungs. The blood also transports glucose from the liver to the muscle, and lactic acid from the muscle to the liver where it can be converted back to glucose. Further functions include the transportation of enzymes, hormones and other chemicals all of which have a vital role to play in the body.

The blood protects the body by containing cells and chemicals which are central to the immune system. When damage to blood vessels occurs, the blood clots in order to prevent cell loss.

The blood is vital in maintaining the body's state of equilibrium; eg, through hormone and enzyme activity, and the buffering capacity of the blood, the blood's pH should remain relatively stable. In addition the blood is involved in temperature regulation and can transport heat to the surface of the body where it can be released.

Blood composition

1 **Plasma** (55% of blood composition) – this is a pale yellow fluid composed of water (90%), proteins (8%) and salts (2%).
2 **Erythrocytes** – these are red corpuscles which contain **haemoglobin**, an iron rich protein which is responsible for all the oxygen transport in the blood. The ability of the blood to carry oxygen is determined by haemoglobin concentration, which may be increased through endurance training.
3 **Leucocytes** – these are white blood cells, and are involved in combating infection. Although larger than red blood cells, white blood cells are fewer in number.
4 **Thrombocytes** – thrombocytes or platelets are small bits of cytoplasm derived from the bone marrow, which play an important role in blood clotting, and so limit haemorrhaging.

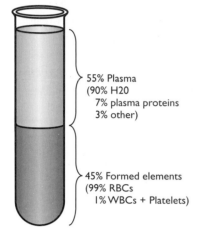

55% Plasma
(90% H20
   7% plasma proteins
   3% other)

45% Formed elements
(99% RBCs
   1% WBCs + Platelets)

Fig. 3.7 THE CONSTITUENTS OF BLOOD

Blood viscosity

Viscosity refers to the thickness of the blood and its resistance to flow. The more viscous a fluid, the more resistant it is to flow. The greater the volume of red blood cells, the greater the capacity to transport oxygen. However, unless it is accompanied by an increase in plasma, viscosity may also increase, and restrict blood flow. Viscosity may also increase when plasma content decreases due to dehydration (which may accompany endurance based exercise).

Haematocrit is the percentage of the total blood volume composed of red blood cells and typically varies between 40% and 45%.

- Haemoconcentration is an increase in the proportion of red blood cells in the blood, and is usually as a result of a decrease in blood plasma volume.
- Haemodilution is a decrease in red blood cell volume, due to a decrease in plasma volume.

List the functions and characteristics of blood.

Blood vessels

The vascular network through which blood flows to all parts of the body comprises of arteries, arterioles, capillaries, veins and venules.

Arteries and arterioles

Arteries are high pressure vessels which carry blood from the heart to the tissues. The largest artery in the body is the aorta which is the main artery leaving the heart.

The aorta constantly subdivides and gets smaller. The constant subdivision decreases the diameter of the vessel arteries, which now become arterioles.

Arteries are composed of three layers of tissue:

1 an outer fibrous layer – the tunica adventitia or tunica externa
2 a thick middle layer – the tunica media
3 a thin lining of cells to the inside – the endothelium or tunica intima.

The tunica media is comprised of smooth muscle and elastic tissue, which enables the arteries and arterioles to alter their diameter. Arteries tend to have more elastic tissue, while arterioles have greater amounts of smooth muscle; this allows the vessels to increase the diameter through **vasodilation** or decrease the diameter through **vasoconstriction**. It is through vasoconstriction and vasodilation that the vessels can regulate blood pressure and ensure the tissues are receiving sufficient blood – particularly during exercise. Arteries and arterioles have three basic functions:

• to act as conduits carrying and controlling blood flow to the tissues
• to cushion and smooth out the pulsatile flow of blood from the heart
• to help control blood pressure.

Veins and venules

Veins are low pressure vessels which return blood to the heart. The structure is similar to arteries, although they possess less smooth muscle and elastic tissue. Venules are the smallest veins and transport blood away from the capillary bed into the veins. Veins gradually increase in thickness the nearer to the heart they get, until they reach the largest vein in the body, the **venae cavae**, which enters the right atrium of the heart.

The thinner walls of the veins often distend and allow blood to pool in them. This is also allowed to happen as the veins contain pocket valves which close intermittently to prevent back flow of blood. This explains why up to 70% of total blood volume is found in the venous system at any one time.

Capillaries

Capillaries are the functional units or the vascular system. Composed of a single layer of endothelial cells, they are just thin enough to allow red blood cells to squeeze through their wall. The capillary network is very well developed as they are so small; large quantities are able to cover the muscle, which ensures efficient exchange of gases. If the cross-sectional area of all the capillaries in a muscle cell were to be added together, the total area would be much greater than that of the aorta.

Distribution of blood through the capillary network is regulated by special structures known as pre-capillary sphincters, the structure of which will be dealt with later in this chapter.

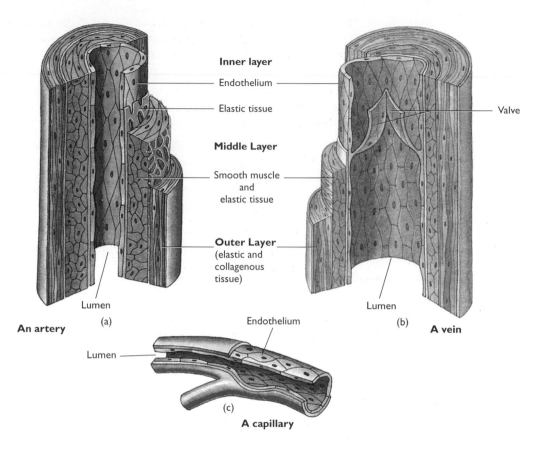

Fig. 3.8 THE STRUCTURE OF BLOOD VESSELS
Source: Tortora (1991)

The circulatory system

The blood flows through a continuous network of blood vessels, which form a double circuit. This connects the heart to the lungs, and the heart to all other body tissues.

The double circulatory system

Pulmonary circulation transports blood between the lungs and the heart. The pulmonary artery carries blood low in oxygen concentration from the right ventricle to the lung, where it becomes oxygen-rich and unloads carbon dioxide. The pulmonary vein then transports the freshly oxygenated blood back to the heart and into the left atrium.

The blood returning to the left atrium is pumped through the left side of the heart and into the aorta, where it is distributed to the whole of the body's tissues by a network of arteries. Veins then return the blood which is now low in oxygen and high in carbon dioxide concentration, to the heart where it enters the right atrium via the venae cavae. This circuit is known as **systemic circulation**.

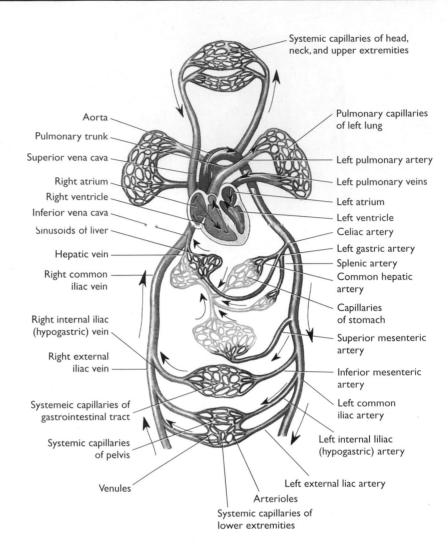

Fig. 3.9 THE DOUBLE CIRCULATORY SYSTEM
Source: Tortora (1991)

The venous return mechanism

Venous return is the term used for the blood which returns to the right side of the heart via the veins. As mentioned above, up to 70% of the total volume of blood is contained in the veins at rest. This provides a large reservoir of blood which is returned rapidly to the heart when needed. The heart can only pump as much blood out as it receives, so cardiac output is dependent upon venous return. A rapid increase in venous return enables a significant increase in cardiac output due to Starling's law.

There are several mechanisms which aid the venous return process:

1 **The muscle pump** – As exercise begins, muscular contractions impinge and compress upon the veins, squeezing blood towards the heart. Pocket valves prevent any backflow of blood that might occur.

2 **The respiratory pump** – During inspiration and expiration, pressure changes occur in the thoracic and abdominal cavities which compress veins and assist blood return to the heart.

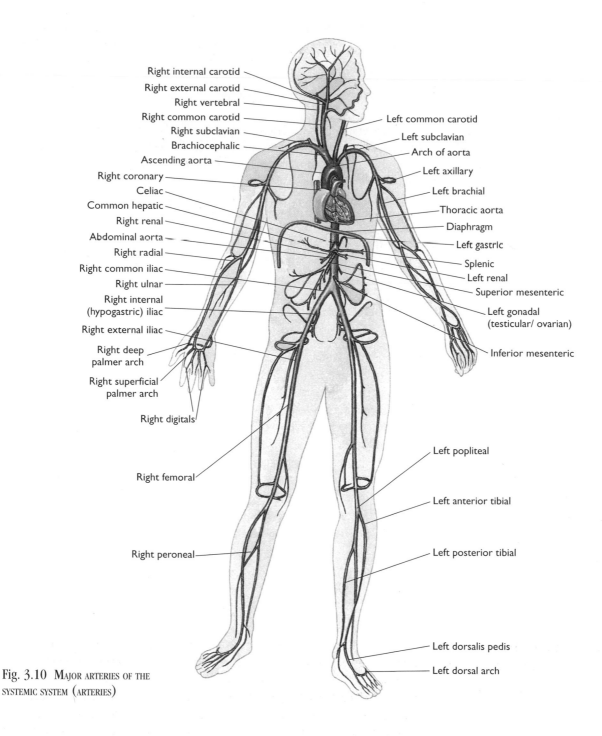

Fig. 3.10 MAJOR ARTERIES OF THE
SYSTEMIC SYSTEM (ARTERIES)

Blood pressure   Blood pressure is the force exerted by the blood against the walls of the blood
vessels. It is necessary to maintain blood flow through the circulatory system and is
determined by two main factors:

1 Cardiac output – the volume of blood flowing into the system from the left
ventricle.

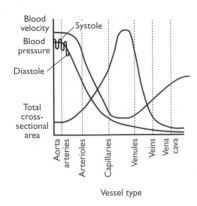

Fig. 3.11 THE RELATIONSHIP BETWEEN BLOOD VESSEL TYPE, TOTAL CROSS-SECTIONAL AREA, BLOOD VELOCITY AND BLOOD PRESSURE

2 Resistance to flow – the impedance offered by the blood vessels to the blood flow.

Blood pressure $=$ cardiac output $\times$ resistance

Therefore, blood pressure increases when either cardiac output or resistance increases.

Blood pressure in the arteries also increases and decreases in a pattern which corresponds to the cardiac cycle during ventricular systole, when blood is pumped into the aorta and lowest during ventricular diastole.

Blood pressure is usually measured at the brachial artery using a **sphygmomanometer**, and is recorded as millimetres of mercury (mmHg) of systolic pressure over diastolic pressure.

- **Systolic** pressure is experienced when the heart pumps blood into the system
- **Diastolic** pressure is recorded when the heart is relaxing and filling with blood.

The typical reading for a male at rest is:

$$\frac{120 \text{ mmHg}}{80 \text{ mmHg}}$$

During exercise, blood pressure changes and is dependent upon the type and intensity of the exercise being performed. During aerobic exercise, the systolic pressure increases as a result of an increased cardiac output, while diastolic pressure remains constant, or in well trained athletes may even drop as blood feeds into the working muscles. During isometric and anaerobic exercise, both systolic and diastolic pressure rise significantly due to increased resistance of the blood vessels. The vasomotor control centre outlined in the following section is responsible for regulating blood pressure.

To investigate blood pressure.

Equipment: digital blood pressure meter or sphygmomanometer

1 **Under the guidance of your teacher, wrap the cuff around the brachial artery.**
2 **Pump air into the cuff up to approximately 190 mmHg.**
3 **Slowly release the air inside the cuff by pressing the attachment on the bulb. The systolic pressure can now be read and recorded.**
4 **Continue to release air from the cuff until the diastolic pressure is displayed on the screen. Record your diastolic pressure.**
5 **Discover your blood pressure by placing the systolic reading over the diastolic reading, ie, $\frac{\text{systolic}}{\text{diastolic}}$.**
6 **Follow the above procedure after completing two minutes of intense exercise.**
7 **Account for any differences in your readings.**

Explain the importance of blood pressure with regard to sporting activity.

Redistribution of blood during exercise

Blood flow changes dramatically once exercise commences. At rest, only 15–20% of cardiac output is directed to skeletal muscle; the majority goes to the liver (27%) and kidneys (22%). During exercise however, blood is redirected to areas where it is most needed. For example, during exhaustive exercise the working muscles may receive up to 80% of cardiac output. This increased blood flow to the muscle results from a restriction of blood flow to the kidneys, liver and stomach. This process is known as **shunting** or **accommodation**.

Table 3.1   BLOOD FLOW CHANGES DURING EXERCISE IN CM^3/MIN
(Source: Clegg, Exercise Physiology, Feltham Press 1995)

ORGAN	AT REST	% BLOOD FLOW	MAXIMUM EFFORT	% BLOOD FLOW
skeletal muscle	1,000	20	26,000	88
coronary vessels	250	5	1,200	4
skin	500	10	750	2.5
kidneys	1,000	20	300	1
liver/gut	1,250	25	375	1.25
brain	750	15	750	2.5
whole body	5,000	100	30,000	100

Vasomotor control

The redistribution of blood is controlled primarily by the vasoconstriction and vasodilation of arterioles. It reacts to chemical changes of the local tissues. For example, vasodilation will occur when arterioles sense a decrease in oxygen concentration or an increase in acidity due to higher CO_2 and lactic acid concentrations. Vasodilation will then allow a greater blood flow, bringing the much needed oxygen and flushing away the harmful waste products of metabolism.

Sympathetic nerves also play a major role in redistributing blood from one area of the body to another. The smooth muscle layer (tunica media) of the blood vessels is controlled by the sympathetic nervous system, and remains in a state of slight contraction known as vasomotor tone. By increasing sympathetic stimulation, vasoconstriction occurs and blood flow is restricted and redistributed to areas of greater need. When stimulation by sympathetic nerves decreases, vasodilation is allowed which will increase blood flow to that body part.

Further structures which aid blood redistribution are pre-capillary sphincters. Pre-capillary sphincters are ring shaped muscles which lie at the opening of capillaries and control blood flow into the capillary bed. When the sphincter contracts, it restricts blood flow through the capillary, and deprives tissues of oxygen; conversely when it relaxes, it increases blood flow to the capillary bed.

1 **Name the major blood vessels in the body, beginning with those affecting the heart. In each case, state how the structure is suited to their function.**
2 **Explain how vasoconstriction and vasodilation function in the body and how they can affect the athlete whilst exercising.**
3 **What are the major differences between the heart of a trained athlete and that of an untrained person?**
4 **Discuss how the vasomotor centre operates.**

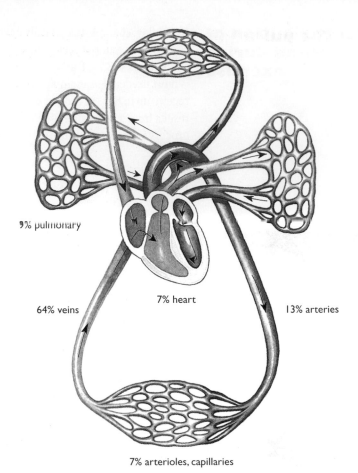

9% pulmonary

7% heart

64% veins

13% arteries

7% arterioles, capillaries

Fig. 3.12 THE DISTRIBUTION OF BLOOD IN THE BODY AT REST

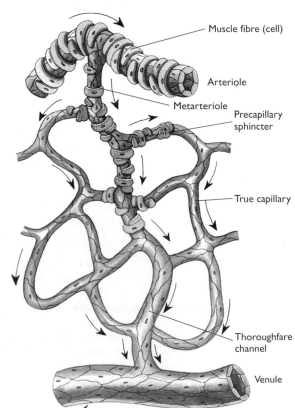

Muscle fibre (cell)

Arteriole

Metarteriole

Precapillary sphincter

True capillary

Thoroughfare channel

Venule

Fig. 3.13 A PRE-CAPILLARY SPHINCTER

The pulse rate

The pulse is a pressure wave which is generated from the heart each time the left ventricle pumps blood into the aorta. The increased pressure causes slight dilation of the arteries as the blood travels through the arteries around the body and this can be felt at various sites on the body. The most common sites where the pulse can be palpated are:

- the radial artery
- the carotid artery
- the femoral artery
- the brachial artery
- the temporal artery.

1 Record your pulse for a 10 second count at each of the following sites:

- carotid artery
- radial artery
- brachial artery.

Remember to start counting from zero.

2 Multiply your scores by six to achieve your heart rate score in beats per minute.
3 Account for any differences in your heart rate scores at the different sites.
4 Why should you never use your thumb to measure your pulse?

An investigation to examine heart rate response to varying intensities of exercise.

Equipment: stop watch, gymnastics bench, metronome

1 Record resting heart rate for a 10 second count at the beginning of the class.
2 Record heart rate for a 10 second count at the carotid artery immediately prior to exercise.
3 Start exercising by stepping onto and off the bench at a low intensity, keeping in time with the metronome.
4 Record your pulse after one, two and three minutes of exercise. After the third minute of exercise, stop the test. Continue to record your pulse each minute during recovery.
5 Once your heart rate has returned to its resting value (or within a few beats) repeat the test at a medium intensity. Record your results as before.
6 Repeat the exercise for a third time but at a very high intensity. Once again record your results.
7 Convert your heart rate scores into beats per minute by multiplying by six.
8 Now use your results to plot a graph for each of the three workloads. Plot each graph using the same axes, placing heart rate along the 'Y' axis and time along the bottom 'X' axis. Don't forget to show your resting heart rate values on the graph.
9 For each of your graphs explain the heart rate patterns prior to, during and following exercise.

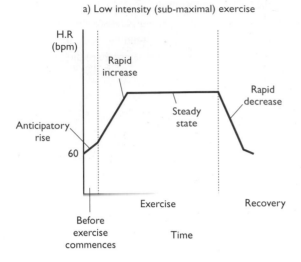

Fig. 3.14 EXPECTED HEART RATE CURVES
FOR DIFFERENT INTENSITIES OF EXERCISE

The lymphatic system

The lymphatic system is a network of vessels that carry lymph, a fluid derived from interstitial fluid (tissue fluid). This carries water, electrolytes and proteins from the tissues. At the capillary bed, some blood plasma is squeezed out of the capillaries into the tissues, which becomes interstitial fluid. Some of the fluid is returned to the capillaries following exchange, but some of it enters the lymph capillaries which drain the excess fluid away from the tissues. Removal of excess fluid is essential to prevent swelling as in oedema or ascites which can cause death.

The lymph vessels merge to form progressively large vessels that drain into large veins, re-entering the blood circulatory system. At certain points the lymph passes through lymph nodes, which filter the lymph removing micro-organisms and foreign bodies. In this way, the lymphatic system forms part of the body's defence system.

The major roles of the lymphatic system are to maintain appropriate fluid levels in the tissues as well as maintaining proper blood volume, preventing excess swelling (through removal of fats and proteins) and fighting infection.

List the basic functions of the lymphatic system.

Summary

- The structure of the heart is specially adapted to its function.
- Valves within the heart ensure a unidirectional flow of blood.
- The sounds of the heart are a result of these valves snapping shut. The Lub sound results from the closing of the atrioventricular valves, whilst the Dub results from the closure of the semi-lunar valves.
- Typically the heart is composed of three layers. An outer pericardium, a thick muscular layer called the myocardium, and a smooth inner endocardium.
- Coronary arteries ensure the heart receives an adequate supply of blood.

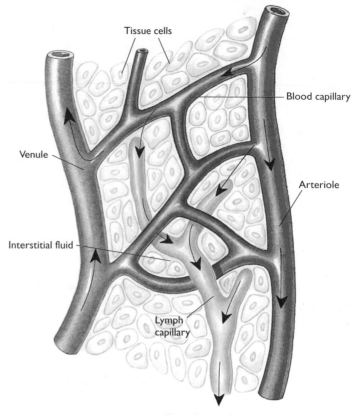

Fig. 3.15 RELATIONSHIP OF LYMPH CAPILLARIES TO TISSUE CELLS AND BLOOD CAPILLARIES

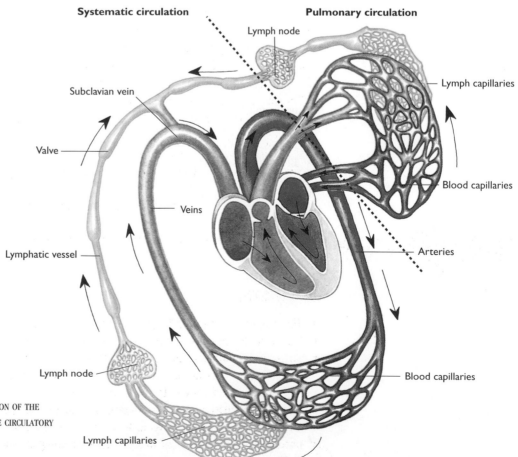

Fig. 3.16 THE INTERACTION OF THE LYMPHATIC SYSTEM WITH THE CIRCULATORY SYSTEM

- The cardiac cycle explains the passage of blood through the heart. It consists of four stages: Atrial Diastole, Atrial Systole, Ventricular Diastole and Ventricular Systole.
- The heart is myogenic – it creates its own impulses.
- The impulse is emitted from the SA Node the surrounding fibres are innervated causing the atria to contract. The impulse eventually arrives at the AV Node, where it is dispersed down the Bundle of His and throughout the Purkinje fibres, causing the ventricles to contract.
- The heart rate is governed by the parasympathetic and sympathetic nervous systems. The sympathetic nervous system increases heart rate by releasing adrenaline and noradrenaline, whilst the parasympathetic nervous system slows the heart down through the action of another hormone acetylcholine.
- Increases in heart rate during exercise is largely the result of increased metabolic activity increasing the concentration of carbon dioxide.
- Cardiac output is the volume of blood pumped out of one ventricle in one minute. Stroke volume is the volume of blood pumped out of one ventricle in one beat and heart rate the number of times the heart beats per minute.
- Cardiac Hypertrophy is the enlargement of the heart often resulting from endurance training.
- Bradycardia is the reduction in resting heart rate (usually below 60bpm) which accompanies cardiac hypertrophy.
- The vascular system encompasses the blood and blood vessels.
- The blood's main functions are the transportation of oxygen and the maintenance of homeostasis.
- Typically blood is composed of Plasma (water, proteins and salts) Erythrocytes, Leucocytes, and thrombocytes.
- Major blood vessels consist of arteries, arterioles, capillaries, venules and veins.
- The continuous network of blood vessels in the body is known as the circulatory system, which is composed of the pulmonary and systemic circuits.
- Blood returning to the heart via the veins is known as venous return. It is aided by the muscle and respiratory pumps.
- Blood pressure is the force exerted by the blood on the inner walls of the blood vessels. It is a product of cardiac output and resistance of the vessel walls.
- Blood flow is controlled by the vasomotor centre which causes blood vessels to vasodilate and vasoconstrict and determines the degree of blood reaching various parts of the body.
- The lymphatic system maintains blood volume, appropriate fluid levels, and fights infection.

chapter 4

Respiratory Considerations

T his chapter examines the structure and function of the respiratory system, including detail on the lungs and the respiratory airways. It also looks at the mechanics of breathing, the process of inspiration and expiration and definitions of lung volumes and capacities. Simple investigations of measurement of these volumes are also included.

The chapter studies gaseous exchange, partial pressures and the transport of gases in the body; factors that may influence oxygen delivery and uptake; and oxygen consumption and the response of the respiratory system to training. Links can be made to other chapters of the book, particularly Chapters 7 and 8, on training and fitness.

Respiration during exercise

The respiratory system is often studied in combination with the cardiovascular system, since the two systems work together to ensure an efficient and continuous supply of oxygen to the body's cells.

Respiration can be divided into two processes – external respiration and internal respiration.

External respiration

External respiration involves the movement of gases into and out of the lungs and the exchange of gases between the lungs and the blood known as pulmonary diffusion.

On its journey to the lungs, air drawn into the body passes many structures:

Nasal passages

Air is drawn into the body via the nose. The nasal cavity is divided by a cartilaginous septum, forming the nasal passages. The interior structures of the nose help the respiratory process by performing the following important functions:

1 the mucus membranes and blood capillaries moisten and warm the inspired air
2 the ciliated epithelium filters and traps dust particles which are moved to the throat for elimination
3 the small bones known as chonchae increase the surface area of the cavity to make the process more efficient.

The oral pharynx and larynx

The throat is shared by both the respiratory and alimentary tract. Air entering the larynx passes over the vocal chords and into the trachea. In swallowing, the larynx is drawn upwards and forwards against the base of the epiglottis, thus preventing entry of food.

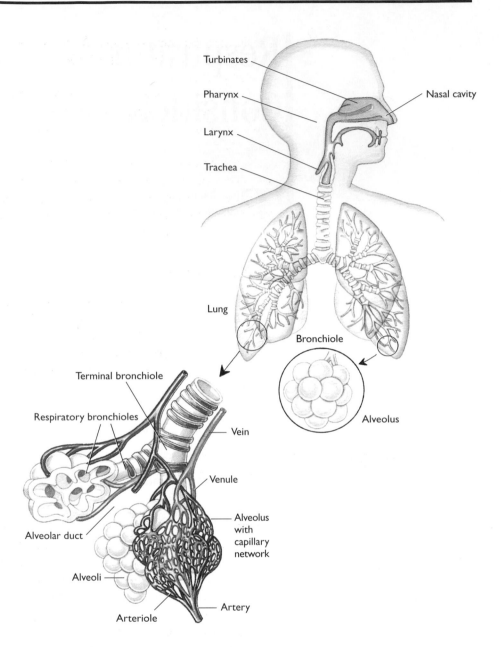

Fig. 4.1 THE STRUCTURE OF THE
RESPIRATORY SYSTEM

The trachea

The trachea or windpipe is approximately 10 cm in length and lies in front of the
oesophagus. It is composed of 18 horseshoe shaped rings of cartilage which are
also lined by a mucous membrane and ciliated cells which provide the same
protection against dust as the nasal passageways. The trachea extends from the
larynx and directs air into the right and left primary bronchi.

The bronchi and bronchioles

The trachea divides into the right and left bronchus which further subdivide into
lobar bronchi (three feeding each lobe on the right, two feeding each lobe on the
left). Further subdivision of these airways form bronchioles which in turn branch

into the smaller terminal or respiratory bronchioles. The bronchioles enable the air to pass into the alveoli via the alveolar ducts, and it is here that pulmonary diffusion occurs (see page 56).

The alveoli are responsible for the exchange of gases between the lungs and the blood. The alveolar walls are extremely thin and are composed of epithelial cells which are lined by a thin film of water, essential for dissolving oxygen from the inspired air.

Surrounding each alveolus is an extensive capillary network which ensures a smooth passage of oxygen into the pulmonary capillaries. It has been estimated that each lung contains up to 150 million alveoli, providing a tremendous surface area for the exchange of gases. The alveoli walls also contain elastic fibres which further increase the surface during inspiration.

Breathing mechanics

The lungs are surrounded by pleural sacs containing pleural fluid which reduces friction during respiration. These sacs are attached to both the lungs and the thoracic cage, which enables the lungs to inflate and deflate as the chest expands and flattens. The interrelationship between the lungs, pleural sacs and thoracic cage are central to the understanding of the respiratory processes of inspiration and expiration.

Inspiration   The process of inspiration is an active one. It occurs as a result of the contraction of the respiratory muscles, namely the external intercostal muscles and the diaphragm.

The external intercostal muscles are attached to each rib. When they contract, they cause the rib cage to pivot about thoracic vertebral joints and move upwards and outwards, much like the handle of a bucket as it is lifted. The diaphragm, a dome shaped muscle separating the abdominal and thoracic cavities, contracts downwards during inspiration, increasing the area of the thoracic cavity. As the chest expands through these muscular contractions, the surface tension created by the film of pleural fluid, causes the lungs to be pulled outwards along with the chest walls. This action causes the space within the lungs to increase and the air molecules within to move further apart.

As pressure is determined by the rate at which molecules strike a surface in a given time, the pressure within the lungs (intrapulmonary pressure) decreases and becomes less than that outside the body. Gases always move from areas of higher pressure to areas of lower pressure, so that air from outside the body rushes into the lungs via the respiratory tract. This process is known as **inspiration**.

During exercise, greater volumes of air can fill the lungs since the sterno-cleidomastoid and scaleni muscles can help increase the thoracic cavity still further.

Expiration   The process of expiration is generally a passive process and occurs as a result of the relaxation of the respiratory muscles used in inspiration. As the external intercostal muscles relax, the ribcage is lowered into its resting position, and the diaphragm relaxes and domes up into the thoracic cavity. The area of the lungs is thus decreased and intrapulmonary pressure increases to an extent where it is greater than atmospheric pressure. Air inside the lungs is forced out to equate the pressure inside and outside the body.

During exercise, the process of expiration becomes more active as the internal intercostal muscles pull the ribs downwards to help increase the ventilation rate. These muscles are ably assisted by the abdominals and the latissimus dorsi muscles.

1 **Name the respiratory muscles used both at rest and during exercise.**
2 **How might training affect them?**

Pulmonary diffusion

Pulmonary diffusion is the term used to explain the process of gaseous exchange in the lungs. It has two major functions:

1 to replenish the blood with oxygen where it can then be transported to the tissues and muscles
2 to remove carbon dioxide from the blood which has resulted from metabolic processes in the tissues.

Partial pressure of gases

Central to the understanding of gaseous exchange is the concept of partial pressure. The partial pressure of a gas is the individual pressure that the gas exerts when it occurs in a mixture of gases. The gas will exert a pressure proportional to its concentration within the whole gas. Thus the partial pressures of each individual gas within a mixture of gases should, when added together, be equal to the total pressure of the gas.

For example, the air we breathe is composed of three main gases: nitrogen (79%), oxygen (20.9%) and carbon dioxide (0.03%). The percentages show the relative concentrations of each gas in atmospheric air.

At sea level, total atmospheric pressure is 769 mmHg which reflects the pressure that atmospheric air exerts. For example:

- The concentration of CO_2 in the atmosphere is approximately 21%
- The concentration of nitrogen in the air is approximately 79%
- Together they exert a pressure of 760 mmHg at sea level.

Therefore the PO_2 (partial pressure of oxygen) is calculated as:

$$PO_2 = \text{Barometric pressure} \times \text{fractional concentration}$$
$$= 760 \times 0.21$$
$$= 159.6 \text{ mmHg}$$

Partial pressure of gases explain the movement of gases within the body, and account for the processes of gas exchange between the alveoli and the blood, and between the blood and the muscle or tissue.

Gaseous exchange at the lungs

It is the imbalance between gases in the alveoli and the blood that causes a pressure gradient, which results in a movement of gases across the respiratory membrane (which facilitates this movement by being extremely thin, measuring only 0.5 μm). This movement is two way, with oxygen moving from the alveoli into the blood and carbon dioxide diffusing from the blood into the alveoli. The partial pressure of oxygen (PO_2) in the atmosphere is approximately 159 mmHg (0.21×760 mmHg), which drops to 105 mmHg in the alveoli since the air combines with water vapour and carbon dioxide which is already present in the alveoli.

Blood in the pulmonary capillaries which surround the alveoli has a PO_2 of 45 mmHg, since much of the oxygen has been already used by the working muscles. This results in a pressure gradient of approximately 60 mmHg which forces oxygen from the alveoli into the blood, until such a time that the pressure is equal on each side of the membrane.

In the same way, carbon dioxide moves along a pressure gradient from the pulmonary capillaries into the alveoli. With a PCO_2 of 45 mmHg in the blood returning to the lungs and a PCO_2 of 40 mmHg in the alveolar air, a small pressure gradient of 5 mmHg results. This causes CO_2 to move from the pulmonary blood into the alveoli, which is later expired. Although the pressure gradient is relatively small, the CO_2 can cross the respiratory membrane much more rapidly than oxygen, as its membrane solubility is 20 times greater.

Endurance athletes, with larger aerobic capacities will have greater oxygen diffusion ability (the rate at which oxygen diffuses into the pulmonary blood from the alveoli) as a result of increased cardiac output, increased alveoli surface area, and reduced resistance to diffusion.

ACTIVITY 2

1 **Explain what is meant by the partial pressure of a gas.**
2 **State how this affects gaseous exchange around the body.**

The transport of oxygen

The majority of oxygen is carried by the red blood cells combined with haemoglobin; this is an iron-based protein which chemically combines with oxygen to form oxyhaemoglobin.

Haemoglobin	+	Oxygen	→	Oxyhaemoglobin
Hb	+	O_2	→	HbO_2

Each molecule of haemoglobin can combine with four molecules of oxygen, which amounts to approximately 1.34 ml. The concentration of haemoglobin in the blood is about 15 g per 100 ml, thus each 100 ml of blood can transport up to 20 ml of oxygen (1.34×15). However, the amount of oxygen that can combine with haemoglobin is determined by the partial pressure of oxygen (PO_2). A high PO_2 results in complete haemoglobin saturation, while at lower PO_2, haemoglobin saturation decreases.

Haemoglobin is almost 100% saturated with oxygen at a PO_2 of 100 mmHg (which is the PO_2 in the alveoli). Therefore, at the lungs, haemoglobin is totally saturated with oxygen, and even if more oxygen were available, it could not be transported. As the PO_2 is reduced, haemoglobin saturation decreases accordingly. This is largely due to the increased acidity of the blood (decrease in blood pH),

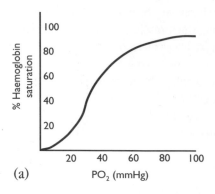

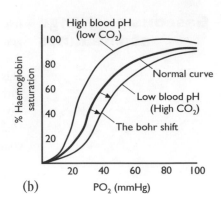

Fig. 4.2 THE OXYGEN–HAEMOGLOBIN
DISASSOCIATION CURVE (A) A NORMAL
OXYGEN-HAEMOGLOBIN DISASSOCIATION CURVE
(B) THE EFFECTS OF BLOOD pH ON OXYGEN-
HAEMOGLOBIN SATURATION

caused by an increase in CO_2 content or lactic acid, and causes a shift in the haemoglobin saturation curve to the right. This is known as the **Bohr shift**, and explains how oxygen is disassociated from haemoglobin at lower pH values in order to feed the tissues.

During exercise, increased CO_2 production causes a greater disassociation of oxygen due to the decrease in muscle pH. A further cause is the increase in body temperature that accompanies exercise; as oxygen unloading becomes more effective, the disassociation curve shifts to the right.

The overall efficiency of oxygen transport is therefore dependent upon haemoglobin content, and many athletes have sought to increase haemoglobin content through the illegal practice of blood doping. By removing blood which is subsequently replaced by the body, the athlete reinfuses it, to increase blood volume and more importantly haemoglobin content. Results of research on the practice of blood doping are conflicting, and it should always be remembered that it is illegal under the current Olympic Committee doping rules.

The transport of carbon dioxide

Carbon dioxide produced in the body's tissues is also transported in the blood in various ways:

- approximately 8% is dissolved in the blood plasma
- up to 20% combines with haemoglobin to form carbaminohaemoglobin
- up to 70% of carbon dioxide is transported in the form of bicarbonate ion.

Initially carbon dioxide reacts with water to form carbonic acid. However, carbon anhydrase, an enzyme found in red blood cells, quickly breaks down to free a hydrogen ion (H+) and form a bicarbonate ion (HCO_{3-}).

$$CO_2 + H_2O \rightarrow H_2CO_3 + CA \rightarrow H+ + HCO_{3-}$$

The hydrogen ion (H+) combines with haemoglobin to form haemoglobinic acid. This causes oxygen to disassociate from the haemoglobin, and shifts the oxygen disassociation curve to the right (the Bohr shift):

$$H+ + HbO_2 \rightarrow HHb + O_2$$

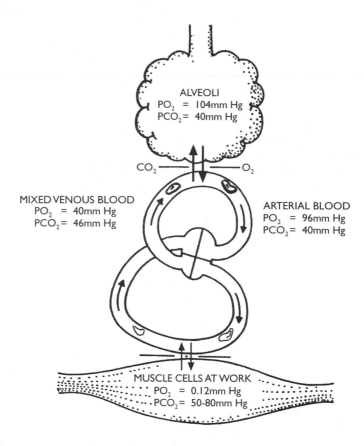

Fig. 4.3 PARTIAL PRESSURES OF OXYGEN AND CARBON DIOXIDE AT VARIOUS SITES IN THE BODY

In this way, the bicarbonate ion frees oxygen for tissue respiration and can aid in the removal of carbon dioxide and other metabolites such as lactic acid. As the blood returns to the lungs, the PCO_2 is low and the $H+$ and bicarbonate ion reassociate to form carbonic acid once again. The instability of this acid causes it to split further into water and carbon dioxide, where particles can diffuse into the alveoli and be expired:

$$H+ + HCO_{3-} \rightarrow H_2CO_3 \rightarrow CO_2 + H_2O$$

1 **Explain how the oxyhaemoglobin disassociation curve can aid our understanding of gaseous exchange. How might increases in blood acidity affect the curve?**

2 **Outline how CO_2 is transported in the body. What is the role of the bicarbonate ion in this process?**

Gas exchange at the muscles and tissues

We have seen how oxygen is brought into the lungs and transported to the capillary beds on the muscles. We now need to turn our attention to how the oxygen can enter the muscle cell.

The process is similar to the exchange of gases at the lungs: the partial pressure of the gases in the blood and tissues determines the movement of oxygen and carbon dioxide into and out of the tissue cells. The high partial pressure of oxygen

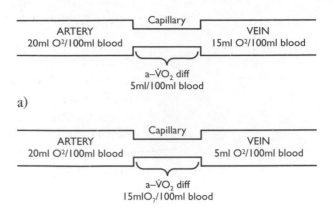

a)

b)

NOTE THAT DURING INTENSE EXERCISE
OXYGEN CONSUMPTION HAS INCREASED AND
A GREATER a–$\dot{V}O_2$ diff RESULTS

Fig. 4.4 THE ATRIOVENOUS OXYGEN
DIFFERENCE BEFORE AND DURING EXERCISE
(A) AT REST (B) INTENSE EXERCISE

in the arterial blood and the relatively low PO_2 in the muscles causes a pressure gradient which enables oxygen to disassociate from haemoglobin and pass through the capillary wall and into the muscle cytoplasm. Conversely, the high PCO_2 in the tissues and low PCO_2 in the arterial blood causes a movement of carbon dioxide in the opposite direction. The production of carbon dioxide in fact stimulates the disassociation of oxygen from haemoglobin as we learned in the previous section, and this (together with greater tissue demand for oxygen) increases the pressure gradients during exercise.

Once oxygen has entered the muscle cell, it immediately attaches to a substance called **myoglobin**, which is not dissimilar to haemoglobin and transports the oxygen to the mitochondria, where **glycolysis** can take place. The concentration of myoglobin is much higher in the cells of slow twitch muscle fibres, as these are more suited to aerobic energy production. Myoglobin has a much higher affinity for oxygen than haemoglobin and also acts as an oxygen reserve, so that when demand for oxygen is increased, as for example during exercise, there is an available supply.

The arterial-venous oxygen difference (a-$\dot{V}O_2$ diff) is the difference in oxygen content between the arterial blood and venous blood, and can measure how much oxygen is actually being consumed in the muscles and tissues. At rest only about 25% of oxygen is actually used; this however increases dramatically during intense exercise to up to 85%.

Draw diagrams to show how and why gases move between:
• **the alveoli and the pulmonary capillaries**
• **the systemic capillaries and the muscle.**

Lung volumes and capacities

Lung volumes

During normal quiet breathing, we inspire approximately 500 ml of air; the same amount is exhaled during the process of expiration. This volume of air inspired or expired is known as **tidal volume**. Of this 500 ml, only about 350 ml makes its way to the alveoli. The other 150 ml remains in the passageways of the nose, throat and trachea and is known as **dead space**. The volume of air which is inspired or expired in one minute is called **minute ventilation**, and is calculated by multiplying tidal volume by the number of breaths taken per minute. On average we breathe 15 times per minute, so our resting minute ventilation can be calculated as follows:

$$VE = T.V. \times f$$
$$= 500 \text{ ml} \times 15$$
$$= 7,500 \text{ ml/min } (7.5\text{l/min})$$

However, at rest we can still inspire much more air than our normal tidal volume. This excess volume of air inspired is the inspiratory reserve volume. It can be defined as the maximum volume of air inspired following normal inspiration, and measures approximately 3,300 ml. Following normal expiration at rest we can also expire more air; this volume is known as the expiratory reserve volume and measures approximately 1,200 ml. The lungs can never completely expel all the air they contain. Approximately 1,200 ml remains in the alveoli to keep them slightly inflated and regulate pressure; this volume is called the reserve volume.

Lung capacities

Lung capacities can be calculated by adding together the different lung volumes. For example:

1 inspiratory capacity is the sum of tidal volume and the inspiratory reserve volume, and amounts to 3,800 ml.

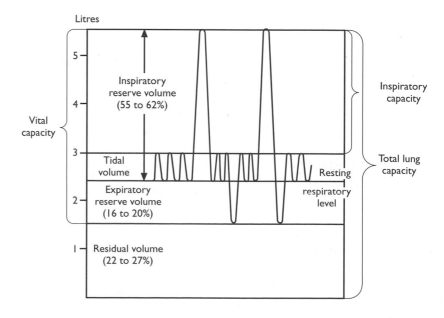

Fig. 4.5 Lung volumes shown by a spirometer trace

2 functional residual capacity is the sum of expiratory reserve volume and residual volume, and accounts for approximately 2,400 ml.

3 vital capacity is the amount of air that can be forcibly expired following maximal inspiration and is the sum of tidal volume, inspiratory reserve volume and expiratory reserve volume; this measures about 5,000 ml.

4 total lung capacity is the sum of all volumes and on average is approximately 6,000 ml.

The Forced Expiratory Volume (FEV1) is the percentage of vital capacity that can be expired in one second. This is approximately 85% and gives an indication of the overall efficiency of the airways. A low reading may assume that the airways are resisting the passage of air during expiration and consequently the efficiency of the gaseous exchange process at the lungs may decrease. A summary of lung volumes and capacities, their values and the effect of exercise is outlined in table 4.1.

Define the lung volumes and capacities. Discuss how and why each changes with exercise.

Ventilation during exercise

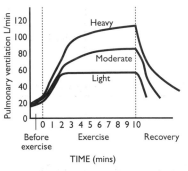

NOTE: The anticipatory rise prior to exercise and the continual increase in ventilation during intense exercise

Fig. 4.6 RESPIRATORY RESPONSE TO VARYING INTENSITY OF EXERCISE

During exercise, both the depth and rate of breathing increases. The tidal volume increases by utilising both the inspiratory reserve volume and the expiratory reserve volume; consequently both these volumes decrease during exercise, while tidal volume may increase six-fold. Since both tidal volume and the frequency of breathing increase during exercise, minute ventilation increases dramatically – values up to 180L/min have been recorded for trained endurance athletes.

Changes in ventilation occur before, during and after exercise as shown in fig 4.6. Before exercise starts there is a slight increase in ventilation; this is called the **anticipatory rise** and is the result of hormones, such as adrenaline stimulating the respiratory centre. Once exercise begins there is a rapid rise in ventilation caused by nervous stimulation. During submaximal exercise this sudden increase in ventilation begins to slow down and may plateau into what is known as the **steady state**. This assumes that the energy demands of the muscles are being met by the oxygen made available, and that the body is expelling carbon dioxide effectively. During maximal exercise however, this steady state does not occur, and ventilation continues to increase until the exercise is finished. This is thought to be due to the stimulation of the respiratory centre by carbon dioxide and lactic acid, and suggests that it is the body's need to expel these metabolites rather than its desire for oxygen which determines the pattern of breathing.

During recovery from exercise, ventilation drops rapidly at first, followed by a slower decrease. The more intense the preceding exercise, the longer the recovery period and the longer ventilation remains above the normal resting level. This is largely due to the removal of bi-products of muscle metabolism such as lactic acid and will be discussed further in Chapter 4.

Respiratory regulation

Ventilation is controlled by the nervous system, and this enables us to alter breathing patterns without consciously thinking about it. The basic rhythm of respiration is governed and co-ordinated by the respiratory centre, situated in and around the medulla area of the brain. During inspiration nerve impulses are generated and sent via the phrenic and intercostal nerves to the inspiratory muscles

Table 4.1 LUNG VOLUMES AND CAPACITIES DEFINED; RESTING VALUES AND CHANGES DURING EXERCISE

LUNG VOLUME OR CAPACITY	DEFINITION	CHANGES DURING EXERCISE	APPROXIMATE NORMAL VALUES (ML)
tidal volume (TV)	volume inspired *or* expired per breath	increase	500
inspiratory reserve volume (IRV)	maximal volume inspired from end-inspiration	decrease	3,300
expiratory reserve volume (ERV)	maximal volume expired from end-expiration	slight decrease	1,000–1,200
residual volume (RV)	volume remaining at end of maximal expiration	slight increase	1,200
total lung capacity (TLC)	volume in lung at end of maximal inspiration	slight decrease	up to 8,000
vital capacity (VC)	maximal volume forcefully expired after maximal in spiration	slight decrease	5,500
inspiratory capacity (IC)	maximal volume inspired from resting expiratory level	increase	3,800
functional residual capacity (FRC)	volume in lungs at resting expiratory level	slight increase	2,400
dead space	volume of air in the trachea/bronchi etc. that does not take part in gaseous exchange		150
minute ventilation	volume of air inspired/expired per minute $VE = TV \times F = 500 \times 15 = 7,500$ ml		7,500

(external intercostals, and diaphragm) causing them to contract. This lasts for approximately two seconds after which the impulses are ceased and expiration occurs passively by elastic recoil of the lungs.

During exercise however, when breathing rate is increased, the expiratory centre may send impulses to the expiratory muscles (internal intercostals) which speeds up the expiratory process.

It is however the chemical composition of the blood which largely influences respiration rates, particularly during exercise. The respiratory centre has an chemosensitive area which is sensitive to changes in the blood acidity. Chemoreceptors located in the aortic arch and carotid arteries assess the acidity of the blood and in particular the relative concentrations of CO_2 and O_2. If there is an increase in the concentration of CO_2 in the blood, the chemoreceptors detect this and the respiratory centre sends nerve impulse to the respiratory muscles which increase the rate of ventilation. This allows the body to expire the excess CO_2. Once blood acidity is lowered, fewer impulses are sent and respiration rates can once again decrease. This regulation of breathing is aided by a series of stretch receptors in the lungs and bronchioles, which prevent over-inflation of the lungs. If these are excessively stretched the expiratory centre sends impulses to induce expiration – this is known as the **Hering-Breur reflex**.

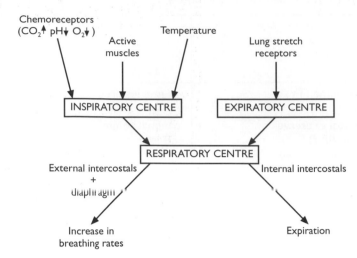

Fig. 4.7 THE RESPIRATORY REGULATION
MECHANISM

1 **Explain the process of increased breathing rates during exercise.**
2 **Why do breathing rates remain high following exercise, even though exercise has ceased?**

Summary

- Respiration can be divided into external and internal respiration.
- External respiration is the process of getting air into and out of the lungs.
- Inspiration occurs when the respiratory muscles contract, lifting the ribcage upwards and outwards and lowering the diaphragm. The resultant pressure differential causes air to rush into the lungs.
- Expiration at rest is a passive process, simply a result of the intercostals and diaphragm relaxing. This once again causes a pressure differential and air is forced out of the lungs.
- Oxygen enters the blood stream at the alveoli through the process of diffusion.
- Gaseous exchange occurs as a result of differences in concentration of oxygen and carbon dioxide around the body.
- The partial pressure of a gas is the individual pressure the gas exerts when in a mixture of gases and explains the movement of gases in the body.
- Oxygen is transported around the body by combining to haemoglobin to form oxyhaemoglobin.
- Carbon dioxide is largely transported as a bicarbonate ion. Some however combine with haemoglobin to form carbominohaemoglobin and some dissolves in the blood's plasma.
- Respiration is governed by various levels within the brain. The main regulatory mechanism is performed by chemoreceptors within the aortic arch and carotid arteries. These assess the concentration of carbon dioxide within the blood.

chapter 5

Energy for Movement

Where do muscles get the energy to provide movement? This chapter aims to answer this and other questions that may arise from the study of muscle physiology.

Energy is fundamental to the study of sport and as such, this chapter will examine the sources of energy for muscular contraction and in particular the role of adenosine triphosphate, carbohydrates and fats in energy provision.

We will see how the resynthesis of ATP occurs via the alactic, lactic and aerobic energy systems, and how, training can enhance the energy output from the three energy pathways.

The body's energy sources

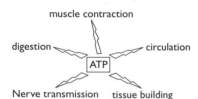

Fig. 5.1 ATP PROVIDES THE ENERGY FOR ALL ENERGY-REQUIRING PROCESSES IN THE BODY

Fig. 5.2 THE SPLITTING OF ATP

All movement requires a series of coordinated muscle contractions, which in turn requires a supply of energy. The energy requirement of a cell is supplied by the breakdown of adenosine triphosphate – a high energy compound.

Molecules of ATP consist of atoms held together by a set of bonds which store energy. It is the breaking or splitting of the outermost bond that releases the energy used to fuel all the processes within the body, and in particular, the contraction of skeletal muscle which facilitates movement.

There is, however only a limited amount of this high energy compound in the muscle cell, which is sufficient only to produce several contractions; or in a practical context, to run as fast as you can for a few seconds. ATP must therefore be constantly resynthesised in order to provide a continuous supply of energy.

ATP resynthesis at rest or during prolonged steady state exercise occurs via aerobic metabolism – the breakdown of carbohydrate and fat in the presence of oxygen. But, this process is rather slow, and cannot meet the demands of high intensity exercise, such as a 100 m sprint where the body requires energy very rapidly. The body has therefore adapted several ways in which to resynthesise ATP to ensure a continuous supply of energy.

There are three basic **pathways** or **energy systems** which govern the replenishment of ATP and therefore energy supply. Which system operates is largely dependent upon how immediate the energy is required, how intense the activity, and whether or not oxygen is present. The three energy systems are:

1 the alactic or ATP-PC system
2 the lactic acid system
3 the aerobic system.

The alactic/ATP-PC system

This is the first of the anaerobic pathways, implying that oxygen is not directly used. This pathway involves the rapid regeneration of ATP through another energy rich compound existing in the muscles, named creatine phosphate (also known as phosphocreatine, PC). Unlike ATP, the energy derived from the breakdown of phosphocreatine is not directly used for muscle contraction, but instead rebuilds ATP to maintain a constant supply of energy.

Once ATP has been broken down to give adenosine diphosphate, a 'free' phosphate and energy which is used for muscular work, it must be resynthesised for further use.

Since ATP resynthesis requires energy itself, phosphocreatine is broken down almost simultaneously to provide the energy for ATP resynthesis; ie, by using this energy to rejoin the free phosphate back on to ADP to once again form ATP.

Features of the system

The most important feature of this system is the speed and immediacy that ATP can be resynthesised through PC. This system is therefore used during the initial stages of very intense muscular activity, such as sprinting, throwing, jumping, or indeed to provide the energy to start exercising after rest.

The main problem with this system however, is that like ATP, PC is very limited within the muscle (although there is approximately four times the amount of PC than ATP), and its levels fall as it is used to replenish the depleted ATP. Fatigue occurs when phosphocreatine levels fall significantly and they can no longer sustain ATP resynthesis. This usually occurs after 8–10 seconds of maximum effort, such as that which occurs in a flat out 100 m sprint.

Since the resynthesis of phosphocreatine also requires energy (using energy from ATP again), it can only be replenished when there is sufficient energy available in the body; this is usually through the aerobic pathway or during recovery once exercise has stopped.

If exercise continues after the 8–10 second threshold of the ATP-PC system, the muscles must rely on other sources of energy available for ATP resynthesis.

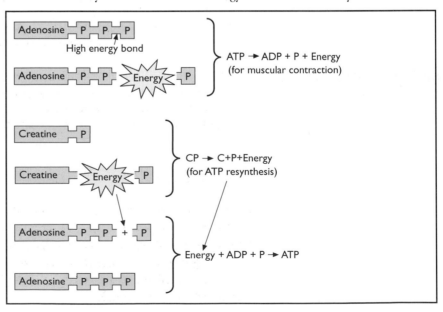

Fig. 5.3 ATP RESYNTHESIS VIA THE ATP-PC SYSTEM

Data collection

The parameters of this task would be:

- **Mark out a 100 m track.**
- **Position a student with a stopwatch at *each* 10 m interval.**
- **A starter will start the 100 m sprinter by waving his/her arm.**
- **At this point all the timers start their stopwatches.**
- **As the sprinter passes each 10 m interval, the timer should stop the stopwatches, keeping the time on the display until it has been written down and recorded.**

We now have our primary data which can now be used and recorded in table 5.1.

Graph of distance against time

1 **Plot a graph of distance (Y axis) against time (X axis) – second column of table 5.2.**
2 **Mark on your graph any straight (or almost straight) portions – note that when drawing a line through your graph points *do not* connect up the points but draw a smooth curve or line which best fits the motion that is represented.**
3 **Mark on your graph any obviously curved portions.**
4 **Write a brief description of what you understand may be happening during the straight and curved bits of the graph.**
5 **If you know how to, work out the slope (gradient) of the graph at 1.0 and 5.0 seconds after the start. What do these values tell you about the action of the runner?**

Computation of speed of runner

1 **Using the information that** $speed = \dfrac{distance\ moved}{time\ taken}$,

using a calculator calculate the speeds of the runner at successive 10 m intervals. Record this value in the second column of table 5.1. (Remember that the distance moved is always 10 m and the time taken is the time recorded in the third column of table 5.2.)
2 **Now work out the average time at which this speed was taken by for example, for the 10–20 section of the table, working out a time half way between the 10 m time and the 20 m time. This then should be done for all sections of the run, and entered in column 3 of table 5.1.**

Analysis of speed and energy production

1 **At what point did the athlete start to slow down?**
2 **Account for this slowing down.**
3 **Explain the process of energy production through the run.**

The lactic acid pathway

Once phosphocreatine has been depleted within the muscle, ATP must be resynthesised from another substance – **glycogen**. Carbohydrate is eaten in the form of sugar or starch and is stored in the muscles and the liver as glycogen.

Before glycogen or glucose can be used to provide energy for ATP resynthesis, it must be converted to the compound glucose-6-phosphate; a process which in itself requires one molecule of ATP.

Table 5.1   Speed against time for the runner

SECTION OF RACE	SPEED FOR THE SECTION MS^{-1}	TIME AT THE MIDDLE OF THE SECTION/S
0–10 m		
10–20 m		
20–30 m		
30–40 m		
40–50 m		
50–60 m		
60–70 m		
70–80 m		
80–90 m		
90–100 m		

Table 5.2   Times at 10 m intervals during the run

DISTANCE MOVED/M	TIME AT THIS POINT/S	TIME FOR PREVIOUS 10 M
0	0.0	
10		
20		
30		
40		
50		
60		
70		
80		
90		
100		

The degradation or breaking down of a glucose molecule to liberate energy is known as **glycolysis**, and since the initial stages of the process are performed in the absence of oxygen, it has become technically known as **anaerobic glycolysis**.

Once glycogen has been converted to glucose-6-phosphate, glycolysis can begin. Glycolytic enzymes work on breaking down the glucose molecule in a series of reactions (12 in total) in the cytoplasm of the cell. Glucose-6-phosphate is downgraded to form pyruvic acid, which in the absence of oxygen is converted to lactic acid. This process frees sufficient energy to resynthesise three moles of ATP, but this process uses up energy, so a net gain of 2ATP results:

a) $C_6H_{12}O_6 \rightarrow 2C_3H_6O_3 + \text{Energy}$
b) $\text{Energy} + 2P + 2ADP \rightarrow 2ATP$

Features of the system

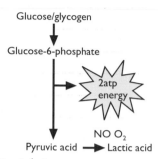

Fig. 5.4 A summary of anaerobic glycolisis (the lactic acid system)

The lactic acid system only frees a relatively small amount of energy from the glycogen molecule (approximately 5%), as the lactic acid produced inhibits further glycogen breakdown. Lactic acid levels may increase from 1 mmol/kg muscle at rest to 25 mmol/kg muscle during intense exercise.

This system does however release energy relatively quickly and is therefore responsible for supplying ATP in high intensity, short term exercise such as a 400 m run or a 100 m swim.

Although the lactic acid system is used between 10 seconds and three minutes, it peaks in those events lasting about one minute. It also comes into play at the end of aerobic events when the intensity increases, as it does during the sprint finish of a 10,000 m race.

To see how the remaining 95% of energy is released from the glucose molecule, we must look at the aerobic system.

Fig. 5.5 A 400 m hurdler will be working predominantly in the lactic acid system

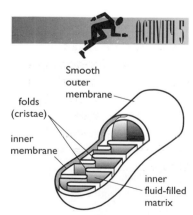

ACTIVITY 5

- **Run 400 m as fast as you can.**
- **At what point did your legs start feeling tired?**
- **Account for this onset of fatigue.**

The aerobic system

As the name suggests, this energy system differs from the previous two, as it requires the presence of oxygen. It takes approximately three minutes to extract the remaining 95% of energy from the glucose molecule, and therefore the aerobic system has a tremendous energy yield (18 times greater than the anaerobic processes).

Fig. 5.6a (a) A mitochondraan

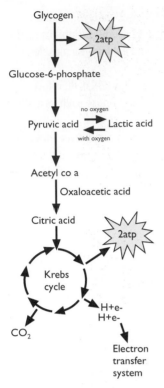

Fig. 5.6b (B) THE KREBS CYCLE

The initial stages of the aerobic process are similar to those of the lactic acid system, except that the fate of pyruvic acid changes when oxygen becomes available. Pyruvic acid is converted to lactic acid in the absence of oxygen, which has a fatiguing effect upon the muscles. In the presence of oxygen, however, pyruvic acid is converted into a compound called acetyl-coenzyme-A, which is further converted to oxaloacetic acid and finally citric acid before it enters the **krebs cycle**.

Under these aerobic conditions, the glucose molecule is broken down further in special powerhouses or factories existing in the muscle cell, known as **mitochondria**. These lie adjacent to the myofibrils and exist throughout the sarcoplasm. Slow twitch fibres possess a greater number of mitochondria than fast twitch fibres, to ensure a continuous supply of energy over a long period of time.

The krebs cycle

Once formed, citric acid enters the krebs cycle in the matrix of the mitochondria, where it is subject to a series of chemical reactions.

1   Citric acid is *oxidised* hydrogen is removed from the compound.
2   As a result, carbon and oxygen are left; they combine to produce carbon dioxide which is eliminated via the lungs.
3   In addition energy sufficient to resynthesise 2ATP is released.

During the krebs cycle process, the glucose molecule has been downgraded to release hydrogen and carbon dioxide. The carbon dioxide is eliminated via the lungs, but what happens to the hydrogen? It is in fact taken to the **electron transport system** (respiratory chain via hydrogen carriers NAD and FAD – see below), which is the final stage of the aerobic pathway and where most of the energy is produced for ATP resynthesis.

The electron transport system

The hydrogen given off at the krebs cycle is carried to the electron transport system by hydrogen carriers (NAD and FAD). In doing so, the hydrogen atom is split into hydrogen ions (H+) and electrons (e−). This occurs in the cristae of the mitochondria. The hydrogen ions (H+) combine with oxygen to form water which is used in various ways in the body, while the hydrogen electrons (e−) provide the energy to resynthesise ATP.

The amount of ATP resynthesised in the electron transfer chain is 34ATP. Each pair of hydrogen electrons provide sufficient energy to resynthesise two or three molecules of ATP, depending upon their carriers ($NADH_2$ provides 3ATP, while $FADH_2$ generates 2ATP). In total, 12 pairs enter the electron transfer chain; 10 via NAD carriers, and 2 through FAD carriers. The total yield is therefore 34ATP:

$$(10 \times 3) + (2 \times 2) = 34$$

Using this figure, it can be shown that the total downgrading of one molecule of glycogen can provide enough energy to resynthesise **38**ATP:

- **2** during anaerobic glycolysis
- **2** during the krebs cycle
- **34** during the electron transfer chain.

Because of the vast energy supply gained through aerobic metabolism, this system is mainly used in the endurance based activities where energy is required over a long period, as well as supplying the energy required by the body at rest.

Fig. 5.7 A CYCLIST WILL WORK PREDOMINANTLY IN
HIS/HER AEROBIC SYSTEM

1 **State and explain the process of energy production during a 10,000 m run. Give precise details of energy systems used at various stages of the run.**
2 **Construct a graph to illustrate the food fuels used against time in this event.**

Complete table 5.3, giving the predominant energy system used for the following activities.

Energy systems and training

Table 5.3   PREDOMINANT ENERGY SYSTEMS

ACTIVITY	ENERGY SYSTEM USED	FUEL DURATION	APPROXIMATE
a gymnastic vault			
a 100 m butterfly swim			
throwing a cricket ball			
a squash rally			
a steady 5 mile run			
running a marathon			

Table 5.4 TRAINING: PRINCIPLES AND PRACTICE

ENERGY SYSTEM USED	ENDURANCE	TIME IN USE	EXAMPLES	TRAINING AIMED AT	EXAMPLES
ATP-PC	speed or power	3–8 sec	• 100 m • tennis serve • badminton smash • weight lifting • fast sprints	increasing stores of ATP-PC increasing size of specific muscles	• repetition sprints • acceleration sprints • short sprint interval training • run in weighted belts • running up hills • running up stairs • high weight/few reps
lactic acid	local muscular endurance anaerobic	10 s–3 mins peaks at 1 min	• 400 m run • 'kick' phase in etc). 1,500 m • full court press in basketball • canoeing	overloading the system, causing large amounts of lactic acid to be produced. increasing lactate tolerance. increase rate of lactate removal.	• repeated bouts of intense exercise (eg, run, swim, etc) • short recovery • work relief • programmes should last several months
aerobic	aerobic endurance	excess of 3 mins	long distance running team games 5,000 m marathon	• increasing aerobic energy stores of: a) muscle glycogen b) triglycerides • mitochondria • enzyme capacity • increasing myoglobin	• long duration training – up to two hours • swimming • long distance running • cycling • little rest

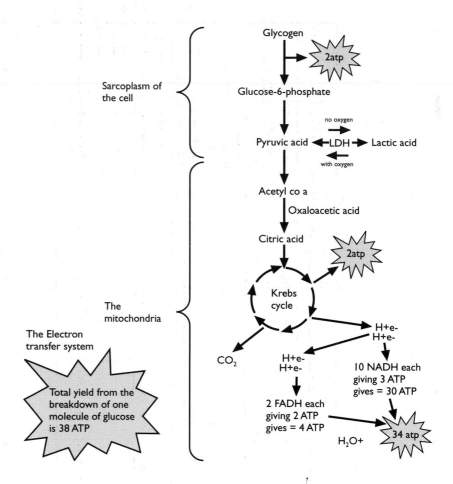

Fig. 5.8 The complete breakdown of glycogen into carbon dioxide, water and energy

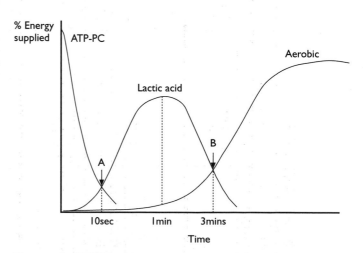

A = ATP - PC - LA THRESHOLD
The point at which ATP-PC energy system is exhausted and Lactic Acid system prevails

B = LA - O₂ THRESHOLD
The point at which Lactic Acid system is exhausted and the Aerobic system takes over

Fig. 5.9   Energy supplied against time

Table 5.5   MAJOR CHARACTERISITICS OF MUSCLE ENERGY SYSTEMS (*Source: Williams, 1989*)

	ATP-CP	LACTIC ACID	AEROBIC (CARBOHYDRATE)	AEROBIC (FAT)
main energy source	ATP, CP	muscle glycogen	muscle glycogen	muscle fats fatty acids
exercise intensity	highest	high	lower	lowest
rate of ATP production	highest	high	lower	lowest
power production	highest	high	lower	lowest
capacity for total ATP production	lowest	low	high	highest
endurance capacity	lowest	low	high	highest
oxygen needed	no	no	yes	yes
anaerobic/aerobic	anaerobic	anaerobic	aerobic	aerobic
characteristic track event	100 m sprint	800 m run	5–42 km run	ultramarathon
time factor at maximal use	1 to 10 sec	30 to 120 sec	more than 5 mins	hours

Food fuels used for ATP resynthesis

Food is the basic source of energy for cellular activity in the human body. It is ingested, digested, absorbed and stored in the form of various nutrients, which can then be used to resynthesise Adenosine Triphosphate.

The main energy providing nutrients include:

1 **Carbohydrates** which are stored in the body as glycogen.
2 **Fats** which are broken down to provide energy.
3 **Proteins** or amino acids which can be utilised for energy once converted to glucose.

Carbohydrates

As shown via the aerobic system, one molecule of glycogen can resynthesise up to 38 moles of ATP, given its complete downgrading.

Carbohydrate occurs in the body as glycogen or glucose. Some glucose is available in the blood, but this is rarely used for muscle contraction. It is more widely used to supply the brain and energy requirements of the nervous system.

Energy for muscular contraction stems from the muscle and liver glycogen.

Table 5.6   A RECOMMENDED CARBOHYDRATE LOADING REGIMEN (*Source: Williams, 1989*)

day 1	moderately long exercise bout (should not be exhaustive)
day 2	mixed diet; moderate carbohydrate intake; tapering exercise
day 3	mixed diet; moderate carbohydrate intake; tapering exercise
day 4	mixed diet; moderate carbohydrate intake; tapering exercise
day 5	high-carbohydrate diet; tapering exercise
day 6	high-carbohydrate diet; tapering exercise or rest
day 7	high-carbohydrate diet; tapering exercise or rest
day 8	competition

note   the moderate carbohydrate intake should approximate 200 to 300 g of carbohydrate per day; the high carbohydrate intake should approximate 500 to 600 g of carbohydrate per day

However, these stores are limited – the human body can only store approximately 80 g of glycogen in the liver and approximately 15 g of glycogen per kilogram of muscle in the muscle tissue. This provides a substantial amount of energy, sufficient to fuel a 10 mile run. By far the most abundant source of energy in the body is stored as fat.

Fat

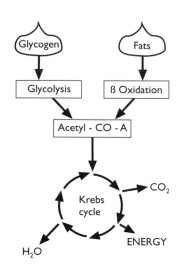

Fig. 5.10 BREAKDOWN OF A FAT MOLECULE

Fat is also a valuable source of energy and takes several forms in the body. The main energy source derived from fat is triglycerides. Before it can be used to liberate energy, however, stored triglyceride must be converted to free fatty acids (FFA). The transport of free fatty acids to the muscle fibres is slow, and the breakdown requires a greater amount of oxygen than that required to breakdown glycogen. This puts added stress upon the oxygen transport and delivery system, hence glycogen is the preferred source, particularly when there is a lack of oxygen available.

During the complete breakdown of a fat molecule, the free fatty acids must go through a process of Beta (β) oxidation before it enters the krebs cycle. It can now follow the same path as glycogen metabolism.

During endurance exercise, such as a marathon run, the body will have to use a mixture of carbohydrate and fats. At the beginning of the race the athlete will be predominantly using glycogen, but since free fatty acids constitute the preferred fuel under these conditions, the quicker the athlete can introduce fat as a source of fuel, the greater capacity of the body to conserve glycogen for later in the race. The body cannot use fat alone and the athlete must use glycogen sparingly throughout the race so that s/he avoids 'hitting the wall'. This is the stage where the body has depleted all glycogen reserves.

Similarly, hypoglycaemia occurs when stored liver glycogen is depleted and is unable to sustain blood glucose levels. This is also more likely to occur in endurance based events such as the marathon or a cycling tour. This condition is more readily remedied by ingesting sugary drinks as soon as possible; these will rapidly increase blood sugar levels and energy supply to the brain.

One of the major effects of training is an increased reliance on fatty acids for ATP production during prolonged exercise. This is largely due to an increase in the number of mitochondria (those factories for aerobic energy production).

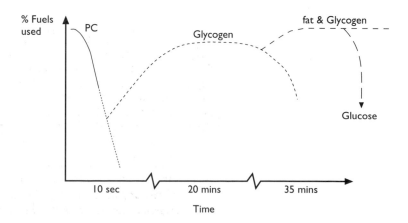

Fig. 5.11 FOOD FUELS SUPPLIED AGAINST TIME

Protein   Protein is the third of the energy-providing nutrients. It is not as significant as the other two energy providers, supplying approximately 5–10% of total energy, and is mainly used when glycogen stores in the body are low.

Typically, protein provides the building blocks for muscle growth and repair, and this is its primary function. By using protein as an energy source, we may be detracting it from its main purpose and cause little muscle adaptation. It is much more advisable to keep glycogen stores replenished by following a high carbohydrate diet.

Further reading

Clegg, *Exercise Physiology* (Feltham Press, 1996)

Davis, Bull, Roscoe and Roscoe, *Physical Education and the Study of Sport* (Wolfe Medical Publishers, 1991)

Fox, *Sports Physiology*

Katch and Mcardle, *Nutrition, Weight Control and Exercise* (Lea and Febiger, 1988)

Seeley, Stephens and Tate, *Anatomy and Physiology* (Mosby Year Book Inc., 1992)

Sharkey, *Physiology of Fitness* (Human Kinetics, 1990)

Wilmore and Costill, *Physiology of Sport and Exercise* (Human Kinetics, 1994)

Summary

- Energy is the capacity to perform work.
- All energy required within the body is directly provided by a high energy compound called Adenosine Triphosphate, which is present in all muscle cells.
- The energy required to resynthesise ATP comes from the breakdown of food and other chemicals within the body.
- The ATP-PC or alactic system is the energy system used for extremely short bursts of high intensity exercise – up to 10 secs of activity. It is an anaerobic pathway.
- The Lactic acid system is another anaerobic system. This system uses energy from the breakdown of glycogen to resynthesise 2ATP. This energy system is predominantly used for activities lasting 1–3 mins in duration.
- The aerobic system is the most efficient means of providing energy to resynthesise ATP. With oxygen the glucose molecule can produce a total gain of 38ATP. The krebs cycle occurs in the matrix of the mitochondria and removed hydrogen and releases carbon dioxide. Sufficient energy to resynthesise 2ATP is also released at this stage. Further breakdown of the glucose molecule takes place in the cristae of the mitochondria via the electron transport system, where sufficient energy to resynthesise 34ATP molecules is released.
- The mitochondrion is the powerhouse of the muscle cell and is where all energy is supplied aerobically within the body.
- The main energy providing nutrients are glycogen, fats and proteins. For endurance based events the body relies upon fats and glycogen, whilst for shorter activities the body will rely solely on glycogen.

chapter 6

Fatigue and Recovery

This chapter is a natural successor from the energy systems. It examines:
- the causes of fatigue
- the relationships between metabolic by-products and fatigue (including a detailed study of the effects of lactic acid)
- how the athlete can recover from fatigue.

The concepts of oxygen deficit and debt will be studied, along with ways in which the coach and athlete can speed up the recovery process, including training.

The recovery process following exercise

Why is it that a sprinter breathes and pants so deeply after a race, even though they may only have run 100 metres? Compare this to a 400 m runner or even a marathon runner. What conclusions can you draw about the pattern of recovery?

Whatever the prior exercise, rapid and deep breathing is commonplace during recovery. It happens because recovery from exercise is dependent upon oxygen, and the increased breathing rate helps to increase oxygen consumption. The oxygen utilised during this recovery period is used to rebuild muscular stores of ATP and PC that may have been depleted, and to remove any lactic acid that may have accumulated in the muscle during the preceding exercise.

The oxygen debt

This is sometimes referred to as **EPOC**: Excess Post-exercise Oxygen Consumption.

The oxygen **debt** can be defined as the amount of oxygen consumed during recovery above that which normally would have been consumed at rest in the same period of time. An oxygen debt will accrue when the body has undertaken some form of exercise anaerobically. This will occur at quite intense levels of exercise, lasting up to three minutes or until the anaerobic threshold has been exceeded (see p 92 for further discussion). The debt can be measured by analysing oxygen consumption pre- and post-exercise, or more simply by examining heart rate scores before and after exercise.

The oxygen debt is used to compensate for the oxygen **deficit**. This deficit is the amount of extra oxygen required to complete the exercise if all the energy could have been supplied aerobically. As oxygen is not available for approximately the first three minutes of exercise, a deficit will always accrue.

The oxygen debt does not always equal the oxygen deficit, because during recovery the oxygen debt must also:

- supply oxygen to provide energy for restoration of the oxymyoglobin link
- supply energy for the increased cardiac and respiratory rates that remain elevated during the recovery phase.

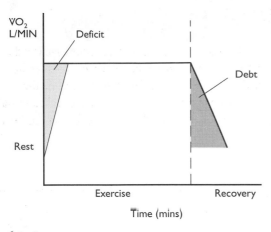

Fig. 6.1 OXYGEN DEFICIT AND DEBT DURING LOW INTENSITY (SUB-MAXIMAL) EXERCISE

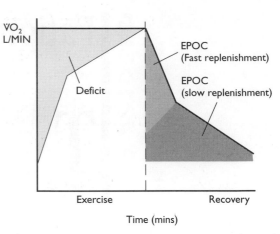

Fig. 6.2 OXYGEN DEFICIT AND DEBT DURING HIGH INTENSITY (MAXIMAL) EXERCISE

Consequently the amount of oxygen consumed during the oxygen debt is greater than that which might have been consumed during the oxygen deficit.

Typically the oxygen debt consists of two components:

1 the **alactacid** debt
2 the **lactacid** debt

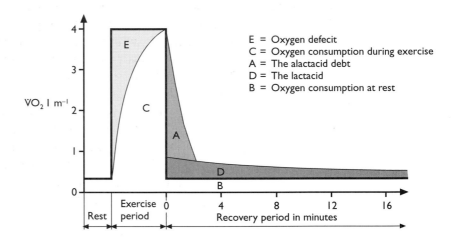

E = Oxygen defecit
C = Oxygen consumption during exercise
A = The alactacid debt
D = The lactacid
B = Oxygen consumption at rest

Fig. 6.3 OXYGEN CONSUMPTION DURING EXERCISE AND RECOVERY

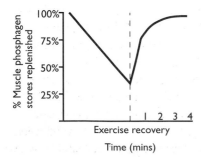

Fig. 6.4 MUSCLE PHOSPHAGEN REPLENISHMENT FOLLOWING EXERCISE

The alactacid debt

The alactacid debt is the first component of the oxygen debt that is replenished. As the name suggests, it is the volume of oxygen required to restore phosphagens used in the **alactic energy system** – namely phosphocreatine. It takes a fairly short period of time to resynthesise phosphocreatine: approximately 2–3 minutes, in which time 2–3 litres of oxygen can be consumed and used to provide the energy for this resynthesis.

This assumes that following a bout of intense work, such as a maximum lift, where the predominant energy system used is the alactic energy system, the body should be recovered sufficiently after three minutes of rest to repeat the exercise.

The lactacid debt

The lactacid debt is the volume of oxygen consumed used to remove lactic acid from the muscles, which has accumulated during anaerobic work. Most of the lactic acid is removed into the blood or oxidised in the mitochondria via the aerobic system with oxygen from this component, to give carbon dioxide and water. Lactic acid is also converted into muscle and liver glycogen, glucose and protein – see table 6.1.

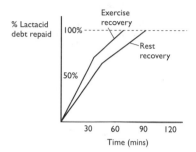

% Lactacid debt repaid

Note that repayment of the lactacid debt can be accelerated by following a period of exercise recovery (cool down) following exercise

Fig. 6.5 REPAYMENT OF THE LACTACID OXYGEN DEBT DURING REST RECOVERY AND EXERCISE RECOVERY

Table 6.1   THE FATE OF LACTIC ACID

conversion into carbon dioxide and water	65%
conversion into glycogen	20%
conversion into protein	10%
conversion into glucose	5%

The process of lactic acid removal takes approximately one hour, but this can be accelerated by undertaking a cool down or some form of exercise recovery, which ensures a rapid and continuous supply of oxygen to the muscles.

Removing lactic acid

Removal of lactic acid also relies upon the buffering capacity of the body, which weakens the effect of lactic acid. The blood is fairly efficient at buffering lactic acid due to the hydrogen carbonate ion produced by the kidneys; this absorbs the lactate and forms carbonic acid, which is eventually degraded to form carbon dioxide and water, both of which are eliminated via the lungs. Indeed, some athletes seek to improve their buffering capacity by 'soda loading' which involves drinking sodium bicarbonate several minutes before an event. Although evidence suggests that performance may be improved through this practice, side effects include vomiting and diarrhoea.

Training with small amounts of lactic acid in the system may improve the resistance and buffering capacity of the body. By improving blood flow to the muscle, the body becomes more efficient at moving lactic acid from the muscle into the blood, which can degrade it and prevent the associated fatiguing effects. For a fuller explanation of exactly how training can improve the buffering capacity of the body, see Chapter 8.

The effect of lactic acid accumulation

Even though the blood will always contain a small amount of lactic acid even at rest (approximately 1–2 millimoles/litre of blood), during high intensity work (such as a 400 m run) this may increase ten fold to 20 millimoles/litre of blood. The following discussion examines just what the effects of such an increase have on the performer.

During high intensity exercise, muscle fatigue occurs at a pH of 6.4 and noticeably affects muscle function. Nobody knows exactly how such acidity causes fatigue, but it is thought that protons disassociate from lactic acid and associate with glycolytic enzymes, thus making them acidic. In this state, the enzymes lose their catalytic ability and energy production through glycolysis ceases. Muscle contraction may also be impaired, as high acidity may inhibit the transmission of neural impulses to the contractile elements of the muscle and obstruct the contraction process. This is particularly true of very high intensity exercise lasting between 30–120 seconds.

Measurement of lactic acid

Lactic acid and lactate, usually used interchangeably, are not actually the same substance:

- Lactate is a *product* of lactic acid which splits to give lactate molecules and hydrogen ions.

Since blood lactate measurement is much easier than taking muscle biopsies, it is the most widely used method of assessing lactic acid accumulation.

Reasons for measuring lactic acid

The measurement of lactic acid has several practical uses to the coach and athlete:

1 It can determine and assess training intensities to ensure the athlete is working at suitable levels and is producing energy by the most effective energy system for their activity.
2 The data provides information on the athlete's current work capacity and fitness levels.
3 The data also assesses the effectiveness of the current training regime.
4 The principal use of lactate measurements in the laboratory is to establish the anaerobic threshold or point of 'Onset Blood Lactate Accumulation', which gives an indication of endurance capacities. (OBLA).

Onset Blood Lactate Accumulation (OBLA)

The concept of OBLA or anaerobic threshold can be explained by using the following example:

- If a person takes part in a task of progressively increasing intensity, such as the multistage fitness test, a point is reached where energy can no longer be sustained completely by aerobic means.
- If intensity increases further, the deficit of energy requirements must be met by anaerobic metabolism.
- By doing so, blood lactate concentration rises, until such a point is reached where lactate concentration is sufficiently high to cause complete muscle fatigue.
- The point at which lactic acid begins to accumulate in the muscles is the point of onset of blood lactate accumulation or anaerobic threshold, and is measured as a percentage of $\dot{V}O_2$ max reached before this rise in acidity (see Chapter 7 for further discussion).

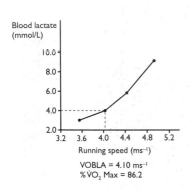

Running speed (ms^{-1})
VOBLA = 4.10 ms^{-1}
% $\dot{V}O_2$ Max = 86.2

	Running speed (ms^{-1})			
	3.58	4.02	4.47	4.92
HLa (mmol/L)	2.9	3.7	5.7	9.1
HR (bpm)	166	179	187	197

The test shows that this squash player is using a large percentage of his $\dot{V}O_2$ max, resulting in a more successful endurance performance

Fig. 6.6 THE OBLA OF A NATIONAL U19 SQUASH CHAMPION

1 **Take and record your resting pulse rate.**
2 **Complete a 400 m run at maximum pace.**
3 **Record your pulse for a 10 second count every minute after the race, until your heart rate returns to its original level.**
4 **Convert your heart rate values into beats per minute by multiplying your results by six.**
5 **Plot a graph depicting your results. Describe and explain the pattern of recovery.**

Fig. 6.7 AN 800 M RUNNER WILL ACCRUE
A LARGE LACTACID DEBT COMPONENT

Other factors affecting recovery

It was previously mentioned that some oxygen consumed during the oxygen debt may not be attributed to oxygen deficit which has accrued during exercise. One such factor is the restoration of the **oxy-myoglobin link**, so that oxygen can once again be transported to the mitochondria for energy provision.

Through exercise, oxygen is disassociated from myoglobin to enable aerobic glycolysis and therefore aerobic energy supply. During recovery the oxygen must be reassociated with myoglobin. To ensure a continuous supply of energy this replenishment occurs very rapidly, and therefore forms part of the alactacid debt.

Restorating muscle glycogen stores

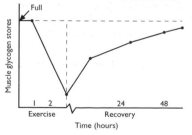

During exercise glycogen may have been depleted in order to provide energy. The repletion of muscle glycogen is a long process and can take up to 48 hours, depending upon the duration and intensity of the preceding exercise.

It is now widely agreed that refuelling with a high carbohydrate diet within one hour of exercise will speed up the recovery process. The energy for glycogen replenishment is made available from the aerobic pathway.

Note that pre-exercise glycogen stores may not be gaine
the marathon runner may have followed a programme of
glycogen loading prior to the event

Fig. 6.8 RESTORATION OF MUSCLE
GLYCOGEN STORES FOLLOWING A MARATHON

1 What may be responsible for the decreased effect of lactic acid accumulation during exercise, following a training regime?
2 Immediately following high intensity exercise what happens to the following:

• **Blood and muscle pH**
• **Blood lactate levels**

3 What is meant by 'buffering'? How can a knowledge of this help the performer and coach?
4 Outline the recovery patterns for:

• **A weight lifter who has just completed a maximum lift.**
• **A 400 m hurdler who has just achieved a personal best time.**
• **A cyclist completing a 50 km training ride.**

5 An athlete is to compete in two events at an athletic meeting: an 800 m run, followed by 1500 m run about one hour later. What advice would you give concerning recovery?

Summary

• The body requires oxygen to recover from exercise.
• An oxygen debt will accrue when some form of anaerobic exercise has taken place.
• Oxygen breathed in during the recovery period is known as the excess post exercise oxygen consumption.
• An oxygen debt can be defined as the amount of oxygen consumed during recovery above that which would normally have been consumed at rest during the same period of time.
• The oxygen deficit is the amount of oxygen that an anaerobic task would require if the task could be undertaken aerobically.
• An oxygen debt consists of two components, the alactacid debt and the lactacid debt.
• The alactacid debt is the oxygen consumed to resynthesise ATP and PC and takes approximately 2–3 minutes.
• The lactacid debt is the oxygen consumed to remove lactic acid from the muscles.
• Lactic acid can be broken down to form carbon dioxide and water, converted to muscle and liver glycogen, converted into protein, and converted into glucose.
• Effective removal of lactic acid relies upon the buffering capacity of the muscle and blood.
• Some oxygen consumed during the recovery period will be used to reinstate the oxymyoglobin link.
• Glycogen depletion through exercise may take up to 48 hours to restore.

chapter 7

Physical Fitness

S ports physiology is the study of how the body's structures and functions adapt in response to exercise, and in particular how training can enhance the athlete's performance.

Fundamental to sports physiology is a knowledge of fitness and training. This chapter explores the whole realm of fitness, and in particular, the complexities involved in defining fitness. A detailed investigation into the components of fitness and fitness testing is the main crux of this chapter, using information gathered from my own research and case studies from the fitness testing laboratory at Lilleshall National Sports Centre. This provides a complete guide to fitness measurement and assessment.

This chapter will form an excellent introduction to Chapter 8, training.

Fitness considerations in physical activity

The term 'fitness' is difficult to define, since it means many different things to different people. For example one individual may see themselves as being 'fit' if they can run for the bus without getting too out of breath, whereas a physically active person may seek a quick heart rate recovery as a measure of fitness, following a distance run. However in the search for an acceptable definition that encompasses most individuals, Dick (1989) has defined fitness as

'... the successful adaptation to the stressors of one's lifestyle ...'

This suggests therefore that all of us must look closely at the stressors of our everyday activities, and see how well we cope with those stressors if we are to gauge our fitness levels satisfactorily.

When considering physical activity however, it would not be acceptable to rely solely upon this definition, since the fitness requirements of various activities differ dramatically from each other. We therefore need to be a little more specific in our definitions. For example: the different fitness requirements of a 100 m sprint and a marathon run:

1 The sprint requires a tremendous amount of power, strength and speed in order to travel a relatively short distance in the quickest time possible. It also requires the muscles to work in the absence of oxygen and as such the composition of the muscle tissue will need to be specialised to accommodate this.
2 The marathon run requires the body to work for an extended period of time, and therefore relies upon the endurance capabilities of the cardiovascular and muscular systems. Oxygen consumption is essential in this instance and similarly the body will have become adapted to take in, transport and utilise as much oxygen as possible during the run.

Fig. 7.1 A 100 M SPRINTER

The components of fitness

The components of fitness relate to the requirements of a given sporting activity, and can help to explain success or failure in sport.

A distinction can be made between components which are generally considered to be **health-related** (health benefits may be gained through improvements in these components), and those that are **skill-related**, although both will affect performance in sport.

Health-related factors are physiologically based and determine the ability of an individual to meet the physical demands of the activity; the skill-related factors are based upon the neuromuscular system and determine how successfully a person can perform a specific skill. Both are required in all activities, but the relative importance of each dimension may differ. For example, a person may be physically suited to tennis, possessing the necessary speed, endurance and strength requirements, but may not possess the hand-eye co-ordination needed to strike the ball successfully. In this instance the individual may be best advised to switch to an activity that requires less skill-related components.

Table 7.1   COMPONENTS OF FITNESS

HEALTH RELATED FACTORS	SKILL RELATED FACTORS
• strength	• agility
• speed	• balance
• cardio-respiratory endurance	• co-ordination
• muscular endurance	• reaction time
• flexibility	• power
• body composition	

Health-related components of fitness

Strength

– the maximum force that can be developed in a muscle or group of muscles during a single maximal contraction.

Strength is directly related to the cross-sectional area of the muscle tissue as well as the type of muscle fibre within the muscle. Fast twitch (white fibres) can generate greater forces than slow twitch (red fibres).

The optimum age to develop strength appears to be in the early to mid-twenties. As the body ages, less protein becomes available in the body for muscle growth, and the stress and anaerobic nature of strength training also makes it an inappropriate method of training during old age.

In this age of gender equality it is highly appropriate to dismiss the notion of a weaker sex. In fact, relative to cross-sectional area of pure muscle tissue, men and women are equal in terms of strength. It is the greater fat content of women and the higher testosterone levels in men that can create the difference in the cross-sectional area of muscles and therefore strength, to the advantage of males.

Fig. 7.2 A WEIGHT LIFTER – STRENGTH IS VITAL TO SUCCESSFUL PERFORMANCE

Speed

– the ability to put body parts into motion quickly, or the maximum rate that a person can move over a specific distance. Speed tends to be genetically determined due to the physiological make up of the muscle. Once again, fast twitch (F.T.G.) muscle fibres tend to be beneficial in activities where speed is essential. However the role of body mechanics and the efficiency of the body's lever systems are also integral in determining speed of the body or body part.

Cardio-respiratory endurance

– the ability to provide and sustain energy aerobically. It is dependent upon the ability of the cardiovascular system to transport and utilise oxygen during sustained exercise.

Muscular endurance

– the ability of a muscle or group of muscles to sustain repeated contractions against a resistance for an extended period of time. Slow twitch muscle fibres will ensure they receive a rich supply of blood to enable the most efficient production of aerobic energy.

Flexibility

– the range of movement possible at a joint. Flexibility is determined by the elasticity of ligaments and tendons, the strength of surrounding muscles and the shape of the articulating bones. Often the degree of movement is determined by the type of joint, since joints are designed either for stability or mobility. The knee joint for example has been designed with stability in mind. It is only truly capable of movement in one plane of direction (it is uniaxial), allowing flexion and extension of the lower leg. This is due to the intricate network of ligaments surrounding the joint, which restricts movement. The shoulder joint on the other hand allows movement in many planes (it is polyaxial) since fewer ligaments cross the joint. However, the free movement at the joint comes at a price, as the shoulder joint can become easily dislocated.

Body composition

– the component parts of the body in terms of the relative amounts of body fat compared to lean body mass. For an average 18-year-old, men range from 14–17% fat, while women range from 24–29%.

   The relative shape of the body or **somatotype** can also be mentioned at this point. Somatotyping is a method used to measure body shape. Three extremes exist:

1 **Endomorphy** – the relative fatness or pear-shapeness of the body.
2 **Mesomorphy** – the muscularity of the body.
3 **Ectomorphy** – the linearity or leanness of the body.

The characteristics of a performer's body can be categorised according to these somatotypes and plotted on the delta shaped graph.

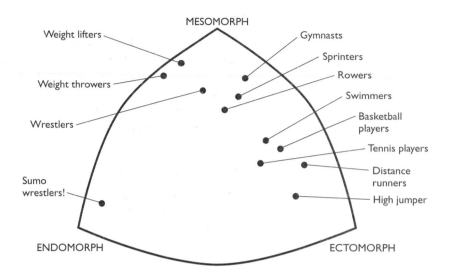

FIG. 7.3 SOMATOTYPING RELATES BODY
COMPOSITION TO SPORTING ACTIVITY

Skill-related components of fitness

Agility

– the ability to move and change direction and position of the body quickly and effectively while under control.

Balance

– the maintenance of the centre of mass over the base of support. This can be while the body is static or dynamic (moving).

Co-ordination

– the interaction of the motor and nervous systems and is the ability to perform motor tasks accurately.

FIG. 7.4 A GYMNAST ON A BEAM REQUIRES
BOTH STATIC AND DYNAMIC BALANCE

Table 7.2   COMPONENTS OF FITNESS FOR DIFFERENT ACTIVITIES

ACTIVITY	SPEED	STRENGTH	CARDIO-VASCULAR ENDURANCE	MUSCULAR ENDURANCE	FLEXIBILITY	POWER	REACTION TIME	AGILITY	BALANCE	COORDINATION	BODY COMPOSITION
swimming											
squash											
marathon											
tennis											
cycling											
rugby											
sprinting											
x-country skiing											
aerobics											
basketball											
judo											
gymnastics vault											
badminton											
netball											
cricket											

Reaction time

– the time taken to initiate a response to a given stimulus.

Power

– the amount of work done per unit of time; the product of strength and speed.

Complete table 7.2 by ticking one health-related and one skill-related component of fitness that you consider to be the most important for each activity listed.

Having established the various requirements and components of fitness of a given activity, an athlete must constantly assess and measure the components in order to gauge improvement.

The measurement and assessment of fitness

In order to measure fitness levels, a battery of recognised tests have been developed, which are easily administered and evaluated. These tests are outlined below.

Through testing it is possible to:

1 identify the strengths and weaknesses of the athlete
2 provide baseline data for monitoring performance
3 provide the basis for training prescriptions

4 assess the value of different types of training and help to modify training programmes
5 predict physiological and athletic potential
6 provide comparisons with previous tests and other elite performers in the same group
7 enhance motivation
8 form part of the educational process.

Measuring your fitness levels: complete the tests outlined below and record your results. Make sure you warm up thoroughly and perform the tests under the guidance of your teacher.

Strength

Strength can be measured with the use of dynamometers which give an objective measure of the force generated within various muscles or muscle groups. The easiest strength test to administer is using the Handgrip Dynamometer which measures grip strength generated by the muscles in the forearm; see fig 7.5.

Record the maximum reading from three attempts for both left and right hands. See Appendix 3 for grip strength norms.

Speed

The simplest measure of speed is a 30 m sprint. Mark out 30 m on a non-slip surface and sprint as hard as you can from a flying start over the course. Record the time taken. See Appendix 3 for 30 m sprint test ratings.

Cardiovascular endurance

Cardiovascular endurance can be assessed by measuring a person's $\dot{V}O_2$ max: the maximum amount of oxygen that an individual can take in, transport and utilise per minute (for a fuller explanation, see page 92). A simple prediction of $\dot{V}O_2$ max can be made through the NCF multistage fitness test. This is a progressive shuttle run test which means that it starts off easily and gets increasingly difficult. See Appendix 3 for test ratings.

Equipment

- 20 m track (or flat non slippery surface)
- NCF cassette tape
- Tape player
- Tape measure and marking cones

Follow the instructions given on the tape. Subjects are required to run the 20 m distance as many times as possible, keeping in time to the bleeps emitted from the tape. Each shuttle of 20 m should be timed so that the individual reaches the end line as the bleep is emitted.

The difficulty increases with each level attained, and speed of running will need to be increased accordingly. Continue to run as long as possible until you can no longer keep up with the bleeps set by the tape. If you fail to complete the 20 m shuttle before the bleep is emitted you should withdraw from the test, ensuring that the level and shuttle number attained has been recorded.

Fig. 7.5 The handgrip test

Muscular endurance

A test for muscular endurance will assess the ability of one muscle or muscle group to continue working repeatedly. A simple test to measure the endurance of the abdominal muscle group is the NCF abdominal conditioning test. See Appendix 3 for test ratings.

Equipment

- NCF abdominal conditioning tape
- Tape recorder
- Stopwatch
- Gym mat

Follow the instructions given on the tape. Subjects are required to perform as many sit ups as possible, keeping in time to the bleeps emitted from the tape. Get a partner to count the number of sit-ups completed correctly, and time the duration of the work period. Subjects should withdraw from the test when they can no longer keep in time to the bleeps, or when technique deteriorates noticeably.

Flexibility

The sit and reach test can be easily administered. It gives an indication of the flexibility of hamstrings and lower back. See Appendix 3 for test ratings.

Equipment

- Sit and reach box

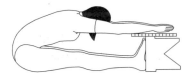

Fig. 7.6 THE SIT AND REACH TEST

Sit down on the floor with your legs out straight and feet flat against the box. Without bending your knees, bend forwards with arms outstretched and push the cursor as far down as possible and hold for two seconds. Record your score.

Body composition

Body fat is measured in a variety of ways:

1 Hydrostatic weighing considers water displacement when the body is submerged in water.
2 Biolectrical impedance is another popular objective measure whereby a small electrical current is passed through the body from wrist to ankle. As fat restricts the flow of the current, the greater the current needed the greater the percentage of body fat.
3 Skinfold measures using callipers: by far the simplest measure. On the left side of the body, take measures at the following sites:

- biceps
- triceps
- sub scapular
- supra iliac

Add the totals together in millimetres and record your results.

At this stage, you may wish to make some other anthropometrical measures such as length of bones and overall height, muscle girths or circumferences, and condyle measures at the joints.

As well as measuring these physical or health related factors, it is also possible to assess skill related components.

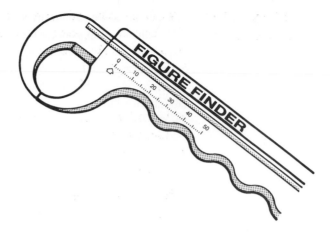

Fig. 7.7 SKINFOLD CALLIPERS

Agility

Agility is most commonly measured via the Illinois agility run. See Appendix 3 for test ratings.

Equipment

- tape measure
- cones
- stopwatch

Place four cones 3.3 m apart. Starting by lying flat on the floor, then run the course as fast as you can on the signal issued by a partner. Ask your partner to time you and record your results.

Reaction time

Although the most accurate measures of reaction time will involve the use of a computer programme, a simple test is the stick drop test. See Appendix 3 for test ratings.

Equipment

- A metre ruler

A partner holds a metre rule in front of you. Place your index finger and thumb either side of the 50 cm calibration without making contact with the ruler itself. Without warning the partner should release the ruler, and you must catch it with your finger and thumb as quickly as possible. Record the calibration at the point your index finger lies.

Power

Power can be measured with the help of a jump metre. See Appendix 3 for test ratings.

Equipment

- jump metre

Standing with your legs straight on the mat of the jump metre, pull the string taut. In one smooth movement, bend the knees and explode upwards, record the score. Repeat and take the highest score. If a jump metre is not available, the vertical jump test is similar.

The above fitness measures are well recognised and simple to administer which makes them very appropriate for this level of study. However, elite athletes may require greater objectivity in their results if they are to compare themselves accurately with other elite performers in their group. Specialised laboratories have therefore been established which dedicate themselves to sports testing. One such laboratory is the Human Performance Centre at Lilleshall; another is the National Sports Medicine Institute at St. Barts Hospital, and what follows is an example of some of the tests they now administer on the elite sports performer.

The anaerobic capacity test

This test is designed to assess each player's ability to exercise anaerobically without experiencing the effect of fatigue through lactic acid build up. The longer an individual is able to work flat out at high intensity, the greater their anaerobic capacity. See Appendix 3 for test ratings.

Each subject is required to perform a maximal 30-second bout of exercise (sprint) on a bicycle ergometer which has been specially linked to a micro computer. During the bout of exercise the computer records the peak power reached, which relates to the body's explosive power ability as well as the mean power. This is an indication of the body's ability to sustain high intensity effort. The percentage of fatigue sustained can also be recorded. Those subjects who are able to sustain and achieve high levels of power throughout the test are those with the greatest ability in anaerobic events.

OBLA test (Onset of Blood Lactate Accumulation)

The lactate threshold, or point of onset of blood lactate accumulation, is the point at which the body appears to convert to anaerobic energy production. Below the lactate threshold the body works aerobically and prolonged exercise can take place, with a blood lactate volume of 2–3 mmol per litre of blood. Exercise above the lactate threshold (which usually occurs at 4 mmol per litre of blood) can only usually be sustained for approximately one minute. (To highlight this, think of how your legs feel at the end of a flat out 400 m run!)

The test is performed in four stages where subjects are required to run at speeds of 8, 9, 10 and finally 11 miles per hour. At the end of each stage blood samples are taken by a small prick on the finger, and analysed for blood lactate. The point at which blood lactate rises significantly indicates the point of onset of blood lactate accumulation, and the running speed which corresponds to this is recorded. Improvements in endurance ability can be observed where lower lactate levels are recorded for the same intensity of exercise; this shows that the body has adapted to cope better with this intensity of exercise through buffering lactic acid.

Maximum oxygen uptake test ($\dot{V}O_2$ max test)

The multistage fitness test gives a reasonable prediction of $\dot{V}O_2$ max, but it *is* purely a prediction and not a truly objective measure of the volume of oxygen that the body can take in, transport and utilise.

There are a wealth of tests to achieve this objective measure, but the most accurate is gas analysis. Subjects are measured at progressively increasing intensities on one of many laboratory ergometers (treadmills, cycle or rowing machines tend to be the most popular), while breathing through respiratory apparatus which is linked to a computer. The computer analyses the relative concentrations of oxygen and carbon dioxide inspired and expired. Since the concentrations of these in the surrounding environment are known, it is fairly simple to calculate the amount of oxygen consumed and the amount of carbon dioxide produced over time.

The subject continues to work at increasingly higher work intensities, until such a time is reached when the body's oxygen consumption does not increase further with increasing workloads. At this point the subject's body is working at its aerobic limit, and any further increments in workload must be met through anaerobic means. This is the point of maximal oxygen uptake, and the amount of oxygen being consumed can now be recorded. $\dot{V}O_2$ max can be measured in absolute terms: ie, 1/min for non-weight bearing activities such as swimming, cycling and rowing, or relative to body weight in ml.kg.min^{-1} (millimetres of oxygen per kilogram of bodyweight per minute). The higher the value of $\dot{V}O_2$ max, the more efficient the body at exercising under aerobic conditions.

The results of the lactate threshold test and maximal oxygen uptake test can be used in conjunction, to determine the percentage of maximum oxygen uptake the subject uses when exercising at the point of lactate threshold (an individual will rarely be able to exercise a 100% of $\dot{V}O_2$ max). The higher the value, the better the subject will be able to sustain exercise at fairly high intensities for long periods of time without getting fatigued, since they can delay the onset and effects of lactic acid which can inhibit muscle action.

Haematology

Haematology is the study of blood and its component parts which can significantly affect our performance during exercise. The functions of blood are well documented in Chapter 5.

The first part of this test considers haemoglobin content at rest. This component transports oxygen from the lungs to the muscle site and other organs. Low haemoglobin levels can lead to premature fatigue as there is a limit to the oxygen carrying capabilities of the body. Low levels can easily be rectified by increasing the amount of iron consumed in the diet. Recommended normal values for males are 14.0–18.0 grammes per decilitre of blood.

This test involves taking a sample of blood via a simple thumb prick which is then analysed.

Haematocrit

Haematocrit measures the amount of fluid in the blood – ie, its current state of hydration, which concerns the proportion of solids (blood cells) to plasma in the blood. Normal haematocrit for males occur in the region of 42–45%. If blood haematocrit is too high, there may be too many red blood cells in the blood relative to plasma; as a result the blood viscosity increases which slows down the flow, and hinders oxygen transport to the muscles. This high value can also reflect that dehydration has occurred, which is obviously a problem in endurance events. Drinking plenty of fluids is essential to prevent performance from deteriorating and to keep the body in an adequate state of hydration.

Muscle power and strength

Muscle force can be tested by an isokinetic dynamometer linked to a computer. It measures muscle strength at different angles and speeds of contraction and can be linked to the speeds most appropriate to the athlete's event. By exerting a force against the dynamometer, muscle strength and power can be assessed.

See table 7.3 for each of the components of fitness; give a recognised test, a brief description of the test and how each test can be evaluated.

Table 7.3   TESTS FOR COMPONENTS OF FITNESS

FITNESS COMPONENT	RECOGNISED TEST	DESCRIPTION OF TEST	EVALUATION
aerobic fitness			
anaerobic fitness			
strength			
muscular endurance			
flexibility			
body composition			
speed			

Discuss the merits of fitness testing. Outline some tests you may use to assess an athlete's level of fitness and how you would evaluate them.

Validity of testing

When any type of testing is undertaken, it must be remembered that many things contribute to performance, and fitness tests are looking solely at one aspect. Other factors to be considered when testing include motivation and the testing environment – is the athlete really pushing themselves in the tests, particularly when some tests require the athlete to work to near exhaustion? – are the tests truly replicating the sporting environment accurately? In order to maximise the validity of a specific test, it may be necessary to repeat the test several times in order to minimise the possibility of human error.

Maximal oxygen uptake ($\dot{V}O_2$ max) and the anaerobic threshold

In the previous section we learnt how to measure an athlete's aerobic capacity, through testing their $\dot{V}O_2$ max. We are now going to look in detail at how maximal oxygen uptake can be specifically related to successful endurance performance. Maximal oxygen uptake can be defined as the maximal amount of oxygen that can be taken in, transported and consumed by the working muscles per minute. It is largely dependent upon the difference in oxygen content of inspired and expired air.

When exercise commences, the volume of oxygen increases sharply at first, and then plateau out into a steady state. This steady state in oxygen consumption represents a balance between the energy demands of the muscle and the amount of oxygen supplied to the muscle to meet these demands. At this steady state, a cyclist (for instance) should be able to continue exercising for a long period of time, theoretically until his energy stores are depleted. If the cyclist then comes up against a hill, oxygen consumption must increase in order to meet the increased energy demands (assuming the cyclist remains at the same speed).

Steady state may once again occur when energy demands are met by oxygen supply. If the cyclist subsequently comes up against a steeper hill, oxygen consumption will again need to increase until steady state is reached once again. If exercise intensity continues to increase in this manner, oxygen consumption will continue to increase, until such a point is reached where the body cannot consume any more oxygen – this point is known as the maximal oxygen uptake or $\dot{V}O_2$ max.

Once this point has been reached, if there is a subsequent increase in intensity (such as cycling up a steeper slope or increasing speed), then the body must meet the extra energy requirements through anaerobic means. This causes severe problems to the cyclist or athlete since anaerobic respiration causes an onset of lactic acid and ultimately fatigue. The only way that this can be prevented is by reducing the intensity of the exercise so oxygen consumption can fall below the point of $\dot{V}O_2$ max. However this may decrease all chance of a successful performance.

The point at which lactic acid starts to accumulate in the body is known as the anaerobic threshold, or onset of blood lactate accumulation (OBLA). It is measured as the percentage of $\dot{V}O_2$ max reached before lactic acid starts to accumulate.

$$\%\dot{V}O_2 \text{ max utilised} = \frac{\dot{V}O_2 \text{ (amount of } O_2 \text{ used)}}{\dot{V}O_2 \text{ max (maximum potential)}}$$

For example:

$$\dot{V}O_2 \text{ used} = 30 \text{ ml/kg/min} = 30$$
$$\dot{V}O_2 \text{ max} = 60 \text{ ml/kg/min} = 60 = 50\% \text{ of } \dot{V}O_2 \text{ max used}$$

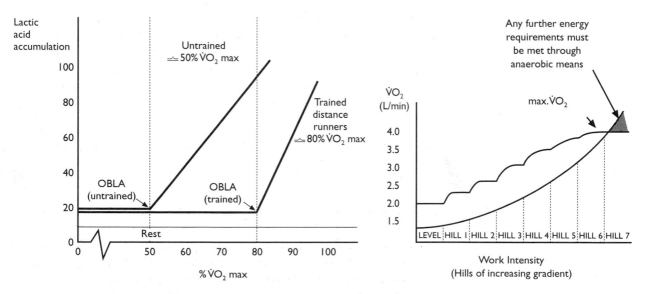

With appropriate endurance training the anaerobic threshold (OBLA) can be heightened, so that a greater amount of aerobic capacity can be utilised. Aerobic performance therefore improves

Fig. 7.8a A COMPARISON OF THE ANAEROBIC THRESHOLD (OBLA) BETWEEN THE TRAINED AND UNTRAINED

Fig. 7.8b OXYGEN CONSUMPTION DURING A CYCLE RIDE OF PROGRESSIVE INTENSITY

The athlete in this example is not utilising his aerobic capacity efficiently, which could be a result of poor training methods or a lack of training.

$\dot{V}O_2$ can only increase by 10–20% through training as it has a 93% genetic component. This assumes that an athlete with a $\dot{V}O_2$ max of 50 ml/kg/min may expect to increase this to 60 ml/kg/min through training.

However, the anaerobic threshold or OBLA is a product of training and can be heightened through following an appropriate training programme, so that aerobic efficiency is improved by utilising a greater percentage of $\dot{V}O_2$ max before the onset of lactic acid. The reasons for this are discussed in Chapter 8.

 **ACTIVITY 5**

1 **How could a knowledge of maximal oxygen uptake ($\dot{V}O_2$ max) help the coach and athlete in the design of training programmes?**
2 **Outline the $\dot{V}O_2$ max scores expected from a rugby player, a shot putter and a triathlete.**
3 **Explain the concept of the anaerobic threshold (OBLA). How would a knowledge of this help to improve endurance performance?**

Summary

- Fitness requirements differ tremendously between athletes and activities.
- Health related components of fitness are largely physiologically based and include strength, speed, cardiorespiratory endurance, muscular endurance, flexibility and body composition.
- Skill related components of fitness include agility, balance, co-ordination, reaction time and power and are dependent upon the interaction of the nervous system with the muscular system.
- Fitness testing is imperative for the elite athlete since it can identify weaknesses and assess the value of the training programme.
- Any fitness tests conducted should be repeated regularly to ensure validity.
- Maximal Oxygen Uptake of $\dot{V}O_2$ max is the maximum amount of oxygen that can be taken in, transported and consumed by the working muscles per minute. It is the best predictor of aerobic capacity and can only increase through training by 10–20% since it has a 93% genetic component.
- The anaerobic threshold or onset of blood lactate accumulation (OBLA) is the point at which lactic acid starts to accumulate. It is measured as a percentage of $\dot{V}O_2$ max reached before lactic acid accumulation. The anaerobic threshold is a product of training and therefore increases through endurance training.

chapter 8

Training Implications

Drawing upon knowledge gained from Chapter 7, this chapter seeks specifically to investigate how training can improve and enhance fitness levels.

The chapter consists of two main sections. The first discusses the principles and types of training that can be employed in a training regime, culminating in considerations needed when designing long-term training programmes. Having acquired this knowledge it is hoped that the reader will be able to design such a programme for the athlete. Throughout this section, the benefits of training on the body systems are highlighted; the second part of this chapter synthesises this information, so that a complete picture is given of the adaptive responses of the body to exercise.

The principles of training

Specificity

The law of specificity suggests that any training undertaken should be relevant and appropriate to the sport for which the individual is training. For example, it would be highly inappropriate for a swimmer to carry out the majority of their training on the land. Although there are certainly benefits gained from land-based training, the majority of the training programme should involve pool-based work.

The specificity rule does not govern just the muscles, fibre type and actions used but also the energy systems which are predominantly stressed. The energy system used in training should replicate that predominantly used in the event. The energy systems should also be stressed in isolation of each other so that high intensity work (stressing the anaerobic systems) should be done in one session, whereas more aerobic and endurance based work should be completed in a separate session.

Progressive overload

This rule considers the intensity of the training session. For improvement and adaptation to occur, the training should be at an intensity where the individual feels some kind of stress and discomfort – this signifies overload and suggests that the old adage 'no pain, no gain' has some truth in it, especially for the elite athlete. If exercise takes place on a regular basis the body's systems will adapt and start to cope with these stresses that have been imposed. In order for further improvement to occur, the intensity of training will need to be gradually increased – this is progression and can be done by running faster, lifting heavier weights, or training for longer.

Reversibility

Also known as 'regression', this explains why performance deteriorates when training ceases or the intensity of training decreases for extended periods of time. Quite simply, if you don't use it you lose it!

Seven weeks of inactivity has been shown to have the following physiological effects. Significant decreases in maximum oxygen uptake have been recorded – up to 27%, which reflects a fall in the efficiency of the cardiovascular system. In particular, stroke volume and cardiac output can decrease by up to 30%. During exercise, increases in both blood lactate and heart rate have been shown to increase for the same intensity of exercise. Muscle mass and therefore strength also deteriorate but at a less rapid rate.

Individual differences

These suggest that the benefits of training are optimised when programmes are set to meet the needs and abilities of an individual. What may help one athlete to improve may not be successful on another. The coach must therefore be very sympathetic to the needs of the athlete.

The F.I.T.T. regime

The coach may also wish to consider the F.I.T.T. regime when designing the training programme. These letters stand for:

- F = frequency of training
- I = intensity of exercise
- T = time or duration of exercise
- T = type of training.

'F'

– the frequency of training. The elite athlete will need to do some sort of training most days, depending upon the activity being undertaken. Endurance or aerobic type activities can be performed five or six times per week, but more intense or anaerobic activities such as strength work should be performed three or four times per week, as sufficient rest days are required for the body tissues to repair themselves following this high intensity work.

'I'

– the intensity of the exercise. This also depends upon the type of training occurring, and can be quite difficult to objectively measure. For aerobic work, exercise intensity can be measured by calculating an individual's 'training zone'; this is represented by the training heart rate and so involves observing heart rate values, which has become much easier with the advent of the heart rate monitor.

The most established method of calculating the training zone is known as the **Karnoven Principle**. Karnoven developed a formula to identify correct training intensities as a percentage of the sum of the maximum heart rate reserve and resting heart rate. Maximum heart rate reserve can be calculated by subtracting resting heart rate (HRrest) from an individual's maximum heart rate (HRmax):

Maximal heart rate reserve = HR(max) − HR(rest)

Where an individual's maximal heart rate can be calculated by subtracting their age from 220:

Maximal heart rate = 220 − age

Karnoven suggests a training intensity of between 60–75% of maximal heart rate reserve for the average athlete, although this can obviously be adapted to account for individual differences.

Training heart rate 60% = 0.60 (maxHR reserve) + HRrest

Consider the following example to illustrate the value of this measure of intensity:

A twenty year old rower, with a resting heart rate of 65 bpm is aiming to build up his endurance capacities for a forthcoming event. He is advised to train between 60–75% of his training heart rate reserve in the weeks prior to the event. To calculate his training zone, the rower used the Karnoven formula as follows:

Training heart rate 60% = 0.60 (HRmax − HRrest) + HRrest
= 0.60 (200 − 60) + 65
= 81 + 65
= 146 beats per minute

Training heart rate 75% = 0.75 (HRmax − HRrest) + HRrest
= 0.75 (200 − 65) + 65
= 101 + 65
= 166 beats per minute

Thus the rower now has some precise figures to measure and ensure that he is training at the correct intensity. In order for some kind of aerobic adaptation to occur, the rower must be exercising within his target zone, between 146 and 166 beats per minute.

This is a valued measure of exercise intensity since it relates closely to both the stress being imposed on the heart and the vascular system and the percent of $\dot{V}O_2$ max at which the athlete is working.

'T'

– the time or duration that the exercise is in progress. For aerobic type activities, the athlete should be training within his/her training zone for a minimum of 20–30 mins. However duration should not be considered in isolation since intensity of training often determines the duration of the training session.

'T'

– the type or mode of training that is undertaken. This is explained on page 101.

1 **Using table 8.1, calculate your training zone (between 60 and 75% of your maximum heart rate reserve).**
2 **Now complete a 15 minute run, ensuring your heart rate lies at 70% of your MHR.**
3 **Sketch the heart rate curve expected.**

Table 8.1 THE TRAINING ZONE

AGE		20	26	30	35	40	45	50	55	60	65	70	75	80
55%	19	18	18	17	17	17	16	16	15	15	14	14	13	13
60%	21	20	19	19	19	18	18	17	17	16	16	15	15	14
70%	24	23	23	22	22	21	20	20	19	19	18	18	17	16
80%	27	27	26	25	25	24	23	23	22	21	21	20	19	19
90%	29	28	28	27	26	26	25	24	23	23	22	21	21	20

Use this table as a calculator to work out your target training zone at various intensities. All scores reflect your heart rate for a 10 second count. Don't forget to start counting from zero! If you fall between age ranges take the next stage group up. Eg, if you are 18 and wish to train at 70% of your maximum heart rate, find the age group 20 along the top of the table and move down until you come to 70% of MHR. Your target 10 s pulse rate should be 23 beats. You may wish to convert this to beats per minute, in which case multiply the figure in the box by six.

Warm ups and cool downs

Warm up   Before embarking upon any type of exercise, it is imperative to perform a warm up. As it is fundamental to safe practice, it has often been considered as a principle of training and thus seems appropriate to discuss here.

A warm up should make the body ready for exercise. It can prevent injury and muscle soreness, and has the following physiological benefits:

- The release of adrenaline will increase heart rate and dilate capillaries, which in turn enable greater amounts and increased speed of oxygen delivery to the muscles.
- Increased muscle temperatures associated with exercise will facilitate enzyme activity; this increases muscle metabolism and therefore ensures a readily available supply of energy.
- Increased temperatures also lead to decreased viscosity within the muscle. This enables greater extensibility and elasticity of muscle fibres which ultimately leads to increased speed and force of contraction.
- Warm ups also make us more alert, due to an increase in the speed of nerve impulse conduction.
- Increased production of synovial fluid ensures efficient movement at the joints.
- Certain psychological benefits can also occur through a warm up, particularly if the individual has certain superstitions or rituals they follow.

Furthermore, it should not be forgotten that warm ups should be specific to the activity that follows, and include exercises which prepare the muscles to be used and activate the energy systems required for that particular activity.

To ensure the athlete gains as much from the warm up as possible, the following stages should be followed:

1 The first phase of a warm up has the purpose of raising the heart rate, increasing the speed of oxygen delivery to the muscles, and of course raising the body temperature. This can be achieved by performing some kind of cardiovascular exercise such as jogging.
2 Now that muscle temperature has increased, the athlete can perform some flexibility or stretching exercises. It is essential that both static stretches and some calisthenic type activities are performed where the muscle is working over its full range.
3 The final stage of a warm up should involve a skill related component where the neuromuscular mechanisms related to the activity to follow are worked. For example, practising serving in tennis, tumble turns in swimming or shooting baskets in basketball.

Cool down

After exercise, a similar process must be followed in order to prevent unnecessary discomfort; this is a cool down. It involves performing some kind of light continuous exercise where heart rate remains elevated. The purpose is to keep metabolic activity high, and capillaries dilated, so that oxygen can be flushed through the muscle tissue, removing and oxidising any lactic acid that remains. This will therefore prevent blood pooling in the veins which can cause dizziness if exercise is stopped abruptly. The final part of the cool down period should involve a period of stretching exercises, which should hopefully facilitate and improve flexibility as the muscles are very warm at this stage.

You are aiming to compete in a marathon. Outline some of the principles of training you would employ to ensure your training regime is successful.

Design a warm up programme for a sport of your choice. What activities would you include in your programme, and why?

Now that we understand the basic laws which govern training, the next stage in our search for a beneficial training programme is to determine the method or type of training that is best employed.

Training methods

Continuous methods

Continuous methods of training work on developing endurance and therefore stress the aerobic energy system. Central to this method of training is the performance of rhythmic exercise at a steady rate or low intensity which use the large muscle groups of the body over a long period of time (between 30 mins and two hours). Good examples of such activities include jogging, swimming, cycling or aerobic dance. The intensity of such exercise should be at approximately 60% to 80% of HRmax, as outlined in the Karnoven Principle so the body is not experiencing too much discomfort while exercising.

The great advantage of this type of training however is that great distances can be covered without the lactate build up associated with anaerobic training methods. Distance runners, for example, may total up to 140 miles per week, a distance equivalent of London to Lincoln.

With such high mileage comes the danger of injury, particularly to the muscles and joints, so any programme should be thoroughly scrutinised. The health-related benefits of continuous training have been well documented; jogging and aerobics are very popular, and as long as individuals are made aware of the injury risk factors, there is no reason why the majority cannot participate safely.

Fartlek, or speedplay

This is a slightly different method of continuous training. It is a form of endurance conditioning, where the aerobic energy system is stressed due to the continuous nature of the exercise. The only difference however, is that throughout the duration of the exercise, the speed or intensity of the activity is varied, so that both the aerobic and anaerobic systems can be stressed. Fartlek sessions are usually performed for a minimum of 45 minutes, with the intensity of the session varying from low intensity walking to high intensity sprinting. Traditionally Fartlek training has taken place in the countryside where there is varied terrain, but this alternating pace method could occur anywhere and you could use your local environment to help you; for example:

- Easy jog for three lamp posts
- Sprint for one lamp post
- Easy jog for three lamp posts
- Sprint for one lamp post
- Repeat three further times
- Walk for one minute
- Jog at 75% of MHR for five minutes.

This type of training can be very individual and the athlete can determine the speed or intensity at which they wish to work. It can also be fun and offers variety to what some regard as the monotony of continuous jogging. Since both aerobic and anaerobic systems are stressed through this method of training, a wealth of sportspeople can benefit. It is particularly suited to those activities that involve a mixture of aerobic and anaerobic work; eg, field games such as rugby, hockey or soccer.

Intermittent training

Intermittent methods of training involve periods of work or exercise interspersed with periods of recovery. Athletes appear to be able to perform considerably more work when the session is broken down into short intense periods of effort and recovery breaks, and the physiological benefits are great.

Interval training

This is probably the most popular type of training used in sport for training the elite athlete. It is very versatile and can be used in almost any activity, although it is most widely used in swimming, athletics and cycling. Interval training can improve both aerobic and anaerobic capacities and enables the athlete to exercise at the specific intensity necessary to train the relevant energy system for that activity.

In order for the correct system to be stressed, several variables have been identified which can be manipulated. These variables include:

1 Distance of the work interval (duration)
2 Intensity of the work interval (speed)
3 The number of repetitions within a session
4 The number of sets within a session
5 Duration of the rest interval
6 Activity during the rest interval.

In order to train the relevant energy system, the coach must ensure that the variables have been adjusted appropriately:

1 For the ATP-PC system, the duration of the work period should last for 3–10 seconds, or an equivalent distance that can be covered in that time at the highest intensity (depending upon the activity being performed).
2 Intensity should be assessed by the athlete working at a percentage of their maximum effort or personal best time for the distance. For the ATP-PC system this should be 90–100%.

3 Generally, the number of repetitions depends upon the length of the work period. For the ATP-PC system, the work interval is relatively short and we can expect to perform up to 50 short intense bouts within a session.

4 These 50 repetitions may be divided up into a number of sets (a group of work and rest intervals), to ensure that the athlete does not get unduly fatigued; eg, 5 sets $\times$ 10 reps.

5 Between each repetition is a period of rest which can be determined by the time it takes for the heart rate to return to about 150 beats per minute. It can be compared to the work interval time, expressed as the work:relief (rest) ratio. For the ATP-PC system where the work interval is relatively short, the rest period may take three times that before the heart lowers to 150 bpm this would be expressed as a work:relief ratio of 1:3.

6 The type of activity that takes place during these rest intervals differs, depending upon the energy system being trained. The ATP-PC system for example requires no activity apart from perhaps some light stretching during the recovery phase, whilst the lactic acid system will require active recovery involving light jogging or walking.

For the lactic acid system, an exercise period of between 15 seconds and 90 seconds should be performed at a moderate intensity. Up to twelve repetitions may be completed over two or three sets with a work to relief ratio of 1:2. This should give time for some although not all lactic acid to be removed. Thus in successive work intervals, the body must work with some lactic acid already present within the system, which should improve the buffering capacity of the body. To speed up the removal of lactate during the relief period, some light exercise should be performed, such as rapid walking or jogging.

To train the aerobic system, the work interval should be much longer, perhaps up to seven or eight minutes in duration. The intensity should again be moderate (and certainly faster than any pace undertaken during continuous training) and measured as a percentage of personal best times for the distance. The longer exercise periods mean that fewer repetitions are needed, maybe only three or four in one session, which can be performed in one set. In order to put extra stress on the aerobic system the recovery time is usually much shorter in comparison to the work period. A work:relief ratio of 1:1/2 may be used where the athlete rests for half the time it took to complete the work period.

The requirements of an interval training session can be expressed as the **interval training prescription**. For example, a swimmer may have the following session prescribed:

$$2 \times 4 \times 200 \text{ m W:R } 1:1/2$$

where: 2 = number of sets
4 = number of repetitions
200 m = training distance
1:1/2 = work to relief ratio

Some examples of interval training regimes are outlined in table 8.2. Sprint interval training sessions are specifically designed to stress the ATP-PC system, improving its capacity and increasing the muscle stores of ATP and PC. This obviously has a direct effect upon sprinters or any activity where bursts of speed are required.

Fast interval training sessions develop anaerobic endurance and therefore stress the lactic acid system. The buffering capacity of the body improves, which delays the onset of fatigue and decreases the effect of lactic acid. This training is of particular importance to 400 m runners and sprint swimmers.

The aerobic system is stressed by performing slower intervals which improves the oxidative capacity of the body. Any endurance based event such as distance running or swimming will benefit from this type of training, in addition to field games such as rugby and hockey.

Follow an interval training programme for a minimum of eight weeks. Note any improvements in performance.

Circuit training

Circuit training involves performing a number of calisthenic exercises in succession, such as press ups, abdominal curls, step ups etc. Each exercise is usually performed for a set amount of time or a set number of repetitions, and the circuit can be adapted to meet the specific fitness requirements of a given sport or activity.

When planning a circuit there are several factors that need consideration. The first of these is the most fundamental – what do you require the circuit for? Once you have answered this you can choose the exercises to include (see examples of exercises in table 8.3 below). You will also need to consider:

- the number of participants
- their standard of fitness
- the amount of time, space and equipment that are available.

Having considered all these points you can now go ahead and plan the layout of your circuit.

One golden rule when devising the layout of the circuit is that the same body part should not be exercised consecutively. Therefore the sequence of the exercises should be as follows: arms, trunk, cardiovascular, legs, arms, trunk, cardiovascular etc. The exception is for experienced athletes performing an 'overload' circuit where the endurance of one muscle group is being trained.

The great benefit of circuit training is that it is extremely adaptable, since exercises can be included or omitted to suit almost all activities. It also enables large numbers of participants to train together at their own level. With regular testing, improvements in fitness are easily visible through circuit training as current work can be compared to previous test scores.

Design a circuit training session for an activity of your choice. Give reasons for the exercises you have chosen.

Strength training

Strength gains are sought by many athletes and usually occur either through weight or resistance training methods, or through a further type of training known as plyometrics.

Table 8.2 INTERVAL TRAINING PRESCRIPTIONS

MAJOR ENERGY SYSTEM	TRAINING TIME (MIN:SEC)	REPETITIONS PER WORKOUT	SETS PER WORKOUT	REPETITIONS PER SET	WORK:RELIEF RATIO	TYPE OF RELIEF INTERVAL
ATP-PC	0:10	50	5	10		rest-relief (eg, walking, flexing)
	0:15	45	5	9		
	0:20	40	4	10	1:3	
	0:25	32	4	8		
ATP-PC-LA	0:30	25	5	5		work-relief (eg, light to mild exercise, jogging)
	0:40–0:50	20	4	5	1:3	
	1:00–1:10	15	3	5		
	1:20	10	2	5	1:2	
LA-O$_2$	1:30–2:00	8	2	4	1:2	work-relief
	2:10–2:40	6	1	6		
O$_2$	2:50–3:00	4	1	4	1:1	rest-relief
	3:00–4:00	4	1	4	1:1	rest-relief
	4:00–5:00	3	1	3	1:$\frac{1}{2}$	rest-relief

MAJOR ENERGY SYSTEM	TRAINING DISTANCE (M) RUN	SWIM	REPETITIONS PER WORKOUT	SETS PER WORKOUT	REPETITIONS PER SET	WORK:RELIEF RATIO	TYPE OF RELIEF INTERVAL
ATP-PC	50	10	50	5	10		rest-relief (eg, walking, flexing)
	100	25	24	3	8	1:3	
ATP-PC-LA	200	50	16	4	4	1:3	work-relief (eg, light to mild exercise, jogging)
	400	100	8	2	4	1:2	
LA-O$_2$	600	150	5	1	5	1:2	work-relief
	800	200	4	2	2	1:1	rest-relief
O$_2$	1,000	250	3	1	3	1:$\frac{1}{2}$	rest-relief
	1,200	300	3	1	3	1:$\frac{1}{2}$	

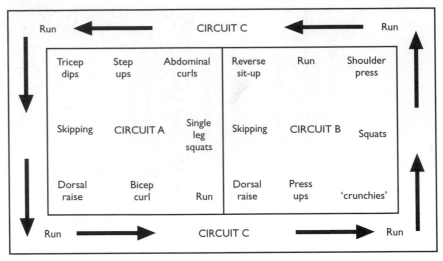

Each participant is to complete each circuit.

Circuit A = 8 exercises x 30 secs = 4 mins
Circuit B = 8 exercises x 30 secs = 4 mins
Circuit C = Run around outside = 4 mins
Repeat 2 or 3 times

Fig. 8.1 A GENERAL FITNESS CIRCUIT

With advances in technology and the improvement in the quality of weight machines, weight training has increased in popularity in both athletic and recreational training regimes. It can be used to develop several components of fitness, including strength, strength endurance and explosive power. Which of these are stressed at a particular time is determined by manipulating the weight of resistance, the number of repetitions and the number of sets.

For activities where maximum strength is required, such as power lifting or throwing the hammer, training methods which increase muscle strength and size will be required. Essentially this will involve some form of very high resistance, low repetition exercise. For example:

Table 8.3   EXERCISES TO INCLUDE IN A CIRCUIT

cardiovascular exercises	running around the gym skipping step ups cycling on an ergometer bounding exercises on a mat
trunk exercises	abdominal curls crunchies dorsal raises trunk twists
arm exercises	press ups/box press bicep curls tricep dips shoulder press squat thrusts chin ups to beam
leg exercises	single leg squats any of the cardiovascular exercises outlined above

FIG. 8.2 STRENGTH TRAINING: LEG
EXTENSION

- Performing 3 sets of 2–6 repetitions at 80–100% of maximum strength, with full
  recovery between sets.

To train for activities which require strength endurance, such as swimming or
rowing, a different approach to training will be required. In order to perform more
repetitions, a lighter load or resistance is needed and the following programme
might be described:

- 3 sets of 20 repetitions at 50–60% of maximum strength with full recovery
  between sets.

Plyometrics

Power is determined by the force exerted by the muscle (strength) and the speed at
which the muscle shortens:

Power = Force × Velocity

It thus follows that by improving either strength or speed of shortening, power may
be improved. One method of training which may improve the speed at which a
muscle shortens is plyometrics.

It has long been established that muscles generate more force in contraction
when they have been previously stretched. Plyometrics enables this to occur by
taking the muscle through an eccentric (lengthened) phase before a powerful
concentric (shortening) phase. This stimulates adaptation within the
neuromuscular system and produces a more powerful concentric contraction of the
muscle group. This has important consequences for sprinting, jumping and

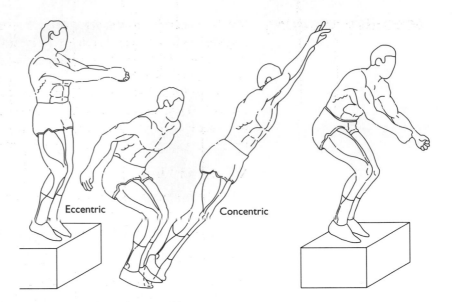

Fig. 8.3 EXAMPLES OF PLYOMETRIC
EXERCISES

throwing events in athletics, as well as in games such as rugby, volleyball and
basketball where leg strength is central to performance.

Exercises that might form part of the plyometrics session include:

- bounding
- hopping
- leaping
- skipping
- depth jumps (jumping onto and off of boxes)
- press ups with claps
- throwing and catching a medicine ball.

The strength gains and muscle hypertrophy associated with strength training may
only start to become evident after about eight weeks of training, and are largely due
to the increase in size and volume of the myofibrils.

**A triple jumper requires some advice on improving leg strength.
Design a strength programme, stating which type of strength is
being developed.**

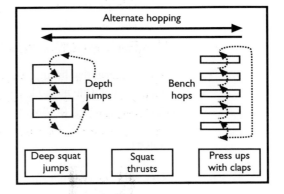

Fig. 8.4 A PLYOMETRICS CIRCUIT

Rotate around the circuit twice one minute on
each exercise stretch off during rest intervals

Mobility training

Mobility training is the method employed to improve flexibility. It is often a neglected form of training, but should be incorporated into every athlete's training programme. Effective flexibility training can improve performance and help prevent the occurrence of injury.

The method of stretching used in mobility training should centre on the connective tissue and the muscle tissue acting upon the joint, as these tissues have been shown to elongate following a period of regular and repeated stretching. Two types of stretching have been identified and outlined below.

Active stretching

The athlete performs voluntary muscular contractions, and holds the stretch for a period of 30–60 seconds. By consciously relaxing the target muscle at the limit of the range of motion, muscle elongation may occur following regular contraction.

Passive stretching

This refers to the range of movement which can occur with the aid of external force. This is generally performed with the help of a partner who can offer some resistance, although gravity and body weight can also be used.

One method of flexibility training that has emerged from passive stretching is **proprioceptive neuromuscular facilitation** (PNF). This seeks to decrease the reflex shortening of the muscle being stretched, which occurs when a muscle is stretched to its limit. A simple PNF technique is now outlined:

1 Move slowly to the limit of your range of motion with a partner aiding.
2 Just before the point of discomfort, isometrically contract the muscle being stretched for between 6 and 10 seconds.
3 After the hold, the muscle will release, having stimulated a golgi tendon organ (GTO) response which causes further relaxation of the muscle and enabling further stretching of the muscle.

With continued practice of PNF, a new limit of the muscle stretch may occur, But, don't forget that pain is the body's signal that damage is occurring, and athletes should not stretch beyond the slight discomfort.

Furthermore, stretching and mobility training should only be performed after a thorough warm up where an increase in body temperature has occurred. This is easily achieved by performing a period of light cardiovascular exercise, centering upon those muscle groups that are to be stretched. In addition, wear warm clothing while performing the stretches to maintain body temperature; if possible, perform in a warm environment.

Responses and adaptations to training

We have already mentioned that the reason behind training is to improve our components of fitness, the capacity of each energy system and overall performance. The body responds to the stresses that training imposes upon it and subsequently adapts and adjusts to meet the demands of the exercise that is occurring.

Table 8.4   THE DEVELOPMENT OF DIFFERENT TYPES OF STRENGTH

OBJECTIVE	INTENSITY OF TRAINING LOAD	REPETITIONS IN EACH SET	NUMBER OF SETS	RECOVERY BETWEEN SETS	EVALUATION PROCEDURES	TRAINING OF VALUE FOR
development of maximum strength	85–95%	1–5	normal 2–4 advanced 5–8	4–5 mins	maximum lift dynamometer	weight lifting, shot, discus, hammer, javelin, jumping events rugby and contact sports men's gymnastics
development of elastic strength	75–85%	6–10	(4–6)	3–5 mins	standing, long and vertical jump capability	all sports requiring 'explosive' strength qualities – sprinting, jumping, throwing, striking
development of advanced level of strength endurance	40–60%	50–75% of maximum	(3–5)	30–45 s	maximum reps possible	rowing, wrestling, skiing, swimming, 400 m, steeplechase etc.
development of a basic level of strength endurance	30–40%	25–50% of maximum	(4–6)	optimal	maximum reps possible	generally required for all sports suitable for young and novice competitors and fitness participants

Source: Leeds University, 1988

Short term responses

Short term responses to exercise are the ways in which the body's systems adjust to cope with the exercise *during* a training session. At the end of the exercise period the body will return to its normal resting state.

Cardiovascular and respiratory responses to exercise

We have established in Chapters 5–6 that many adjustments are made by the cardiovascular system during exercise to ensure adequate delivery of oxygen and nutrients to the muscle and efficient removal of metabolites from the muscle. Such adjustments include an increased heart rate of between 60–80 bpm at rest to between 160–180 bpm during exercise.

We also see a slight increase in stroke volume during exercise, with the elite athlete increasing stroke volume from 110 ml/beat to 170 ml/beat while exercising; this is due to Starlings Law.

There is also an increase in cardiac output (cardiac output is a product of heart rate and stroke volume). Cardiac output may increase from 5–6 L at rest to 30 L during exercise.

More importantly, however, is the adjustment made in the redistribution of blood being pumped around the body. At rest, only about 20% of the cardiac output is distributed to the working muscles. During exercise however, when there is greater demand for oxygen up to 85% of cardiac output may be distributed to the working skeletal muscles. This can occur through accommodation and shunting of blood from inactive tissues such as the stomach and kidneys to the working muscles. Adjustments in blood pressure are also seen during exercise due to the increased blood flow and vasoconstriction of blood vessels which ensure a rapid flow of blood to the working muscles.

Respiratory responses occur largely because of the increase in muscle metabolism which takes place as a result of the increased activity. Increased muscle glycogen breakdown results in greater amounts of carbon dioxide production, which decreases blood pH and stimulates the respiratory centre to increase ventilation. With higher exercise intensity (usually exceeding 60% of $\dot{V}O_2$ max), increased production of lactic acid may occur. This also increases acidity and again stimulates the respiratory centre to increase ventilation.

Long term adaptations

Long term physiological adaptations are those changes that occur in the body as a result of following a long term training programme.

Muscular adaptations

Depending upon the type of the prior training, different adaptations will occur in the muscle. We are first going to look at the changes that occur following a period of aerobic training and then take a look at the anaerobic changes that may arise.

Aerobic adaptations

These occur in the muscle as a result of following an endurance based training programme. Examples of activities that can be performed include swimming or jogging, although any continuous type activity will lead to some adaptation.

Regular stimulation of the muscle through aerobic based exercise will cause changes to occur within the muscle cell. In particular, the structure of the muscle fibres may alter. Since the performance of endurance exercise stresses the slow twitch muscle fibres, these respond by enlarging by up to 22%. This gives greater potential for aerobic energy production since larger fibres mean a greater area for mitochondrial activity.

Indeed, endurance training leads to an increase in both size and number of mitochondria. Some studies have reported mitochondria size to increase by up to 40% and the number by over 100%. Since the mitochondria are the factories that produce our aerobic energy, increases in size and number can be associated with the economies of scale achieved by large businesses and an increase in production of energy will result.

Endurance training may also increase the activity of our **oxidative enzymes** which work on breaking down our food fuel to release the energy stored within. As a result, there is more scope to use glycogen and fat as a fuel. The oxidation of both these fuels increase, providing greater amounts of energy. With hypertrophy of slow twitch muscle fibres there is a corresponding increase in stores of glycogen and triglycerides which ensures a continuous supply of energy, enabling exercise to be performed for a longer period of time.

A further benefit of aerobic training is the increase of up to 80% in **myoglobin** content within the muscle cell. Myoglobin is the substance within the muscle that carries oxygen to the mitochondria, and is similar in structure to haemoglobin. With greater amounts of myoglobin, more oxygen can be transported to the mitochondria which further improves the efficiency of aerobic energy production.

All of these aerobic adaptations associated with endurance training ensure that a higher percentage of $\dot{V}O_2$ max can be attained before the anaerobic threshold is reached and thus the onset of fatigue can be delayed. Generally, $\dot{V}O_2$ max is not a product of training as it is largely genetically determined but these metabolic adaptations within the muscle that occur as a result of training may slightly increase an individual's $\dot{V}O_2$ max (maximum oxygen uptake) in the region of 10–20%.

Anaerobic adaptations

The anaerobic or lactate threshold is a product of training, and improvements in this will certainly improve endurance performance.

While training at very high intensity, eg, sprint or strength training, **hypertrophy** of fast twitch muscle fibres takes place. Increases in levels of ATP and PC within the muscle occurs which increases the capacity of the ATP-PC or alactic energy system. The efficiency of this system is further improved through increased activity of the enzymes responsible for breaking down ATP and PC. These include creatine phosphokinase and myokinase.

Training at high intensities for up to 60 seconds has also been shown to increase the **glycolytic** capacity of the muscle, largely through increasing the activity of glycolytic enzymes. This improves the muscles' ability to break down glycogen in the absence of oxygen and means that the athlete can exercise for longer periods of time before feeling the effects of fatigue.

This is further aided by improvements in the **buffering** capacity of the muscle, which enables the muscles to tolerate lactic acid more effectively. When lactic acid accumulates in the muscle, hydrogen ions (H+) are released, inhibiting glycolytic enzyme activity and interfering with the contractile elements of the muscle. Bicarbonate existing in the muscle and the blood mop up these hydrogen ions reducing acidity. By following an anaerobic training programme, the buffering capacity of the body increases substantially, and enables the body to work for longer periods of time and at higher levels of acidity.

Cardiovascular adaptations to training

Following endurance training, many cardiovascular adaptations arise. In the first instance, the actual size of the heart may increase – **cardiac hypertrophy**. This enables the heart to work more efficiently, particularly at rest. The increase in thickness of the myocardium (cardiac tissue) enables the left ventricle to fill more completely with blood during the diastole phase of the cardiac cycle. This allows the heart to pump more blood per beat since the thicker walls can contract more forcefully, pumping more blood into the systemic system and ultimately to the muscles.

Consequently, stroke volume increases both at rest and during exercise. With an increase in **stroke volume at rest**, the heart will no longer need to pump as many times per minute to achieve the same amount of blood flowing to the body's tissues.

Since the heart seeks to work as efficiently as possible resting heart rate decreases as a result of the endurance training that has taken place.

When resting heart rate falls to below 60 beats per minute, **bradycardia** results, which explains the very low resting heart rates often experienced by top endurance athletes; for example, Indurain, the many times Tour de France champion is reported to have a resting heart rate of around 30 bpm!

As an athlete's stroke volume increases, the cardiac output of the trained athlete also increases. Cardiac output may increase by up to 30–40 lmin- in trained individuals. However it is important to note that there is little or no change in the values of resting cardiac output, due to the decrease in resting heart rate that accompanies endurance training.

The adaptations mentioned above have centred on the structure and function of the heart. We now need to discuss those training-induced changes that occur in the **vascular** and **circulatory** systems:

1 One reason that accounts for greater performances in aerobic events following training is the increased **capillarisation** of trained muscles. New capillaries may actually develop which enables more blood to flow to the muscles and enables more oxygen to reach the tissues. Furthermore, existing capillaries become more efficient and allow greater amounts of blood to reach the muscles, which also become more efficient at extracting the oxygen due to the muscular adaptations mentioned above.
2 Improvements in the vasculature efficiency (especially the arteries) to vasoconstrict and vasodilate, improve the redistribution of blood by shunting the supply to the active muscles and tissues, so that there is a greater supply of oxygen for energy production in these working muscles.
3 These efficiency gains also result in a **decreased resting blood pressure** following endurance training, although blood pressure during exercise of a sub-maximal or maximal nature remains unchanged.
4 Increases in blood volume following training can be attributed to an **increase in blood plasma** (the water component of the blood). This has the important function of decreasing the blood viscosity and enabling the blood to flow around the body easier, thus enhancing oxygen delivery to the muscles and tissues.
5 An increase in **red** blood cell volume and **haemoglobin** content is also higher in the trained athlete which further facilitates the transport of oxygen around the body. However although haemoglobin content increases, the increase in blood plasma is greater and consequently the blood haematocrit (the ratio of red blood cell volume to total blood volume) is reduced, which lowers the viscosity of the blood and facilitates its progress around the body.

Respiratory adaptations to training

Endurance performance is dependent upon oxygen transportation and utilisation, but no matter how good the functioning of these are, improvements in performance will not happen unless we can get oxygen into the body. The respiratory system is responsible for receiving oxygen into the body and dealing with the waste products associated with muscle metabolism. Respiratory functioning does not usually hinder aerobic performance, and the adaptations that take place merely aid the improved cardiovascular functioning.

Following training, there is a reduction in both resting respiratory rate and the breathing rate during submaximal exercise. This appears to be a function of the overall efficiency of the respiratory structures induced by training.

Surprisingly there are only very small increases in lung volumes following training. Vital capacity (the amount of air that can be forcibly expelled following maximum inspiration) increases slightly, as does tidal volume during maximal exercise. One factor to account for these increases is the increased strength of the respiratory muscles which may facilitate lung inflation.

Pulmonary diffusion (the exchange of gases at the alveoli) will become more efficient following training, especially when working at near maximal levels. The increased surface area of the alveoli during exercise together with their increased capillarisation, ensures that there is ample opportunity for gaseous exchange to take place, and thus guarantees sufficient oxygen is entering the blood.

A student decides to take up distance running and joins a local running club. After following a training programme for three months, a distinct improvement in performance is noted. From a physiological standpoint, account for these changes.

We have seen from this chapter that training will induce changes in the muscular, cardiovascular and respiratory systems which make their functioning more efficient and hopefully improve endurance performance. We now need to discuss how a coach or an athlete can design a training programme to guarantee and maximise the effects of these adaptations.

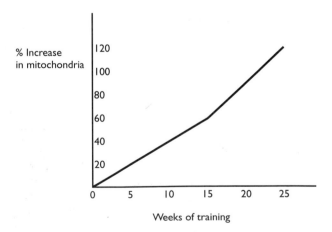

Fig. 8.5 THE INCREASE IN THE SIZE AND NUMBER OF MITOCHONDRIA AS A RESULT OF ENDURANCE TRAINING

A 120% increase in the number of mitochondria following a 25 week endurance programme. Size of mitochondria may also increase in size by up to 40%

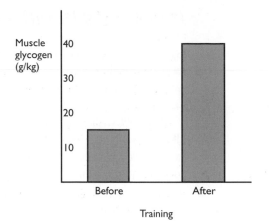

Fig. 8.6 THE INCREASE IN MUSCLE
GLYCOGEN CONTENT FOLLOWING ENDURANCE
TRAINING

A 20 week, 4 day/week endurance training
programme.

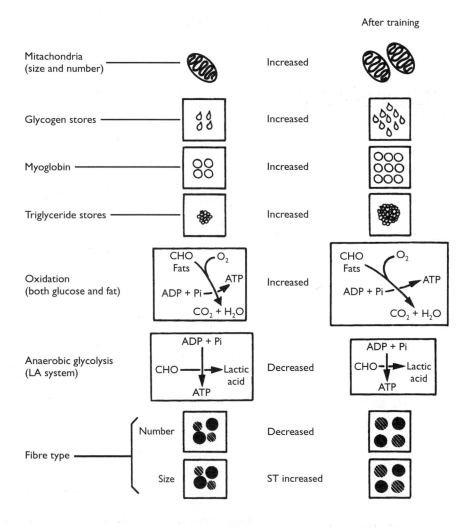

Fig. 8.7 A SUMMARY OF PHYSIOLOGICAL
EFFECTS OF ENDURANCE TRAINING ON THE
MUSCLE

Source: Davis, Kimmet and Auty (1986)

Key:
■ FT fibres
▨ ST fibres

Designing a training programme

Training programmes do not come in a standard package that suit everybody; they have to be made to measure and designed specifically for the individual. For example, Linford Christie would need a very different programme to one designed for a marathon runner.

The problem that a coach faces when designing a programme is that not only are all athletes different but each sport requires different components of fitness at varying levels of importance. A programme should therefore be balanced yet specific enough to ensure that the demands of both the athlete and sport are being met.

When planning a training programme, the following factors should be considered to ensure a worthwhile experience for the athlete:

- the performer's needs
- the sport and related fitness components
- the principles of training
- the types of training that can be employed
- the training year.

We have discussed the first four considerations earlier in this chapter. There now follows a short explanation of how a training programme can be structured to ensure optimal performance of the athlete.

The training year

It is important to structure the training programme so that the athlete can achieve the best possible improvements in performance, and that optimal performance occurs in the climax of the competitive season. To ensure this, the training programme should be viewed as a year-long process divided into specific periods designed to prepare the athlete for optimal performances. This is known as **periodisation**.

Typically the periodised year has three periods:

- the preparation period
- the competition period
- the transition period.

The preparation period

The preparation period includes the off-season and pre-season aspects of the periodised year.

During the off-season stage, general conditioning is required through a well rounded programme of aerobic endurance training, mobility training and training to maintain strength.

During the pre-season stage there is a significant increase in the intensity of training. This is the time when much of the strength work should be undertaken, through lifting heavier weights or working against greater resistances, and working at higher speeds. Towards the end of this period the coach should employ some competition specific training; eg, working on sprint starts for the sprinter.

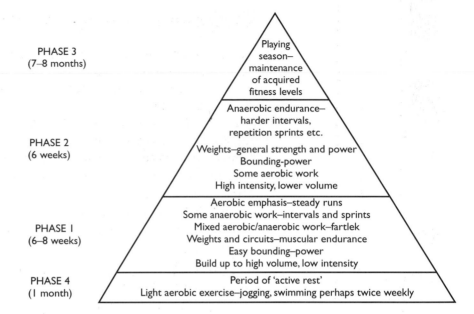

PHASE 3
(7–8 months)

Playing
season—
maintenance
of acquired
fitness levels

Anaerobic endurance—
harder intervals,
repetition sprints etc.

PHASE 2
(6 weeks)

Weights–general strength and power
Bounding-power
Some aerobic work
High intensity, lower volume

PHASE 1
(6–8 weeks)

Aerobic emphasis–steady runs
Some anaerobic work–intervals and sprints
Mixed aerobic/anaerobic work–fartlek
Weights and circuits–muscular endurance
Easy bounding–power
Build up to high volume, low intensity

PHASE 4
(1 month)

Period of 'active rest'
Light aerobic exercise–jogging, swimming perhaps twice weekly

Fig. 8.8 THE PERIODISED YEAR FOR A RUGBY PLAYER

The competition period

Training during the competition period should be aimed at maintaining levels of conditioning achieved during the pre-season phase. Maximum strength training is reduced and much of the training should be centred on competition specific aspects. For the endurance athlete however, training at high intensity is still important in preparation for competition.

The transition period

Following a hard season of competition the body needs to recuperate, and the transition period bridges the gap between the season passed and the next training year. Essentially the transition period should be a period of active rest with some low intensity aerobic work such as swimming or cycling. The transition period is vital and should not be omitted; as well as giving the body a break from all the hard work in psychological terms, it can enhance motivation for training during the following periodised year.

ACTIVITY 8

1 **What structural changes are brought about within a muscle as a result of:**
    - **a strength training programme using weights**
    - **an endurance training programme?**
2 **State the importance of flexibility to sporting activity. How might you begin to improve flexibility? Use sporting examples where necessary.**
3 **Discuss ways in which training intensity can be determined.**
4 **Design a circuit training programme for a specific group of people. State the exercises you would use and explain why. What other considerations might be necessary?**
5 **Outline some training regimes designed to improve**
    - **the aerobic system**
    - **the anaerobic systems.**

Summary

- In order for a training programme to be successful the athlete must follow the laws or 'principles of training'. These include specificity, progressive overload, reversibility, individual differences, frequency, intensity, time, type, warm ups and cool downs as well as many others.
- There are a number of training methods that can be employed by an athlete. These include continuous methods such as fartlek or intermittent training methods such as interval training, circuit training, weight training and plyometrics. Mobility training is often neglected and athletes should incorporate some form of stretching activity into every session.
- A well planned training programme will cause the body to adapt positively. The adaptive responses can be categorised into the following categories: Aerobic muscular changes, anaerobic muscular changes, cardiovascular adaptations, and respiratory adaptations.
- When designing a training programme the coach must ensure that it is tailor made for the athlete. The training year should be structured initially into three main phases: the preparation period, the competition period and the transition period.

chapter 9

Nutritional Implications

In addition to following a well-planned and organised training programme, it is now widely recognised that diet and nutrition is vital to successful performance. Many athletes now employ the services of nutritional experts.

Since the physical demands of training and competition on the athlete are high, much research has been undertaken concerning the extent to which diet can ease these demands. This chapter will explore the dietary requirements of the high level performer, and the use of diet as an ergogenic performance enhancing aid (through supplementation and diet manipulation).

Nutritional effects upon performance

Whatever the sport or activity, it has now become widely recognised that nutrition is of great importance. A well-balanced diet is essential for optimum performance in both training and during competition. Athletes place enormous demands on their bodies when competing at the highest level, and to enable the body to function at its peak during the daily training regimes, an adequate diet is needed. Not only should the athlete's diet be designed to provide the energy required during exercise, but it should also provide the necessary nutrients for tissue growth and repair and those needed to keep the human machine functioning at its optimal level.

Essentially there are six groups of nutrients that should be included in the athlete's diet:

1 Carbohydrate
2 Fat
3 Protein
4 Vitamins
5 Minerals
6 Water.

Carbohydrate

Carbohydrate comes in various forms, including:

- simple sugars (glucose, fructose)
- complex starches (rice, pasta, potatoes).

Carbohydrate is vital to the athlete since it is the primary energy fuel (particularly during high intensity exercise), it is essential for the nervous system to function properly and also determines fat metabolism in the body. Intake should comprise approximately 60% of the athlete's diet.

Carbohydrate is stored in the muscles and liver as glycogen, but the amount that can be stored here is limited and therefore regular refuelling is needed. Excellent sources of carbohydrate include cereals, fruit and vegetables and confectionery – the latter should only be included in the athlete's diet in moderation.

Fat   Fat is also a major source of energy in the body, particularly during low intensity exercise such as endurance activities. Up to 70% of our energy is derived from fat during our resting state.

Typically fat exists in the body as:

- triglycerides (the stored form of fat), or
- fatty acids (the usable form of fat for energy production).

When sufficient oxygen is available to the muscle cell, fatty acids constitute the favoured fuel for energy production, as the body tries to spare the limited stores of glycogen for higher intensity bouts of exercise and this can delay the effects of fatigue. Through training, the body adapts by increasing its ability to use fat as a fuel. The body however cannot use fat as its sole fuel source, so energy production in the muscle is usually fuelled by a combination of glycogen and fat. One explanation for marathon runners 'hitting the wall' is that glycogen stores are completely depleted, and the body attempts to supply all the energy required by metabolising fat. The hydrophobic (low water solubility) quality of fat however inhibits this metabolism, energy production is slow and the muscles fail to contract.

Eating fat alone does not improve the muscles ability to use it as a fuel source and the problems associated with excessive fat consumption are well documented such as the cardiovascular diseases outlined in Chapter 10.

It is recommended therefore that the athlete should keep the consumption of fatty foods low (at a maximum of 30% of total calories consumed) which will ensure adequate energy stores, good health and a greater proportion of calorie intake to be supplied by carbohydrate.

Protein   Proteins are chemical compounds composed of chains of amino acids. They provide the building blocks for tissue growth and repair (including muscle tissue), produce enzymes, hormones and haemoglobin, and can provide energy when glycogen and fat stores are low.

Typically protein should constitute approximately 15% of total calorie intake. Good sources include meat, fish, poultry, dairy products and beans and pulses.

The use and worth of protein supplementation as an ergogenic aid remains unclear, but it is generally thought that sufficient protein can be gained from the athlete's diet. Excessive protein consumption may in fact pose some health risks, as the kidneys may become overworked in excreting any unused amino acids.

Vitamins   Vitamins are chemical compounds required only in small amounts by the body. However they perform a vital role in energy production and metabolism. A list of the major vitamins is shown in table 9.1.

Generally the body can gain the required amounts of vitamins through a well balanced diet. Vitamins are largely found in fresh fruit and vegetables and wholegrain cereals, although some athletes believe that supplementation will enhance energy production and subsequently lead to improved athletic performance. Taking a multivitamin pill may prove useful as a precaution for some athletes, but megadoses of up to 100 times the recommended daily allowance (often expressed by athletes) are definitely not needed and may in fact cause some health problems.

Minerals   These nutrients are also required in relatively small amounts by the body, but are vital for tissue functioning. Many of the minerals are dissolved by the body as ions and are called **electrolytes**. These have the important function of maintaining the permeability of the cell, and also aid the transmission of nerve impulses and enable effective muscle contraction. Some of the major minerals are outlined in table 9.2.

Many minerals may be lost through sweating during exercise. These must be replaced quickly and there are now a vast array of fluid replacement products on the market designed for just that purpose.

Water   Water is a nutrient whose importance is sometimes neglected. It is essential for the sportsperson, as it carries nutrients to and removes waste products from the body's cells, and helps to control body temperature. Water makes up about 50–60% of a young person's body weight, up to a third of which is contained in the blood plasma. (Plasma carries oxygen via the red blood cells to the working muscles, transports nutrients such as glucose and fatty acids, transports hormones vital to metabolism and removes waste products such as CO_2 and lactic acid.)

Water loss through sweating is accelerated during prolonged exercise and in hot conditions, and it is essential that this fluid is replaced in order to maintain a good state of hydration. Even small losses of water can impair performance and adversely affect work capacity in a number of ways. These include:

- reducing the efficiency of the circulatory functioning largely by a drop in blood pressure, which reduces blood flow to the active muscles
- inhibiting the thermoregulatory centre which can lead to problems such as heat stroke.
- the loss of electrolytes such as sodium, chloride and calcium. Although it was once believed that this loss may induce muscle cramps, it is still an area of contention; many studies show that such losses may not have a direct effect on performance.

The athlete's diet

What you eat before, during and after exercise will have a direct effect on how you perform, either in training or in competition. Athletes undertaking daily training sessions need a high energy intake through eating carbohydrates, which should form up to 60% of total energy intake. Research points to the athlete having 4–6 small meals a day rather than 2–3 larger ones. This ensures that muscle and liver glycogen stores are kept topped up throughout the day.

On the day of competition or if there is going to be a particularly hard training session, the athlete should eat a meal high in glycogen 3–4 hours before competing to keep blood glucose levels high throughout the duration of the competition.

If you are involved in heats or bouts of work over the day, it will be necessary to top up glycogen stores by consuming small amounts of carbohydrate through snacks such as dried fruit or one of the many carbohydrate drinks on the market. Fluids such as water should also be taken during competition to prevent dehydration.

Following the competition or training, it is necessary to refuel the body as soon as possible in order to resynthesise muscle and liver glycogen stores. A high carbohydrate meal should be eaten within two hours of the cessation of the exercise to start this refuelling process. Water and isotonic supplements should also be taken to replenish those lost through sweating and aid in rehydration.

Table 9.1   The major vitamins

VITAMIN	RDA FOR HEALTHY ADULT MALE AND FEMALE (MG)	DIETARY SOURCES	MAJOR BODY FUNCTIONS	DEFICIENCY	EXCESS
water-soluble vitamin B-1 (thiamine)	1.4–1.5 1.0–1.1	pork, organ meats, whole grains, legumes	coenzyme (thiamine pyrophosphate) in reactions involving the removal of carbon dioxide	beriberi (peripheral nerve changes, edema, heart failure)	none reported
vitamin B-2 (riboflavin)	1.6–1.7 1.2–1.3	widely distributed in foods	constituent of two flavin nucleotide coenzymes involved in energy metabolism (FAD and FMN)	reddened lips, cracks at corner of mouth (cheilosis), lesions of eye	none reported
niacin	18–19 13–14	liver, lean meats, grains, legumes (can be formed from tryptophan)	constituent of two coenzymes involved in oxidation-reduction reactions (NAD and NADP)	pellagra (skin and gastrointestinal lesions, nervous, mental disorders)	flushing, burning and tingling around neck, face, and hands none reported
vitamin B-6 (pyridoxine)	2.2 2.0	meats, vegetables, whole-grain cereals	coenzyme (pyridoxal phosphate) involved in amino acid metabolism	irritability, convulsions, muscular twitching, dermatitis near eyes, kidney stones	none reported
pantothenic acid	4–7 4–7	widely distributed in foods	constituent of coenzyme A, which plays a central role in energy metabolism	fatigue, sleep disturbances, impaired coordination, nausea (rare in man)	none reported
folacin	0.4 0.4	legumes, green vegetables, whole-wheat products	coenzyme (reduced form involved in transfer of single-carbon units in nucleic acid and amino acid metabolism	anaemia, gastrointestinal disturbances, diarrhoea, red tongue	none reported
vitamin B-12	0.003 0.003	muscle meats, eggs, dairy products (not present in plant foods)	coenzyme involved in transfer of single-carbon units in nucleic acid metabolism	pernicious anaemia, neurologic disorders	none reported
biotin	0.10–0.20 0.10–0.20	legumes, vegetables, meats	coenzyme required for fat synthesis, amino acid metabolism, and glycogen (animal-starch) formation	fatigue, depression, nausea, dermatitis, muscular pains	none reported
vitamin C (ascorbic acid)	60 60	citrus fruits, tomatoes, green peppers, salad greens	maintains intercellular matrix of cartilage, bone, and dentine important in collagen synthesis	scurvy (degeneration of skin, teeth, blood vessels, epithelial haemorrhages)	relatively nontoxic possibility of kidney stones
fat soluble vitamin A (retinol)	1.0 0.8	provitamin A (beta-carotene) widely distributed in green vegetables retinol present in milk, butter, cheese, fortified margarine	constituent of rhodopsin (visual pigment) maintenance of epithelial role in mucopolysaccharide synthesis	xerophthalmia (keratinisation of ocular tissue), night blindness, permanent blindness	headache, vomiting, peeling of skin, anorexia, swelling of long bones
vitamin D	0.075 0.075	cod-liver oil, eggs, dairy products, fortified milk, and margarine	promotes growth and mineralisation of bones increases absorption of calcium	rickets (bone deformities) in children osteomalacia in adults	vomiting diarrhoea, loss of weight, kidney damage
vitamin E (tocopherol)	10 8	seeds, green leafy vegetables, margarines, shortenings	functions as an antioxidant to prevent cell-membrane damage	possibly anaemia	relatively nontoxic
vitamin K (phylloquinone)	0.07–0.14 0.07–0.14	green leafy vegetables small amount in cereals, fruits, and meats	important in blood clotting (involved in formation of active prothrombin)	conditioned deficiencies associated with severe bleeding; internal haemorrhages	relatively nontoxic synthetic forms at high doses may cause jaundice

Source: Fisher and Jensen, 1990

Table 9.2 THE MAJOR MINERALS

MINERAL	AMOUNT IN ADULT BODY (G)	RDA FOR HEALTHY ADULT MALE AND FEMALE (MG)	DIETARY SOURCES	MAJOR BODY FUNCTIONS	DEFICIENCY	EXCESS
calcium	1,500	800 / 800	milk, cheese, dark-green vegetables, dried legumes	bone and tooth formation, blood clotting, nerve transmission	stunted growth, rickets, osteoporosis, convulsions	not reported in man
phosphorus	860	800 / 800	milk, cheese, meat, poultry, grains	bone and tooth formation, acid-base balance	weakness, demineralisation of bone, loss of calcium	erosion of jaw (fossy jaw)
sulphur	300	(provided by sulphur amino acids)	sulphur amino acids (methionine and cystine) in dietary proteins	constituent of active tissue compounds, cartilage and tendon	related to intake and deficiency of sulphur amino acids	excess sulphur amino acid intake leads to poor growth
potassium	180	1,875–5,625	meats, milk, many fruits	acid-base balance, body water balance, nerve function	muscular weakness, paralysis	muscular weakness, death
chlorine	74	1,700–5,100	common salt	formation of gastric juice, acid-base balance	muscle cramps, mental apathy, reduced appetite	vomiting
sodium	64	1,100–3,300	common salt	acid-base balance, body water balance, nerve function	muscle cramps, mental apathy, reduced appetite	high blood pressure
magnesium	25	350 / 300	whole grains, green leafy vegetables	activates enzymes, involved in protein synthesis	growth failure, behavioural disturbances, weakness, spasms	diarrhoea
iron	4.5	10 / 18	eggs, lean meats, legumes, whole grains, green leafy vegetables	constituent of haemoglobin and enzymes involved in energy metabolism	iron-deficiency anaemia (weakness, reduced resistance to infection)	siderosis, cirrhosis of liver
fluorine	2.6	1.5–4.0	drinking water, tea, seafood	may be important in maintenance of bone structure	higher frequency of tooth decay	mottling of teeth, increased bone density, neurologic disturbances
zinc	2	15	widely distributed in foods	constituent of enzymes involved in digestion	growth failure, small sex glands	fever, nausea, vomiting, diarrhoea
copper	0.1	2	meats, drinking water	constituent of enzymes associated with iron	anaemia, bone changes (rare in man)	rare metabolic condition (Wilson's disease)
silicon vanadium tin nickel	0.024 0.018 0.17 0.010	2 not established	widely distributed in foods	function unknown (essential for animals)	not reported in man	industrial exposures: silicon – silicosis, vanadium – lung irritation, tin – vomiting, nickel – acute pneumonitis
selenium	0.013	0.05–0.02	seafood, meat, grains	functions in close association with vitamin E	anaemia (rare)	gastrointestinal disorders, lung irritation
manganese	0.012	not established (diet provides 6–8 per day)	widely distributed in foods	constituent of enzymes involved in fat synthesis	in animals: poor growth, disturbances of nervous system, reproductive abnormalities	poisoning in manganese mines: generalised disease of nervous system
iodine	0.011	0.15	marine fish and shellfish, dairy products, many many vegetables	constituent of thyroid hormones	goiter (enlarged thyroid)	very high intakes depress thyroid activity
molybdenum	0.009	not established (diet provides 0.4 per day)	legumes, cereals, organ meats	constituent of some enzymes	not reported in man	inhibition of enzymes
chromium	0.006	0.05–0.02	fats, vegetable oils, meats	involved in glucose and energy metabolism	impaired ability to metabolise glucose	occupational exposures: skin and kidney damage
cobalt	0.0015	(required as vitamin B_{12})	organ and muscle meats, milk	constituent of vitamin B_{12}	not reported in man	industrial exposure dermatitis and diseases of red blood cells
water	40,000 (60% of body weight)	1.5 litres per day	solid foods, liquids, drinking water	transport of nutrients, temperature regulation, participates in metabolic reactions	thirst, dehydration	headaches, nausea, oedema, high blood pressure

Source: Fisher and Jensen, 1990

Fig. 9.1 REHYDRATION WHILE PERFORMING

Glycogen loading

Some athletes seek to manipulate dietary intake before competition in order to optimise performance. One method of doing this is by glycogen loading or **supercompensation**. This process involves depleting the glycogen levels seven days prior to the event by doing endurance-based training, and then starving the body of carbohydrate over the following three days by omitting such foods from the diet. For the remaining days leading up to competition the athlete will consume high carbohydrate meals to boost muscle glycogen stores up to twice that normally stored.

This method of manipulation is widely practised in endurance events and maximises energy production via the aerobic pathway. Recent research has shown however that total depletion of glycogen may not be necessary for trained athletes and simply resting for three days prior to competition and eating high carbohydrate meals may maximise glycogen stores. It is important to point out however that storage of glycogen requires a greater ingestion of water and water intake must increase accordingly.

ACTIVITY 1

1 **What nutritional advice would you give to a triathlete both in training and preparing for competition?**
2 **Why might increased muscle glycogen stores increase performance? How would you increase the muscle glycogen stores of your athletes?**
3 **Explain how diet may be used as an ergogenic acid.**

Summary

- A well balanced diet is essential for successful performance in sport both whilst training and in preparation for competition.
- Six groups of nutrients should be included into an athlete's diet. These are carbohydrate, fat, protein, vitamins, minerals and water.
- Carbohydrate in the form of sugars and starches is the main energy provider for the high intensity athlete – it is stored in the muscles and the liver.
- Fat is the major source of energy in the body and is mainly used during low intensity endurance based activities. Stored fat is broken down into free fatty acids – its usable form. The body cannot use fat alone but uses a combination of fat and glycogen.
- Proteins are composed of amino acids, the body's building blocks. They are also an energy provider, but are only used when glycogen stores are very low.
- Vitamins can aid in the production of energy. Given a well balanced diet there should be no need for supplementation.
- Minerals are vital for tissue functioning, transmission of nerve impulses and enable effective muscle contraction.
- Water is an essential nutrient. Water loss during exercise can impair performance in a number of ways. It certainly contributes to heat stroke and can induce muscle cramps.
- Athletes should ensure they receive adequate energy supplies. A high carbohydrate diet of up to 60% of total energy intake is essential. Many small meals are better than 2 or 3 larger ones.
- Glycogen loading or supercompensation is a form of diet manipulation to ensure the energy stores of the body are at their greatest prior to a competition.

Health-related Implications

O ur study has so far been confined to the use of exercise physiology as an aid to the high level performer, to improve performance. This chapter seeks to illustrate how exercise and physical activity can be used for health-related reasons; in particular, how exercise can be used to prevent and control common health problems, including cardiovascular disease, obesity and diabetes. We discuss how to design exercise programmes used specifically to improve health and rehabilitate individuals.

This chapter also covers the importance of exercise for the young and elderly people, and gender issues that arise from the study of sports physiology.

Health-related fitness

It has long been known that exercise can lead to a healthier lifestyle. Below is a discussion of the role of exercise in the prevention of disorders of the heart and vascular system, and how it can be used as an important element in weight control. It focuses on prescribing exercise programmes for the general population, as opposed to the elite athletes discussed in Chapter 8.

Cardiovascular disease

Cardiovascular disease is the main cause of death in the industrialised nations of Western civilisation, and accounts for an estimated 40% of all deaths in the United Kingdom. There are several forms of cardiovascular disease, which include:

- atherosclerosis – a laying down of fatty deposits in the arteries
- coronary heart disease – may lead to angina pectoris (coronary thrombosis) or a myocardial infarction (heart attack)
- cerebral infarction (stroke)
- hypertension – constant elevated blood pressure.

Atherosclerosis is a degenerative disease. It is typified by a thickening and hardening of the arterial walls, as a result of atheroma or plaque being deposited.

By the laying down of atheroma, the lumen of the vessel is decreased in diameter. This is further narrowed by the formation of blood clots on the rough edges of the plaque. With continual deposition of atheroma, the walls of the arteries harden and lose their elasticity; this reduces their ability to vasoconstrict and vasodilate – two important mechanisms in regulating blood pressure. Consequently, blood pressure rises permanently as the resistance to blood flow has increased – the body suffers **hypertension**. This is clinically defined as blood pressure consistently above 160/100 mmHg, and can increase the risk of stroke, heart attack and kidney failure.

When atherosclerosis occurs mainly in the coronary arteries (which supply the myocardium with blood), parts of the heart become deprived of oxygen and a **myocardial infarction** or heart attack may ensue. For severe cases of coronary heart disease, a heart bypass operation may be required which enables blood to bypass the blocked part of the vessel and reach the oxygen deprived tissue. Similarly, severe blockages of the cerebral arteries supplying the brain may cause oxygen deprivation, resulting in a **cerebral infarction** or stroke.

The incidence and severity of the disease is dependent upon the following independent and dependent risk factors.

Independent risk factors

Independent or primary risk factors are so called because the presence of any one of them can cause the development of such vascular diseases. These include smoking and a high fat intake.

1 **Smoking** increases the risk up to 20 times, and is a dose-related factor: the more you smoke, the more the risk. However, ceasing smoking can reduce this risk greatly within a few years.
2 A high fat diet can cause an increased risk, due to the deposition of **cholesterol** in the arteries.

Cholesterol is used by the body to form cell membranes and hormones. It is transported in the blood by protein molecules called **lipoproteins**. Generally a high level of blood cholesterol is associated with an increased risk of coronary heart disease.

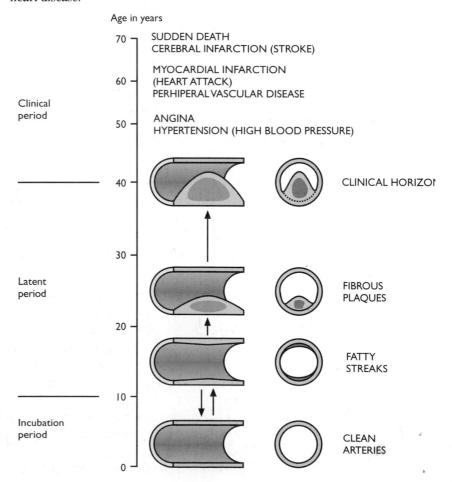

Fig. 10.1 THE DEVELOPMENT OF ATHEROSCLEROSIS

More importantly, however, is the *type* of lipoprotein that carries the cholesterol. The inflated risk is largely linked to a high proportion of *low* density lipoproteins (LDL) to *high* density lipoproteins (HDL). The quantity of low density lipoproteins is increased when a diet high in saturated fats is followed. These lipoproteins have a tendency to deposit cholesterol in the arteries, whereas high density lipoproteins act as waste disposal units – they remove cholesterol from the arterial wall and carry it to the liver where it can be metabolised.

Consequently, a high proportion of high density lipoproteins to low density lipoproteins can substantially reduce the risk of atherosclerosis onset.

Dependent risk factors

Dependent risk factors are those which do not necessarily cause CVD alone, but when in combination with other factors, may substantially increase the risk.

1 **Heredity:** there appears to be a genetic link in the development of cardiovascular diseases. The easiest way to determine if this factor is appropriate is to look back at your family history for the incidence of this disease.
2 **Personality** or **stress** is also widely accepted as a contributing factor. Although almost everybody will experience stress, how the individual deals and copes with that stress is the vital point. Type A personalities (characteristics of impatience, aggression and ambition) have a higher risk than type B individuals with the opposite characteristics.
3 **Lack of exercise:** studies show that people who habitually exercise at an intensity of 70% of their predicted maximum heart rate have a much lower risk of heart and vascular diseases; the reasons for this will be dealt with later in this chapter.

LDL–Cholesterol
The higher it goes, the higher the risk

HDL–Cholesterol
The higher it goes, the lower the risk

Coronary Heart Disease and Lipoproteins

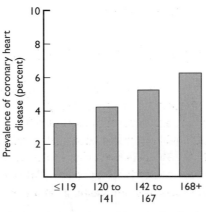

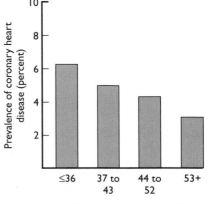

LDL-Cholesterol (mg per deciliter.)

HDL-Cholesterol (mg per deciliter.)

Fig. 10.2 CORONARY HEART DISEASE AND LIPOPROTEIN CONCENTRATION

Source: CPC International Best Foods Division

Case history:
A 53-year-old male with a two-year history of severe angina had a serum cholesterol level of only 237 mg/dl, and a triglyceride level of 136 mg/dl, both of which are considered "normal." However, his LDL-cholesterol value of 181 mg/dl, and HDL-cholesterol value of 31 mg/dl, placed this patient at higest risk (see graphs). The LDL and HDL measurements can be made by any laboratory equipped to measure cholesterol and triglycerides.

4 Other factors that are uncontrollable yet increase the risk are increasing age (due to the progressive narrowing of arteries through atherosclerosis) and gender (men have historically had higher incidences of CVD than women).

Atherosclerosis is not confined to the middle aged. Research has found that fatty streaks can start appearing in the arteries of early teenage children; by the mid-twenties these may develop into fibrous plaques and by the early forties, severe blockages of the arteries can start to occur. The rate at which the disease progresses is largely determined by the heredity factor and the lifestyles that individuals choose to enjoy.

The role of exercise in the prevention of cardiovascular disease

Numerous studies have been conducted into how exercise can prevent cardiovascular diseases. The installation of an exercise programme together with the cessation of smoking can go some way in the prevention of such diseases. A summary of the major findings now follows:

- Exercise tends to reduce the overall risk of developing some form of cardiovascular disease by about 30%, largely due to the adaptation of the cardiovascular system discussed in Chapter 8. By exercising, improvements occur in the contractility of and blood supply to the heart. By causing blood vessels to vasoconstrict and dilate regularly, exercise can prevent the arteries from hardening and losing their elasticity, and so ward off the effects of atherosclerosis. This will also prevent hypertension and the associated dangers.
- Exercise can also reduce the level of fatty deposits in the blood and increase the proportion of HDL:LDL, as well as reducing overall cholesterol levels. The laying down of fatty deposits in the arteries is therefore significantly reduced.
- Exercise can also reduce body fat and reduce the strain upon the circulatory system.
- The increased breakdown of blood glucose as a result of exercise, reduces blood sugar content and decreases the incidence of adult onset **diabetes**.
- Vigorous activity can also have a cathartic effect, reducing stress and generally instilling 'the feel good factor'.

Obesity and weight control

Obesity is a condition which accompanies a sedentary or inactive lifestyle, and is an excessive increase in the body's total quantity of fat. Typically, men with more than 25% body fat and women with more than 35% are clinically defined as obese.

One method frequently used to estimate the extent of obesity is the Body Mass Index (BMI). This does not solely consider a person's weight, but also takes into account body composition. A person's BMI can be calculated by dividing body weight in kilograms by the square of body height in metres. For example:

- A man weighing 110 kg and measuring 1.83 m in height will have a BMI of 33 kg/m^2.

1 **Calculate your body mass index.**
2 **Compare it with results from the rest of your group and comment upon your findings.**

Obesity can lead to an increased risk of atherosclerosis, hypertension, heart disease and strokes. This is largely due to low density lipoprotein proliferation in the blood plasma, which will increase the level of fatty deposits in the arteries around the body, including the coronary and cerebral arteries. Other complications may include the development of gall bladder disease and diabetes. This is characterised by increased blood sugar levels, resulting from insufficient insulin production from the pancreas.

The control of body weight

The rate at which the body uses energy is termed the **metabolic** rate, and is an important factor in weight control. At rest the body still requires energy; the rate of energy expenditure at rest is known as the **basal metabolic** rate and may vary from 1,200–2,400 Kcal per day.

The amount of food required by an individual above that which is required for the body's essential physiological functions, is dependent upon the amount of physical activity in which the individual is engaged throughout the day.

For body weight to remain constant, energy *input* via food must equal energy *expenditure*. This is the basis of weight control and is known as the **energy equation**. Too much food consumed for energy requirement will lead to a positive energy balance and a gain in weight. Conversely, if energy expenditure is greater than the energy derived from the food consumed, a negative energy balance occurs, the body will draw upon its energy stores in the form of fat, and a decrease in weight will be seen.

In order to cure obesity, it is necessary to shift the energy balance from a positive to a negative one, so that energy expenditure is greater than energy input. The body will then draw upon its fat stores for the missing calories; as fat mobilisation and consumption occurs, body weight decreases. The formation of a negative energy balance is best achieved by a combination of decreased calorie intake and increased activity.

Other benefits of performing exercise as part of a weight control programme include the suppressing of appetite, and an increase in the resting metabolic rate, which assumes that more calories are used up in the body even if exercise is not taking place!

The best type of exercise to perform in order to lose weight would be aerobic exercise, using large muscle groups that continues for a minimum of 30 minutes. It is also an idea to prescribe non- or partial-weight bearing activities such as swimming or cycling for the overweight individual, since this will prevent undue stress being placed on the joints.

Exercise and ageing

Most of us reach our peak of physical fitness in our mid twenties or early thirties. The extent to which our fitness declines is largely due to increased inactivity which accompanies the ageing process. Numerous studies have concluded that there are many physiological changes that occur with age, and exercise can decrease the rate at which this decline occurs.

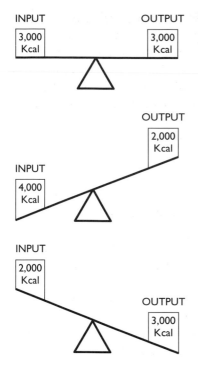

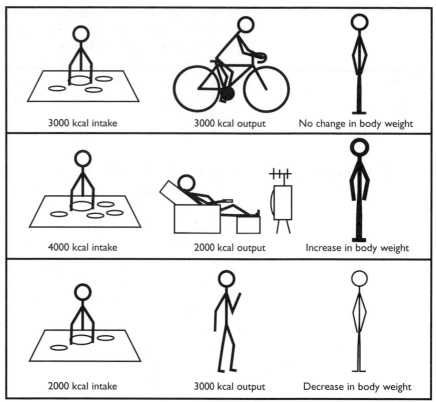

Fig. 10.3 THE ENERGY EQUATION

The effects of ageing

Cardio-respiratory functioning decreases for many reasons:

1 Maximum heart rate decreases by approximately one beat per minute, every year. This has a knock-on effect to cardiac output which consequently decreases as we age.
2 Stroke volume also decreases, due to the laying down of collagen fibres in the myocardium of the heart. This reduces the heart's elasticity and contractility.
3 The formation of fibrous plaques in the arteries is associated with the ageing process, and so peripheral resistance to blood flow is increased.

These factors result in a reduced blood flow around the body and a decreased ability to transport oxygen to the working muscles. Aerobic capacity therefore decreases at an estimated rate of 10% per decade, largely due to a reduced $\dot{V}O_2$ max and a decreased a-$\dot{V}O_2$ diff (less oxygen is being taken from the blood and utilised in the muscles).

Table 10.1 ENERGY EXPENDITURE IN DIFFERENT SPORTS

SPORT	DURATION	ENERGY EXPENDITURE
swimming	60 mins	5/25 kcal/min
jogging	30 mins	7–8 kcal/min
soccer	90 mins	9 kcal/min
rugby	80 mins	6–9 kcal/min
tennis	60 mins	6–9 kcal/min
sprinting	15 secs	90 kcal/min

4   Lung tissue loses some elasticity with age, which decreases some lung volumes and capacities. This further reduces oxygen availability to the muscles.
5   Changes in the effectiveness of the musculo-skeletal system also occur with ageing. Decreased muscle strength, mass, and fibre cross-sectional area, and an increased percentage of slow twitch muscle fibres can all occur with an increase in age.
6   There is a decrease in the ability of the nervous system to initiate and respond to stimuli. This is largely due to a loss of nerve cells in the brain.
7   Decreased bone mineral content causes the bones to become more brittle and less resilient. Bones are unable to withstand too much stress, and fractures may occur; this increased porosity of the bone is known as *osteoporosis*. This is particularly seen in postmenopausal women, and is a function of oestrogen deficiency that may accompany the menopause. Hormone Replacement Therapy (HRT) can improve this disorder.

Exactly how much of the decline in fitness levels is a direct result of the ageing process is not really known. However, studies have shown that continuing exercise into old age can decrease the rate at which this decline occurs.

The effects of regular exercise on the ageing process

Exercise has positive benefits for a person's health whatever their age. The improvements in physiological functioning associated with regular exercise have been clearly documented earlier in this book, and here they are related to the ageing process:

1   Cardiovascular improvements include a reduction in heart rates at rest and sub-maximal workloads, and a reduced blood pressure for those who have suffered from mild hypertension.
2   Exercise can prevent the formation of blood clots occurring in the arteries, and therefore reduces the risk of a thrombosis.
3   Blood cholesterol levels decrease, and can thus hinder the development and progress of atherosclerosis.
4   Exercise reduces the depletion of protein and slows the rate of strength loss.
5   Through exercise, muscle tissues will keep its elasticity; this will improve flexibility, enabling greater independence and mobility for the older athlete.
6   The incidence and severity of osteoporosis is also greatly reduced as a result of following a regular exercise programme.

Designing an exercise programme

Before prescribing an exercise programme, participants should be screened, and should preferably have a medical examination by their doctor.

The intensity of exercise should be light at first, with a gradual introduction of increments. Ideally, all fitness elements should be included in the exercise programme, although it is advised to keep high intensity work to a minimum; anaerobic work should never be advised for those with cardiovascular defects. Consequently, the aerobic system should be predominantly stressed, using the large muscle group rhythmically at fairly low intensity. Try to avoid high impact activities, as undue stress on the bones and joints could cause skeletal complications.

It is necessary to monitor everyone for signs of distress during the exercise. Care should also be taken to ensure the environment is conducive to such exercise.

Older individuals can overheat and dehydrate quickly in hot conditions, and a cold temperature can deprive the heart of oxygen (respiratory and vascular vessels may constrict).

You are asked to prescribe a 10-week exercise programme for a group of middle-aged men who have been relatively inactive for some years.

1 What factors do you need to consider in preparing the programme?
2 State the type of exercises you would include and give reasons for your choices.

Summary

- Cardiovascular disease is the biggest cause of death in the Western world.
- Forms of cardiovascular disease include, atherosclerosis, coronary heart disease, angina, strokes and hypertension.
- Independent risk factors for a cardiovascular disease include smoking and a high fat diet.
- Dependent risk factors include genetics, personality and stress, lack of exercise, age and gender.
- Exercise can help prevent cardiovascular disease in many ways. It improves the whole functioning of the cardiovascular system, it reduces fatty deposits in the arteries by stimulating HDL concentrations, and reduces stress.
- Obesity is an excessive increase in the body's total quantity of fat. Men with an excess of 25% body fat and women in excess of 35% body fat are clinically defined as obese.
- Obesity can lead to an increase in the incidence of cardiovascular diseases and diabetes.
- The basis of weight control is known as the energy equation. A positive energy balance occurs when energy input is greater than energy output, and results in an increase in weight. A negative energy balance occurs where energy input is less than energy output resulting in a decrease in weight.
- Exercise will increase energy output and therefore shift towards a negative energy balance. Exercise can also suppress appetite and increase metabolic rate.
- The decline in fitness with age is largely due to a reduction in activity.
- Ageing decreases maximum heart rate, stroke volume and cardiac output. Lung tissue loses elasticity and bones become more brittle through osteoporosis. Exercise can limit the extent of the ageing process.
- When designing a health related exercise programme, participants should be screened and preferably given the all clear by their doctor. Exercise should be of light intensity and therefore aerobic in nature. High impact exercise should be kept to a minimum.

chapter 11

Fundamental Biomechanics

In order to fully understand human motion, a basic understanding of mechanics is required. The term 'biomechanics' literally means 'the mechanics of living beings' and biomechanists analyse human performance from a scientific standpoint with the aim of achieving optimal sporting techniques, improving the design of equipment and determining the stresses imposed on the body during performance in order to prevent injury. This chapter provides a comprehensive yet digestible guide to mechanical factors contributing to sports performance.

Central to the study of biomechanics are Newton's laws of motion, and this chapter will use these laws as the primary focus.

There follows an investigation of linear and angular motion through practical experimentation, enabling students to relate specifically to sporting situations.

Force

Force is the 'push' or 'pull' exerted upon an object or body, which may either cause motion of a stationary body or a speeding up, slowing down or even a change of direction of a moving body. Generally, forces can either be generated internally to the body via muscular contractions or externally through gravity, friction and the forces of air and water. Without such forces, movement would not be possible, but optimal performance can take place when all forces are understood and adapted to the same aim. For example:

- Jonathan Edwards' world record triple jump at the 1995 World Championships: everything from the run up, the hop phase, the step phase, the angle of the jump and the landing were all at an optimal level, resulting in a gold medal and world record jump. Central to this performance were the internal and external forces exerted upon his body.

Force is a **vector quantity** – it has both magnitude and direction which, when considered with the point at which the force is applied, determines the resultant action or direction of the resultant force. Where forces act in different directions, the resultant can be found by constructing a parallelogram of forces, with the resultant force lying along the diagonal of the parallelogram.

All forces are measured in Newtons. One Newton represents the force required to give a 1 kg mass an acceleration of 1 m per second squared. To illustrate the forces acting on a body, see fig 11.3: a free body diagram is drawn which also shows the magnitude of such forces (by length of the line drawn) and the point at which the force is applied.

Fig. 11.1 Jonathan Edwards' world record-breaking triple jump in the 1995 World Championships

Linear motion

Velocity

With reference to sporting performance, we are always concerned with how fast a body or an object is travelling – ie, their **speed**. However, speed is a **scalar quantity** and direction is never really considered. When considering linear motion, biomechanists normally require a direction, and as **velocity** is a vector quantity and has both size and direction, this is the preferred term.

$$\text{Speed} = \frac{\text{distance travelled}}{\text{time taken}}$$

$$\text{Velocity} = \frac{\text{displacement}}{\text{time taken}}$$

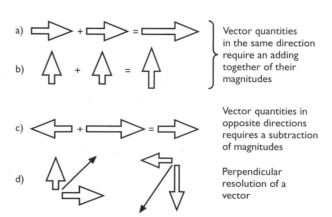

Fig. 11.2 Vector quantities
Adapted from Hay and Reid, 1988

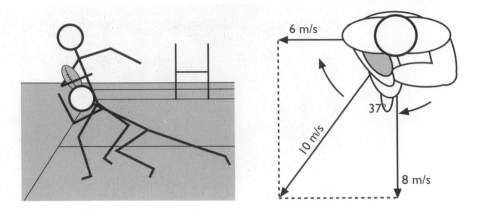

Fig. 11.3 THE PARALLELOGRAM OF FORCES.
THE RESULTANT OF TWO VECTORS IS CALCULATED
VIA THE PARALLELOGRAM OF FORCES

Both quantities are generally measured in metres travelled per second.

Acceleration

In many sporting situations, such as 100 m sprint, acceleration should also be considered in order to analyse an athlete's successful performance. Acceleration represents the *rate* of change of velocity; as such it is a **vector** quantity, possessing both magnitude and direction.

$$\text{Acceleration} = \frac{\text{change in velocity}}{\text{time taken}}$$

Newton's laws of motion explain the principles of acceleration and movement, and are explained below, using the example of a 100 m sprinter.

The law of inertia

At the beginning of the race, an athlete remains stationary in the blocks. According to Newton's **first** law of motion:

Every body at rest, or moving with constant velocity in a straight line, will continue in that state unless compelled to change by an external force exerted upon it.

This suggests that a body or an object has a tendency to resist any change in its state of motion – if a body is travelling in a straight line at constant speed, it will continue to do so unless acted upon by a force.

The same is true for the sprinter in the set position in the blocks. S/he will remain stationary unless a force is exerted upon the blocks. The force exerted must be great enough to overcome this inertia, and in doing so the sprinter will move forward out of the blocks. However the inertia of an object is directly proportional to its mass, so a body with a greater mass will need a larger force to overcome its inertia than a body with less mass. Once out of the blocks, the athlete will quickly accelerate as there has been a change in velocity (which is zero when the sprinter is in the blocks).

Fig. 11.4 LINFORD CHRISTIE IN THE
BLOCKS

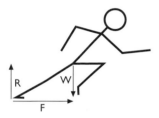

R   W

F

a) beginning

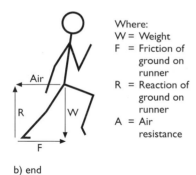

Where:
W = Weight
F = Friction of
    ground on
    runner
R = Reaction of
    ground on
    runner
A = Air
    resistance

Air

R   W

F

b) end

Fig. 11.5 A FREE BODY DIAGRAM SHOWING
THE FORCES ACTING ON A SPRINTER AT THE
BEGINNING AND END OF A RACE

The law of acceleration

In order to generate a greater acceleration, the athlete must generate a greater force. This is Newton's **second** law of motion, which states that

The acceleration of a body is proportional to the force causing it, and the acceleration takes place in the direction in which that force acts.

This is expressed as $F = ma$:

- F = force generated
- m = mass of body or object
- a = acceleration

If the mass and acceleration of the sprinter are known, it is simple to compute the force required to give that acceleration. For example:

mass of athlete = 74 kg
acceleration   = 4.6 m/s^2
F   = ma
F   = 74 kg $\times$ 4.6 m/s^2
F   = 340 Newtons

Remember, a Newton is the force which gives a mass of 1 kg an acceleration of 1 m/s^2.

After about five seconds of the sprint we would expect the sprinter to have reached maximum velocity, and (according to Newton's first law) to remain at this constant velocity, so why does the athlete start to slow down? The explanation is relatively simple:

- the effects of air resistance (although negligible)
- physiological effect of the sprint – this is the main cause. The muscle stores of ATP and PC which provide the energy for muscular contraction are depleted.

This slowing down of the athlete represents a change in velocity and therefore is known as **deceleration**. In fact most sprinters will start to slow down after 80–90 m and the winner will often be the person who takes longer to slow down!

The action/reaction law

Newton's **third** law of motion states that:

When one object exerts a force on a second object, there is a force equal in magnitude but opposite in direction exerted by the second object on the first.

More simply, to every action there is an equal and opposite reaction. The sprinter on the blocks experienced a force propelling him/her forward. From Newton's third law we can deduce that as the athlete pushed backwards and downwards on the blocks, the blocks pushed the athlete upwards and forwards out of the blocks.

Reaction forces can easily be seen in the field of sport:

* A footballer kicking a ball exerts a force upon it in order to set it in motion (N1); according to Newton's third law, the ball will exert an equal and opposite force onto the kicking foot.
* The high jumper exerts a force upon the ground in order to gain height, by the ground exerting an upward force upon him/her.

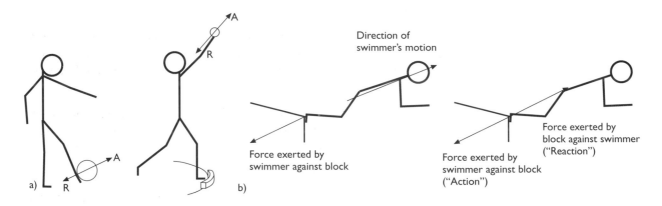

Fig. 11.6 ACTION AND REACTION FORCES (A) WHEN AN ATHLETE APPLIES A FORCE TO THE FOOTBALL OR PUTS A SHOT, THE BALL AND SHOT EXERTS AN EQUAL FORCE ON THE ATHLETE'S FOOT OR HAND (B) ACTION AND REACTION FORCES IN A SWIMMING START

Frictional force

Friction is a force which acts on the interface of surfaces which are in contact, and acts in the opposite direction to the direction of motion. The magnitude or size of the frictional force will determine the relative ease or difficulty of movement for the objects in contact.

The coefficient of friction indicates the ease of movement and is determined by the amount of molecular interaction between the two surfaces in contact. For example:

* The coefficient of friction between a rugby boot and grass will be much larger than that between an ice skaters skate and an icy surface.
* In order to increase the coefficient of friction, a rugby player might remove mud and grass from his boots before packing down for a scrummage.
* The volleyball court is regularly swept to remove perspiration which will enable a firmer grip between shoe and court.

The coefficient may also be increased by increasing the force that presses the surfaces together:

- Mountain bikers often sit back over the driving wheel when riding up a muddy slope in order to gain a better grip of the tyre on the surface.

Friction forces can further be increased by increasing the surface area in contact with another:

- An athlete wears spikes when running on a tartan track
- A racket player may wear a glove in order to maintain a firm grip.

Momentum, impact and impulse

Momentum

Momentum is the amount of motion a moving object possesses and is the product of its mass and velocity:

$$Mo = m \times v$$

- A sprinter with a mass of 75 kg and a velocity of 10 m/s has a momentum of 750 kg m/s.

From the above equation it can be seen that a body's momentum can be changed by altering either its mass or velocity. However, in sporting activity the mass of a body or object generally remains constant, so any change in momentum must be due to a change in velocity (acceleration). For example:

- a long jumper may increase velocity by changing their approach run, in order to increase their momentum before take off. Once in the air, the velocity and mass of the jumper remains constant, so momentum is said to be conserved.

This extends Newton's first law of motion:

In any system of bodies that exert forces on each other, the total momentum in any direction remains constant unless some external force acts on the system in that direction.

Impact

Momentum becomes more important in sporting situations where collisions or impacts occur. The outcome of the collision depends largely upon the amount of momentum each of the bodies possessed before the collision took place. The body with greater momentum will be more difficult to stop. For example:

- if a prop forward weighing 90 kg and a scrum half weighing 60 kg were both travelling at the same velocity, the prop forward would have a greater momentum and would require a large force to stop his path to the try line.
- the speed at which the squash ball is struck is determined by the momentum of the racket head at the time of impact.

A change in momentum is synonymous with a change in acceleration and as such relates to Newton's second law of motion (page 000). This is expressed as:

$$F = ma$$

In order to work out the acceleration (a), the following equations must be used:

$$a = \frac{v - u}{t}$$

thus:

$$F = \frac{m(v - u)}{t}$$

$$F = \frac{mv - mu}{t}$$

$$Ft = mv - mu$$

$$Ft = \text{change in momentum}$$

Impulse

This final equation suggests that any change in momentum is dependent upon the product of the force and the time that that force is applied to an object, known as **impulse**. It therefore follows that any increase in the force applied or the time over which the force is applied, will increase outgoing momentum. This has important implications for sporting situations where acceleration of a body or object is essential. For example:

- a follow through of a racket or hockey stick will ensure that the time over which the force has been applied is at its maximum; the change in momentum or acceleration of the ball will be greater than if a follow through had not been performed.
- the shot putt: over time the technique of this event has been transformed. Originally a sideways stance was adopted before the putt. However the **O'Brien** technique aims to apply a force over a longer period of time by incorporating a one and three-quarter turn and increasing the acceleration of the shot. Again by performing a follow through the athlete can ensure that the time of contact has been maximised. Of course in addition to developing this technique the athlete still requires the necessary physical attributes in order to apply a large force to the implement.
- water polo: a player catching the ball with one hand will aim to decrease the velocity over a long period of time and so decrease the force exerted by the ball on the hands. S/he does this by meeting the ball early and withdrawing the catching hand in the direction of the ball's motion, thus cushioning the impact; this will prevent the ball hitting the hand and bouncing off uncontrollably.
- cricket: when catching a fast moving cricket ball, the same principle applies, which can prevent injury to the hands.

Other examples include the use of crash mats in activities such as gymnastics and high jump.

Fluid forces

We are now going to turn our attention to fluid forces such as those offered by air and water. When a body or object moves through air or water, it is affected by **fluid friction** which acts in the opposite direction to the motion of the moving body. The amount of air resistance or fluid friction experienced depends upon the shape of the object and the speed at which the object is moving.

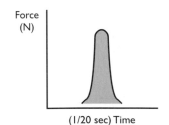

Force (N)

(1/20 sec) Time

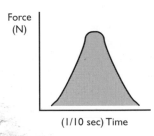

Force (N)

(1/10 sec) Time

Fig. 11.7 THE EFFECT OF A FOLLOW THROUGH ON THE OUTGOING MOMENTUM OF A HOCKEY BALL (A) FORCE EXERTED WITHOUT A FOLLOW THROUGH (B) FORCE EXERTED WITH A FOLLOW THROUGH

Air resistance

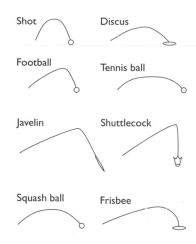

Fig. 11.8 THE EXPECTED FLIGHT PATHS OF A VARIETY OF PROJECTILES

Air resistance is prevalent in most sporting activity, although its affects on performance vary greatly. Air resistance can affect the performer in flight; for example:

- the long jump
- projectiles such as balls, shuttlecocks and javelins
- cyclists
- sprinters.

Air resistance offered to a projectile while in flight may change the **parabolic flight path**. Some examples of flight paths expected from a variety of projectiles are illustrated in fig 11.8. Flight paths can be categorised as:

- parabolic (a uniform symmetrical shape)
- nearly parabolic
- asymmetric.

To discuss the effect of air resistance on flight paths, we will examine more closely the flight of a shot putt and badminton shuttlecock.

Fig. 11.9 THE O'BRIEN TECHNIQUE

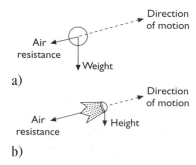

Fig. 11.10 THE FORCES ACTING ON (A) A SHOT AND (B) A SHUTTLECOCK IN FLIGHT

Flight is governed by the ratio of weight to air resistance. Since air resistance is dependent upon the size, shape and speed of an object, all slow moving objects have little air resistance. The weight of the object will be the determining factor and will almost form a parabolic arc. This is illustrated in fig 11.10a, which shows the flight path of a shot putt.

Faster moving objects have greater air resistance. This causes rapid deceleration and slowing down of the projectile until a point is reached where weight once again becomes the determining factor, leading to an asymmetric flight path. Observe the flight of a badminton shuttlecock from a high serve: it will decelerate rapidly and drop vertically – hopefully on the back baseline.

Fluid dynamics

When an object which is uniform in shape, such as a football, travels slowly through the air, the layers of air flow past the object in smooth symmetrical flow lines. This is known as **laminar flow**; see fig 11.11.

However, many objects in sport are fast moving and do not allow laminar flow. This is because as air travels around an object, the layer of air directly in contact with the object's surface is slowed down by surface friction. On a fast moving object, the air is unable to keep in contact with the surface and breaks away to form fast moving eddies of air. This is termed **turbulent flow**; see fig 11.12.

Because the air is fast moving at the back of the object, it has relatively lower pressure in comparison to that at the front. This causes a force pulling the ball back, since objects will always move from areas of higher pressure to lower pressure. This force is known as **drag**.

In activities where maximum speed is the aim, drag must be minimised and this is achieved through **streamlining**. The clearest example of this is cycling:

1　A new cycle helmet was designed which aimed to encourage laminar flow around the head; see fig 11.13.
2　The shape of the racing bike has changed dramatically to minimise the area of the cyclist in contact with the air. Lotus developed the bike on which Chris Boardman won the 1992 Olympic title – this had a lightweight carbon fibre frame and numerous aerodynamic design effects.
3　Graeme Obree, the 1995 world pursuit champion, adopted the following position on the bike in order to improve streamline and reduce the drag force: his head was positioned far out in front of the handlebars, low over the front wheel, while his arms were tucked in under his chest.

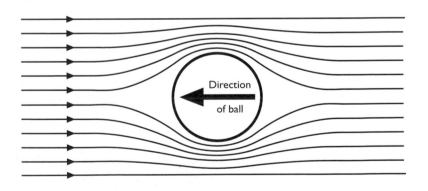

Fig. 11.11 LAMINAR FLOW OF AIR AROUND A SLOW MOVING BALL

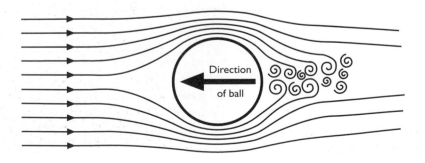

Fig. 11.12 TURBULENT FLOW OF AIR AROUND A FAST MOVING BALL, CAUSING A DRAG FORCE

The Bernouilli effect

A series of experiments conducted by Bernouilli demonstrated that when flow lines get closer together, velocity increases and there is a resulting drop in pressure. This had important implications for the design of objects in flight, the most noticeable being the design of aeroplane wings.

Figure 11.15 shows that the flow lines on the upper surface of the wing have to travel further than the flow lines on the lower surface, and must increase in velocity in order to reach the back at the same time as those on the bottom. As the velocity increases, pressure decreases. A pressure differential exists between the upper and lower surfaces, and a lift force results, keeping the plane in flight.

This principle has also been applied to Formula 1 racing, but the aerofoil is inverted, causing a downward force enabling the car to hold the bend much better.

The Bernouilli effect applied to spinning objects is known as the **magnus effect**. When an object in fluid (including air) spins, the air molecules in contact with the object spin with it, creating a boundary layer; see fig 11.16. When air

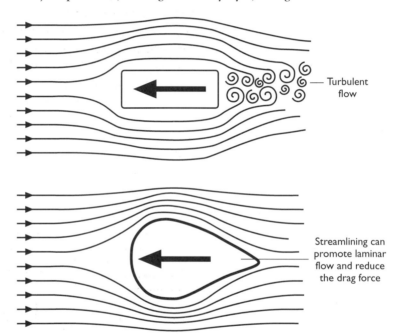

Turbulent flow

Streamlining can promote laminar flow and reduce the drag force

Fig. 11.13 Streamlining a cycle helmet can reduce drag, and promote laminar flow

Fig. 11.14 A cyclist tries to reduce the effects of drag by streamlining

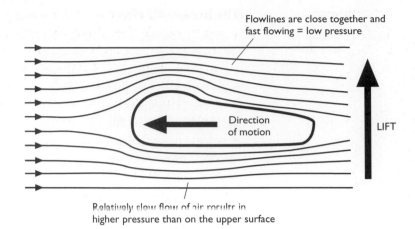

Flowlines are close together and
fast flowing = low pressure

Direction
of motion

LIFT

Relatively slow flow of air results in
higher pressure than on the upper surface

Fig. 11.15 THE BERNOUILLI EFFECT
EXPLAINS HOW AEROPLANES CAN STAY IN
FLIGHT

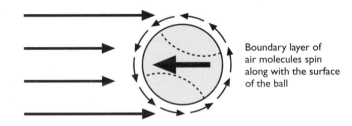

Boundary layer of
air molecules spin
along with the surface
of the ball

Fig. 11.16 THE BOUNDARY LAYER

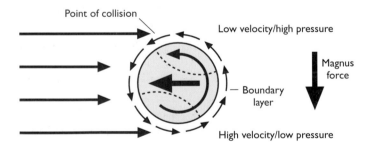

Point of collision

Low velocity/high pressure

Magnus
force

Boundary
layer

High velocity/low pressure

Fig. 11.17 MAGNUS FORCE ON A BALL
HIT WITH TOP SPIN

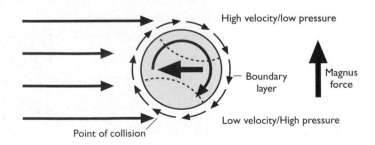

High velocity/low pressure

Magnus
force

Boundary
layer

Low velocity/High pressure

Point of collision

Fig. 11. 18 MAGNUS FORCE ON A BALL HIT
WITH BACK SPIN

Fig. 11.19 A SOCCER PLAYER CAN USE THE MAGNUS EFFECT BY PLACING SIDE SPIN ON A FOOTBALL TO CAUSE THE PATH OF THE BALL TO CURVE

molecules spin *with* the object, they eventually collide head on with the mainstream air flow on one side of the object only; see fig 11.16. This head-on collision causes a decrease in velocity and a higher pressure results.

This causes a pressure differential with the opposite side of the ball, since on this side the boundary layer flows in the same direction as the mainstream air flow. The pressure differential causes a **magnus** force, directed from the high pressure region to the area of low pressure; see figs 11.17 and 11.18.

- The magnus effect is heightened when new balls are used in tennis, since the nap or fuzz of the ball traps a much larger boundary layer of air and causes a greater pressure differential.
- Soccer players use the magnus effect from free kick situations or corners to curve the flight path of the ball. The kicker places a side spin on the ball, curving it around the wall of defensive players in front of goal; see fig 11.19.

Fluid resistance

The effect of fluid resistance is most clearly illustrated by the forces that act upon the swimmer; see fig 11.20. The drag force shown is dependent upon four main factors:

FIG. 11.20 THE FORCES ACTING UPON A SWIMMER

Where B = Bouyancy
            (reaction)
        W = Weight
        D = Drag due to
            (fluid friction)

1 The forward cross section of the swimmer. To reduce drag, the swimmer should adopt as streamlined a position as possible: maintain a flat position close to the surface, without dropping the feet.
2 The surface area in contact with the water. This concerns the swimmer's body shape – elite swimmers tend to be very lean (verging on ectomorphic), which reduces the friction derived from body contact.
3 Surface effects. Swimmers attempt to minimalise turbulent flow by wearing shiny swimsuits, wearing swimming hats and 'shaving down' – the practice of removing body hair. These practices allow the water to flow past the body more smoothly and limit the drag force.

Fig. 11.21 A SWIMMER IN ACTION

4 Speed of the swimmer. The relationship between speed and drag is positive – the faster you swim, the greater the drag. As in competitive swimming, the aim is to swim as fast as possible. There is little swimmers can do to prevent this, but adopting an efficient technique that minimalises drag yet enables fast swimming should be a priority for all swimmers and coaches.

Gravity

Gravity is an external force that naturally occurs and pulls a body or object towards the centre of the earth. Newton's law of gravitation states:

All particles attract one another with a force proportional to the product of their masses, and inversely proportional to the square of the distance between them.

Due to the immense difference between the mass of the earth and objects involved in sporting activity (including human bodies), the gravitational force of attraction between the two bodies is large, and has a significant effect upon performance.

Centre of gravity

An important feature of gravitational pull is that it always occurs through the centre of mass or weight of an object, which is where the weight tends to be concentrated. This point is known as the **centre of gravity** and signifies that point about which the object or body is balanced in all directions. For spherical objects such as a shot the mass is distributed symmetrically around its centre, which therefore indicates its centre of gravity or mass. Due to irregular body shapes however, the centre of gravity is not so obvious for humans. For a person standing erect with hands by their sides, the point of centre of gravity is approximately at naval height, but this point is constantly changing during movement. For example:

- if a person raises one arm above their head, the centre of gravity will move further up the body
- if the person adducts their arm to the right of the body, the centre of gravity will move slightly to the right.

Thus depending upon the shape of the body the centre of gravity will vary.
Athletes and coaches can use their knowledge of this concept in order to improve performance. A perfect example is the high jump:

- The development of the Fosbury flop was developed so that greater heights could be achieved. By arching the back, the centre of gravity will move outside the body, and may pass underneath the bar while the jumper actually travels over the bar! The jumper using the Fosbury technique will therefore not need to raise their centre of gravity as high as someone performing a western roll technique when clearing the same height.

The position of the centre of gravity is also important for maintaining balance. An object or person will remain in balance as long as the centre of gravity remains directly over its base of support (because the force of gravity will always act directly down). As soon as the centre of gravity moves away from the base of support, the object will become more unstable. For example:

- a gymnast on a balance beam: as soon as the centre of gravity moves outside the beam, the gymnast will become unstable and fall.

If the centre of gravity is lowered or the base of support is increased, the more stable the object or body:

- Rugby players forming a platform for a ruck take a large step and lower their hips. This ensures a stable platform and enables them to stay on their feet.
- A judo player has a wide stance, in order to resist attacks from their opponent.

Levers, turning effects and angular motion

Levers   Efficient and effective movement is made possible by a system of **levers**. These are mechanical devices used to produce turning motions about a fixed point (called a **fulcrum**). In the human body, bones act as levers, joints act as the fulcrum and muscle contractions provide the force to move the lever about the fulcrum.

A basic understanding of lever systems can be used to explain rotational motion, and help athletes develop the most efficient technique for their sport.

There are three types of levers, and each is determined by the relationship of the fulcrum (F), the point of application of force or effort (E) and the weight or resistance (R).

1 **First** class lever: the fulcrum lies between the effort and the resistive force.
2 **Second** class lever: the resistance lies between the fulcrum and the effort.
3 **Third** class lever: the effort is between the fulcrum and the weight – see fig 11.22.

The majority of movements in the human body are governed by third class levers.

Functions of levers

Levers have two main functions:

1 increase the resistance that a given effort can move.
2 increase the speed at which a body moves.

First class levers can increase both the effects of the effort and the speed of a body; **second** class levers tend only to increase the effect of the effort force; **third** class levers can be used to increase the speed of a body. An example of a third class lever in the body is the action of the hamstrings and quadriceps on the knee joint, which

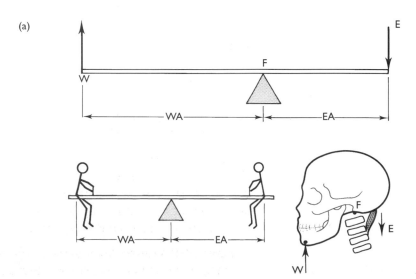

Fig. 11.22a THE FIRST ORDER OF LEVERS

(b)

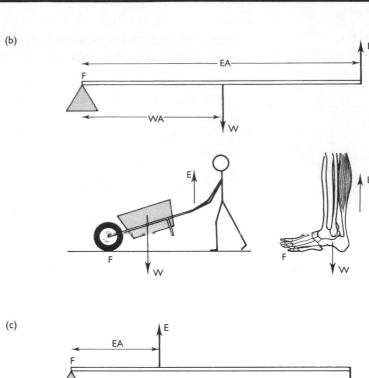

Fig. 11.22b THE SECOND ORDER OF LEVERS

(c)

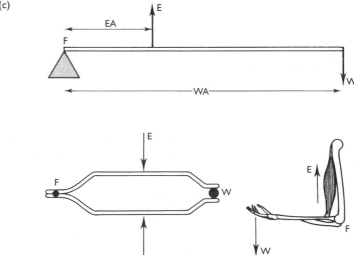

Fig. 11.22c THE THIRD ORDER OF LEVERS

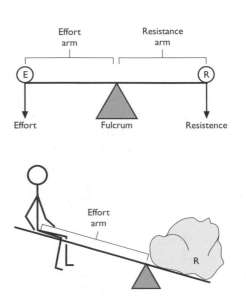

Fig. 11.23 COMPONENTS OF A LEVER

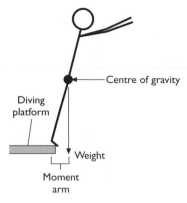

Fig. 11.24 THE MOMENT ARM OF A DIVER
— BY LEANING OUT IN PREPARATION FOR A
DIVE, THE MOMENT ARM IS INCREASED
(LENGTHENED), INCREASING THE ROTATIONAL
EFFECT

causes flexion and extension of the lower leg. The extent to which this can increase, depends upon the relative lengths of the **resistance arm** and the **effort arm**:

1 The resistance arm (RA) is the part of the lever between the fulcrum and the resistance: see fig 11.23. The longer the resistance arm, the greater speed can be generated.

2 The effort arm (EA) is the distance between the fulcrum and the resistance; the longer the effort arm, the less effort required to move a given resistance. In sport, implements are often used such as rackets or bats to increase the length of the effort arm which will increase the force that an object such as a ball is struck. However the optimal length of an implement should be determined by the strength of the person handling it which is why, for example, junior tennis rackets have been designed.

The relative efficiency of the lever system is expressed as the mechanical advantage (MA) which can be determined as follows:

$$MA = \frac{\text{effort arm}}{\text{resistance arm}}$$

Levers and turning effects

The levers of the human body are capable of rotational movement only, so the majority of movements in sporting activity are of an angular nature about a joint (fulcrum). The twisting or turning effect of an applied force is known as the **moment of force** or **torque**, and is directly related to the distance between the point of application of the force (muscle insertion) and the fulcrum (joint). This is the **moment arm** (MA) and can be applied either to the effort arm or the resistance arm.

The largest turning effect or rotation will occur where the moment arm is at its longest or the force applied is at its greatest. For example:

• when preparing to dive from a platform, by leaning out before the dive the moment arm is lengthened and the rotational effect is increased — see fig 11.24. The moment of a force is equal to the product of the force applied multiplied by the length of the moment arm:

Moment of force =   magnitude of force × the perpendicular distance between the line of action of the force and the pivot

$$M = F \times MA$$

Eccentric force

The turning effect of the diver is produced by a force which is not passing through the centre of gravity. This off centre force is called the **eccentric force**, and is vital for rotation to occur. Look at fig 11.25. When the force is applied through the centre of gravity as in figure (a) the resulting motion will be **linear**, but when the force is applied outside the centre of gravity as in figure (b), the resulting motion will be **angular**. By moving the centre of gravity, the diver can produce an eccentric force to perform either a clockwise rotation (front somersault) or an anticlockwise rotation (back somersault).

Look at fig 11.26. When holding such a weight, there is a tendency for this moment to turn the lever clockwise. In order to balance the lever at the fulcrum and hold the weight in a static position, the bicep must produce a force equal to the clockwise moment.

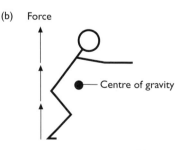

Fig. 11.25 ECCENTRIC FORCES (A) WHEN
APPLYING A FORCE THROUGH THE CENTRE OF
MASS, THE RESULTING MOTION WILL BE
LINEAR (B) WHEN APPLYING A FORCE WHICH
DOES NOT PASS THROUGH THE CENTRE OF
GRAVITY, THE RESULTING MOTION WILL BE
ANGULAR

Total clockwise moment = total anticlockwise moment

Clockwise moment = force × distance to fulcrum

Anticlockwise moment = force (of muscle) × distance of muscle insertion from the joint

y (force of resistance) = z (force of muscle)

This is commonly known as the **principle of moments**, and explains how a system can be balanced about a fulcrum.

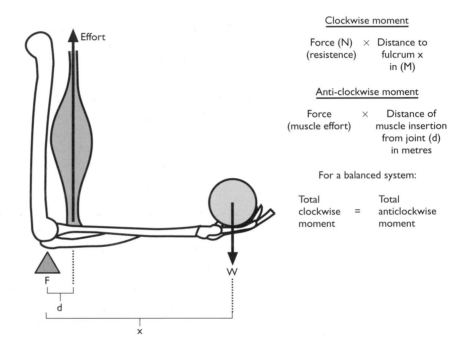

Fig. 11.26 THE PRINCIPLE OF MOMENTS

Angular motion

Quantities used to explain linear motion also apply to angular motion: displacement, velocity and acceleration. However, in rotating bodies we consider these quantities in their angular forms, namely angular displacement, angular velocity and angular acceleration.

Angular displacement

Just as the distance travelled by a body moving linearly can be measured, so can the distance of an object rotating around an axis. Angular displacement is usually measured in degrees; where there is one complete rotation, the body will have passed through 360°. If the direction of rotation is stated when describing angular distance, the term angular displacement is used.

Angular velocity

The angular velocity of a body is the angle through which a body rotates about an axis in one second. It is calculated as the angle described in a given time divided by that time. For example: if a trampolinist performing a tucked back somersault, turns through 360° in 2 seconds, their resulting angular velocity will be 180° per second. However the standard unit for angular motion is radians per second (rads/sec) and so we must convert degrees turned into radians.

2π radians $=$ 360°

1 radian $=$ 57.2958°

1 degree $=$ 0.017453 radian

Angular acceleration

This is the rate of change of angular velocity, and is measured in radians/second².

Moment of inertia

The moment of inertia of a body is its resistance to rotational or angular motion. When already rotating, the moment of inertia is the resistance of a body to a change in the state of rotation; this can be compared to its linear counterpart.

The moment of inertia of a body is determined by its mass and the distribution of its mass around the axis of rotation. The further its mass is away from the axis, the greater its moment of inertia and the more force is required to make it spin or stop it spinning if rotation is already occurring. Where the body's mass is concentrated about the axis, the lower the moment of inertia and the faster the rate of rotation.

In a sporting context this can be seen when comparing the rate of spin of a layout somersault and a tucked somersault:

- In a layout somersault the mass is distributed away from the axis of rotation. The gymnast will have a large moment of inertia and the rate of spin is slow.
- In the tucked position the gymnast's mass is concentrated around the axis of rotation, the moment of inertia is decreased and the rate of spin is increased.

Similarly, an ice skater will rotate much faster when the arms are pulled into the body, since the moment of inertia is decreased.

The moment of inertia can be calculated as follows:

Moment of inertia $=$ the sum of (mass of body part $\times$ distance from the axis of rotation, squared)

$$= \Sigma(m \times r^2)$$

Fig. 11.27 A SLALOM SKIER ROUNDING A FLAG

- By decreasing the value of r, the moment of inertia is decreased and angular velocity increases.
- If r doubles, the moment of inertia increases by $2^2 = 4$.
- If r increases four-fold, the moment of inertia increases by $4^2 = 16$.

Newton's first law of angular motion

A rotating body will continue to turn about its axis of rotation with constant angular momentum unless an external couple or eccentric force is exerted upon it.

This law is also know as the law of conservation of angular momentum.

Angular momentum is the product of the moment of inertia (MI) and angular velocity (ω).

Angular momentum =   MI × ω

This equation demonstrates the inverse relationship between the moment of inertia and rate of spin; if one increases, the other decreases, and vice-versa. For example:

- during a tumble, the only external force acting on a gymnast is her weight which acts through her centre of gravity and cannot affect her angular momentum.

Angular momentum is therefore conserved and remains the same. In order to decrease the rate of spin, a gymnast must therefore redistribute her mass in order to increase the moment of inertia. This is done by extending out of the tuck position before landing.

The inverse relationship between angular velocity and moment of inertia and it's effect upon angular momentum is illustrated in fig 11.29.

Position	Axis	Moment of inertia (kgm²)
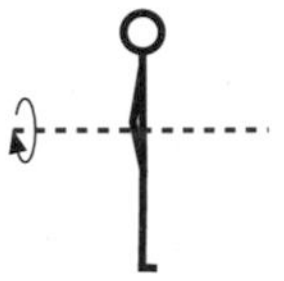	Frontal	12.0–15.0
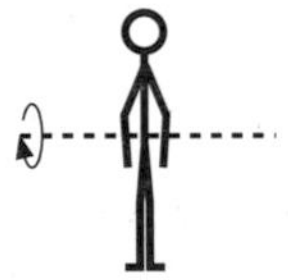	Transverse	10.5–13.0
	Transverse	4.0–5.0
	Long	1.0–1.2
	Long	2.0–2.5

Fig. 11.28 COMPARISONS OF BODY
POSITION AND MOMENT OF INERTIA
Source: Hay & Reid, 1988

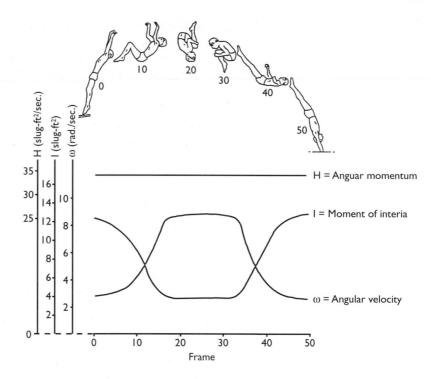

Fig. 11.29 The relationship between angular velocity moment of inertia, and angular motion

Newton's second law of angular motion

The angular acceleration of a body is proportional to the torque causing it and takes place in the direction in which the torque acts.

By increasing a turning effect or torque, greater angular acceleration can be achieved. For example:

- a gymnast increases angular momentum on a high bar when building up for a dismount that includes a number of somersaults.

Newton's third law of angular motion

For every torque that is exerted by one body on another, there is an equal and opposite torque exerted by the second body on the first.

This is another action-reaction law and can easily be seen in sporting activity:

- In the long jump, as the legs are brought forward and upward to land, a reaction force causes the arms to be brought forward and downward.
- When a trampolinist performs a pike jump, the legs are brought up clockwise as the arms are brought down anticlockwise to meet them.

Summary

Newton's laws

First law
Every body continues in its state of rest, or of uniform motion in a straight line, except in so far as it may be compelled by impressed forces to change that state.

Second law

The rate of change of momentum is proportional to the impressed force, and the actual change takes place in the direction in which the force acts.

Third law

To every action, there is an equal and opposite reaction; or the mutual actions of the two bodies in contact are always equal and opposite . . .

Linear motion

$$\text{Speed} = \frac{\text{distance moved}}{\text{time taken}} = \frac{d}{t}$$

Acceleration = change of speed per second $a = \dfrac{v - u}{t}$

$$V^2 = U^2 + 2as$$
$$S = Ut + \tfrac{1}{2} at^2$$

(where V = final velocity, U = initial velocity)

Force = mass × acceleration, f = ma

Kinetic energy = $\tfrac{1}{2}$ × mass × (velocity)^2

Weight = mass × gravity, w = mg

Impulse + impact

Momentum = mass × velocity, momentum = mv
Impulse = force × time, f × t
Impulse ∴ = change of momentum, mv

Levers

Moment of force =   force × distance to fulcrum
(couple)
Total anti-clockwise moment = total clockwise moment

Angular motion

1 radian = 57.2958 degrees
1 degree = 0.017453 radians

$$\text{Angular velocity} = \frac{\text{angle turned through in radians}}{\text{time taken}}$$

(angle turned per second)

Moment of inertia = the sum of [(mass of body part) × (distance from the axis of rotation)^2]
∴ MI = $\sum(m \times r^2)$

Rotational energy = $\tfrac{1}{2}$ × moment of inertia × (angular velocity)^2

Angular momentum = angular velocity × moment of inertia

ACTIVITY 1

1 **A weight lifter exerts an upward force of 2000N on a bar bell of 170 kg. What is the vertical acceleration?**
2 **Draw free body diagrams of the following, showing all the forces acting upon them:**

a) A high jumper at take off
b) A gymnast performing a handstand
c) A diver at take off

A knowledge of centre of mass can be of great benefit to the sports person. Using examples from sport show how the centre of mass and its adjustment can enhance performance.

Analyse the human lever system. Classify the type of lever in operation at as many joints as possible. Give sketch diagrams to show the lever system in action.

1   **What factors affect the degree to which air resistance influences the flight path of projectiles?**
2   **Give at least three examples from sport where fluid friction affects**
    a) an object
    b) a sportsperson
3   **State the effects of this fluid friction in each case.**
4   **What do you understand by the term Magnus Effect? Explain how a knowledge of Magnus forces can assist a tennis player.**

1   **What do you understand by the term Moment of Inertia?**
2   **Using diagrams to support your answer, show how body shape and angular velocity are related in the performance of a trampolining routine.**
3   **Give examples from sporting situations where changes in the moment of inertia affects performance.**
4   **Sketch pin-men diagrams of body positions which generate high rates of spin and compare with those body positions which lead to low rates of spin.**
5   **Sketch a graph to show angular velocity against time as a trampolinist travels through a tucked front somersault. Add to your graph a corresponding line showing the moment of inertia.**

1   **How would the resultant force of a person performing a vertical jump differ from the high jumper performing the fosbury flop technique?**
2   **Explain why the 'hitchkick' technique has developed in the long jump.**

Further reading

Davis et al., *Physical Education and the Study of Sport* (Wolfe Publishing Ltd, 1991)

Davis, Kimmet and Auty, *Physical Education: Theory and Practice* (MacMillan, 1986)

F W Dick, *Sports Training Principles*, 2nd edn (A & C Black, 1989)

G Dyson, *The Mechanics of Athletics* (University Press, Cambridge, 1977)

T Ecker, *Basic Track and Field Biomechanics* (Tafnews Press, 1985)

J Watkins, *An Introduction to the Mechanics of Human Movement* (MTP Press, 1986)

R Wirhed, *Athletic Ability and the Anatomy of Motion* (Wolfe Publishing Ltd, 1984)

chapter 12

The Organisation of Sport in the United Kingdom

Sport sociology is an approach which attempts to determine the place of physical activity in the cultural hierarchy. Society is a dynamic concept as it is constantly changing and adapting, sometimes gradually evolving over centuries, and in other instances revolutionary changes are experienced almost overnight. Sport will reflect and influence the society of which it forms an integral part.

Cultural research in this area has expanded to include other societies which are modelled on different plans and motivated by different ideals. Societies ranging from primitive to modern industrial are now studied: the organisation of physical activities and type of participation are viewed as an essential part of that society.

The social situation involving sport with which you are most likely to be familiar, is that of the United Kingdom. We will therefore attempt an overview of the system of sport and physical education in the UK, trying to account for the present using a historical approach, focusing on the important issues, and outlining a system with which to compare other societies.

This chapter identifies organisations which are significantly involved in the administration of, and policy making decisions for, sport and physical recreation in the United Kingdom. These will include government organisations such as the Department of National Heritage, the Minister for Sport, and local authorities; and Quangos (Quasi Autonomous Non Government Organisations) such as the Sports Council, Countryside Commission, Forestry Commission and the Nature Conservancy Council.

Figure 12.1 on page 158 shows how the range of physical recreation and sporting activities are organised in the UK. It is important that you continually refer to this figure in order not to lose sight of the overall links between each unit.

Interrelating aspects of society which affect the system of sport:

- Economic
- Educational
- Historical
- Political
- Religious
- Social and Cultural
- Demographic
- Ecological

The role of central government

The role that a national government adopts towards any social factor can be indicative of the importance placed upon it. The government of the UK has tended to have legislation which is **permissive** rather than **mandatory** in matters regarding sport and recreation. An example of this is that local authorities provide for sport but are not required by law to do so.

In 1960, following the Wolfendon Committee report on the state of sport and recreation, both major political parties rejected the idea of a Ministry for Sport, preferring the idea of a Sports Council which would be under the jurisdiction of a Minister of Sport instead. The significance of this is that sport would only be part of the minister's responsibility, and it would not have cabinet status as in other European countries.

The movement away from political control of sport was highlighted in 1972 when the recently formed Sports Council received a Royal Charter. This means it should be free from political control.

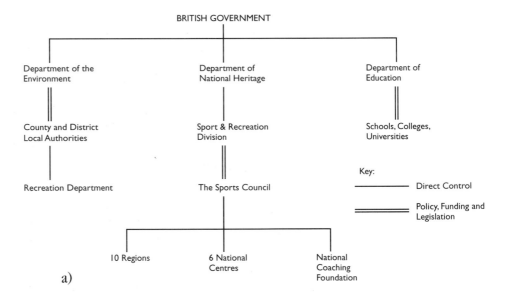

a)

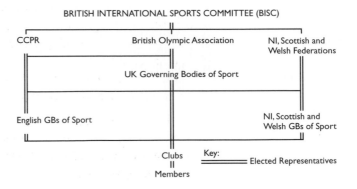

Fig. 12.1   THE STRUCTURE OF SPORT (A) GOVERNMENT (B) BRITISH INTERNATIONAL SPORTS COMMITTEE (BISC)

b)

A decentralised political system has also contributed to this position (ie, dividing the organisation of government amongst local authorities). Greater powers were given to local authorities after World War II; they were able to make their own policy decisions, relating to their own unique regional characteristics. However, successive Conservative governments in the 1980s and '90s have implemented a shift towards centralising power again, and this has affected policy for sport among other social factors. A brief summary of these changes:

- increasingly centralised policies, eg, the National Curriculum and the Educational Reform Act 1988. Previously much of the responsibility for education had rested with the local authorities
- a gradual reduction in emphasis on the welfare state
- market solutions to service provision, ie, privatisation of leisure services management and Compulsory Competitive Tendering (CCT).

Minister for Sport

In the 1960s, the creation of the post of Minister for Sport provided a focus for the coordination and formulation of policy. This was long overdue as six government departments previously had a significant responsibility for sport and recreation; for example:

- Sports council matters – Minister of Sport
- Tax exemptions for sports clubs – Junior Minister for DoE
- Safety at football grounds — Home Office Minister
- Schoolchildren and sport – Department of Education

The involvement of so many government departments posed considerable problems of coordination for the Minister for Sport.

The creation of the position had two main purposes:

1 to enable sport and recreation to perform a key role across a wide range of government policy: to improve the nation's health, to alleviate social deprivation, and to channel the energies of the young.
2 to enable governing body representatives and volunteers to serve sportsmen and women, providing a financial, advisory and legal framework.

Structure

The Minister for Sport has a Sport and Recreation Division (referred to from now on as SARD). The allocation of responsibility can be seen in fig 12.2. Coordination is mainly gained through informal contacts – but not many issues have affected all departments at the same time. SARD is administered by civil servants, and sport policy can sometimes be overshadowed by other issues, such as health, education and defence. This has led to an ad hoc approach, with SARD having little contact with the main providers of sports opportunities for the majority of the public, that is, the local authorities.

This fragmentation of responsibility and interest is apparent at all levels of sports policy. Certain limitations are apparent with the role of the Minister for Sport:

1 The role of the Minister is to advise and consult, not to direct.
2 S/he coordinates sport rather than controls it.
3 S/he now comes under the Department of National Heritage, which also has competing responsibilities.

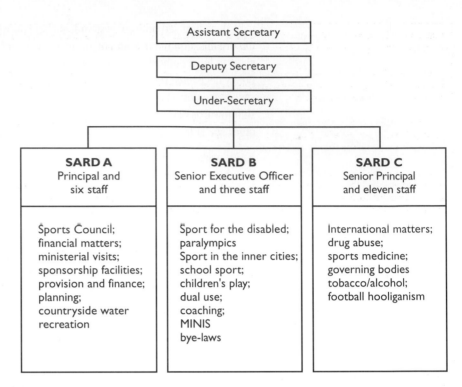

Fig. 12.2 THE ORGANISATION OF THE SPORT AND RECREATION DIVISION AND THE ALLOCATION OF RESPONSIBILITY

However, these limitations should not be overstated for the Minister *can* exert considerable influence on policy, when required. This would mainly depend on:

- the prominence of sporting issues to the government
- the quality, ambition and style of the Minister in office.

Research some instances of the involvement of specific Ministers of Sport; for example, Denis Howell, Neil McFarlane, Colin Moynihan.

Department of National Heritage

The Department of National Heritage was founded in 1992, and the Minister for Sport moved to it from the Department of the Environment. There are two main advantages:

1 Sport is located firmly within a wider cultural and leisure brief.
2 Sport now has a voice at cabinet level.

However, the department also has responsibility for the arts, broadcasting, films, tourism and heritage. It is also responsible for the funding of national galleries and museums, and sport has to compete in this arena.

In 1995 the Prime Minister, John Major, produced a statement laying out his aims for the development of Sport in the UK, entitled 'Raising the Game'. Figure 12.3 relates the most important sections.

I set up the Department of National Heritage to protect, enhance and develop the arts, leisure and sport. That is why we are publishing ideas to rebuild the strength of every level of British sport.

These new plans are the most important set of proposals ever published for the encouragement and promotion of sport. I want us to bring about a seachange in the prospects of British sport – from the very first steps in primary school right through to the breaking of the tape in an Olympic final.

The existence of the National Lottery has transformed forever the prospects of British sport. Indeed, this was one of my principal aims when I decided to create the Lottery. It was a way to provide resources for sport – and other good causes – that would be unlikely ever to come directly from the taxpayer.

The £300 million a year that the Lottery in full flood will provide for sport will revolutionise it over the years ahead. It will make possible the creation of a new British Academy of Sport for the best of our young men and women. It will help generate the resources for some of our other targets – for example, to achieve the target I am setting today, to bring every child in every school within reach of adequate sports facilities by the year 2000.

In this initiative I put perhaps highest priority on plans to help all our schools improve their sport. Sport is open to all ages – but it is most open to those who learn to love it when they are young. Competitive sport teaches valuable lessons which last for life. Every game delivers both a winner and a loser. Sports men must learn to be both. Sport only thrives if both parties play by the rules, and accept the results with good grace. It is one of the best means of learning to live alongside others and make a contribution as part of a team. It improves health and opens the door to new friendships.

My ambition is simply stated. It is to put sport back at the heart of weekly life in every school. To re-establish sport as one of the great pillars of education alongside the academic, the vocational and the moral. It should never have been relegated to be just one part of one subject in the curriculum. For complete education we need all of those four pillars of school life to be strong.

Sports education is only the first step to a lifetime's enjoyment of sport. Sporting opportunities must continue after school. So we shall be looking to colleges and universities to do more to promote sport among their students. At present, too many teenagers find it difficult to transfer their sporting interests to the world outside school. So we will also aim to improve the sporting links between school and club sport. In that way we can improve access to high quality coaching and promote sensible arrangements to share facilities and equipment. There is much to gain in this, both for clubs and for schools.

Fig. 12.3   EXCERPTS FROM JOHN MAJOR'S ADDRESS, 12 JULY 1995

1   **What values did John Major assign to participation in sporting activities?**
2   **What four 'pillars' of education does he refer to?**
3   **Give reasons why there may be a significant drop out rate in sport participation on leaving school.**
4   **John Major refers to a continuum from the primary school to Olympic standard. What suggestions does he make to realise this transition?**

Quangos

A large number of quangos exist outside government departments, with varying degrees of independence. They have clearly defined functions specialising in their own area, but this has tended to increase the problem of coordination rather than improve it.

Quangos are not under the direct control of Parliament but linked to the government in some way, either financial, policy accountability or its statutory obligations. Some common characteristics can be identified:

- Quangos tend to be funded directly by the Treasury.
- The board in control is usually elected by the appropriate Minister.
- They tend to perform promotional or developmental activities.
- They tend to have specialist expertise not found elsewhere in the government.
- They remain slightly politically detached from sensitive issues such as racial and

sexual equality, creating a 'buffer zone' for the government.

- Paradoxically, they could help the former Conservative government to bypass contentious local authorities (usually under Labour control).

However, quangos are often fragmented, lack coordination, are administratively cumbersome and contain increasing numbers of interested and sometimes competing parties.

An example of a quango is the Sports Council.

Sports Council

The Sports Council has five main functions:

1 to encourage people of both sexes and all ages and abilities to take part in sport and physical education.
2 to assist and advise on the design and distribution of sports facilities by making grants to appropriate organisations.
3 to provide sportspeople with help and advice to enable them to reach their full potential.
4 to allocate financial and physical resources to relevant groups and individuals.
5 to provide information for and about sport.

Figure 12.4 shows the structure of the Sports Council.

There is a strong emphasis on allocating its government grant of approximately £49.8m (1994/95). This money is supplemented by the Council's own activities and non-governmental sources, and is spent in various ways:

- staff costs
- sport development
- the running of the six national sports centres

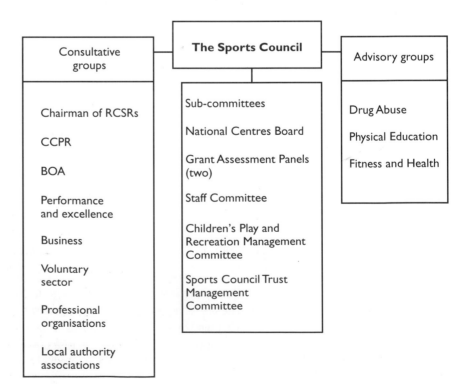

Fig. 12.4 THE STRUCTURE OF THE SPORTS COUNCIL

- expenditure such as research, training courses, children's play and publicity.

Some of the achievements of the Sports Council are now listed.

'Sport for all'

This campaign in 1972 was on a nationwide basis regardless of sex, age, race or social class. To achieve this aim they targeted groups with low participation such as 13–24 years; 45–59 years; women; people with disabilities and the unemployed. Within the wider campaign certain specialist campaigns were set up.

Research the Sports Council's campaigns from 1975 onwards.

Policy for excellence

The broadening of the base of participation has always been viewed as feeding the apex of the triangle; ie, the broader the base, the more top sportspeople are likely to be developed. In this area emphasis has been placed on improving coordination between relevant agencies. The Sports Council has a Performance and Excellence team, and funds governing bodies to assist with administration costs incurred by the training of elite athletes, staff costs, travel, coaching schemes and so on, in order to help raise performance standards.

The National Coaching Foundation

This was established in 1983 to provide a range of educational and advisory services for all coaches and to complement the award schemes of the individual governing bodies. This has enjoyed increasing success. It oversees the running of the 16 National Coaching Centres which are primarily based in Institutions of Higher Education (see fig 12.5).

Fig. 12.5 THE LOCATION OF NATIONAL COACHING CENTRES IN THE UK

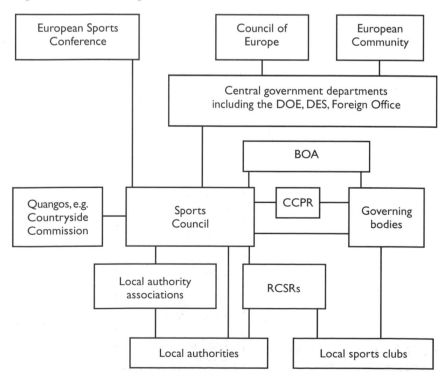

Fig. 12.6 CONTACT BETWEEN THE SPORTS COUNCIL AND OTHER ORGANISATIONS

Regional offices

Nine (later ten) regional offices of the Sports Council were set up to provide the means by which Council policy is promoted at local level; as such, they represented the local authorities and sports interests in each region. In 1996 they were abolished as part of a restructuring programme. Their functions included:

1 advising the Sports Council of their regional needs and how grants should be allocated
2 reviewing existing sports facilities and making effective maximum use of them
3 encouraging the work of local councils and other local community action
4 liaising with relevant organisations such as tourist boards, the National Parks Authority, the Countryside Commission and the Waterways Boards.

One of the organisations the National Sports Council has traditionally liaised with is the Central Council of Physical Recreation (the CCPR).

Central Council of Physical Recreation

Interested organisations

Outdoor Pursuits

Games and Sports

CCPR Executive Committee

Major Spectator Sports

Water Recreation

Movement and Dance

Fig. 12.7 STRUCTURE OF THE CENTRAL COUNCIL OF PHYSICAL RECREATION

This organisation was originally founded in 1935 to have responsibility for sport and recreation in the UK. It had three main objectives:

1 to encourage as many people as possible to participate in physical activity
2 to provide the governing bodies with a separate organisation to represent their collective interests to the Sports Council
3 to increase public awareness and knowledge of the importance of sport.

They set up regional offices and the first national sport centres, and as such, the organisation was a precursor to the Sports Council. In 1972, the Sports Council took over the overall responsibility for sport, and the personnel of the CCPR were merely transferred from one to the other. It was inevitable perhaps that similar policies would be adopted, at least until each organisation defined their individual roles more clearly. Thus, the CCPR became the **representative** and **consultative body** to the Sports Council. It became the chief means of preserving the traditionally voluntary and independent nature of organised sport in the UK.

A useful way of simplifying one of its roles is to visualise it as the middle man between the Sports Council and the autonomous governing bodies whose interests it represents. The CCPR can liaise across a wide range of sporting activities and bring together specialist bodies. There are however some limitations, mainly the organisational weakness and the rivalry between the CCPR and the Sports Council.

The CCPR Executive Committee has divided sport and recreation into six divisions: see fig 12.7.

ACTIVITY 4

Write a list of specific physical activities which would come under each category heading.

CCPR policy towards current issues

It supports 'dual use' policy: this recommends increased access to sporting facilities but protests against Compulsory Competitive Tendering, viewing it as a threat to the British tradition of the provision of public sporting facilities. This emphasises the nature of the CCPR – an organisation which looks after the interests of sport for the people.

CCPR achievements

The **Community Sports Leaders Award** was initiated in 1982 and is an effective qualification in promoting the concept of leadership roles in sport for young people. It can be promoted by schools, colleges and community groups, and is also recognised by the Duke of Edinburgh Award.

Financing the CCPR

The CCPR is financed from five main sources:

1 subscriptions and donations from its members
2 support from industry and commerce
3 sponsorship by individuals or companies of particular events and projects under the CCPR
4 sales of its own publications and research findings
5 contractual support from the Sports Council.

Countryside Commission

This is a public body with a wide range of responsibilities in England and Wales, and was formed under the National Parks and Access to the Countryside Act 1968. It has various functions, including:

1 the selection and designation of National Parks, AONB (Areas of Outstanding Natural Beauty) and country parks
2 the establishment of long distance footpaths and bridleways
3 the provision of information services about the countryside
4 advice on the use of the countryside for open air recreation balanced by a concern for conservation
5 carrying out research and experimental projects
6 giving grants and loans to non-public bodies.

The Forestry Commission

This has two main organisations:

1 The Forestry Authority – the main advisory and grant aiding arm of the Commission.
2 Forest Enterprise – covers the forests and woodlands. Walking and sometimes cycling is encouraged. They encourage private landowners to allow public access through special grants.

Local authorities

We have already mentioned the burden on local authorities to provide leisure facilities in their area. This is decreed under mainly permissive legislation, such as the Physical Training and Recreation Act 1937 and the Local Government Miscellaneous Act 1976, which stated that a local authority 'may provide . . . such recreational facilities as it thinks fit'.

The following factors stimulated local government involvement:

• The creation of the Sports Council (1972), the Tourist Boards (1969) and the Countryside Commission (1968).

- The creation of new sporting and recreational facilities, in particular leisure centres and country parks.
- Increased leisure and a steady rise in the standard of living.
- Increase in the rate and frequency of sport and recreation participation.
- Creation of 'service' departments within local authorities following the restructuring of local government in 1974, eg, a leisure service department.

A two-tier structure emerged, of District and County Councils. Leisure provision assumed greater importance, but a lack of coordination halted its progress. Recreational planning was encouraged through government reports, particularly the 1975 White Paper 'Sport and Recreation'.

Leisure, by the 1990s, is mainly the responsibility of one specialist department. Excluding educational provision, authorities' net expenditure on revenue support for sport exceeds **£400 million** a year in England and Wales. In addition, **£100 million** capital expenditure is incurred.

 **Write to your local leisure officer, asking them for a list of their objectives for leisure provision in your area.**

Pressures on local authorities

Local authorities operate within certain restrictions:

1 The community charge and the capital control regimes affect the ability of local authorities to fund new developments and their attitudes to subsidies.

2 Increased competition from the private sector, partly due to the establishment of Compulsory Competitive Tendering and the effects on dual use policies following the Education Reform Act 1988 require improved management on behalf of local authorities.

3 Sport and physical recreation also has to compete with nine other departments: the arts and cultural provision, libraries, entertainment and catering services, museums, heritage and conservation, tourism, youth and community services, adult education and selective social services.

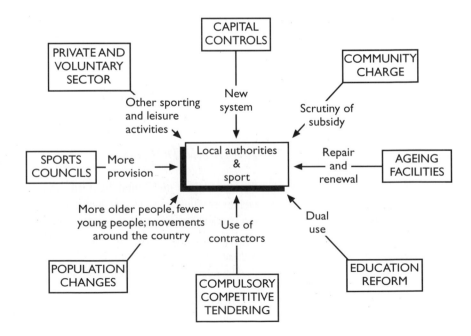

Fig. 12.8   PRESSURES ON LOCAL
AUTHORITY SPORTS POLICY

Table 12.1   VARIOUS LEISURE ACTIVITIES

SPORT	EDUCATION	TOURISM	SOCIAL	CULTURAL
sports centres playing fields ski slopes	libraries swimming pools	museums conservation country parks	youth clubs community centres	theatres art galleries

4 The term 'leisure' encompasses a wide range of activities, like sport and physical recreation, education, tourism, social and cultural. This is illustrated in table 12.1.

As legislation is mainly permissive, it is not surprising that wide variations in provision and expenditure can be found between local authorities.

 **ACTIVITY 6**

In the light of some of the problems highlighted, what procedures would you suggest to a local authority in order to improve the level and effectiveness of its leisure services?

Positive aspects

Positive features emerge, nonetheless:

- Financial expenditure has remained reasonably steady.
- Leisure is a popular demand by local residents.
- Leisure is increasingly valued for its own benefits and not just as a means of meeting other policy objectives like reducing vandalism or improving the nation's health.

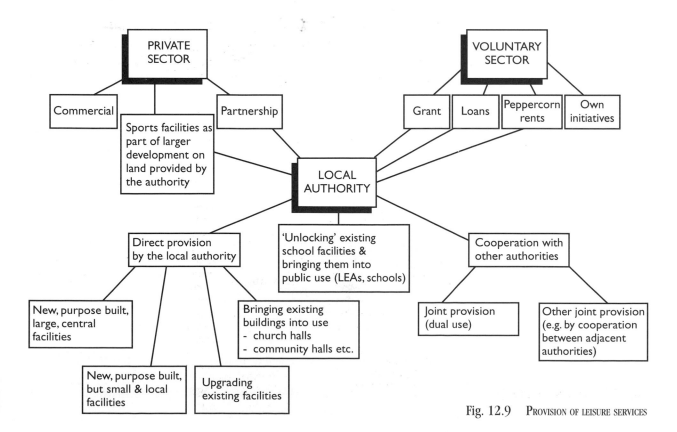

Fig. 12.9   PROVISION OF LEISURE SERVICES

- Leisure in the 1990s was also perceived to be of economic benefit to a local area, particularly in its ability to attract tourism.

Research some of the work of the Institute of Leisure and Amenity Management (ILAM).

Autonomous organisations

Governing bodies of sport

History

With the increasing popularity of sport during the late nineteenth century, it became necessary for individuals and clubs taking part to agree on a common set of rules or laws. In most areas this led directly to the formation within each sport of a governing body, with the task of agreeing rules for the sport so that all clubs and individuals could compete on equal terms.

The persons responsible for the establishment of the governing bodies were mainly the educated, middle and upper classes, and there is still a tendency for sport administration in the UK to be the domain of the middle classes.

Structure

It is difficult to generalise across all the governing bodies, as some are extremely wealthy (eg, the Football Association), while others are still heavily reliant on grants. However, there are some common characteristics:

- executive boards and officers
- elected by clubs through local, regional and county representatives
- many have separate organisations in the four home nations (England, Scotland, Wales, Northern Ireland)
- many still have separate organisations for men and women.

Below is a list of the professional staff of the Badminton Association, as an example of a governing body. See fig 12.10 for the hierarchical structure.

- Chief Executive
- Accountant
- Director of Coaching and Development
- Coaching Manager
- Events Director
- Tournament and County Liaison Officer
- Press and Public Relations Manager
- P.A. to the Chief Executive
- Coaching Secretary
- Secretarial Staff

There are approximately 300 governing bodies in the UK. Many are unpaid volunteers, though this situation has improved somewhat by the appointment of paid administrators (largely dependent on the size and scale of the individual governing body).

These organisations proudly retain their autonomy from political control and each other. They become a more collective voice when represented to the Sports Council by the CCPR, though we have already voiced some concern over this rather strained relationship. Their main functions are to:

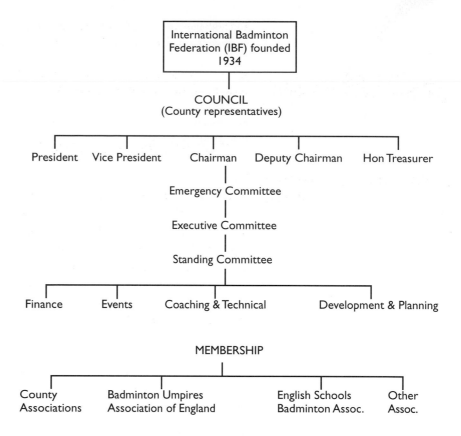

Fig. 12.10   ORGANISATION AND
ADMINISTRATION OF THE BADMINTON
ASSOCIATION

- establish rules and regulations (in accordance with the International Sports Federations, ISF)
- organise competitions
- develop coaching awards and leadership schemes
- selection of teams for country or UK at international events
- liaise with relevant organisations such as the CCPR, Sports Council, local clubs, British Olympic Association and the International Sports Federation.

Recent changes for governing bodies

Examples of some changes are:

- growth of new sports, setting a challenge to the older traditional sports
- the decline in extra-curricular school sport and a dependence on the governing bodies to try and fill this gap
- the blurring in definition of amateur and professional sport
- the need to compete internationally with countries who have developed systematic forms of training have made the governing bodies develop the coaching and structuring of competitions and devote more money to the training of their elite sportspeople.

Governing bodies have a variety of **finance** sources: drawing from member clubs, associations and individual members, or receiving grant in aid from the Sports Council. The last two decades have seen the dominance of television sports coverage and consequently sponsorship affects many sports. Governing bodies have had to meet this challenge and market themselves in the modern world if they wish to take advantage of these opportunities. Sports like snooker, badminton, squash and athletics have moved into the arena of big business. **Commercial sponsorship** is now a desirable form of income.

Research in your class the development of a particular governing body. Choose from different categories, eg, traditional, professional, a new growth sport, or a sport which has recently experienced rapid change etc.

The British Olympic Association

Structure

The International Olympic Committee (IOC) requires that each country organise a National Olympic Committee (NOC). Each governing body of the competitive olympic sports (recognised by the IOC) should be represented, alongside officers of the British Olympic Association and the two IOC representatives.

Function

Their function is to:

- encourage interest in the olympic games through undertakings such as liaison with schools
- foster the ideals of the olympic movement
- organise and coordinate British participation; the BOA needs to organise the participation of 500 athletes and officials including all travel arrangements or equipment and horses
- assist the governing bodies of sport in preparation of their competitions
- advise on public relations with the press (a relatively recent function)
- provide a forum for consultation among governing bodies
- organise an Olympic Day in the UK
- raise funds through the British Olympic Appeal, mainly from private sources, business sponsors and the general public.

You have probably already noted the absence of a government grant. This is the tradition of the BOA: to be independent of government. Preparations for the 1996 Olympic Games in Atlanta began early in order to raise the required £4 million. Sponsors included:

- Aquascutum – formal uniform
- Adidas – sport and leisure clothing
- Delta Airlines/Sportsworld Travel – free travel

Since 1988, the BOA has also had to adapt to changes as have other organisations already mentioned, and since 1992 have added the following to their list of duties:

- advice on training on nutrition and sports psychology for olympic coaches
- medical and careers advice for athletes
- sponsoring medical research into fitness and athletic injuries.

The British Olympic Medical Centre at Northwick Park was restructured, and athletes were to have access to all the medical support they required over the four years in preparation for Atlanta. A sport-specific strategy was developed to help athletes cope with the problems of jet lag, acclimatisation and dehydration. The BOA had a training camp at Tallahassee to allow athletes to experience training in a climate similar to Atlanta, while team managers and coaches also benefited from support services.

National Playing Fields Association

Founded in 1925, this body aims to ensure that there are opportunities for all to participate in their chosen activities, by stimulating the provision of playing fields and other facilities for indoor and outdoor recreation. It encourages the adoption of Play Leadership Schemes for children.

National Rivers Authorities (NRA)

The NRA protects and improves inland and coastal waters of England and Wales. It has responsibility for pollution control and water-based recreation activities. An important initiative in this area is the river canoeist's guide to responsible enjoyment of rivers. British Waterways covers similar ground but mainly around the canal networks.

English Tourist Board

Its primary aim is to encourage tourism; as interest increases in activity holidays, the tourist board are continually having to improve standards. The national governing bodies of the relevant sports are being asked to assist in the quality assurance initiative piloted in Wales.

International organisations

It would be superficial to treat the organisation and administration of sport from a purely national level, therefore a brief view of the international links will be made.

International Olympic Committee

This organisation generates almost all international sporting activity. There are two organisations:

1 The Session takes decisions on issues such as drug abuse, political boycotts, television contracts and world sport development.
2 The Executive Board is responsible for the organisation of those policies. Attempts are made to make representation as balanced as possible, ie, from wealthy and poor countries.

This organisation is free from national government pressure, probably due to its enormous financial reserves, and so is a very powerful organisation. It aims to raise its reserves to $100 million. If the IOC gives a sport eligibility status (ie, the requirement for inclusion into the Games programme), it can boost that sport considerably.

The IOC is under a lot of pressure from NOCs, international sports federations and national governments. The ability to withstand this will be tested as the world of sport becomes increasingly complex and sophisticated.

The Minister for Sport in the UK has links with the IOC and other international organisations, and this is an increasingly regular contact as much of the pressing concerns have an international dimension, eg, football hooliganism, the current issue of drug abuse.

Council for Europe

This was established in 1949 and focuses on cultural, sporting, educational and environmental issues; for example:

- the use of drugs in sport
- economic effects on sports investments
- football hooliganism
- developing support for the Paralympics.

International Sports Federations (ISF)

The ISF's main responsibilities are

- to organise events
- to arrange sponsorship and television contracts
- to formulate the rules which will be adhered to by the national governing bodies.

At the Olympics, they are responsible for the technical aspects of their sport and the officials.

Commonwealth Games Federation (CGF)

After the Olympic Games, the CGF is the next most important multi-sport competition in the world, involving 65 countries with a range of 25 sports (no team sports). It maintains a strong British influence.

The role of the CGF is to promote and organise the four-yearly games, establish satisfactory conduct guidelines and encourage amateur sport. The Federation is not as wealthy as the IOC and depends heavily on voluntary help. Sports seeking acceptance to the Olympics often try to be accepted by the CGF first.

Facilities

Our sporting experiences are only made possible by the wealth of public facilities which have developed during the twentieth century. Prior to this, specialised sporting activities had been mainly the preserve of the privileged classes who owned land and built the necessary facilities, eg, real/lawn tennis courts, croquet, etc. Social changes began to take the needs of the lower classes into account, beginning with public baths, urban recreational parks and followed by the provision of facilities for physical education in state schools. From then on there was a rapid expansion in local authority provision of public recreational facilities.

Local authorities

They are the main providers of land and large scale facilities for community recreational use:

1 They maintain playing fields, gymnasia, tennis courts, golf courses, boating lakes, swimming baths and sports centres.
2 Local authorities are able to borrow capital to finance facilities within an overall allocation for 'locally determined schemes'.
3 The Sports Council is able to support local authority sports projects, costs of national centres and local facilities provided by voluntary organisations.

Local education authority

It is a legal requirement for all publicly maintained schools to provide for the physical education of pupils. Considering that the vast amount of recreation facilities available at most schools, it makes sense to maximise their use. Most LEAs and district councils now have policies to share facilities. Private schools and Higher Education Institutions also have facilities available.

Outdoor pursuit centres

Local education authorities established up to 400 residential outdoor centres between 1960 and 1970. The main aims of these centres were:

- to provide experiences in support of physical education
- to offer residential experience of outdoor adventure activities, to broaden the personal and social development of youth.

They are also widely used in the training of teachers and instructors in the pursuit of national governing body awards.

The primary users of the centres are undoubtedly schools (64%). Other users are the commercial sector, and they are used for leadership training. In a recent survey, 65% of centres felt that the user base could be broadened. Thirty per cent of centres operate for about 39 weeks per year. They may need to change this policy as they move into the unprotected, competitive market due to the decline in local authority financing of the centres, eg, the summer holiday period could be an opportunity to promote activity holidays. Most of the full time employed staff are qualified (93%).

Suggest some potential markets which could best increase the usage of these centres.

Community sport centres

They often cater for a range of interests and those with high quality facilities often attract national interest. Examples of these are: the Meadowbank Sports Centre; Harrison's Rock in Kent; Bowles Rocks Outdoor Pursuit Centre; Birmingham National Indoor Arena; Lord's Cricket Ground; Wimbledon Tennis Club.

However, the majority of us are more familiar with a local leisure centre.

Research your local centre (eg, a sports centre, a country park, a water based recreational facility etc).
Note carefully:

- **its provision of a variety of activities**
- **its costing system**
- **access for the disabled**
- **opportunities for the Sports Council's target groups**
- **ease of access for the local catchment area**
- **opening hours**
- **social areas**
- **club use**
- **competition use of the centre, etc.**

Be as thorough as you can.
Following your findings write a report which concentrates on the positive as well as the negative, with any recommendations.

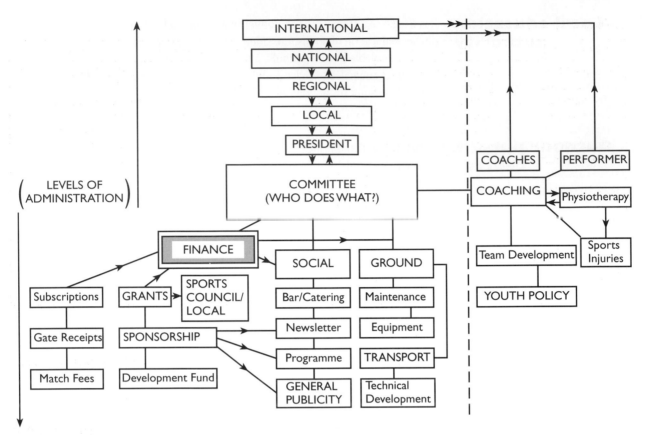

Fig. 12.11   Administrational
FRAMEWORK OF A LARGE ATHLETIC CLUB

Write a list of the possible aims and objectives of a leisure centre manager.

Local voluntary sports clubs

These would normally be affiliated to the national governing body, eg, football, cricket, hockey. However, private clubs may be linked to business firms. Figure 12.11 and table 12.2 give examples of sports club administration and organisation.

Commercial facilities

For example: ten pin bowling; ice and roller skating rinks; squash clubs; golf courses; driving ranges; riding stables.

National sports centres

These are run by the Sports Council – see fig 12.12. The Sports Council recognises that only by providing appropriate training facilities for the elite performers will it be possible for the UK to compete effectively in international sport. This aspect of the national sports centres has become more important within the last decade, requiring governing bodies to become equally involved in order for these centres to become the flagships of sporting excellence.

Plas y Brenin

Based in Snowdonia, this is the national centre for mountain activities. It trains

Table 12.2 ADMINISTRATION OF A SPORTS CLUB

ROLE OF OFFICERS	CLUB MEETINGS	FINANCE	PRACTICAL MANAGEMENT	CLUB SAFETY

club president
vice president
club chairman
club secretary
club treasurer
fixtures secretary
social secretary
press officer
club groundsman
captains
bar manager
membership
  secretary
training & coaching
junior section
senior members
	management comm.
	agenda
	minimum attendance
	voting procedures
	minutes
	regularity of meetings
	a.g.m.
		income
		subs
		match fees
		sale of clothing
		bar
		social events
		lotteries
		capital costs
		loans/grants
		breweries
		banks
		local auth.
		sports council
			admin
			staffing
			finance
			bar management
			legal
			facility care
			insurance
				Health & Safety at Work
				  1974
				injuries (rel. to facilities)
				accidents
				governing body reg.
				training awards
				insurance

leaders and offers courses in the Alps, Scotland and in Snowdonia. They run award schemes and employ full time instructors who work with the governing bodies.

Holme Pierrepont

This centre offers an artificial canoe slalom course, a 200 metre regatta lake and an artificial ski tow, amongst its facilities. The key governing bodies (the British Canoe Union, the British Water Ski Federation and the National Federation of Anglers) make extensive use of this facility.

Lilleshall Hall

This is a multi-purpose centre with a particular specialism in gymnastics and football. Governing bodies account for 75% of use. The human performance fitness testing centre is open to all and signifies the attempt to coordinate the fields of sports medicine, physiotherapy and rehabilitation.

Crystal Palace

Also a multi-purpose facility, it has a world famous stadium, swimming pool, and a variety of indoor facilities and artificial surfaces. A sports injury clinic provides for individual treatment.

Bisham Abbey

The main activities include tennis, squash, hockey, weight lifting and golf. An Excellence partnership has been forged with the British Amateur Weightlifters Association. Elite squads account for approximately 70% of use.

Manchester

This is the most recent addition to the Sports Councils National Facilities. It contains the velodrome for cycling, and has been accredited an Olympic training centre by the BOA. This is in recognition of the fact that it provides the very best training opportunities and services for British cyclists. It is managed by the British Cycling Federation on behalf of the Sports Council.

National
Sports Centres

Manchester

Plas y Brenin

Holme Pierrepont

Lilleshall Hall

Bisham Abbey

Crystal Palace

Fig. 12.12 NATIONAL SPORTS CENTRES IN THE UK

Olympic Accreditation Scheme

This scheme was set up in 1992 by the BOA in order to raise the standard of training facilities for elite athletes. The passport scheme was further developed – 403 athletes now enjoy free access to local training facilities. The result is improved facilities and a reduction in costs for Olympic sports using accredited centres.

British Academy for Sport

The idea of an Academy was raised by the government in its policy statement 'Sport: Raising the Game', July 1995. A consultation paper has sought the views of sports administrators, coaches and top level performers. The idea is to focus on the needs of top level performers and those with talent and commitment to succeed. It is intended to be more than just a world class training facility, it will also provide a support structure to give selected sports and their respective governing bodies everything they need to develop excellence and future British world champions.

A regional network of facilities with direct services operating beneath it is also envisaged.

National Cities of Sport

The Sports Council are developing a more coordinated approach toward a coherent sports facilities plan, and as such, have designated Birmingham, Sheffield and Glasgow as the first National Cities of Sport. The Cities of Sport Programme aims to create a network of cities with the vision, commitment and resources to bid for and stage major sporting events. It hopes to bid by using a planned, coordinated approach supported by an infrastructure at both local and national level, management expertise; it is very important to develop partnerships among councils, universities, media and business community as well as sports organisations.

New national stadium

Creating a new national stadium is a decision of national importance. Millions of pounds of National Lottery money will be spent with the intention of providing a stadium which will cope with modern day seating capacities (80,000) and spectators expectations (easily accessible, safe and comfortable), and with the capability of attracting European and world single or multi-sports events. The major users, rugby, football and athletics, have had a major input.

Finance

Government

Sport in the UK is financed in various ways. We have already mentioned the central government grant in aid given to the Sports Council (£49.8 million in 1994/95), which the Council then distributes to the CCPR, local authorities, and governing bodies etc. It is interesting to note that the government receives more money from sport than it distributes (income £2443 million, expenditure £545 million; 1985 figures, Henley Centre for Forecasting).

In contrast, local government spends more money than it receives from sport. Government funding is justified by benefits to the whole society. Success in sport is of national benefit though it may not always produce a commercial return, often a prerequisite for private funding.

The voluntary sector

This is the area in which most sporting activity occurs. Individuals come together to form clubs and associations which are run to benefit the participants. They are generally self-financing; annual subscriptions and match fees provide the bulk of the revenue and indicates the 'grass roots' development of sport in the UK.

Governing bodies

An example of a national governing body is the All England Women's Hockey Association. Their general income for 1995 totalled approximately £393,833 and was gained from the Sports Council grant, sponsorship (England squads and championships), affiliation fees, donations, insurance, commission and royalties, marketing, interest receivable and profit on sale of investments. Its expenditure was £371,903, leaving a yearly surplus of £21,930. Money was spent on items such as elite squads, matches, publications, salaries and personnel expenses, international affiliation fees (Fédération Internationale de Hockey and the English Hockey Federation), promotions, press and publicity, development officers etc. In financial terms, it is a medium-sized governing body, and a breakdown of its income and expenditure gives us some idea of its range of needs.

Sports Aid Foundation

The Sports Aid Foundation was set up in 1976, to enable top amateur athletes (at both junior and senior level) to train with similar privileges enjoyed by state sponsored athletes abroad. It is another self-financing organisation which draws funds from commercial, industrial and private sponsors and fund raising projects. Outstanding competitors generally receive the money. They receive grants according to their personal needs, cost of their preparation, training and competition and are usually recommended by their governing body. Since 1976, over £5 million has been given to over 5,000 competitors. Grants are awarded through its charitable trust to talented athletes who are in education, on low income or disabled.

Gambling in sport

Commercial betting and gaming is allowed under strict licensing regulations. This includes card games and casinos, but the bulk comes from greyhound and horse racing, and football matches.

With the aim of putting money back into sport, the Football Trust has been set up to supervise the levying of money from football pools and 'Spot the ball' competitions. Its income is over £32 million a year. Much of this money will be used to improve facilities for both performers and spectators (in line with the Taylor Report recommendations).

The Trust has announced plans to establish a nationwide Grass Roots Facilities Scheme. Over £1 million has been allocated and will be available for pitch and changing facilities for local authority owned, non league clubs, schools, voluntary bodies and other organisations.

The National Lottery

At the time of writing (1997), £10.5 billion has been raised from National Lottery ticket sales. Nearly £4 billion has been equally divided between the five good causes: the arts, heritage, the millennium fund, charities and sports. The sports share to date is £796 million, shared by the Sports Councils in the UK. The Lottery

Sports Fund has provided grants for projects ranging from village halls, athletic clubs, new major sports venues and the individual sports themselves. The knock on effect is also positive as these new developments create jobs for builders, planners etc. The income is making a difference at local, regional and national level.

SCSI School Community Sports Initiative

This has been established to help schools apply for increased levels of funding from the National Lottery Sports Fund, to develop good school/community sports facilities.

The National Lottery has had a considerable moral, economic and social impact. What do you consider to be the advantages and disadvantages of the good causes scheme and what suggestions for change would you make?
What opportunities exist for the funding of amateur athletes?

Foundation for Sport and the Arts

This organisation was set up by the pools promoters in 1991 to channel funds into sport and the arts. The pools provide approximately £43.5 million p.a. which can be used for the benefit of sport. It works closely with the Sports Council and administers grants. Its main aims are to

- support the improvement of existing facilities
- assist the construction of new sports venues
- help with appropriate sports projects (schools, disabled, Olympic and Paralympic teams).

The sums involved are quite substantial, eg, £1 million to Northern Ireland's Sports Training Centre, £100,000 to Widnes Rugby League FC to assist with the upgrading of the facilities following the Taylor recommendations, £200,000 to Yorkshire & Cleveland Riding for the Disabled.

Sponsorship

The private sector contribute approximately £230 million a year to sport, involving more than 2,000 British companies assisting schemes from national excellence programmes to local grass roots schemes. See Chapter 16 for further information on sponsorship.

Tax

The introduction of the Uniform Business Rate in 1990 meant that rates for some sports clubs tripled. This is generally considered as unfair, as they are non-profit making and in addition provide a social service. The British Olympic Association, which receives no Government assistance, have to pay approximately £750,000 on £5 million raised. Britain is the only country to tax its Olympic fund raisers.

Summary

- Sports policy is characterised by a high degree of fragmentation between central government departments. There is heavy reliance on local government to provide facilities and opportunities for sport and recreation.
- SARD is considered to have a reasonably low status within DoE policy, so most Ministers have tended to leave sport policy to the Sports Council – but they may intervene on strategic issues.
- The future of the CCPR is probably not secure, as the continuing bureaucracy surrounding the relationship between two such similar organisations is heavily criticised.
- In local authorities, there is a decentralised approach towards the organisation of sport and recreation, reflecting the political system in the UK. There is a slender thread of cohesion through the organisations, but there are also areas of overlap and conflict.
- As with much of the administration of sport in the UK it is a mixture of tradition and compromise.
- There has been a steady expansion in the internationalisation of sport and it has brought challenges for the National Governing Bodies to adjust their rules and take note of the international sporting calendar.
- The influence of the IOC causes some concern as Third World Countries attempt to gain recognition.
- The establishment of the British International Sports Committee (ie, the combined voices of the Sports Council, the BOA and the CCPR) is the beginning, hopefully, of a more coordinated approach towards national and international sporting matters.
- The pattern of funding for sport in the UK will be dominated by sponsorship. Government grants (local and central) and funds from the governing bodies and private individuals make the next share. Relatively small but important market niches are funded by the SAF and the BOA.
- British sports bodies must cast off their traditional amateur, elitist approach to join the modern, professional sports world, if this country is to allow its athletes the same opportunities as those from rival countries.

chapter 13

Concepts of Physical Activity

The aim of this chapter is to explore the various concepts of physical activity: play, leisure, physical education and sport. We have already used some of these terms, but it is necessary at this stage to explore each term in its own context; ie, what characterises each concept, its uniqueness and also its common elements. We will also follow the theory of each concept with a brief look at how the theory has affected the development of the activity in society.

For ease of study we will start from the least organised, play, and move on to the most highly organised, sport: see fig 13.1.

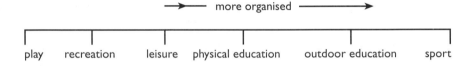

Fig. 13.1 THE PHYSICAL ACTIVITY CONTINUUM

Play

Play is something which children *and* adults do. It takes different forms and has different motives and benefits for each, but it can assume a great significance and importance to people's lives. A quick look in the dictionary to investigate what we mean by the word 'play', reveals that it conjures up many different meanings; eg, 'to occupy or amuse oneself in a sport; to fulfill a particular role – he played defence; a dramatic production; play fair'. It is very difficult to extract one meaning alone, but we must attempt to tease out the common characteristics which are relevant to our field of study and have been developed by psychologists such as Huizinga, Piaget, Callois and Ellis.

Play to the Ancient Greeks was associated with childhood. Play served to integrate children into Greek culture, acting as a form of social control, as well as developing the mental, physical and social well-being of the youngsters. The philosopher Aristotle believed children should have an early diet of games, tales and stories. These would better serve the developing child than formal lessons.

In the Middle Ages, the Church focused on the preparation of the soul for the after life. Play was therefore given a low status, being seen as a threat to the social order and a waste of time. Work for salvation attained high status and the two concepts were separated. This coincided with the harsh life many children experienced, which carried on into the nineteenth century where many were sent to work at a very early age. However, it was also at this time that French Philosopher Rousseau reinstated play as an important part of 'getting back to nature' in the text *Emile*. He claimed that simplicity and freedom should be an important part of a child's development into an adult, allowing spontaneity and self expression. However, it would be some time before most children experienced this concept.

Classical theories of play

1 **Surplus Energy**
2 **Preparation**
3 **Recapitulation**
4 **Relaxation**

These theories tend to concentrate on the instinctive nature of man and tend to reflect only certain aspects of play behaviour.

Play

is spontaneous

is voluntary

is fun

is serious

has intrinsic value

brings satisfaction

heightens arousal

is creative

is uninhibitive

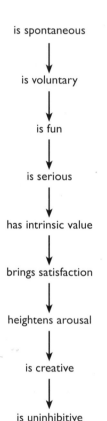

Fig. 13.2   VALUES OF PLAY

J Huizinga

The contribution of Huizinga, a Dutch cultural historian, lies in the detailed way he describes play; he provides observations but does not attempt an explanation of play. His descriptions include the following:

- Play is creative; it is repeated, alternated, transmitted; it becomes tradition.
- Play is a stepping out of real life.
- Play is uncertain. The end result cannot be determined.
- All play has rules, and as soon as the rules are transgressed, the whole play world collapses.
- Play is social. A play community generally tends to become permanent, encouraging the feeling of being together in an exceptional situation, of mutually withdrawing from the rest of the world.

'Play is a voluntary activity or occupation exercised within certain fixed rules of time and place, according to rules freely accepted but absolutely binding, having its aim in itself and accompanied by a feeling of tension, joy, and the consciousness that this is different from ordinary life' *(Huizinga, 1964).*

Piaget

Piaget, a Swiss psychologist, claimed that play is:

- an end in itself
- distinguished by the spontaneity of play as opposed to the compulsion of work
- an activity for pleasure
- devoid of organised structure.

Piaget believed that play was the most effective aspect of early learning. Much educational thinking has been influenced by this thought. Play is crucial for development and intelligence: the child uses its intelligence in play and is manipulative; s/he adapts to the environment by modifying feelings and thoughts through:

- assimilation – child imposes own knowledge on reality, thus can change reality
- accommodation – child fits into environment.

Callois

Callois, a French sociologist, developed a theory which suggested that play is a reflection of society. He used Greek terms to develop four forms of play:

1 **Agon** (competition) – contest or struggle, eg, competitive games.

2 **Alea** (chance) – the end is determined by chance or fate.

3 **Mimicry** (role taking) – eg, children playing mummies and daddies.

4 **Ilynx** (vertigo) – eg, fast-moving activities which induce giddiness.

These can all be distinguished from each other by two other aspects:

- **Paidia** – the pure ideal of children's play, where fun is the key element
- **Ludus** – when activities become more organised.

When we move from play to sport, the ludic element becomes more prominent.

Place the following activities on table 13.1:

- **lottery, children dressing up, theatre, skiing, abseiling, fencing, merry go rounds, tag, mummies and daddies, hockey, kite flying, chess.**

Try to think of other activities to fill in the table.

Table 13.1   CATEGORISING ACTIVITIES

	AGON	ALEA	MIMICRY	ILLYNX
paidia ludus				

Ellis

Recent theories of play tend to be concerned with the 'individual' explanation of play. Ellis summarises five major theories:

1 **Generalisation** and **compensation** – people select activities which will either reflect or compensate for their world of work.
2 **Catharsis** – the purging and consequent release of strong emotions. It suggests that aggressive tendencies can be subdued, but research suggests that experiencing aggression, such as involvement in sport, can lead to more aggression.
3 **Psychoanalytic** – the Freudian idea that play is motivated by pleasure.
4 **Development** – Erikson's idea that children can learn through play, the ability to master reality.
5 Play is ritualised to provide social traditions.

Modern theories

Play is regarded as stimulus-seeking behaviour. In his book, *Why people play?*, Ellis developed the notion that play involves the integration of three theories:

- learning
- developmental
- arousal seeking behaviour (behaviour is motivated to maintain an optimal level of arousal).

He claims that:

'When the primary drives are satisfied the animal continues to emit stimulus seeking behaviour'.

However, when the situation is too complex it reduces arousal; at the opposite end, if the outcome is too predictable, the lack of uncertainty will also reduce arousal. Imagine a sporting contest where the opponents are not well matched. Both know the result is a foregone conclusion, so an intermediary level is sought. This theory has the advantage of incorporating work and play, rather than separating them.

The following definition is a useful amalgamation of the different theories of play.

'Play is activity – mental, passive or active. Play is undertaken freely and is usually spontaneous. It is fun, purposeless, self initiated and often extremely serious. Play is indulged in for its own sake; it has intrinsic value; there is innate satisfaction in the doing. Play transports the player, as it were, to a world outside his or her normal world. It can heighten arousal. It can be vivid, colourful, creative and innovative. Because the player shrugs off inhibitions and is lost in the play, it seems to be much harder for adults, with social and personal inhibitions to really play'.

(Adults play but children just play more *G. Torkildsen*).

Implications of play

Education

The importance given to play in terms of children's ability to learn more effectively, has been taken seriously by many educationalists. Certainly in the early years there is a focus on play activities through which children will learn.

Exploratory learning led to a more **heuristic** teaching style (a device or strategy that serves to stimulate investigation). The teacher's role changed from being purely instructional to one of initiating a guidance form of learning.

Physical education lessons

There are aspects of physical education which do not match the concept of play. For example: it is compulsory; the content is chosen by the teacher; the teacher is in authority over the group; the group does not initiate the activity spontaneously.

Recreation

Recreation managers should also take note of the positive experiences which play can generate in everyone's lives, not only children's.

ACTIVITY 2

1 **What strategies as a teacher could you use to help inject a more playful element in a PE lesson, while achieving your educational objectives? (The following section on physical education may give you some ideas).**
2 **What possible constraints can operate on the play world of children?**

Recreation

The word 'recreation' originates from the Latin word 'recreatio', which means to restore health. Recreation has long been connected with relaxation and recuperation of the individual. It has been particularly valued during the nineteenth and twentieth centuries, with the emergence of an industrialised, machine controlled workforce. Recreation is thought to be useful in restoring people's energies for work. However, as with other concepts of physical activity, people participate for many different reasons. Many sections of the community are not in paid employment and yet participate in recreation.

Other ideas focus on recreation as being: activity based; not an obligation; socially acceptable; morally sound; an emotional response; an attitude; a way of life.

Theories of recreation

Serving the needs of human beings

J. B. Nash evaluates recreation as creative social contribution and a way of satisfying human inner urges. He developed the participation model where the recreative lifestyle is 'active participation experience'. Nash regards play as the childhood preparation for recreation in adult life and as a practice for work.

A leisure time activity

The most widely accepted view of recreation is simply activities in which people participate during their leisure time. One problem with this viewpoint is that many people are biased towards thinking that recreation can only be sport or physical activity.

1 **List the numerous activities that you, your family and peers take part in, as recreation.**
2 **Can you classify these in any way? For example, physical and non physical; individual or team/group situations; creative or informative?**

M. Neumeyer describes recreation as any activity, either individual or collective, which is pursued during one's leisure time. Recreation has four elements:

1 behavioural expression
2 intrinsically valuable
3 rewards found within the activity
4 socioculturally conditioned.

Valuable to individual and society

Many theorists (H. Meyer; C. Brightbill; G. Butler) espouse the idea that recreation must be of 'value', either to the individual or society. This is always a problem area, because whose values are more important? This is particularly significant when considering the provision for recreation by the public and voluntary agencies. What are the presumptions under which they organise their services?

Recreation as re-creation

J. S. Shivers concentrates on the idea of recreation as an 'experience'. Recreation wholly absorbs the individual at any one moment and helps provide 'psychological homeostasis', ie, the satisfying of psychological needs, and the process of mental re-balancing. Recreation is the harmony and unity experienced between mind and body. This occurs at the *time* of the experience; the *value* is felt later.

The degree to which individuals feel this 'completeness' of recreation will vary, probably will only occur in its purest sense on a few occasions. Those occasions would undoubtedly be extremely memorable and personally uplifting. Do you have any such experiences?

A social process

J. Murphy believes recreation is a *process*, which requires exploration, investigation, manipulation and learning behaviour. This theory is similar to theories of play, examined earlier. He claims that the physical, psychological, social and educational processes are the outcome of recreation, and lead to self realisation.

A social institution

R. Kraus takes a different slant:

- Voluntary activities must to some degree be determined by the choices made available. This involves the social institutions and agencies which have developed, eg, churches, schools, industries, voluntary agencies, government departments, etc.
- Skill levels associated with many activities take time to master.
- Motivation to participate is rarely completely intrinsic.

Recreation planning

- Services should be developed so that people can find recreation and fulfil individual needs.
- Programmes should take a holistic approach, ie, concern for the whole person.
- Access should be available to all citizens
- Planning for recreation *activities* can be measurable and operable, but planning cannot guarantee a recreation *experience* (a particular incident or feeling).

Recreation planning certainly has its place within this modern and rapidly changing society, but for many people, true recreation is not about having their leisure time organised in the same way that the world of work is organised, as this brings its own constraints. Improvements can be made:

1 **Recreation managers** need to create an environment where recreation is most likely to occur.
2 **Work** conditions can be improved to give people greater chances of self expression, recreation activity and recuperation.
3 **Education** can be extended to include leisure skills, helping people to realise and achieve their potential.

 ACTIVITY 4

Discuss the following:

1 **Why is play a more important aspect of a child's life and recreation more significant for adults?**
2 **What is the significance of the word 'process'?**
3 **What are the suggested outcomes of participating in recreational activities?**
4 **Give an example of a distinct value orientation of a stated institution.**

Summary of theories of recreation

'Recreation consists of activities or experiences carried on within leisure, usually chosen voluntarily by the participant – either because of satisfaction, pleasure or creative enrichment derived, or because he perceives certain personal or social gains to be gained from them. It may also be perceived as the process of participation, or as the emotional state derived from the involvement.'
(R. Kraus, 1971)

Recreation can be viewed as:

- an extension of the 'play' experience
- a personal experience – the value to the individual
- the nature of an activity

- an institution and structural framework
- a process – what happens to an individual.

Leisure

The Ancient Greeks regarded 'leisure' as important for the development of the 'whole' man, his mind and body. This, however, was a state reserved only for the wealthy members of society. The growth of Christianity had a negative effect on leisure time, believing it to have little value in the preparation of the soul for the later life. The Puritan work ethic is a concept developed in the sixteenth and seventeenth centuries which valued the benefits of labour as opposed to the temptations of idleness. It has had far reaching effects on how we view leisure; even today, work is given a much higher status than leisure activities.

Theories of leisure

There are four major approaches to looking at leisure.

Leisure as time

This refers to **surplus** time; ie, time left over when practical necessities have been attended to. These necessities were referred to by the Countryside Recreation Research Advisory Group in 1970 as 'work, sleep, and other needs' (including family and social duties). C. Brightbill claims that people need the time, opportunity and choice to enjoy true leisure. He contrasts true leisure with enforced leisure, such as illness, unemployment or forced retirement.

1 **Fill in a weekly timetable with all the 'necessities' mentioned above, including sleep, paid work, college/school work, domestic responsibilities etc. Then try and approximate the amount of time you have left as leisure.**
2 **Fill in the activities you consider to be part of your leisure time.**

Leisure as activity

Leisure activities can be subdivided into different categories of interest: sport; home entertainment; hobbies and pastimes; reading; public entertainment; holiday activities such as sightseeing.

J. Nash believes that leisure activities occur on four levels:

1 passive
2 emotional
3 active
4 creative involvement.

Each is attributed a value; those at the apex are considered more worthy as leisure than those at the base.

Other theories claim that it is the meaning the activities have for the individuals participating which is more important than the activities themselves.

J. Dumazadier believes that leisure must be freely chosen and should benefit the individual in terms of relaxation, diversion or broadening of horizons. He uses the term 'semi leisure' to include such activities as DIY which can be pleasurable as well as being functional.

Leisure as an end in itself

This contradicts the idea of free time being leisure. The state of mind with which a person approaches this free time is crucial. In its ideal state, leisure should be an opportunity for self expression (J. Pieper; C. Brightbill; S. de Grazia).

The holistic approach

J. Dumazadier believes leisure has three main functions:

1 relaxation
2 entertainment
3 self fulfillment

In other words, leisure holds a meaning for people and this is what is most important. It can relieve stress, be an antidote to boredom and allow freer movement than is allowed in many work places.

The concept of leisure is still undergoing changes. Many people are now motivated to work, not for the sake of work but to allow them the opportunity to enjoy their leisure status. Many feel their true identity is not that which occurs at work, but that which emerges during leisure.

Leisure and work

- Leisure is generally something people do not have to do, whereas most people have to work to earn a living.
- Work and leisure can both create a sense of self worth, creativity and personal development within a person.
- The common belief that people have more free time for leisure in the modern world, can be challenged by the fact that economic circumstances can force people to take on extra work.

In modern industrial societies, work can determine:

- how much time a person has for leisure
- how much energy they can bring to their leisure
- whether leisure can be pursued through work.

'Purposeful leisure' is a term used by communist governments who, as they operate an authoritarian system, require as much control over their population in leisure in the same way as other areas of social life. This is social control, extolling the belief that rebellious tendencies can be curbed and political messages can be equally learnt through the leisure situation.

Growth and change in leisure time

There are many reasons for the growth and change in leisure time in the UK:

- working hours have been reduced by the application of technology
- labour-saving gadgets enable people to spend much less time on domestic chores in the home
- increase in life expectancy
- increase in disposable incomes

- decline in the role of traditional social structures like the church and family
- education for everyone
- mobility of a large section of the population
- public provision of leisure facilities including the ability to hire equipment which would otherwise be out of reach of the majority of the population
- early retirement
- high unemployment.

Popular (low) culture

Individuals choose their own leisure within the context of their own culture, values and identity; the majority of the population will also be exposed to marketing forces of leisure. Popular culture is therefore defined by what is available and what represents social development.

Popular culture can also create change and trends, eg, skateboarding, public marathons. Different aspects are given prominence at different times but generally there is less of a tendency to maintain traditional established practices. The far-reaching effects of the mass media as it transmits Western popular culture across the world can however result in a uniformity of cultures, rather than the richness and variety of cultures which characterise different countries.

Consider the following factors and suggest how they can affect and be affected by leisure:

- **occupation**
- **trends**
- **levels of participation**
- **leisure provision in society**
- **women's lives**
- **media**

High culture

This traditionally refers to the cultural pursuits of the higher social classes and they usually reflect the privileged lifestyles of wealth, education and more free time. Activities pursued by this group of people are often not made easily accessible to the lower social classes, and there is a sense of cultural separation. These activities are often considered to operate on a more intellectual and refined manner to those of popular culture.

1 **Select activities which can be categorised as popular or high culture.**
2 **Discuss the elements which make them different.**
3 **Investigate the different approaches taken by the media towards activities from the two ends of the spectrum.**

Summarise theories of leisure.

Integrating play, recreation and leisure

Each concept has its own distinct nature, but that they also have similarities; they are multi-dimensional and link together.

Similarities

- freedom
- self expression
- satisfaction
- quality
- self initiated
- no pressure or obligation to take part
- range of activities
- experiential

Differences

- emphasis, eg, play has a strong emphasis on childlike spontaneity and unreality.
- functions, eg, for learning, refreshing, recreating or just being!

Interrelationships

Leisure can be the pivot upon which the other two concepts can be embraced

> *'leisure can conceptually embrace the freedom of play, the recreation process and the recreation institution. Leisure can be presented as the opportunity and the means for play and recreation to occur.'* (Torkildsen).

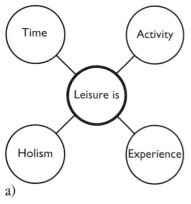

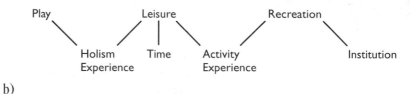

b)

a)

Fig. 13.3 (A) MULTI-DIMENSIONAL CONCEPT OF LEISURE (B) A SIMPLE PLR DIAGRAM

A recreation programme combines planning, scheduling, time tabling and implementation, using resources, facilities (eg, swimming pools, parks, natural resources etc) and staff to offer a wide range of services and activities. The activities will range from allowing spontaneity to being completely structured.

ACTIVITY 9

1 **What factors should recreation managers take into account when building and planning services?**
2 **Explain the difference between the terms 'leisure' and 'recreation'.**
3 **Name two home based leisure activities and two non-home based leisure activities.**
4 **Select two categories of people who are known to have low participation rates in the non-home based activities. For each category explain why their participation is low and suggest strategies which could help to rectify the situation.**

Fig. 13.4   PLAY, RECREATION, LEISURE
OR SPORT?

Fig. 13.4   PLAY, RECREATION, LEISURE OR SPORT?

Physical education

What is physical education?

Physical education is an academic discipline (an organised, formal body of knowledge), which has, as its primary focus, the study of human movement. It may be viewed as a field of knowledge, drawing on the physical and human sciences and philosophy, with its main emphasis on physical activity. As this field of knowledge has broadened, the subject specific areas have increased. Sub-disciplines have emerged which have diversified the subject and related it to career opportunities; examples are – sport sociology, biomechanics, sports medicine, exercise physiology, sport philosophy, history, psychology, sports management. You will probably recognise some of these from your own 'A' level physical education course.

Physical education at this level may seem a far cry from what you have experienced over the last twelve years at school. At this stage it is necessary to know what is meant by the term and to appreciate that a philosophy has developed over the last century, and will continue to do so, sometimes changing radically the practice of our subject.

Consider these philosophical viewpoints:

- All participants, regardless of athletic ability, should have equal amounts of playing time on the school curriculum.
- Physical educators should be role models and practise on the playing fields what they preach in the classroom.
- Physical education is only useful in that it provides a break from academic lessons.
- Physical education should be compulsory.

Physical education is an educational process which aims to enhance total human development and performance through movement and the experience of a range of physical activities within an educational setting. Total development means acquiring activity specific skills and knowledge, as well as fostering positive attitudes and values which will be useful in later life. Physical education can help us to achieve a quality of life and a vitality which can be lacking in sedentary lifestyles.

The key words are:

- **Range of physical activities**
- **Movement**
- **Activity specific skills**
- **Knowledge**
- **Values**
- **Educational setting.**

Aims and objectives

Physical activity involves doing, thinking and feeling. Children need to know *how* to perform or express themselves, know *about* physical activities and also benefit from the enriching experience of knowing how it *feels* to perform.

Already we have given physical education some very difficult challenges. We are assuming that all the outcomes are positive, but this is clearly not the case. Among your peers are those who have enjoyed their physical education experiences but also those who definitely did not! Before we can hope to achieve the positive benefits, we must clarify the aims, objectives and desired outcomes from the physical education curriculum.

Aims

Physical education aims to:

- develop a range of psycho-motor skills
- maintain and increase physical mobility and flexibility, stamina and strength
- develop understanding and appreciation for a range of physical activities
- develop positive values and attitudes like sportsmanship, competition, abiding by the rules
- help children acquire self esteem and confidence through the acquisition of skills, knowledge and values
- develop an understanding of the importance of exercise in maintaining a healthy lifestyle.

Objectives

Physical education can affect different areas of development. For example:

- The children will be able to complete a 20 minute run – physical development.
- The children will execute the correct technique for a gymnastic vault – motor development.
- The children will be able to explain the scoring system in badminton – cognitive development.
- The children will display enthusiasm and enjoyment and participate in the extra-curricular activities – affective or emotional development.

Ask a group of your peers about their experiences of physical education (including the types of activities, what they enjoyed most or least). You can ask general or more specific questions.

Table 13.2　The structure and function of a practical session: definition of terms, relating to a practical session

TERM	DEFINITION	RELATED TO EDUCATIONAL SETTING
structure	the way in which something is constructed or organised; the arrangement and interrelationship of parts	a lesson within a school timetable; compulsory; age, size, sex and ability of group; location; authority structure
function	the special activity or purpose of a thing or person	
objectives	something one is trying to achieve or reach	transmit knowledge and skills; safety; success for all abilities; enjoyment; fitness
strategies	the planning and directing of the whole operation of a curriculum or lesson; a plan to achieve something (such as the objectives)	effective grouping; personal knowledge; varied teaching styles (instruct, guide); discipline; differentiated tasks to cater for varying abilities; rewards systems
content	the substance of a thing or occasion	change kit; warm up; skills; small/conditioned game; full game
constraint	to confine, restrain, inhibit, restrict	duration of a lesson; ability of group; condition of facility or equipment
evaluation	to set the value of; to judge or assess the worth of something	to test (physical, verbal, written) at end of session or block; own feeling or judgement of lesson (should be ongoing)
authority	the power or right to control; a position that commands power	headteacher, teacher, prefect, captain
conflict	a state of opposition between ideas, which can lead to tension	relationships (teacher/child, child/child, teacher/teacher); ideas (compulsory, kit, showers)
dysfunction	any disturbance or abnormality in the function of a group	discipline problems

Imagine you are taking a practical session with Year 9; a team game within the physical education timetable. Using table 13.2 as a guide, draw up a detailed plan of your lesson.

(This could assist students following the CCPR Community Sports Leaders Award or on teaching practice, and can be used as a role play situation within your academic group.)

A balanced physical education programme

A balanced programme should attempt to offer a variety of activities selected from each group in table 13.3, in order to maximise fully the opportunities to be gained from the different activities. There should be a balance of activities which are:

- team orientated
- individual
- competitive
- non-competitive movement based.

Table 13.3 A BALANCED PHYSICAL EDUCATION PROGRAMME

GAMES				MOVEMENT
INVASION	NET	STRIKING/FIELD	REBOUNDING	gymnastics dance trampolining athletics swimming
football netball hockey rugby	tennis volleyball table tennis	cricket rounders softball	squash	

1 **Study the aims of physical education and see how you might link these to the activities shown in table 13.1.**
2 **Tick the activities which you experienced during your secondary education. Do you think that you received a balanced physical education programme?**
3 **Conduct a survey of approximately six schools in your local area. Try and find out what they offer their pupils. Can you find parallels or many variations? Does what is on offer reflect the different nature of the schools?**

Who chooses the physical education programme?

In the United Kingdom there is a decentralised system where the teacher and individual school has the power to produce its own programme, though it is increasingly bound by government guidelines. The National Curriculum now sets out which subjects are to be taught at each Key Stage of a pupil's schooling. Physical education is compulsory from Key Stage 1 (ages 5 to 7) through to Key Stage 4 (up to age 16).

1 **Find out from your teacher what the general requirements and programmes of study for each Key Stage are.**
2 **What factors may a teacher have to take into account when devising a syllabus?**

Assessment in physical education

Aims and objectives will depend on how achievement is evaluated and how well the children have progressed is one element within the evaluation. Several types of assessment are used in physical education departments, such as longitudinal student profiles, purely quantitative data like fitness tests or generalised comments.

Children need to be able to show what they know, what they can do and what they understand. They can show this through written and verbal language, and in a performance situation.

Assessment should be made of the whole person, not just physical skills. Aspects of their personality such as their ability to work with groups or individually, and their ability to abide by rules should be assessed.

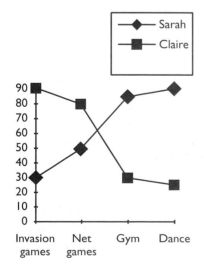

Fig. 13.5 AN ASSESSMENT GRAPH

Study fig 13.5, which gives the results of two students' assessment tests.

1 **What comments might you make about the strengths and weaknesses of the two candidates?**

2 **What does an average score for each reveal?**

Administration of physical education in the UK

The UK has a system of private and state school education, and of comprehensive and grammar schools. The nature of schools can be as diversified as the people they house. As shown in Chapter 12, local authorities used to have a large influence on how education operates in their areas; they would be the middle man between the schools and the government. During the 1980s, the government implemented increasingly centralised policies, such as the National Curriculum, the Local Management of Schools (LMS) and the growing number of grant maintained schools (GMS), which resulted in them leaving local authority control. The government sought more direct control of education, and through the Education Reform Acts of 1986 and 1988, they have restricted the freedom of teachers, schools and local authorities to construct their own syllabus.

How has this affected physical education? At the beginning of the century, the Board of Education produced syllabuses which schools were required to follow. These laid out the content and style of teaching, and set guidelines for teachers to follow. Little interaction was required by the children, and there was a strong emphasis on the teacher's authority. Physical fitness at this stage was the primary goal.

As training for teachers improved, and the subject developed, there was less need for the syllabuses to be used, and they eventually became defunct. Changes in educational thinking also had an impact; the emphasis changed from a focus on the physical or organic requirements to concentrating on the development of the 'whole' child. This included opportunities for self expression, socialisation, problem solving and experimentation, and the performance outcome was not considered quite so important as the process. The schools now made their own decisions on what should be taught.

This remained the case until the implementation of the National Curriculum.

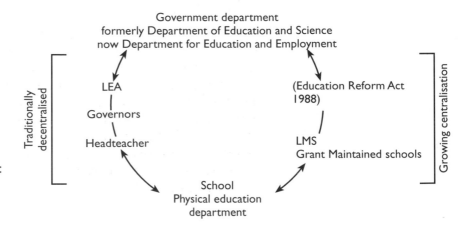

Fig. 13.6   Changes in administration: the government can now deal directly with the school, rather than through the LEA

What are the advantages and disadvantages of a decentralised education system?

National Curriculum

The National Curriculum attempts to raise standards in education and make schools more accountable for what they teach. Physical education continues to be one of only five subjects which pupils of all abilities must pursue, from their entry to school at age 5 until the end of compulsory schooling at age 16.

Attainment targets and programmes of study have been written for physical education. Children are required to demonstrate the knowledge, skills and understanding involved in areas of various physical activities, including dance, athletics, gymnastics, outdoor and adventurous activities and swimming. There are four Key Stage Tests, which take place in years 1, 3, 7 and 10.

In the document 'Sport: Raising the Game', the government went one step further, and produced a revised PE curriculum which took effect in August 1995 (see page 160 for further discussion of this document). It contained the following points:

- an enhanced role for team games
- a minimum requirement of two hours per week of PE and sport in formal lessons
- teaching standards to be regularly monitored by OFSTED (Office for Standards in Education)
- all 5–7-year-olds to be taught the skills and rules of competitive team games
- all 7–11-year-olds to play the mini versions of adult recognised games
- all 11–14-year-olds to progress to play the full game
- all 14–16-year-olds to play a competitive team game alongside other sports and physical activities of their choice.

This initially sounds encouraging and positive but fig 13.7 shows data published by the European Union of Physical Education Association. The survey shows the amount of time spent per week on physical education in schools, in the USA and the UK. At the primary level the UK is ninth out of ten and at secondary level the UK is placed at the bottom of the table.

The Department of Education also conducted a survey in 1995, which showed that some schools are still not devoting two hours a week to physical education as recommended.

Private schools

Education in this country began with private schooling for the social elite. Pupils enjoyed extensive facilities and focused on the 'character building' aims of education, as preparation for responsibilities in later life as employers, officers, members of the clergy and so on. Competitive team games developed to serve these aims. There was always a concentration on sport rather than a physical education emphasis and this is still prevalent today. As a result sport coaches still tend to be employed often for their specialist sporting prowess. This is particularly evident for schools wishing to continue a sporting tradition. Competitive fixtures are a recognised feature and the prestige which arises from winning helps to distinguish it from other schools.

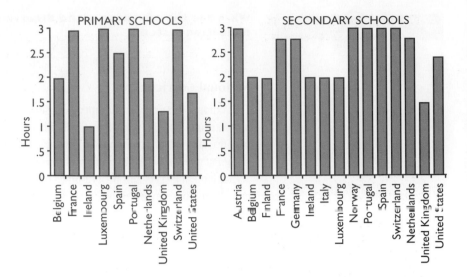

Fig. 13.7   THE AMOUNT OF TIME
DEVOTED TO PE IN SCHOOLS IN THE UK
COMPARED TO THE REST OF EUROPE AND
USA

Source: European Union of PE Associations

State education – primary schools

State education began after the Forster Education Act 1870 which initiated
compulsory schooling for all. Compulsory schooling begins at the age of five. As
mentioned above, in the state system physical education is compulsory and is a core
subject of the National Curriculum: students must spend at least two hours a week
on this subject. The class teacher is usually in charge, though is not usually a
specialist. Some schools may hire in specialist help for certain activities, eg,
swimming.

The content of the lessons is usually based on movement and ball skills.
Learning by moving and doing is considered essential to the physical, emotional,
intellectual and social education of young children. Children's own play is generally
very physical and enjoys a lot of repetition, as this enables them to master skills
which increases their sense of worth. The physical education programme can use
this as a foundation. Variety is also important as their concentration span can be
limited and they need to be stimulated by interesting situations.

In addition to the curriculum, many schools also offer club activities like
gymnastics, netball, soccer, country dancing, etc. This tends to be at the discretion
and goodwill of the teachers.

Secondary education

As children approach the end of the compulsory years of schooling, it is necessary
to foster in them an awareness of the opportunities available in the community. As a
result of the philosophy of educating children for their leisure time, schools began
to offer options programmes in the later years where a wider variety of activities,
sometimes using community facilities, could be experienced. Smaller groups
guided by additional non-specialist staff made this possible. Students should be
informed about and put into contact with local clubs and sports centres. This is an
area of weakness in the United Kingdom; there are traditionally poor links between
schools and community sport, as a result of trying to keep a distance between sport
and physical education. This will be discussed in more detail later.

Physical education as an examination subject has flourished. A rapidly growing
number of students opt to take GCSE and 'A' level examinations, and some GNVQs
offer sport and physical education as a focus.

Developments in school sport

The term 'sport' refers to the 'physical activities with established rules engaged in by individuals attempting to outperform their competitors' (Wuest, Bucher, 1991). Its main focus is on improving performance standards rather than the educational process and mainly takes place outside the formal curriculum. It is usually viewed as an opportunity for children to extend their interest or ability in physical activities.

The changes in society and education in the last 20 years have affected school sport (ie, the extra-curricular opportunities), with a reduction in emphasis on the sporting elite, which sometimes required a disproportionate amount of resources for a few children. Extra-curricular clubs, open to all, became more acceptable. The situation did not change overnight, however; many teachers continued to focus on competitive sports, and extra-curricular activities were affected by these factors:

1 The teachers' strikes in the early 1980s – the contractual hours and lack of monetary incentives tended to diminish teachers' goodwill, and clubs were disbanded.
2 Financial cuts were felt in terms of transport.
3 The local management of schools allowed schools to supplement their funds by selling off school fields.
4 The increasing amount of leisure and employment opportunities for children meant they were less attracted to competing for their school team.
5 The anti-competitive lobby became more vocal: they espoused the theory that competition in sport was not good for children's development.

This all led to the claim that school sport was in decline, although the report produced in 1995 by the Office of her Majesty's Chief Inspector of Schools, 'Physical Education and Sport in Schools – A Survey of Good Practice', concluded 'that there was little to support the notion of irrevocable decline'.

Fig. 13.8   SCHOOL SPORT ENCOURAGES TEAMWORK

Table 13.4   ADVANTAGES AND DISADVANTAGES OF COMPETITIVE SPORT

ADVANTAGES	DISADVANTAGES
Children have natural competitive instinct, and as more motivated to practise, enjoyment of sport increases	Continued feelings of failure can cause stress and anxiety
Can raise self esteem and learn how to cope with failure and success	The need to win can encourage unsporting behaviour

What strategies would you use in order to teach a competitive game situation to a group of mixed ability 11-year-olds, producing the more positive aspects of competition?

'Sport: Raising the Game'

The focus of the 1995 document is mainly on reinstating the status of school sport within school life. It formed part of the Conservative government's overall strategy to develop an effective sporting continuum.

The publication of this document showed a recognition that school sport had declined, and the government wanted to rectify the situation:

1 The **Sportsmark** scheme recognises the best schools with additional gold star awards for the most innovative. Teachers who make an extra commitment to school sport can, *at the governors' discretion* receive additional salary points.

2 The weak links with community sport has already been highlighted. To attempt to overcome this the government welcomed the idea of improving links by accepting and encouraging the voluntary assistance offered by coaches. However, this is dependent on the initiative of the individual teachers and schools. Finance, needless to say, is also limited.

3 Schools must record in their annual prospectuses their sporting aims and their provision for sport.

Review the extra-curricular provision for sport in your education institution, and lay it out as a timetable as suggested below.

	Lunch	After school
Monday		
Tuesday		

Physical education or sport?

This is an ongoing debate, which re-surfaced in this document with the government's decision to give competitive sport a higher status. The terms 'physical education' and 'sport' are complex. There is an overlap between them but their central focuses are different. The aim of former is to educate the person, while the latter has other purposes, eg, achieving excellence, fitness, earning an income, etc. A good physical education programme can be the foundation on which the extra-curricular opportunities can be extended and enhanced. However, physical education teachers should not necessarily feel pressured into allowing a 'sport' ethos to creep into the curriculum.

ACTION
Agenda

SPORTSMARK CRITERIA

To achieve a Sportsmark schools might expect to:

i. offer a minimum of two hours a week of formal PE lesson time;

ii. offer at least four hours each week of structured sport outside formal lessons: schools will be expected to provide all interested pupils with the opportunity to participate in sport at lunch-times, in the evenings and at weekends;

iii. devote at least half the time spent on PE both inside and outside formal lessons to sports which, if not the full game, should be played in a form judged appropriate for the year group by the relevant sports governing body;

iv. encourage teachers and others involved in extra-curricular sport to gain coaching qualifications or leadership awards enabling them to lead sports matches;

v. encourage teachers to improve their individual coaching skills by taking advantage of the different levels of awards/qualifications provided by the national governing bodies of sport;

vi. ensure in secondary schools that pupils of all ages have the opportunity to take part in competition if possible, and promote competition within their own school and against other schools;

vii. have established links with local sports clubs: schools will be expected to have developed links with a number of local sports clubs as a way of providing pupils with further sporting opportunities outside school hours. Sportsmark schools are likely to be among those successfully competing for the Sports Council's challenge fund for school–club links; and

viii. encourage pupils to take part in sports governing bodies' award schemes.

Fig. 13.9 EXCERPTS FROM *PLAYING THE GAME*

Some people were concerned that the Conservative government's agenda appeared to be about the winning of major international and World Cup events. Is it the aim of schools to set the foundations for success at international level? If so, the professional coaches should perhaps have as much contact with school teams as the physical education teacher has.

The problem of liaison and contact with outside agencies appears to be more of a problem. Initiatives have begun and are being successful, such as TOP Play, BT TOP Sport, and Champion Coaching (which involves 145 local authorities). The aim is to guide the young person from school to community sport and provide coaching training and experience for teachers and coaches involved. This is a top priority for the Sports Council and National Coaching Foundation, and the traditional notion of keeping sport coaching out of schools is being challenged.

The National Council for School Sport

Membership is open to national sports organisations in England and Wales responsible for the development of their sport in schools. The aims of the Council are to: coordinate the work of the school's national sports associations; encourage the formation of new associations; provide a forum for discussion; encourage involvement in the International School Sport Federation.

The official journal is the *Sports Teacher* magazine.

Outdoor education

Outdoor education and recreation refers to the participation in outdoor pursuit activities within the natural environment. The difference between the two is that recreation is done in one's own free time, while outdoor education takes place within an educational setting.

 **ACTIVITY 18**

1 **List as many activities as you can which take place in the natural environments of water, mountains, air and countryside.**
2 **Where people do not have easy access to these areas, how could you adapt the urban environment for them to learn the basic skills of some of these sports?**

These activities can place the individual in situations which are dangerous and challenging, and which induce exhilaration, fear and excitement. They can be competitive, but more often against the elements or the human body, than against another person. Generally, there are no officials with rules, though there are codes and ethics of practice which are usually adhered to.

The personal qualities required for and enhanced by these activities include:

- self reliance
- decision making
- leadership
- the ability to trust others
- the ability to be trusted.

These activities are not usually done alone, and the ability to work with others to overcome obstacles and find solutions is important; so too is the need to conquer fear of danger and the unpredictable. They often create unique situations which cannot be found playing in sports such as netball or soccer.

Risk and adventure

There has been a considerable growth both in the traditional (eg, canoeing, rock climbing, abseiling, climbing) and 'new' (eg, jet skiing, snow boarding, mountain biking) adventure sports. The reasons for this growth can be explained by:

- increasingly sedentary lives, which makes some people seek a more active and exciting leisure time
- increased leisure time and standards of living, which make these activities more accessible
- the development of new and exciting technology sports
- the appreciation of the natural environment particularly as a release from urban pressures.

According to Mortlock, there are four broad stages of adventure:

1 **Play**
2 **Adventure**
3 **Frontier adventure**
4 **Misadventure.**

I If you were a leader of a mixed ability group, which stages would you aim to achieve for your group and which factors would you aim to avoid?
2 Plan an activity which could come under the outdoor education umbrella. Note the pitfalls which could arise.

Are outdoor pursuit activities for everyone?

These activities should be available to everyone, regardless of wealth, race, sex or health. Many of these activities are being made more available to people with disabilities in the community, particularly through organisations such as the Calvert Trust; at their centres near Keswick, Exmoor and Kielder Water, the emphasis is on ability, achievement and enjoyment, and a range of disabilities such as physical, mental and sensory disabilities, are catered for. The Commission concluded that more information about these activities should be directed towards people from ethnic minorities to increase their participation. 'A Countryside for Sport' (1993) sets out the Sports Council's policy on encouraging newcomers. Established in 1994, 'The Foundation for Outdoor Adventure' should assist in providing information to ethnic community leaders.

Outdoor education and the school curriculum

There are strong reasons why outdoor education should be included in the school curriculum; namely, the benefit to the personal and social education of children, through experiential learning. The National Curriculum does not require that outdoor education is taught, though schools can arrange for it to be included. The skills which can be directly experienced and learned are an intrinsic element of Key Stages 3 and 4 of the adventurous activity option in physical education.

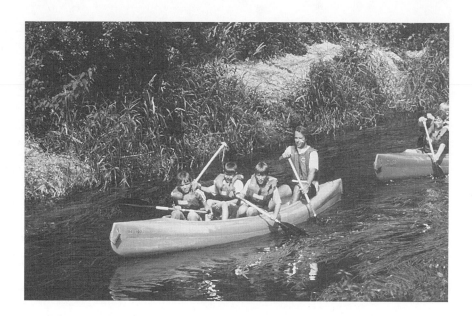

Fig. 13.10 OUTDOOR ACTIVITIES
SHOULD BE AVAILABLE TO EVERYONE

In an already constricted timetable, few schools have the commitment to the subject to support and sustain outdoor education:

1   The Education Reform Act 1988 increased the problems schools experienced in offering these activities.
2   The fundamental changes to the way in which schools are funded have also seriously affected the opportunities for teachers to gain valuable in-service training in order to achieve the appropriate qualifications.
3   Local education authorities may no longer have access to sufficient funds to provide for this training.
4   The law regarding charging pupils for out of school activities may cause schools to limit or abandon such activities, as voluntary contributions may not be sufficient. This could mean that only the wealthier schools are able to participate, so these activities would retain their elite image.
5   The increasing concern over safety issues is another problem for schools.

Other subjects could also utilise and benefit from outdoor education as it has useful cross curricular implications; environmental issues which can be highlighted are inequalities in wealth distribution, land use, forestation and deforestation, energy sources and the problems caused by people and pollution. However, it must not lose its own unique contribution in its own right. The United Kingdom lags far behind many other countries in its provision, and many outdoor education residential centres have been threatened with closure.

Tourism and environmental safeguards

Outdoor pursuit activities are growth sports, but there are also some problems which need to be addressed. The areas in which they often take place are country parks, nature reserves, green belt areas, areas of outstanding natural beauty and national parks. Conflicts can emerge between the sport participants, land owners and the environment. The UK is a relatively small island with a high density population. Problems caused by the growth in tourism and outdoor activities will be

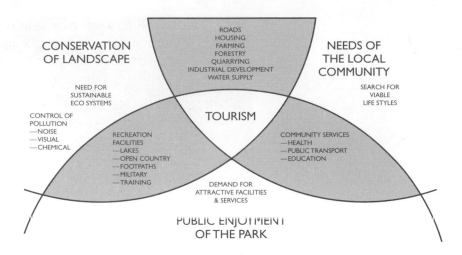

CONSERVATION
OF LANDSCAPE

NEEDS OF
THE LOCAL
COMMUNITY

ROADS
HOUSING
FARMING
FORESTRY
QUARRYING
INDUSTRIAL DEVELOPMENT
WATER SUPPLY

NEED FOR
SUSTAINABLE
ECO SYSTEMS

SEARCH FOR
VIABLE
LIFE STYLES

CONTROL OF
POLLUTION
—NOISE
—VISUAL
—CHEMICAL

TOURISM

RECREATION
FACILITIES
—LAKES
—OPEN COUNTRY
—FOOTPATHS
—MILITARY
—TRAINING

COMMUNITY SERVICES
—HEALTH
—PUBLIC TRANSPORT
—EDUCATION

DEMAND FOR
ATTRACTIVE FACILITIES
& SERVICES

PUBLIC ENJOYMENT
OF THE PARK

Fig. 13.11   CAUSES OF CONFLICT IN A
NATIONAL PARK

more keenly felt than in much larger, low population density countries such as the USA and France.

Some of the problems caused are:

- erosion of land and river banks
- pollution caused by motor sports
- the increase in the number of vehicles disturbing wildlife and local residents.

The most radical solution would be to *ban* the activities, but it might be more viable to *plan* for these activities in order to minimise the damage done to the environment. The agencies concerned need to liaise together to produce effective strategies. These would include the Sports Council, the CCPR, the governing bodies of the individual sports, the local authorities, the Countryside Commission and the National Parks Authorities.

National parks

There are ten national parks in the United Kingdom: the Brecon Beacons, Dartmoor, Exmoor, the Lake District, Snowdonia, the Norfolk and Suffolk Broads, the North York Moors, Northumberland, the Peak District, the Pembrokeshire Coast and the Yorkshire Dales.

Locate the national parks on a map of the United Kingdom.

These areas are governed by the national park authorities, which are local government bodies consisting of local councillors plus members appointed by the Secretary of State for the Environment. They have two statutory duties:

1 to protect and enhance the character of the landscape
2 to enable the public to enjoy the recreational opportunities of the area.

They also need to protect the social and economic well being of the local community.

National parks cater for a wide range of interests: they provide walkers with pleasant open countryside for enjoyment, accommodation for tourists and a livelihood for farmers and foresters, quarrymen and gamekeepers, rangers. The movement to establish these parks came from two main sources:

- access to mountains and moorlands (ramblers in the North of England)
- landscape preservation (Southern England middle class amenity lobby).

Increasing industrialisation and urbanisation amidst the changing relationships between rural and urban areas were important factors in the formation of the parks. See Chapter 17 for further information.

The Outward Bound Trust

The Outward Bound Trust began to pioneer outdoor activities in the 1940s. It has five centres in Britain, including Aberdovey in Wales, Ullswater in the Lake District and Loch Eil in Scotland. The organisation is now worldwide. Outward Bound works in partnership with the Duke of Edinburgh's Award Scheme. Its main aim is to promote personal development training for young people, placing them in challenging situations, such as physical expeditions, skill courses and the city challenge which is the urban equivalent. The challenging and often rugged activities include living in the wilderness, mountain climbing, canoeing, skiing and touring on bicycles. The first school was founded in Wales in 1941 by Kurt Hahn, an educator, to help young sailors who were 'outward bound' to sea.

Sport

What is sport? We know that the Sports Council refers to numerous activities as sport; we have sports clubs; hunting is called a sport; a person can be referred to as 'a good sport', and so on. In general we use the term loosely in normal conversation, but when we are relating important sociological concepts to sport (such as discrimination, concepts of femininity and its relationship to physical education), it is necessary to focus quite specifically on what we mean by the term. See Chapter 17 for a comprehensive history of sport.

A definition of sport would be useful, to examine the key elements. Sport can be defined as:

'institutionalised competitive activities that involve vigorous physical exertion or the use of relatively complex physical skills by individuals whose participation is motivated by a combination of intrinsic and extrinsic factors'
(Coakley, 1993).

What do we mean by some of these terms?

Institutionalised:
- A standardised set of behaviour recurs in different situations.
- Rules are standardised.
- Officials regulate the activity.
- Rationalised activities involve strategies, training schedules and technological advances.
- Skills are formally learned.

Physical activities:
- skills, prowess, exertion
- balance, coordination
- accuracy
- strength, endurance

The extent of the physical nature of the activity can vary and can lead us to question whether an activity such as darts, is a sport. Darts is referred to as a sport via the media, but the fact that it does not require much physical exertion can place it lower down on the sport continuum, even though it meets other criteria for inclusion as a sport. Any activity which does not meet all the criteria listed above would have less status as a sport.

Intrinsic:	*Extrinsic:*
• self satisfaction	• money
• fun	• medals
• enjoyment	• fame
• own choice	• obligation
• 'play spirit'.	• praise.

Most people will combine both of these motivations in the approaches they adopt towards sport participation. Think of an activity you regularly participate in. Are there occasions when you have been motivated in both ways?

Consider arguments for and against call synchronised swimming a sport.

The following situation may help clarify this complex concept as we have developed the argument so far:
Two friends who kick a football in the street are involved in an informal, social occasion. Physical exertion is present and skills are developing, but the people are involved in recreation rather than sport. If they challenged two other friends to a competition, this has moved to a situation called a contest or match. It is competitive but still under informal conditions. Only when they follow formalised rules and confront each other under standardised conditions can their situation be called sport.

Using a variety of equipment, devise a game within a group.

- **What characterised the development of this game?**
- **What would you have to do to change it into a PE lesson?**
- **What would you have to do to turn this game into an Olympic activity?**

Merely playing a recognised physical activity is not enough to allow us to call it sport. The situation under which it is operating is also important and needs consideration.

1 **Suggest other activity situations where this level of analysis could be applied.**
2 **How can the institutionalised sporting activities, such as football and hockey, be made more enjoyable for young children, creating a more educational environment?**

Amateurism and professionalism

There are two types of sports performers:

1 A person who competes as an **amateur** does so on the grounds that they will not receive monetary reward for their involvement in sport.
2 A **professional** sportsperson is one who earns an income from their sport.

See Chapter 17 for more information on this issue.

Benefits of sport

- Sport can act as an emotional release.
- It can offer individuals an opportunity to express their own individuality.
- Sport can help in the socialisation of people, ie, encourage a collective spirit and persuade people away from social unrest.
- Sport can help people achieve success when other avenues of achievement are not available to them.
- Sport can also help highlight issues which can be changed.

Problematic areas

- Sport can help to retain and reinforce discrimination.
- Too much emphasis can be placed on winning, and financial rewards intensify this.
- Competition, if not handled well can be damaging.
- Excessive behaviour can be encouraged through sport.
- Spectator sport can begin to outweigh active participation.
- Media coverage can dominate sports and their type of coverage can determine the wealth of a sport.

Classification of sporting activities

When we examined the nature of physical education, in particular, the need for children to experience a balanced physical education programme, we referred to activities such as games and movement. These in turn could be classified into further categories: the Council of Europe and the Sports Council have identified four main categories of sporting activity:

1 Conditioning activities
2 Competitive games and sports
3 Outdoor adventure activities (covered on page 000)
4 Aesthetic movement or gymnastic movements.

Conditioning activities

These are activities which are primarily designed to improve the physical and mental condition of the performer. Examples of such activities would be aerobics and also circuit and weight training. A programme of work is set and should be followed on a regular basis if it is to have the desired effect. They are easily adaptable for both the recreational and more serious performer. Some participants will participate purely for the general conditioning effect, while others will use it to achieve fitness for a particular sport. In some cases, they have developed into competition sports in their own right, for example, weight lifting and aerobics. They have competitions at all levels with rules, regulations and scoring systems.

Competitive games and sports

The main aim of competitive participation is to find out who is the best given equal circumstances. For example, athletes are matched within categories of level of ability, such as club, county or national standard; by age, weight and often gender, to make the competition as fair as possible. They adhere to the same standardised rules, which makes the unpredictability of the outcome more exciting. Their skill level, physical and mental fitness will be the main criteria of winning.

1 **Why is a pyramid a useful way of categorising competition?**
2 **What strategies could you use to increase the amount of people who reach the elite level?**

As one unit wins, another must lose. However, during a game an individual can still make successful contributions like winning a contest within the game; eg, the defender who marks an opposing attacker out of the game. A player can enjoy the game even though they lost, simply because the effort, challenge and physical work was worthwhile.

Athletics

This category includes races, field athletics and weight lifting. The athlete who wins the 100 m is the person who reaches the tape first. All race events, whatever the form of locomotion, are decided in this way: the high jumper clears the bar; the thrower achieves the furthest distance in the competition. The explosive or sustained power of the athlete is tested. In order to be fair to their opponents, athletes adhere to strict rules and also may take it in turns. This is called a quantitative, **objective** method of assessment, where scientific criteria is applied. The advances in the level of technology used have allowed extremely fine units of measurement to be used.

List as many ways as you can of scientifically measuring the outcomes of athletic contests.

Games

This category includes ball, fighting and target sports. Within a game situation, competitors interact with each other, and in the case of team games, with their own team mates. Interaction will take the form of verbal communication like calling out, coding messages and in preparing strategies; non-verbal communication takes place through signals, signs and facial expressions. Players need the ability to process a lot of information which is constantly changing and this requires them to make decisions either quickly, or more slowly, as in a strategic approach to the activity. Players will bring to the game situation their own skill level, attitudes, and previous experiences. They will have certain expectations also. They will want to play well and have their achievements recognised, will want to win and socialise with other players.

In a game of hockey, identify situations where a player is
- **processing information**
- **aiming at a stationary and moving target.**

The wide variations of activities existing in this category enable us to sub-divide them further.

Invasion games

These are games where one team invades the territory of their opponents. Examples would be hockey, netball, basketball and football. Scoring is usually in the form of goals and points, and the winner is the team who achieves the most goals or points within the allocated time period. The contest can last for one match or extend over a longer period of time, as in a league.

Invasion games are about maintaining possession of the ball by passing effectively within your team or creating possession by tackling or intercepting. Some invasion games allow personal *contact*, while others have strict rules forbidding it. The principles of play are based mostly on attacking and defending, and numerous strategies will be worked on to achieve the advantage. A range of skills and techniques are developed. They are usually 'open' (flexible) skills, as the game situation is always changing and the player is usually reacting to another's move. However, in situations like a penalty stroke in hockey, the skill could be described as closed.

Net games

This category includes tennis, volleyball and badminton, and constitutes a situation where opponents are separated by a net. These can be individual or team games. The winner is decided by who wins the most games, sets or rubbers. Domination in this instance is achieved by playing shots which the opponent is unable to return. The skills are again mainly 'open' except in the serve situation where the server has control; this is why so much importance is placed on the serve. All net games start with a serve, though they vary as to how points are scored in relation to the serve.

Rallies involve opponents hitting the object into each other's territory. The players must return the object immediately and on the rebound. Only in volleyball does a team have the option to move the ball around before returning it over the net.

A further category of net games are called 'rebounding' games, where the principles of play are the same but where a net is not used. Such activities include squash, fives, racquetball and rackets.

Innings games

Games such as cricket, baseball, softball and rounders are included in this category. An innings is the opportunity a team has to score. The playing area is defined as infield and outfield. The infield gives the opportunity for striking the ball in order to score runs, while the outfield is used to field or defend the ball and cut down on the opportunities for the opposing side to score runs. The aim is to get the other team out. A contest will occur between the bowler and batter who are put in a one-on-one situation.

Target games

The main characteristic of these games (archery, snooker, golf, darts, ten pin bowling) are that they require a high degree of accuracy when aiming at a target, which may be stationary or moving.

Gymnastic movements

These activities rely on the repetition of a movement pattern. Technical expertise (technique) and artistic interpretation are the two main factors which are assessed. The body is used as an art form, with appearance and individuality forming an important element. The 'performance' is assessed.

In activities such as ice skating where the winners are chosen by judges, there can be more questionable outcomes, than in competition sports. External motivation factors such as those listed on page 000, can sometimes play a part. This type of assessment is called qualitative or **subjective** assessment.

Analysis

Beashel and Taylor (1996) analyse each sporting activity by breaking the activity down into component parts.

- **Structural**
- **Strategic**
- **Technical**
- **Physical**
- **Psychological**.

Take a sport you have an intimate knowledge of and analyse it, using the above criteria.

Summary

- You should have a clearer picture of differences between the concepts of play, recreation, leisure, physical and outdoor recreation/education and sport; their unique features and also features which complement and relate with each other.
- People become involved in sport for various reasons and at various levels; each activity provides different challenges and experiences.

Using an A3 sheet of paper, list as many key words as you can under play, recreation, leisure, physical education, outdoor recreation and sport.

chapter 14

Levels of Sport Participation

This chapter investigates the various levels of participation in sporting activities. This will range from the broad base of the pyramid where the main emphasis is on participation, to the apex of the pyramid where the focus is on the standard of performance. For ease of study, society will be categorised into distinct groups based on age, disability, gender, socio-economics, culture and race, and each will be studied in relation to their sporting participation.

We will concentrate on the Sports Councils Target groups and the policies developed to increase their levels of physical activity, and try to establish some of the reasons for low participation.

Many of the qualities assigned to sport are well recognised – opportunity for self knowledge, personal achievement, good health, enjoyment, skill acquisition, social interaction, responsibility, development of confidence and so on. We should therefore be concerned that certain sections of the population are missing the chance to benefit from such an enriching experience.

The issue of participation

The need for a more coordinated and fair approach to the provision of sporting activities was addressed in the Sports Council's report *Better Quality Sport for All*, 1996. It looks at two main areas:

1 **sports development:** enabling people to learn basic sports skills with the possibility of reaching a standard of sporting excellence.
2 **sports equity:** redressing the balance of inequalities in sport ie, equality of access for everyone, regardless of race, age, gender or level of ability.

The Sports Council has a sport development continuum:

- **Foundation:** learning basic movement skills, knowledge and understanding; developing a positive attitude to physical activity.
- **Participation:** exercising one's leisure option for a variety of reasons – health, fitness, social.
- **Performance:** improving standards through coaching, competition and training.
- **Excellence:** reaching national and publicly recognised standards of performance.

Firstly it is important to understand the sociological basis for inequality in sport. It is not intended to be a thorough sociological review – merely a tool to help us achieve a greater understanding of the issue.

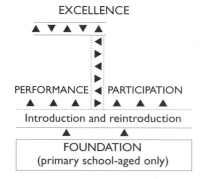

Fig. 14.1   Sports development continuum model

EXCELLENCE

PERFORMANCE ◄► PARTICIPATION

Introduction and reintroduction

FOUNDATION
(primary school-aged only)

All men are equal?

In the descriptive sense this is patently untrue: human beings do not possess the same amount of physical, mental or moral qualities. In the prescriptive sense, however, people ought to treat one another with equal respect, dignity and consideration.

Stratification of society

Society can be divided into layers, as are rocks (ie, rock strata). The divisions are based on biological, economic and social criteria, eg, age, gender, race and social class. The dominant group in society, which controls the major social institutions like the media, law, education and politics, can exercise control over the more subordinate groups. This need not be the majority – take the case of previous minority white rule in South Africa. Using this classification, the dominant group in the UK could be described as white, male and middle class; the subordinate groups would be women, ethnic minorities, people with disabilities and belonging to the working class.

Discrimination can occur when opportunities available to the dominant group are not available to all social groups.

Discrimination means 'to make a distinction: to give unfair treatment especially because of prejudice', and it occurs when a prejudicial attitude is acted upon. Discrimination can be **overt**, eg, laws which form part of the structure of a society, such as the former political system of apartheid, or a membership clause for a private sports club. This can be officially wiped out by changing the law, but **covert** discrimination (hidden or less obvious), eg, people's attitudes and beliefs, can be very hard to dislodge.

When subordinate groups in society are discriminated against, their opportunities are limited, including opportunities of social mobility (the pattern of movement from one social class to a higher or lower one). This can also be affected by whether the social system is closed (an extreme example is the Hindi caste system in India), or open (a true egalitarian democracy).

Sport and stratification

Sport is often described by sociologists as a microcosm of society: it reflects in miniature all facets of society. This includes the institutionalised divisions and inequalities which characterise our society. Sporting institutions are equally controlled by the dominant group in society, and stratification in sport is inevitable when winning is highly valued. It is highlighted even more when monetary rewards are on offer.

Sport is often cited as an avenue for social mobility:

- physical skills and abilities – professional sports requires little formal education
- sport may create progression through the education system eg, athletic scholarships
- occupational sponsorship may lead to future jobs
- sport can encourage values such as leadership and teamwork skills, which may help in the wider world of employment.

Race

Race is the physical characteristic of an individual, while ethnicity is the belonging to a particular group, eg, religious, lifestyle. Racism is a set of beliefs or ideas based on the assumption that races have distinctive cultural characteristics determined by hereditary factors, and that this endows some races with an intrinsic superiority.

Examples of racism in sport

In sport, racism can be seen in a system called 'stacking'. This refers to the disproportionate concentration of ethnic minorities in certain positions in a sports team, which tends to be based on the stereotype that they are more valuable for their physical skills than for their decision making and communication qualities. In American football there has been a tendency to place ethnic players in running back and wide receiver positions. In baseball, until fairly recently, they have tended to be in outfield positions. According to Grusky's theory of centrality (1963), this restricts them from more central positions which are based on coordinative tasks and require a greater deal of interaction and decision making. Significantly, coaches who make these decisions are generally white. Sociological studies have revealed the self-perpetuating coaching sub culture which exists in American sport (J Coakley, 1994). When existing coaches need to sponsor a new coach, they are likely to select one with similar ideas.

Attempts to overcome racism in sport

'Lets stamp racism out of football'

This was a large scale, national campaign begun in 1993–4, intended to cut racial harassment out of football. It was supported by CRE/PFA (Commission for Racial Equality and Professional Footballers Association) and supporters' groups, the FA, the Football Trust, the Premier and Ensleigh Leagues. In 1994–5, over 10% of clubs took specific action.

It is a recognition that clubs who reap financial benefits of fielding players from ethnic minorities should also show a greater responsibility and consideration for all its customers or members. It was highlighted in the media as a serious issue requiring action, with particular regard to Paul Ince, Mark Stein and Andy Cole. Concern is also felt that ethnic minority players should experience equal opportunities in reaching the administerial levels of the game.

Imagine you are in charge of a football club. What comprehensive measures would you take to eliminate racism from the game!

Educational study

There has been a tendency for teachers to act upon a stereotype; they had labelled a group of children and developed certain expectations of them. This can be self-perpetuating, as children can internalise these misconceptions and regard the sport side of educational life as the only successful route for them.

Studies of ethnic minority participation in sport

The Greater Manchester Conurbation was selected as a region to try to identify the relationship between ethnicity, culture and participation in sport, in 1991. African, Bangladeshi, Caribbean, Chinese, East African, Asian, Indian, Pakistani and a comparable British white group were studied. The striking results were the **gender** differences:

- to be female and a Muslim, Hindu, or Sikh is likely to result in a lower participation rate. The higher the importance placed on religion, the more this trend increased, as a strong patriarchal structure operates (Carroll and Hollinshead, 1992–3).
- Women in these research studies did express a wish to increase their participation and this should have implications for sport policies.

Respect for **cultures** must also be considered:

- Asian groups do not rate sport and PE as highly as some of the other groups, and there are a lack of role models.
- Some cultural traditions can conflict with active sport participation habits, such as showing parts of the body, sharing changing facilities, attending co-educational classes.

The biggest provider of facilities for all groups was the local authority. Problems the ethnic groups encountered were 'feeling an outsider', racism, and lack of single sex provision.

To summarise the results of the study:

- Sport is generally popular with ethnic groups – the Asian Games attract thousands of people.
- Special assistance is needed.
- Clubs should be supported but integration not forced.
- Information should be available about sport provision.
- Ease of access is important.
- Group leaders who may persuade other members to participate should be encouraged to train.
- Sport development officers from ethnic minorities should be appointed.
- Greater media coverage, such as Channel 4's Kabbaddi have helped to raise the awareness of the general population.

Using your knowledge of a local sports centre, explain why the Sports Council should give special attention to ethnic minority users.

Gender

Gender means the biological aspect of a person, either male or female; gender roles refer to what different societies and cultures attribute as appropriate behaviour for that sex. These can vary from culture to culture and also change historically within a culture. We learn our expected role through a process called **socialisation**, which simply means the learning of cultural values and is equally applicable to table manners! We learn firstly through primary socialisation (mainly from our close family group at an early age), and then through secondary socialisation from the wider world of institutions. What emerges are the terms **masculinity** and **femininity**.

1 **Write a list of what you consider to be the dominant characteristics of these two gender roles.**
2 **Write a list of the qualities necessary to succeed in sport at a high level.**
3 **Which gender role best fits the sport role model?**

Sexism in sport

Sexism is the belief that one sex is inferior to the other, and is most often directed towards women. It is sometimes based on the idea that women are not best suited to roles which carry prestige and influence. Traditionally women have been denied the same legal, political, economic and social rights enjoyed by men.

Don't underestimate the long lasting effect of attitudes which are handed down through the generations. Sexism against women operates in sport in numerous ways:

The Barr Sex Test

This requires a sample of cells to be scraped from the inside of a woman's cheek to determine the amount of 'Barr Bodies' present (chromatins). If the count drops below a minimum percentage, the athlete is disqualified. Princess Anne was the only female Olympic athlete who was not required to take this test.

The Sex Discrimination Act (SDA) 1975

This act made sex discrimination unlawful in employment, training, education and the provision of goods, facilities and services; ie, a female should be treated in the same way as a male in similar circumstances.

- Competitive sport is excluded by section 44 of the Act. Separate competitions for men and women are allowed where 'the physical strength, stamina or physique puts her at a disadvantage to the average man'. Problems have occurred where female referees and PE teachers have been denied promotion on the grounds of being a woman, and some successful appeals have been made.
- Private sports clubs can legally operate discriminatory policies, under Sections 29 and 34. After an appeal in 1987, the EC recommended that all clubs which are not genuinely private must remove any barriers which discriminate against men or women.

Women and professional sport

The Womens Sports Foundation (WSF) is a voluntary organisation promoting the interests of women and girls in sport and recreation. There is a network of regional groups and a wide range of activities and events are organised. Their regular publication is 'Women in Sport Magazine'.

Professional sport still tends to favour men, even in activities such as pool, where physical strength differences could be questioned.

Only women who are very dedicated and committed move through from participation to performance sports. Myths and negative stereotypes still abound, and the media give much less coverage to women's sport:

- Surveys have shown that national newspapers give less than 6% of total sport space to women's sport.
- The Women's Sport Foundation found in a 4-week period in 1991, a 90% male bias in photographs and articles in newspapers.
- Television rarely covers women's team games which the majority of school girls play, even though the national teams are internationally quite successful.
- There are more sport competitions for men.
- Financial constraints affect women more than men, as they attract less sponsorship to help with training, equipment, travelling and general fees.

Female power in sports organisations and levels of administration have not matched the rise in female sport participation.

- Few women reach the top levels of coaching: in 1992 there were only eight

Table 14.1   PERCENTAGE OF MALE/FEMALE ATHLETES AND COACHES IN THE GREAT BRITAIN SUMMER OLYMPIC TEAMS

	% OF ATHLETES		% OF COACHES	
	MALE	FEMALE	MALE	FEMALE
1976	73	27	96	4
1980	68	32	91	9
1984	68	32	96	4
1988	64	36	90	10
1992	61	39	92	8

Official reports of Olympic Games British Olympic Association.

female coaches at the Olympics, compared with 92 male coaches (see tables 14.1 and 14.2)
- Mixed governing bodies, such as swimming, badminton, tennis, riding and cycling all show a poor ratio of female decision makers in proportion to the amount of female participants. A similar situation occurs in the Sports Council, and in 1992, only six of the 95 members of the Olympic Committee were women.

The problem has increased with a more professional and bureaucratic environment, and perhaps reflects the inappropriateness of the male model of sport, women's lack of access to political systems and the poor recruitment mechanisms operating in these institutions.

Female participation in recent years

The percentage of women over the age of 16 years participating in both indoor and outdoor sport increased from 52% in 1987 to 57% in 1990. Men's participation increased from 70% to 73%. Women's *indoor* participation increased more than men's, which can mainly be accounted for by the rapid increase in keep fit and aerobics (up 33% in three years). However, indoor sport for women still lags 14% behind men. Numbers for women's outdoor sport fell, with outdoor team games still very much a male preserve.

Table 14.2   PERCENTAGE OF MALE/FEMALE ATHLETES AND COACHES IN THE SUMMER OLYMPICS GREAT BRITAIN TEAMS

	% OF ATHLETES		% OF COACHES	
	MALE	FEMALE	MALE	FEMALE
1976	73	27	96	4
1980	68	32	91	9
1984	68	32	96	4
1988	64	36	90	10
1992	61	39	92	8

Official reports of Olympic Games British Olympic Association.

Table 14.3   SPORT PARTICIPATION RATES BY SEX, 1987–1990

1987–1990	proportion of women participating in sport or physical activity rose from 52% to 57%
1986	women comprised 26% of participants in outdoor team games
1988	women comprised 6.7% of participants in outdoor team games
1989	39% of women participated in sport and physical activity, excluding walking women comprised 60% of those who participated in indoor sport only

 ACTIVITY 4

Women continue to face social, political and prejudicial barriers to sport. Identify as many examples of inequalities as you can under these three categories.

The Brighton Declaration on Women and Sport

In Brighton on the 5–8th May 1994, sport policy and decision makers at both national and international level met. It was organised by the British Sports Council and supported by the British Olympic Committee; 82 countries took part. There was a wish to increase the momentum that had already begun to narrow the gap between male and female sport participation across many continents.

The following points were developed:

1 Equal opportunity should be available through all social structures, and anti discrimination legislation should be implemented.
2 Facilities should take into account the needs of women, particularly in the provision of childcare and safety.
3 Physical education in particular should take into account the differing approaches and aspirations of girls to active sport involvement, compared with those of boys.
4 Women involved in high performance sport should be supported in terms of competition opportunities, rewards, incentives and recognition.
5 Sporting organisations should develop policies and programmes to increase the number of women coaches, advisors, decision makers, officials, administrators and sports personnel at all levels. Particular attention needs to be directed at recruitment, development and retention.
6 Research and information in sport should equally reflect women's involvement.
7 Action for change must be coordinated. Women themselves can do much to improve the situation but this can only really be effective if they are helped through the social structures operating.

What women can do:

• Develop a positive attitude to a healthy lifestyle; find out what is available locally and encourage a friend to go with them; be determined!
• Having developed an interest, join a club to gain access to coaching and facilities; lobby a governing body, local authority and the media to increase availability and opportunity of coaching, facilities, competition and coverage.

Fig. 14.2   WOMEN CAN BE JUST AS AGGRESSIVE AS MEN

- Attend courses to improve career prospects; apply for senior positions; become a coach or administrator; gain relevant qualifications.
- Be aware that family responsibilities can coexist with other aspirations.

What organisations can do:

- Ensure equality of opportunity to acquire sports skills.
- Adopt policies on child care, transport, access, pricing, and programming of facilities.
- Recognise that women do not form an homogeneous group. Women who are disabled, are members of an ethnic minority, have heavy domestic responsibilities, have busy working lives, or school leavers, will all require some specific action directed at them.
- Positive images of women should be widely seen in a variety of sport promotional material and not only the traditionally female sports. This will help provide much-needed role models for young girls.
- Redress inequalities in competition, coaching, financial assistance and improve the talent identification process.
- Review recruitment practices and establish appropriate training and allow flexible working hours.
- Publicise the achievements of women's contributions to sport.

The Sports Council recently investigated the specific needs and preferences of women and they came up with five principles called the '5c's':

- promote **confidence**
- a **comfortable** atmosphere
- **choice** of activity
- **convenience** of programmes
- **consultation**

Outline the Sports Council's sports development continuum. What do the four levels of foundation, participation, performance and excellence mean? Discuss the main issues which affect women's involvement in sport.

Sport and people with disabilities

A national survey in 1988 suggested that there are 6.2 million adults with disabilities in Britain; 14.2% of the population. Approximately 5 million have a disability severe enough to limit everyday activities, 1 million have a learning disability, 69% are over the age of 60 and only 5% are under 30 years of age.

Many people experience discrimination which effectively excludes them from active social participation. Yet sport can help to integrate them into the rest of society and add to their quality of life. In the UK the special needs of disabled athletes are catered for by six national disability sports organisations:

1 The British Amputee Sports Association
2 The UK Sports Association for People with Mental Handicap
3 Cerebral Palsy Sport
4 The British Les Autres Sports Association

5 The British Sports Association for the Disabled (probably the most important organisation for people with disabilities in the UK)
6 The British Paralympic Association.

A growing number of opportunities exist; the National Federation of Gateway Clubs has over 660 affiliated clubs, giving 40,000 disabled people an opportunity to take part in leisure activities.

Research some of these organisations and pool the information within your group.

Current trends tend to focus on the sport rather than on the disability, to allow closer involvement with mainstream sport which previously has not catered for the needs of disabled athletes. The increasing numbers of participation should provide role models for people with disabilities. It is very important that all these organisations, both mainstream and special needs, cooperate and pool their resources in joint programmes of work; the creation of one federated organisation might help the situation.

Integration into mainstream sport does not have to mean participating at the same time as everyone else. It is more significant that facilities, competitions, training and coaching should be equally available to people with disabilities as to able-bodied people.

Improving opportunities

The Sports Council

The Sports Council has implemented various projects aimed at improving sporting opportunities for disabled people.

1 The campaign 'Every Body Active' was set up following research which highlighted several major problems encountered by people with disabilities; in particular a lack of awareness amongst mainstream leisure providers and PE teachers as to the special needs of this group of people.
2 The 'Pro-motion' campaign established in 1990 is now a national programme intending to raise awareness, training, liaison and resources.

Much of the Sports Council's work is regionally developed and coordination is therefore difficult to achieve. However, several common features emerge:

- promotion and development of training programmes
- inclusion of information about disabled sport in publications
- liaison with relevant organisations
- encourage local authorities and governing bodies to consider the needs of people with disabilities
- develop coaching opportunities
- appointment of sport development officers with special interest in this area.

The Sports Council's policy document 'Sport and People with Disabilities' was published in 1993, and is a national statement of intent for which it will be accountable.

The former Conservative government carried out research and published a report, 'Building on Ability'. As a result, the following initiatives were set up:

- the development of a national disability equality training course
- the identification of examples of good practice involving the participation at a local
- level of young people with disabilities
- a national governing bodies liaison project, involving 40 schemes and promoting integration with 23 governing bodies
- support the Pro-motion programme which seeks to develop sport and recreational opportunities for those with a multiple disability.

Finance

1 The British Paralympic Association (BPA) was given £500,000 to establish a trust fund to support a variety of disabled sport initiatives.
2 The Sports Council received an additional £300,000.
3 Substantial grants have also been given by the Foundation for Sport and the Arts.
4 In 1993 the Sports Council gave 10% of the £1.5 million raised by the National Swimathon to the BPA. This was then matched by the government, for use in grass roots development of sport for people with disability.

Local authorities

Local authorities play a crucial role at local level, because of their leisure departments. The planning and architects departments are also important when trying to build functional and imaginative facilities. When facility tenders are reviewed and renewed under the compulsory competitive tendering regulations, the needs of the disabled must be considered.

Excellence

Excellence in sport performance has grown substantially, both in the number of competitions and variety of activities. The Paralympics (so called because it runs parallel to the Olympics) and the World Championships are the notable examples. The 1992 Barcelona Paralympics for people with a disability attracted over 3,000

Fig. 14.3   THERE ARE MANY SPORTS WHICH CAN BE ADAPTED FOR PEOPLE WITH DISABILITIES

competitors from 86 countries. The British team finished in third place behind the United States and Germany. They were held one month after the able bodied games and athletes were able to use the Olympic Village for the first time, as they shared the same organising committee.

As knowledge about training, coaching and the input of sport science increases, the performance levels of disabled athletes will undoubtedly improve.

Facilities

Facilities are gradually improving for disabled users, partly under the Safety at Sports Grounds Act 1975, and also through a growing desire to provide access. The programming of activities and the attitude of staff are also important considerations.

Outdoor facilities are increasing provision, for example, those run by the Calvert Trust and Scope. Several important sports centres exist, such as the Ludwig Guttman Sports Centre at Stoke Mandeville and the Midland Sports Centre for the Disabled in Coventry.

The Sports Council's National Sports Centres have also been advised to draw up a strategy to enable disabled athletes to use their facilities.

- **Make a checklist to see how a local leisure facility is designed to cater for the needs of the disabled people in your area.**
- **Once you have agreed a comprehensive list, visit a variety of facilities (ie, indoor, countryside, water) and review their effectiveness.**
- **Suggest cheap but effective modifications which could be made.**

Sport for people aged 50 and over

Statistics show that over 50% of the adult population will be over 45 in the year 2000. This age group is increasingly affluent as personal pensions have improved during the twentieth century and people may have more disposable income to spend. They are also generally more active and healthy than ever before, and an increase in physical activity can help to prevent the inevitable onset of ageing. Approximately three slightly strenuous sessions per week of 20 minutes duration is advised. Medical advice may need to be sought, particularly if the person has not participated in physical activity for some time. The important checks are cardiovascular, respiratory and orthopaedic.

In 1990 an Allied Dunbar Survey produced a survey on the physical capabilities of over 2,000 men and women; it was published in 1992. Research some of the findings. (This could link in with your Exercise Physiology unit.)

Social benefits of sport are also stressed, because this can be a time of dramatic change for many people. Some may become widowed; some may retire or be made redundant, and family obligations may change. Active lifestyles can help people overcome great social change. Thus, this group of people comprises a potentially rich market for sport.

Since the Sports Councils campaign, '50+ All to Play For' in 1983, more activities have been promoted for this age group. Here are some of the most popular ones:

1 Indoors – keep fit; aerobics; dance; carpet and short mat bowls; table tennis.
2 Outdoors – walking/rambling; cycling; jogging; archery; canoeing; golf; tennis; swimming; cricket; hockey; bowls.

Many other more adventurous activities are also enjoyed.

Select some of the activities mentioned and suggest why they are particularly suited to people over 50. Think about the physiological and social aspects of the activity.

Competitive days need not be over; many sports have veteran and 50+ sections. Other ways of getting involved are as sports leaders, such as coach, referee, club officials. Organisations which should be involved in developing this kind of activity are: local authority departments responsible for sport and recreation; sports centres and swimming pools; adult education classes; the national and regional sports councils; the governing bodies of sport.

Sport for young people

First of all we must recognise that not all young people share common lifestyles; they may have different socio-economic backgrounds, parental attitudes, social experiences and so on. Physical activities are promoted by a wide range of individuals and agencies, such as:

- the education system, in particular the physical education programme
- sports clubs and governing bodies
- play workers
- the youth service
- local authorities

It is necessary for these agencies to coordinate their efforts. For example, national governing bodies and schools associations need to jointly plan programmes which will support a common youth sport policy.

In previous years, the Sports Council have targeted the age band 13–24 years. However, recent research (General Household Survey) suggested that low participation was not the problem, but that young people do not play as many sports as children. However, young females still participate less than their male counterparts. On leaving school, more casual sports are enjoyed, alongside adventure sports and health related activities.

Consider the following groups of young people and suggest some of the *advantages* and *disadvantages* they face in terms of sports participation:

- **full time education**
- **full time employment**

- **unemployed**
- **young women**
- **young mothers**
- **young people in rural areas.**

The National Junior Sports Programme was launched in February 1996 by the Sports Council, working alongside the Youth Sports Trust. Its aim is to encourage young children from the age of four to become involved in sport. It will provide kit, coaching and places to play, and the more talented performers can be identified from a wider base. It will be a rolling programme and many teachers will be trained. The advantage is that it can fit neatly into the current physical education system. There are four main elements:

- Top Play (4–9-year-olds)
- Top Sport (7–11-year-olds)
- Champion Coach
- Top Club (11 years+)

Funding will come from the National Lottery, the Sports Council, Youth Sports Trust and business sponsorship (£14 million in total).

Socio-economic groups

The term 'social class' can refer to a person's income, status in society, family background and educational experiences. The development of sport in the nineteenth century was initially in the powerful and influential hands of the upper and middle classes. The working class male stamped his presence on the new mass spectator sports of football, boxing and horse racing, but administrational control was still in the hands of the middle classes. The working classes had to wait for the provision of recreational rights and public facilities.

Much research has concluded that lower socio-economic backgrounds do lead to a lower participation rate in sporting activities. This can be attributed to a variety of reasons:

- the cost of facilities
- the dominant middle class culture which operates in sport centres
- the lack of leadership roles
- a general lack of health
- the lower self esteem of low income groups (in particular the unemployed) which can encourage feelings of helplessness, inferiority, and isolation from major social institutions.

A working class 'sub culture' can operate where norms and values are different from the dominant group, and are passed down from one generation to the next. This has been termed the 'cycle of poverty' – where one form of deprivation tends to reinforce another. It is a very complex area which the sport initiatives need to address if they are to be successful in mobilising this section of the community.

We have looked at categories of people within society and particularly at the participation base of the sports pyramid. Now it is time to discover how some people manage to extend beyond the recreational and performance end of the sports continuum, and onwards to sporting excellence.

Excellence

What does 'excellence' mean?

Excellence can be defined as a 'special ability beyond the norm, to which many aspire but few go on to achieve'. There are some problems with using words like this. For example, we often talk about personal excellence, but this may not mean according to national or international standards. The athletes who broke records half a century ago were still excellent for their era, even though today their times or distances would not measure up. A performer could have excellent technique but not achieve the highest scores in top competition. For our purposes, excellence means the superior, elite athletes at both amateur and professional level, who reach the pinnacle of performance in their chosen sport.

The 'sport for all' base, ie, the provision of sport for the masses and the elite, is a compatible system; the wider the base of the pyramid, the greater the apex. This was very much the philosophy of the former USSR, who promoted sport with a compulsory national fitness campaign, which was a coherent talent identification system followed by a rigorous training and coaching schedule. They believed that success at the highest levels could help reinforce the policies, lifestyles and attitudes of the political state, and were prepared to fund a centralised approach to the achievement of a sports excellence programme, which would draw from the widest base of participants as possible.

Excellence usually suggests a specialism of one activity, and is judged by international and world standards.

The providers of excellence in sport are mainly: the Sports Council; national governing bodies; the National Coaching Foundation; the Sports Aid Foundation; the centres of excellence; sports schools; local authorities; sports clubs; school sport associations; schools.

The Sports Council have developed numerous strategies for various sections of the community, not only to encourage participation but also to enable talented and committed people to strive for excellence. Historically, the UK has not had a nationally organised plan for identifying talent, and it has mostly been an ad hoc approach with luck playing a large part. The support system for the development of excellence is mainly located outside schools.

Coaching

One of the traditional weaknesses in the UK is the coaching system. Only in 1983 was a national organisation established which was responsible for meeting the needs of coaches and athletes – the National Coaching Foundation. Their remit was to develop a comprehensive, national, coach education programme, and their main achievement has been to awaken many of the governing bodies of sport to the importance of coaching.

However, funding has always been a problem, as British governing bodies have been relatively slow to joint the competitive market, with the old loyalties of amateurism proving hard to shake off. The majority of sports coaches in this country are voluntary and unpaid. Consequently, in the world of employment, coaching has low status. These enthusiasts are the last bastions of amateur sport, but changes are required if the UK is to compete internationally. Local authorities also have varying degrees of success in their contribution to coaching in sport, but it will depend on the interest and funding available.

The coach education schemes contain six important elements:

- sport specific knowledge (techniques/tactics)
- performance related knowledge (fitness/nutrition/mental preparation)
- ethics and philosophy (codes of practice)
- management/vocational skills (planning/time/money)
- teaching/coaching methodology (communication skills)
- practical coaching experience.

The National Coaching Foundation has recently launched 'Coaching for Teachers', to raise the profile of coaching with PE teachers and non-PE teachers.

Sports schools

There are a small selection of specialist sports schools in the UK, but again there is no centralised approach. Some examples are Millfield, Kelly College, Reeds School and Lilleshall. The advantages of such institutions are the combination of top quality coaching, education, accommodation, medical science, a pool of similar talent, an organised competition structure and links with professional clubs. However, there are some disadvantages also. They form a private network of schools which result in an exclusive system drawing inevitably from a limited pool of talent; young people may have to experience residential, institutionalised life away from home, and the physical and psychological demands are high.

A project called 'The Training of Young Athletes' (TOYA) was established in 1987 by the Institute of Child Health. Its remit was to 'examine the effects, both positive and negative which prolonged training and competition can have on the development of youngsters'. Some of the positive aspects highlighted were a high level of fitness and self esteem, but negative aspects included injuries and 'burn out'.

Why pursue excellence in sport?

- Sport represents a challenge in peoples' lifestyles which have become increasingly sedentary and controlled.
- Many people are also curious about their own and the human species' potential; sport is sometimes called the last frontier, as our limitations are still not yet known.
- Sport can provide an alternative employment path with the added attraction of high social status if high level success is achieved.
- It gives individuals a high self esteem, a feeling of worth and quality in their lives.

Social advantages of pursuing excellence

Sporting success can boost national pride and morale (governments are usually keen to be connected with this); a reduction in anti-social behaviour; the role models of sport attract a large spectator audience; economic benefits; the excellence end of the continuum feeds the base of sport for all.

Disadvantages of excellence

- It is elitist – it can only serve the interests of a few
- Costly resources are required for a minority of sports participants.
- Over-specialisation and obsession with a physical activity can occur, which may have damaging physiological and psychological effects.
- The moral value of sport can be lost due to the 'win at all costs' attitude, which is made worse when the stakes become higher.

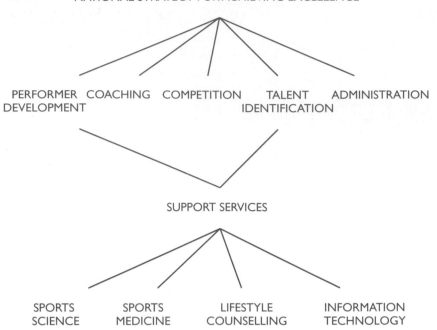

NATIONAL STRATEGY FOR ACHIEVING EXCELLENCE

PERFORMER COACHING COMPETITION TALENT ADMINISTRATION
DEVELOPMENT IDENTIFICATION

SUPPORT SERVICES

SPORTS SCIENCE · SPORTS MEDICINE · LIFESTYLE COUNSELLING · INFORMATION TECHNOLOGY

Fig. 14.4 NATIONAL STRATEGY FOR ACHIEVING EXCELLENCE

1 **What problems could comprehensive schools face in pursuing sporting excellence, and what do they have in their favour?**
2 **Three key words have been mentioned: opportunity, provision, esteem. Suggest factors to be considered under each heading, applying specifically to sporting excellence.**

Study *The Development of Tennis in Great Britain 1996–2001*, by The Lawn Tennis Association, October 1995. It is a comprehensive document, and is an attempt by one of the most exclusive sports cultures in the world to open its doors in order to widen the sporting base, improve competition structures to identify talent more easily, and train officials at all levels. It should radically change the nature of the sport at both the grass roots level and consequently at the elite level.

During the last decade there has been an increasing pressure from all sections of British sport for the administrators to concentrate more resources into the pursuit of excellence. A national strategy for achieving excellence has begun to take root (see fig 14.4). The key to achieving a nationally coherent programme lies in linking together all the complex jigsaw pieces which currently operate in isolation. The support services of sport science, sports medicine, lifestyle counselling and information technology must also be integrated to produce an effective multi-disciplinary approach. The days of the coach being the sole provider of support to the athlete are almost gone – particularly at the highest levels of performance. The coach–athlete relationship is still a crucial element, but other people who hold specialist knowledge also play their part in the development of the athlete. Consistency from all the support team is paramount. The value of sport science is unquestioned but it must work alongside coaching expertise.

1 **Write an account of your own experiences in sport, from the early days to the time when you began to take a more serious interest.**
2 **Make a note of your role models, family background, sex, race, schooling, sports club, peer group, and relate how each might have contributed positively or negatively towards your involvement in sport.**

Summary

- The broader the base of sport participation, the greater the talent pool from which to draw in order to increase the chances of sporting excellence.
- Unequal access to the 'sport for all' ideal will negatively affect the sports pyramid.
- Sport initiatives must take careful note of the complex nature of the various groups they seek to help.
- A nationally coordinated approach towards excellence needs to be further developed if Britain is to compete on equal terms with other nations.

Sport, Politics and Culture

This chapter explores the role that sport and physical education assume in the political arena. It examines the organisation, administration and policy making process of sport in different cultures, which should help you to reflect on major issues such as policies for school sport, the use of drugs in sport and spectator violence.

The politics of sport

Before we explore the concept of how sport and politics interact, we may find it useful to begin with a definition of politics:

'the science and art of government; dealing with the form, organisation and administration of a state or part of one, and of the regulation of its relations with other states ... Political [means] belonging to or pertaining to the state, its government and policy'.

(Oxford English Dictionary).

Let's take some of the key words and look at their possible meaning to sport.

Administration

The administration of sport can be seen as developing from the community, for example, a local sports club forms the base of the pyramid, and is surmounted by its regional, national and international counterparts. The international governing bodies of sport (the International Olympic Committee, the Commonwealth Games Federation and the European Sports bodies) are political bodies. They are concerned with governing sport, making decisions, creating and distributing finances and resources, and often their dealings must reflect the political climate in which they operate.

Relations with other states

The relationships between states with regard to sport began as soon as worldwide travel and unified rules of competition developed. Sport can provide international goodwill: it can promote cultural empathy and understanding between nations, and athletes are seen as ambassadors of their country. The Olympic Charter promotes the view that sport promotes world peace by improving international understanding and respect.

However, sport can also reinforce conflict: the sense of belonging to a country encourages a sense of patriotism and nationalism, and thus is all the more powerful when conflict is prevalent, be it war or sport. Sport represents and reinforces images and feelings of communal, regional and national identity. Powerful symbols are used, eg, national anthems, team colours, flags and ceremonies. Sporting conflict results in winners and losers. Winners can be viewed as superior and powerful, whereas losers are inferior and powerless. Sport is often portrayed as being more than just a contest between two opposing sides, and success is attributed to countries as much as to the athletes themselves. For example, the Scottish rugby ground at Murrayfield evokes vivid messages and images of Scottish identity and nationhood, and England is often portrayed as the 'old enemy'.

Policy

Policy suggests decision making based on the ideology (set of ideas) or philosophy of those in power. This is relevant from local to international situations. Numerous indicators can be used to determine the importance a government places on sport:

- the expenditure for sport
- the position or status of sports ministers within a government
- the type and amount of sport legislation produced.

Politics reflects the power systems within a culture – who has the power and how do they use it? Sport and physical activities have sometimes been used by various governments, individuals and administrators for political reasons. The British government used to be in control of many of the world's sports organisations, but there has been a shift in power, and Britain is no longer so prominent.

The commercial world plays an extremely important role in sports decision making, at local, national and international level. The cost of staging sports events, particularly at international level, is extraordinarily high:

1 The constructing of stadiums requires capital which often only governments can raise.
2 The running of events increasingly involves those who pay international television fees.
3 Revenue for major events requires huge commitment from governments.

Equally, sport is now a major market for governments, and the trend in the United Kingdom has been for the government to receive more money from sport than it contributes.

Political uses of sport

Social factors

Sport can be used to introduce or reinforce social harmony. Government inquiries into inner city riots usually include reference to the need to provide better sporting facilities. This can be taken to have various meanings:

1 Boredom creates dysfunctional activity; by providing the highest standard of sporting facilities and by educating people to use them constructively in their leisure time, we can help to improve people's quality and enjoyment of life, giving them less reason to involve themselves in anti-social activities.
2 The 'bread and circuses' theory: this is more controversial, and claims that sport can be used to divert the attention and energy of the masses away from the problems of the political and social system in which they live.

Sport as 'character-building'

Sport would also seem to have socialising qualities, which can be used as a political tool. In the nineteenth century, English public schools placed great importance on the values gained from the boys' involvement in team games, such as the ability to work in a team, cooperation, leadership and the response to leadership, obeying rules, respecting authority and so on. See Chapter 17 for further information.

Propaganda

Sport can be used as political propaganda; eg, in the 1930s, the Nazi Youth groups aimed to indoctrinate young people in the values of Nazi Germany.

Defence and work

Sport has also been used to raise the fitness level of populations in order to better prepare them for defending their country and to make them more productive in the workplace:

1 Following heavy losses in the Boer War, attention was focused on the physical deterioration of the British troops in the nineteenth century.
2 Physical fitness among the working classes became official policy in Britain by introducing compulsory fitness exercises in state schools in the early twentieth century.
3 In the old Soviet Union, a national fitness campaign called 'Ready for Labour and Defence' was compulsory for its citizens and was still operational in the latter half of the twentieth century.

Thus, we can see there are various reasons why national governments become involved in sport. See fig 15.1 for a summary of these points.

Fig. 15.1   NATIONAL GOVERNMENT INVOLVEMENT IN SPORT

Choose four functions of sport from fig 15.1. Explain in detail how each operates.

State intervention

We have already established that it is extremely difficult to keep sport and politics separate. However, a crucial point can be the nature of the involvement and the *type* of political system which operates:

Centralised political system

A centralised system at a simple level means to draw under central control – the central government directs policy across the country. An example of this is the former Soviet Union. The Soviet Union under Communist rule was not initiating a 'new' use of sport when it sought to make use of sport's ability to improve the health and hygiene of the population, boost morale, production and military effectiveness, integrate a diverse nation of peoples with varying cultural backgrounds, and to provide an international image for their regime. What *was* new was the extent of the **central control**, with state legislation to coordinate and support policies. Sport and its usefulness was considered too important to be left to chance. Sport would have the same attention, assistance and planning as other social agencies, such as education.

Decentralised political system

A decentralised system is one where the administration of government is reorganised into smaller, more autonomous units. Examples are local authorities in the United Kingdom; and the individual States of America, who control their own affairs while the federal government becomes involved in matters of national importance. The government in power can give guidelines, but would not normally enforce them. The local authority could then use the guidelines to suit their particular needs.

What are the advantages and disadvantages of:

1 **a decentralised system**
2 **a centralised system?**

Sport and politics in the United Kingdom

We have been suggesting that sport cannot be seen as an activity which only has relevance to those who practise it; it also serves various functions of a society. The rest of the chapter will study a variety of different countries and cultures, and their relation to sport.

In the United Kingdom, sport and politics have traditionally been kept separate. The reverse side of the coin is that many people genuinely defend the right of sport to be free from direct political control, seeing it as a danger to the autonomy of the traditional sporting governing bodies and not necessarily having the best interests of sport at heart. Many wish sport to be above the concerns of politics; they do not wish sporting heroes to be the object of sociological analysis, or for sport to be tarnished by political concerns – sport should be an escape from the everyday world.

Traditional social class barriers, the development of sport through the 'grass roots' and the dominant sporting ethos of amateurism, have had an important impact on the relationship between the political and sporting agencies in the UK. The amateur code was an important part of the nineteenth century tradition of team games in public schools: sport was regarded as important for the individual benefits rather than for financial gain. However, it must not be forgotten that amateurism itself was a code based on a political model. It was the privilege of the gentry to be able to participate in sport for 'the love of it', while other social classes were excluded, lacking the time and money. The ideals of amateurism should be viewed in this light: we have clung on to this tradition in a modern and fast-changing society, and sportspeople are having to fight for their right to earn a living from sport. They are often in conflict with their own sports administration; eg, the lengthy negotiations in 1996 between the English Rugby Football Union and the English rugby clubs.

Local government involvement in sport

As we saw in Chapter 12, local government has traditionally had an important role to play in the provision of recreational and sporting facilities for its local area. However, its responsibility has been permissive, rather than mandatory; by law, it is not required to provide for recreation.

Compulsory Competitive Tendering

Following the Local Government Act 1988, a range of local authority services were tendered, including the management of local authority leisure services. The Conservative government wanted to ensure a more competitive market in order to reduce costs.

Compulsory Competitive Tendering is slightly different from privatisation of large companies. The local authority would still:

- own the facilities
- control the prices
- set quality standards
- influence programming
- retain the ability to decide policy.

The Minister for Sport, Colin Moynihan, preferred the local authorities to become 'enablers' rather than providers. An 'enabler' needs to plan, coordinate, and facilitate the provision of leisure services. To do this they must think strategically, to identify and make explicit their objectives when planning new capital projects. This is not to suggest they were not doing this before the legislation. Four main areas need to be considered: planning and research; development within the community, eg, Action Sport; management, eg, accessibility, price range and quality experience; marketing, eg, to ensure that target groups are identified on the basis of market research.

Table 15.1   ADVANTAGES AND DISADVANTAGES OF CCT

ADVANTAGES	DISADVANTAGES
Reduce unit costs by 20%	Could result in worse pay and conditions for employees
Free local authorities from the day to day running problems	Sport no longer regarded as a social service
Help to review the use of manpower	CCPR felt it was a serious attack on traditional provision of sports facilities

Law and order

Players

There has been an increase in sports legislation and legal challenges to the administrators of sport. Sport has traditionally been perceived as being outside and

Drink related offences	1,414	Section 2 Football Offences	
Section 5 Public Order Act: Disorderly behaviour	713	Act: Throwing missiles	28
		Assault on police	26
Section 4 Public Order Act: Threatening behaviour	580	Deception	25
		Breach of Exclusion Order	22
Prevent breach of peace	337	Motor vehicle crime	16
Section 4 Football Offences Act: Running on pitch	206	Section 3 Football Offences Act: Racial/indecent chanting	13
Criminal damage	129	Going equipped to steal	11
Section 3 Public Orde Act: Affray	124	Handling stolen goods	9
		Forgery	9
Assault	115	Street trading	8
Miscellaneous offences: Breach of bail/ Obstruct police/Bye laws	114	Highway obstruction	8
		Burglary	7
Theft	95	Arrested on warrant	6
Possession of drugs	61	Sporting events: Fireworks offences	5
Section 2 Football Offences Act: Violent disorder	60	Sex offences	2
Ticket touting	47	Robbery	2
Possession of offensive weapons	35	Total	4,227

Fig. 15.2   ARRESTS AND OFFENCES AT FA PREMIER LEAGUE AND FOOTBALL LEAGUE MATCHES, 1993/94
Source: Digest of Football Statistics, 1994

almost above the law, and as such has retained autonomy for a greater length of time than most other social agencies. But the number of prosecutions of sports players for assaults which occurred within the confines of the game, has increased. Should assaults be viewed separately to a similar occurrence outside a sports setting? On one hand, players have understood the activity they are taking part in, and in signing a contract they have accepted that the rules of the game control the extent of physical contact which is allowed. On the other hand, a foul could be considered outside the rules and therefore, no contract was entered into.

The results of this type of judicial reasoning have led to convictions of assault. Yet many people would also accept that the rules are not taken literally and terms such as the 'professional foul' are a part of the game. Rugby referees have been prosecuted for allowing a situation to develop which caused harm to a player. Whatever the rights or wrongs of these cases, they evidently have far-reaching consequences for the world of sport.

Supporters

The attitude and behaviour of supporters has also been controversial in the eyes of the law. The growth of hooliganism in the 1970s and 1980s brought into question the ability of the football clubs to regulate the behaviour of their supporters.

Education

As we have seen, the Education Act 1988 affected physical education within the wider education system. The traditionally decentralised system of education was being challenged by a Conservative government seeking more control. This necessitated cutting the powers of the local authorities. The capacity for schools to manage their own budgets and the introduction of the National Curriculum reinforced a growing centralisation of policies. The new National Curriculum specified in general terms the content of physical education teaching. This went further in 1995 with the government report 'Raising the Game'.

Politics and international sporting events

Across the different countries of the world, sport commands a similar passion and interest. It may take a different form in some areas but its make up is quite similar. Travel and mixing of cultures has led to this situation. In the UK, we are becoming more exposed to sport from other countries, and their sports are being transplanted into our own culture; for example showing American Football on British television has led to a massive increase in participation.

Incidents involving sport and international politics are well known. We will mention a few briefly, but it would be useful for you to research these in more detail.

South Africa and apartheid

In 1956 the South African Government made sport a formal part of its apartheid policy: non-whites were excluded at all levels. They did not only enforce this policy at home. They also rejected the New Zealand cricket side which was to field Maoris in 1960. The New Zealanders agreed not to send any Maoris within their touring side, but this continuing contact with South Africa led to their own isolation, culminating in a boycott of the 1976 Montreal Olympics, after New Zealand were admitted.

A world ban on South African sport was declared in 1964, and was considered by some to be an effective punishment. South African teams were denied the opportunity to display their sporting excellence, something which was extremely important to them. However, they went to great lengths to attract world class competition: in 1969–70, the English Rugby Union entertained a Springbok touring team but suffered from widespread public demonstrations against their decision.

There have been many instances of pressure being exerted by those in political power over sportspeople. Choose any two from the list below and find out as much detail as you can:

- **Gleaneagles Agreement 1977**
- **1980 Moscow Olympics**
- **1984 Los Angeles Olympics**
- **Apartheid**
- **Blood sports**
- **Football hooliganism.**

The Olympic Games

The Olympic Games are among the world's greatest sporting events. The modern games were established by Baron Pierre de Coubertin in 1896. He visited England in the nineteenth century and was impressed with the amateur code of public school team games, and the athleticism of the students. He revived the ancient Olympic Games of Greece which had originally been a religious festival in honour of Zeus. They had lasted over 1000 years, and the competition had been fair, but their decline began when the need to win became stronger as the rewards became greater.

De Coubertin wished to draw countries together in healthy competition, the new games to be above political issues and for the importance of winning to be kept in perspective.

'To enable and strengthen sports, to ensure their independence and duration, and thus to enable them better to fulfil the educational role incumbent upon them in the modern world. For the glorification of the individual athlete, whose muscular activity is necessary for the community, and whose prowess is necessary for the maintenance of the general spirit of competition.'

(1894).

Fig. 15.3 COLLECTION OF EARLY OLYMPIC PROGRAMMES, DATING FROM 1896

He elected the first members of the International Olympic Committee, hoping they would continue the spirit of the games he re-created. Ever since, they themselves have elected new members, which is perhaps another instance of a sports governing body with a self perpetuating set of values.

The games have successfully survived but not without cost. They have been affected by wider political situations, and are often remembered as much for the political events surrounding them as the athletic feats. One of the key reasons is that the games have provided a focus for the country hosting the event. Their political systems are given prominent media coverage and instances have occurred where governments have used this to promote their own political message. The 1936 Olympics were held in Berlin, and Adolf Hitler used this opportunity to promote the values of the Third Reich on a world stage.

Equally, when opponents to the government wish to make a political protest, they also have a prime opportunity when the eyes of the world are watching. The result is often a boycott of countries from the Games. A boycott is the refusal of a faction to participate in a sporting event in order to deliver a political message, and is usually the rejection of a political regime. The Soviet Union boycott of the Los Angeles Olympic Games in 1984, had a large effect on the event. The reasons for the boycott were complex but involved:

- a reaction to the American boycott of the Moscow Olympic Games in 1980
- fear of defection of their own athletes to the West
- the ability of the men's track and field team
- the ideological problem of being part of a successful 'capitalist games'.

Table 15.2 charts some of the political situations which have surrounded some of the Olympic Games. Select one of those listed and find out information in greater detail.

Apolitical aspects of the Olympic Games

The following **message** appears on the scoreboard at every Olympic Games:

'The most important thing in the Olympic Games is not to win but to take part, just as the most important thing in life is not the triumph but the struggle. The essential thing is not to have conquered but to have fought well.'

The Olympic **flag** shows five interconnecting rings, all in different colours, displayed on a white background. It was designed by Baron Pierre de Coubertin in 1913. The rings represent the five continents involved in the Olympic Games – Europe, Asia, Oceania, Africa and the Americas.

The Olympic **motto** is 'Citius, Altius, Fortius', which means 'swifter, higher, stronger'.

The six **goals** of the Olympic movement are:

- personal excellence
- sport as education
- cultural exchange
- mass participation
- fair play
- international understanding.

Table 15.2 OLYMPICS AND POLITICS

YEAR	VENUE	POLITICAL ACTIVITY AND AFFECTED COUNTRIES
1936	Berlin	Germany used Games for Nazi propaganda Hitler's Aryan race theory discredited – Jesse Owen, black athlete won four gold medals
1956	Melbourne	Soviet Union invaded Hungary, Spain and Holland withdrew in protest China withdrew because of Taiwan's inclusion Egypt and Lebanon did not compete because they were fighting for the Suez Canal
1964	Tokyo	South Africa's invitation cancelled in 1963 Indonesia and North Korea not allowed to compete because they had taken part in an international tournament considered unsatisfactory by the ioc
1968	Mexico City	South Africa's invitation withdrawn because of threatened boycott by other countries, over apartheid 2001 Mexicans killed and many more injured by army during demonstration against use of Government money for the Games – widespread poverty in the country Black American athletes gave clenched fist salute – against treatment of Black Americans
1972	Munich	Rhodesia's invitation withdrawn because of apartheid other countries threatened to boycott if they competed Israeli athletes and officials assassinated by Palestinian terrorists
1976	Montreal	30 nations in total did not attend African nations boycotted Games because New Zealand rugby team had toured South Africa French Canadians were angered that the Queen was to perform the opening ceremony Taiwan withdrew several competitors banned for using anabolic steroids two Romanians and one Soviet athlete asked for political asylum in Canada
1980	Moscow	Soviet Union had invaded Afghanistan and because of the Soviets record on Human Rights and their refusal to withdraw troops, 52 nations boycotted the games led by the usa
1984	Los Angeles	Soviet Union withdrew, along with many Eastern European countries, Cuba and others some felt that it was in retaliation, but official reasons given, was over 'concern for the safety of their teams' it was felt that the organisers had violated the Olympic charter
1992	Barcelona	South Africa returned to Olympic competition after abolition of apartheid Germany competed as one nation Soviet Union had ceased to exist and the individual countries competed in their own right

Read this extract from George Orwell's 'The Sporting Spirit' taken from *Shooting an Elephant*, which gives a personal account of what he considers to be the link between sport and politics.

'I am always amazed when I hear people saying that sport creates goodwill between the nations and that if only the common peoples of the world could meet one another at football or cricket, they would have no inclination to meet on the battlefield.

Nearly all the sports practised nowadays are competitive. You play to win and the game has little meaning unless you do your utmost to win. On the village green, where you pick up sides and no feeling of local patriotism is involved, it is possible to play simply for the fun and exercise, but as soon as the question of prestige arises, as soon as you feel that you or some larger unit will be disgraced if you lose, the more savage instincts are aroused. Anyone who has played even in a school football match knows this. At the international level, sport is quite frankly mimic warfare. But the significant thing is not the behaviour of the players but the attitude of the spectators, of the nations who work themselves into furies over these absurd contests and seriously believe at any rate for short periods – that running, jumping and kicking a ball are tests of national virtue.

As soon as strong feelings of rivalry are aroused, the notion of playing the game according to the rules always vanishes. People want to see one side on top and the other side humiliated, and they forget that victory gained through cheating or through the intervention of the crowd is meaningless. Even when the spectators don't intervene physically, they try to influence the game by cheering their own side and rattling opposing players with boos and insults. Serious sport has nothing to do with fair play. It is bound up with hatred, jealousy, beastfulness, disregard of all the rules and sadistic pleasure in witnessing violence; in other words it is war minus the shooting'.

Consider the following questions:

- **What is the author's opinion of competition?**
- **How does the author make a distinction between two types of physical activity?**
- **What elements of conflict, cohesion and expectancy are given in the passage?**
- **What vocabulary does the author use to reinforce the view that modern sport is merely 'mimic warfare'?**

Does sport reflect culture?

This final section will explore the effect of different cultures on the development of sport and physical activities. Physical activity or games are cultural institutions determined by the culture in operation, but may also influence how a culture operates. Discovering the meanings and significance of games in various cultures and their function with regard to cultural values and related social structures is an interesting project.

When we take part in a game or sport, we subject ourselves to special rules and behaviour, which may reflect opinions and values held in other areas of life. Two key values which operate in society and also in games, are **competition** and **cooperation**. The former can be described as trying to achieve what another person is trying to achieve at the same time; the latter can be defined as working with others to achieve the same end. Four main factors can determine which is dominant within the culture:

1 the natural environment which 'houses' the culture
2 the level of technology
3 the dynamics of the social structures
4 the education system.

Using this level of categorisation, a social system which is dependent on the initiative of the individual, where property is valued for individual ends, where there is a single scale of success and where a strong development of the ego is in operation, would be conducive to competitive behaviour.

Conversely, a social system which does not depend on the initiative of the individual, or on exercise of power over people, has a fairly rigid social hierarchy and a weak emphasis on status, will be conducive to cooperative behaviour. Various cultures such as the Samoans could be regarded in this light.

Samoa

The Samoan culture has been described as cooperative by Mead (1976). An attempt was made to study this society before the culture was exposed to outside influences and began to change. The Samoan economy depended primarily on agriculture, with land held by the household groups. Each individual within this group contributed to the total result, which was then shared by all. Property was valued for groups, not individuals. The individual was only important in terms of the position which he or she occupied in the overall scheme. The individual also held multiple roles and therefore did not develop a fixed response to himself or others. Casting lots was used to help selection for various tasks. Matters were decided by 'wheeling round the coconut'.

Rivalry between districts acted as a cohesive force within the group. This unity increased the communities' strength which enabled them to succeed in warfare. Tribal war was quite frequent, so strength and endurance were valued qualities.

Children were viewed as aggressive, violent and destructive, and in need of discipline which they gained from nurses, themselves also children. Conforming to the society was an integral part of learning, and failure to do so could mean expulsion from the group.

Competitive games gave people an outlet for their intense spirit of rivalry, but individual prowess did not determine the successful outcome. Success would be decided by the result of a large number of simultaneous contests, and the victory of the community would be sought to the extent that particularly talented individuals would be kept apart so as to prevent a decisive contest. Contests would be used to gain as many victories as possible against inferior opponents. Prizes were not given though success was highly valued.

Games involving teamwork did not appear in Samoan life until contact with Britain, America, Germany and New Zealand; cricket then became the sport for the Samoans. It was initially adapted to reflect their own values – there could be two hundred on a side, and the game could last from four to twelve days in order to let everyone have a bat. Rugby and baseball were also modified to make them more compatible to the Samoan way of life.

The Maori culture

Before New Zealand was colonised by Britain, the native Maori people were an integrated, cooperative political society. Their cooperative nature was dictated by their system of having a fixed status from birth. This rank in the society could not be changed, thus preventing the necessity for competition. This is an example of a 'closed' social structure, similar to the Indian caste system, which keeps the individual in his/her place in society.

The most valuable personality traits were generosity, individual achievement and resourcefulness, innate abilities and talents. The individual identified with his tribe; the means of production were collectively owned and the returns of the labour

Fig. 15.4   THE HAKA IS PERFORMED BY THE NEW ZEALAND RUGBY TEAM AT ALL INTERNATIONAL FIXTURES; IT IS A MAORI WAR CHANT

belong to the group. This fostered cooperative attitudes through work.

Recreation was an important element in Maori life. Many games and amusements developed from tribal myths, and the people relied heavily on games, pastimes and vocal music to conserve the ancient folklore. Any social occasion was a signal for children and youths to have scheduled contests. Many of the games involved manual dexterity like knucklebones, where throwing and catching was important, or distance throwing.

In Maori culture, games seemed to serve various functions:

- training for war
- acquiring grace and skill
- contributing to economic efficiency
- recreation
- promoting tribal loyalty
- an outlet for healthy competition in an otherwise cooperative social structure.

It seems that cooperative societies do develop competitive games, but the way in which the results are treated distinguishes them from modern day competitive societies.

How do such societies compare with a modern society like the United States?

United States of America

The USA is the strongest power in the American continent and is a **pluralist** and **egalitarian** society; the former means that all the different ethnic groups are autonomous but interdependent and have equal power; the latter is a belief that mankind should have the opportunity for equality – politically, socially and economically.

The dominant sporting ethos in the USA is that of professional sport, reflecting the capitalist drive of American society. Competition became accepted as early as the 1870s as a basic principle in sound economics and therefore part of the great

American enterprise. Competition has become a prime value in education, politics and the military. The traditional pioneering background of America has led to a favouring of physical strength and ability to 'play the game'. Americans also value cooperation which is reflected in their desire to form voluntary associations. Many of the pioneers sought companionship in collective effort, and it is through team sports that Americans combined their desire for individualism within a collective endeavour.

The term 'antagonistic cooperation' describes a situation where two units are in conflict but within a wider system of cooperation (Sumner 1940). Huizinga describes it as 'two groups standing in competition but bound by a spirit of hostility and friendship combined.' Sutton Smith believes that competitive games can only take place when opponents respect and have confidence in each other: in anatomical terms, muscle movement is dependent on two antagonistic muscle groups in balance.

An interesting point to note is that during the nineteenth century, America inherited many team games from the UK, yet their team games developed along different lines. The Americans rationalised and systematised sports, when the British were trying to resist this trend.

Summary of differences between cooperation and competition

In many cooperative cultures:

- competition played an essential part in the enjoyment of games, but there was little emphasis on the part played by the individual.
- the games reflected the culture and in the case of Samoa, exposure to modern games led to an early adaptation and modification of games, to integrate with Samoan culture.
- there was a lack of specialisation and hierarchy in their games, which perhaps reflected their simplified social structures.

In modern competitive societies:

- games were valued for the character traits they were thought to foster.
- cooperation was valued but individual achievements highly rewarded.
- there was a sharp division of labour and intense specialisation.

The former USSR

The former Soviet Union was governed according to a communist philosophy. The class divisions were supposedly broken down, private ownership was abolished, and equality for all was a high priority. However, their system of sport appeared to contradict their general political theories. The regime which gained power in 1917 after the overthrow of the Russian monarchy, viewed sport as a vehicle to promote a new, worldwide identity for the country, and targeted success at the Olympic Games as its primary aim. A massive sporting programme was set up which required huge resources, in a country which lacked some of the most basic amenities. The government was willing to pour resources into elite sport, which ultimately meant vast funding for a few, and *not* equality for all. Elite athletes were given special privileges, and although competition was not generally encouraged in society, it was justified in sport as success enhanced the value of communism to other world powers.

Sport in this instance is *not* seen to reflect the culture; it was directly used to serve a particular political purpose.

Developing countries

Some countries in Africa, Latin America and South East Asia can be referred to as developing countries, or more recently, as less economically developed countries (LEDC); these countries were previously referred to as the Third World. They do not necessarily come under either the communist or capitalist system, but they were all colonised by wealthier countries in the West. As a result, the culture of the colonising nation was imposed on these countries. Their games and rituals were considered inferior to games such as cricket, soccer and netball, and youths were encouraged to discard their cultural heritage. These countries faced common social and sporting problems:

- Their economies were land-based, yet they were experiencing a shift towards an industrial economy.
- An increase in urban populations led to a less active society.
- Their sport infrastructure could not initially match the West in terms of organisation and facilities.
- Western sport tends to be more specialised, requiring more resources.
- Discrimination under colonial rule usually excluded native participation in sport at a high level. Independence helped to produce a democratisation of sport, where the masses can experience activities previously enjoyed by the governing elite.

New, independent governments faced a difficult decision in relation to sport: should they:

1 provide scarce resources for the mass of the population, or
2 fund an elite group of athletes in order to compete on the world stage?

The greater status given to Western sport tended to demote the rural areas in - terms of financial resources, and the towns and cities would be given consideration first.

The prestige, international standing and potential financial gain, achieved through a successful elitist sport programme, has proved hard for governments to ignore. If they follow this route, they are well advised to select carefully the sporting activities which will help them realise their aims, basing their selection on their scarce resources and the experience of the population.

Ancient Greece

Much of the character of modern day sport originated in Greece, about 1000 BC. The Ancient Greeks institutionalised the need of humans to compete and be the best, to discover the limits of man's powers. The athletes of Greek society were revered as earthly gods: they received monetary rewards, could be appointed military generals, and their names were recorded for posterity. The word 'athlete' comes from the Greek word 'athlos' which means prize: the result of contests involving hard physical endeavour and suffering. Athletes were supposed to train seriously for their event which included following a strict diet.

The Greeks held a national event, the Panhellenic games, every four years. The oldest recorded was in Olympia, 776 BC. However, they were religious festivals and the athletic enclosure would be surrounded by shrines. Military contests would be postponed in order for the games to be held.

By the sixth century BC specialisation had begun to take place, with intensive training for a specific event. The trainer had also assumed a place in this process. The professionalisation of sport was also underway. Athletes competed *for* money rather than being rewarded for a successful games. Corruption and bribery soon followed.

Ancient Rome

The vast colosseums served the same function for the Romans as the Panhellenic games. In AD 1, there were 76 religious festival days celebrated by 'ludi', comprising shows, plays (mimicry) and games (agon). The spectators enjoyed real conflict, finding athletics dull in comparison. Their most exciting sport was the 'naumachia' where criminals would reenact naval battles until they killed each other, and the winners could be given their freedom. Animals in direct contest with gladiators were prestigious occasions. Gladiators were highly trained, but would often have to fight to the death. Men were also killed for entertainment purposes.

Sport was a way of keeping the masses of people occupied and therefore gave them less reason or chance to rebel. The wealthy competed in their donations to their society and sponsorship to sport. This culture used sport as a spectacle; play had moved on to become display, and a patriotic sense was aroused when watching a difficult contest where the ultimate price of life would be paid. This was an era coming to an end.

Summary of different cultures and sport

Examining different cultures and their relation to sport shows that games have been developed to perform various functions, including:

- bonding community groups
- providing socially approved outlets of aggression and opportunities to compete
- acknowledging important human events such as birth, marriage and death
- communicating with the gods (Ancient Greece)
- preparing children for later adult roles, and developing skills which would become economically important for the society
- training people for war and the workplace.

Summary

- The type of political and economic system is crucial in determining the nature of state intervention; centralised or decentralised, capitalism or communist.
- A range of cultures was studied, highlighting the two key values of competition and cooperation. A common factor emerged between different cultures: human beings naturally take the utilitarian aspect of physical activity, and transform it into a social experience.
- You should appreciate the complexity of games, recreations and sports to a variety of societies and not presume them to be a coincidental or superficial aspect of human life.

chapter 16

Issues and Concerns in the Modern Day Sports World

This chapter covers areas and issues in the sports world which cause concern and media interest. In order to gain a deeper insight into these issues, you will need to draw upon information and knowledge gained from other chapters, particularly Chapters 15 and 17.
The following areas are explored:

- the commercialisation of sport
- sport and the media
- deviancy in sport through spectator violence and drug abuse.

The commercialism of sport

Globalisation is the process whereby different nations are more closely interrelated; this has its advantages for sport, but there is a danger of different cultures losing their true identity as the Western values of sport become increasingly dominant across the world. The influx of international players into home teams is also a reflection of globalisation.

Historically, sport has sometimes been used as a way of entertaining the public. As it developed the qualities to attract large crowds, the term 'spectator sports' emerged. Initially, sports would generate money on a more personal level. The participants could receive some monetary reward and the spectators would wager on the event, partly to increase the excitement of the event but also to have the opportunity to win more money than they could from their everyday occupation. When these entertainments became more regular, certain individuals recognised the opportunity to make more money using an organised approach. Promoters and patrons started to accrue more profit than the participants, and even the wagering became more structured.

Today this has evolved into a situation where sport is heavily commercialised, packaged and presented to world wide audiences. Countries with a market economy have been most open to this kind of development; capitalism encourages its population to work in competitive conditions to create profitable enterprises. The availability of widespread television coverage has attracted large scale businesses who can use sport to promote their products, and the development of technology has meant that sports which had once been national pastimes, eg, basketball in the USA, are now able to look further afield and seek global audiences.

The development of commercialisation

The large audiences needed to give support in the form of live spectators for gate receipts and possessing television sets to view the sports at home, tend to be found predominantly in advanced technological societies who possess enough free time, disposable income, and the means to travel easily to different sporting venues. It is no coincidence, therefore, that commercial sports originally began in the nineteenth century in Britain – the country to first develop industrialisation and communication networks. Professional sport grew steadily and included activities such as cricket, ball games, prize fighting and pedestrianism. Competitors could be paid for their efforts and coaching and training methods developed alongside; more detail can be found in Chapter 17.

It is interesting to see this development in Britain, which had, as its ruling class, the elite upper class who developed the 'amateur' concept which was aimed at keeping monetary values out of sport. The business side of sport was delayed in Britain in comparison to the USA, who had no compunction about putting sport and money together. By the 1990s, even in Britain, sport has become big business.

Sporting goods

The manufacture of sports goods which had once been a specialist market producing equipment and clothing for the participants, has now become a sports industry providing mainstream fashion items for people who may never get out of breath! The development of trainers as a status symbol for young people, is the result of a very successful advertising campaign.

Changing the rules

Some sports have changed as a result of commercial interest. For example, rules to speed up the action to prevent spectator boredom, changes in scoring to create more excitement, evenly balancing competitors to achieve uncertain outcomes (as this has been proved to increase spectator interest) and providing breaks in play so sponsors can advertise their products. Reassuringly, however, the basic structure of most sports (ie, the format and goals) has remained the same.

Research a sport and trace any changes made which could have been as a result of commercial input; examples are ice hockey, lawn tennis, squash and cricket.

Changing organisations

The organisations in charge of individual sports have found that their remit has changed over the years. This again can be highlighted in Britain where the governing bodies were originally based on the principle of amateurism. They have had to adapt to commercial pressures, if they have wanted their sport to maintain its status. Amateur sport receives its main funding from sponsorship and individual donations. Some sports are wealthier than others, but they all need to pay for athletes' training, operating expenses and the staging of events. Staff with expertise in financial management and publicity are hired rather than those purely with an interest in the sport itself, and decisions related to revenue are not necessarily made with the good of the athletes at heart. This has led to some athletes seeking more control, 'taking on' the organisations concerned, and setting up their own players' association in order to project a collective voice; eg, the PGA (Professional Golf Association) the ATP (Association of Tennis Professionals). Athletes' protests include rule changes, the competitive season being extended or the need to create more revenue for themselves.

Revenue for athletes

The public image is that athletes are grossly overpaid. However, this is only the case for a minority of athletes. In the USA, the courts decided that professional athletes

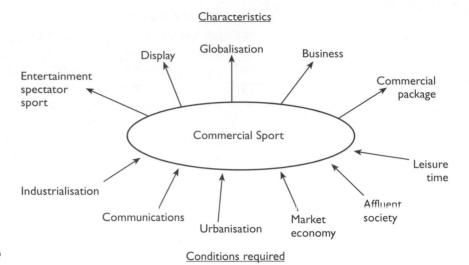

Fig. 16.1   WHAT IS COMMERCIAL SPORT?

who were likely to have short careers were not really overpaid. Athletes have also traditionally not enjoyed many rights within their employment contracts. This was legally challenged by the athletes in the 1970s, when it was found that the majority of athletes did not earn as much as television entertainers. To attract endorsements, athletes need a strong public image so that people will recognise and identify with them. Women and black sports persons may be the victims of prejudice against them.

Research the changes in rugby union and rugby league since 1994. (The CD Roms of *The Guardian* and *The Times* newspapers are useful sources of information.)

Summary

- Commercial sports have developed under certain social and economic conditions – urbanisation, industrialisation, effective communications, surplus disposable income and a large population with high living standards and sufficient leisure time.
- The basic structure of sports have remained the same but commercialisation has been influential.
- Mass audiences sometimes demand drama and excitement rather than aesthetic appreciation.
- Control of sport needs to be balanced between the owners and athletes.
- Amateur sports are becoming pressurised by the need to generate more money.

Sponsorship

Sponsorship is the provision of funds or other form of support to an individual or event in return for a commercial return. It is of mutual benefit to both parties.

Sponsorship is now an intrinsic aspect of sports funding. Through the medium of television, business sponsors of sport can create the images they want, allow identification with the sports stars and introduce the 'new' populations into the game to their product.

The Olympic Games

The International Olympic Committee (IOC) has expanded its investments to include 200 nations, and has made the Olympic Games one of the biggest media events in the world. Sponsorship for the Games is set up on a global basis. The Olympic Programme (TOP) involves approximately 44 companies, including Coca Cola, Adidas and Kodak (Adidas actually brought the idea to the IOC). Sponsorship is necessary, as the staging of the event is enormously expensive, well recognised after the 1976 Games in Montreal almost went bankrupt. Tax payers were unwilling to shoulder the burden of cost, while television companies were willing to pay large sums to transmit. Without international coverage (167 countries) the sponsors would not be willing to invest so much, and events might not be able to take place.

Aspects of sponsorship

Fig. 16.2   SPORTS TEAMS OFTEN ADVERTISE A SPONSORING COMPANY ON THEIR KIT

A **sponsorship agency** is an agency which specialises in advising on or organising sponsored events and programmes, and which may be employed either by a sponsor or a sports body. It acts as a broker, bringing together the sponsor and the sports body to create or organise an event or programme which is mutually beneficial to both parties (The Howell Report); eg, West Nally and Mark McCormack International Management Organisation.

An individual athlete may also have an **agent** who promotes the competitor to gain financial benefits for each of them. The **marketing** of athletes or events is an integrated and professionally planned promotion.

Trust Funds are a means for an amateur athlete to receive money from their sport. They are managed by the governing body and accept money from subventions, for advertising services or as participation money. It will be held until retirement from the sport, but funds for athletic expenses can be withdrawn before retirement.

Athletes will often display companies names on their equipment, clothing and vehicles. This is known as **endorsing** a product. The performers are contracted to declare publicly their approval of a product or service. When Eric Cantona was at Manchester United Football Club, he endorsed Nike products, but his team mate Ryan Giggs endorsed Reebok goods. Sports stars in the 1990s have emerged as 'personality advertising', and are used as a big sell. Gary Lineker and Paul Gascoigne teamed up to a partnership of a different kind – an advert for Walkers crisps. It has been suggested that sports performers are beginning to resemble 'human billboards'.

Perimeter advertising is where advertising boards surround pitches and are sold off in meters to commercial organisations, providing a stationary form of advertising.

The Institute of Sports Sponsorship (ISS)

This is one of the main national organisations concerned with sport sponsorship. It was set up in association with the CCPR Sports Sponsorship Advisory Service, and acts as a grouping of commercial companies and public bodies with an interest in sport.

Sportsmatch

The Conservative government's £1 for £1 Business Sponsorship Incentive Scheme (for grass roots sport) was established in 1992. It will provide funding for over £3.7 million a year in UK to match funds for the private sector.

It is administered by the ISS in cooperation with the Sports Council, and provides an excellent opportunity for sports bodies and sponsors to double the value of the project investment or to mount extra events or activities. The Sportsmatch Awards Panel which considers grants is particularly interested in developing projects for rural and inner cities which lack sporting resources. The events must be competitive, challenging and physically skillful.

Advantages and disadvantages

Sponsorship and advertising have been key factors in the redevelopment of many sports. They provide capital to sport, while at the same time:

- securing an appropriate image for the sponsor. For example: Gillette sponsor cricket, creating an 'English' image for their product; Coca Cola sponsor the Olympics and school sport, conveying fun and liveliness.
- achieving specific marketing objectives.

There are some disadvantages though. There has been uneven development across sports. Sponsors tend to come forward where there are already large audiences; a diversion of sponsor money away from the minority sports can cause a decline in those sports. For example, in 1978 the World Squash Championships were cancelled due to a lack of sponsor and no guaranteed television coverage; in the case of football, increased television coverage helped to cause a reduction in live attendances. Elite sport can be promoted at the expense of the grass roots due to its ability to attract media coverage.

There can be sensitivity about political advertising which can cause problems; Thames Television blocked out coverage of the 1985 Edinburgh Games when the organisers, Edinburgh Council, refused to move an anti apartheid banner. Some sports have been adapted to suit TV coverage. In cricket, the one day game has developed to increase the pace, which has placed priority on certain skills. The tobacco company, Rothmans, encouraged attacking and batting skills and defensive bowling, and paid more in sponsorship when the ball was driven to the boundary – so that their adverts appeared more frequently!

Sponsors sometimes withdraw when their objectives are not achieved or where there is no perceived gain. There can be contradictory messages when a product being advertised is considered dangerous to people's health. Tobacco companies were banned from general advertising on British television in 1965. Sport, which achieved a significant percentage of a network's output, was therefore a good advertising proposition for the tobacco companies. The main sport beneficiaries of tobacco sponsorship have been motor racing, tennis, cricket, golf, show jumping and snooker. However, the Sports Council did not accept tobacco sponsorship and did not make its Sport Sponsorship Advisory Service available to it. Tobacco has in the past contributed 10% of total sponsorship, and the government could not compensate for this amount, should tobacco advertising be banned from sport. This poses the question: is tobacco bad for health but good for sport?

List the positive and negative effects of tobacco sponsorship and account for the factors you mention.

An example of sponsorship – Coca Cola

Coca Cola has made a heavy impact on the sports sponsorship scene. The company views sport sponsorship as a way of gaining access to their customers.

Coca Cola provide the customer with things in which they can participate, eg, signed footballs, days out at training grounds, good seats at prestigious sports events. This is the world of corporate hospitality.

- Coca Cola prefer to be synonymous with a sport, rather than a team. They have a five year contract at Wimbledon tennis championships, which started in 1997. They occupy the suite next to the Committee suite to entertain their major customers, VIPs, editors of key opinion-forming journals and so on. In addition they secured the advertising and 'pouring rights', which means that any drinks used by players or officials is contained in a Coke receptacle, whether or not it is a drink of Coke. In other words, they are involved in 'presence marketing' which is a term used to mean the saturation of a venue with their product.
- The slogan 'Eat Sleep Drink Football' created by Ivan Pollard is now being reworked as an advert to appeal to the Brazilian market.
- Within a country, the company selects the most popular sport and chooses sport personalities with clean cut, wholesome images, like Glen Hoddle, Les Ferdinand and Alan Shearer. Ryan Giggs and singer Peter Andre have been sponsored as a route into the fashion world.
- They also provide benefits to an area hosting an event. The Olympic Stadium at Atlanta (which interestingly is 'the home of Coke') was almost rebuilt by Coca Cola – including the roads, hotels, athletes' accommodation and Centennial Park.

Look at an event through a sponsor's eyes: what strategies would you adopt to attract a potential sponsor? Be detailed in your response.

The Howell Report (1983)

We have already addressed some of the problems sponsorship can create for sport. The Howell Report sought to make recommendations. Here are some examples:

1   The Sports Council, CCPR and individual governing bodies should seek control and accept responsibility for the application, provision and practice of sponsorship in sport.
2   Governing bodies should establish sponsorship committees to help regulate sponsorship, and these should include competitor representatives. Governing bodies should not rely too much on business sponsorship, and should diversify approaches if the sponsors pull out.
3   Proper ethical standards and policies to protect sports performers from exploitation should be ensured.
4   Sponsors should aim to support sport both at the grass roots and at the elite level. They can gain experience at local and regional levels, while also providing a social service. They should aim to give prior notice of their intention to withdraw their support.
5   Trust funds should be monitored carefully by the governing bodies.
6   The Sports Aid Foundation should market itself more efficiently to achieve its targets.

7   High ethical standards should be everyone's main concern: influential sponsorship deals should be compatible with the interests of sport; full knowledge of all arrangements should be made available.

Though sponsorship has provided much needed capital for sport, the bedrock of funding in the UK is still a combination of public funding and the massive voluntary and unpaid commitment of sports enthusiasts.

The media

The media includes newspapers and radio and television broadcasting, by which information is conveyed to the general public.

Newspapers The early types of sports news sheets, notably *Bell's Life* (1822) and *Sporting Life* (1865), provided short, detailed sports reports. General newspapers gradually begun to include sport sections, bringing sport to those people who may have had little contact with sport but who now were able to recognise sports performers. By the 1920s, the mass audience for sport had emerged. Sports reports in newspapers could summarise events and appeal to a wide range of audiences at different times (unlike television coverage). Today there are two major types of newspapers:

1   The **tabloids**, such as *The Sun* or *The Mirror*, tend to have a large section devoted to sport, but focus on particular types of sport – mainly those with broad appeal and male dominated.
2   The **broadsheets** such as *The Guardian* or *The Times* tend to cover and analyse sport in more depth; they offer slightly more variety of sport, but there is still a predominance on male sport.

Take a selection of newspapers. Estimate the ratio given over to sport and the ratio of different types of sport. Can you come to any conclusions? Is there a difference in emphasis between the tabloids and broadsheets as suggested here?

Radio Radio started to report live events in the 1920s, which gave the broadcast an immediacy; this was strengthened by the advent of television broadcasting. The BBC traditionally has shown sports events without the advertisers' influence whereas in the USA they scheduled events to maximise advertisers' demands.

Television Television has the advantage of being able to broadcast instantaneous sporting action to a large audience, relatively cheaply. Because of the relatively low cost of sports broadcasting compared favourably with drama and light entertainment, and the high ratings gained, it is not surprising that sport features so heavily on television schedules, particularly at weekends.

Television has helped to bring lesser known or rarely watched sports to the foreground; it has helped participants to reach superstar status, and consequently raised the performers' earnings. This has sometimes put athletes under great pressure to make more performance appearances than is good for them, physically or mentally.

However, television reporting can also over-dramatise problems within the sports world. Also, deals made between sporting bodies and the media can favour certain sports, such as the alliance between Adidas and FIFA.

The effect on sport

Some sports have changed to make them more amenable to media coverage. Television coverage can also influence positively or negatively the participation rates in a sport. Over the last fifty years, terrestrial television in the UK has expanded from one channel to five. The new channels need to seek out new markets, and when the new Channel 4 arrived, it boosted the viewing and participating figures for volleyball and table tennis, and gave significant coverage of the ethnic game kabbadi.

* Volleyball became a regular sports feature between 1980 and 1984 – the number of affiliated players rose by 70%.
* Conversely, when table tennis no longer received television coverage, its membership of participating players dropped by a third. The governing bodies in both cases were convinced that the changed rates of participation were not coincidences. If women's sports received more coverage, would we see the rise in female participants that so many organisations are trying hard to achieve?

Chart the changes in a sport of your choice which have occurred as a result of commercial pressures.

Sports commentators

The media reports on what actually happens and as such is objective; yet as readers, viewers or listeners, we must take into account the values and beliefs of those who commentate on the events. The commentators are the mediators who describe and analyse the action for the viewer at home. They can become celebrities in their own right and are sometimes associated with just one sport; eg, Murray Walker (motor racing), John Motsam (football), the late Dan Maskell (tennis at Wimbledon), Harry Carpenter (boxing). The style of presentation has become closely related to the culture of the mass audience. Events are hyped up, where the commentators discuss the likely outcome of an event for hours before, advising viewers on how to interpret the situation.

Influence of technology

The increase in technology has enabled an effective combination of detailed coverage with fast action tension. The use of zoom lenses has meant less reliance on fixed angle lenses, and makes possible close ups of players, catching facial and verbal expressions which spectators at live events could not hope to capture; it is possible to fit cameras in a racing car, under water, and in a goal, which give the viewer at home a privileged viewing position. Action replays and freeze frames enable a detailed analysis to take place.

Communication satellites enable live transmission around the world. This has had a growing impact on viewing audiences. Television rights can be granted to companies who do not transmit to many homes. The Broadcasting Act 1990 in the UK declared that all rights to broadcast sport can be sold to the highest bidder.

Media coverage and social values

* Television coverage concentrates on the conduct of the participants and spectators, and is generally sympathetic to officials. Different sports receive

different emphasis of coverage; eg, tennis players who behave badly are often described as 'brats' which has a very middle class tone, whereas in soccer, the language used might be 'thugs', possibly showing more intolerance of working class behaviour.

- Gender inequalities in sport can be reflected by the media. Men figure more as participants and media sport professionals, whereas women tend to comment on women's sports, if at all. There have been recent challenges to this position, eg, Sue Barker for the BBC. Non-contact sports for women are given more positive media coverage, such as tennis, gymnastics and track athletes. The massive inequality in coverage tends to reaffirm the stereotype that sport is for men, and women have little to comment on. See fig 16.3.

- The media can help generate a sense of nationalism, particularly since the development of international coverage of events where the symbols of nationalism are displayed for all to see – rituals, flags, ceremonies, parades, uniforms and anthems – making them highly emotive events.

- In the UK, sportspeople from ethnic minorities can become potent role models for young people, and their representation can promote equality of opportunity. However, the media can also promote the stereotype that black people can excel in sport and physical activity but not in other areas of life. Similarly to women, people from ethnic minorities are not prominent in the controlling positions of power in the media, like commentators and directors, writers, producers, photographers etc.

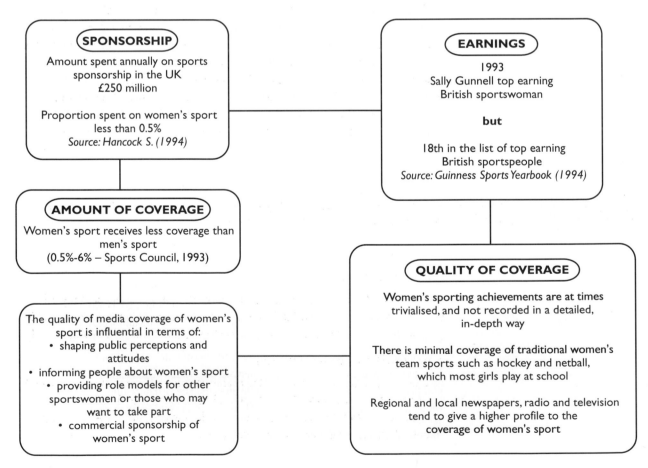

Fig. 16.3 WOMEN'S SPORT

Watch a sport event on television and record it. Then analyse in detail for a particular aspect; eg, comments made by the commentators, the language used, reference to certain players. This will be time-consuming, but if done as a class activity you could each report on a different event and compile some interesting information.

Deviance

Behaviour which goes against the society's general norms and values is called 'deviant' behaviour. This can include behaviour which is against the law and therefore **criminally** deviant, eg, burglary, or against the **moral** values of the society but which is not criminally deviant, eg, promiscuity.

Can you think of a criminal and immoral example of deviancy in a sporting situation?

Approaches to deviancy

Relative deviancy

Deviant behaviour can reflect the balance of power in a society. Who decides what is lawful and what is morally right? Usually those with the most control, ie, the dominant culture. Right and wrong can mean different things to different people and is sometimes dependent on culture, gender and social class. Those who do not conform to the rules and identify as a group with similar interests, acting in a manner which is not conventional in the dominant culture, can be classed as members of a sub culture. Examples are the special group of athletes bonded by a sense of commitment; football hooligans; rugby clubs. This view suggests that deviance can be relative, and that deviants are victims of a power system which makes the rules.

What characterises a rugby club as a sub culture? For further reading, see Loy and Kenyon (1981).

Absolute deviancy

Another view of deviancy takes an absolute view of right and wrong, and regards deviant behaviour as morally bankrupt. The solution is to establish more control by creating more rules and punishing the perpetrators more successfully and publicly.

Normal distribution approach

An alternative to the absolute and relative approach is proposed by Coakley (1993). He suggests there is a 'normal distribution' of behaviour which falls into a range of acceptances. Deviance occurs when behaviour falls outside this range, *on either side*; ie, there can be under- and over-conformity.

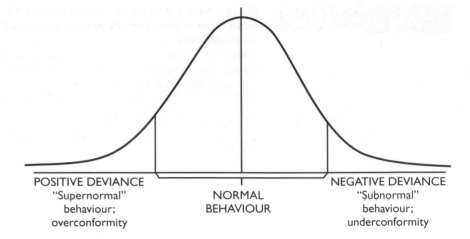

Fig. 16.4   A NORMAL DISTRIBUTION
APPROACH TO UNDERSTANDING DEVIANCE
Source: Coakley (1993)

Deviance in sport

Athletes are encouraged to behave in ways that would not be allowed in other areas of life. This can pose special problems for sport. 'On the field' deviance includes 'violations of norms that occur while preparing or participating in sports events' (Coakley, 1993). It can be caused by the pressure of media coverage or commercialism, or the pressure to win. Similar behaviour outside of the sport situation could result in arrests and prosecutions.

Under-conformity and negative deviancy

This is a situation where an athlete rejects rules; at the extreme extent, this could be anarchic. Negative deviancy involves cheating and deliberately harming another player, and should be easy to control because a rule violation can be punished appropriately.

Over-conformity and positive deviancy

This is a situation where an athlete goes too far in conforming with the rules. Examples are, where training becomes obsessive; where performance-enhancing drugs are taken; when normal life suffers or where athletes participate in sport despite injury, and are praised by the organisers and media. The athlete takes risks, makes sacrifices and pays the price, in order to conform to the norms of the group. This form of deviance can be harder to control and would benefit from a reassessment of the sport ethic and the meaning given to sport by those in control – the organisers, sponsors and media.

According to Coakley (1993), the sport ethic has four core elements:

- athletes make sacrifices for the game
- athletes strive for distinction
- athletes accept risks and play through pain
- athletes accept no limits in the pursuit of possibilities.

 **Have you ever been in a situation where you were expected to adopt 'positive' forms of deviance? What was the outcome? How did you feel?**

We will now look specifically at the following issues:

1 Aggression in sport by athletes
2 Spectator violence, in particular football hooliganism
3 Drug taking by athletes.

Aggression in sport

The various theories of aggression are covered in greater detail in the Psychology section of this book. Aggression includes any behaviour which *intends* physical or psychological harm to another person. This distinguishes it from other terms used in sport situations, such as assertive, rough, competitive. Intimidation is the threatened intent to harm, using verbal or physical means. Sports vary in their nature, and so the extent through which aggression can be expressed also varies. Activities involving physical contact are more easily open to shows of aggression than activities where players are separated from each other. However, a game like netball which according to the rules, is a non contact game, can often involve aggression.

Theories that sport helps to cause aggression are based on the following:

- participating in or spectating sport leads to frustration, which leads to violence
- sportspeople learn to associate violence as a means to achieve success
- the dominance of 'male' behaviour in sport leads people to believe that men are naturally superior to women because they have greater strength and more violent tendencies.

People care about the result of sporting action, and victory can be used to reflect superiority in other aspects of life. Frustration can lead to the emotional response of anger which can, in the sporting arena, be expressed as a violent response. The cause of frustration could be an official's decision during a game or environmental conditions. Frustration can be stimulated when athletes use equipment which are associated with violence.

 **Which sports do you think would be most likely to lead to aggression in sport?**

Aggression is likely to be prevalent when spectators identify strongly with one particular side and are likely to feel anger quite easily, where similar opportunities for aggression and frustration are present. Contact sports are therefore most likely to lead to violence on the pitch, and this is compounded when large rewards are available for winning and when expectations of coaches and fans are high. Tolerance of rule violations seem to increase as the level of competition increases.

An extreme case is ice hockey, where 'enforcers' are employed to act as hit-men. Yet these are players who do not necessarily feel anger or frustration associated with the game. They intimidate and carry out violent acts because that is their primary task in the game.

As female participation in contact sports has increased, it has become apparent that they also use violence as a strategy, but research (though limited as yet) generally concludes that they are not as violent as men. Sport has long been a male preserve, and mistakes made during a game often result in sexist comments such as 'playing like a girl'. Thus, some sportsmen feel the need to prove their masculinity beyond doubt, by using violent means; this implies that aggressive behaviour can be the result of social conditioning, and is not merely a natural masculine trait.

Spectator violence

A number of general approaches to deviance can be applied to the specific form of deviant behaviour which is termed 'football hooliganism'. Football hooligans have been defined by the Sports Council as 'those people who were dealt with by the police for offences occurring in connection with attendance at football matches'. A dictionary definition of a hooligan is a 'disorderly and noisy young person who behaves in a violent and destructive way'. A distinction needs to be made between supporters, fans and hooligans. Supporters and fans manage their emotions effectively; Guttman (1986) concluded that spectating at sports events did not result in an increase in violent behaviour. Hooligans on the other hand go to matches to engage in aggressive and violent behaviour before, during or after the game. Considering the amount of sports events and the number of people spectating on a regular basis, it is clear we are dealing with a minority of people, albeit a media-attracting minority.

Sociological approaches to hooliganism

Early theories of hooliganism concentrated on social class, and tried to explain the behaviour of hooligans in terms of their social status. However, it is no longer a useful way of describing people, as class distinctions are not clear-cut in modern society. Furthermore, whereas early theories were based on the premise that most football hooligans were uneducated, less well off members of society, recent studies have discovered that a large number of people who cause trouble at football matches are highly educated professional people, who often need to keep their identities as football supporters separate from their working lives. It is in fact difficult to find any one single factor to explain deviancy as it applies to football hooliganism; a synthesis of approaches is required.

Hooliganism at football matches has been exaggerated and distorted, and should be seen in a wider socioeconomic and historical context. The media has a tendency to sensationalise the news and to amplify the problem being reported.

Football has had a long, fluctuating history of crowd disorders, and Pearson (1983) suggests that such problems date back to the seventeenth and eighteenth centuries.

Marsh (1978) argued that aggravation at football matches is effectively a 'highly distinctive, and often ceremonial system for resolving conflict'; behaviour at football matches is a ritual action. Behaviour is structured and ordered rather than chaotic; the fighting itself has rules, and much of it is not serious.

Taylor (1971) argues that football is now a passive spectator sport rather than a participatory one. The increasing professionalism, control by wealthy directors and change from grounds to stadiums, have taken away any sense of control or participation from the spectators, and football hooliganism could be a response to resist these changes.

Arousal seeking and risk taking appear to be compensatory acts. This idea links with Elias and Dunning's theory (1970), who suggested in their title, *The quest for excitement in unexciting societies*, that in industrialised societies there are fewer opportunities for people to express themselves freely.

Brown (1991) believes that some hooligans become addicted to the activity just as gamblers and alcoholics do. Increasing stimulation is needed to generate high arousal because of psychological deprivation. People who have not had enough opportunity to experience a wide range of rewarding experiences can be forced to use narrower strategies to deal with life's problems.

Practical factors which contribute to hooliganism

There are a number of important factors which can contribute to the *level* of violence at sports events:

- Violence shown by the players seems to transmit itself to the spectators.
- Pre-event hype can also increase the level of violence, so the media and organisers should take some responsibility for the way they promote the event.
- Controversial officials' decisions can sometimes cause an increase in violence, particularly if the situation is at a crucial stage. The need for competent officials is essential.
- The supporter group dynamics, ie, the size and structure of the group, their social and cultural backgrounds, the importance associated with the event and the historical relationships of those attending.
- The authorities' strategies for controlling the event.
- The amount of alcohol consumed before the match.

In Britain, the short distance between sporting locations has enabled the establishment of a tradition of away fans travelling to every game. The two sets of fans openly display their allegiance through the symbols of colours, flags, scarves, songs and so on. This is not possible in larger countries where supporters have further distances to travel.

Fig. 16.5   SPECTATOR VIOLENCE

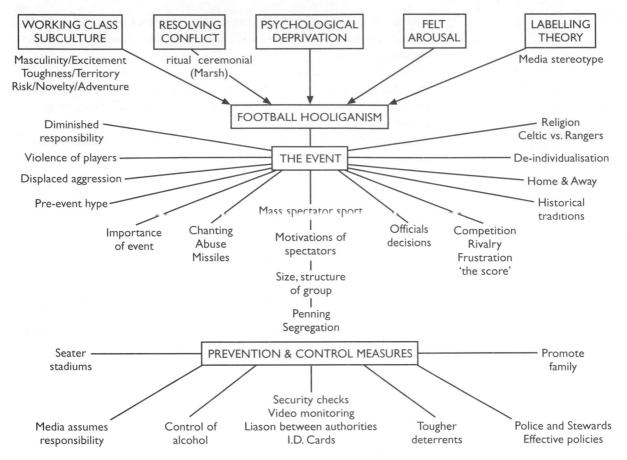

Fig. 16.6 POINTS TO REMEMBER ABOUT
HOOLIGANISM

Taking all the factors mentioned above, discuss comprehensive measures which could be employed to control the level of violence amongst participants and spectators.

Dealing with hooliganism

Hooliganism initially took place in football grounds. These were easily accessible, spectators were not segregated and matches occurred at regular intervals. Trouble generally erupted when goals were scored. However, when the authorities began to use strategies like fenced pens with close police scrutiny, the violent activity began to move away from the grounds.

The Taylor Report following the Hillsborough disaster led to measures such as abolishing the soccer terraces. By 1994–5 season all Premier League and First Division clubs had to upgrade their stadiums to be all seater facilities. This has led many people to complain of the lack of atmosphere, as they feel that the excitement generated by large crowds is being eradicated.

Video monitoring has been installed at most grounds so that police can closely monitor crowd movement. Freeze frames can highlight particular trouble makers. Information is stored on computer in the National Criminal Intelligence Service and allows police liaison in England and Europe.

Perimeter fencing was not successful in preventing violence, and neither was the identity card scheme. However, the level of hooliganism has decreased in the last few years. Some have complained that the police measures reduced much of the fun element and increased the risk element too much.

Summary

The relationship between sport and aggression has been covered in some detail. It is a complex social phenomenon which requires a synthesis of perspectives.

Putting time between the player and the frustration seems to be a more substantial argument than sport either increasing or decreasing the level of 'natural' violence found in humans.

- Frustration combined with anger, opportunities and stimulus cues lead to aggression.

Drugs in sport

The history of drug abuse is as old as sport. Athletes in Greece and Rome took substances to improve their athletic performance. However, drug use in modern sport has become regular and systematised. Research shows that it is more than a peripheral problem, and operates at both amateur and professional levels, among male and female athletes and across a wide variety of sports. Factors which led to an increase in the use of drugs include:

- advances in biology and medicine
- the use of drugs in World War II
- the development and availability of testosterone, steroids and growth hormones in the 1950s.

Weight-trainers in particular demonstrated the possible results of using these drugs, other athletes who recognised their potential capitalised on this. Drugs allow athletes to control their bodies; they can alter their bodily functions, though this will result in a *loss* of power if used unwisely. The 'substance availability hypothesis' ties

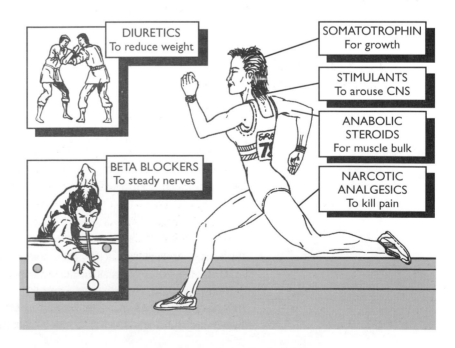

Fig. 16.7   THE EFFECT OF DRUGS ON THE BODY

in closely with the type of positive deviance mentioned earlier, where an athlete is over-committed to the sport ethic and is willing to risk all for the opportunity to perform at their highest level.

In the last 20 years, drug taking has become a very common part of top class sport. This in spite of the efforts of various national and international doping committees, and the establishment of the International Olympic Committee Medical Commission in 1967. It appears that the chemists supplying sportspeople with drugs, are trying to keep one step ahead of the chemists working to keep sport free from the effects of drugs. One of the problematic areas is defining an illegal drug, and the effects they have on the performer and performance; what is artificial, natural, foreign, fair or abnormal?

The organisations responsible for their sport generally have to take control of the testing for drugs in their sport. This will take place at both the national and international levels. Below is an example of the action taken over a period of time and the links between the domestic and international organisations.

Which drugs are used?

The International Amateur Federation Rule 144 on doping states:

1 doping is forbidden
2 doping is the use by or distribution to an athlete of certain substances which could have the effect of improving artificially the athlete's physical and/or mental condition and so augmenting his athletic performance.

It lists a total of over 80 individual drugs classified under **stimulants**, **narcotic analgesics** and **anabolic steroids**, and states that chemically or pharmacologically related drugs are also forbidden.

'Ergogenic aids' refer to any substance that improves performance.

Amphetamines (stimulants)

- most widely used manufactured stimulants
- used to improve *endurance performance*, ie, enable people to continue working at high levels for prolonged periods of time.
- increases mental and physical alertness
- decreases fatigue
- increases metabolism
- increases heart rate and blood pressure

The more an athlete uses stimulants, the less effect it has on the body as it gets used to it, so the athlete has to take more to have an effect. Side effects increase if more stimulants are taken.

Narcotic analgesics

- narcotics put people to sleep
- analgesics kill pain

These drugs are highly addictive. Their possession is a criminal offence in most countries; this group of drugs includes: morphine, heroin, methadone, codeine.

Cyclists have been known to take morphine towards the end of a hard day's ride. They receive an initially powerful stimulating effect from the drug which enables them to finish strongly. This stimulating effect is then followed by a longer sedating effect, during which the cyclist would sleep, being refreshed for the next day's cycling.

Codeine is a difficult drug to detect, as it is used in normal medical complaints.

Anabolic steroids

These are artificially produced male hormones. Our natural hormones help to repair body after periods of stress; these have the same effect.

- anabolic means protein building
- steroids means hormones

Sports people use them to build up their power and increase their recovery rate after training.

Androgenic properties

Steroids minimise properties of the hormone – male characteristics, eg, facial hair, deep voice etc. If taken in large doses artificially, it can lead to impotency, infertility etc.

Anabolic properties

- Rapid healing of body tissues is increased by steroids and can make athletes more aggressive and competitive.
- They promote muscle growth and therefore increase lean body weight.
- They can cause such problems as liver damage, or acne. Taking steroids makes athletes bigger, stronger and more powerful.
- It enables them to train harder with less fatigue and much shorter recovery time; so, increased quality training gives rise to greater power.

Testosterone

- A male hormone, produced naturally in body of both males and females.
- A natural compound, so not so easy to detect in drug testing.
- Anabolic steroids can be taken until a few weeks before competition then to clear them for testing; testosterone can take over and be undetected.
- Side effects – body sometimes stops producing own supply of testo.
- Ratio in normal body for test to epitesto is 1:1; when ratio reaches 6:1, then the result is achieved. Some athletes then inject more epit to boost ratio up.

Blood doping

This is the removal and reinfusion of a person's blood to improve the aerobic capacity by increasing the numbers of red blood cells. This increases the blood's oxygen-carrying capacity. There is a danger of increasing the viscosity (thickness) of the blood and overcrowding the capillaries and blocking them, which can lead to heart failure.

A survey of 100 top runners in the USA found that 50 of them said they would take a certain drug knowing that although it could make them Olympic champions, it could kill them in a year. Discuss the issues involved in this situation.

1 **Find out information about a well documented case of an athlete charged with taking drugs; eg, Ben Johnson, Diane Modahl.**

2 **What are the problems for defining a drug for normal purposes and those for sport?**

3 **How would you persuade an up-and-coming young athlete not to take drugs?**

Summary

- Sport, sponsorship and the media are all interdependent on each other for their success and popularity.
- The media can transform sport into a crucial part of people's lives. Without coverage, sport would have a much lower profile.
- The concept of masculinity tied up with sport success, achieved through violent means, could have consequences outside of the sport setting.
- Violence amongst spectators can be determined by the event, the crowd dynamics and other social factors.
- Drug-taking conforms with the positive deviance model and can be the result of the over commitment to the sport ethic rather than a reflection of declining moral standards. Athletes mostly make their own decisions and cannot be seen wholly as victims of a power system.
- The *greater use* of drugs is due more to the wider availability of drugs.
- Testing has not developed sufficiently to counteract the use of drugs.
- New norms need to be created for sport and athletes should have some participation in this process.

chapter 17

The History of Sport

So far we have examined the present day situation regarding sport and physical education. We have occasionally referred to how the past has influenced the present. Now it needs a more in-depth analysis. In other words, how and why have we arrived at the present day situation? We will:

- chart some social changes which have been influential to our everyday lives and see how recreational activities have been affected
- look carefully at education – the public schools and the state schools system
- apply knowledge gained in order to analyse a variety of physical recreational and sporting activities.

Whatever we discover about sport must not be seen in isolation. Remember Chapter 15: the system of sport influences and is in turn influenced by the social system – economic, geographical, educational, social and political factors.

You will need to have a basic grasp of British history. It is not useful to refer to Regency or Victorian times if you have no idea of where they fall in the overall scheme. English Heritage has produced a useful ruler charting the different eras in chronological order – see fig 17.1. Looking at the origins of sports and pastimes, it is clear that they were initially *functional*, eg, for military and hunting purposes. When societies depended less on survival, many activities took on a *recreational* dimension, such as children's play and the feasts and festivals which often had *religious* associations, either pagan or Christian.

The Norman conquest

The Norman conquest of the Anglo Saxons in 1066 is an extremely important event in British history, as this was the last time that Britain was successfully invaded. William the Conqueror was both Duke of Normandy and King of England. He introduced the feudal system, by which rulers granted land in exchange for military service. The Doomsday Book in 1085 was the first official public record of the Kingdom's holdings. William gave the land to his own nobles, and the Anglo Saxons became serfs to the Norman lords; a serf was not a free man but was part of the property of the manor.

The forest laws restricted the privileges of the commoners, and their hunting activities were curtailed. With the Norman conquest, the 'Age of Chivalry' reached its peak. The jousting tournament was characterised by the privilege of the elite to participate, its functional purpose for military training and the unquestioned code of honour among knights. The popularity of the tournament declined as did the culture from which it sprang. It survived in a more base form, as a sporting contest without the military overtones. This type of activity took place in the Whitsuntide ales, May Day festivals and church wakes, where the elite in society had withdrawn to a spectating role, rather than a participatory one.

43-450AD	Roman Britain
450-613	Anglo Saxon invasion
613-1017	Division into Kingdoms
1017-1066	Danish Rule
1066	William I
1087	William II
1100	Henry I
1135	Stephen
1154	Henry II
1189	Richard I
1199	John
1216	Henry III
1272	Edward I
1307	Edward II
1327	Edward III
1377	Richard II
1399	Henry IV
1413	Henry V
1422	Henry VI
1461	Edward IV
1483	Edward V
1483	Richard III
1485	Henry VII
1509	Henry VIII
1547	Edward VI
1553	Mary I
1558	Elizabeth I
1603	James I
1625	Charles I
1649	Commonwealth
1660	Charles II
1685	James II
1689	William III & Mary
1702	Anne
1714	George I
1727	George II
1760	George III
1820	George IV
1830	William IV
1837	Victoria
1901	Edward VII
1910	George V
1936	Edward VIII
1936	George VI
1952	Elizabeth II

Fig. 17.1   HISTORICAL DATES

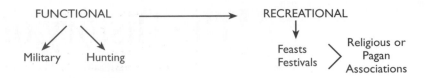

Fig. 17.2   FUNCTIONAL AND RECREATIONAL ORIGINS OF SPORT

Medieval England

The years between 1066 and 1485 are generally known as the Middle Ages. This period saw a change in fortunes for most people in England. The first half was prosperous allowing for the development of churches and universities. The bulk of the population were peasants in rural areas but there was an increase in the townsmen who were mainly merchants, lawyers and doctors. Their wealth increased as trade was made possible, due to fewer private wars between the different lords. The townsmen were above the serfs because they were free but below that of the lords, so they formed the beginnings of the middle class, who were to later grow even more powerful. They formed guilds which were special organisations to safeguard the rights of craftsmen and merchants to practice their trade within the town walls. As the middle class grew richer the kings began to choose them as their lawyers and officials. Their sons would then study in order to be able to make their way in the world. The Church was responsible for the basic education available. Boys were taught to read and write in Latin. Bishops established cathedral schools. Much of this was to change after the Reformation.

Festivals and feasts played an important part of life in the Middle Ages. Much recreational pastimes took place at this time. The horse was a significant feature for the nobility, who used them for hunting and the tournaments (see above). Military activities were favoured over purely recreational ones and archery became a compulsory aspect of young men's lives. Some sports and games were banned as they were becoming so popular that it was feared they would interfere with men's archery practice, essential for the defence of the realm.

Festivals were held in honour of events that were important to people's daily lives; eg, the change of seasons, harvest, and the summer and winter solstices. As the pagan customs were taken over by the Church they were given new religious meanings. 'Holy days' were put aside for feasting, which is how the word 'holiday' originated. In many countries towns and villages had their own special festivals and saints' days which celebrated the death of a saint.

Fig. 17.3   FRONTISPIECE TO *THE BOOK OF FALCONRIE*, 1498

Easter is the most important feast of the Christian Church, and its date fixed the dates of the holy days connected to it – Lent, Shrove Tuesday, Ash Wednesday. Shrove Tuesday is the last day before the fasting of Lent, and was a time for feasting and fun. Recreations took place within a wide social pattern, and activities included mob football, wrestling, animal baiting, skittles and bowls. The minstrels provided entertainment, and were dancers, acrobats, composers and performers of music.

The Tudor and Stuart era (1485–1714)

The Tudors

England changed rapidly under the Tudors. Religious disputes developed as people could not agree on how the Church should be run. Some wanted services similar to the old Catholic ways, while others wanted a 'purer' type of service. These people became known as Puritans; see below.

Under Henry VIII's rule, there was greater prosperity and more time for cultural pursuits like music, literature and the theatre. Henry was a great sports lover, and created one of the liveliest courts in Europe. He participated in all-day hunts and wrestling, and ordered his own real tennis court to be built at Hampton Court (it is still well worth a visit). Access to education, equipment and facilities enabled the upper classes the privilege of exclusive recreational activities.

Under Elizabeth England was growing richer. Games and sports flourished at this time. This was the age of the Renaissance gentleman, who was knowledgeable, partook in the appropriate physical activities, and was appreciative of all art forms.

The mass of the population also enjoyed their traditional pastimes. Activities like mob football continued to develop, allowing for conjugal and territorial conflicts to be sorted out in an enjoyable manner. They were often disorderly and violent, allowing energies to be vented. Many activities were still regional, were played with a few simple rules (or none at all) and were passed down to future generations by word of mouth.

The baiting and killing of animals was also a great treat. People lived in harsh conditions, and held different attitudes about the treatment of animals from modern values. Activities like cock fighting, bull baiting, bull running were all popular. They originated in rural areas but were also enjoyed in the towns; there is an account of bull running in London as late as 1816. Again however, there were distinct social class divisions in physical activities.

Fig. 17.4 STAGHUNTING WAS A POPULAR PASTIME DURING THE SIXTEENTH AND SEVENTEENTH CENTURIES

The Stuarts   After the death of Elizabeth I, James VI of Scotland (the son of Mary Queen of Scots) became James I of England. He had been brought up a Protestant, and in 1617, issued a declaration known as the 'Book of Sports' which encouraged the notion of traditional pastimes, so long as they did not interfere with church attendance.

Following the civil war and execution of Charles I (James I's son) in 1646, Oliver Cromwell was made protector of Britain. He was intent on establishing Parliamentary rule allied with a Puritan lifestyle. Puritanism particularly objected to:

- practising sport on a Sunday
- inflicting cruelty on animals
- the idleness, drinking and profanity generally associated with sport and the public houses.

The effect of the Puritans on the development of sport was to be significant. They believed that people should concentrate on working hard and praying for salvation, and were opposed to recreational activities which they considered as sinful and a waste of time. As many of the traditional activities took place after church services on a Sunday, and many derived from pagan traditions, they came under fierce attack from the Puritans.

Cromwell failed to unite all the different factions, and Charles II returned as monarch in 1660. This period was known as the Restoration. Charles II was in favour of many sports. His Court enjoyed a lifestyle of ease, affluence and leisure; they occupied themselves lavishly on sporting pursuits, and there was an immediate revival of the 'courtly mould'. The Restoration helped to restore many of the previously banned popular activities, but never again to their past glories. The Cotswold Olympian games were revived by Robert Dover, who was both a supporter of the athleticism of the gentry but also longed for a return to 'merrie England', where all social classes had enjoyed recreations together. This was an annual sports event which was held with activities for the gentry and the peasantry. However, the influence of Puritan rule continued to be felt, and many recreational pursuits were slow to revive.

The Hanoverian era (1714–1790)

The Industrial Revolution began in England in the middle of the 1700s and developed over a hundred years. It signified a dramatic movement of people from rural areas to the towns. Farming had become less important as small farms had been taken over by large landowners as a result of the enclosure system. The efficiency of the urban factories also put many people employed in the cottage industry out of work. Factory work required unskilled workers, who worked long hours in cramped, dirty conditions six days a week; young children were often employed in difficult and dangerous conditions.

Moving from rural areas to the new towns and cities had an enormous impact on people's lifestyles, not least on their recreational pursuits.

- Their previous games were increasingly difficult to accommodate, for example, mob football.
- Space was at a premium and so were facilities, so there was to be a shift in emphasis from a participation base to a more spectator based pursuits.
- The economic conditions of people had changed, and their long working hours also curbed their opportunities for recreation.

Some activities such as cricket, racing, rowing and pugilism (forerunner to boxing) had already begun their first phases of organisation. Rules developed in activities which began to occur more frequently, where the upper classes had control and when the moral climate within society began to change. Sports clubs and governing bodies developed to meet the recreation needs of 'Old Boys' who had left their public school and university and wanted to continue participating in sport. Evidence for this:

- the publication of the Racing Calendar from 1727
- the formation of the Jockey Club in 1752
- the rules for cricket, which were first drawn up in 1727.

In the eighteenth century, the Methodists continued the Puritan work ethic; they strengthened the attack on popular sports, believing that sport and drinking on a Sunday would lead to an after-life in hell. The violence associated with many of the pastimes, like wrestling, football and animal sports was believed to be the cause of social unrest; employees would use them as an excuse to miss work, at a time when eighteenth century employers required a more disciplined workforce in the mills.

Victorian Britain

Victoria became Queen in 1837. Her reign was a period of dramatic social change, which is reflected in the development of games and sport during the nineteenth century.

The working class

Under Queen Victoria's reign, social reformers campaigned for improvements in the physical and mental health of workers in society.

Parliament passed many laws and reforms to address the problems of women and children being employed in factories under terrible conditions and for long working hours, eg, the Reform and Factory Act 1832, the Ten Hours Act 1847 and the Factory Act 1878. The custom of a half-day Saturday began early in her reign, followed by the movement for early closing for shop workers on Wednesdays.

Factory owners created factory sports facilities and sponsored work teams. The development of the railways enabled them to send their workers on recreational trips, such as to the seaside. Employers hoped to gain the goodwill of their workers, increase morale and encourage the moral benefits of participating in team games.

From the 1870s onwards, there was a move to encourage a healthy, moral and orderly workforce, illustrated by the provision of parks, museums, libraries and public baths. Sport developed into an important part of working life. The Municipal Reform Act 1835 led to the building of parks in the towns and cities; the general public were encouraged to use these parks for recreational use after 1870. The reasons for providing parks were:

- to improve the health of the population
- to discourage crime on the streets
- as part of the Temperance movement, to wean people away from the evils of alcohol and gambling
- to instil morality in workers by following the rules of rational, organised sport
- to demonstrate a sense of social justice.

The skilled workforce gradually shifted their attentions and interests away from the traditional popular sports, taking up pastimes such as reading and quieter exercise in the park:

The decline of traditional sports, especially those which involved fighting, was not simply a question of pressure from well-organised groups of evangelicals and businessmen; in addition to the agitation from abolitionists there was evidence of a gradual shift in public taste, especially amongst the literate and more highly skilled elite of working people themselves.   *(R. Holt).*

By 1900, working people were heavily involved in sporting activity. There was a continuity between the traditional and modern sports; bowls, darts, billiards, fishing, pigeon racing and dog racing provided sporting entertainment.

Sport for the upper classes

The upper classes were wealthy and powerful, possessed vast tracts of property and dominated Parliament well into the nineteenth century. They enjoyed a life of leisure, and were waited on by their army of servants. The aristocracy took part in local sports and affairs, usually in the form of patronage of prize fights (forerunner to boxing) and pedestrianism (road walking). A **patron** is a person who sponsors any kind of artist of athlete from their own private funds. Patronage tends to occur amongst a privileged class within a hierarchical society. Wealthy aristocrats who wanted to be associated with new styles and trends, would sometimes spend large amounts of money on sporting events and particular athletes. It was an age where some aristocrats could lead and others would follow. Examples are:

- the Duke of Cumberland's association with racing and prize fighting
- Lord Orford and coursing
- the Earl of Derby and cock fighting, and the hunt.

A group of patrons would join together and form an association, eg, the Pugilistic Club, which would then organise the sport. When patrons withdrew their funds, preferring to sponsor different, perhaps more elite, sports, the effect was similar to modern day commercial sponsors pulling out of sports events; it usually led to a

Fig. 17.5   PRIZE FIGHTING, *c.*1840

decline in the activity. With regard to animal sports, on the one hand they supported the ban on cock fighting, while maintaining their own passion for fox hunting; another example of the powerful safeguarding their own interests?

The French Revolution had shown the possible results of a breakdown in relations between the aristocracy and the ordinary people. The English gentry were not now so confident of the complete acceptance of the respect shown them by the lower classes.

The new rich (or nouveau riche) who emerged from the Industrial Revolution, became a strong 'middle class' section of society. They wished to emulate the upper classes by buying old estates, educating their children in the established public schools, and establishing their own recreations which would separate them from the working classes. They also brought Christian morality to their recreation.

Inns and pubs

The inn had always been a social rural meeting place, and was used as a stopping place for the gentry on long journeys. A tradition of games developed, which was encouraged by the inn-keepers to increase their business; examples are fives, rackets, boxing, coursing, quoits. Many of the new sports clubs met in pubs, and they formed mutually beneficial partnerships:

- The village cricket teams would often use the field next to the pub.
- The hunt would have their stirrup cup at the pub followed by dinner.
- Liquor tents would be provided by publicans at sporting events.
- Bowling greens and boxing rings were built on to pubs, and pubs often organised a football team.

Those associated with sports were often regulars at the inns, so it was in the interests of the publican to encourage sport.

The English alehouse had to adapt to the new urban recreational needs. The pub became a focal point for workers trying to maintain a sense of identity, which was being eradicated in the new urban culture. As early as 1879, there were strings of clubs in Blackburn which were the culmination of the formalising of street corner teams. Boxing took over from the previous animal baiting sports of cock fighting and ratting.

Religion

The Victorian era was a climate of suppressing vice and encouraging religion and virtue. Non-conformism and the Protestant ethic became more firmly entrenched. Sports became less brutal, gambling was driven underground and there was a decline in blood sports.

Muscular Christianity

Muscular Christianity was an evangelical movement, and Charles Kingsley was one of its most influential exponents. Kingsley helped to combine the Christian and the chivalric ideal of manliness. It was the return of the Platonic concept, the 'whole man'. It improved one's ability to be gentle and courteous, brave and enterprising, reverent and truthful, selfless and devoted.

Kingsley believed healthy bodies were needed alongside healthy minds. Neglect of health was as lazy as a neglected mind. He also led the hygienic movement which was to have a deep effect on the working conditions of the poor.

There was little or no support for sport for its own sake at this time; sport should increase physical health and military valour, and create Christian soldiers. It was a fusion of **physical** with **moral** training.

Evangelical developments were directly linked with two philosophies – the Muscular Christians were promoting what the non-conformists were sceptical of:

1 Muscular Christians regarded cricket, boating and football as positive recreation.
2 The Church was attempting to attract workers from the pubs by forming alternative social clubs, such as Hand in Hand clubs.

Eventually there was a strong link with the club development of working class sport, particularly football; eg,

- Barnsley: 1887, Rev Preedy appointed.
- QPR: 1881, Rev Young appointed.
- Aston Villa: 1874, a Wesleyan Chapel built.

In Birmingham approximately a quarter of football clubs were explicitly connected to religious organisations between 1870 and 1885.

The YMCA

The YMCA is a non-sectarian, non-political Christian lay movement. Its aims are to develop high standards of Christian character through group activities; improve the spiritual, social, recreational and physical life of young people. It began in London in 1844, led by George William, and initially concentrated on young men in the drapery and other trades. On the construction of the YMCA Gym at Liverpool in 1887, William claimed:

'The aim of the founders was not to furnish the public of Liverpool with increased facilities for athletic exercise, or intellectual development, important as these may be in themselves; but to multiply the number of Christ's true followers among the young men of our city, and to aid in strengthening their Christian character.'

'No sport on Sunday'

The proclamationists and muscular Christians were united by their desire to observe Sunday as a day of complete rest, without physical activity. This signified a slow development of working class sports, as workers were prevented from joining the elite sports, and parks were closed on Sundays. Wealthy people, who usually had private facilities, seemed to escape from the Sunday ban on sport; golf, tennis and croquet were regularly played on Sundays.

Alternative Sunday pastimes were encouraged by the muscular Christians, such as cycling, rambling and boating. The bicycle had revolutionised the English Sunday, and the clergy might with advantage arrange short services for cyclists passing through their parishes.

The Romantic Movement

The work of Romantic poets such as Wordsworth and Coleridge had a considerable influence on recreation in the countryside; their poems made the countryside attractive to town and city folk. The excursions began as exclusive pastimes, as time and money were required. Rambling was regarded as recreational, while mountaineering was taken more seriously, with the Alps being a favourite location.

Ramblers tended to be drawn from the liberal, educated professions, who approached the activity with educational aims: an appreciation of the topography and local knowledge, and an aesthetic appreciation of natural beauty. Excursion tickets on the rail networks later helped the lower social classes participate.

The transport revolution

The roads and canal systems in Britain were vastly improved during the eighteenth centuries. People, ideas, services and goods were mobile and could be transported around the country. Areas which had hardly been influenced by the outside world, were now open to change. In terms of sport, inter-town fixtures could be held and spectators could travel to watch the spectacles. This tendency was to be transformed in the nineteenth century with the advent of the railways.

- Increased wealth and mobility enabled the sports of hare, stag and fox hunting to be more easily accessible to the middle classes. Animals could be transported with relative ease and comfort, and competitions changed from being on a local club level, to national competitions between England, Ireland and Scotland.
- Ramblers, cyclists and mountaineers could access the countryside and more isolated areas.
- Fishing was revolutionised. In 1867 a book titled *The Rail and the Rod* was published; a guide to angling spots which could be reached within a 30 mile radius of London.

The major spectator sports of racing, cricket and football became national sports. Special excursion trains would carry spectators. William Clarke of Nottingham formed the first All England Cricket XI and transported them about the country, playing games against a variety of sides. The railways enabled them to play 30 or more matches a season, and allowed a high level cricket to be enjoyed by those who would otherwise have been unable to experience such an event.

The game of soccer flourished, particularly in the newly industrial counties of Lancashire and Yorkshire. The teams and supporters travelled by rail. A team started by the Lancashire and Yorkshire Railway became Manchester United Football Club.

National sporting events then developed into international events, and foreign competition improved standards further. The re-birth of the Olympic Games in 1896 was only made possible by rail travel.

 **ACTIVITY 1**

Using a variety of sports, explain how the communications by water, road and rail influenced the development of different sports.

- **Consider the importance of rivers for sports and developments of towns.**
- **Consider the development of roads to the present day.**
- **Consider the railway for transport and animals, and for bridging the link between rural and urban areas.**

The British Empire

In the nineteenth century, British imperialists believed they had a duty to spread their forms of government, religion, and culture to those nations they considered less advanced or civilised. Some of the British colonies benefited by the growth of an infra-structure of roads, schools and hospitals, but the imposition of colonial rule permanently altered the cultures and traditions of the colonised countries.

The influence of the British Empire was felt across the world. Western culture (including sport and recreation) was spread via numerous groups of people – soldiers, administrators, missionaries, young men on the Grand Tour, engineers and businessmen. The public school ethos which viewed sport as a character-building vehicle was imposed on the colonies. British subjects imported and exported sports, usually modifying them to suit their own needs:

- Croquet came to England from Ireland, and was successfully transported to India.
- Polo was enjoyed by British soldiers in India, with the first polo match being played in England in 1871.
- Shooting was an experience which most of the gentry participated in and their interest was fired up with the prospect of big game shooting in Africa, where they could collect and transport home their enormous trophies.
- Thoroughbred horses were exported to most of Britain's colonies, and with them the English style of racing.
- Football did not spread so easily within the Empire, perhaps because the colonial administrative staff preferred other activities.

Professionalism and amateurism

The concept of amateurism was thought to reflect the Ancient Olympian spirit, placing the ideals of fair play and team spirit high above any material objectives. In the 1850s Dr Penny Brookes founded the Much Wenlock Olympic Games and formed a National Olympic Association. He had a pure sense of amateurism, and encouraged the citizens of Much Wenlock to delight in the challenge of sport with no thought for a reward. The first Games were held in 1850, and included events such as football, cricket, quoits, a blindfold wheelbarrow race, and chasing a pig through the town. It had all the trappings of a rustic festival, and perhaps reinvented the Cotswold Games first started in 1612 in Chipping Camden. By 1870 the events included track and field athletics, such as the pentathlon and tilting at the ring (a version of the jousting tournament).

The public school influence established its own definition of amateurism, which superseded the Much Wenlock version. Much of the public school version of athleticism was Olympian in outlook: combining physical endeavour with moral integrity, where the struggle was fought for the honour of the house or school. Baron Pierre de Coubertin visited both Much Wenlock and Rugby School in 1890, in the years preceding the foundation of the modern Olympic Games. He looked forward to a time when anyone would be able to participate, regardless of social standing or race.

In England there were two distinct phases of amateurism:

1 Originally, amateurs were gentlemen of the middle and upper classes who played sports in the spirit of fair competition.
2 There was a shift in definition of an amateur, from a straightforward social distinction, to a monetary one. Originally there had been no problems perceived by earning money from amateur sport.

Fair play was the bedrock upon which amateurism was based. It was important to adhere to the rules of the game, but it was expected that a player would discipline himself rather than wait for a referee's decision. A situation was recorded that the

Corinthian Casuals, founded in 1882, would withdraw their goalkeeper on the awarding of a penalty to the opposing side, on the principle that they should accept the consequences of a foul.

There were advantages and disadvantages to the amateur code. It promoted restraint in victory and graciousness in defeat; the acceptance of rules and consequent respect for decisions. However, it excluded the working classes which was a moral argument for its abolition. In 1894 the Rugby Football Union and the Northern Union split due to the refusal of the authorities to allow northern players to have enough leisure time to compete on the same basis as players in the south. Employers could not accept 'broken time payments' (compensation for loss of wages), and by so doing, excluded manual workers who needed time to train and travel for sport. Similar conflicts were felt in rowing and cricket.

Trace the pattern of change in physical activities so far. Give reasons to account for the change.

The public schools

The sons of the gentry were educated at large, prestigious, fee-paying boarding schools. Separate schools for daughters were founded much later, and catered for very different needs; boys' schools were academic while girls' schools concentrated on social accomplishments like sewing and managing a household.

There were originally nine elite institutions, which were called 'Barbarian' schools as they maintained the gentry tradition: Eton, Harrow, Rugby, Shrewsbury, Charterhouse, Westminster, Winchester, St Paul's and Merchant Taylor's.

The emergence of the middle classes has already been mentioned as a major change in the social structure. When they acquired the necessary funds for their sons to attend these prestigious schools, they were unfairly rejected as the schools wished to remain exclusive, and so began to build their own proprietary colleges which were based on the elite schools. Examples of these 'Philistine' schools are Cheltenham College, Marlborough and Clifton.

The development of sport in the public schools radically changed previous concepts of sport. The boys brought to their schools their experiences of games like cricket and mob football and country pursuits such as fishing and coursing. Before the formalisation of team games, the boys would leave the school grounds, and participate in rowdy behaviour; this often involved poaching, fighting and

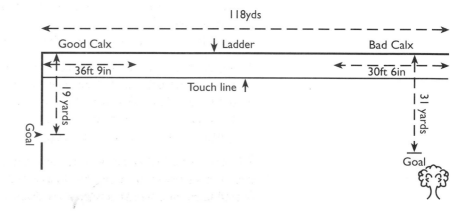

Fig. 17.6   THE ETON WALL GAME

trespassing, drinking alcohol and generally bringing the school's reputation into disrepute, causing conflict with local landowners and gamekeepers.

However, during this stage, they had began the process of organising their own activities and devising new ways of playing; these were often associated with individual architectural features of the different schools, eg, cloisters for fives, and the Eton wall game. This is an old form of football, and survives to this day. It developed from the unique architectural feature of a long red brick wall which separates the school playing fields from the Slough road. Ten players per side work the small ball along a narrow strip, 4–5 yards wide and 118 yards long. The players are assigned their playing position and specialised role according to their physique. The wall was built in 1717, but the game became popular in the nineteenth century.

Can you think of reasons why a game peculiar to this school should continue to be played?

Thomas Arnold, the head of Rugby School encouraged the boys to develop activities which could be played on the school grounds and which would also highlight the more moral features of teamwork, such as self discipline, loyalty, courage; character-building qualities suitable for the prospective leaders of society.

The government was forced to intervene in public school education in 1861, when the Clarendon Commission was set up to 'inquire into the revenues and management of certain colleges and schools and the studies pursued and the instruction given there'. When the Clarendon Report was published in 1864, it strengthened the position of the headmasters by stressing the positive, educational features of team games as agents of training character. It did not place too much emphasis on skilled performance, but stressed moral qualities such as group loyalty. It also highlighted sports which were less useful, including hare and hounds, and gymnastics – both activities which focused on individual qualities. However, the report also revealed the extent to which games were becoming central to the school lives of the boys.

The Taunton Commission published in 1868 which examined other schools, also regarded gymnastics as inferior and less lively than the indigenous English games, which they recognised as having educational value. The headmasters rallied together at a conference in 1869 under the leadership of Edward Thring (see page 275), and agreed that sport should encourage conformity in the boys' lives.

The Victorian public schools can be described as total institutions:

- The schools had institutional frameworks.
- The boys took part in regulated activities.
- The boys behaved in a way that was different to their role outside the school; eg, the fagging system placed younger boys in a subservient role to older boys. These were the sons of the gentry and would not normally be subservient to anyone.
- The boys were admitted and released on a termly basis.
- They had to assimilate the institutionalised values and rules in order to conform.

Can you think of any other social institutions which could match this type of analysis?

Cricket was already a fairly well established game in society and as such was considered suitable for the boys; mob football, on the other hand, was played by the lower classes in society and was not so acceptable, until the boys devised a more organised format. The game of rugby supposedly began at Rugby School, when William Webb Ellis picked up the ball during a game of football and ran with it.

The boys were in charge of organising the games, and senior bands of boys (normally called prefects) would be in control, reflecting the fagging system. Games committees were formed, eg, the Harrow Philathletic Club. The masters actively discouraged some activities (poaching and gambling) while others were allowed to exist on an informal recreational basis among the boys (fives and fighting). They actively encouraged the boys to organise team games.

Initially, inter-school fixtures were not feasible as no two schools had the same rules. However, by the mid nineteenth century, the headmaster and staff started to organise sports. Games were seen as a medium for achieving educational aims with a moral social sense; they could also help combat idleness and as such were a form of social control. Boys who excelled in games were admired by the other pupils.

Athleticism

The cult of athleticism stressed the physical and social benefits of sports:

- The physical benefits were seen to counteract the effects of sedentary lifestyles, and sport was viewed as therapeutic, invigorating and cathartic. It was also seen as a break from work.
- Sport would take place within a competitive situation which would help the boys learn how to cope with winning and losing all in a dignified manner. It helped to develop leadership qualities, and the Captain was a high status office to hold.

The House system was instrumental to the competitive sport events, in which the manner of the performance was considered more important than the result.

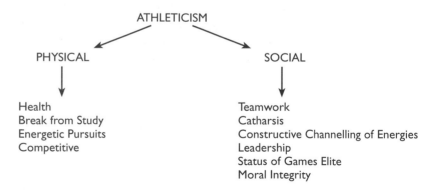

Fig. 17.7   THE BENEFITS OF ATHLETICISM

Consider the following areas and compare the situation in a state school today with a public school in the nineteenth century:

- **Physical education curriculum and the latest Government proposals**
- **Physical education exams**
- **Student lifestyles (part time work, increase in leisure activities, etc).**

There were also opponents of this emphasis on athleticism, with many people believing it was becoming more important than the boys' studies, and could lead to a regimentation of boys' thoughts and behaviour with a destruction of individuality.

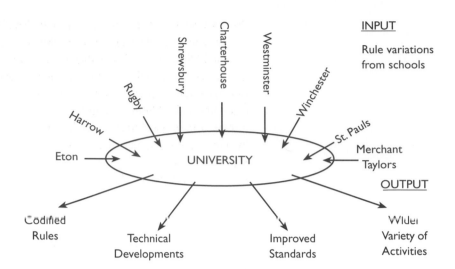

Fig. 17.8   THE INPUT AND OUTPUT OF
THE UNIVERSITIES

Old boys who returned as teacher after university were often employed for their games prowess as much as for their intellectual teaching contribution. They brought to the schools the new sports they had learnt at university, the fully codified versions of the games and also the philosophy to excel at their sport.

The public schools instituted the idea of the Sports Day, which operated as a public relations exercise to the old boys, parents and governors of the school. The funds of the school could benefit from generous donations and valuable publicity could be gained.

'The public schools were the first centres of excellence for sport and resembled modern day sports schools.' Discuss.

Thomas Arnold

Thomas Arnold became headmaster of Rugby School in 1828 where he directed a crusade against personal sin, eg, bullying, lying, swearing, cheating, running wild. They were to remain on the school grounds, he forbade shooting and beagling as

Fig. 17.9   THE EARLY DAYS OF RUGBY

these activities encouraged poaching, and fights should only occur within his presence and supervised by the prefects who enforced his authority.

Arnold is known for his contribution to Muscular Christianity, but he valued games only for what they could contribute towards the social control of the boys. The development of athleticism followed the cooperation of the boys in maintaining discipline and achieving Arnold's reforms.

Tom Brown's Schooldays by Thomas Hughes was published in 1860 and highlighted the Victorian ideal towards the physical side of the Christian gentleman. Hughes expanded the manliness ideals of Charles Kingsley – moral manliness became extrovert masculinity.

Edward Thring of Uppingham

Uppingham rose from being an obscure grammar school to a famous public school in the nineteenth century under its headmaster, Edward Thring. From the start he encouraged the playing of games:

- He played fives and football with the boys.
- The school day began early and finished at midday to accommodate games.
- He was the first to open a gymnasium in 1859 and incorporated swimming and athletics as part of the physical education programme.

"Huzza, there's going to be a fight between Slogger Williams and Tom Brown!"

The news ran like wildfire about, and many boys who were on their way to tea at their several houses turned back, and sought the back of the chapel, where the fights come off.

"Just run and tell East to come and back me," said Tom to a small School-house boy, who was off like a rocket to Harrowell's, just stopping for a moment to poke his head into the School-house hall, where the lower boys were already at tea, and sing out, "Fight! Tom Brown and Slogger Williams."

In another minute East and Martin tear through the quadrangle, carrying a sponge, and arrive at the scene of action just as the combatants are beginning to strip.

Tom felt he had got his work cut out for him, as he stripped off his jacket, waistcoat, and braces. East tied his handkerchief round his waist, and rolled up his shirt-sleeves for him: "Now, old boy, don't you open your mouth to say a word, or try to help yourself a bit,—we'll do all that; you keep all your breath and strength for the Slogger." Martin meanwhile folded the clothes, and put them under the chapel rails; and now Tom, with East to handle him, and Martin to give him a knee, steps out on the turf, and is ready for all that may come: and here is the Slogger too, all stripped, and thirsting for the fray.

It doesn't look a fair match at first glance: Williams is nearly two inches taller, and probably a long year older than his opponent, and he is very strongly made about the arms and shoulders,—"peels well," as the little knot of big fifth-form boys, the amateurs, say; who stand outside the ring of little boys, looking complacently on, but taking no active part in the proceedings. But down below he is not so good by any means; no spring from the loins, and feeblish, not to say shipwrecky about the knees. Tom, on the contrary, though not half so strong in the arms, is good all over, straight, hard, and springy, from neck to ankle, better perhaps in his legs than anywhere. Besides, you can see by the clear white of his eye, and fresh bright look of his skin, that he is in tip-top training, able to do all he knows; while the Slogger looks rather sodden, as if he didn't take much exercise and ate too much tuck. The time-keeper is chosen, a large ring made, and the two stand up opposite one another for a moment, giving us time just to make our little observations. The combatants, however, sit there quietly, tended by their seconds, while their adherents wrangle in the middle. East can't help shouting challenges to two or three of the other side, though he never leaves Tom for a moment, and plies the sponges as fast as ever.

Fig. 17.10   Extract from *Tom Brown's Schooldays*

Other public schools tended to ignore Thring's innovations and continued with their diet of games. Thring did not place so much importance on the games elite, and believed that non-athletic boys could enjoy games. Thring had attended Eton as a boy which is where he developed his love for physical activity; he truly promoted sports for the love of it.

Read the extract from *Tom Brown's Schooldays*, and consider the following questions:

1 **Comment on the level of technical development of the physical activity described.**
2 **Explain the different social relationships being identified.**
3 **Discuss the values being reinforced as part of a character-building process.**

Female education

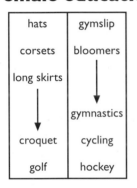

hats	gymslip
corsets	bloomers
long skirts	
	gymnastics
croquet	cycling
golf	hockey

Fig. 17.11 As sport for women developed, so did their clothing

In the late 1800s the education of girls was very poor. It was pretentious and costly, with an emphasis on accomplishments for society rather than for the intellectual development of the girls. Music and dancing counted as the highest priorities, with writing and arithmetic being the lowest. 'Medical' reasons to limit women's sports participation were legitimised; it was believed that women who participated in strenuous physical activity would become muscle bound, which would be detrimental to childbearing. As physical activity and educational examinations incorporated a degree of competitiveness, this was not conducive to the social image of how women should behave.

In the Victorian era, constructive education for women was regarded as a threat to the norms for behaviour for that society. As the struggle for women's rights developed, their increased wealth in the nineteenth century enabled women even greater leisure time. The pioneers of female education had to overcome mountains of prejudice. These were hard-headed, common sense groups of middle class women, stirred by a sense of women's duties rather than their rights. Two of these pioneers were Frances Mary Buss and Dorothea Beale. The former founded the North London Collegiate School and Camden School for Girls, while the latter transformed the derelict Cheltenham Ladies College and turned it into a serious educational establishment for the upper and middle classes. They started the process of changing the Victorian ideals, and public day schools for girls were modelled on these schools.

Miss Beale wanted to teach the rudiments of science but had to call it 'physical geography' to escape condemnation. The introduction of physical education caused the most controversy. At this time girls were not supposed to exercise at all. Allowing girls to run and jump, and the removing of corsets was as culturally radical as the unbinding of Japanese women's feet.

The Schools Inquiry Commission 1868 was important for women's education, suggesting that girls' foundation schools would soon become a reality. By 1881, the universities recognised that girls had fulfilled the degree requirements of boys. By 1898, following the Endowed Schools Act, there were 80 endowed girls schools and by 1900 there were 36 girls' public day trust schools. The 1918 Act gave the same educational advantages as boys.

The improvement in general education was paralleled by the development of physical education for girls. There was a need for specialist physical education teacher training colleges; the first was established by Miss Bergman in 1885 at Broadhurst Gardens, using the Hampstead Gymnasium. She later moved to Dartford Heath in 1895, where physical education on a full-time specialist basis began. The object of the College was to teach gymnastics and swimming in girls' schools, to conduct outdoor games and to spread the knowledge of physiology and hygiene. Other training colleges soon followed:

- Anstey College, 1899.
- Chelsea College, 1898.
- I.M. Marsh College, 1899.

Miss Bergman was appointed Lady Superintendent of Physical Education in 1881 on the London School Board. The main emphasis came from Swedish Gymnastics with its focus on health rather than educational values. Miss Bergman modelled female education on that of the boys and was keen to implement some of the games available in schools. She wrote in the 'Teacher's Encyclopaedia' that the principal games represented in the English girls schools were hockey, cricket, basketball and lacrosse. She also saw the benefit of tennis but felt her students were already reasonably proficient from their social backgrounds.

The Board of Education Syllabuses however paid scant attention to games, and of 11 publications issued between 1919 and 1927, only one was devoted to non-gymnastic activities. The games which were advocated were those where speed of eye, foot and hand combined with team play and cooperation.

Despite these restrictions, women athletes began to emerge in the last quarter of the nineteenth century, such as Lottie Dodd, Mary Outerbridge and Constance Applebee. They tended to shine in sports where they did not have to overcome heavy objects and where spatial barriers and rules prevent bodily contact with the opponent.

Thus, physical activities for girls developed much later than those for boys, and its gradual development was linked to sociological factors and the development of female education in general. When prejudicial attitudes began to change, girls began to participate in activities such as tennis, hockey, gymnastics and cricket. They then developed their activities along similar lines to the boys; they established clubs and entered competitions. There was a concentration on female sports developing a separately to boys, partly due to the single sex developments in schools, but social games like tennis allowed a mixing of the sexes.

State education

Prior to 1870, the education of the masses had been the responsibility of the parish, and was very inconsistent. The Forster Education Act 1870 was a great milestone in social welfare, as it created a state system of education. There was a developing initiative to build more schools and the Act was the result of some radical changes in social thinking by philanthropists and social reformers.

Ever since the first Board Schools were built in 1870, teachers in the poorest districts were faced with the extreme poverty of many of its pupils. As many as three to four million children were living below the poverty line.

There were two main principles of state education:

1 There shall be efficient schools everywhere throughout the United Kingdom.
2 There would be compulsory provision of such schools if and where needed, but not unless proved to be needed.

The existing British schools, foreign schools, under the Foreign Schools Society 1808 and national schools, under the National Schools Society 1811, would continue to provide the bulk of the nation's education, provided they were good enough. The main points of the Education Act were as follows:

- England and Wales divided into 2,500 school districts.
- The Churches were to decide if they needed to build new schools.
- Failing this, a School Board had to be elected by local people, to finance schools from the rates.
- The children would pay a small fee, with an increase in government grants. The very poor could receive free education.
- The school age was not less than five years but no more than thirteen years. In London they were exempt at age 10 if they passed grade V and were needed to work for the family income.

Mundella's Education Act of 1880 made education compulsory for all children between the ages of five and ten, without exception. In 1893 the compulsory school leaving age was raised to eleven and in 1899 to twelve years.

1 **What faults could you find with the Education Act 1870?**
2 **What effect do you think the Education Acts had on poor children, teachers and parents?**
3 **Explain why there would have been a problem of non-payment of school fees.**

Experiences of children at state schools were very different from those of their gentry counterparts. Small buildings with little space and no recreational facilities allied with a philosophy which denied any recreational rights to the working class, and placed its own constraints on the physical activities available to the state school system.

Gymnastics formed the bedrock of early state school physical exercise. Foreign influences, in the form of Swedish and German gymnastics, combined with the English style under Archibald Maclaren. Guts Muths from Germany wrote the first text which gained significant recognition, called *Gymnastik fur die Jugend* in 1793. This was to influence Per Henrik Ling in Sweden and together they can be called the 'fathers of modern gymnastics'. The Schools Boards tended to favour the Swedish system for its free flowing, free standing exercises possibly due to the employment of Swedish inspectors; whilst the strength based German gymnastics which utilised apparatus developed within the club structure.

The lack of fitness and discipline and the poor general health of the working classes had been noted in the Boer War (1899–1902) and blamed for the heavy loss of life suffered. Swedish gymnastics also came under threat as not being effective enough in improving the fitness of the working classes sufficiently for the hardships of war.

A policy of drill and physical training were initiated but had little recreational value. In 1902 the model course was instituted by Colonel Fox of the War Office. The main aim of the course was to

- improve the fitness of the working classes for military preparation
- increase their familiarity with combat and weapons
- improve discipline and obedience amongst the working classes.

Drill was characterised by commands issued by the teacher or NCOs (non commissioned officers) to the children who would be standing in uniform military style rows and obeying the commands in unison. Large numbers could be catered for in a small space, and as the movements were free-standing and required no apparatus, they were cheap. After 1873 boys and girls received drill.

The problems with this approach were that they were essentially adult exercises for children. They did not take children's needs and physical and mental development into account. There was no educative content and individualism was submerged within a group response. The use of NCOs also reduced the status of the subject as it did not use qualified teachers.

1 What qualities were required by the teacher and the pupils in military drill?
2 How do the pupil requirements compare with those being generated through team games within the public school system?

Due to the problems and concerns over the model course, the Board of Education established a syllabus of physical training in 1904, 1909, 1919, 1927 and 1933. They stressed the physical and educative effect of sport:

1 The physical content would have been very much influenced by their primary concern for the medical and physiological base from which they approached the subject. As such the therapeutic effect, the correction of posture faults, and exercises to improve the circulatory systems would have been foremost in their aims.
2 The educational aims would try to develop alertness and decision making.

The 1919 Syllabus took into consideration the loss of life of the First World War, and the flu epidemic which hit the country shortly afterwards. Sir George Newman had recognised the beneficial effects of recreational activities in helping to rehabilitate injured soldiers. By 1933 there was more freedom of movement and a more decentralised lesson. This was a recognition of the increasing rights of the working classes and the educational value of group work.

Consider the 1904 and the 1933 syllabuses in fig 17.12 and trace the similarities and differences.

Post-Second World War developments

After the war there was an extensive rebuilding programme and facilities were more sophisticated than before. The therapeutic effect of recreational activities was again valued. The commando training during the war had developed the use of obstacle training, and this was how the first apparatus began to appear in schools – scramble nets, rope ladders, mats and frames, hoops, wooden tables and benches.

The 'movement' approach began in physical education lessons; children were required to use their initiative and learn by discovery. This also demanded new teaching methods and there was the development of a more heuristic style which placed the teacher in the role of *guiding* the children rather than being purely *instructional*.

The influence of Isadora Duncan and Laban with their form of dance using the body as an expressive medium, was taken up by women teachers. Modern Educational Dance 1948 gave 16 basic movement themes and rudiments of free dance technique and space orientation. The word 'Movement' came to reflect the 1940s and 1950s as 'posture' had reflected the 1930s.

The Butler Education Act 1944 planned to reform education in Britain. It was a major social reform; it aimed to remove special privileges and ensure equality of opportunity for all. Its main provision were as follows:

- There were to be 146 local education authorities to replace the previous 300. They were required to provide recreational facilities to specific sizes.
- The school leaving age was to be raised to 15 from 1947.
- All education in state maintained grammar schools was to be free. To attend grammar schools children now needed to pass the eleven plus exam, rather than pay.
- All children would leave the elementary school at 11 and move to a secondary school – either grammar or secondary modern. This was a complete separation of the primary from secondary education, and meant that new schools had to be built.
- More mature forms of physical education were required to suit the higher ages of the children. The HMI (Her Majesty's Inspectorate) for PE now reported to the Chief Inspector, not the Chief Medical Officer.
- The 1944 McNair Report gave PE teachers the same status as other teachers.

I PLAY RUNNING OR MARCHING	Play or Running about. The children should, for a minute or two, be allowed to move about as they please.
II PRELIMINARY POSITIONS AND MOVEMENTS	Attention. Standing at Ease. Hips Firm. Feet Close. Neck Rest. Feet Astride. Foot Outward Place. Foot Forward Place. Stepping Sideways. Heels Raising. Right Turn and Right Half Turn. Left Turn and Left Half Turn.
III ARM FLEXIONS AND EXTENSIONS	Arms Downward Stretching. Arms Forward Stretching. Arms Sideways Stretching. Arms Upward Stretching.
IV BALANCE EXERCISES	Heels Raising. Knees Bending and Stretching. Preparation for Jumping. Heels Raising (Neck Rest). Heels Raising (Astride, Hips Firm). Heels Raising (Astride, Neck Rest). Head Turning in Knees Bend Position. Knees Bending and Stretching (Astride). Leg Sideways Raising with Arms Sideways Raising. Knee Raising.
V SHOULDER EXERCISES AND LUNGES	Arms Forward Raising. Arms Sideways Raising. Hands Turning. Arms Flinging. Arms Forward and Upward Raising. Arms Sideways and Upward Raising.
VI TRUNK FORWARD AND BACKWARD BENDING	Head Backward Bending. Trunk Forward Bending. Trunk Backward Bending. Trunk Forward Bending (Astride). Trunk Backward Bending (Astride).
VII TRUNK TURNING AND SIDEWAYS BENDING	Head Turning. Trunk Turning. Trunk Turning (Astride, Neck Rest). Trunk Turning (Feet Close, Neck Rest). Trunk Sideways Bending. Trunk Sideways Bending (Feet Close, Hips Firm). Trunk Sideways Bending (Feet Close, Neck Rest).
VIII MARCHING	Marking Time (From the Halt). Turnings while Marking Time. Quick March. Marking Time (From the March). Changing Direction.
IX JUMPING	Preparation for Jumping. *Note* Work from this Column should be omitted until above exercise has been taught under IV.
X BREATHING EXERCISES	Breathing Exercises without Arm Movements. With Deep Breathing, Arms Sideways Raising.

Note Exercises bracketed should be taken in succession.

(a)

PART ONE

I

Introductory Activity 1. Free running, at signal, children run to 'homes' in teams. (Four or more marked homes in corners of playground.) All race round, passing outside all the homes, back to places and skip in team rings.

2. Free running, at signal all jump as high as possible and continue running. Brisk walking, finishing in open files, marking time with high knee raising.

3. Aeroplanes. (Following the leaders in teams.)

Rhythmic Jump 1. Skip jump on the spot, three low, three high (continuously) *(Low, 2, 3, high, 2, 3, etc.)*

2. Astride jump. *Astride jumping—begin! I. 2. I. 2. etc. stop!*

3. Skip jump, four on the spot, four turning round about (8 counts) and repeat turning the opposite way (8 counts)

2

1. (Astride [Long sitting]) Trunk bending downward to grasp ankles. Unroll. *(With a jump, feet astride—place! [with straight legs—sit.!] Grasp the ankles—down! With unrolling, trunk upward—stretch! With a jump, feet together—place!*

2. (Astride [Astride long sitting]) Trunk bending downward to touch one foot with opposite hand.

3. (Feet close [Cross-legged sitting].) Head dropping forward and stretching upward. *(Feet—close!) Head forward—drop! Head upward—stretch!* (Crouch) Knee stretching and bending. ('Angry Cats') *(Crouch position—down!) Knees— stretch! bend! up! down! etc. stand—up!*

3

1. As small as possible, as tall as possible. [(Crook sitting, Back to wall) Single arm swinging forward-upward to touch wall.] [(Crook sitting) Drumming with the feet, loud and soft.]

2. Single arm circling at a wall. (Run and stand with side to wall, nearest hand supported against wall about shoulder height. Circling with free arm. Turn about and repeat.)

4

1. Free running like a wooden man. Finish in open files in chain grasp. (One foot forward, heel level with the other toe). Knee full bending and stretching with knees forward. (Several times. Move the back foot forward and repeat.) (Lean standing) Hug the knee. [(Crook lying) Hug the knees. (Lower the feet quietly.)]

2. Running in twos, change to skipping, finish in a double ring facing partner holding hands. Knees full bend. Knee springing. Hands on ground and jump up. *Knees full bend! Knee springing—begin! I, 2, I, 2, etc. Stop! Placing the bands on the ground, with a jump stand—up!*

3. Form a ring. Gallop step left and right, at signal, run and stand with side to wall, nearest hand supported against wall (the other arm sideways). Kick the hand. (Turn about, or run to opposite wall and repeat several times with each leg.)

5

1. Brisk walking anywhere, change to walking on heels or toes, at signal run to open files facing partners. (Feet-close, Arms forward, Fists touching.) Trunk turning with single elbow bending. (Elbow raised and pulled back. 'Drawing the bow.') *(Feet—close! With fists touching, arms forward—raise!)* With the right arm, draw the bow— pull! Let go! With the left arm—pull! Let go! etc. Arms—lower!

2. Race to a wall and back to centre line and join right hand across with partner. Tug of war with one hand.

3. (Informal lunge with hand support.) Head and trunk turning with arm raising to point upward. (Left (right) *foot forward with knee bent and left (right) hand on knee (informal lunge)—ready!) With arm raising to point upward, head and trunk to the right, (left)—turn! With arm lowering, forward—turn. (Repeat several times.) With a jump, feet change!*

6

Class Activity

1. Running, jumping over a series of low ropes. (In ranks of six or eight in stream.)

2. Frog jump anywhere.

3. Free running or skipping, tossing up a ball and catching it. (A ball each. Who can make the greatest number of catches without missing.)

Group Practices

1. Running or galloping with a skipping rope. (A rope each.)

2. Running Circle Catch, with a player in the centre, throwing, or bouncing and catching a ball.

3. Sideways jumping over a low rope, partner helping. (Partner astride rope, performer holding partner's hands does several preparatory skip jumps on the spot and then a high jump over the rope landing with knees bent and standing up again.)

4. In twos, crawling or crouch jump through a hoop, held by partner.

Game

Odd Man.

Free Touch with 6 or 7 'He's.' ('He's' carry a coloured braid or bean bag as distinguishing mark.).

Tom Tiddler.

7

Free walking, practising good position, lead into school.

(b)

Fig 17.12   (A) 1904 SYLLABUS FOR PHYSICAL EDUCATION (B) 1933 SYLLABUS FOR PHYSICAL EDUCATION — EXCERPT

Moving and Growing, and Planning the Programme

These two publications were issued by the Ministry of Education in 1952 and 1953 respectively. They replaced the old syllabuses and were to be implemented in primary schools. They combined the two influences of:

- obstacle training from the army
- movement training from centres of dance.

Running parallel to these changes were:

1. Circuit training (devised by G T Adamson and R E Morgan at the University of Leeds)
2. Weight training – progressive resistance exercises
3. Outward Bound Schools promoting adventurous activities to develop the personality within the natural environment in challenging conditions.

These publications developed as a result of changes in educational thinking which was to make learning stem from a more child-centred approach. The activities included agility, playground and more major game skills, dance and movement to music, national dances and swimming. The key words which separate them from earlier forms of physical activity in state schools are:

- exploratory
- creative
- individual
- fun.

 **ACTIVITY 11**

Trace the involvement of government in education from 1870 to the present day. Concentrate on political aspects like centralisation policies, the intended aims of education and the use made of physical activities. Consider also the social factors operating at each stage.

Summary

What elements of sport and physical education from the nineteenth century are still with us today?

There have been great social changes, which have affected the types and opportunities of sports participation available.

- a higher ratio of spectator based interest in sport as opposed to a participation base
- a dominance of male sports both in terms of participation and media coverage
- the Victorian concept of femininity has had far reaching effects – the feminine type of sports are given the most positive media coverage
- there is still a middle class dominance in positions of power in the sporting organisations
- continuing problems between the two concepts of amateurism and professionalism.

The use of the different terms used over the years (drill, physical training and then education) reflect the gradual development of certain ideas. Not only were there different activities but also a different relationship between the teacher and the class, with a changing concept of discipline. An account began to be taken of the childrens' emotional, mental and physical needs.

Physical Activities

chapter 18

T

he development of various physical activities within their overall social context should now make more sense. Always try and see the historical, political, economic, geographical, educational, and social and cultural aspects – as they will affect the pastimes and sports that we will study.

Popular	Rational
• occasional	• regular
• few, simple rules	• complex, written rules
• limited structure and organisation	• highly structured
• participation sport	• spectator sport
• physical force	• refined skills
• lower class development	• upper class development
• local	• regional/national
• limited equipment and facilities	• sophisticated equipment and facilities

MOB FOOTBALL REAL TENNIS

Fig. 18.1   DEFINITION OF POPULAR AND RATIONAL SPORTS

Contests inspired by military aspects

Rise in popularity:

• Such physical activities had an original utilitarian purpose, such as effective defence, fitness of armies, and survival. They were often developed into competitions for training which could also serve as entertainment, eg, gladiators in the arena.
• Some required only the physical body (boxing, wrestling), while others made use of equipment (archery, fencing, quintain, jousting)
• These sports reflected the level of technology of a particular era.
• They often had social class distinctions which reflected the culture of the particular era, eg, medieval, pre- and post industrial society.

They were often associated with concepts such as wagering, spectatorism, competition/training, professionalism, amateurism.

Decline in popularity:

These activities often declined in popularity when the original purpose was no longer necessary: this was often caused by an advancement in technology. When moral atmospheres changed within a society, the activities either became obsolete, remained or were revived in some adapted form through education, as sports and as pastimes. Sometimes they became governed by associations, formed by interested persons.

Quintain   The quintain was originally a tree or post and is associated with military activity – 'running at the quintain'. Roman soldiers would run at the quintain on foot, on horseback, on each other's backs and in boats. It was an activity enjoyed across the social classes, and continued into the seventeenth century, although it had merely become a ritual for festivals and wakes.

Water quintain was popular, and played frequently on the River Thames. The boats were either manned with rowers or allowed to drift with the current. The activity required skill, a careful and accurate aim, and a steady eye.

Tournament and jousting

Jousting was a medieval form of combat between horsemen armed with lances. There were occasional boat jousts (similar to quintain). The word 'tournament' comes from the French word 'tournoi' – the wheeling motion of the competitors as they turned and returned to enter the lists (large open space with ropes and railings). Generally two men would fight in a joust, but any number could fight in a tournament.

Early tournaments were very bloody – knights on foot could be trampled underfoot by other charges. The Church disapproved of tournaments, but no amount of papal decrees could decrease their popularity. They became important social events for the wealthy section of society, and provided military training for young knights.

The popularity of jousts and tournaments declined during the Tudor era, as the ethos of society changed. They became relics of the age of chivalry and courtly love.

Archery

There is evidence of bows and arrows being used over 50,000 years ago, and as such, archery claims the oldest ancestry of any sport actively pursued today. It was originally practised for hunting purposes, but became important for military training, and as recreation.

From the reigns of Henry I to Elizabeth I, archery practice was compulsory for men from youth to advanced middle age, for reasons of defence. The traditional longbow was made of yew, and the arrow was normally made of wood with a steel point and a reinforced string notch.

In the eighteenth century George IV encouraged the sport, and was patron of several societies of elite bowsmen. During the Victorian period, archery became an activity for the leisured classes, and many clubs were established. It was considered a suitable recreation for women due to the lack of strenuous exercise, and became a popular social event. In 1861, the Grand National Archery Society was established as an official governing body for archery in the United Kingdom.

Boxing

Boxing is an ancient sport: it was enjoyed in Ancient Egypt, Greece and Rome. Pugilism (pugus is the Latin word for fist) was introduced into the Olympic Games in 686 BC, in which boxers wore soft leather coverings on their hands and used primitive punching bags and head guards. The Romans used boxing for gladiatorial combat. They introduced a stud into the primitive boxing glove called a cestus, which led to the banning of boxing and its disappearance as a spectator sport.

Boxing was revived in England towards the end of the seventeenth century. The first organised bare knuckle fight was in 1681, as entertainment for the Duke of Albermarle. There were initially very few rules, and participants could even kick their opponents. However, boxing was one of the first sports to have a written code of rules and rudimentary kind of national championship run by a coterie of sporting aristocrats, the London Publicans and Patrons. James Figg opened an Academy of Boxing, and his pupils were skilled in numerous forms of self defence: boxing, wrestling, quarter staff, broadsword and cudgel. Jack Broughton is referred to as the 'father of boxing'. He opened an amphitheatre in Tottenham Court Road in 1740, and regulated the practice of prize fighting which remained in force for 100 years, and added respectability to the game:

1 wrestling above the waist only
2 no hitting below the belt
3 gloves used for sparring
4 you can't hit a man when he's down.

These formed the basis of the London Prize Ring Rules drawn up in 1838. The Marquis of Queensbury lent his name and patronage to new rules laid down at the end of the nineteenth century.

   Working class boxers often received patronage from the upper classes; they would become folk heroes, as their fights were reported in the newspapers. Boxing was popular at fairs, races and other public occasions. Famous venues include the Fives Court in St Martin's Lane in London. In the early 1900s arenas like Wonderland and Premierland were established in the East End of London, where boxing was actively promoted.

Wrestling

Wrestling is an individual combat activity; strength, skill and stamina combine to make it one of the most basic sports. Its origins are ancient, and are illustrated in wall paintings in ancient Greece, Egypt and China. There was a wrestling event in the Olympic Games in 704 BC, but an element of corruption crept in, and competitors were sometimes bribed to lose fights.

   The popularity of wrestling was revived in the nineteenth century, as part of the prize fights. Events took place on raised platforms with sloping sides – no ropes were used. The sport later became more safety conscious, with the introduction of weight categories, rules, training, preparation and the control of a referee. Wrestling was popular from the village green to the Royal Court; during the era of the music halls, it emerged as one of the most popular entertainments of the day.

Fig. 18.2   WRESTLERS FROM THE *QUEEN MARY PSALTER*, *C*.1810

Fencing

The dextrous use of a sword for attack or defence has a long history, and has its roots in the traditions of knightly chivalry. Today it is a sport practised increasingly throughout the world with three weapons: the foil (sporting purposes), the epée (infantry fighting), and the sabre (cavalry weapon).

   During the Middle Ages, a fencing style was developed by travellers who carried daggers in case of attack en route. A battle axe, mace or long double-handed sword was used; these weapons were heavy and clumsy. Prize fights took place in the sixteenth century, which were very popular and patronised by the Royal Court. A stage would be erected in a hall or public garden, and champions challenged each other to bouts with a variety of weapons. In the eighteenth century, the 'fisticuffs' bout was introduced, and the use of a sword gradually died out.

Fencing became popular in the public schools and universities during the nineteenth century. In 1861, it was included in the curriculum of the army school of physical training. It became part of a gentleman's education, and developed an elite image.

For each activity inspired by the military:

- **describe the rise and fall of the activity or phases of the activity.**
- **which social conditions affected the activity?**
- **what was the role of a patron?**
- **which would be suitable for women and why?**

Field sports

These include numerous activities. We will concentrate on the following:

- fox hunting
- hare coursing
- angling
- shooting and deer stalking
- horse racing.

Fox hunting

Fox hunting is the pursuit of the wild fox with a pack of hounds. Each hunt has its own designated area called the hunt country. The hunt meets at a predetermined place and moves off to a 'draw' – a particular woodland or other habitat where foxes are likely to be found. The hounds work as a pack and are bred for their intelligence, speed, stamina, voice and sense of smell.

By the turn of the eighteenth century fox hunting had become one of England's premier sports with a fashionable following. It represented a status symbol: 'The Field' made a regular public display of the power structure of the countryside, and 'The Master of Foxhounds' was a prestigious title. One of the most famous was Hugo Meynall, Master of Quorn. The tenant farmers followed the squirearchy as did the rich businessmen from the towns from the towns and cities. Smart Midland packs like Quorn and Pytchley attracted large numbers of rich young men who lavished money on horses and servants – the Regency bucks. By the late Victorian and Edwardian times, subscription packs developed where members of the hunt would contribute significantly to the Master's expenses. In 1810 there were 24 such packs but by 1854 this had risen to over 100. The railways, though initially regarded with suspicion by the hunts, enabled wealthy urbanites to join.

Women and children were also included. The hunt was very much a social occasion with balls and dinners connected to it. The dress was hunting pink with correct buttons and tight fitting leather boots with immaculately polished top boots. By the 1870s, at least 10,000 people were riding to hounds, with a similar number on foot.

Give a counter argument for the following statements:

- **'We do it for the ride. It's the best way to get a good gallop.'**
- **'We've been hunting for hundreds of years – its a fine old tradition.'**

- 'Fox hunters conserve the countryside.'
- 'Foxes are pests. They need to be controlled.'

Hare coursing

Hare coursing dates back to 1500 BC in the Valley of the Nile, and was probably introduced to Britain in 500 BC. Its original function was to obtain food for human survival, and the competitive element (between two dogs) was introduced during Elizabeth I's reign.

It became a popular social event in rural England in the nineteenth century. Hares were 'flushed' out of cover and two greyhounds were 'unleashed' by the 'slipper' – the official responsible for releasing the dogs simultaneously. The gentry rode on horseback, and private ground was often crossed by people on foot. The correct dress was jodhpurs, boots, hard hat and jacket.

In the 1920s circuit tracks were built, in which greyhounds trailed an artificial hare on the track. The speed and agility of the dogs are tested. Gambling on these races soon became very popular.

Angling

Angling is an ancient practice which developed initially to provide food. By the fifteenth century it was practised as a sport in England and was popular with the Tudors in the sixteenth century. There was a clear distinction between the commercial and sport aspect of fishing; fishing for sport required much leisure time.

Two main forms of sport fishing emerged:

1 Coarse fishing, which generally took place in urban areas, often in polluted waters.
2 Game fishing, a more expensive pursuit enjoyed on country estates. The fish sought would be salmon and trout.

- Women were also involved in this pastime.
- Charles Cotton wrote 'The Complete Angler' in 1653 which established the activity and influenced its development.
- A Royal Society was formed in 1660.

Shooting

The Game Laws of the eighteenth and nineteenth centuries were implemented by the landowners whose sole aim was the protection of their own shooting interests, the pheasants and partridges. They were primarily used to exclude both the lower classes and the rent paying tenant farmers who were not wealthy enough. These laws were more easily enforceable due to the Enclosures Act which divided the country into large estates. People were refused permission to kill game on the landowner's land and this caused much hostility in rural areas where poverty often required the killing of wild game for food.

Clearance of woods, scrub and marsh land increased the opportunity for hare and partridge shooting, but reduced pheasant shooting. In the 1880s, scientific incubating breeding was mastered; birds could be specifically bred for shooting purposes.

Deer stalking

Deer stalking was the most prestigious of all field sports. Developments in the rifle in the nineteenth century enabled hunters to kill a stag from a distance of 300 yards or more. This was later reformed to 'carted stag', which became popular on the fringes of London. The deer were domesticated and so the activity was almost like an artificial sport. A deer was taken to the venue in a cart and then set loose; the hounds were laid on for a fast and furious hunt.

Horse racing

This equestrian activity derived from warfare, chariot racing and hunting. The first permanent racecourse with an annual fixture is thought to be in Chester, in 1540. By the 1750s, the Jockey Club was in existence which struck a new commercial and bureaucratic control over the activity. Systems of mating horses produced faster horses, so racing became confined to thoroughbreds descended from Arabian, Turkish or Barbary steeds imported into England during the seventeenth and eighteenth centuries. The races were initially small annual occasions, and as they were held mid-week, this restricted the participation of working people. They formed casual competition, and the gentry sometimes participated in the races. It was very much a male pursuit, with a great Royal interest.

The railways enabled the activity to become more of a national and regular event, as spectators and animals could be transported with ease, comfort and safety. As the activity began to attract more spectators, the usual structures to divide the social classes were erected in the form of private boxes and public stands. It became a highly organised event with owners and trainers; jockeys and officials; a handicap system; the 'bookies' emerged as professional commission agents.

Two main types of racing emerged:

1 'Across the flats' – point to point. It gains its name from its original straight run across country.
2 'Over the Sticks' – steeplechasing under national hunt rules. The riders went over ditches, birch fences and water.

The Derby held at Epsom Downs is a mixture of ancient festivity and sporting innovation. At the turn of the century, 100,000 people would congregate on the Downs as a mass exodus from London; the race is part of the Cockney folklore.

Blood sports

Blood sports as entertainment were a part of British life up to the end of the nineteenth century. In a violent society where minor offences were punishable by hanging, little moral consideration was given for the suffering animals.

Characteristics of blood sports: physical violence; gambling was usually involved; vicarious interest in the infliction of pain; popular in rural and urban areas; involved all social classes.

Reasons for **popularity** of blood sports: excitement; limited entertainment available; to win money by gambling; accessible, easy to stage; ancient notion that animals exist merely as a resource for humans; to strengthen the mentality of soldiers before entering warfare.

In the nineteenth century, blood sports was banned because of:

- a new era of evangelical and humanitarian concern
- increase in concern over correct ways of behaviour; blood sports were not considered to be suitable in a civilised society

- the urban revolution stimulated new concepts of recreation
- complaints of breaches of the peace by the assembly of large, rowdy crowds
- employers discriminated against employees likely to suffer injuries due to violent pursuits.

Legislation included:

- 1822: to prevent ill treatment of horses and cattle (not including the bull)
- 1824: Royal Society for the Prevention of Cruelty to Animals established
- 1835: baiting sports banned, including the bull
- 1840: Cruelty to Animals Act (cockfighting now illegal).

Bull and bear baiting

This sport was first recorded in the reign of Henry II. A bull or bear would be tied up and terriers would set at it, with the aim of hanging on to them without being dislodged; the dogs would fail if tossed away by the bull or bear. The dogs would eventually win, but betting took place on the performance of individual dogs. The bulldog was so-called because of its talent at this sport: with its thick set body, short legs and powerful jaws, it would cling to the bull and tear off chunks of flesh. It became a national symbol for British strength and determination.

Bear gardens were popular in the sixteenth century under the Tudors; there was one behind the Globe Theatre (where Shakespeare's plays were performed), and another in the Royal Palace. Four or five dogs would be let loose at the bear at the same time, and the fight ended when the supply of dogs ran out or the bear was too badly injured to carry on. Parliament tried to ban the practice in 1802, and were finally successful in 1835.

'Bull running' was a sport in which a bull was let loose in the streets of a town, and would be goaded by spectators with sticks; eg, at Tutbury and Stamford. The run usually ended on a bridge, and the bull would be spared if the crowd failed to toss it into the water. In rural areas, this sport was restricted to special festivals, but was more common in urban areas.

Cock fighting

This was the most popular blood sport which set animal against animal; it was thought that cocks' natural aggression made for a fair fight, and each had an equal chance of victory if well matched. Cocks were bred and trained to fight, and metal spurs were added to their feet during the seventeenth century. Breeds included Piles, Blackreds, Pollcats, Pirchin, Ducks, Gingers and Shropshire Reds.

This was a sport popular across all social classes in urban and rural areas, for its entertainment value and gambling potential. Large towns had cockpits where regular contest took place; in 1800, there were seven cockpits in Newcastle. Failure to pay bets could result in the offender being hauled up in a basket above the pit (as in the Royal Cockpit at Bird Cage Walk).

'Throwing at cocks' was a favourite sport for Shrove Tuesday. Birds would be tethered, and people paid to throw stones or sticks at them. The birds' legs would usually break, and they would be killed.

Dog fighting

This was a traditional sport in the Midlands. Contests were held secretly, and dogs would be matched in pubs. It was banned by Parliament in 1911, but it still continues illegally as a subculture; there was a conviction in 1985 for dog fighting.

Aquatic activities

Spa towns

Britain's inland spa resorts became fashionable in the nineteenth century when it became popular for the upper classes to 'take the waters', and railways helped their mobility. Spa towns have their origin in Roman times where they developed from mineral springs or holy wells. The Tudors established taking the waters as a standard medical practice, which was a tradition continued by the Georgians towards the end of the eighteenth century.

They also offered rest and relaxation away from the growing industrial towns. Some of the notable towns are Bath with its Roman remains and impressive Georgian architecture, Buxton with thermal springs high up in Derbyshire, and Harrogate.

 **ACTIVITY 3**

Can you think of any modern practices which seem to try to recreate these kind of atmospheres?

Rowing

Leander Club is the oldest amateur rowing club in the world, believed to have been founded in 1818. Membership is a mark of distinction in the rowing world and a large proportion are former Oxford and Cambridge oarsmen. Leander's golden era came in the years between 1891 and 1914, during which they recorded 30 Henley wins (including 13 in the Grand Challenge Cup) and also won the Olympic eights in 1908 and 1912, and the Olympic pairs in 1908.

The art of propelling a boat is practised as a sport in most countries, but it began as a utilitarian activity when it provided power for war ships and transport in industrial towns.

The River Thames formed one of the main highways in medieval times; wealthy people had their own state barges and the professional watermen plied for trade. Watermanship refers to the skill of handling a boat. By the beginning of the eighteenth century, there were more than 40,000 licensed watermen. There were frequent contests between the watermen, and betting on the barges was common.

The earliest account of a regatta on the River Thames was in 1775. This occasion was derived from the Italian regata, originally boat races on the Grand Canal in Venice.

The standard of rowing increased in the nineteenth century due to an increasing professionalism. Rowing races attracted an enormous following and were widely reported in the press. Many rowers became coaches of amateur crews and eventually, due to the rapid and powerful rise of amateurism and the First World War, professional contests gradually died out.

Dogget instituted in 1715 what is now the oldest sculling race in the world. Crews race for an orange livery with a silver badge, hence the title 'Dogget's Coat and Badge'. (Broughton the prize fighter was an early winner.) Rowing clubs which emerged were mostly amateur; one of the most famous was Leander in 1818.

Bumping races were a traditional form of racing, especially in narrow stretches. Crews would attempt to touch or bump the crew in front and crews would change place according to the number of bumps scored. The crew finishing first would take the title 'Head of the River'. The public schools took to rowing, as it met their values of athleticism.

 **ACTIVITY 4**

What qualities of athleticism would be evident in a rowing fixture?

The need to win these fixtures led to the hiring of professional watermen, but due to the amateur ethos they reported that they were hired merely to provide competition! Rowing became competitive at Oxford and Cambridge Universities in the early years of the nineteenth century. The first University Boat Race took place at Henley in 1829; the Henley Regatta was established ten years later.

Fig. 18.3   Swimming and rowing on
the River Thames

Henley Regatta

This soon became a great traditional event, reflecting the Victorian love of
combining sporting events with a grand social occasion.

* Initially, only amateurs could compete.
* Non-British competitors were briefly banned in 1908.
* The Manual Labour clause excluded anyone who by trade or employment is a
  mechanic, artisan or labourer'.

However, it became less exclusive; the Manual Labour clause was abolished in
1890, and the Leander Club began to compete against teams such as the
Thames Tradesmen and the Metropolitan Police. The Amateur Rowing
Association was formed in 1882, followed by the National Amateur Rowing
Association in 1890.

**How do you think that Henley Regatta has reflected English
society in the nineteenth and early twentieth century?**

The seaside

The fashion for sea bathing began in the eighteenth century when it was regarded as
serving medical purposes, rather than for fun. The seaside resort took over in
popularity from the spa towns. Bathing became popular in the 1720s and the first
bathing machines made their appearance in Scarborough in 1753. Bathing nude
was not uncommon at this time and the bathing machine afforded some privacy
when costumes were heavy and uncomfortable. These would be pulled by men or
horses to the seaside. They would later be replaced by bathing tents at the turn of
the twentieth century. Men and women would have separate bathing areas. Mixed
bathing and the wearing of costumes came in the nineteenth century.

During the Victorian era, the railways and steamers with their cheap excursion
fares made the seaside resorts accessible to large numbers of people. Thomas Cook
established his travel company in 1841 and laid on excursion trains. This resulted

in the exodus of the upper classes to more isolated areas like the west country resorts. The creation of Bank holidays in 1871 resulted in even more people visiting the seaside, sometimes as day trippers.

Swimming for recreation developed in the eighteenth century when rowing and yachting became popular:

- In 1734, the first open air swimming pool was built in London.
- Captain Webb swam the English Channel in 1875.
- Public baths were built following the 1840 Act.

Racket sports

Real tennis

This game originated in France, as suggested by the terminology: 'dedans', 'tambour', 'grille'. It was an activity of the French Royal court, and was made popular in England by the Tudors. One of the most famous courts is still in use at Hampton Court. This was the sport of the noblemen and royalty and in 1536 there were restrictive acts which forbade servants and labourers to play. This helped to retain the privileged status of the elite. The game was originally played with the hand, 'le jeu de paume', until the sixteenth century when rackets were used.

This was a very sophisticated, exclusive game requiring expensive facilities, equipment and an understanding of the complex rules and social etiquette of the game. The emphasis was on the individual's skill and tactical and strategic awareness; as ever, wagering was evident. It was the epitome of rational sport.

Rackets

This game began in fairly humble circumstances in England. Open courts existed in the back yards of taverns and inns, and in many towns. They were social meeting

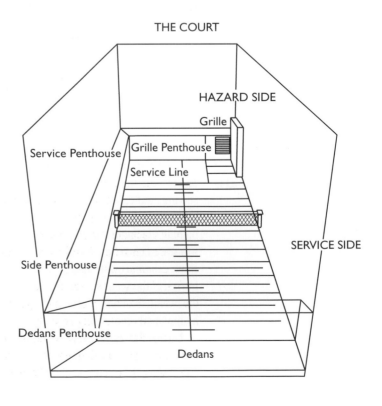

THE COURT

HAZARD SIDE

Grille

Service Penthouse

Grille Penthouse

Service Line

SERVICE SIDE

Side Penthouse

Dedans Penthouse

Dedans

Fig. 18.4   A REAL TENNIS COURT

Fig. 18.5 An early version of tennis, taken from *Orbis Sensualium Pictus* by John Comenius, 1659

places and there was always a wall to be used. Equipment could also be hired from publicans wishing to make the most of their business opportunities. They had all the requirements – willing opponents, alcohol and wagering.

The game was a test of strength and accuracy. In a four-handed match the players took alternate 'out' and 'in' games, which would lead to exciting rallies.

Rackets was taken up by the public schools for its simple qualities and the possibilities of using architectural features within the school grounds. It was a game which suited the cult of athleticism, containing rules, etiquette and sportsmanship.

Fives

Fives was played with the palm of the hand, wearing a glove, and the ball was hit against the wall. It was played in inns and other public places, and was a much more individual game than rackets. In the public schools it tended to be played more in the boys' recreation time and consequently did not establish well-known formal rules. As the game was not taken up at the universities, individual schools' variations continued. These qualities tended to make it a less favourable game than rackets as far as the staff were concerned.

Lawn tennis

Real or Royal tennis was an aristocratic pastime and was not conducive to the lives of the middle and lower classes. However, in the nineteenth century the middle classes with their increasing wealth and leisure time wanted to establish their own form of recreation which would set them apart from the lower classes. The game became enormously popular midway through Queen Victoria's reign.

Major Wingfield took most of the credit for the game's popularity. His invention, which he called Sphairistike had an hour-glass shaped court. He provided a commercial product which could be bought in kit form making it attractive to the middle classes whose wealth was often determined by trade. The Marylebone Cricket Club (MCC) then took it one stage further, calling it lawn tennis and adopting an oblong shaped court.

It ousted croquet from the lawns of the middle classes, and proved to be an ideal game for large suburban gardens to be played by both social classes, in their increasingly leisured society. There were few recreational activities at this time that both sexes could enjoy together. The ladies were able to play privately away from the public gaze, and it was a game which helped to remove some of the stereotypes. They could run around becoming increasingly energetic and clothing began to be slightly less restrictive. Their schools also accepted the game as it was non-contact, had rules and was acceptable to the parents.

The middle classes also ensured its club development and the administrative structures. The lower classes had to wait until there was public provision, so their participation was delayed.

Cycling

This was an activity which reflected the technological advances and social changes in the nineteenth century.

- The **Hobby Horse** (1818) was the forerunner to the bicycle. It was propelled by the rider who sat astride and pushed alternate feet on the ground.
- The **Boneshaker** (1868) was invented by the Michaux brothers in Paris.
- The **Penny Farthing** (1870–1890) – The large front wheel was developed to obtain more speed for every turn of the pedals, so that the wheel covered more ground.
- The **National Royal Tricycle** (1884) was developed from the Penny Farthing to make a safer ride.
- The **Rover Safety** (1885) was the machine that set the fashion and was built with the first Diamond frame.

The bicycle was developing during the machine age, and could be produced in large numbers. It was an alternative mode of transport to the horse and cart, and consequently more appealing to the middle classes. The gentry initially retained their preference for the horse and were disdainful of 'new fangled' machine. The roads initially were poor, but improvements were gradually made.

The gentry ladies however were keen to take on this new form of transport which gave them a sense of freedom from their claustrophobic lives which required that they were chaperoned everywhere and were expected to fulfil rigid social roles. Further encouragement was given by the Royal daughters' use of the bicycle.

The growing interest in the countryside also made the bicycle useful, as a route out to the country lanes. The railways offered Rover tickets which would take the cycle and the cyclists further afield. Club developments became hugely popular, particularly the touring branch. Bicycles were expensive however, and the majority of people had to wait for the second hand trade to develop.

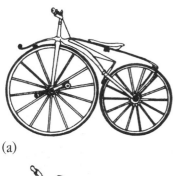

(a)

(b)

(c)

(d)

(e)

Fig. 18.6   (A) The hobby horse, 1818; (B) the boneshaker, 1868; (C) the penny farthing, 1870; (D) the national royal tricycle, 1884; (E) rover safety 1885

Fig. 18.7   ENGLAND V SCOTLAND AT THE OVAL, 6 MARCH 1875

Football

Football began as a mob game. It lacked the organisational features of the modern game and was characterised by large numbers of players, exclusively male and from the lower classes, involved in a territorial struggle. The game tended to be played occasionally on annual holidays like the wakes as the people had limited free time, and would cover distances between villages. Due to only being played a few times a year there were limited rules, and hence violence, injury and sometimes death, were common as the game was determined by force rather than skill. There was no division of labour; players had no particular roles, and there was a loose distinction between participating and spectating. This was originally a rural activity and reflected the harsh way of life lived by uneducated, rural people.

What changed the game out of all proportion to its original character? The gentry sons in the public schools began to play the game regularly on the school grounds. Though they started with variations in rules from school to school, they gradually began to develop them in the form of shape of goals, boundaries, limits on the size of the team and so on. A competitive structure emerged with inter-house and inter-school matches. Some variations remained and were distinctive to individual schools; the unique facility features like the Close at Rugby with soft turf and the Quad at Charterhouse, where the dribbling game emerged. There is also the Eton Wall game which still exists today (see page 000).

University graduates further codified the game and established associations; the Football Association was established in 1863. When university graduates became employers they encouraged the game among the workers, partly to boost morale and loyalty, and also to instil middle class values and discipline. They also established their middle class sports clubs based on amateurism.

The roads and pavements were the playgrounds of working class children and they devised numerous types of street games. Football was one of them and most streets had a football team associated with a strong community feeling. The cramped living conditions and shortage of facilities led to a more spectator-based interest in the game. Developments in transport opened up the rest of the country for fixtures further afield.

There was therefore a curious development across the different social classes. The game began as a mob game by and for the lower classes. The public schools made it popular with the gentry in the south of England, who also incorporated middle class values within the game as it developed along strictly amateur lines – the southern amateurs. However, in the north of England it developed in the industrial towns, and professionalism soon crept in with clubs like Sheffield Wednesday establishing, when Wednesday became early closing day. The Football League was established in 1885. When the two sides met there was a culture shock!

Cricket

Cricket is one of the oldest established games and was played from the outset by both social classes; the aristocrats and the commoners played together. There were not many activities which both social classes played together, though they had particular roles within the game to signify their status. The game reflected the feudal structure of the village. The early clubs emerged from the rural village sides, with the gentry acting as patron. There were a variety of reasons for this: the game took place in the summer season when light was at its premium, allowing the workers time to participate, and because of its non violent nature, there were no threats to the gentry in playing with the peasants. The early rules and gentlemanly behaviour ensured a level of respectful behaviour.

Games would attract spectators in their thousands. The first written rules were drawn up by the Duke of Richmond in 1727 to help control country house games where sometimes large sums of money would hinge on the outcome. The MCC emerged as an organisational feature comparatively early in the game's

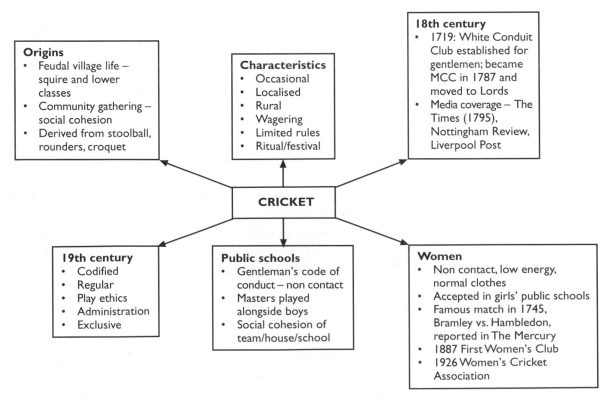

Origins
- Feudal village life – squire and lower classes
- Community gathering – social cohesion
- Derived from stoolball, rounders, croquet

Characteristics
- Occasional
- Localised
- Rural
- Wagering
- Limited rules
- Ritual/festival

18th century
- 1719: White Conduit Club established for gentlemen; became MCC in 1787 and moved to Lords
- Media coverage – The Times (1795), Nottingham Review, Liverpool Post

CRICKET

19th century
- Codified
- Regular
- Play ethics
- Administration
- Exclusive

Public schools
- Gentleman's code of conduct – non contact
- Masters played alongside boys
- Social cohesion of team/house/school

Women
- Non contact, low energy, normal clothes
- Accepted in girls' public schools
- Famous match in 1745, Bramley vs. Hambledon, reported in The Mercury
- 1887 First Women's Club
- 1926 Women's Cricket Association

Fig. 18.8 THE DEVELOPMENT OF CRICKET

development. The terms 'gentlemen' and 'players' emerged to distinguish the amateurs from the professionals.

Though it was a game to appeal to all social classes, county cricket remained quite exclusive, holding matches mid-week. The suburban middle classes began to take out county membership and the large grounds began to take over from the smaller, more portable fixtures. This would detach it even more from the working classes. The Lancashire League was established similarly to the football league, to cater for the needs of the working classes.

Cricket was immediately acceptable in the public schools as it matched all the criteria for social control for the masters and athleticism for the boys. The rules meant a code of behaviour by the boys who would be expected to behave within the spirit of the game. The fags, or younger boys, would help the older boys in practice and the assistant masters would also play. When fixtures became prestigious and important to win, professionals were employed to raise the standards of play amongst the team.

The first official women's cricket match is recorded as having taken place in 1745, between Bromley and Hambleden. It grew in popularity during the nineteenth century, as women's clothing began to adapt to sporting conditions. The Women's Cricket Association was formed in 1926.

Athletics

Many athletic activities developed from functional activities like the throwing events, while others from agricultural pursuits like hunting and clearing obstacles. Pedestrianism was similar to race walking, and developed in Stuart and Georgian Society where young men were sent ahead of a coach to warn the inn keeper of their imminent arrival. Wagers were placed and the gentry acted as patrons. It developed into an endurance event covering long distances against the opponent or the clock. Can you see the similarities between the sculling races like the Doggett Coat and Badge and the Prize Ring? It involved a working class performer and a gentry patron, but it was often a corrupt activity. Pedestrianism was a commercial attraction, with notable characters like Deerfoot the American earning large sums of money.

Hurdling is said to have evolved from the boys at public schools improvising in their leisure time and re-enacting events they saw at home like the association between hunting and hare and hounds and hurdling with horse racing. Other events were included like high and standing broad jumps, and athletics meetings began. They developed athletics clubs, eg, the London Athletic Club.

In 1896 the revival of the modern Olympic Games heralded an international appeal for athletics. Specialisation was taking over from the traditional all-round English amateur sportsman; play had moved on to competition and winning.

Golf

The origins of golf are thought to derive from ancient activities played by the Patagonian Indians, from a game called jeu de mal in France and het kolven in Holland. However, the Scots claim that they were the first responsible for the game developing to its present form. It was banned in 1457 as it was feared that it interfered with people's archery practice.

The Stuarts made golf a Royal pursuit and Mary Queen of Scots was frowned upon for playing the game following her husband's death. The French Royal connection also brought the term 'caddy' which derived from the word cadets – the younger sons of the French aristocrats who came over to England as her pages. The Scots adopted this to mean loafers and scroungers! Many monarchs to follow were interested in the game.

The competition for the Silver Golf Club in 1744 was the first ever held in golf, and a Code of Rules was agreed.

However, golf originally seems to have been for the ordinary people, eg, the Fish Wives of Musselborough. From the seventeenth century onwards, equipment changes meant increased prices which effectively priced the fishermen and labourers out of golf. The first balls were made of turned boxwood followed by a feathery ball. Rubber balls wrapped in gutta perch, in the nineteenth century, were much more expensive. The shafts were made from hickory which had to be imported from the USA. This led to the situation where the gentry played and the commoners carried the clubs as caddies. With the enclosure of land and the cost of laying out courses on expensive land near suburban areas, it soon became the exclusive preserve of a wealthy minority.

The proliferation of clubs meant an equal proliferation of local rules. By 1919 the matter of rules was passed to the Royal and Ancient Society. The clubs were governed by the upper and middle classes, and women were admitted on the understanding that a level of internal segregation was accepted. They could not vote or be shareholders.

Golf helped to foster a community life in the suburbs. Women from all social classes had played the game from its early days, and by 1898 there were 220 ladies' clubs. However, as the Victorian stereotype of female behaviour took hold of society, they met with problems. They were considered physically inferior to men, which led to a miniature version of the course or from the forward tee on men's courses. They were advised to attempt no more than 70 yards for a drive.

In order to carry out research on activities and games, referring to a checklist can help to organise the information in a manageable format. Table 18.1 shows the checklist applied to badminton; research some details about the development of hockey using this approach.

Summary

From this selection of activities, you can see how sport within society is a dynamic experience, constantly changing to adapt to new pressures and sometimes exerting its own influence on society.

- From brutal and blood sports to a system where legislation curtailed activities or caused modifications.
- The change in emphasis from rural to urban sport with a philosophy of participation was hindered by lack of facilities and space.
- From watching in small local groups to mass spectatorism; business enterprise; improved communications and a national interest in sport.
- From local rules to fully codified rules formulating governing bodies.
- Control passed from the aristocracy to the middle classes.

- Bribery, corruption and vice largely eliminated, and with it the old concept of professionalism.
- Recreation was no longer the privilege of the nobility. By the end of the nineteenth century, the working class had won the same right to recreation.
- With the spatial restrictions of urbanisation came the desire to escape to the country. The weekend exodus became a national characteristic.

Table 18.1   GATHERING INFORMATION ABOUT BADMINTON

PRINCIPLE	INFORMATION	REASON
origin	evolved about 1870 from ancient childrens game of Battledore and Shuttlecock army officers exported/imported – India	British Empire
social event	derives its name from the seat (estate) of the Duke of Beaufort at Badminton, Gloucestershire played in Victorian salons by men and women	leisure activity, ie, upper class
social class	upper class	• leisure time • space and equipment
influences	• Duke of Beaufort • army	played game on estate imported/exported games
early game	• hour glass shaped court • doubles popular but 3, 4 and 5 a side usual	to accommodate doors of Victorian salon singles considered selfish
later game	1870 Poona 1st laws; 1893 Badminton Association 1899 All England Championships; 1901 court made rectangular	regulate court size and rules for competitions
sporting atmosphere	equipment (net; rackets; shuttle); court (boundaries); spectators; recreation in leisure time	
education	not initially popular in either public or state schools	• no team game values • lack of facilities
clothing	men – informal day wear women – formal restrictive long dresses	modesty
amateurism professionalism	originally amateur	developed by Victorians – amateur code
clubs	250 clubs were members of the Badminton Association by 1914	Victorians developed the club ethos; competitions made possible
other	1934 International Badminton Federation	

chapter 19

Comparative Studies

Having studied the United Kingdom and its approach towards sport and physical education within the context of the overall culture, we will now undertake a similar study looking at the United States of America, France and Australia. A comparative approach is widely used in many other academic disciplines and is an attempt to describe, analyse and explain factors occurring within society. A reformative approach occurs when different cultures borrow and adopt ideas which may prove of benefit to their society.

Problems with initial attempts at comparative research lay in isolating a topic of study and not viewing it in the context of the whole system. It was recognised by the turn of the twentieth century that the individual aspect being studied needed to be seen as an integral part of that society. Only then can the value orientations which surround the particular parts of a culture be fully understood. Thus, a multi-disciplinary approach emerged involving economics, history, philosophy, sociology, psychology, anthropology, social science and science. This was pioneered by George Bereday and he presented four main stages:

- **description** – the systematic collection of data
- **interpretation** – analysis in terms of social sciences
- **juxtaposition** – a review of similar systems to determine the framework to be used to compare
- **comparison** – first of select problems and then the relevance to the various cultures.

Comparative physical education and sport is still a fairly recent field of study; the International Society on Comparative Physical Education and Sport (ISCPES) was formed in 1980. Their publications can be useful sources of information.

You may well find it useful, at this stage, to summarise what you already know about the British system, under the major headings of politics, geography, discrimination, socio economics, physical education, sport, as a reference point. A spider diagram presentation could be used. This would be a good brain storming exercise for your class.

United States of America

Consider the impact of the factors in fig 19.1 on the system of sport in the USA.

Imagine the trek west to settle in uninhabited wilderness areas, with a hostile indigenous population to overcome.

- **What personal qualities would be most likely to prove successful?**
- **Can you relate any of these qualities to success in sport?**

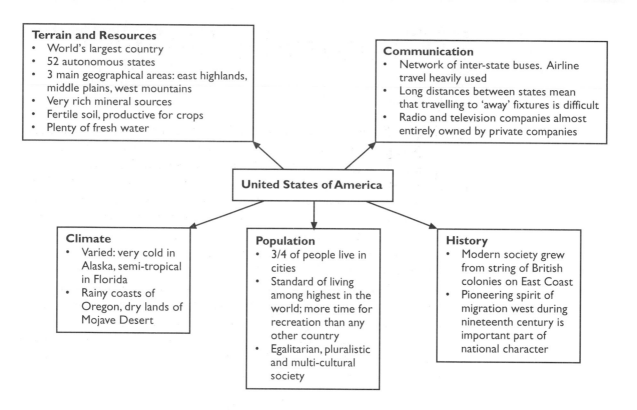

Terrain and Resources
- World's largest country
- 52 autonomous states
- 3 main geographical areas: east highlands, middle plains, west mountains
- Very rich mineral sources
- Fertile soil, productive for crops
- Plenty of fresh water

Communication
- Network of inter-state buses. Airline travel heavily used
- Long distances between states mean that travelling to 'away' fixtures is difficult
- Radio and television companies almost entirely owned by private companies

United States of America

Climate
- Varied: very cold in Alaska, semi-tropical in Florida
- Rainy coasts of Oregon, dry lands of Mojave Desert

Population
- 3/4 of people live in cities
- Standard of living among highest in the world; more time for recreation than any other country
- Egalitarian, pluralistic and multi-cultural society

History
- Modern society grew from string of British colonies on East Coast
- Pioneering spirit of migration west during nineteenth century is important part of national character

Fig. 19.1 THE UNITED STATES OF AMERICA

Development and structure of government

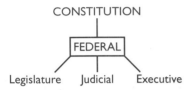

CONSTITUTION

FEDERAL

Legislature　　Judicial　　Executive

Fig. 19.2 THE AMERICAN GOVERNMENT

Following the War of Independence in 1776, the colonies achieved their objective of freedom from Britain in 1781. They wished to detach themselves from the British elitist, closed social class system, which excluded the majority of people from opportunities of self improvement, on the grounds that they did not possess the preferred social status. This new, competitive, capitalist economy aimed to provide people with the determination, talent and drive with the opportunity to be successful. This is popularly called 'The American Dream' – in theory, people can experience upward social mobility regardless of social class – that is, 'rags to riches'. Professional sport was given an extra boost in this rapidly expanding industrial and commercial country.

A new government with a federal constitution was founded, effectively creating a republic. A federal constitution is where the powers of government are divided between the national and the state or provincial governments. This was an important concept: the people had just broken away from a distant system of power over which they had little control, and did not want to replace it with another, so they sought to restrict the powers of the new national government via the constitution of the United States which serves as the Supreme Law of the Land. The Bill of Rights guaranteed the basic rights of American citizens. The constitution establishes federalism with three separate branches:

- legislative (responsible for creating laws)
- executive (power to enforce laws)
- judicial (power to dismiss laws)

The government operates on three different levels – national, state and local:

- national government – with delegated powers
- state government – residual powers (where they work together, it is called concurrent power).

It is a

- **democracy** with a representative government which means the people elect leaders who will represent them.
- **republic**, which is where the chief of state is also elected by the people, unlike a monarch who inherits the title.
- **constitutional** government operating under a set of laws and principles outlined in the constitution.
- **federal** system with a sharing of power between the national, state and municipal governments.

The spread of white American culture was not without a price. The indigenous population of Indians were defeated and resettled, losing many of their ancient pastimes. Reference to the ancient game of lacrosse as played by the Iroquois Indians, is often made as one example of a tradition that survived, albeit in a new form. This may have survived because it was a fast and exciting game, similar to other developing rational games, and was introduced to England at a time when these developments were occurring. It was adopted in the girls' public schools in the nineteenth century.

In the mid 1800s, the plantations in the South produced huge cotton crops, and black slaves were relied upon to do the manual labour. The different values held in the North finally led to the Civil War in 1861; Abraham Lincoln issued the Emancipation Proclamation in 1863, pronouncing all slaves in the confederacy to be free. However, the Southern states continued to limit the rights of black people, and the experiences of black people are still not equal to those of white people, even in the late twentieth century; legal rights do not always mean equal opportunity; see page 000.

Sport in the United States

As with Britain, in the nineteenth century there was an increasing rationalisation of sport:

- club membership was exclusive
- spectator sports were developing
- social class distinctions were introduced and reinforced through the amateur/professional divide
- organised sport carried the burden of achieving social and economic objectives and became serious in its orientation
- positive male character traits were closely allied to those needed to be successful in sport, as well as being useful in serving God and country.

By the 1920s these cultural links had become clearly defined, with the growth of spectator sports cleverly marketed in order to raise money and create profits. This occurred at both professional and intercollegiate level and national organisations were being established to control the rapid growth, eg, the National Collegiate Athletic Association (NCAA).

The powers of the federal government have expanded since the constitution was first designed. By 1983, the American government had involved itself in matters concerning sport in 11 areas – antitrust, criminal activities, restructuring sport, discrimination, capital support, tax/duty exemption, social work projects, sponsored publicity, health/fitness promotion, boycott and international athletic tours. Some of these areas are outlined below:

- **Antitrust** – this is where the US government regulates or opposes trusts, monopolies, cartels or similar organisations in an attempt to prevent unfair competition. Some incidences have involved the NCAA.
- **Criminal activities** – this involves organised crime in horse racing and betting. The 'fixing' of events was made a criminal offence in 1963.
- **Restructuring sport** – numerous attempts have been made to curb the violence in boxing, but efforts have failed as Congress is unwilling to impose sanctions on what is effectively a privately owned sport business. However, in 1978 the Amateur Sports Act was passed as an attempt to solve problems between the NCAA and the AAU. They had been unable to agree and this led to the establishing of the United States Olympic Committee. It effectively streamlined the amateur sports scene and allowed federal intervention.
- **Discrimination** – Title IX or the Education Amendment of 1972; see page 306. In 1975, the Education for All Handicapped Children Act was passed which ensured the inclusion of children with special educational needs to regular physical education programmes.
- **Capital funding** – generally, Congress does not directly support sporting events, though this has become more prevalent, particularly for the Olympic Games and other prestigious events.
- **Tax exemptions** – these have also been granted in the area of sport. About three-quarters of the stadiums and arenas have been funded from federal

sources. Few managers own the facilities, because if they are owned by the federal government, the owners are exempt from taxes, maintenance and insurance costs – this is picked up by the tax payer.

- **Promoting health and fitness** – with escalating health costs, the government has turned its attention to preventative medicine and established the Office of Health Information, Health Promotion and Physical Fitness, and Sports Medicine. Its role is to coordinate all matters relating to education for health.
- **Boycott** – the most famous boycott was the one ordered by President Carter in 1980, to pressurise the National Olympic Committee to boycott the Moscow Games. It was successful in its campaign.

Overall, the government *will* act in sports matters but generally prefers to maintain a low profile; it intervenes only when deemed necessary.

Concepts of American sport

There are three main sporting concepts operating in the United States.

1 The dominant concept is the **Lombardian** ethic which is based on the Protestant work ethic of self-discipline, clean living and mental alertness. The popular image of this ethic is taken from the saying of the coach, Vince Lombardi, 'Winning isn't the most important thing, it's the only thing'. This emphasises the competitive, achievement-orientated, reward-based type of sport behaviour.

2 The **Counter culture** is an attempt by some sections of American society to change the emphasis in sport to one where the process is the important thing and the outcome is unimportant. It comes from Grantland Rice's slogan, 'It's not whether you won or lost but how you played the game'. This tends to take an anti-competitive viewpoint and Eco Sport has evolved from it – cooperative rather than competitive games. The New Games Foundation aims to change the way people play by reducing the amount of equipment and skill and replacing them with informal situations, emphasising group effort rather than group reward.

3 The middle line is the **Radical** ethic and is perhaps the nearest to the British stance, where the outcome is important but so too is the process. The quest for excellence can be strived for and achieved, but not at the expense of other values.

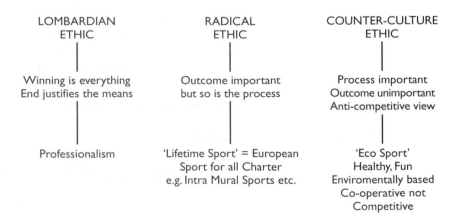

Fig. 19.3 CONCEPTS OF AMERICAN SPORT

Physical education

The American system houses a private and a public sector, with the former being self-financing and often associated with Church groups. A decentralised system operates, which means each state is in charge of its own education, administration and jurisdiction. This has the advantage of being more likely to meet the needs of each state, as considerations of wealth and climate can be catered for. The state is responsible for providing a free education, teaching programmes, certification of teachers, building standards and financial support.

Children begin nursery (kindergarten) aged four to five years, which aims to prepare them for their elementary education to educate them from the age of 6–12 years. Advancement to each grade is based on achieving specialised skills in a number of subjects. The secondary schools allow much choice in the upper grades, as subjects are career-based. The final aim is to pass the high school diploma.

In one sense, the system is similar to the UK, where local authorities have some input. However, the teacher in the USA does not have the same amount of freedom as the British teacher in choosing their teaching programme, as the superintendent of the local school board draws up a programme which the teachers implement.

ACTIVITY 4

What are the advantages and disadvantages of a local school board, with some teacher representatives, creating the physical education programme?

Physical education is an essential and basic part of the total educational programme from kindergarten to age 12. Physical activities are valued for their ability to enhance the unique characteristics of students on a physical, mental, emotional and social level. Children are encouraged to develop motor skills, knowledge and attitudes necessary to help them function within their society. You may well recognise some similarities to the British philosophy. Physical education is an integral part of most of the curriculums' content, and is seen as part of the whole sporting continuum.

There are similarities in primary education with the UK, where the movement approach towards physical education is adopted with a more heuristic teaching style and is taken by the classroom teacher who is usually a non-specialist. This is not common in the secondary sector in the USA as a fitness testing approach takes over, whereas teachers in the UK tend to take the child-centred approach for a greater length of time. Fitness testing tends to suit a culture which is based on objectivity, accountability, quantification and the determination to produce the best they can. The Physical Fitness Movement was influential in introducing fitness tests.

The physical education teacher in the USA is separate to the sports coach and generally has a lower status. Teachers in the USA are experiencing similar moves to improve the physical education experience as in Britain, and the thrust of America 2000 is TQM: total quality management where valuing and respecting the needs of the learners is essential. It is a long term plan to help all schools achieve the National Education Goals adopted in 1991. Other initiatives include OBE, outcome based education, and the Neighborhood Schools Improvement Act which will also involve a shift from traditional values.

Ages	4–5	6–12	12–17	17–19	17–22
	Kindergarten	Elementary Grades 1–6	High School	College	Uni
			Junior Senior Grades 7–12	Junior Technical	

Fig. 19.4 THE AMERICAN EDUCATION SYSTEM

There are various organisations which have responsibility for sport in schools. The State Athletic Association coordinates and regulates inter-scholastic athletic competition; the National Federation of State High School Associations (NFSHSA) established uniform rules for competition and gives guidelines and advice.

Title IX

Women in the USA have historically experienced similar gender inequality as their British counterparts. Sport evolved along the male and masculinity concepts of competition, achievement, aggression and dominance which led to poorer opportunities for women and resulted in lower participation rates. Their positive female sporting images have tended to be similar to other western cultures: activities which require grace, and have little physical contact and so a lower level of aggression, and those in the supporting or cheerleading role which has its own high status, based on a glamorous, entertainment approach to women in the sporting arena.

The female participation rate did not radically change until the 1970s when a sudden rise in female participation in sports occurred and was visible at all levels from the youth sports to intercollegiate to amateur and professional. This can be attributed to several factors:

* the women's movement
* federal legislation
* the fitness movement
* an increased public awareness of women athletes helped by increased media coverage of female sport.

Fig. 19.5 Gail Devers takes the gold medal at the World Athletic Championships in Gothenburg, 1995

Federal legislation in the guise of Title IX, the Education Amendment of 1972, was one of the most influential factors as it made compulsory the equal treatment of men and women in education programmes which were in receipt of federal funding. It was enacted in 1972 by the Department of Health Education and Welfare and released in 1975. Women could take a case as far as the Supreme Court, and since then, numerous cases and judgements have been made. It stated that no discrimination should occur at either the programmes offered, the quality of teaching and availability of facilities, medical services, travel allowances and so on. All efforts should be made to teach coeducationally, though for heavy contact sports separation could occur. The equality should be proportional to the number of men and women participating.

At an administrative level, the previous governing of women's sports was the preserve of the Association of Intercollegiate Athletics for Women (AIAW), and they had the usual responsibilities of establishing policies and procedures governing competition and championships. In 1982 the NCAA and NAIA took over.

* **If there is a scholarship fund of $200,000 with 70 men and 30 women athletes, how much would the male and female athletes be entitled to?**
* **What problems do you think Title IX has caused within the educational institutions? Refer to both teaching staff, students and administrative details.**
* **What are the arguments for and against the UK adopting a similar policy to Title IX?**

Fig. 19.6 THE STRUCTURE OF USA OLYMPIC SPORT

Adaptive sporting programmes

Adapted physical education is an umbrella term used to encompass areas such as dance, sport, fitness and rehabilitation for individuals with impairment across the lifespan. It has evolved from two major areas – the medical and educational perspectives – and was integrated in the 1950s. It recognised that teaching styles, facilities and equipment should be adapted to meet the individual needs of both regular and special students. The USA has again led the way in terms of legislation – federal legislation in 1975 required that there should be more inclusion in regular classes; in other words the mainstreaming of children with special educational needs – a movement from a medical to educational emphasis, with specialist training for teachers to help them deal more effectively with these children, and consultant monitoring. The Joseph F. Kennedy Jr. Foundation has been active in this area. The Sport for All and the Paralympics movement continue to exert pressure for change, in the way that people view disability and the possibilities for physical education and sport programmes.

Intra-mural activities

These include highly structured competitive sports and games played to a high level, as well as sports participation of a recreational nature, where the emphasis is more on the social experience. They occur outside regular school classes or hours with teams organised on the basis of grade, class, house etc.

Extra-mural activities

These generally refer to inter-school competitions, which again can be informal or highly organised and serious. The students go through a more selective process, the activities are widely reported by the press and considerable interest is taken by the local community.

Inter-scholastic sports

Schools belong to the State High School Athletic Associations, which in turn belong to the National Federation of State High School Associations. This organisation coordinates and regulates contests in sport, as well as other activities.

Inter-scholastic competition achieves its greatest emphasis in grades 10 to 12. Those who are carefully selected practise a few hours each day. Rivalry in the local school leagues is intense, and competitions from local, district and regional levels occur which culminate in the championship of the state. State tournaments exist but the size of the country inhibits national school tournaments. (It is worth noting here that the size of each state is comparable to a European country.) Schools can be classified into divisions, depending on the size of enrolment. The coach is a member of the high school faculty, and money comes from donations from local booster clubs and local taxes.

These programmes are an accepted and high status part of the school and college system, and are thought to deliver positive educational goals. There are however critics who believe that their effects are more negative than positive. The table below offers both arguments.

Table 19.1   THE ADVANTAGES AND DISADVANTAGES OF INTER-SCHOLASTIC SPORT

ADVANTAGES	DISADVANTAGES
• Encourages pride and loyalty to school	• Too much emphasis on competition and winning
• Improves fitness levels	• Most students are spectators, while players are often seriously injured during play
• Develops teamwork skills, valuable for later life	• Takes too many resources away from other educational programs
• Strengthens links between school and community	• Can assume too much importance, academic studies could suffer
• Encourages students to become involved in school activities	• Encourages outdated 'macho' ideals

Inter-collegiate sport

America based its colleges and sporting activities on the nineteenth century English universities and public schools. Harvard and Yale reflected the developing traditions of their British counterparts, Oxford and Cambridge. Professionalism hit inter-collegiate sport very soon and possessed the following characteristics:

- competition for non-cash prizes or for money prizes
- competition against professionals
- money was charged at the gates
- the costs of a training table (food costs) was not borne by the athlete
- athletes were recruited and paid, and professional coaches employed.

American students soon abandoned the British ideal of amateurism. There was a feeling that the college students were being distracted from the primary aims of a college education, and the management of college athletics was becoming too large for the students to handle. By 1900 nearly every college had an athletic committee,

Fig. 19.7 Junior College Soccer, Costa Mesa, USA

with control of athletics shared between the students and alumni, or the sole prerogative of the institution. Then with further development and expansion, inter-college regulation was needed. The National Collegiate Association was established in 1906 to control and create order in collegiate athletics; the National Association of Intercollegiate Athletics in 1952; and the Association of Intercollegiate Athletics for Women in 1972.

Inter-collegiate athletics is based on two foundations:

1 the NCAA Division III for small institutions where sport and physical education are an integral part of students' lives.
2 Division I, where sport is run as an entertainment business and a training ground for professional and high level amateur sport, namely the Olympic Games.

Division II is a transition ground between the two. The lack of an effective club structure in the USA has made this an inevitable route for athletes wishing to pursue a career in sport.

'Big time' programmes

Generally it would be the responsibility of the principal to ensure that educational objectives are adhered to and that winning does not become over-stated. The problems become more obvious at the inter-collegiate 'big time' programmes where incentives can distract athletes from academic work and are characterised by commercialism, poor rights of athletes and distorted views of gender and race; in such instances these are more negative in their outcomes. Criticisms have been made about the lip service paid by some athletes and college administrators to the academic courses being undertaken by the high level college athlete. A difference needs to be made between the 'big time' collegiate sports and the lower profile levels which do not have scholarships and do not have the entertainment label tagged on; research has shown that academic studies do not suffer at this level.

What is the benefit of a system which develops such interest in college sport? Consider the value placed on the British colleges sport scene.

Sport and entertainment

There are four major popular sports in the USA – football, baseball, basketball and ice hockey. Sport in this instance has become a business and athletes are marketed as assets who are well known and who can help generate funds and advertise products with their skill, showmanship and positive health images. The sports are packaged and presented to the public, and sports tend to be loud, brash, energetic and involve huge productions – a show rather than a game, display rather than play?

Baseball

In comparison to football, basketball and ice hockey, baseball is not a territorial game and is not governed by time. Its roots are rural, it has a slower pace and more of an individual focus. It is thought to have evolved from the game of rounders, though it has left this game far behind in the modern day sports world. It began as a more working class sport and developed in inner cities; as such it has similar social parallels to soccer in England, with more aggressive supporters than are found in American football.

What are the main differences between baseball and rounders in the present day?

American football

American football sums up the country's character – technological, territorial, physically violent and intimidating, a team effort and the epitome of specialisation. It originated from the game of rugby in Britain, but developed along different lines within its new culture. It developed further in the elite colleges and universities and was therefore a more middle class game. Its development reflected America's attempts to create a new identity, separate from Europe, and the game was influenced by many other different cultures. It was not constrained by the amateur traditions and the 'win' ethic emerged alongside professionalism.

Contrast football in the UK with its counterpart in the USA. Suggest cultural and historical differences which have resulted in two very different games.

Why is there less violence amongst the American supporters?

Basketball

Basketball has more potential for improvisation than either baseball or football due to the fluidity of play. The players are free to execute their own individuality and can perform cunningly deceptive moves. It was deliberately created rather than gradually evolving, as did baseball from rounders and football from rugby. The game was created by James Naismith to channel young men's energies and develop their moral character, and yet the game manipulates the rules by balancing the risk of penalty against the advantages to be gained. Basketball has become a symbol of black identity and black social power.

Ice hockey

Ice hockey is the most violent of team games – fighting is part of the action, and is expected. The physical speed of the game and the implement used have made this game fast, brutal and violent. The players are dressed for protection but carry injury with pride and are willing to play on when injured. Team members play in a confined area with close and vocal supporters to whom winning has an intense emphasis. In contrast to basketball, ice hockey is predominantly a white game and this is probably due to its origins in sub-arctic Canada.

Though these dominant sports possess their own characteristics, they also contain common elements such as high scoring and fast play, requiring skill and power:

- They create entertainment through the media and sponsors, and tend to attract families rather than have single sex traditions.
- The facilities are extensive and of a high standard, both in terms of players and spectators.
- They operate as businesses controlled by owners, and are heavily marketed with their accompanying merchandise.

- They can carry racial identity and preferences.
- The games are very competitive and draws do not feature.
- The professional ethos of the Lombardian ethic with material rewards for success reflects the capitalist system.

Because of the size of the USA, there is not the tradition of home and away fans as in Britain, and the crowds are therefore less partisan.

Coaching

Sports coaching emerged as a specialised profession in the 1870s and coincided with the growth of competitive sport. Similarly to Britain at the same time, the elite institutions had a vested interest in achieving team records and individual achievements. A split occurred between sports coaching and physical education. The former concentrated on competitive success, rewards for success, culminating in an intense pressure to win, particularly at inter-collegiate and professional levels. The latter, on the other hand, stressed the health, enjoyment and personal development as its major goals.

The role of the coach will often determine the type of behaviour which will most successfully achieve the desired outcome. Coaches are generally assertive, tough and focused on high achievement. As athletes progress up the sporting ladder, from high school to the youth leagues, to inter-collegiate and professional ranks, these

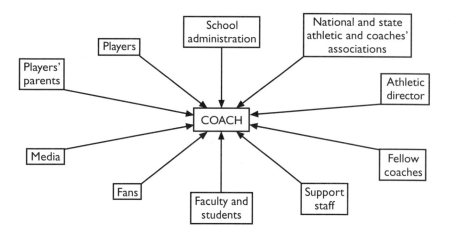

Fig. 19.8 ROLE STRAIN FOR THE COLLEGE COACH

aspects of a coach's behaviour would be expected to increase. As coaches are held accountable for the results and the results are scrutinised and publicly reported, they have a lot of pressure to succeed. This can lead to 'role strain' and ultimately to role conflict (Coakley, 1993). The coach has to interact with many different people, each with different expectations, and can find it difficult to meet everyone's needs. In America, young coaches need a mentor and they usually rely on the sponsorship of established coaches. This has tended to reinforce the perpetuation of values and can exclude women and ethnic groups.

- **Compare the role of the sports coach with that of the physical education teacher in the USA.**
- **How would you change this situation in order to attract minority groups into coaching for a long term effect?**

Ethnicity and sport

A 'race logic' was developed by the early colonialists in America, that black people were physically superior but mentally inferior to white people. Historically, the sports associated with black people during the slavery era were boxing and horse racing.

- In boxing, the white owners would train up a black boxer, and use the fight as a way of entertainment and opportunity for wagering. The boxer would have gained considerably less from the situation, and parallels can be drawn to the gladiatorial concept.
- In horse racing, white owners were involved in the training and planning but the jockeys were usually black, fulfilling a role which required a more mechanical and physical input.

These racial prejudices have been difficult to overthrow, and are still common within the social institution of sport. The tennis player Arthur Ashe was not allowed to play in certain parts of America, as tennis was at that time still a white, middle class sport. A similar situation was highlighted in 1997 with the emergence of Tiger Woods in the golfing arena, who has also experienced prejudice and discrimination. Racial stacking in sports teams is a well reported issue, where players from a certain racial group are either over- or under-represented in certain positions in a sports team. Black players traditionally have not occupied positions which require decision making but have been placed in positions which rely on the physical attributes of speed, reflexes and strength. In football there have been few black quarterbacks, though in recent times when the role of quarterback has become more physical, there has been a corresponding increase in black quarterbacks. It does not necessarily mean that there has been an improvement in equal opportunities within the sport.

In baseball, black people have tended to occupy the outfield positions, despite the fact that there used to be a highly successful black baseball league when they would have fulfilled all those roles themselves! It was only when the white owners moved in that their status within the game began to change. There is a parallel with cricket in the nineteenth century, when the lower classes would occupy more physical positions, leaving the central positions requiring thinking, strategy and closer social interaction to the upper classes. This is also closely tied to Grusky's theory of centrality. A vicious circle is created and these beliefs perpetuated, as few black people become coaches or sports administrators.

The lower sport participation rates and ethnic sport preferences have also been determined by these ideological factors. The dominant group determines the access and opportunities available, and it is not easy for minority groups to challenge those social determinants, despite the exception who manages to create the American dream. They can become role models for their ethnic groups, but this can reinforce the stereotypes that only a particular type of sport is suitable for black people, and that sport rather than education is the most suitable avenue for social mobility.

Children's organised sports programmes

If sporting activities carry socially desirable values, it is not surprising that a culture will try to develop such qualities in its young. An example of a well organised sports programme for children is **Little League Baseball**, which was established in 1939 and is now a business organisation employing full time professional employees and volunteers. It was initially set up by parents who wanted a well structured sporting programme. The league caters for 8–18 year olds and is the largest of its kind in the world attracting media coverage. A senior division for youngsters aged 13–15 and a big league for the 16–18 year olds is also part of the programme.

Children are selected by competitive trials for their specified age range, and the winning of leagues and tournaments is highly valued. Following local and regional playoffs, an annual world series is held where foreign teams can also enter.

The league is based on adult leagues, with some modifications: the diamond is two thirds the size and the games are limited to six innings. The season lasts 15 games, with no more than two games a week being permitted.

Table 19.2   PRINCIPLES OF PLAY, ADULT SPORTING PROGRAMMES AND LITTLE LEAGUE

PURE CHARACTERISTICS OF PLAY	ADULT-ORGANISED SPORTS PROGRAMMES	DESCRIPTION OF LITTLE LEAGUE
spontaneous	organised	established in 1930s
creative	serious	business organisation
developmental	institutionalised	full time professionals and volunteers involved
experimental	rationalised	world's largest sports league for children
enjoyable	socialisation	television coverage
use initiative	bureaucracy	specified age groups
rule making and enforcing	competitive	highly competitive
develop moral judgements	success valued highly	high degree of commitment required

ACTIVITY 10

What are the characteristics of adult organised children's sports programmes, and what problems can be associated with them?

Senior programmes

At the other end of the age spectrum, is the U.S. National Senior Sports Classic VI, the Senior Olympics. The U.S. National Senior Sports Organisation promotes the image of healthy old age, aiming to establish positive role models for health and physical fitness. The opening ceremonies usually attract 10,000 athletes.

Outdoor education and recreation

The importance attached to the 'great outdoors' in American society is evident in its literature and films. The links go back to the days of the pioneers and their efforts to overcome numerous obstacles in their attempts to push back the geographical frontiers. The scale and size of the country, with its varied land relief and climates, make for rich and exciting experiences. The character-building qualities which emerge from such experiences are still considered as important to America's future.

The National Parks are administered by the Bureau of Outdoor Education, which has developed a coherent structured approach. The land is classified according to its level of isolation; Class I would be close to towns and would be widely used, while Class V would be classed as wilderness areas where it is possible to wander undisturbed for days. There is nothing comparable to this latter section in Britain.

There has been an increase in the participation of high risk sports in the USA since the 1970s. These sports can be classed as a counter culture, because they oppose the social values of competition and chance, favouring stimulation and vertigo. The rise in popularity of such sports can be attributed to several factors: see Chapter 13.

Concerns over safety have led to action to regulate these sports in the form of The Federal Aviation Administration, and the National Park Service of the Department of the Interior which controls rock climbing and mountaineering. However, isn't this sort of regulation exactly what people may be trying to get away from?

Outdoor education camps

07.15	Reveille. Short optional dip or jog.
07.45	Flag raising and personal inspection.
08.00	Breakfast, followed by clean-up of the cabin or tent.
09.30	1st activity period.
10.30	2nd activity period.
11.45	Optional general swim.
12.30	Lunch.
13.30	Rest hour supervision.
14.30	1st afternoon activity period.
15.30	2nd afternoon activity period.
16.30	Free time supervision.
18.00	Dinner.
19.00	Flag lowering– followed by special evening events.
21.00	First Bell– lights out for younger children.
22.00	Lights out for the seniors.

'While some routine is essential there is always something different planned to bring new experience into a busy, happy, healthy existence'

Fig. 19.9 A TYPICAL DAY AT CAMP

The camping movement did not gain acceptance until 1900. The first 100 camps were initiated by teachers and were supplemented by the YMCA, the Boy and Girl Scouts, Campfire Girls etc. The American Camping Association was formed, and camping programmes gradually gained educational acceptance and helped to raise the status of welfare and general camps.

There are several thousand summer camps for children throughout the USA and Canada, mostly permanent camps where children can reside for one to eight weeks. The camps take children from 6–16 years, and are responsible for their welfare 24 hours a day. 'Going to camp' for an extended period of time is a well established tradition in the USA. There has been a tradition of sending urban children to the natural environment, and in a country where the summer holidays last three months, it is accepted for children to spend time away from their parents.

There are different types of camps:

- **Private residential** – these are privately owned and cater for the high/middle income families. They run on a profit-making policy, providing permanent residential facilities, and operate all over the country. They have a range of facilities for various sports and crafts.
- **Day camps** – these can also be privately owned or run by organisations such as the YMCA or local towns.
- **Organisational camps** – these are run by Christian based organisations like the Girl and Boy Scouts and the YMCA, though the emphasis on religion can vary.
- **Camps for underprivileged children** – these are operated by various social, philanthropic or religious agencies like the Salvation Army, and aim to give inner-city children a break from the urban environment. It is very heavily subsidised, with families paying little or nothing at all towards the cost. The facilities are more basic and the emphasis is on the recreational experience and appreciating the environment.
- **Special needs camps** – these are for people with physical or mental disabilities (adults as well as children), diabetics, people who are overweight (often termed Fat Camps), or who have special learning or behavioural problems.

Summary

- There is a decentralised system – each state operates its own administration.
- There are exclusive, private clubs, but which are different from British sports clubs.

- Careers in sport tend to take the route of collegiate sport as a feeder for the professional leagues as well as maintaining amateur eligibility.
- Inter-scholastic and collegiate sport is run on business and commercial lines, with control exerted by cartels.
- There is still discrimination in sport for female and black athletes, though legislation has laid the foundations for change.
- The dominant sports reflect the capitalist culture from which they evolved.
- The government tries not to become too involved in sport, but has produced much legislation in particular areas. Where business interests occur, the government tends to favour the sports bodies which will bring revenue and civic prestige.
- Children's sports programmes stress the dominant sporting values of adults and there is a tendency for an over-emphasis on winning.

France

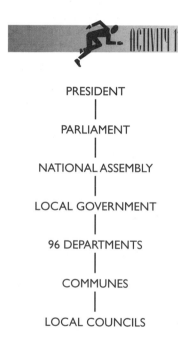

Consider the impact of the factors in fig 19.11 on the system of sport in France.

PRESIDENT
|
PARLIAMENT
|
NATIONAL ASSEMBLY
|
LOCAL GOVERNMENT
|
96 DEPARTMENTS
|
COMMUNES
|
LOCAL COUNCILS

Fig. 19.10 FRENCH GOVERNMENT

Politics

Political power is shared between the President and Parliament. The former is elected by the people, and is head of state and the chief executive; the latter consists of the National Assembly comprising 577 deputies, and is also elected. It is a democratic system in which numerous parties have an opportunity to gain seats. The President appoints the Prime Minister who deals with the day-to-day running of the country's affairs.

Local government is divided into 96 departments which in turn are divided into communes (towns and villages), governed by elected mayors and councils. The departments are grouped into 22 regions. France used to be highly centralised with the national government wielding power in the regions, through the prefects, who controlled police and law and order. However, since 1982, locally elected bodies such as town and regional councils have had more power, and the prefects's influence has started to decline. This was a result of the socialist policies of President Mitterand (1981–1995) who advocated the decentralisation of government. He was ousted from power by the Conservative Jacques Chirac.

Physical education

Children are taught in primary schools from the age of 6–10 years, then in a secondary school from 11–18 years. Schools and universities are state controlled and the traditional links between them make them inter-dependent.

Physical education comes under the control of the Secretary of State for Youth and Sport. The central administration comprises four sections, one of which is the Physical Education and Sports section. This section deals with two branches – the Physical Education and Sports Department and the Department of Sport Activities. There is a clear hierarchical system of role responsibility which can ease the planning and implementation of policy. The Department of Sports Activities oversees the national sport federations, which coordinate at local, regional and national level. There are two kinds of federation – the single and multi sport. The local clubs however, still form the basis of French sport, similar to the UK.

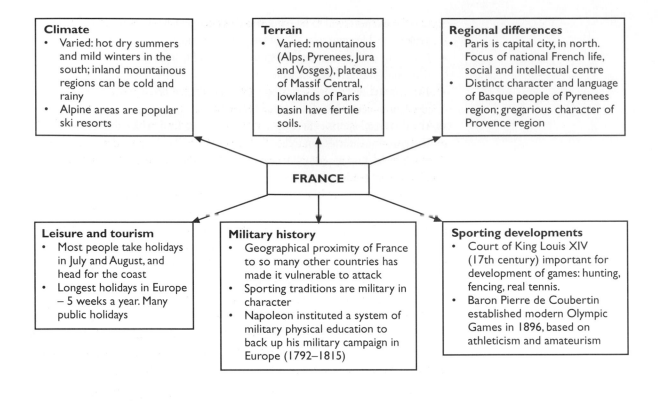

Climate
- Varied: hot dry summers and mild winters in the south; inland mountainous regions can be cold and rainy
- Alpine areas are popular ski resorts

Terrain
- Varied: mountainous (Alps, Pyrenees, Jura and Vosges), plateaus of Massif Central, lowlands of Paris basin have fertile soils.

Regional differences
- Paris is capital city, in north. Focus of national French life, social and intellectual centre
- Distinct character and language of Basque people of Pyrenees region; gregarious character of Provence region

FRANCE

Leisure and tourism
- Most people take holidays in July and August, and head for the coast
- Longest holidays in Europe – 5 weeks a year. Many public holidays

Military history
- Geographical proximity of France to so many other countries has made it vulnerable to attack
- Sporting traditions are military in character
- Napoleon instituted a system of military physical education to back up his military campaign in Europe (1792–1815)

Sporting developments
- Court of King Louis XIV (17th century) important for development of games: hunting, fencing, real tennis.
- Baron Pierre de Coubertin established modern Olympic Games in 1896, based on athleticism and amateurism

Fig. 19.11 FRANCE

The French have strong traditions for intellectual rigor. The state lycées offer free tuition to all, but some are more exclusive. The state secondary school or colleges are similar to British comprehensive schools. The Baccalaureat is taken at 18 years and is a rigorous exam, essential for higher education (note the possibility that the British government may move towards a Baccalaureat system). There are also technical lycées for the more middle ability range. There are a mixture of state and private schools which are Catholic. The education system is centralised – decisions made by the government are transmitted across the country. However, in reality, the further from Paris, the less adherence is made to governmental decisions.

Primary education

Primary school focuses on the child's physical and psychological development. The 1969 decree instituted the 'one third teaching time' system, or 'Le Tiers Temps Pedagogique', which is a fixed weekly quota of 27 hours to be spent at school. Of these 27 hours, six are devoted to PE and sport. This was believed to be the most flexible way of arranging sessions to meet the needs of individual schools and to break down the subject barriers.

The children are put in an exploratory situation which will help them discover things for themselves. High priority is placed on the fundamental motor skills of swimming and athletics. However, the reality does not always reflect the ideal. The primary school teacher, though given access to specialist help, is often not specialist trained, and facilities vary enormously. It is only in a few schools that the suggested time is given to PE and sport.

The institutionalised implementation of this system has allowed for the development of experimental classes in winter, by the sea and in the country; these are known as 'half time teaching classes'. The children spend two to three weeks in the natural environment while continuing their education. The classes are literally transplanted to a special centre, and have two main objectives:

1 to give the children an opportunity to get away from urban pollution
2 to discover and appreciate the natural environment.

They allow the children a wider appreciation of the variations within their own country. The class teacher is fundamental to the success of this system as they must plan and prepare according to the needs of their children.

Secondary education

The Official Instructions of 1967 came from the Ministry for teachers of PE and sport. They consist of four main parts:

1 the place of PE and Sport in education as a whole
2 a categorising of activities and their intended benefits to the children
3 the role of the teacher
4 the practical organisation of teaching PE.

These documents were intended as a guide to help the teacher plan the syllabus, while respecting the spirit of the instructions. Each school was expected to produce a programme of work which should include: floor or apparatus gymnastics, athletics, ball skills, combat sports, team sports.

In addition to the compulsory PE and sports sessions on the timetable, a pupil must practise a sport either within a school sports association, or at a sports centre (Centres d'animation sportive, CAS), under the direction of the Department for Youth and Sport, or in a municipal or private club. The aim is to spend approximately five hours a week on physical activity and sport. The optional sport programme is very different from the class situation, and creates affinity groups.

The generally poor sports facilities at secondary schools hinder the implementation of an effective programme, and the choice of activities is much narrower than in Britain. From 1954, all schools were to be built with a gymnasium or sports field, but funds for this ambitious plan soon dried up. The government has encouraged the use of council facilities; but these are heavily used by many school groups, and the logistics of planning the time and transport creates problems for the teachers. Another inhibiting factor is the need for pupils to practise the restricted number of activities which will form part of their leaving certificate, taken at 15 at the end of the first phase of secondary schooling and the Baccalaureat at 18. The school sport system is perceived as more important than the physical education by parents and pupils. They view PE more as a way of passing the exam. The club allows them the access to develop greater skill and prowess, more so than in Britain.

In this respect France is quite different from Britain. In France, there is a definite trend towards prioritising sport rather than PE, creating strong links between schools and clubs.

Sports afternoons are supposed to be an official part of the school curriculum but the ongoing problems of administrators not having sufficient interest in physical education limits their effectiveness. The policy of sports afternoons is centrally controlled by a State Federation through to a Regional and Local Federation. The pupils must have a licence (membership card), so statistical evidence of sport participation is available. Team games like soccer and rugby and individual sports like tennis, skiing and mountaineering are among the most popular sports according to the membership numbers. These statistics provide evidence of trends and projections which can be used for policy making, a medical reference point and can help to monitor standards for selection purposes.

Table 19.3   THE STRUCTURE OF THE EDUCATION SYSTEM

AGE	EDUCATION	ESTABLISHMENT
2–5	Pre-School (non compulsory)	Nursery School
6–10	Primary	Primary School
11–14	Secondary – 1st stage	College
15–17	Secondary – 2nd stage	Lycée
18	Higher	University, Grandes Ecoles

Table 19.4   THE WEEKLY HOURS OF PE AND SPORT IN SCHOOLS

PRIMARY		SECONDARY	
		Stage 1	Stage 2
PE and Sport (Compulsory)	1/3 teaching time 6 hrs	PE & Sport 3 hrs	PE & Sport 2 hrs
		Sport (CAS) 2 hrs	Sport (CAS) 3 hrs
Sport (Optional)	USEP half day	UNSS half day School Sports Association	

Optional = the pupil may select a sport of his choice. Takes place either in school, in CAS (sports centre), or in a club authorised by the Regional Directorate for Youth and Sport.

Organisations for school sport

Historically, school and university sport have been closely allied in France. The Association of School and University Sport (ASSU) was formed in 1963. They then separated in 1975, with the creation of the UNSS, Union Nationale du Sport Scolaire for school sport, and the FNSU for university sport.

Schools formed sport associations whereby children could practise on a voluntary basis the sport of their choice at the times allocated on the timetable. The school sports associations are therefore the fundamental unit which gives access to a maximum number of young people. The association aimed to provide competitive educational events for both junior and senior high schools. The PE teachers are directly involved in the sport process as well as their main priority of PE, which provides a natural continuity.

The creation of 'mass formulae' are a proper introduction to competitive sport. They are a system of multi-sport competitions involving over a period of eight half days, the class as a social unit. The licence allows pupils to register for all sports. Competitions are based on a pyramid structure with losers offered further competitions adapted to their level. This provides good preparation for helping students join the federal or civil clubs, but there can be conflict between the clubs and schools as they compete for the most talented children. Teachers can also sometimes feel that sport poses a threat to physical education.

 ACTIVITY 12

What parallels can you draw between physical education and school sport in the UK and France? What are the advantages of the 'license' system?

'Sport Pour Tous'

In 1972, the French National Olympic and Sports Committee was given responsibility for a campaign to promote sport for all, following France's participation in the proceedings held by the Council of Europe. The State Department for Youth and Sport supplied a teacher of physical education and sport

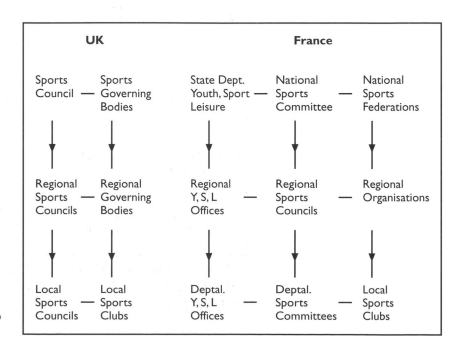

UK		France		
Sports Council —	Sports Governing Bodies	State Dept. Youth, Sport — Leisure	National Sports Committee —	National Sports Federations
↓	↓	↓	↓	↓
Regional Sports Councils —	Regional Governing Bodies	Regional Y, S, L — Offices	Regional Sports Councils —	Regional Organisations
↓	↓	↓	↓	↓
Local Sports Councils —	Local Sports Clubs	Deptal. Y, S, L — Offices	Deptal. Sports Committees —	Local Sports Clubs

Fig. 19.12 COMPARISON OF FRENCH AND BRITISH SPORTS ADMINISTRATION

to advise the Committee. The campaign was intended to convince the public of the necessity for a minimal participation in physical pursuits and sport, and to enable their access irrespective of their social status. It was specifically aimed at non-participating adults, and there were three levels at which intervention could occur:

1 Leisure time: adults were encouraged to practise a sport.
2 Place of work: it was stressed that workers needed to be in better physical condition for their own safety.
3 Place of residence: the development of sport has greater potential where facilities are organised close to places of residence. Making amenities more accessible was therefore a prime aim.

The administration of sport, in both the UK and France is split between national, regional and local levels. Both countries operate 'sport for all' campaigns. However, France is more bureaucratic at the sporting level, and financial aid is more substantial. The state finances sport to a greater degree than in the UK and yet the British are experts in financing their own sport; and as such, are perhaps more enthusiastic about sport, than a people who rely on state aid for their recreation.

The slogans of French 'Sport for All' are:

- **Within Everyone's Reach**
- **Need to be Physically Active**
- **A Noble Lifestyle**
- **Mass Participation in a wide range of Activities**
- **Socialisation of the Family and Continuity through sport**
- **Instil a Love of the Open Air**
- **Spontaneity.**

Excellence in French sport

Excellence in sport is often taken up by national governments in its attempts to gain international prestige, and the realisation that sport has its place within international politics in the twentieth century. Sport was initially a preparation for the military and subsequently a substitute for military conflict.

France concentrated on elitism more perhaps than any other European nation. France has a long history of physical excellence – its elite academies in the Renaissance era promoted the cultural development of aristocrats. Military defeats in the nineteenth century led to a reassessment of physical preparation in military and civic terms. As we have mentioned, Baron Pierre de Coubertin set out to revitalise the French nation in its approach towards physical activity.

This type of philosophy was taken up by de Gaulle, post World War II, as part of his nationalist policies in which he wanted political, economic and sporting success. Following the poor French results in the Rome Olympics 1960 which dented national pride and prestige, he was reported as saying 'if we want medals we must pay for them. We (the state) must take up the organisation and financing of sport'. In 1966 he awarded the Legion of Honour to six champions. State aid was granted to improve facilities and administration support as part of a centralised approach. Ministerial decrees and instructions were supported by regional and departmental offices to coordinate the national policy.

In the 1970s INSEP, the National Sports Institute, was created from the merging of the National Sports Institute (INS) and the teacher training establishment

Fig. 19.13 WOMEN'S RUGBY
INTERNATIONAL MATCH BETWEEN FRANCE AND
ENGLAND

(ENSEPS), which aimed to produce the adult elite performer. It is a centre of
excellence:

- It undertakes scientific research.
- It produces highly qualified teachers, coaches and administrators.
- Selection is undertaken by the federations (governing bodies) and there is
  constant feedback of the medical screening to coaches.
- It provides a venue for national team training in their quest for excellence.
- There is a permanent sport study section for over 100 children which caters
  specifically for swimming, gymnastics and tennis.

The process of talent identification begins with the Brevet d'Aptitude Physique
for 8–12 year olds. Another initiative is 'Amenagement du Rhythme de Vie de
l'Enfant' (ARVE), which targets young people primarily to participate in sporting
activity. At club level, the Carnet de Valeur Physique tests more specific skills for
10–18 year olds. The Regional Sports Study Sections involve 11–29 year olds in
further laboratory screening, culminating at INSEP where medical, psychological,
sociological, biomechanics measurements, physiology and physical training tests,
take place.

Allied with this are the sport study sections. They provide special classes for
talented children and certain schools offer certain sports. These have the usual
advantages of sports schools – excellent facilities, coaching, medical and
physiological tests, structured competition – while normal schooling continues. The
pupils would still work towards the Baccalaureat ABCD or G and reach a certain
level in their chosen sport. One was established at Lycée Font Romeu, high up in the
Pyrenees for high altitude training.

The boarding school concept was favoured by the French and easily administered due to the national philosophy, direction and coordination by the Ministry of Sport and the centrally directed and uniform system of education. They have generally achieved moderate sporting success with good academic success.

Sport study sections are a part of the normal school system with specialised groups working in certain sports. High quality teaching and coaching is drafted in and movement on to specific centres is possible for specific sports excellence. By 1975 there were over 106 sport study sections catering for 2,000 pupils in 23 sports. In 1980 there were 145 catering for 3,400. There is heavy competition for places, and they are popular with parents and pupils.

Outdoor education and recreation

The varied climate and land forms offer excellent choices in outdoor pursuit activities both within and outside of the school system. As in the USA, French people place a strong emphasis on getting children away from the cities to appreciate country life. There is a similar tradition in France as in the USA of parents taking separate holidays to their children, and the camp experience is a high priority.

This priority begins at school as part of the curriculum with the transplant classes where children are taken into the country to appreciate the variety of regions in France as well as developing the outdoor pursuit skills of skiing, sailing, climbing and so on. The teacher accompanies the class, to combine normal teaching in the morning with an outdoor activity in the afternoon. They can cater for over a million children every year.

The 'colonie de vacance' are mainly aimed at low income, disadvantaged groups and the costs are subsidised. There are also camps for the wealthier sections of society, and they are very similar to the USA camp schools.

The Union Nationale des Centres de Plein Air (UCPA) is a world leading organisation for training in outdoor pursuits. It runs 51 centres, which can accommodate 60,000 per year and has extensive facilities, equipment and instruction. They concentrate on eight sports – skiing, climbing, underwater swimming, riding, sailing, coastal cruising and canoe-kayak. They also specialise in more general open air activities such as Safari Photo which is like orienteering with a camera, and 'discovery of the mountains' in the Alps and Pyrenees.

British–French sport exchanges are popular as France offers a wider variety of terrain, climate and sports facilities than the UK. Governing bodies, the Sports Council and LEAs have long established links.

 ACTIVITY 13

Consider the place of outdoor education on the National Curriculum, the mainly fee-paying outdoor pursuit holidays which are available in the UK and British specialist Outdoor Pursuit Centres, in order to better understand the differences between France and Britain.

Sport and ethnicity

Ethnic communities in France have generally maintained their own cultures and pastimes, which include pelota, bull fighting and boule or petanque. Cultural traditions which have survived the rapid changes in the modern world tend to have common factors:

• They tend to be in isolated geographical areas which are less prone to outside influences and where changes take much longer to occur.

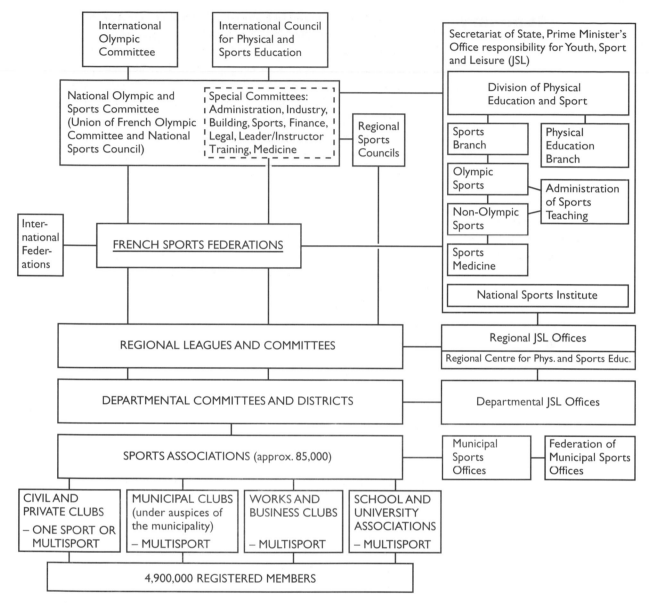

Fig. 19.14 THE STRUCTURE OF SPORT IN FRANCE

- They tend to be rural and agriculturally-based, reflected in the strength-based activities, and activities which may once have had an initial utilitarian purpose.
- The connection to a particular area also gives it a cultural identity and local pride.
- Local competitions began as communities gathered together for recreation purposes.
- They often require simple, unsophisticated facilities and equipment.

ACTIVITY 14

Compare the Highland Games to the French ethnic festivals.

ACTIVITY 15

- **Research some information on the Tours de France.**
- **What characteristics have made boules a popular game in France?**

Summary
- There is a centralised political approach to education and sport.
- The Federation (akin to British governing bodies) is the fulcrum of French sport, and is answerable to the Minister for Sport.
- There is a tradition of multi-sport federations like the UNSS, unlike the British tradition of single sex clubs.
- Elite sport was encouraged by the policies of Charles de Gaulle, and has received state aid and support with the development of elite centres like INSEP.
- There are strong links between schools and civil clubs.
- The facilities in schools are generally poor and have led to more use of municipal facilities.
- Physical education is an examination subject on a compulsory basis and a rigid programme is followed.
- A programme of 'Sport pour Tous', similar to our Sport for All campaign, is aimed at improving the health of the nation.

Australia

Consider the impact of the factors in fig 19.15 on the system of sport in Australia.

Politics

Australia is a member of the Commonwealth of Nations. The federal government is located in Canberra and conducts the national affairs. Similar to the United States, the Australian states have their own parliament and governor. It is a society based on democracy, with each citizen entitled to vote once they reach the age of eighteen.

Legislative authority is held by the Federal Parliament, and political power rests with the Prime Minister who heads the government.

Education

Education is compulsory for all Australian children between the ages of 6 and 15. Infant classes however, are available from age five. A free education is provided by the government in schools in all populated areas of the country. Similar to most other countries, fee-paying schools also operate and are often associated with religious denominations. Similar to the USA, the individual states have overriding responsibility for education, therefore generalisations are dangerous, although a centralised system does operate. Some funds are allocated by federal government from levied taxes, but the government does not have control over the states' spending. New policies show some similarities to the British model of Local Management of Schools where responsibility for salaries and maintenance, among other issues, has passed from the central administration to the individual schools.

The State Department of Education lays down the educational content of syllabuses, trains the teachers and acts as a final authority.

Children who live in the outback are too far away from official schools, so they receive instruction over the air waves and send work to be graded. This operates under a programme called School of the Air. They can also attend a school which travels to them by railroad.

There are approximately 20 universities and a number of colleges that offer courses leading to undergraduate and advanced degrees.

History and population
- Indigenous Aboriginal community, migrated to Australia in pre-historic times
- Attractive country for immigration since World War II, resulting in diverse, multi-cultural society
- 85% of population live in cities

History
- European settlers arrived in 1788; Australia became a British colony
- Free settlers began to arrive in 1820s, finding fertile land in the west
- Colonies became self-governing during end of nineteenth century, formed Commonwealth of Australia

AUSTRALIA

Geography
- Made up of six states: New South Wales, Victoria, Queensland, South Australia, Western Australia, Tasmania
- Major cities are located in the costal areas
- Isolated by seas and oceans

Climate
- Seasons are reversed from northern hemisphere
- Tropical climate in the north, temperate climate in the south
- Pacific coasts receive highest rainfall; non-coastal regions are very dry

Communication
- Transport is well developed – extensive network of roads along coast, modernised train service and internal air service
- Use of satellite has allowed television access to previously remote areas

Fig. 19.15 AUSTRALIA

Physical education

Each state develops its own physical education. In some states, a considerable integration of school and council personnel and facilities has been realised. Local committees with sub committees made up of voluntary youth organisations and junior sport organisations have developed a number of play centers, recreation leadership programmes and coaching clinics.

Teachers are trained at colleges in two or three year diploma courses. Degree programmes have taken longer to establish. The teacher training programmes require the students to enter into a contract to complete the course and to serve as teachers for a certain period of time.

Outdoor activities are the norm in this favourable climate. Schools generally have good playing field facilities, swimming pools and outdoor gymnasia. In elementary schools, the emphasis tends to be on posture, gymnastics games and movement activities. At secondary level, conditioning or fitness activities, gymnastics, track and field games and swimming are integral parts of the programme. Girls participate more positively than their American counterparts.

Similarly to France, the sports afternoon, morning coaching session or sports day supplement physical education lessons. All pupils and teachers are expected to participate, with the more specialised teachers taking inter-scholastic teams. In reality however, there is a high absentee rate from students who are not interested.

Competitive sports are controlled by amateur athletic associations and annual state championships are held in separate sports. In 1975 the National School Sports Council was established, which signalled the growing formalisation of school sport.

There is strong interest in the international Outward Bound Movement and the Duke of Edinburgh Award Scheme. Mountain areas which have the benefit of snow are popular venues for weekenders and holiday enthusiasts. Swimming is the most

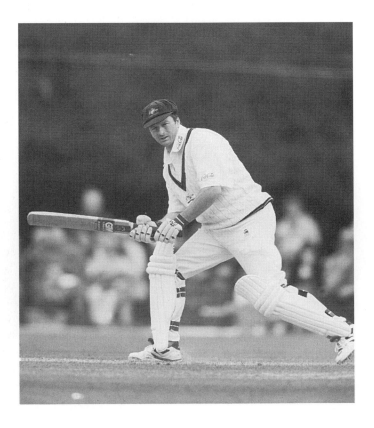

Fig. 19.16 STEVE WAUGH, ONE OF
AUSTRALIA'S HIGHEST SCORING BATSMEN

popular sport – heavy emphasis is placed on this within the school curriculum, and it is the most popular participant sport.

The Government commissioned a state-wide physical education and sport survey which was completed in 1993 but data and findings have been slow to emerge. The Federal Response to the Report has been disappointing.

Important bodies such as the Australian Council for Health, Physical Education and Recreation (ACPHER) have agreed that all government schools should have weekly timetabled physical education lessons. However, constraints limited the schools' implementation of the recommended compulsory 60 minutes of physical education every day.

ACPHER has also proposed that all primary schools should have access to trained physical education specialists whether it be a permanent or peripatetic resource.

Physical education in Victoria

It is useful to study a particular state as this can give more specific information about physical education as well as allowing a more general understanding of sport in Australia to take place. There has generally, across Australia, been a lack of political will to put in place coordinated and well funded sports policies. However, there are exceptions and the state of Victoria is one of them.

With a new government, physical education has been viewed as a priority area by the Ministers of Education and Sport and Recreation as well as the Chief Executive of Education.

The Review of Physical and Sport Education in Victorian Schools was begun in 1993 by the Minister for Education in an attempt to develop a coordinated approach towards improving children's experiences and participation in physical and sport education. This resulted in the implementation of the Physical and Sport Education in Schools Policy in 1995, and has proved to be a watershed for Australian policy. Victoria received $2 million for the professional development and additional staffing for 'model' schools. Other schools were to share $1 million, to support efforts for improvements in facilities and participation.

The main recommendations were as follows:

1 PE and sport to be a high priority in the school charter and to receive accreditation for courses.
2 The training of non specialist teachers to be upgraded. Already, approximately 8,000 teachers have attended new PASE courses.

The DSE also produced 'Health and Physical Education – Curriculum Standards Framework' in 1995. However, the level of bureaucracy may well cause some problems, especially for the non specialist teachers. Tests have begun in mathematics and English, and physical education should be tested in the near future. As in France, the problems which can occur from schools teaching 'for the tests' have caused concern.

- The Victorian Primary and Secondary School Sports Associations organise inter-school sports throughout the state, benefiting from federal government grants.
- The Directorate of School Education supports staff development, and helps with the promotion of sport through these associations.
- School Sports Awards recognise excellence in major school sports and can be given to individuals, teams and coaches, and those who help the school in its

attempts to improve the standards of school sport. You may recognise a similarity here between the Sportsmark Awards the Conservative government promised to those schools who meet the criteria laid out in the document 'Sport: Raising the Game', in 1995.

- Similarly to the United States, the national television networks are becoming involved to show features on school sport, from school initiatives to information on individual students and sports events. This can encourage a community interest in school sport.
- Victoria has its own state 'Aussie Sport' programme (see below).
  - 'Be Your Best' Aussie Sport aims to help students and teachers learn the modified sports with the help of a Sport Development Officer.
  - 'Be Your Best' School Club Activity Days encourage links between schools and clubs
  - 'Be Your Best' Allsports programme is an after school/weekend programme involving local sporting clubs and youth coaches.

'Aussie Sport'

'Aussie Sport' is a national sporting initiative committed to the development of young people through sport. The ASC and the state departments of sport and education work closely together in order to foster positive community relationships, to ensure a coordinated approach to junior sport in their area.

'Aussie Sport' is about

- supporting quality teaching and coaching
- promoting and developing quality sport for young people
- making sport more accessible, easier to play and enjoyable
- developing essential sporting skills in young people
- fostering greater community involvement in junior sport

Various programmes are tailored to suit different needs:

Sportstart

This is aimed at working with young children through very informal play activities, such as simple games and activities, and playshop courses to help parents understand their children's play habits.

'Sportit'

This is designed for primary school children to learn the basic motor skills used in the major sports. Packages have been designed to help teachers promote this area within the timetable allocation. The Modified Sport Programme is a way of reducing or putting in miniature, adult sport programmes. Examples are Netta Netball, Minkey and RooBall. Over 40 national sporting organisations have developed modified versions of their sport.

'Sport – Everyone's Game'

This aims to reach all groups within society and particularly those with lower active participation ratios. Examples include 'The Active Girls Campaign' and 'Willing and Able' (for disabled people). A computer program to help children select activities appropriate to them is available through 'Sport Search'. They can identify their own characteristics and gain information about sports and the associated organisations.

Players	Parents	Teachers
• Play by the rules • Never argue with an official • Control your temper • Work hard for yourself and for your team • Applaud good play from the opposition • Treat all players with respect • Cooperate with your coach and team-mates • Play for fun, not just to please parents and coaches	• Remember that children play sport for their enjoyment • Encourage children to participate • Focus on the child's effort rather than winning or losing • Never ridicule a child for losing • Applaud good play by the opposition • Support efforts to remove verbal and physical abuse from sport • Respect official's decisions • Support volunteer coaches, officials and administrators	• Encourage children to explore different kinds of sport • Teach appropriate sports behaviour as well as skills • Give priority for primary school children to free play activities, rather than highly structured games • Keep up to date with the latest coaching practices • Help children understand that playing by the rules is their responsibility • Give children equal opportunities to participate

Fig. 19.17 AUSSIE SPORT CODES OF BEHAVIOUR

Aussie Sport also runs leadership programmes for secondary school children, which can be compared to the British CCPR Community Sports Leaders Award.

'CAPS'

Challenge, Achievement and Pathways in Sport (CAPS) is a community club based scheme for 14–20 year olds and enables them to acquire skills in the associated fields of coaching, management, officiating and so on.

Talent identification

Attempts to screen for talented sports people has tended to focus on athletes who are already in the system and who have already shown a commitment to their particular activity. The Australians have recently tried to take this one step further by looking for potential talent in those not currently participating.

Sport specific profiles have been instigated, ie, the requirements from both a physiological and psychological viewpoint for a particular sport. Testing has then moved on to the schools to try and match the child to the sport they have been deemed most suited for. The teachers within the school environment carry out the initial tests on 14–16 year olds covering physical measurements and psychological assessments. The top 10% then progress to Phase 2 where more sport specific testing would take place in laboratories.

These children (approximately 10%) become part of a squad within the talent development programme. The state and the individual sporting associations are then responsible for the funding, and variations occur depending on the resources of facilities and coaching. Children who do not make the grade are encouraged to join local clubs to develop their talents.

In order to reduce the duplication of testing for a variety of different sports, each with their own interests at heart, the federal government has released funds for the development of elite athletes, under the Olympic Athlete Programme. The talent search is carried out by a national coordinator and eight state coordinators. These then liaise with the sport specific agencies, academies and school/recreation departments. Perhaps it was no coincidence that this followed the awarding of Sydney for the Olympic Games, in 2000. The sports most suited to this type of testing and most likely to achieve 'quick' results are reflected in those chosen for the search. These are athletics, canoeing, cycling, rowing, swimming, triathlon, water polo and weightlifting.

What do you think makes these particular sports suitable for the talent identification programme?

The response has been very encouraging. In 1995, 40% of all schools eligible to take part did so. At Phase 1 100,000 children took part; Phase 2 10,000; Phase 3 1,000. The aim of the programme is about improving the international standards of performance but there have been positive developments for individuals who have been tested and introduced to the sports they may best be suited to, and has encouraged a national interest for the Olympics in 2000.

Types of sport

The English influence is evident in the sporting traditions of the Australians, both in the type of game such as cricket and rugby, but also in the attitudes of how you play the game, dress codes, etc.

- One of the first recorded cricket games was between two teams of the HMS Calcutta in 1803, and today Australian cricket attracts thousands of spectators. Competition against England (the Ashes) incites nationalist fervour.
- The Australian tennis teams are renowned and have won several Davis Cup competitions.
- Horse racing is an Australian passion.
- Swimming is popular perhaps inevitably as a result of the climate and extensive coasts. The 'Australian crawl' was introduced at the turn of the twentieth century.

It is also interesting to note the recent tendency for Britain to emulate the Australian system for sport, eg basing the British Academy of Sport on the Australian model.

Australian football

This game dates back to 1858 when two men, Harrison and Wills decided to design a purely Australian game. The game which emerged showed signs of influences from cricket (oval pitch), Gaelic football (being played by Irish troops) and the English game of rugby. The cricket pitches were used and were controlled by the cricket clubs. The Melbourne club is the oldest, founded in 1858. This game also helped to keep cricketers fit in the winter months. The size of the playing area even today is not a set distance but has minimum and maximum dimensions. The reason for this game not being successful internationally is the size of the pitch. It is difficult for already established pitches to be converted. The areas in Australia where the game flourishes are reported as having extensive facilities.

Government involvement in sport

The Report of the Australian Sports Institute Study Group 1975 concluded that Australians 'spend an enormous amount of time and money on sport – thinking, talking, reading and writing about it, saving and spending for it and above all, loving it'.

The response of governments to the funding and provision of sport has been mainly ad hoc with a complex network of agencies operating at public, private and shared sectors. Prior to the formation of the Federal Department of Tourism and Recreation in 1972, funding for sport usually came from the sports organisations themselves, apart from sending athletes to international competitions. There was a need to formalise national, state and local plans for sport.

After 1972, a Capital Assistance Programme was to help provide sporting facilities at the local level, and a Sports Assistance Programme was to help national associations with travel, coaching, and administrative costs. A national fitness awareness campaign came under 'Fitness Australia'.

The need for federal involvement in promoting a national sports policy has been addressed. Both major political parties have produced policy statements; mass participation and the pursuit of excellence are important objectives.

The Australian Institute of Sport was established in 1981 in Canberra in cooperation with the Canberra College of Advanced Education, and is an

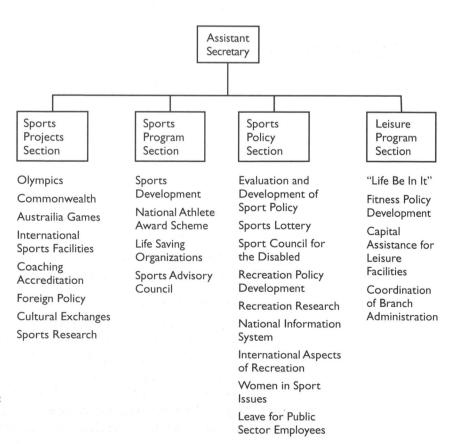

Fig. 19.18 SECTION RESPONSIBILITIES FOR SPORT AND RECREATION BRANCH WITHIN THE MINISTRY OF HOME AFFAIRS

opportunity for talented sports persons to pursue their interest in sport to the highest level without risk to their education. This was the vision of Bob Ellicot, which was given impetus by overseas visits to China, England and America. The federal government funds this initiative. The aims of the Institute are:

1 to provide top level specialist coaching for talented athletes at the same time continuing their education.
2 to support the athletes with sports science and sports medicine back up.

Athletes of both sexes and all ages work under full time national and international coaches.

The Victorian Institute of Sport

Each state has its own Institute of Sport, intended to promote excellence in sport. The Victorian Institute of Sport (VIS) was established in 1990. It is supported financially by the government and private sectors, and a Board of interested and influential sports people establishes its philosophies. For example, individual sports federations can apply for admission, and acceptance will be based on whether they have the required number of registered athletes, how high their athletes are ranked, the selection procedures they operate from local to state level and their potential for attracting sponsorship which will partly be determined by the media profile they have developed. They can be included in the major VIS programmes or one year courses.

Athletes have access to

* advanced coaching – fitness, skill, tactical and psychological aspects of their chosen sport
* competitive opportunities – national and international events
* career development – personal skills, education, future employment prospects

Compare the plans for the British Academy Sport with the Australian model.

Other initiatives include the National Coaching Accreditation Scheme and the International Standard Sports Facilities Programme.

Mass participation

The Australian 'Life Be In It' campaign used the media heavily to promote mass participation. The model starts at the person and aims to assist them in the learning process of making them aware of the need for physical activity, helping them to participate in physical activities and evaluating the participation to assess behavioural changes.

The national sport federations supported by the government carry much of the responsibility for organising mass activities. In contrast, the participant in America has to bear the main cost of participating.

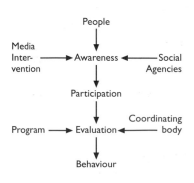

Fig. 19.19 Basic model used in Australian and Canadian programs

The Aborigines

Aborigines were the first original inhabitants of Australia. They lived in nomadic tribes and over the centuries they spread out across the continent, creating and maintaining their own territory in which they had freedom to hunt and fish, though they established only temporary accommodation. They lived in clans and several clans made up an extended family. The spiritual world was an integral part of the philosophy of the Aborigines. Boomerangs were used for hunting (non-returning) and sport (the returning boomerang). The Aborigine population has been decimated by military action, disease and exile into remote areas.

Referring back to Chapter 15, what types of activities would you expect to operate in a primitive nomadic tribe? Chapter 4 in Calhoun (1987) will also help.

Sport and people with disabilities

The first opportunities for disabled athletes in Australia occurred in 1954 under the Australian Deaf Sports Federation; wheelchair sports began in 1972. The Australian Confederation of Sports for the Disabled speaks on behalf of all handicapped sport groups to the government. Associations represented include paraplegic and quadriplegic people, deaf people, those suffering with cerebral palsy, amputees and so on. They generally have national governing bodies, with state associations.

Sport for people with learning difficulties follows a different route. Sport depends on access, awareness, attitudes, acceptance, ability (Little, 1987). There are segregated and integrated programmes depending on these factors, and can be unique to the sport, the club and the individual.

Summary

- Geographically, Australia is similar to the USA, and a variety of scenery and climate allows for wide variations in sports, though with less opportunities for winter sports.
- Australia has felt the influence of the British sports scene and has maintained links with the old country for a longer period of time.
- Australia has similar government administrations to the USA and France.
- Mass participation and the pursuit of excellence are important objectives, though the latter has recently attracted more world attention.
- The original characteristics of sports have been adapted within the more isolated continent and now have their own unique character.
- Sport and physical education are given time on the timetable and outside sports coaches are used within the school setting.

Comparative examination techniques

Having studied each country within its own context, you will need to find a method of directly comparing aspects of sport and physical education across all four countries. A useful method would be to take a topic such as 'the preparation of physical education teachers'. You need to pull aspects of the topic together and then draw up a table and place key words under each country. This can be an effective way of revising.

The preparation of physical education teachers

Having considered how the subject of physical education is taught, we can assess how the teachers are prepared for their future role.

It is important that when you are asked to compare or contrast between different countries, that you clearly state each, rather than assuming that by mentioning one, the examiner will know that you understand the other. The examiner must be able to see a direct comparison in order to link the two together.

Example 1

Question:

What are the different values inherent in school sport in the UK and the USA?

Answer:

USA
- success in victory
- male games playing elite/female cheerleader
- elite sports persons separate to main stream
- heavily financed
- professional/deviance orientation

UK
- value from playing/intrinsic
- equality between girls and boys
- less status for games elite
- no cheerleaders in UK
- no financial privileges
- amateur/PE 'value' system

Example 2

A response to a question about teaching and extra curriculum responsibilities in the UK and the USA could be shown as:

UK
- teacher responsible
- goodwill/no extra pay
- job security
- low community profile
- range of activities

USA
- coach responsible
- coach highly paid
- hire and fire
- high media/community profile
- specialist

A descriptive account will usually gain minimum marks. You will need to show a deeper understanding by applying knowledge gained from each country and showing what effects this will have had on physical education and sport. Thus, political and sociological analysis is required. Terms which you should incorporate in your responses are:

- decentralised/centralised
- democracy/egalitarian
- pluralist/assimilation/ethnic groups
- dominant culture/sub culture
- legislative
- nationalism
- functional/utilitarian/recreational
- autonomous/state-controlled
- capitalist/socialist
- republic/federal

Give a definition and brief example of the above terms.

Conclusion

Issues

Globalisation

It is important to recognise the globalisation of sport due to the technological developments of transport and the media. Countries learn from each other and the issues of human rights are slowly being addressed. Sports like baseball and American football are gaining acceptance outside of the USA.

A 'Core' programme

Despite the many differences existing across the countries we have looked at, there are also many similarities, such as mass participation, elite sport programmes, compulsory physical education and the development of sports for people with disabilities. A wider variety of sports has taken over from the traditional sports of gymnastics, football and track and field.

Commercial sport

Sport is big business and forms a significant income for governments. The development of the consumer market for sports goods, as well as sports events given extensive coverage by the media, contribute to this.

National government involvement in sport

This was summarised by Semoutiak as being for:

- political indoctrination
- labour and military efficiency
- national prestige
- international goodwill
- individualising and socialising function
- economic and legislative functions.

The reasons for different governments becoming involved in sport can reveal a lot about the values of that government and its opinion of physical education and sport.

Values

- The old concept of amateurism has undergone many changes, and abuse is prevalent in many systems, where eligibility for the prestigious Olympic Games is at stake. Situations like trust funds have changed the nature of amateur athletics and the full time training of student athletes for the inter-collegiate competitions are examples of double standards operating. This begs the question – is there a place for amateurism in the twenty-first century?
- Physical education or sport? This is a question of educational philosophy – if the achievement of sporting excellence is the primary aim, the sport ethic can become too dominant and consequently damaging to children's personal development.

- The preparation of the sports professionals is consequently highlighted. Can the physical education teacher, with their primary concern being the individual development of each child through a variety of physical activities, really take on board the win ethic associated with sport and the increasing specialisation required for each individual sport? Consider the priority given to sport in the 1995 publication, 'Sport: Raising the Game'. Do they need to separate and remain with different aims? Does a system where there is a strong link developed between the school and community sport associations, such as in France, show an effective balance?

- Activity versus study? In an era when the industrialised countries of the world are concerned for the increasingly sedentary lifestyles of its citizens, physical education is showing a greater tendency to be examined on a theoretical level, possibly reducing the amount of physical energy expended?

- Nationalist tendencies can be reinforced through sport and can move from a unifying constructive factor to one which incites hatred, exploitation of athletes, unequal distribution of resources.

- The Olympic Games have moved from the original Coubertin aims of reviving French nationalism based on the English tradition of athleticism, to one of providing a world stage for governments to raise their prestige and for political power groups to vent their tensions.

- Is the sports business world beginning to edge out the ordinary supporter, with the increased admission prices? The characteristics of these sports may well continue to change.

- The deviant acts of aggression, drug abuse and lack of respect for sports officials is becoming all too prevalent as the win ethic assumes greater prominence.

Let's hope that in the future we can learn the best practices from each other and keep the positive nature of physical education and sport high on the agenda, for the development of future generations.

Further reading

L Allison (ed), *The Politics of Sport* (Manchester University Press, 1986)

D Anthony, *A Strategy for British Sport* (C Hurst & Co, 1980)

T Arlott, *Oxford Dictionary of Sport* (Oxford University Press, 1975)

P Bailey, *Leisure and Class in Victorian England* (Cambridge University Press, 1981)

P Beashel, J Taylor, *Advanced Studies in Physical Education* (Nelson, 1995)

B Bennet, Howell & Simri, *Comparative Physical Education and Sport* (Lea & Febiger, 1983)

D Birley, *Sport and the Making of Britain* (Manchester University Press, 1993)

B Buford, *Among the Thugs* (Mandarin, 1992)

C Brightbill, *The Challenge of Leisure* (Prentice Hall, 1963)

C Bucher, D Wuest, *Foundations in Physical Education and Sport* (Mosby, 1991)

G Butler, *Introduction to Community Recreation* (McGraw-Hill, 1968)

D W Calhoun, *Sport, Culture and Personality* (Human Kinetics, 1987)

R Callois, *Man Play and Games* (Free Press of Glencoe, 1961)

E Cashmore, *Making Sense of Sport* (Routledge, 1991)

J Coakley, *Sport in Society: Issues and Controversies* (Mosby, 1993)

J F Coghlan, *Sport and British Politics* (J Roscoe Publications, 1990)

Cohen, *Folk Devils and Moral Panics* (Blackwell, 1972)

F W Cozens, *Sports on American Life* (University of Chicago Press, 1953)

V Dalen, B Bennet, *A World History of Physical Education* (Prentice Hall, 1971)

J Dumazadier, *Toward a Society of Leisure* (WW Norton, 1967)

E Dunning, *Quest for Excitement: Sport and Leisure in the Civilising Process* (Blackwell, 1986)

M Ellis, *Why People Play* (Prentice Hall, 1973)

J Ford, *This Sporting Land* (New English Library, 1977)

Gardiner, *Greek Athletic Sports and Festivals* (Brown, 1970)

S de Grazia, *Of Time, Work and Leisure* (Doubleday, 1962)

R Holt, *Sport and the British* (Oxford University Press, 1990)

B Houlihan, *The government and politics of sport* (Routledge 1991)

J Huizinga, *Homo Ludens* (Beacon Press, 1955)

— *The Play Element in Contemporary Sport* (Frank Cass, 1971)

J H Kerr, *Understanding Soccer Hooliganism* (Open University Press, 1994)

R Krause, *Recreation and Leisure in Modern Society*, 2nd ed. (Goodyear Santa Monica, 1978)

A Langley, *World Issues: Sports and Politics* (Wayland, 1989)

J Lieberman, *Playfulness, its Relationship to Imagination and Creativity* (Academic Press, 1977)

Loy, Kenyon, *Sport, Culture and Society* (Lea & Febiger, 1981)

J A Lucas, *The future of the Olympic Games* (Human Kinetics, 1992)

T Marsh, *The Illusion of Violence* (Dent, 1978)

T Mason, *Sport in Britain* (Faber & Faber, 1988)

— *Only a Game* (Cambridge University Press, 1993)

N McFarlane, *Sport and politics – a world divided* (Willow books, 1986)

P McIntosh, *Physical Education in England since 1800* (Bell & Hyman, 1952/78)

M Mead, *Cooperation and Competition among primitive peoples* (Gloucester Mass Peter Smith, 1976)

H Meyer, *Community Recreation* (Prentice Hall, 1964)

C Mortlock, *The Alternative Adventure* (Cicerone Press, 1984)

J Murphy, *Recreation and Leisure Service* (William C Brown, 1975)

J Murphy, Williams and Dunning, *Football on Trial* (Routledge, 1990)

J Nash, *Philosophy of Recreation and Leisure* (C V Mosby, 1960)

M Neumeyer, *Leisure and Recreation* (Ronald Press, 1958)

Pearson, *A History of Respectable Fears* (Macmillan, 1983)

J Piaget, *Play, Dreams and Imitation in Childhood* (Norton, 1962)

J Pieper, *Leisure, the Basis of Culture* (New American Library, 1952)

G Redmond (ed), *Sports and Politics; the 1984 Olympic Scientific Congress Proceedings*, vol 7 (Human Kinetics, 1984)

G Sage, *Power and Ideology in American Sport* (Human Kinetics, 1993)

J Shivers, *Principles and Practices of Recreational Service* (Macmillan, 1967)

W Sumner, *A Study of the Sociological Importance of Usuages, Manners, Customes, Mores and Moral* (Boston Ginn, 1940)

G Torkildsen, *Leisure and Recreation Management* (Spon, 1991)

Taylor, *Soccer Consciousness and Soccer Hooliganism*

M Tozer, *Physical Education at Thring's Uppingham* (University of Leicester, 1974)

British Journal of Physical Education

Central Office of Information, *Aspects of Britain 'Sport and Leisure'* (1994)

Audit Commission, *Sport for Whom?* (1989)

The Hillsborough Stadium Disaster Final Report (HMSO, 1990)

Sports Council publications:

Fifty Plus and All to Play for (1994)

People with Disabilities and Sport (1993)

Sport in the Nineties – New Horizons (Willow, 1986)

Sport – Raising the Game (1995)
What is the Sports Council? Fact Sheet (1994)
Women and Sport (1995)
CCPR publications
The Organisation of Sport and Recreation in Britain
The Howell Report (1993)

chapter 20

The Nature of Skilled Performance

This chapter will give you a basic understanding of the terminology that is used by those involved in physical education and sport in relation to skill development and learning. You should be able to:

- understand the terminology of skill development and learning
- use it in the correct context
- relate it to practical examples.

Here is a list of the terms to be covered in this chapter. It is important that you understand them.

- Motor skill
- Perceptual skill
- Cognitive skill
- Simple skill
- Ability
- Psychomotor ability
- Gross motor ability
- Perceptual ability

- Continuum
- Gross and fine skills
- Discrete, continuous, serial skills
- Self paced/externally paced skills
- High/low cognitive skills
- Feedback
- Complex skill

Once you have read this chapter you should gain an understanding of:

- the phrase **skilled performance**
- the phrase **acquisition of skill**
- the term **skill**.

What is skilled performance?

 **ACTIVITY 1**

In most occupations, sports, daily activities and in the development stages of young children the results of skill learning are evident.

1 Discuss with your fellow students what you think makes a human activity a skilled performance.
2 Try to come up with a short list of examples from various walks of life.

In discussion with your fellow students you will all have been able to suggest various examples of skilled performances, recognising perhaps that a:

- concert pianist may be said to be performing skillfully
- ballet dancer's co-ordination and timing are skillful
- perfect pass by a quarterback in American football is skillful
- long range three point score in basketball is skillful
- well executed off drive in cricket is skillful
- gymnast performing a vault in the Olympic Games is skillful
- pole vaulter completing a vault is skillful
- potter using a potting wheel is skillful.

In other words we can all recognise the outcome or the end product of a skillful performance. However, as students of physical education and sport you need to know:

- how does this end product come about?

What process underlies the acquisition of skill and control of movement? How is skill acquired? What influences its attainment and how is it retained? The following chapters will help you develop a better understanding of the underlying processes involved in acquiring skill.

As a student of physical education and sport you should then be able to:

1 Analyse movement situations.
2 Recognise any faults or problems.
3 Recognise good practice and performance.
4 Solve any problems of how to improve skill levels and overall performance.

As you read through these chapters you will realise that the study of the acquisition of skill is not an exact science. There are no one hundred percent 'correct' or right ways of acquiring skill. Having been made aware of the various related theories, concepts, principles and methods you should be able to:

- use this information to support your understanding
- develop your own ideas
- think about the implications for teaching and coaching.

Using the term 'skill'

You may have noticed in the list of examples given or in your own discussions that the word 'skill' can be used in two slightly different ways. We can use the word to relate to skill as an **act** or **task** or use it as an indicator of **quality** of performance.

Skill as an act or task

The word in this context is used to denote an act or a task that has a specific aim or goal to achieve, for instance a gymnast performing a vault. Further examples are:

- taking a penalty flick in hockey
- shooting a free shot after a foul in basketball
- serving in tennis.

If we observed players carrying out any of the examples given above on a regular basis and they were achieving a high percentage success rate then we would consider them as being skillful players. The use of the word in this context refers to a physical movement, action or task, involving some or all of the body, that a person is trying to carry out in a technically correct manner.

Skill as an indicator of quality of performance

The word in this context is probably a little more ambiguous than skill as an act or task. The word **well** added to the description of the skill infers a qualitative judgement of the skill being made by you as the observer, for instance you may remark on a well-executed off drive during a cricket match. Very often we make judgements between players comparing performances, looking at players' achievements in the context of the class or school team or against set criteria. Thus we measure or assess in either relative or absolute terms.

Defining different types of skill

Psychologists have considered *different types of skill*, trying to differentiate for instance between **motor skills** and **verbal skills**. Examples of three different types of skill are:

1 **Intellectual skills or cognitive skills**
   Skills which involve the use of a person's mental powers, eg, problem solving, verbal reasoning (verbal skill).
2 **Perceptive skills**
   Interpreting and making sense of information coming in via the senses.
3 **Motor skills**
   Smoothly executing physical movements and responses.

 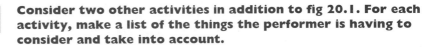

Consider two other activities in addition to fig 20.1. For each activity, make a list of the things the performer is having to consider and take into account.

When National league basketball players are performing a 'skillful' dribble and 'driving' the basket they are not only showing technically good movements (ie, showing motor skill) but in carrying out the action the player has had to make many decisions including:

- how to dribble
- whether to dribble or pass
- position of opposition
- position of own team mates
- context of game
- situation in game – winning or losing?
- time in game (how long to go?)
- do we need to score or keep the ball?
- what are the odds of making the dribble, drive and possible shot?

Fig. 20.1 NATIONAL LEAGUE BASKETBALL PLAYER DRIBBLING

This obviously involves a whole host of both **cognitive skills** and **perceptual skills**, as only after having taken into account all the various information (cues, signals, stimuli) being received from around them can a basketball player then carry out the necessary skill to any degree of proficiency. Therefore, as we can see, although many psychologists have tried to define the ways in which motor, cognitive and perceptual skills are independent of one another, from a physical educational and sporting point of view when we talk of skill we usually mean a combination of all three areas. In your further reading around this topic you will come across the phrase 'perceptual motor skills' or very often just 'motor skills' – the perceptual or cognitive involvement is usually implied.

Complex skills and simple skills

In your consideration and discussions for activity 2 you will have concluded that in carrying out movement we are rarely just 'doing'. Some level of thought and decision making has usually taken place. However, as you develop your understanding in this area you will come to realise that certain sporting activities and physical movements require *more* thought, conscious control and decision making than others. These are known as **complex skills** whereas those activities and movements requiring very little conscious thought or decision making and only basic movement patterns are called **simple skills**.

Acquisition of skill

In the phrase 'acquisition of skill' the word 'acquisition' infers that skill is something that you can gain as opposed to something that you already have.

'Skill is said to be gained through learning. Skill is said to be learned behaviour!'
(B. Knapp).

Definitions of skill

You will have a better understanding of the nature of skill if you consider a variety of definitions and see how those definitions have developed.

In your group either individually or in twos and threes select one of the following definitions and consider what it is trying to imply or say and then feedback your understanding of the definition to the rest of the class.

1 Professor GP Meredith, *Information and Skill*

'Excellence of performance – the successful integration of a hierarchy of abilities (all the abilities we have) appropriate to a given task under given conditions.'

2 Oldfield, *The Analysis of Human Skill – New Biology*

'The behaviour which tends to eliminate the discrepancy between intention and performance.'

3 Guthrie, from *Skills in Sport*: modified by B Knapp

'The learned ability to bring about pre-determined results with maximum certainty often with the minimum outlay of time, energy or both.'

4 Argyle and Kendon, *The Experimental Analysis of Social Performance*

'An organised, coordinated activity in relation to an object or a situation which involves a whole chain of sensory, central and motor mechanisms.'

5 M Robb, *The Dynamics of Skill Acquisition*

'While the task can be physical or mental, one generally thinks of a skill as some type of manipulative efficiency. A skilled

movement is one in which a predetermined objective is accomplished with maximum efficiency and with a minimum outlay of energy. A skillful movement does not just happen. There must be a conscious effort on the part of the performer in order to execute a skill.'

6 R Magill, *Motor Learning: Concepts and Applications*

'An act or a task that has a goal to achieve and that requires voluntary body or limb movements to be properly performed.'

Skill is a learned behaviour

From your discussions and feedback sessions relating to activity 4 you will have realised that the term 'skill' is a complex term to define. Any definition should, however, involve several important points. The better-known definitions which tend to be referred to are the ones by B Knapp (after Guthrie), R Magill, and M Robb.

Overall, you can see that, according to these various definitions, skill involves learning to be effective and efficient in:

- achieving a well defined objective
- maximising – being consistently successful
- minimising – maintaining the physical and mental energy demands of performance at an optimum level
- minimising – taking only the minimum time required.

Using an example from either the individual or game activities you have covered, work through the above definitions trying to give in depth practical examples of how they might apply to physical education and sport.

Using the term 'ability'

It is important at this stage to consider another term which is very often synonymous with the word skill and is often used in definitions of skilled behaviour. The term is **ability**.

In your discussions of what constitutes skill, the term ability has probably often been used in the wrong context. Often in a variety of sports, players from abroad are referred to as having higher levels of ability than our 'home' developed players. When what we mean is that their skills in terms of technique are of a higher quality. It is the word 'ability' which is being used in the wrong context. We often talk of players as having 'lots of ability' when what we mean is they have developed high levels of skill.

Definitions and characteristics of ability

It is important that you understand the differences between skill and abilities. The study of abilities comes under the umbrella of 'differential psychology'.

'Motor abilities are relatively enduring traits which are generally stable qualities or factors that help a person carry out a particular act.'

(E. Fleishman).

'Motor abilities are innate inherited traits that determine an individual's coordination, balance, ability and speed of reactions.'

(R. Arnot and C. Gaines).

It is sufficient at this stage for you to realise that abilities are said to be enduring capacities or qualities and characteristics that a person has within themselves. A person is therefore born with these qualities. Abilities are said to be innate, inherited traits, factors that help, for instance, a persons agility, coordination, balance and speed of reactions.

A person trying to carry out a sporting activity will *learn to use* these underlying innate qualities or characteristics in an organised way in order to carry out coordinated movement.

Taxonomy of human perceptual motor abilities – Fleishman, 1972

The work of Fleishman (1972), which is one of the better-known pieces of research, developed a taxonomy of human perceptual motor abilities. He carried out extensive testing of over 200 tasks, the results of which led him to propose that there seemed to be 11 identifiable and measurable perceptual motor abilities. In addition he identified nine physical proficiency abilities. These differed from perceptual motor abilities in that they are more generally related to gross physical performance.

1 **Limb coordination** – the ability to coordinate the movement of a number of limbs simultaneously.
2 **Control precision** – the ability to make highly controlled and precise muscular adjustments where large muscle groups are involved.
3 **Response orientation** – the ability to select rapidly where a response should be made as in a choice reaction time situation.
4 **Reaction time** – the ability to respond rapidly to a stimulus when it appears.
5 **Speed of arm movement** – the ability to make a gross, rapid arm movement.
6 **Rate control** – the ability to change speed and direction of response with precise timing, as in following a continuously moving target.
7 **Manual dexterity** – the ability to make skillful, well directed arm hand movements, when manipulating objects under speed conditions.
8 **Finger dexterity** – the ability to perform skillful controlled manipulations of tiny objects involving primarily the fingers.
9 **Arm hand steadiness** – the ability to make precise arm, hand positioning movements where strength and speed are minimally involved.
10 **Wrist finger speed** – the ability to move the wrist and fingers rapidly, as in a tapping task.
11 **Aiming** – the ability to aim precisely at a small object in space.

Fleishman's proficiency abilities

Typically these more general athletic abilities could be considered physical fitness abilities.

1 **Static strength** – maximum force exerted against an external object.

2 **Dynamic strength** – muscular endurance in exerting force repeatedly, eg, pull ups.

3 **Explosive strength** – the ability to mobilise energy effectively for bursts of muscular effort, eg, high jump.

4 **Trunk strength** – strength of the trunk muscles.

5 **Extent flexibility** – the ability to flex or stretch the trunk and back muscles.

6 **Dynamic flexibility** – the ability to make repeated, rapid trunk flexing movements as in a series of stand and touch toes stretch and touch toes.

7 **Gross body coordination** – the ability to coordinate the action of several parts of the body while the body is in motion.

8 **Gross body equilibrium** – the ability to maintain balance without visual cues.

9 **Stamina** – the capacity to sustain maximum effort requiring cardiovascular effort, eg, a long distance run.

Additional further abilities which have not been included by Fleishman are such things as:

- **Static balance** – the ability to balance on a stable surface when no locomotor movement is required
- **Dynamic balance** – the ability to balance on a moving surface or to balance while involved in locomotion
- **Visual activity** – the ability to see clearly and precisely
- **Visual tracking** – the ability to visually follow a moving object
- **Eye–hand coordination** – the ability to perform skills requiring vision
- **Eye–foot coordination and the precise use of hands or feet.**

These and others are, however, equally acceptable abilities as they are measurable and quantifiable. In your additional background reading and task analysis you will probably come across many more. It is important to understand that all individuals possess all the above abilities identified, however we do not all possess them at equal or similar levels. If a person has not got the appropriate levels of specific abilities needed for a specific sport then the odds against them making it to the top in that sport may be high. But this does not mean that such a person has to give up all together. Practically no one is born with a package of superior abilities large enough to make for an overall athletic ability. Although researchers have tried to identify the possibilities of an 'all round general athletic ability' results have actually tended to support the view that *specific skills require specific abilities*.

Ability is task specific

Certain skills may use different sets of abilities or they may use the same abilities put together in a different order. Also abilities are not necessarily linked or related; for example a person having high levels of trunk strength may not necessarily have high levels of explosive strength. If a person is good at throwing a cricket ball there is no guarantee that they will be good at throwing a basketball or a javelin. In other words the fact that a person does not have the level of abilities necessary to succeed at one activity does not mean that they do not have the potential to succeed in another activity requiring slightly different abilities or levels.

 ACTIVITY 5

1 **Individually make a list of the abilities required for the following activities:**
- **Badminton**
- **Hockey**
- **Weight lifting**
- **Swimming**

Fig. 20.2 EXPLOSIVE STRENGTH

- **Gymnastics**
- **Table tennis**
- **High jump**
2 **Compare your list with a partner and then try to decide on the ability-level needed in order to excel in these activities:**
- **high level**
- **reasonable level**
- **basic level**

In your discussions you will have found that whilst there is a certain degree of overlap between the requirements of activities, for example strength, coordination and speed, when you came to analyse the level and type of abilities required they became much more specific to the sport being considered, eg, different types of strength. Dynamic strength is used in weight lifting but explosive strength in the high jump.

The implications for teaching and coaching

1 The role of ability identification as predictors of potential achievements in learners has to be considered carefully. Consider the implications, both good and bad, if we were able to measure a beginner's abilities and then 'channel' them into the appropriate sport. Prediction studies have shown, however, that abilities which are important at the early stages of learning (cognitive phase) are not necessarily the same as those which are important at the more advanced stages of learning (autonomous phase). For example, Fleishman's and Rich's 1963 work suggest that:
- a greater number of abilities (more general to the task) contribute to learning a task in the early stages than do so later on
- different and fewer abilities (more specific to the task) contribute more and more to success with practice.
2 The ability to take in information and make sense of it, in other words 'perceptual ability' involving cue selection, concentration attention along with vision spartial orientation, are more important at the early stages of learning than later when learning is replaced more by kinesthesis.

Verbal comprehension is also very important at the early stages of learning as a person is precluded if they cannot understand instructions or what is being asked of them.

It is therefore generally understood that whilst testing a person's abilities to assess future potential can be useful, testing of this kind is not accurate and should not be used in isolation.

Consider the following situation and answer the question.
A coach has a large class for basketball. In order to achieve what they feel might be more effective teaching, they decide to divide the class up into smaller groups. The whole class is first asked to carry out various related tasks, eg, bouncing, catching, dribbling, shooting. As a result of observing the way people carried out these tasks the coach splits the class into groups according to each person's initial performance levels.
What are the possible implications of this approach for the whole class's future success at basketball?

Classification of skills

Having worked your way through the chapter to this point you will be aware of:

- what constitutes a skill
- how specific skills are underpinned by the appropriate abilities.

This gives you a better understanding of the implications for teaching and coaching the acquisition of skills in the widest sense. You will have realised that different skills require different kinds and amounts of abilities and also possibly different patterns. In the same way in which we analyse skills to assess which different abilities are needed we can also analyse skills in relation to things they have in common. Looking at skills in terms of the characteristics that they have in common is called **classification of skill** and is part of the overall process of task analysis. By classifying skills that are involved in sporting activities:

- a teacher or coach is enabled to **generalise** across groups of skills and apply major concepts, theories and principles of learning to types of skills
- a teacher or coach will not necessarily have to consider each specific skill in a unique way
- a teacher or coach will be able to select the appropriate starting point for a learner
- the identification of the appropriate types of practice conditions required will be made easier, eg, whole, part, whole, massed or distributed (see page 398). Similar methods can be applied to skill within the same groupings
- the timing and types of instruction to be given is clarified, eg, verbal feedback, ongoing or terminal – see page 386
- the detection and solving of any problems the learner may be facing is made easier
- a teacher or coach would probably not use the various classifications in isolation but move from one to another, or combine aspects of all of them at the appropriate time.

Classification systems

Several different ways of classifying or grouping skills have been developed in order to try and help our understanding of motor skills. In order to solve the problem of listing skills under certain headings which could lead to confusion over where to list skills made up of several different aspects, the use of a **continuum** was devised. A continuum is an imaginary line between two extremes. This enables you to analyse skills and place them between two given extremities according to how they match the analysis criteria being applied.

Gross and Fine classification

If you used the Gross–Fine classification given in table 20.1 in terms purely of *headings* for lists of skills the criteria for analysing the skills would derive from the 'degree of bodily involvement' or the precision of movement.

As you can see from table 20.1, some skills do not fall easily into specific categories nor can they be listed exclusively under exact headings.

Darts, spin bowling and serving in a game of badminton all involve wrist finger speed and dexterity along with aiming accuracy which would suggest they should be taught as a fine skill. In addition however, in order for these small movements to be

Table 20.1   GROSS – FINE SKILL CLASSIFICATION

GROSS SKILLS	FINE SKILLS

• involve large muscle movements
• major bodily movements skills associated with:
  strength
  endurance
  power
• for instance
  walking
  running
  jumping
  kicking a football
	• involve small muscle movements
	• small bodily movements skills associated with:
	  speed
	  accuracy
	  efficiency
	• associated more with industrial motor skills:
	  writing
	  painting
	  sewing

?←—DARTS—→?	
?←—SPIN BOWLING—→?	
?←—BADMINTON—→?	

made larger movements – particularly in spin bowling – have also had to be made which would suggest they should be taught as a gross skill. Hence the use of a continuum where the complex nature of motor skills can be taken into consideration; they can be placed on the continuum somewhere between the two extremes according to the degree of similarity they have to the various criteria being applied.

Now, using the same Gross–Fine classification (see table 20.1) place darts, spin bowling and badminton along a continuum according to how they match the criteria being applied.

The Discrete, Serial, Continuous continuum

This classification is made on the basis of how clearly defined the beginning and end of the skill is.

    The use of this type of continuum has been popularised by researchers viewing performance from a human engineering perspective.

Table 20.2   THE DISCRETE, SERIAL CONTINUOUS CONTINUUM

DISCRETE skills	SERIAL skills	CONTINUOUS skills
CRITERIA	CRITERIA	CRITERIA
• well defined beginning and end • usually brief in nature a single specific skill • if skill is repeated have to start at beginning eg, ◇ a basketball free throw ◇ kicking a ball ◇ hitting, catching	• a number of discrete skills put together to make a sequence or series • the order the distinct elements are put together is very important • each movement is both a stimulus and response eg, ◇ gymnastic routine ◇ triple jump	• poorly defined beginning and end • activity continues for an unspecified time – (ongoing) • The end of one movement is the beginning of the next eg, ◇ swimming ◇ running ◇ cycling

Table 20.3   THE PACING CONTINUUM

SELF PACED/ INTERNAL PACED SKILLS	EXTERNALLY PACED SKILLS

• Performer controls the rate at which the activity is carried out
• Performer decides when to initiate movement
• Involves pro-action
• more closed skill
  eg,
  ◇ shot put
  ◇ forward roll
	• Action is determined by external sources
	• Involves the performer in reaction
	• more open skill
	  eg,
	  ◇ white water canoeing
	  ◇ receiving a serve in tennis

The pacing continuum

This classification is based on the degree of control that the performer has over the movement or skill being carried out. This classification is synonymous with the next classification open and closed.

The open/closed continuum

This is one of the better-known classifications and is based on the stability of the environment in which the skill is being performed.

DEFINITIONS

Open/externally paced skills:

'At every instant the motor activity must be regulated by and appropriate to the external situation.'
(B. Knapp, 1972)

Closed/skills:

'Conformity to a prescribed standard sequence of motor acts is all important.'
(H. Whiting, 1969)

Table 20.4   THE OPEN/CLOSED CONTINUUM

CLOSED SKILLS	OPEN SKILLS

• not affected by the environment
• stable fixed environment (space/time)
• internally/self paced predominantly habitual stereotyped movements
  eg,
  ◇ headstand in gymnastics
  ◇ weight lifting
	• very much affected by the unstable changing environment
	• externally paced environment
	• predominantly perceptual movement patterns require adjustment (adaptation)
	• very often rapid adjustments, variations of skill needed
	  eg,
	  ◇ passing/receiving in netball or basketball
	  ◇ tackling rugby

Draw an open–closed continuum and place the following skills on it.

Free shot in basketball; serve in tennis; serve in badminton; dribbling in football; rugby tackle; running 1500 m; sailing; backhand defensive shot in table tennis; judo.

Select an open skill from one of the major game activities, for instance:

• **tackling in hockey or rugby**
• **fielding in cricket**
• **passing in netball**

Try and explain in detail all the aspects of the skill and situation that would have to be considered when carrying out the skill. Do not forget to apply all the criteria, showing why it would be classified as an open skill.

More recently, with the emphasis moving towards information processing modules, classifications have been suggested that consider the degree of cognitive/perceptual involvement. Do skills have higher or lower levels?

Examples of high cognitive skills are:

- chess
- batting in cricket

- strategies/tactics.

Decision making is critical.

Examples of low cognitive/motor skills are:

- walking
- power lifting.

Primary determinant of success is the quality of movement.

Task analysis

It is important that the teacher or coach is aware of all the various demands being placed on a learner at any one time within either simple or complex skills.

It has been suggested that the major factors contributing to task difficulty are:

- the degree of perception necessary.
- the degree of decision making involved.
- the nature of the act itself.
- the feedback availability.   (J. Billing).

Therefore you can see that just labelling a task as difficult or easy is not enough. It is necessary to specify the degree and nature of the difficulty if appropriate and effective instructions and strategies are to be developed.

Figure 20.3 shows a task analysis for the tennis serve (executive programme) indicating the appropriate components (subroutines) and identifying some of the underlying perceptual motor abilities necessary for the plan of action to be completed.

Figure 20.4 shows how motor skills can be analysed according to the complexity of each sub component. See Chapter 23 for further discussion of task analysis.

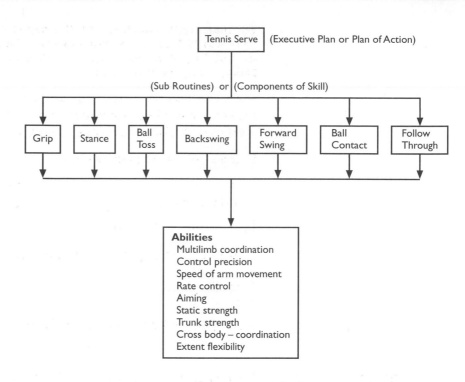

Fig. 20.3 A TASK ANALYSIS FOR THE
TENNIS SERVE

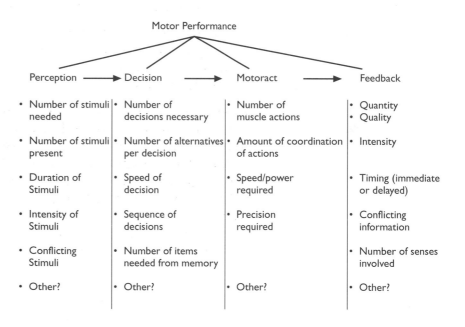

Fig. 20.4 ANALYSING MOTOR SKILLS
Source: Adapted from J Billing, 1980

Summary

Skills

1 Skill can be an act or task.
2 Skill can be used to indicate quality of performance.
3 Motor skills are essentially a combination of cognitive/perceptual and motor skills put together.
4 Skill is learned behaviour.
5 Skills have pre-determined objectives to achieve.
6 Skill involves being able to carry out the action consistently.
7 Skills are performed with an efficient use of time and energy.

Abilities

1 Abilities are innate enduring qualities or capacities.
2 Abilities are task specific.
3 Abilities underpin skill development.
4 The idea of one overall 'athletic ability' is largely a myth.
5 Many other factors contribute to all round athletic development.

Classifying skills

1 It is important to consider all aspects of the skill/task being taught.
2 Classification considers the common characteristics of skills.
3 A continuum is a more effective tool in classifying skills.
4 Teaching strategies are linked to the in-depth analysis of skills.

Revision Questions

1 What is a motor skill and a perceptual skill?
2 What are cognitive skills?
3 What are complex skills and simple skills?
4 What is an ability? What is a psychomotor ability? What is gross motor ability?
5 Differentiate between gross and fine skills. Give examples.
6 What are discrete, continuous, serial skills? Give examples.
7 What are self paced and externally paced skills? Give examples.
8 What are high and low cognitive skills? Give examples.
9 What are open/closed skills?

chapter 2

The Principles of Learning

Learning plays a central role in most of psychology and as such it is one of the most expansively researched and discussed areas in the whole of psychology. Learning is said to be a hypothetical construct, in that it can only be **inferred** from either:

- observing behaviour; or
- testing, measuring and evaluating performance.

All human beings have tremendous capabilities for learning. As a student of physical education and sport it is not enough just to recognise that learning has or has not taken place (the end result or outcome); you should have a more in-depth understanding of the theories and principles associated with the underlying learning process and be able to apply this understanding to the practical learning situation.

Here is a list of the terms to be covered in this chapter. It is important that you understand them.

- Learning definition
- Inference
- Practice observation
- Retention tests
- Transfer test
- Cognitive learning
- Affective learning
- Effective learning
- Cognitive phase

- Associative phase
- Autonomous phase
- Performance curves
- Linear
- Negative
- Positive
- Plateaus
- Learning variables

It would be very convenient to have a list of absolute truths about the learning and teaching of specific motor skills related to every possible sports performance. However, your own individual experiences should help you realise that there are no conclusive statements and guarantees cannot be given. This is because:

- learning is a complex process during which many physical and psychological changes are taking place
- there are many variables to be considered
- it is very difficult to consider the many variables and parts of the learning process in total isolation.

Once you have read this chapter you should gain an understanding of:

- definitions of learning
- different types of learning

- stages/phases of learning
- performance/learning curves
- major factors that can affect learning.

Definitions of learning

As we have discussed in the previous chapter, implicit in the understanding of the term skill is the notion that **learning** has taken place, that skill is **learned behaviour**. To become skillful involves a person's performance changing in line with certain criteria and characteristics associated with skill.

It is generally accepted that for learning to have taken place there has to be a recognisable **change** in behaviour and that this change in behaviour has to be **permanent**. Thus, the performance improves over time becoming more consistent in terms of its:

- accuracy
- efficiency
- adaptability

Learning has been defined as:

'the more or less permanent change in behaviour that is reflected in a change in performance.'   *(B. Knapp).*

'a change in the capability of the individual to perform a skill that must be inferred from a relatively permanent improvement in performance as a result of practice or experience.'   *(R. Magill).*

'a relatively permanent change in behaviour due to past experience.' *(D. Coon).*

'a set of processes associated with practice or experience leading to relatively permanent changes in the capability of skilled performance.'   *(R. Schmidt).*

In discussion with other students in your group consider the four definitions given above and select the main aspects of the definitions.

In your discussion of the four definitions you should have concluded, and psychologists generally agree, that:

- learning is not a 'one-off' lucky effort/performance
- learning is *relatively* permanent
  (This does not mean, however, that the skill is performed one hundred percent correctly each time. It does mean that a learner's capability to perform a particular skill consistently has increased.)
- learning is due to past experience and or practice.

How do we judge if a skill has been learned?

There are various methods of assessing a performance in order that more accurate inferences can be made about learning. The general methodology would be to:

1 **observe** – behaviour/performance
2 **measure/test** – behaviour/performance

3 **evaluate** – behaviour/performance
4 **translate** – the information gained into meaningful conclusion
5 **infer** – that learning has or has not taken place.

Three common methods of measuring and testing which have been used to enable teachers and coaches to make more accurate inferences with regard to learning have been:

- practice observations
- retention tests
- transfer tests

Practice observation

This is when a teacher or coach records a learner's performance over a period of time in an accurate way in order to provide a quantitative means for evaluating progress: eg, results showing more accuracy or consistency in relation to time spent practising (see later section on performance curves).

Retention tests

This is when a teacher or coach tests a student's performance after practice and then re-tests again after a few days and then again in order to check whether the initial levels of performance have been maintained, persisted or improved after a period of little or no practice.

Transfer tests

This is when a teacher or coach determines how well a particular skill has been learned by seeing how well it can be performed in a different situation to that experienced by the student during practice: is the accuracy and consistency maintained from practice to game situation?

Types of learning

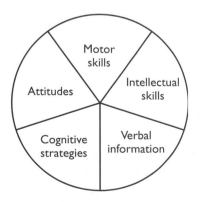

Fig. 21.1 THE CATEGORIES OF LEARNING

As you will have realised in your earlier discussions with regard to types of skill, in order to carry out motor skills at the highest levels more than just pure physical movement is involved. There is usually some cognitive and perceptual involvement to various degrees depending on the skill being carried out. In the same way therefore that motor skills involve more than purely the physical movement of muscles, limbs, etc., then learning can occur in more than just a physical way. There have been many different approaches to the analysis of what form learning can take in relation to the types of skills or situations being experienced.

Robert Gagné (1977) suggested that there are five main categories of human performance that may be developed by learning and that any learned capability whatever it is called, History, Geography, Physics, Football, Swimming, etc. has characteristics from one or other of these categories.

1 **Intellectual skills**
   Dealing with the environment in a symbolic way, eg, reading, writing mathematical symbols, etc.
2 **Verbal information**
   Learning to state or tell ideas or information by using oral, written or body language, ie, communication.

3 **Cognitive strategies**
   Learning to manage one's own learning, ie, use of memory, thinking, problem solving and analysis.

4 **Attitudes**
   Acquiring mental states which influence choices of personal actions, eg, choosing badminton rather than hockey as a preferred recreation.

5 **Motor skills**
   Learning to execute movement in a number of organised ways, either as single skills or actions, eg, catching a ball, or more comprehensive activities, eg, playing netball or basketball.

 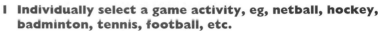

1 **Individually select a game activity, eg, netball, hockey, badminton, tennis, football, etc.**
2 **Using Gagné's categories as a guide, write a list of all the aspects of the activity that you may learn about when being introduced to the game.**
3 **Feedback your list to your member of staff along with everyone else in the group.**

In carrying out activity 2 you will probably have come up with examples of learning under each heading.

For example:
1 Developing particular motor skills, eg, catching, throwing, kicking, hitting/striking etc, depending on the game.
2 Developing tactical awareness, defensive strategies and attacking strategies.
3 Learning the rules and regulations.
4 Learning the ethics/morals of the game, eg, sportsmanship.
5 Developing positive attitudes towards the game and sport in general.
6 Understanding training principles.
7 Learning how the body works and how to make it work more efficiently.
8 Learning how to analyse movement in order to recognise strengths and weaknesses in your own and others' game.
9 Communication skills, both verbal and non-verbal.
10 Learning to interpret information.

All these and probably many more examples will be on your lists. Whilst we are primarily concerned with learning associated with motor skills, it is obvious that in order to learn motor skills we also experience learning in many other ways. Although experimental psychologists have tried, it is difficult to separate learning in its widest sense from motor performance, since all contribute to the level of motor skill achieved.

A more simplistic view of learning experienced within physical education and sport is seen in table 21.1.

In dealing with motor learning, it is often difficult to separate the various aspects as all will contribute in some way at some time to the level of skill. It is therefore necessary to develop all areas in order to make the learning process more meaningful, eg, a sensitive teacher or coach may find that in order to develop a student's high jumping technique (effective learning) they may have to help the student understand the basic biomechanics of the movement and link this to their ability to analyse their own movement (cognitive learning). In addition positive attitudes may be needed with regard to specific physical training and psychological aspects, eg, confidence and focusing (affective learning).

Table 21.1 THE THREE TYPES OF LEARNING

Cognitive	Affective	Effective
to know	to feel	to do

• mental processes eg,
   ◇ tactical awareness
   ◇ strategies
   ◇ problem solving
	• attitudes and values eg,
	   ◇ ethics
	   ◇ sportsmanship
		• motor learning eg,
		   ◇ physical
		   ◇ catching
		   ◇ passing

(inclusive of Gagné's categories 1, 2, 3)	(Gagné's category 4)	(Gagné's category 5)

Phases of motor skill learning

As there are different types of learning associated with the learning of motor skills there are also different stages or phases of the learning process.

In order to gain a clearer understanding of the learning process there have been many attempts to identify the various phases, or stages, that students go through when learning motor skills. It has been agreed that whatever the number and name of phases identified the phases are not separate or distinct, but that they gradually merge into each other as a person moves from being a novice to being proficient.

Having a better understanding of what is happening and what the learner is experiencing during each phase should help you in developing appropriate teaching and coaching strategies to ensure that the learning process is efficient and successful.

Three stage model

Paul Fitts and Michael Posner (1967) identified one of the better-known models which in its turn has been expanded upon by others.

The three phases identified are

1 Cognitive
2 Associative
3 Autonomous

Whilst each of these phases has certain characteristics associated with it, movement from one phase to the other is seen as developmental and gradual along a continuum.

1 Cognitive phase	2 Associative phase	3 Autonomous phase
BEGINNER		HIGHLY SKILLED

Cognitive phase

This is the initial phase in the learning process when, as a beginner faced with a

Fig. 21.2 THE COGNITIVE PHASE: HAVING A
GO! BEGINNERS NEED TO BUILD UP A FEEL
FOR THE ACTION

new skill or set of skills to learn, you want to be told what you need to know, for example:

- what is required of you?
- what task is to be performed?
- what are the basic rules?
- how do I hold the stick?

The emphasis in this phase is very much on early understanding or cognitive involvement (internalising information) in order that initial plans of action can be formulated. Beginners are directed towards important aspects of the new skill to pay attention to. These cues may be intensified in order to help concentration, eg, bigger or brighter bats and balls are often used, and any initial success is enthusiastically reinforced. The length of this phase varies according to the beginner and the strategies being used but it is generally a relatively short phase.

The associative phase

This intermediate or practice phase in the learning process is generally significantly longer than the cognitive phase, with the learner taking part in many hours of practice. The characteristics of this phase are that the fundamental basics of the skill required have generally been mastered and are becoming more consistent.

- the mental or early cognitive images of the skill have been associated with the relevant movements enabling the coordination of the various parts of the skill (sub-routine) to become smoother and more in line with expectations
- motor programmes are being developed
- gross error detection and correction is practised
- the skills are practised and refined under a wide variety of conditions.

Whilst the skills are not yet automatic or consistently correct there is an obvious change in the performance characteristics.

The autonomous phase

After much practice and variety of experience the learner moves into what is considered the final phase in the learning process, the autonomous phase. The characteristics of this phase are that:

- the performance of the skill has become almost **automatic**
- the skill is performed relatively easily and **without stress**
- the skill is performed effectively with little if any conscious control: it is **habitual**
- the performance is consistent with highly skilled movement characteristics.

The performer is able to:

- process information easily, helping decision making
- concentrate on the relevant cues and signals from the environment
- concentrate on additional higher level strategies, tactics, and options available
- detect and correct errors without help.

Once a player has reached this phase of learning it does not mean that learning is over. Although the performer is very capable, small improvements can still be made in terms of style and form, and to the many other factors associated with

Fig. 21.3 IN THE AUTONOMOUS PHASE SKILLED SOCCER PLAYERS CAN DRIBBLE THE BALL HABITUALLY, ENABLING THEIR ATTENTIONAL CAPACITIES TO CONSIDER OTHER ASPECTS OF THE GAME AT THE SAME TIME, EG, MOVEMENTS OF OTHER PLAYERS AND OPTIONS AVAILABLE

psychological aspects of performance which can help develop learning even further.

The relationship between learning and performance

As we have already stated, occasional good or 'one-off' performances are not a true indication of learning having taken place. There has to be a relatively permanent change in performance over time as a result of practice and or experience. One of the more traditional ways of gathering evidence in order to discover if learning has or has not taken place has been by comparing practice/performance observations. Performance levels over a certain length of time are recorded and the results are plotted on a graph, producing **performance curves**. Very often these curves of performance are inaccurately referred to as learning curves. This has been based on the assumption that changing levels of skill closely parallel performance scores. However, it is performance not learning that is being measured. By keeping records of skill performance over a period of time (eg, a lesson, one hour, a term, a season) an individual's, but more often a group's, progress can be plotted. This will provide a graphical representation of the specific aspect of performance being tested. Thus a picture of the relationship between practice and performance is presented from which inferences can be made. It has been suggested that the validity of performance curves as true representations of learning is problematical due to the many variables that may have an effect. However, as long as they are not used in total isolation, such curves do act as useful indicators of general trends in learning. Although they may be used to show changes in an individual's performance of a particular motor skill or skills, performance curves tend to be more widely used to represent composite or group performance.

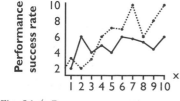

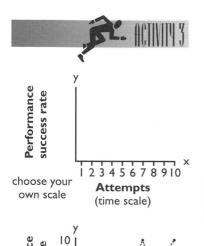

choose your own scale

Fig. 21.4 PERFORMANCE SUCCESS RATE GRAPHS

You are going to undertake a learning experiment in one-handed ball juggling. No practice is allowed beforehand or in between attempts.
1 **Divide yourselves into pairs.**
2 **Have two tennis balls per pair and a piece of graph paper.**
3 **Have ten consecutive goes each at one-handed juggling.**
4 **Count the number of successive throw-ups each person can manage in each of their ten goes.**
5 **Log the results on a table as below.**

Attempts	1	2	3	4	5	6	7	8	9	10
Success										

6 **Plot the performance of both yourself and your partner on a piece of graph paper and compare the graphs.**
7 **Average out your two scores and draw another graph.**
8 **Average out all the scores of the members of your group and draw a composite graph for the whole group.**
9 **What inferences can be drawn from this final graph?**
10 **What variables may have affected the individual and group performances? How could you make this experiment scientifically more valid?**

11 What did you notice with regard to the shape of the curves as you average out more by adding more results?

12 A further way to develop your performance curves would be to treat the ten attempts as a block of trials and average this out. Then, over a period of time, repeat the block of ten attempts on a regular basis. This could be done with various skills, eg, basketball free throws, serving in tennis, target shooting in hockey or football, shooting in netball, etc.

Types of performance curves

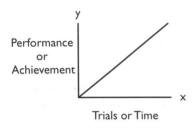

Fig. 21.5 LINEAR CURVE OF PERFORMANCE

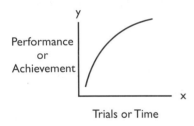

Fig. 21.6 NEGATIVELY ACCELERATED CURVE OF PERFORMANCE

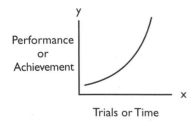

Fig. 21.7 POSITIVELY ACCELERATED CURVE OF PERFORMANCE

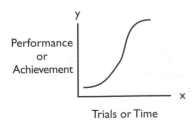

Fig. 21.8 OGIVE OR S-SHAPED CURVE OF PERFORMANCE

When analysing performance curves it has been found that graphs are made up of several different shapes within the overall context of the general performance curve. The curves shown in figs 21.5–21.9 are termed smooth curves. However, as you will have noticed from your own individual graphs and further reading, curves found in research studies are usually erratic in nature.

Figure 21.5 indicates that performance improves directly in proportion to the amount of time or number of trials. In fig. 21.6, the curve of decreasing gain indicates that a large amount of improvement occurred early on in practice and then although improvement usually continues, it is very slight in relation to the continued amount of time or trials. The inverse curve of increasing gain in fig. 21.7 indicates small performance gains early on in practice followed by a substantial increase later in practice. Figure 21.8 is a combination of the previous types of curve. The plateaus in fig. 21.9 indicate that during certain periods of practice or from one particular trial to another there was no significant improvement in performance.

Plateaus

The levelling off in performance preceded and followed by performance gains has been called a plateau. Plateaus in performance and possibly learning have been the subject of considerable research. One of the earliest pieces of research to suggest that plateaus existed was by Bryan and Hunter (1897) when studying the performance of trainee telegraphers learning the morse code. Think of experiences you have had when trying to learn particular skills; there must have been times when initial success was followed by a period of time when, however hard you tried, no apparent improvement was achieved. Then, all of a sudden everything 'clicked' together and you cannot now remember what the problem was. Although such an experience is often described by individual learners and by performers at the highest level, performance curves generally relate to group or class results and therefore experimental evidence to support the existence of plateaus related to individual learning is hard to come by. Whilst we may experience plateaus in practice and performance it has been argued (FS Keller, 1958) that learning continues or at the very least plateaus do not necessarily mean that learning has also plateaued. In terms of learning development it is generally agreed that if plateaus do exist they are something that should be avoided as they can lead to a stagnation in performance and a possible loss of overall interest.

Possible causes of plateaus

It has been suggested that the following factors have to be considered as possible causes of plateaus.

1 Movement from learning lower order or simple skills to higher order or more

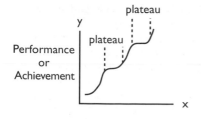

Fig. 21.9 PLATEAU IN PERFORMANCE

complex skills may create a situation in which the learner needs to take time to assimilate more involved information and attend to correct cues and signals.

2   Goals or targets are set too high or too low.
3   Fatigue/lack of physical preparation.
4   Lack of variety in practice.
5   Lack of motivation/interest due to problems associated with the above.
6   Lack of understanding of plateaus.

1   **Individually, consider the possible causes of plateaus given above and try to make some practical suggestions as to how a teacher or a coach might try to ensure that learners do not experience plateaus in their skill development.**
2   **Present your suggestions to the class and compile a full list of suggestions and strategies.**

Considerations in motor learning

There are many different factors called **learning variables** that you have to be aware of, understand and consider; these can influence the effectiveness of the learning process.

There are four main categories of learning variables. In considering these categories you may come across unfamiliar terms, which are explained in later sections.

Category 1: variables associated with the learning process

The basic process that learners go through when faced with a new situation to which they have to respond is usually similar for all.

The learner will:

• observe the situation
• interpret the situation
• make decisions as to what they have to do
• decide on plans of action
• generate movement plans
• take in further information (feedback) as the result of actions becomes available in one form or another.

The learner can experience success or difficulty in any part of this process. Understanding it helps a teacher in the task of presenting useful information to the learner.

For a more detailed coverage of the information processing approach to learning see Chapter 22 page 371.

Category 2: variables associated with individual differences

A sensitive teacher or coach would try to develop a good knowledge of the individual differences listed below, and consider how they might affect the learner, in order to help the learning process.

• ability
• age (chronological and maturational)
• gender

- physiological characteristics, eg, physique (size, shape, weight linked to maturity, fitness)
- psychological, eg, motivation, attitudes, personality
- previous experience
- sociological aspects.

Category 3: variables associated with the task

A teacher would need to consider:

- the complexity of the task, eg, simple or complex?
- the organisation of the task, eg, high or low?
- the classification of the task, eg, open/closed? fine/gross?
- the transfer possibilities.

An understanding of task analysis is essential (see the sections on task analysis, pages 350 and 392) in order that the appropriate teaching strategies can be developed.

Category 4: variables associated with the instructional conditions

Teachers and coaches can manipulate the learning environment in a variety of ways:

- through styles of teaching
- through mode of presentation
- by using different forms of guidance
- by choosing appropriate types of practice.

All the above approaches will have a considerable affect on the learning experience of the individual or group.

Summary

1 Learning is permanent.
2 Learning is due to practice or experience.
3 Learning is inferred.
4 There are different types of learning (cognitive, affective, effective).
5 There are different phases of learning (cognitive, associative, autonomous).
6 Learning develops along a continuum.
7 There are different types of performance curves.
8 Plateaus are to be avoided.
9 Learning is affected by many variables.

Revision Questions

1 Explain the difference between performance and learning.
2 Why can we only infer learning has or hasn't taken place?
3 What are the characteristics associated with the three stages of Fitts and Posner's model of learning?
4 In what ways does a performer in the autonomous phase differ from a performer in the cognitive phase?
5 How is the notion of a continuum related to learning development?

6 Why is the term performance curve used rather than learning curve?

7 What is a plateau in a performance curve?

8 Should we infer that plateaus in performance mean learning is not taking place?

9 How might you learn from performing wrongly?

10 What factors may cause plateaus in performance?

11 Consider an ogive-shaped curve of performance and explain the reasons behind the shape.

chapter 22

Theories of Learning

We have already seen that learning is a relatively permanent change in behaviour. In order to help your understanding of how this relatively permanent change in behaviour comes about it is necessary to consider some of the more important theories and models of learning that have been proposed since the turn of the century. Having an understanding of major theories, together with an historical perspective of their development, should enable you to see the relevance and practical application of teaching and instructional conditions associated with the methods and strategies which are prevalent in physical education and sport today.

Here is a list of the terms to be covered in this chapter. It is important that you understand them.

Theories of learning

- Stimulus
- Response
- Bonding
- Classical conditioning
- Operant conditioning
- Behaviour operants
- Law of readiness
- Law of exercise
- Law of effect

- Trial error learning
- Reinforcement – positive and negative
- Punishment – tangible and intangible
- Drives
- Drive reduction
- Cognitive theory
- Gestaltism
- Insight learning

Information processing

- Display
- Cues/signals/stimulus
- Proprioceptors
- Exteroceptors
- Introceptors
- Kinesthesis
- Selective attention
- Short-term sensory store
- Short-term memory
- Long-term memory
- Reaction time

- Hicks Law
- Psychological refractory period
- Channel capacity
- Motor programmes
- Open loop/closed loop control
- Schemas
- Feedback
- Knowledge of results
- Knowledge of performance
- Intrinsic feedback
- Extrinsic feedback

Once you have read this chapter you should gain an understanding of:

- Behaviouristic/connectionist perspectives
- Hull's Drive Reduction Theory
- Cognitive/gestaltist perspectives
- Information processing models
- Motor programmes

- Open and close loop theories of control
- Schemas
- Feedback.

Conditioning theories

In the early twentieth century **behaviourism** was thought to provide a scientific base for the explanation of human behaviour. This approach placed the emphasis on the learning environment where behaviour in response to specific stimuli could be observed and used to make predictions about future behaviour in relation to similar situations or stimuli. The early behaviouristic approach was based on what became known as **stimulus-response theories** or **theories of association** where the 'outcome' or 'product' was more important than the process. It has been referred to as a very mechanistic and generalised approach inferring that *all* learners can have their behaviour shaped or conditioned through regular association (ie, practice) and manipulation of the learning practice environment by the teacher or coach. The performer learns to associate certain behaviour (response) with certain stimuli from within the environment. Once this connection or bonding together of a particular stimulus and response occurs then the performer's behaviour becomes habitual enabling predictions to be made about that person's future responses to the same or similar stimuli. Although dating from before this century **Stimulus (S)** and **Response (R) theories** as we know them owe much to the work carried out by Pavlov, Thorndike and Skinner. Although both Pavlov (classical or respondent conditioning) and Skinner (operant conditioning) both represent the behaviouristic S–R approach to learning there are some important distinctions that need to be considered.

Classical conditioning (Pavlov 1849–1936)

During his experiments Pavlov noticed that the dogs being used would salivate (unconditioned response) very often before their actual food (unconditional stimulus) would arrive in response to the noise of food being prepared, clanking of buckets, sight of the food, etc. Thus the dogs were learning to associate these other stimuli within their environment with the taste of the food.

In his later experiments Pavlov found that by pairing specific stimuli, ie, a bell, lights, shapes (conditioned stimulus) with the food (unconditioned stimulus) over a period of time he could produce the same salivation (unconditional response).

He found that although ringing a bell (stimulus) would not normally produce the salivation, by this continual pairing or association of food and bell he could eventually produce the salivation in the dogs by merely ringing the bell independently, thus creating a conditional response (CR) to a conditioned stimulus (CS).

It is the principles associated with the theory that are important: Pavlov showed that a certain conditioned response and behaviour could be developed by association with a certain conditioned stimulus. If applied into a learning environment within physical education the teacher or coach can, through repetitive practice, get a beginner to associate a particular type of action or movement with a particular stimulus. It was felt that this approach could be generalised across all learners, with all students being treated the same, experiencing the same repetitive practice and being expected to behave in the same way. The traditional 'drill' technique, whereby all students in a class respond to the same stimulus or cue

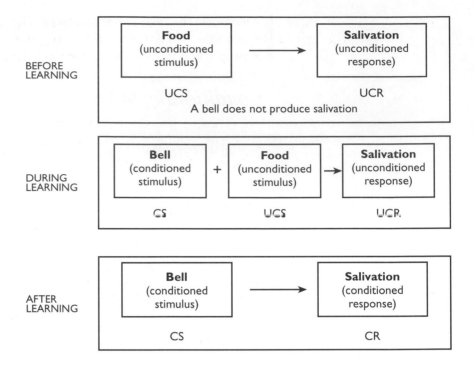

Fig. 22.1 PAVLOV'S EXPERIMENT TO PRODUCE CONDITIONAL RESPONSE WITH CONDITIONED STIMULUS

(almost reflex behaviour) with the students having no real choice, has developed from these basic S–R principles.

This approach relies very much on the teacher manipulating situations within the learning environment (gymnasium, hockey pitch, etc.) in order to create habitual responses. A criticism of classical conditioning is that although behaviour or response may be triggered automatically and may be correct, it is not necessarily linked to understanding – which may be needed if further or more complex skills and strategies are to be developed.

Operant conditioning (Skinner 1904–1990)

In his later work on instrumental or operant conditioning, Skinner drew heavily on Thorndike's (1874–1949) three laws of learning. He did not totally reject the work done on classical conditioning by Pavlov but suggested that this view of how behaviour could be created was too simplistic. He saw the learner as being more involved in the learning process. The learner associates the consequences of their previous actions with the current situation (stimulus) and responds accordingly taking into account whether those previous consequences were satisfactory, pleasing and successful or unsatisfactory, unpleasant and unsuccessful. These consequences would either serve to strengthen the bond between certain stimulus and response or weaken it. Skinner suggested also that these bonds could be further strengthened or weakened by the use of appropriate reinforcement, thus increasing or decreasing the probability of that behaviour happening again in the future. Both **Positive** and **Negative reinforcement** could be used to increase the probability of a certain behaviour happening again and punishment could serve to weaken the bond and thus reduce the probability of certain unwanted behaviour or performance happening again.

Thorndike's laws of learning

Skinner's studies in operant conditioning developed out of considerable early research by Thorndike who, in developing his own research on 'trial and error learning' linked to S–R bond theory, proposed many laws of learning, the most famous of which are as follows.

Law of readiness

In order for learning to be really effective the performer has to be in the right frame of mind psychologically as well as being physically prepared and capable of completing the task, ie, appropriate maturational development, motivation and prerequisite learning.

Law of exercise

In order for the bond between the stimulus and response to be strengthened it is necessary for regular practice to take place under favourable conditions. Repetition of the correct technique is important, sometimes referred to as 'the law of use'. However, he suggests that failure to practise on a regular basis could also result in 'the law of disuse' when the bond is weakened. Appropriate or favourable conditions could be created by the use of reinforcement.

Law of effect

The law of effect is central to understanding the essential differences between classical and operant conditioning. Thorndike concluded that:

1 What happens as a result of behaviour will influence that behaviour in the future.
2 Responses that bring satisfaction or pleasure are likely to be repeated again.
3 Responses that bring discomfort are not likely to be repeated again.

This is not the same as classical conditioning where the stimulus always produces the same response whether it is good or bad. However, his basic premise was that:

• behaviour is shaped and maintained by its consequences.

For example, if a badminton player receives a return which is only half court and not too high he will 'smash'. If this proves to be successful and therefore pleasurable it will serve to strengthen the connection between the stimulus (half court return) and the response (smash) and thus make it more likely that this behaviour will be repeated the next time the same situation occurs. However, a problem sometimes associated with trial and error learning is that a beginner may learn a poor or wrong technique (R) which may be effective in a limited way. This may result in having to re-learn at a later date in order to weaken the S–R bond which they have developed.

Skinner went on to suggest that certain additional reinforcement or motivational techniques such as praise or rewards could serve to support even further his view of the law of effect.

The consequences of operants or behaviour, ie, performance can be:

1 positive reinforcement ⎫ strengthen behaviour
2 negative reinforcement ⎭
or
3 punishment – weaken behaviour

The above reinforcements or punishments can come in various guises.

Definition of reinforcement

Any event or action or phenomenon that by strengthening the S–R bond increases the probability of a response occurring again. In other words it is the system or process that is used to shape behaviour in the future.

Positive reinforcement usually follows *after* a learner has demonstrated a desirable performance, eg, the basketball player has developed the correct 'set shot' technique and receives praise from the coach.

In discussion with a partner try and think of other types of positive reinforcements that may increase the probability of a response being repeated.

Negative reinforcement again serves to increase the probability of a certain desirable behaviour happening again but it is by the withdrawing of a possible aversive stimulus, eg, a teacher or coach constantly shouting at their team from the sideline suddenly stops shouting. The team or players would assume that they were behaving or performing in the correct way and thus try and repeat the same actions or skills again.

You must ensure that you do not confuse negative reinforcement with negative feedback or punishment.

Definition of punishment

An event or action, usually an aversive stimulus, to try and reduce or eliminate undesirable behaviour, eg, a penalty is given in football for a foul within the penalty area or a red card is given to a player who repeatedly infringes the laws of the game. Punishment can be effective but may result in frustration and bitterness and is seen by many as a negative approach.

Fig. 22.2 Punishment is used to eliminate undesirable behaviour. It tells us what not to do, not what to do!

When and how to use reinforcers

In using reinforcement techniques a teacher or coach needs to be aware of the effect that different reinforcers may have and how and when to use them effectively to ensure the appropriate learning and performance of motor skills. Within operant conditioning once the teacher or coach has decided what the desired level of performance or skill level is they will use reinforcers knowledgeably to condition the learner's behaviour in the appropriate way. It may be that the teacher plans the lessons in order that success is gained quite easily in the first part of the session. Success itself can act as the reinforcer. As the skills become more demanding praise for achieving aspects of the desired response may be given. The teacher or coach must ensure that the praise is given soon after the correct behaviour is performed in order that the beginner can link it to their actions (temporal association) and has no doubt what it is for (see the section on feedback, page 385). In using reinforcers a teacher or coach needs to consider the following.

1 How often to use them (too much or too little, partial or complete).
2 Ratio of positive to negative.
3 How soon after response.
4 What type to use.
5 Size and/or value of reinforcer.

All the above will be affected by the teacher's and beginner's interpretation and perception of the reinforcers used.

In discussion with a partner make a list using the table below of both tangible and intangible reinforcers and punishments that could be used with a learner in the associative phase of learning.

Reinforcers		Punishments	
Tangible	Intangible	Tangible	Intangible

Complete the same table for a professional sports performer. Discuss the differences.

Drive reduction theory (C L Hull 1943)

Whilst drive reduction theory is primarily linked to motivation it has strong links to learning and our understanding of S–R bonding; see Arousal, p 442. Hull's theory suggested that continual repetition on its own may not serve to increase the strength of the S–R bond and thus shape the required performance. The strength of the S–R bond (learned behaviour) is affected by the:

- level of motivation or drive
- intensity of the stimulus/problem
- level of incentive or reward
- amount of practice/reinforcements.

Hull believed that learning could only take place if drive reduction (acting as reinforcement) occurred and that all behaviour (learned performance) derived from a performer's need to satisfy their drives.

There have been many criticisms of Hull's work but in relating it to physical education and sport we can see that once the S–R bond is strengthened and performance of the task has become a habit (drive reduction) then in order to develop skills learning or performance levels further and prevent 'inhibition' or lack of drive a teacher or coach must set further goals or more complex tasks to ensure that drive is maintained.

It is also important that the teacher or coach ensures that only correct technique or good performance leads to the drive reduction as it is *this* S–R bond that will be reinforced. Bad technique or habits must not be allowed to achieve drive reduction.

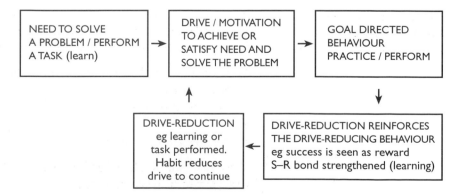

Fig. 22.3 HULL'S DRIVE REDUCTION THEORY

Cognitive theories

As research of human behaviour and performance developed further, many psychologists began to move away from the traditional behaviouristic approaches. Cognitive theorists saw the individual as being central to the process of learning, not merely reacting in a reflex manner (response) to outside influences (stimulus). **Understanding** of the total relationship between the many stimuli within the environment at any one time, and indeed their link to previous and future stimuli, was an essential part of cognitive theory.

The main early supporters of this approach, whose views have become synonymous with the cognitive approach, were known as 'gestaltists'. They believed that 'the whole is greater than the sum of its parts'. Gestaltists such as M Wertheimer (1880–1943), K Koffka (1886–1941) and W Köhler (1887–1967) argued that in the learning situation a beginner will continually organise and reorganise mentally in relation to previous experiences the various aspects that they are faced with in order to solve a problem in the present situation.

This view of learning is known as 'insight learning': a learner suddenly discovers the relationship between the many stimuli they have been faced with and 'it all comes together!' (for instance a learner suddenly gets the timing of a serve correct). Insight learning often results in the performer progressing very quickly after periods of apparently little progress. It is then important that further questions, problems or goals are set in order to motivate the learner to develop their performance further. The association of S–R by 'trial and error learning' (or chance which is then reinforced when correct thus gradually strengthening the bond) has no role to play in the cognitive perspective. Learning is not seen as a random process. What is learned within insight learning is therefore not a set of specific conditioned associations but a real understanding (cognitive) of the relationship between the process and means of achieving the end result. For instance, a defending hockey player who has the reasons explained to them why, when they are the last person in defence, they should not commit themselves, but 'jockey' their opponent, keeping goal-side, as this will enable other players to get back to help or put pressure on the attacker possibly forcing a mistake, is more likely to understand when and why to carry out the coach's instructions in future situations and also see the relevance of their role.

This, it is argued, is better in the long run than simply being told what to do or possibly punished if they do 'dive in' and commit without thinking. In practice, following the cognitive approach it would be important that the teacher or coach had an in-depth understanding and knowledge of both the individual learner and the various coaching strategies relevant to the skills being taught. It seems that a variety of experiences are essential for learners to develop their 'insight' of the present task or problem using knowledge gained from previous situations.

This whole learning approach allows learners to develop their own strategies and routes of understanding alongside general principles thus enabling the quicker learners to progress at their own rate: this has obvious links to the promoting of motivation and the developing of an individual's full potential.

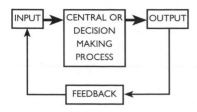

Fig. 22.4 SIMPLISTIC INFORMATION PROCESSING MODEL

Information processing

Information processing is an approach which sees the development of human motor behaviour (motor learning) as a *process* rather than a specific stimulus and response relationship. It has developed under the umbrella of cognitive psychology.

Much of the terminology used in the various models is reflective of the post war computer age in which it developed. The models appear to make comparisons between the ways in which machines function and process information and the ways in which humans 'achieve, retain and transform knowledge' (Jerome Bruner, 1972). Although research and the many models produced tend to suggest that the process learners go through is basically the same the information processing approach recognises the individuality of the learner. Individuals are studied as active beings using knowledge in ways personal to themselves. This involves a whole host of processes. Individuals will be involved in:

- information reception
- information translation
- information transmission
- information reduction
- information collation
- information storage
- information retrieval.

The information processing approach has been traditionally based on two assumptions.

1 That the processing of information can be broken down into various sub-processes or components.
2 That each of these components has limitations in terms of capacity or duration which affect the amount of information that can be processed.

Information processing emphasises that:

- perception
- attention
- memory and
- decision making

play an important part in the overall learning process.

Information processing models

Various psychologists have put forward graphical representations of how they see the various parts of the cognitive process relating together. These models are intended to aid understanding. The learning process is, however, a changing, complex, multi-dimensional process and such models must be seen as hypothetical and flexible. Two of the better-known models which are generally referred to are Welford's (1976) and Whiting's (1970), in figs 22.5 and 22.6.

Both models reflect basically the same process:

- stimulus identification stage
- response identification/selection stage and
- response programming stage

although they use slightly different terminology.

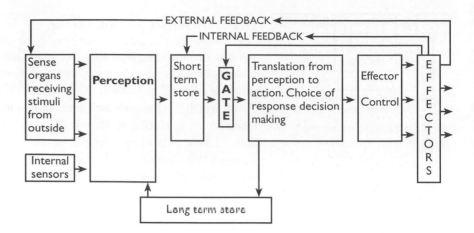

Fig. 22.5 WELFORD'S INFORMATION
PROCESSING MODEL
Adapted from A.T. Welford, 1976

Stimulus identification stage

This stage is mainly a sensory stage where the stimulus (eg, a ball) is detected along with speed, size, colour, direction of movement, etc.

The display

This is the physical environment in which the learner is performing. The display for the player shown above would be her own team mates, opposition, the pitch, ball, goal posts, the crowd and whatever else is going on in the vicinity of the game, whether important or not.

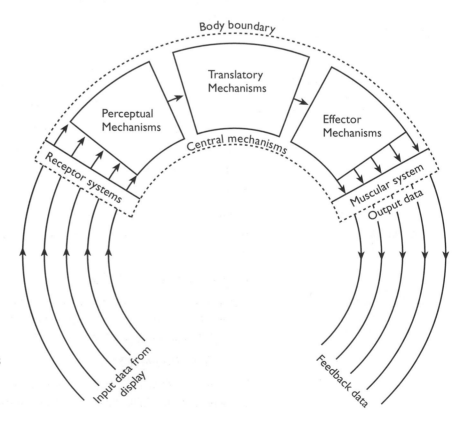

Fig. 22.6 WHITING'S MODEL (1969) IS
A WELL-KNOWN ILLUSTRATION OF THE
INFORMATION PROCESSING THEORY.
Adapted from H.T.A. Whiting, 1970

Fig. 22.7 A PLAYER HEARS HER TEAM-MATES CALL, SEES THE BALL, FEELS HER GRIP ON THE STICK AND BRACES HER LEGS IN READY POSITION TO RECEIVE THE BALL

Stimuli and cues

These are specific aspects of the display that are being registered by the learner's sense organs (eg, a ball being passed to them).

Sense organs, sensory systems and receptors

These are the receptors which take in the sensory information. There are three types.

1 Exteroceptors – **extrinsic** information from outside the body:

- visual
- audition
- touch
- smell
- taste.

2 Proprioceptors – nerve receptors within the body in muscles, joints, etc. providing **intrinsic** information regarding what class of movement is occurring. Kinesthetic information is also provided about the feel or sense of movement. The inner ear also provides proprioceptive information.

3 Introceptors – information from the internal organs of the body, heart, lungs, digestive system, etc. This information is passed to the central mechanism of the brain via the body's sensory nervous system.

Perception

This process involves the interpretation of the sensory input, along with discrimination, selection and coding of important information that may be relevant to the decision making process. The process of selective attention and use of memory are important at this stage.

DEFINITION

Perception is:

**'the process of assembling sensations into usable representations of the world.'
(D. Coon, 1983)**

Response selection stage

Having identified information from the display, this stage involves deciding on the necessary movement in the context of the present situation, eg, does the hockey player receive the ball and pass, change direction and dribble, or hold the ball?

Translatory/decision making mechanism

This involves an individual having to use the coded information received to recognise what is happening around them in order to decide on and select the appropriate motor programme to deal with the situation.

Response programming stage

In this final stage the motor systems are organised in order to deliver the chosen plan of action.

Effector mechanisms/effector control

Motor programmes or schemas (plans of action) are selected and developed. These plans, in the form of coded impulses, are sent via the body's *effector* or motor nerves to the appropriate muscles telling them what action to carry out.

Muscular system/effectors

The muscles receive the relevant 'motor programme' or plan of action in the form of coded impulses, initiate the movement and the action is performed.

Feedback

As a result of whatever action has been carried out the receptor systems receive information in various forms (see input data, page 373). There are many different types of feedback (see page 386) but it can be either extrinsic or intrinsic.

It can be seen that the body's control system (brain) through a series of receptors and effectors, controls our physical movements by evaluating the need for action and then executing it when and where it deems necessary. How effective this processing of information is depends on many variable factors which will be discussed over the following pages.

Memory

The memory is seen as a critical part of the overall learning process. It is central to our ability to receive the relevant information, interpret it, use it to make decisions and then pass out the appropriate information via the body's effector systems.

There has been much debate about the structure, organisation and capacity of the memory process with many modifications being suggested to the basic 'two-process' or 'multi-store' model of memory as described by Atkinson and Shiffrin (1968). It is generally suggested however, that there are two main aspects of memory: short-term memory (STM) and long-term memory (LTM). These two parts of memory are in some way preceded by a third area known as the sensory system or short-term sensory store (STSS) which involves a selection and attention process.

The STSS receives all sensory information provided by sensory receptors. It can hold large amounts of information (it is virtually limitless). Information usually lasts in the STSS for a fraction of a second (maximum 1 second). Unless it is reinforced it will be lost – scanning is a way of reinforcing information.

Selective attention

Due to the apparent limited neurological capacity of the short-term memory suggested by many single channel models (eg, Broadbent 1958, Norman 1969, 1976) it is acknowledged that there is some form of selection system in order to prioritise information, although there are disagreements about the positioning of this filtering system (see Welford's model fig. 22.5, the gating process).

The process of selective attention is responsible for selecting relevant from irrelevant information from the display. This allows the tennis player, for example, to focus on the specific cues being presented by their opponent when receiving serve (the grip, throw up of the ball, angle of racket, position in relation to service

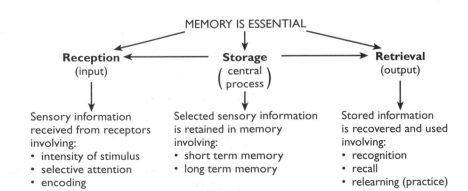

Fig. 22.8 MEMORY IS ESSENTIAL

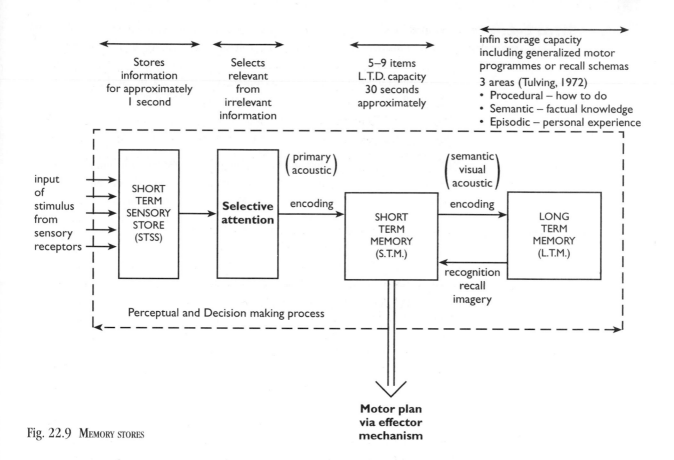

Fig. 22.9 MEMORY STORES

court, etc.) and ignore other aspects of the environment (display) which may distract them (eg, crowd, noise from the next court, ball boys, etc.) thus helping to prevent potential information overload.

The efficiency of the short-term sensory store and the selective attention process is influenced by several factors.

- **experience** – know what to look for – an experienced tennis player will know what to look for when facing an opponent
- **arousal** – the more alert you are the more likely you are to choose the appropriate cues. In cricket, a batsman who is alert is able to pick up on spin, speed and direction of the ball
- **quality of instruction** – as a beginner you don't always know what to respond to. The coach or teacher can direct your attention verbally, visually, mechanically
- **intensity of stimulus** – the effectiveness of the senses (eg, short sighted, poor hearing) when detecting, eg, speed, noise, size/shape and colour.

Selective attention can be improved by:

- lots of relevant practice
- increasing intensity of the stimulus
- use of language associated with or appropriate to the performer in order to motivate and arouse
- use of past experience/transfer to help explanations
- direct attention.

Short-term memory

Because the short-term memory appears to function between the STSS and the long-term memory receiving and integrating relevant coded information from both areas and passing on decisions via the body's effector systems (processing and storing information) it is often referred to as the 'working memory' or 'work space' (Atkinson and Shilfrin, 1971). The information in our STM at any one time is said to be our 'consciousness'.

Capacity of STM

Compared with the two other aspects of memory the STM has very limited capacity hence the need for the process of selective attention (when only relevant information is encoded and passed to STM). Seven plus or minus two items (7 ± 2) appears to be the maximum amount of information 'chunks' that any one person can hold. It has been suggested, however (Miller, 1956) that by practising a process called 'chunking' or grouping together of many items of information, a person can remember several 'chunks' of information rather than just seven individual items. Thus a games player with practice will possibly be able to remember at least seven different tactical moves or options happening around them rather than the seven aspects of a specific skill or strategy. In addition, a performer, by linking various aspects of a particular skill together, eg, a tennis serve, will see it as a whole, once learned, rather than as all the various parts of sub-routines of the service, grip, stance, throw up, preparation of racket, point of contact, follow through and recovery.

Duration of STM

It is generally accepted that unless the 7 ± 2 item of information within the STM are reinforced in some way by practice, repetition or rehearsal then they will only remain in the short-term memory for a relatively short period of time: approximately 30 seconds. If 'attention' is directed away from the information being held in the short-term memory then it tends to be forgotten. In order to keep information 'circulating' within the STM, research has suggested that it is more effective for a person to repeat it verbally. Visual imagery, although slower, can also be used. Important areas of information are passed on to the long-term memory for retrieval and use at a later date.

Long-term memory

The long-term memory is what is generally thought of as someone's 'memory'. Information about past experiences is stored, including learned knowledge, perceptual skills, motor skills, etc. In short, all classes of information associated with learning and experience are retained in the LTM.

Capacity of LTM

The long-term memory is thought to have unlimited capacity. It enables a performer to deal with present situations or tasks by using information that has been specifically learned (either behavioural or factual) or information gained from general past experiences.

Duration of LTM

Information, once learned and stored in the long-term memory, is thought to be there indefinitely, perhaps permanently. The main problem with information stored in the long-term memory is one of retrieval. Once information has been rehearsed, reinforced and linked together in the appropriate manner within the STM (coding) it is passed to the LTM for storage. It is generally thought that once learned and stored in the LTM motor skills in particular are protected from loss. There is evidence to suggest that retrieval is more effective with skills that have been 'overlearned' (practised continually) and become autonomous. Skills that are linked or associated together in a more continuous way (cycling, swimming) rather than individual discrete skills (handstand, headstand) can also be retrieved more effectively.

Retrieval of information

Retrieval of information that has been stored in the LTM for future use can take several different forms. The more common forms are recognition, recall, re-learning.

- **Recognition:** when a tennis player sees something familiar with regard to a style of serve by their opponent or a defender in soccer sees several things happening in front of them and they have to make their mind up which one is the most dangerous and adapt their own movement to it having 'recognised' certain cues or signals (retrieval cues).
- **Recall:** when a performer has to actively search their memory stores for certain previously learned skills or information that may help solve a problem in the present.
- **Re-learning:** if something has previously been learned but then forgotten it will possibly be easier to learn a second time round.
- **Imagery:** when a performer is able to 'hook' their present cognitive or motor situation onto some form of visual image of previously well-performed situation, skill or strategy (see mental rehearsal page 400).

Decision making

In adopting an information processing approach to analysing how a performer uses present information in the form of cues and signals from the environment (display), in conjunction with previously learned or experienced information or movement skills in order to carry out some form of response (decision making), you should now have realised that this process takes time. Being able to select the correct plan of action (make a decision) quickly, is obviously critical in many sports, particularly those classified as using open skills, where adapting to continually changing situations is important, eg, tennis, basketball, hockey. It therefore follows that the quicker a performer can go through the whole process the greater advantage this should have for the motor action being carried out: anticipation becomes possible.

Reaction time

Reaction time is seen as an important performance measure helping researchers to find out exactly what happens prior to a response being made (response preparation time) and what factors can affect the speed and effectiveness of the response.

- **Reaction time** is defined as:

'the time between the onset of a signal to respond (stimulus) and the initiation of that response.' (R. A. Magill).

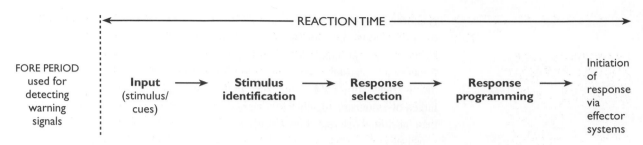

Fig. 22.10 REACTION TIME

This is different to two other time zones very often associated and sometimes confused with reaction time, namely 'movement time' and 'response time'.

- **Movement time** is defined as 'the time from the initiation of the first movement to the completion of that movement'
- **Response time** is defined as the time from the onset of a signal to respond (stimulus) to the final completion of the response or action

In the following diagram complete the missing labels.

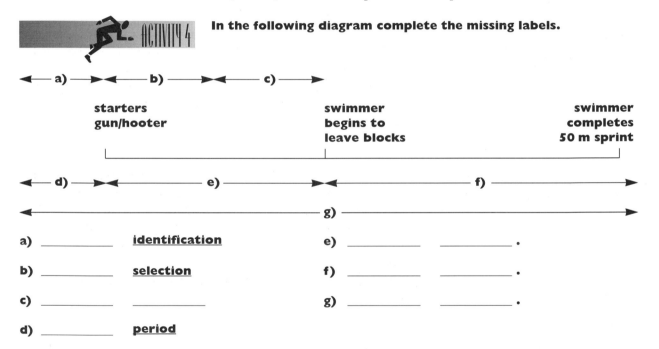

a) _____ **identification**

b) _____ **selection**

c) _____ _____

d) _____ **period**

e) _____ _____ .

f) _____ _____ .

g) _____ _____ .

Individuals differ considerably in their speed of reactions (reaction time – RT) or what has been termed 'response preparation time'. There are many important factors that can affect a performer's reaction time, usually associated with either the

- stimulus
- individual performer
- requirements of the task.

Response preparation time (decision making) can be affected by various factors associated with the amount of information and the number of decisions that have to be made.

Simple reaction time

This is a specific reaction to a specific stimulus (one stimulus – one response), eg, reacting to a starter at the beginning of a race.

Choice reaction time

Fig. 22.11 Darren Gough

This is when there are a number of alternatives: either a performer has to respond correctly when faced with several stimuli all requiring a different response or a performer has to respond correctly to a specific stimulus from a choice of several stimuli. Generally, the more choices a performer has to face with regard to either number of stimuli to deal with, or, more importantly, the number of optional responses, the more information they have to process and the longer or slower the reaction time is. This general 'rule of thumb' is based on Hick's Law (1952).

Hick's Law states that: 'Reaction time will increase logarithmically as the number of stimulus response choices increase.'

The linear relationship implies that reaction time increases at a constant rate every time the number of response choices is doubled. This has obvious implications for a performer when trying to outwit an opponent. A bowler in cricket is better placed to dismiss a batsman if they have more types of delivery at their disposal and can use them at various times to create a feeling of uncertainty in the batsman's mind – RT can be increased by over 50%.

Stimulus–response compatibility

The compatibility of a stimulus and response (S–R) is related to how 'naturally' connected the two are. If a certain stimulus happens, what usual response does it cause? The more 'natural' or usual the response the quicker the reaction time.

Experienced sailors can reduce their reaction time to almost zero as they move the tiller of the boat in relation to wind changes (S–R compatibility). It appears almost natural.

Predictability of stimulus occurring

The more predictable a stimulus is the more effective the response can be in terms of time and accuracy. If a performer can predict in advance what is going to happen by being able to pick up on various cues and signals or advanced information, then RT can be reduced dramatically. This pre-cueing technique, as it is sometimes called, has the similar but reverse relationship caused by Hick's Law regarding choice reactions.

A player's reaction time however, can only be reduced if they pick up on the correct cues and predict the correct stimulus.

In discussion with a partner, consider a badminton or tennis situation. What pre-cueing information might you be looking for when facing a serve? What might this enable you to do?

Previous experience/ practice

The more experienced a performer is and the more practice they have had of making choices, and relating the compatibility and probability of certain responses to certain stimuli, then the more likely it is that their RT will be faster. The effect is obviously greater where choice RT rather than simple RT is involved. Hence the experienced badminton player, when placing the shuttle in various parts of the court, knows, through a good deal of appropriate practice, that only certain types of shot can be played by their opponent from this position. This will allow them almost to pre-select plans of action (see motor programmes, page 382), ie, anticipate, thus reducing their reaction times and response times to what appears to be almost instant processing.

Anticipation

Anticipation is linked very closely to experience. Anticipation, where a performer is able to initiate movement programmes or actions with 'perfect timing' relies very much on a performer using signals and cues and recognising certain stimuli early, thus predicting what is going to happen. The defender in hockey or football who always appears in the right place at the right time to make the tackle or intercept the attacking pass is using their previous experience.

An experienced tennis player receiving a second serve would have picked up on their opponent's angle of racket and subtle positioning of feet, etc., to recognise that a top-spin serve, causing the ball to 'kick' up high and wide to the forehand, was probably coming over the net. He or she then prepares accordingly, thus processing has begun earlier. An inexperienced beginner on the other hand would not understand what a top spin serve can do to the ball or be able to recognise the warning signals/cues (selective attention). Thus they would be totally unprepared for the high bouncing ball when it arrived. Beginners need more processing time in order to organise, prepare and initiate a response.

Psychological refractory period (PRP)

A performer using previous experience in order to help them anticipate certain moves or actions depends heavily on making the correct predictions in order to reduce the time needed to prepare a response. One way a performer can try to increase the RT of their opponent is by presenting certain information, a certain stance or movement of the racket in tennis or stick in hockey which implies to the opponent that a certain shot or movement will occur (predicting). The opponent then processes this information in order to prepare and initiate a response. As the opponent's response to the first 'dummy' or fake action is initiated, the player changes the move or shot causing the opponent to re-evaluate the situation and react to the second set of stimuli. The processing of the new information, for instance a drop shot in badminton rather than the anticipated overhead clear, takes time, creating a slight time delay. This delay in being able to respond to the second of two closely spaced stimuli is termed the **psychological refractory period** (PRP). In practice, if timed correctly, the opponent in tennis or badminton or defenders in hockey or basketball, are made to look foolish as, by the time they have reorganised their movement to deal with the second stimulus, the point has been won or they have been beaten by the attack.

Theoretically the delay is created by the increased processing time caused by a hold-up or 'bottleneck effect' within the response programming stage. Within this stage it is suggested that the brain can only deal with the initiation of one action or response when presented with two closely following stimuli. This is known as the single-channel hypothesis. A PRP will only occur however, if the 'fake' or 'dummy' move or action is significant enough to cause the opponent to think it is actually going to happen.

There must also be no lengthy delay in carrying out the second stimulus or 'real' action as this may negate the whole significance of the PRP.

Intensity of stimulus

There is evidence to support the view that as intensity of stimulus increases reaction time decreases, eg, larger, brighter implements (rackets or balls) for beginners in particular.

Age It is generally accepted whilst being relatively limited in early childhood RT improves rapidly through the developing years up until the optimum level which is thought to be the late teens/early twenties. After this it levels off only to slow down considerably as old age approaches. Lack of experience on which to base quick and effective decisions has been suggested to explain children's limited RT.

Gender Research has tended to support the view that males have shorter reaction times although female reaction times deteriorate less with age. The factors already discussed, however, have much more of an influence than gender.

Arousal, attention and alertness

Here are the three As of information processing.

Arousal

The level of arousal of a performer is seen as a significant influencing factor upon their ability to make decisions quickly (response preparation time). We will consider various arousal theories and their links to motivation and performance in much greater detail within psychology of sport on page 442. As an introduction to the concept, arousal can be viewed as the energy or excitement levels of the individual generated at the time the performance is taking place. These levels can vary from extremely high, almost agitated behaviour to the lowest level, sleep. Both these extreme states are not recommended for the performer in sport as they do not create the 'optimum' state of mental readiness for effective decisions to be made.

Attention

Over-arousal creates 'states of anxiety', causing lack of concentration and lack of attention to important coaching points.

Performing under high arousal conditions has been shown to reduce a performer's ability to pay attention to all the important and relevant aspects from the displays, possibly creating an inadequate response particularly if something unexpected happens. This phenomenon is known as **perceptual** or **attentional narrowing**. See Arousal, p 446.

Alertness

Linked to the concept of optimum arousal and levels of attention is the term alertness. Being continually prepared (alert) to pick up on specific changing cues/signals and thus make correct decisions has been, in the main, linked to the performer's ability to maintain arousal levels or state of readiness. For instance, when a goalkeeper in hockey or football is seen 'prowling' the 'D' or penalty area watching the game, keeping on their toes, they are working on maintaining 'alertness'. While it is relatively easy to maintain optimum levels of arousal and thus attention for very short periods, particularly if you are involved in the game continually, it is sometimes difficult to maintain alertness over longer periods, such as in a full game situation or in repetitive practice situations.

Motor programmes and control of movement

Motor programmes

The traditional view of a motor programme was that it was a centrally organised pre-planned set of very specific muscle commands that, when initiated, allowed the entire sequence of movement to be carried out without reference to additional feedback. This view helped to explain how performers sometimes appear able to carry out very fast actions that have been well learned (particularly closed skills) without really thinking about the action, almost like a computer. In other words, they use very little conscious control. This has obvious links to Fitts' and Posner's autonomous stages of learning in Chapter 21.

In relating this notion of automatic movement to information processing you can appreciate that the limited capacities of the memory process would easily be overloaded, and take considerable time, if every part of every action had to pass via the STM. The notion of a motor programme being decided upon and initiated from the short-term memory appears to solve the overload problem where, in relatively stable situations, movement can be carried out without the need for modification. This type of control of movement is called 'open loop control', without feedback. Two areas of research which support this view are:

1 Reaction time has been found to be longer in actions which involve more complex movements. A tennis serve, for example, has many component parts. This suggests that the action is carried out following a pre-planned organisation.
2 In animal experiments involving **deafferention** where the **afferent** nerve bundles are severed near the spinal cord, it has been shown that even though the brain cannot receive sensory information via the central nervous system (no feedback) the animals are still capable of carrying out movement. This suggests that movement is centrally organised and that feedback is not critical in certain movements.

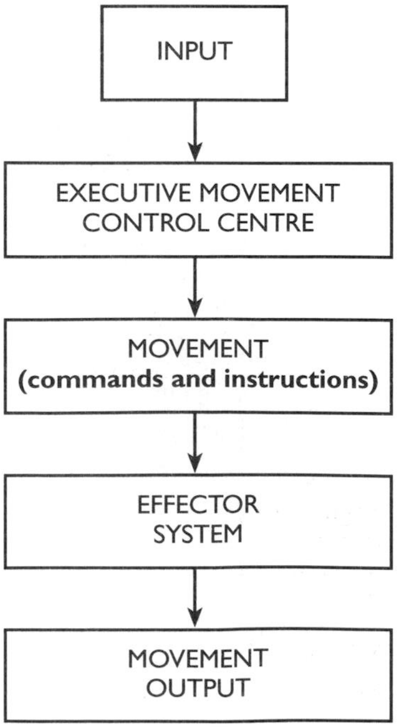

```
┌─────────────────────┐
│        INPUT        │
└─────────────────────┘
           │
           ▼
┌─────────────────────┐
│ EXECUTIVE MOVEMENT  │
│   CONTROL CENTRE    │
└─────────────────────┘
           │
           ▼
┌─────────────────────┐
│      MOVEMENT       │
│(commands and instructions)│
└─────────────────────┘
           │
           ▼
┌─────────────────────┐
│      EFFECTOR       │
│       SYSTEM        │
└─────────────────────┘
           │
           ▼
┌─────────────────────┐
│      MOVEMENT       │
│       OUTPUT        │
└─────────────────────┘
```

Fig. 22.12 SIMPLIFIED MODEL OF OPEN LOOP CONTROL

Open loop control

Motor programmes or pre-learned mastered movements initiated on command are thought to be developed through practice. A series of movements is built up, starting with very simple movements, until certain actions are stored as complete movements. These complete movements or motor programmes can be stored in the long-term memory and retrieved at will; the whole movement to be carried out can then be initiated by one complete command. It is suggested that such skills are built up in a hierarchical or schematic way.

Closed loop control

Within the closed loop model the loop is completed by information from the various sensory receptors feeding back information to the central mechanism or executive.

While it is accepted that there are many types of feedback, in this view of feedback control the feedback is internal (kinesthetic) allowing the performer to compare what is actually happening during the movement with the point of reference, namely the correct or currently learned and stored motor performance. This evaluation of the movement currently being undertaken means errors, if any, can be detected and acted upon. As you can see from fig 22.15, all feedback goes

Fig. 22.13 EXPANDED MODEL OF OPEN
LOOP CONTROL

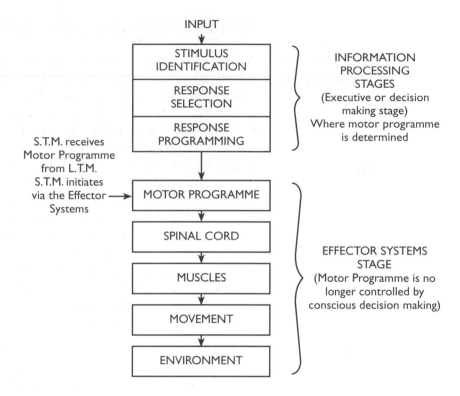

INPUT

STIMULUS
IDENTIFICATION

RESPONSE
SELECTION

RESPONSE
PROGRAMMING

INFORMATION
PROCESSING
STAGES
(Executive or decision
making stage)
Where motor programme
is determined

S.T.M. receives
Motor Programme
from L.T.M.
S.T.M. initiates
via the Effector
Systems

MOTOR PROGRAMME

SPINAL CORD

MUSCLES

MOVEMENT

ENVIRONMENT

EFFECTOR SYSTEMS
STAGE
(Motor Programme is no
longer controlled by
conscious decision making)

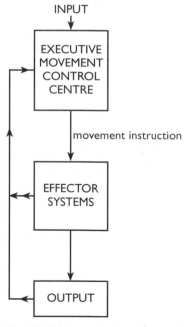

INPUT

EXECUTIVE
MOVEMENT
CONTROL
CENTRE

movement instruction

EFFECTOR
SYSTEMS

OUTPUT

Fig. 22.14 SIMPLIFIED MODEL OF CLOSED
LOOP CONTROL

Fig. 22.15 EXPANDED MODEL OF CLOSED
LOOP CONTROL

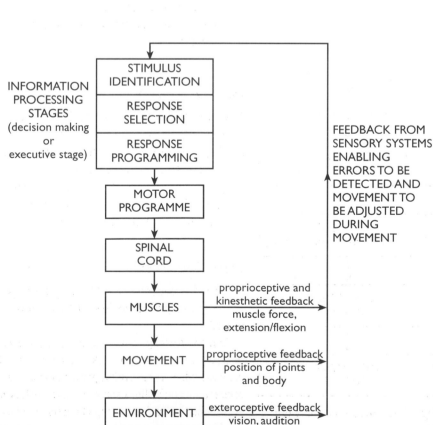

STIMULUS
IDENTIFICATION

RESPONSE
SELECTION

RESPONSE
PROGRAMMING

INFORMATION
PROCESSING
STAGES
(decision making
or
executive stage)

MOTOR
PROGRAMME

SPINAL
CORD

MUSCLES

MOVEMENT

ENVIRONMENT

proprioceptive and
kinesthetic feedback
muscle force,
extension/flexion

proprioceptive feedback
position of joints
and body

exteroceptive feedback
vision, audition

FEEDBACK FROM
SENSORY SYSTEMS
ENABLING
ERRORS TO BE
DETECTED AND
MOVEMENT TO
BE ADJUSTED
DURING
MOVEMENT

back through the processing system, which means that the process of detecting and correcting errors is relatively slow.

Research has shown that the closed loop system of movement control generally works more effectively with movements taking place over longer periods of time (continuous skills, eg, running) or with skills requiring slower limb movements (headstand or handstand).

In practice, while in certain actions one specific mode of control may dominate, the fact is that most sporting activities involve both fast, slow, simple and complex movements in a whole variety of coordinated ways. This suggests that performers are continually moving between open loop and closed loop control, with all systems of control being involved in controlling the performers' actions.

Schema theory

It was stated on page 382 that motor programmes were traditionally considered to be a specific set of pre-organised muscle commands that control the full movement. This suggests that specific motor programmes for all possible types of action are stored in the long-term memory awaiting selection and initiation.

Although the question of how these motor programmes are structured and stored has been considered since the last century, it was not really until Jack Adams presented his closed loop theory specifically related to motor skills in 1971 that more up-to-date research began in earnest.

For Adams the motor programme was made up of two areas of stored information.

1 **The memory trace** – used for selecting and initiating movement, operating as an open loop system of control prior to the perceptual trace.
2 **The perceptual trace** – used as the point of reference (memory of past movements) and also to determine the extent of movement in progress. Thus the perceptual trace is operating as a closed loop system of control.

The quality or strength of all these traces is built up and developed through practice with the performer using both intrinsic and extrinsic feedback. Schmidt presented his well-known **schema theory** as a way of dealing with the limitations, as he saw them, of Adam's closed loop theory. Schmidt proposed that schemas, rather than the memory and perceptual traces suggested by Adams, explained recall of movement patterns. Instead of there being very specific traces for all learned or experienced movement, schemas as Schmidt saw them were 'a rule or set of rules that serve to provide the basis for a decision'.

Schmidt suggested that we learn and control movements by developing generalised patterns of movement around certain types of movement experience, eg, catching, throwing. A performer does not store all the many specific but different types of catching and throwing; rather they collate together various items of information every time they experience either catching or throwing. This helps in building up their knowledge of catching or throwing in general. Performers thus construct schemas which enable them at some future time to successfully carry out a variety of movements.

A schema for throwing can be adapted to:

- returning a cricket ball to wicket keeper
- a long pass in basketball/netball
- a goalkeeper in football setting up an attack
- throwing a javelin
- playing darts.

By collating as much movement information as possible with regard to throwing we can adapt to new situations because we know the general rules associated with throwing long, short, high, low, etc. In order for schemas to be constructed and developed, the performer has to collate information from four areas of the movement: see table 22.1.

Table 22.1   RECALL AND RECOGNITION SCHEMAS

recall schemas information is stored about determining and producing the desired movement (similar to memory trace)	**1** initial conditions (where we are)	• knowledge of environment • position of body • position of limbs
	2 response specification (what we have to do)	• specific demands of the situation • direction • speed • force
recognition schema information is stored enabling evaluation of movement	**3** sensory consequences (what movement feels like)	• information based on sensory feedback • during and after movement • involves all sensory systems
	4 response outcomes (what has happened)	comparisons are made between • actual outcome • intended outcome • KR is important

Feedback

The final part in the information processing system is feedback (FB). Strictly speaking feedback is a processing term referring to information coming from within the system rather than information coming from the outside world. Feedback is now generally referred to as all the information in its various forms that a performer receives as a result of movement (response produced information). When a performer is taking part in physical activity in any shape or form information is fed back into the system either during the activity or after the activity. This information can come from within the performer or from outside relating to the adequacy of their performance. This information is used to either detect and correct errors during the activity or to make changes/improvements the next time the skill is performed. As well as changing performance, feedback can also be used to reinforce learning and motivate the performer. It has been argued that without FB learning cannot occur. Evidence to support this view is provided by research conducted by Bilodeau and Bilodeau (1959, 1961) and G Stelmach (1970).

ACTIVITY 6

1   In discussion with a partner and using practical examples, try and create a list of as many different kinds of feedback that a performer may receive when taking part in sporting activities.

Activity	Type of feedback	Example from sport

2 Try to think of possible methods or classifications that you might use to group together the different types of feedback you have thought of.

Types and forms of feedback (FB)

Intrinsic feedback

Sometimes referred to as internal or inherent feedback, this type of FB comes from within the performer from the propriceptors. When a golfer swings at the ball they can feel the timing of the arm movement and the hip movement in conjunction with a perfect strike of the ball. This is also referred to as kinesthetic FB. The golfer can see and hear their club swing, and hear the ball being struck, which serves to back up the proprioceptive information being received. All this information is inherent to the task.

Extrinsic feedback

Sometimes referred to as external or augmented FB, this type of FB is information received from outside the performer about the performance and is given and used to enhance (augment) the already received intrinsic FB. This is the type of FB that is generally referred to in teaching and coaching. It can however, be received from team mates within the context of a game. Performers usually receive this type of FB by visual or auditory means; for instance the coach or teacher tells or shows a performer the reasons why success or failure has occurred.

Extrinsic FB can obviously be made up of a mixture of several different types and forms:

- Continuous
- Terminal

- Knowledge of results (KR)
- Knowledge of performance (KP)

- Positive
- Negative

Continuous feedback

Sometimes referred to as ongoing or concurrent FB, this type of FB is being received *during* the activity. It is most frequently received as proprioceptive or kinesthetic information, eg, a tennis player can 'feel' the ball hitting the 'sweet spot' of the racket when playing strokes during a rally.

Terminal feedback

This is FB received by the performer *after* they have completed the skill or task. It can either be given immediately after the relevant performance or be delayed and given some time later.

Positive feedback

This type of feedback occurs when the performance of a task was correct or successful. It can be used to reinforce learning, increasing the probability of the successful performance being repeated, eg, a coach or teacher praising a beginner when they catch a ball successfully.

Although positive FB is thought to facilitate perceived competence and help intrinsic motivation, it is important that a teacher doesn't give too much positive FB thereby distorting a performer's perceptions of their own performance and possibly affecting motivation.

Negative feedback

This type of FB occurs when the performance of a task was incorrect, eg, a basketball player will receive negative FB in various forms if they miss a set shot: they see the ball has missed, friends comment, they realise they did not put enough power behind the ball and the teacher or coach may indicate faults and suggest correction. All this should help to ensure that further shots are more successful.

Knowledge of results and knowledge of performance

Knowledge of results (KR) is an essential feature of skill learning. Without knowing what the results of our actions have been we will be unable to modify them in order to produce the precise movements needed for the correct performance of a skill. One of the more important roles of a teacher or coach is to provide this type of information. Knowledge of results is usually given verbally, eg, a netball coach saying 'You missed the net by 10 cm' or an athletics coach shouting out lap times during training. This type of FB about goal or task achievement is thought to be very useful in the early phases of learning when beginners like to have some measure of their successful performance. An eight-year-old child will see her performance in terms of 'I scored a goal today' or 'Our team won all the games', not in terms of the quality of her own performance.

Once KR has been given it is then usually necessary for the teacher or coach to give information as to why or how the result came about. A hockey coach, when trying to develop passing, may give KR as in 'Your pass was far too wide'. They may support this by adding 'The reason it was so wide was because your left shoulder was not pointing towards your partner, your feet were not in the right position and your stick did not follow through in the direction the ball was meant to go'. This gives the performer additional (augmented) extrinsic information in order to help them know not only the result of the action (KR) but also know why the result was incorrect and how to correct the performance. This type of FB about the actual movement pattern is more like the FB given by a teacher and is known as 'knowledge of performance' (KP). Although most of the traditional research has been carried out with regard to KR, due to its ease of measurement, there has been a definite shift in emphasis towards researching KP particularly with the increased availability of more modern computer and video technology allowing greater mechanical analysis of technique and performance.

Knowledge of results (KR) as used in most psychology or coaching texts is referred to as:

'Information provided to an individual after the completion of a response that is related to either the outcome of the response or the performance characteristics that produced that outcome.'   *(R. Magill).*

The use of feedback

Feedback can be used to help with:

- the correction of errors
- reinforcement
- motivation.

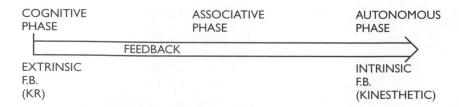

COGNITIVE
PHASE

ASSOCIATIVE
PHASE

AUTONOMOUS
PHASE

FEEDBACK

EXTRINSIC
F.B.
(KR)

INTRINSIC
F.B.
(KINESTHETIC)

Fig. 22.16 How feedback moves the performer through the three stage model

There are numerous studies to support the importance of feedback (KR) in the learning process. In referring back to Fitts' and Posner's phases of learning, feedback can be used to move the performer through the three phases of the learning process.

Once in the autonomous phase the performer should be less reliant on KR and should, through their knowledge and understanding of the activity, be able to detect their own errors and, in conjunction with kinesthetic FB, be able to make corrections to their own performance.

Although skills can be learned without FB it is generally accepted that FB makes the learning process more efficient by improving error correction and developing better performance. Relating this back to the section on motor programmes (page 382), we can see that if a performer receives additional information the quality of his or her generalised patterns of movement (schemas which help initiate and control movement) can be effectively enhanced, particularly in the early phases of learning. When considering the use of FB the teacher or coach needs to be aware of the following:

- current skill levels of the performer (phase of learning)
- nature of the skill (complexity/organisation/classification) and its transferability.

In relation to the above points, the coach or teacher has to decide on the following aspects of FB:

- general or specific
- amount (too much or too little)
- how to present it (visual/verbal)
- frequency, eg, after every attempt, or summary after several attempts (performer must not become dependent on extrinsic FB).
- time available for practice/processing.

Although the quantity, distribution and whether it is positive or negative are important considerations, the most crucial aspects of feedback are *quality* and *appropriateness*.

KR must not provide too much information otherwise the performer will not know what to pay attention to or how to use the FB to help future attempts. Attention must be directed to specific or major errors particularly with beginners. If major errors are left then this could lead to the performer assuming them to be correct, strengthening the incorrect S–R bond and making it much more difficult to deal with later. As well as telling the beginner what the problem is a teacher or coach must provide information on how the performer can correct the error.

Feedback (KR) must be meaningful and relevant to the phase of learning. Beginners might need general information whereas experienced performers may need more specific information. Sometimes however, beginners may need much more specific information: a more experienced badminton player would understand 'Your positioning is not right' and probably rectify the fault immediately. The same statement made to a beginner would be of little value as they need much more specific FB with regard to the position of feet, angle of upper body or preparation of racket prior to the shot, etc. in order for them to make the necessary corrections.

Researchers have found that time intervals after the performance have a bearing on how KR should be used. A teacher needs to be aware that once KR has been given the performer has to have time to assimilate the information and put the KR into action. However, too long a delay could allow the performer to forget what has happened or to lose understanding of the relevance of the KR being given.

Feedback can also be used as reinforcement. Reinforcement, as you already know, increases the probability of certain behaviour being repeated. Using FB to strengthen the bond between stimulus and response is useful.

Positive FB has a great role to play in reinforcement. Both KR or KP can be useful in motivating a performer, maintaining interest and effort (direction and intensity). Seeing performance improve, eg, an athlete improving their personal best or a tennis player increasing the accuracy and percentage of successful first serves, should ensure that performers keep on practising. It is very helpful if this is carried out in a formal way with statistical evidence being logged by the teacher or coach. This information can be used both for the evaluation of current performance (error detection) and for future target setting. In this way, feedback can be used as an incentive. Using feedback in conjunction with goal setting has been recognised as being very effective in the learning process.

Summary

Learning theories

1 The key components of the behaviouristic perspective are stimulus (S) and response (R). The S–R theory is based on the concept that learning involves the development of connections or bonds between specific stimuli and responses.
2 In classical conditioning, drill and habit are very important elements of every lesson.
3 In operant conditioning, reinforcement is central to shaping behaviour.
4 The teacher or coach must try to produce feelings of satisfaction to give strong reinforcements (law of effect).
5 Hull's drive theory links motivation to the strengthening of the S–R bond.
6 Cognitive theories suggest that performers must be able to understand events. The concept of 'insight' is a major aspect of cognitive theories.

Information processing

1 The human motor system can be viewed as a processor of information with sensory information passing through various stages.
2 The effectiveness with which a performer processes various forms of sensory information often affects overall performance.
3 Reaction time is an important measure of information processing speed, and is affected by many factors.
4 Feedback and kinesthesis are imperative in closed loop control.
5 Pre-learned mastery of motor programmes is essential for open loop control, feedback is not integral in motor control.

6   Motor programmes are seen as generalised sets of movements stored in the long-term memory allowing performers to tailor movements to the demands of the environment.

7   Feedback provides information about errors to help make corrections and improve performance. It can act as reinforcement for correct actions and help to develop motivation.

8   The quality of feedback information is important to ensure learning is effective.

Revision Questions

1   What is a theory of association?

2   Explain the S–R bond.

3   What is a major criticism of classical conditioning?

4   In what ways does operant conditioning differ from classical conditioning?

5   What does reinforcement mean?

6   How does positive and negative reinforcement affect the probability of behaviour happening?

7   How does punishment affect behaviour?

8   What is the law of effect?

9   Give a practical example to show your understanding of how behaviour is shaped and maintained by its consequences.

10   How does a teacher or coach prevent 'inhibition' developing?

11   What does 'insight learning' mean?

12   Why is the cognitive approach to learning thought to be more effective?

13   What is meant by information processing?

14   (a) Draw a simple model of information processing.
      (b) Give practical examples from tennis or badminton for each of the parts of your simple model.

15   Draw and label Whiting's model of information processing and explain the terms.

16   What are various parts of the memory process?

17   Draw a simple model to show your understanding of how the parts of memory link together.

18   What is the process of selective attention?

19   What is response preparation time better known as?

20   What other factors affect a performer's speed of reactions?

21   What are good and bad effects of anticipating?

22   What does PRP stand for? Explain a situation in a game where it could be used to benefit performance.

23   What are motor programmes?

24   Explain open loop and closed loop control of movement.

25   What four areas of an action are used to develop schemas?

26   What are KR and KP?

27   When using feedback what does a teacher or coach need to be aware of?

28   In what ways can extrinsic feedback be used to modify performance?

chapter 23

Turning Theory into Practice

In Chapters 20–22, we have considered the nature of skilled performance, principles of learning and theories associated with learning. In general it is accepted that having a better understanding of the principles and theories associated with perceptual motor skill learning helps a teacher or coach prepare and deliver more effective teaching and coaching strategies. In order to create an effective learning environment a teacher or coach needs to consider many variables which can be categorised into several main areas. Here is a list of the terms to be covered in this chapter. It is important that you understand them.

- Complex skills
- Simple skills
- Organised skills
- Unorganised skills
- Sub-routines
- Interrelated skills
- Independent skills
- Transfer
- Positive transfer
- Negative transfer
- Retro-active transfer
- Pro-active transfer
- Bi-lateral transfer
- Near/far transfer
- Inter-task
- Intra-task
- Zero transfer
- Identical elements
- Similarity
- Transfer appropriate processing
- Visual guidance
- Verbal guidance
- Manual/mechanical guidance
- Forced response
- Physical restriction
- Massed practice
- Distributed practice
- Mental practice
- Whole method
- Part method
- Progressive part method
- Variations in teaching styles
- Command style
- Reciprocal style
- Discovery
- Guided discovery
- Problem solving

Once you have read this chapter you should gain an understanding of the considerations related to:

- the learning and performance process
- the learner/individual differences
- the task
- the instructional/practice conditions.

Considerations linked to the learning and performance process

In considering the learning and performance process we have already stated that there is no definitive approach guaranteed to succeed. A teacher or coach needs to be aware of the positive and negative aspects of the many theories and models associated with effective learning. They then need to be able to use and adapt them where appropriate according to the individual needs of the learner and the demands of the situation.

Considerations linked to learner/individual differences

Considerations related to the individual can be identified and researched in isolation but usually they are variables that are interlinked and difficult to separate in real life situations. They include:

- age – chronological age; maturational age (physical and mental)
- gender
- abilities – perceptual and motor (see Chapter 20)
- psychological – motivation, interests, attitude, personality
- physiological – size, shape, weight, fitness components
- sociological
- previous experience – links to transfer, information processing, perception, motor programmes and schemas
- stage of learning (see Chapter 21)
- any personal limitations – sensory, physical, learning problems.

Considerations linked to the task

When considering the task a teacher or coach would have to ask themselves:

- is it a simple or complex task?
- is it an organised or unorganised task?
- what is the classification? (see Chapter 20)
- is transfer possible?

Complex or simple tasks

When deciding on the degree of complexity of a skill/task a teacher or coach will consider the difficulties it could present to the beginner. These difficulties are generally associated with the amount of information that the performer has to cope with when trying to complete the skill/task (cognitive involvement).

Complex tasks have a high degree of cognitive involvement and require a great deal of 'attention' to the skill. Simple tasks have a low level of cognitive involvement

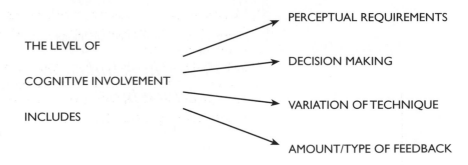

Fig. 23.1 COPING WITH INFORMATION — COGNITIVE INVOLVEMENT

and require a low level of attention. By being aware of the information processing and memory demands placed on a learner a teacher or coach can try to structure practices in order to reduce the complexity of skills.

One way of achieving this is for the teacher or coach to break down the main skill/task into various parts thus reducing the amount of information (cognitive involvement) the performer is having to cope with (see page 000 on presentation and organisation practice). As the performer moves through the various stages of learning (see Chapter 21) the amount of information they have to deal with can be increased.

Organisation of a skill/task

Fig. 23.2 A HANDSTAND IS HIGHLY ORGANISED: THE COMPONENTS ARE INTERRELATED

Fig. 23.3 HIGH TO LOW ORGANISATION CONTINUUM

Having suggested that complex skills can be broken down into their constituent parts to simplify them, some skills/tasks by their very nature are very difficult to break down into sub-routines and therefore have to be taught as a 'whole' movement. Skills or tasks that are difficult to break down are said to be highly organised: there is a very strong relationship between the components of the skill.

If a skill/task is said to be **low in organisation** this means that it can be broken down easily into sub-routines. These sub-routines can be practised in isolation as they are relatively independent of each other.

High in
organisation

Low in
organisation

Skills/tasks can be placed along the continuum according to their degree of organisation

Transfer

Having considered the complexity, organisation and classification of a skill/task a teacher needs to consider structuring the learning environment in order to take into account the concept of **transfer**. The instructional approaches used to introduce and teach skills/tasks to performers very often depend on the relationship between various skills that have either been taught previously or are going to be taught in the future. The transfer of performance and learning from one situation to another has been an essential element of organisational and instructional approaches for many years.

Transfer of learning is seen as being the influence or effect of performing or practising one skill/task on the learning of another skill/task. There is evidence to support the following general points.

1 That different types of transfer possibilities exist.
2 That certain practice conditions can either help or hinder the actual effect or degree of transfer.
3 That the amount and direction of transfer can be affected by many factors.
4 That teachers need to be aware of the principles associated with transfer.
5 That teachers need to be able to apply these principles in order to structure effective teaching or coaching situations.

Types of transfer

The following are types of transfer:

- pro-active
- retro-active
- positive

- negative
- bi-lateral
- near

- far
- inter-task
- intra-task

Pro-active transfer

When a skill/task presently being learned has an effect on future skills/tasks this effect is said to be pro-active. A teacher ultimately aiming to teach basketball may start off by introducing beginners to throwing, catching, passing, moving, dribbling, thus building up skills to be transferred into the future game situation. Simplified forms of more complex activities are introduced.

Retro-active

When a skill/task presently being learned has an effect on previously learned skills/tasks this effect is said to be retro-active.

Positive transfer

Positive transfer, as the term suggests, is when skills/tasks that have been learned/experienced help or facilitate the learning of other skills. This can be positive retro-active or positive pro-active. Similarities in both skill components and information processing characteristics will help increase the possibilities of positive transfer. If these similarities are pointed out, particularly to beginners in the associative phase of learning, the effect of transfer can be enhanced further.

A diver wishing to improve their coordination of turning and twisting may take part in trampolining practice in order to develop more control and possibly understanding of rotation and twisting. The components in the practice situation (trampolining) are very similar, and realistic to the main task, thus improving the likelihood of positive transfer occurring.

It is important, therefore, if we accept this basic principle, that a teacher or coach must ensure that practice situations are as realistic as possible. Research on similarities between the stimulus and response has shown that maximum positive transfer can be produced when the stimulus and response characteristics of the new skill are identical to those of the old skill. Other theories have supported the idea that it is general principles of understanding and movement that are transferred as well as the specific elements of a skill. Thus it is when the information processing requirements (cognitive components) are similar that the effect of transfer is greater.

A player involved in team games, such as either football or hockey, would be able to transfer their spatial awareness, tactical understanding of passing, moving and tackling from one game to another. Having learned to throw a cricket ball the basic principles of the movement can be transferred to throwing a javelin (see the schema theory page 383). This view of positive transfer being more likely between activities having similar cognitive elements (information processing conditions) has been termed **transfer appropriate processing**.

Negative transfer

When one skill/task hinders or inhibits the learning or performance of another skill/task this is known as negative transfer. Sports performers and coaches tend to believe that this happens on a regular basis. Thankfully the effects of negative transfer are thought to be limited and certainly temporary; it is thought to happen when a performer is required to produce a new response in a well-known situation (familiar stimulus). Stimuli are identical or similar but the response requirements are different. Initial confusion is thought to be created more as a result of the performer having to re-adjust their cognitive processes rather than problems associated with the motor control of the movement. The familiar example of tennis having a negative effect on badminton is often quoted, but although the two games have similar aspects, tactics, use of space, court, net, racket, hand eye coordination, etc., the wrist and arm action are very different.

In order to overcome or limit the effects of negative transfer teachers and coaches should be aware of areas that may cause initial confusion. Practices need to be planned accordingly, ensuring that the players are aware (direct attention) of possible difficulties they may experience.

Bi-lateral transfer

In the earlier discussion of transfer we have considered transfer from one skill/task to another. Bi-lateral transfer, however, occurs when learning is transferred from limb to limb, ie, from the right leg to the left leg, etc. When a basketball coach tries to develop their player's weaker dribbling hand by relating it to earlier learned skills with the strong hand they are involved in bi-lateral transfer. This involves the player in transferring both motor proficiency and levels of cognitive involvement. The performer is thought to adjust and transfer the parameters of stored motor programmes linked to one limb action to the other.

Zero transfer

When one skill/task has no effect on the performance of another skill, eg, swimming or horse riding, zero transfer is said to occur.

Research into transfer

Inter-task

The effect of a skill/task on a different or new skill/task is called inter-task transfer. Typical experiments would relate to the amount of time saved in learning, for instance, the lay up shot in the game by using a particular type of drill in basketball practice.

Intra-task

Intra-task transfer occurs when the relationship between two different types of practice or conditions of practice are considered. Comparisons can be made to show how different types of practice conditions might influence the learning of a specific skill/task.

Near transfer

When a coach develops specific practices/skills which are very realistic and relevant to the 'real game' situation in order to try and help players in future games this is referred to as near transfer.

Far transfer

Far transfer is when a teacher or coach tries to develop general skills and understanding which may be used in the future to transfer to more specific games or activities. A teacher working with primary children on developing their coordination, spatial awareness or general throwing and catching skills for future use in basketball or netball is working on far transfer.

Considerations linked with instructional/practice conditions

Finally, a teacher or coach has to consider possible variables associated with themselves and the situation when deciding on curriculum methods and strategies. These considerations can again be categorised into several main areas. When a teacher or coach is aware of all the previously discussed considerations to do with the learning process, the learner and the task, they can then ask themselves, in order to be effective:

1   What types of guidance shall I use?
2   What types of practice/presentation shall I use?
3   What style of teaching shall I use?

Types of guidance   Guidance is information given to the learner or performer in order to help them limit possible mistakes (incorrect movement) thus ensuring that the correct movement patterns are carried off. While guidance or instructions are usually given to beginners when skills/tasks are unfamiliar, it is obviously used continually in various forms at all stages of learning and performance (see feedback and knowledge of results, page 385). The form of guidance given, together with its effectiveness, will depend on several aspects:

- the learner – motivation; stage of performer's experience/learning linked to their information processing capacitation and capabilities
- the type/nature of the skill/task
- the environment or situation.

In order to facilitate the acquisition of skill formal guidance can take several forms:

- visual guidance
- verbal guidance
- manual/mechanical guidance.

If formal guidance does not serve to improve performance through the long-term retention of learning then it cannot be called guidance.

Visual guidance

Visual guidance can be given in many different ways in order to facilitate the acquisition of skill:

- demonstration
- video/film/TV
- posters/charts
- OHTs/slides

Visual modes of receiving information are heavily relied on by beginners. Visual guidance is particularly useful in the early stages of learning (cognitive phase) by helping the learner establish an overall image or framework of what has to be performed. This modelling of the elements involved in skills is an important aspect of skill acquisition. See Chapter 26, p 463 on observational learning.

There are considerable differences of opinion with regard to the long-term effectiveness of visual guidance. However, for the more advanced performer, specific and complex information can generally be provided more readily by modern technology.

Visual guidance can also be used to highlight certain cues or signals from the display helping the selective attention processes of beginners in particular. Equipment in infant and junior schools is often brighter or bigger in order to help performers 'see things' more clearly.

The teacher or coach can **modify the display** more specifically by highlighting areas of the court or pitch that shots should be played into or by making target areas bigger. Routes of movement can also be indicated by markers, etc.

It is very difficult in reality to consider visual guidance in isolation as verbal explanations very often have to accompany the demonstration or visual image being presented.

Verbal guidance

Verbal guidance is again a common form of guidance used by teachers or coaches and can be either very **general** or **specific**. A teacher may talk through a particular strategy in team games in order to give players a general picture of what is required before putting the move into practice. This **priming** helps to reduce the stimulus uncertainty (see decision making and reaction times, page 377). It is also useful to draw learners' attention to specific details of certain movements by giving verbal cues alongside visual demonstrations. **Verbal labelling** of specific aspects of a movement by a performer is also thought to facilitate learning. A teacher may help the beginner link their visual image of the task to certain verbal cues.

It is important that the learner does not become too heavily reliant on verbal guidance thus reducing their own ability to pay attention to aspects of performance, process information, make decisions and solve their own problems when guidance is removed. Verbal guidance is thought to be more effective with advanced performers who, because of increased experience and wider movement vocabulary, are able to transfer or transpose verbal comments into visual images more readily. Teachers or coaches may therefore find difficulty in simply describing certain movements to beginners particularly those involving more complex or highly organised skills. They will have to use a combination of both visual and verbal guidance in order to help the learner to internalise the information being presented.

 **In discussion with a partner try to think of ways you could verbally guide a performer through the pole vault.**

When considering verbal guidance, it is important that it is: clear/precise, relatively short (not too lengthy), appropriate to the level of the learner, and not overdone.

Do not overload. Only a few important points will be taken in during the first few attempts. Children have very short attention spans (see information processing, page 371).

It is also useful to note that when giving verbal guidance:

- everybody should be able to hear

- the pitch and tone of the voice should be varied in order to encourage or emphasise a specific point
- a sense of humour is a great help.

Manual/mechanical guidance

This type of guidance involves trying to reduce errors by in some way physically moving (called forced response) or restricting/supporting (called physical restriction) a performer's movements. This form of guidance is particularly useful in potentially dangerous situations. A performer may initially need physical or mechanical support in order to develop the confidence to 'have a go' themselves. In trampolining a coach may stand on the bed and physically support the beginner through the stages of a somersault (manual/physical guidance). With more advanced performers they may also use a twisting belt which would provide mechanical guidance by physically restricting the performer. A performer may have their response or actions **forced** by the coach or teacher. In taking a performer through an action they will very often take hold of the racket arm in tennis forcing the performer to carry out certain movements, eg, a backswing for early preparation.

While in the initial stages of learning, the use of mechanical aids, such as floats and armbands in swimming, serve a very useful purpose, it is important that beginners do not become over reliant on them and lose their own 'kinesthetic feel' for the movement. There has to come a time, in gymnastics for example, where support for the learner has to be gradually removed once the teacher or coach is sure that the performer is 'safe'.

Types, structure and presentation of practice

What types of practice shall I use? In deciding how to use their allotted time to benefit learners effectively, teachers or coaches need to make decisions about when to practice, and how often. In making these decisions they should consider whether practice is better all at once (massed), or whether breaks are required (distributed). Within these blocks of practice they will consider whether the skill should be taught as a whole, in parts or various combinations. The question of mental practice or rehearsal also needs to be considered.

Massed and distributed practice

For the purposes of this text, **massed practice** is seen as being almost continuous practice with very little or no rest at all between attempts or blocks of trials.

Distributed practice is seen as practice with relatively long breaks or rest periods between each attempt or block of attempts.

Practice and the learner

Although massed practice may appear to save time as the teacher or coach does not have to spend time after long breaks either re-introducing the performer to the task or reducing psychological barriers (fear, anxiety, etc.), this may be a short-sighted policy as distributed practice for beginners is seen as being a more effective learning process. The length of the practice session should be appropriate to both the physical and psychological maturity (state of readiness) of the performer.

Table 23.1 PRACTICE AND THE INDIVIDUAL

MASSED PRACTICE	DISTRIBUTED PRACTICE
Better when the individual is: • experienced • older • fitter • more motivated	**Better when the individual is:** • beginner • less experienced • limited preparation (physical/mental) • less motivated

Beginners are more likely to be affected by lack of attention/concentration and lack of appropriate physical and mental fitness to sustain long periods of practice. Distributed practice with beginners, allowing for greater variation of practice, is seen as essential as it not only allows for better schema developments and transfer possibilities but also helps maintain motivation. Random practice is seen as being more effective than ordered.

Interestingly, research suggests that the learners and performers themselves are not always the best judges of structure and time allocation, generally preferring to rush through things superficially. There is evidence to support the view that for the more experienced/older/fitter performer massed practice is more effective.

Practice and the task

Practice sessions need to be long enough to allow for improvement but should not be overly long. Whilst the effect of fatigue in relatively dangerous situations (gymnastics, outdoor pursuits) could be potentially serious, the effect of fatigue in massed practice can hinder performance in the short term although not necessarily skill learning in the long term. Alternatively, distributed practice for discrete skills may lead to lack of motivation due to the performer's frustration at having delays between attempts. Group or team activities can be practised for longer than individual tasks as players can have rests in between thus lessening fatigue and frustration. At the same time groups should not be so big that rest intervals or waiting times become over long thus de-motivating learners or allowing opportunities for ill-discipline.

The use of rest periods or intervals needs to be considered within distributed practice. They can be used for the following:

• to reduce fatigue
• to reduce short-term inhibition
• to give feedback (KR and KP)

Table 23.2 PRACTICE AND THE TASK

MASSED PRACTICE	DISTRIBUTED PRACTICE

Better when the task is:
• Discrete
  brief in nature
  e.g., hitting a golf ball,
  shooting baskets
• Simple
	Better when the task is:
	• Continuous
	  requiring repetition
	  of **gross skills**
	  e.g., swimming, cycling, running
	• Complex – precision orientated
	• Dangerous

- to offer an alternative activity/novelty game (must ensure no negative transfer)
- to develop positive transfer
- to re-motivate
- to offer mental practice/rehearsal (see section below).

Mental practice

The definition of mental practice is: the mental or cognitive rehearsal of a skill without actual physical movement.

When looking at the various types of practice available for a teacher or coach to use mental practice or mental rehearsal is an area often overlooked. We have mentioned above that time intervals or rest periods between practice can be used for mental practice.

Mental practice or rehearsal is seen as being very beneficial. In the early stages of learning (cognitive phase) mental rehearsal is initially seen as the learner going through a skill/task and building up a mental picture of the expected performance in their mind (a cognitive process). This may involve a performer in deciding how to hold a hockey stick or a gymnast going over a simple vault in their mind. More advanced performers can use mental practice to rehearse possible alternative strategies or complex actions/sequences, thus almost pre-programming their effector systems and possibly helping with response preparation, reactions and anticipation. Mental practice can be a powerful tool in the preparation of the highly-skilled performer. A traditionally-held view has been that through mental practice a performer could slightly stimulate (below optimum threshold) the neuromuscular systems involved in activities and thus simulate (practice) the movement. In addition, mental practice is used regularly by more experienced performers in learning to control their emotional states. Optimum levels of arousal can be reached and maintained for effective performance. Wider developments in sports psychology have meant that mental rehearsal is being increasingly used to reduce anxiety and increase confidence, by getting the performer to focus their attention on winning, or performing successfully.

Although mental rehearsal is now seen as an important element of practice (better than no practice at all), it is not seen as a substitute to be used exclusively; rather it is much more effective when used in conjunction with physical practice.

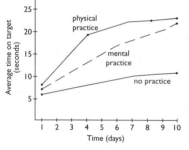

Fig. 23.4 COMPARISON OF EFFECTS OF MENTAL AND PHYSICAL PRACTICE ON PERFORMANCE
Source: Rawlings, Rawlings and Chew Yilk (1972) *Psychonomic Science* 26 page 71. Copyright 1972 by Psychonomic Society Inc.

The use of mental practice prior to performance

The performer needs to be advised to seek out a relatively quiet situation where they can focus mentally on the task. This will probably involve moving away from the competitive or performance situation.

The learner or performer needs to:

- go somewhere quiet
- focus on the task
- build a clear picture in their mind
- sequence the action
- imagine success
- avoid images of failure
- practice regularly.

The use of mental practice between practices

When used in between physical practice a performer must try and re-create the kinesthetic feeling and mental image they recently successfully experienced (remembering what was good). Equally so when a performer makes a mistake, stopping for a few seconds to reason why and then rehearse a good performance may have a positive effect on future performances.

This reviewing mentally of good and bad practice both during and after performance will help in building up good positive images. A golfer, when playing a practice swing, is very often mentally rehearsing the positive feel for the shot, imagining distance, angles of trajectory and power needed.

Whole or part method of practice

Performers differ in their response to whole or part practice. The **whole method** of learning is when the activity or skill is presented in total and practised as a full/entire skilled movement or activity. The **part method** of learning is when the activity or skill is broken down into its various components or sub-routines and each sub-routine is practised individually.

Additional variations have been developed whereby whole-part, part-whole or progressive part methods have been used.

Whether it is effective to teach a skill as a whole or whether it is more effective to break it down into its various sub-routines depends very much on the answers to two questions.

1 Can the skill/task be broken down into its sub-routines without destroying or changing it beyond all recognition? (see complexity and organisation, page 392).
2 What is the degree of transfer from practising the parts (sub-routines) back to the main skill or activity (see transfer, page 393).

Whole approach

It is argued that if a whole approach is used then a learner is able to develop their kinesthetic awareness or total feel for the activity. The learner is usually given a demonstration or explanation of what is required, builds up a cognitive picture and then becomes acquainted through practice with the total skill; they are then able to positively transfer the actions/skills more readily to the competitive or 'real' situation. By being able to link together the essential spatial and temporal elements of the skill the activity/skill quickly becomes meaningful to the performer. This approach is seen as a more effective use of time and should be used whenever possible particularly when skills have low levels of complexity and high levels of organisation, eg, a bench press in weight training. Skills which are very rapid (discrete or ballistic in nature) are also usually better practised as a whole. Although they could possibly be broken down, the parts are usually very much interrelated and therefore if broken down the skill would be changed out of all recognition – with possible negative effects on transfer, eg, hitting a softball.

When a skill is complex, highly organised and thus difficult to break down, very often an easier way to present it to beginners has to be found. Simplifying the activity/task enables the performer to experience the whole activity but with less information and decision making to deal with. Equipment is very often made lighter or bigger/smaller and less technical rules are imposed, or fewer physical demands and dangers, eg, uni hoc, mini hockey, short tennis. In general experienced performers will benefit more from the whole approach as they are better prepared to deal with skills that cannot be broken down or are very complex.

Fig. 23.5 SERIAL SKILLS SUCH AS THE LONG JUMP, WHERE THE SKILLS ARE SEQUENTIALLY ORDERED, LEND THEMSELVES MORE TO A PART METHOD OF LEARNING

Part approach

Skills which are very complex but low in organisation lend themselves to being practised and learned more effectively by the parts method. An additional consideration is again how interrelated or independent the various sub-routines are. Just because sub-routines are easily separated does not mean, however, that they have to be practised by themselves. The part method, while allowing teachers and coaches to work on areas of the skill that a beginner finds difficult, also tends to be more time consuming.

Activities such as front crawl in swimming which are not too complex but low in organisation lend themselves to being taught by the part method. The arm action, leg action, breathing pattern and body position can all be analysed and taught individually. While each can be and usually are practised independently, allowing the performer to experience success and thus gain confidence, it is important that the performer is able to practice synchronising the various sub-routines together. If the beginner does not experience the whole stroke there is a possibility that the kinesthetic feel for the whole action could be lost. When teaching the skills of passing in major team games, eg, soccer, rugby, hockey, it is essential that they are not taught in isolation. The beginner needs time for the interrelated units or sub-routines to be practised together in order that they can make the natural link between the parts. This, therefore, becomes a more progressive part method with combinations of the whole.

The progressive part method

The progressive part method or gradual metamorphosis is where earlier independent actions change their form to become something totally different. A learner being taught complex skills by the progressive part method benefits from the positive aspects of both part and whole methods. A gymnastic coach trying to develop a gymnast's routine would often follow this progressive part method. All the relatively complex but independent parts of the routine, eg, handstand, cartwheel, handspring, somersault, etc. are learned and practised in isolation, but then linked together into small units in order that the gymnast can experience and learn how to fluently link (sequence) the individual skills together. These units or blocks of skills are then linked again until eventually all the various parts of the action have been built up (the chain is completed) into the whole routine. These methods often rely on the operant method of learning discussed in Chapter 21.

 ACTIVITY 2

Consider a golf stroke being carried out and decide how you would teach it taking into account not only its moderate levels of both complexity and organisation, but also the fact that it is a discrete skill. Should you use the whole? part? or progressive part method of practice?

Teaching by an specific method is not guaranteed to work and the better teachers and coaches are generally flexible, using various combinations of the three basic methods discussed at different times. Many teachers begin an activity by allowing the beginner to experience the sequencing of the whole movement. They will then analyse strengths and weaknesses enabling them to develop a part method to deal with any problem areas. Then a progressive part process may develop where chunks or units of actions are practised together in a simplified task or small sided games. The performer is then allowed to return to the whole movement again.

Table 23.3   SUMMARY OF METHODS OF PRACTICE

WHOLE METHOD	PART METHOD	PROGRESSIVE PART METHOD
• Low level of complexity/simple task • High levels of organisation • Interrelated sub-routines • Discrete skills • Short duration/rapid ballistic • Lacks meaning in parts • Allows co-ordination of important spatial/temporal components	• High levels of complexity • Low levels of organisation • Independent sub-routines • Serial tasks • Slow tasks • Lengthy or long duration • Dangerous skills	• Complex task • Helps 'chaining' of complex skills learned independently • Allows for attention demands to be limited • Allows for co-ordination of spatial/temporal components to be experienced • Helps with transfer to whole
Performer is: • experienced • high levels of attention • in the later stages of learning • older • highly motivated • using distributed practice	**Performer is:** • a beginner • someone with a limited attention span • in the early stages of learning • having problems with a specific aspect of skill • someone with limited motivation • using massed practice	

Small problem areas may continue to be practised in isolation in order to refine technique. Complete adherence to one or other method is not advisable or useful.

ACTIVITY 3

In analysing the tennis serve to determine its components you could arrive at the seven sub-routines given in fig 23.6.

I   Where on a continuum would you put the serve?

High   complexity   Low   High or low?

2   Are any of the sub-routines more interrelated than others? (Difficulty in practising in isolation.)
3   Are there more independent sub-routines than others? (Easier to practise in isolation.)
4   Would you practise as a whole? If so, why?
5   Would you practise in parts? If so, why?

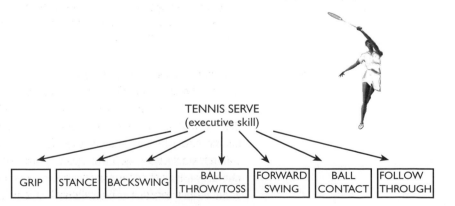

TENNIS SERVE
(executive skill)

| GRIP | STANCE | BACKSWING | BALL THROW/TOSS | FORWARD SWING | BALL CONTACT | FOLLOW THROUGH |

Fig. 23.6   THE TENNIS SERVE — AN EXECUTIVE SKILL

6 **Would you practise via a combination or modified part method? If so, why?**

7 **Discuss your ideas with the rest of the class.**

8 **Choose another skill or activity that you have experience of and carry out the same type of analysis to decide which teaching method or methods would be more effective.**

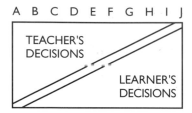

Fig. 23.7 Spectrum of teaching styles
Source: Moston and Ashworth (1986)

Teaching styles

What style of teaching should you use? It is important that you are aware that the style of teaching adopted by a teacher or coach can considerably affect the learning environment. In planning strategies using the various methods already discussed a teacher or coach is trying to create a favourable learning environment. An effective style of teaching aims to present information and thus develop effective learning by promoting achievement, satisfaction and motivation. Teachers invariably adopt different styles in various situations. A teacher's or coach's style of teaching is developed as a result of many factors. These are shown in table 23.4.

In looking at the decisions to be made over what, when and how to teach and learn, Moston and Ashworth (1986) developed their spectrum of teaching styles.

The more teacher orientated position, 'A', is referred to as the **command style**. The other end of the spectrum, where the learner makes more of the decisions, is referred to as **discovery learning**. There are obviously variations between the two extremes.

Command style (A)

Fig. 23.8 Many aerobic classes are taught by a command style of teaching

This style tends to see the teacher adopting a very authoritarian style! Within this rather behaviouristic approach there is little consideration given to the individual with all learners being treated in generally the same way. This style is thought to inhibit cognitive learning as thinking and questioning are not encouraged by the teacher. The teacher makes all the decisions. The learner is not allowed to develop responsibility for their own learning and is in danger of becoming a clone of the teacher by following movements, decisions and strategies dictated by the teacher. This type of learning has limitations for developing open skills as open skills require the performer to be able to adapt.

In addition, due to the formality of the situation there is little opportunity for any social interaction. This traditional approach helps to establish: pupil control, clear objectives/models for pupils, routine/organisation rules, and safety procedures. It is useful when working with beginners, large groups and in dangerous and limited time situations.

Reciprocal style (C/D)

Developing further along the spectrum than command style this approach is based more on cognitive theories. Although what is to be taught or covered is still decided by the teacher, it allows learners to take slightly more responsibility and become more involved in the decision making process. The sessions are structured in order that the objectives are clearly stated to the learners. The learners work in pairs taking alternative goes at being observer and performer. Although there is regular general and specific input from the teacher, the situation lends itself to more social interaction than the command style. Learners are encouraged to give feedback as a result of their analysis and evaluation of the performer's progress. In analysing and

Fig. 23.9 CONTINUUM OF STYLES

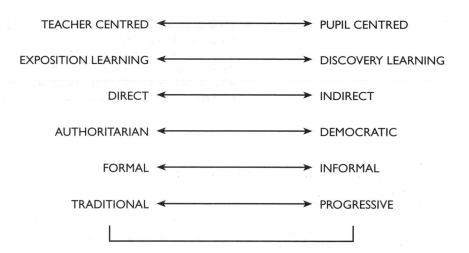

TEACHER CENTRED ←——————→ PUPIL CENTRED

EXPOSITION LEARNING ←——————→ DISCOVERY LEARNING

DIRECT ←——————→ INDIRECT

AUTHORITARIAN ←——————→ DEMOCRATIC

FORMAL ←——————→ INFORMAL

TRADITIONAL ←——————→ PROGRESSIVE

Table 23.4 FACTORS AFFECTING TEACHING STYLE

TEACHING STYLE	**TEACHER**	• philosophy • personality • present experience/training/skill • knowledge of the activity • textbooks/research
	ACTIVITY	• analysis of task • demands being placed on the learner • classification, complexity, organisation • dangerous • distribution of practice
	LEARNER (group or individual)	• individual/group personal characteristics • student's chronological and maturational age • student's level of skill • student's level of ability • student's level of condition/fitness • student's level of knowledge • student's level of interest/attitude/motivation
	SITUATION	• environmental factors • resources/staffing • facilities • equipment • time • dangerous

evaluating their partner's performance the learner is developing a greater understanding of the movement and passing this on to the partner. They should also be able to transfer this to their own performance when their partner has to reciprocate, giving additional individual feedback.

This style of teaching is useful in developing a learner's:

• self image
• confidence

- communication skills
- cognitive strategies.

The teacher does, however, need to monitor the process carefully and interject regularly to ensure that incorrect techniques are not being developed and reinforced. It is also important that the learners are at the appropriate maturational level of development and can cope with both giving and receiving constructive criticism from their peers and not merely focus on the negative or destructive aspects.

Discovery learning/guided discovery

This much more individualistic style of teaching is rather time consuming and is usually developed into guided discovery learning. In guided discovery the teacher generally has to lead the performer by providing the appropriate information, cues and questions in order to get the learner to 'discover' effective and correct movement skills or the understanding associated with certain techniques. The teacher needs to have an in-depth knowledge of each pupil and be constantly evaluating progress. Due to inevitable time limitation, learning will not be uniform for all. Students will progress at different rates, creating extra demands on the teacher.

By using progressive question and answer techniques in association with reinforcement, teachers can guide a learner's greater understanding. In developing greater understanding in one area the performer will also learn to adapt decision making and reasoning processes from previous or correct skills (pro-active positive transfer) to future learning situations. In being more involved with their own learning the learner is thought to gain greater personal satisfaction together with a more positive self image which in turn will help to develop even greater motivation.

Problem solving approach

Very often associated with the guided discovery method discussed above, the problem solving approach encourages students to be creative and develop their individual cognitive and performance processes. According to their different sizes, shapes, abilities and capabilities learners can approach problems set by the teacher individually.

Summary

1 Teachers must be able to adopt and adapt many theories associated with teaching and learning in order to develop a learning environment appropriate to the needs of the learner.
2 Transfer refers to the influence of one activity/skill upon another. There are a variety of types of transfer and transfer can be effective forwards or backwards in time.
3 Transfer between tasks that are very similar is greater than transfer between dissimilar skills.
4 The relationships between skills/concepts and cognitive processes need to be pointed out and explained to learners in order to increase the probability of positive transfer taking place.

5 When deciding on whole or part practice the complexity and organisation of a skill/task needs to be analysed in relation to the individual needs of the learner and the situation.

6 Practice over an extended period with short practice periods and limited rest periods is generally found to be more effective.

7 Teachers or coaches can adapt a variety of guidance techniques appropriate to the individual needs of the learner. Visual, verbal, mechanical/physical are the main types of guidance.

8 The effectiveness of massed or distributed practice depends on the type of task, level of the learner and the situation.

9 Sticking rigidly to one method of either whole or part practice is not generally advised. A combination is often more effective.

10 Research studies have shown that learners can benefit greatly from mental practice. The effectiveness of mental practice is increased considerably if used in conjunction with, rather than instead of, physical practice.

11 It is important that learners are taught how to use mental practice effectively.

12 There are a variety of teaching styles that can be adopted and it is important that teachers are flexible in their approach to teaching and coaching styles.

Revision Questions

1 What are the four categories of variable factors that need to be considered by a teacher before they can develop an effective learning environment?

2 Using examples, explain complex and simple tasks.

3 What is meant by the organisation of a skill/task?

4 What type of task can be broken down into sub-routines?

5 What is meant when sub-routines are said to be interrelated?

6 What are the main types of transfer?

7 Why is variety of practice important for a learner?

8 What use might simulators, eg, tennis ball machines, be in the learning of skills?

9 In what ways can a teacher try and reduce the effect of negative transfer?

10 What are the various types of guidance a teacher can give to a learner?

11 What are the advantages and disadvantages of using visual aids?

12 When a demonstration is given, what important factors must a teacher consider?

13 Why is distributed practice more appropriate for a beginner?

14 What type of practice might suit a more advanced performer and why?

15 Choose two specific skills from an individual and a game activity and explain why you might use whole or part practice.

16 Is it possible to learn a skill by mental practice? Support your answer.

17 Why is it better for a teacher or coach to be flexible in their structuring of practice sessions?

18 What are the main reasons for a teacher adopting teaching style 'A' on Moston's and Ashworth's spectrum of teaching styles?

19 What are the advantages of adopting a more discovery learning or problem solving style of teaching?

Psychology of Physical Education and Sport

During the second half of the twentieth century the status of sport and physical education within society has increased tremendously. This has been linked, in the main, to developing media, commercial and political interest and has resulted in increased pressure and demands being placed on sports performers. Whilst this in turn has led to major improvements in both technological and physiological preparation it has also meant that more recognition has been given to the need to prepare performers psychologically.

It has long been recognised that even if a performer is physically trained to near perfection and supported by the best equipment and technology available this does not guarantee an excellent performance or victory. Research has been carried out by sports psychologists since the early 1960s in order to help us to:

- **understand** — behaviour/performance and situations in sport
- **explain** – behaviour/performance or factors that influence performance/events in a systematic manner
- **predict** – behaviour/events or outcomes/performance
- **influence/control** – behaviour/performance or events.

When observing sport, commentators and the media often use simplistic terms to explain why certain things happen. Phrases like 'there has been a psychological shift in the game', a performer is 'coping with pressure', a performer has been 'psyched out of the game', a performer has the 'wrong temperament', are all used, along with many others, to explain variations in performance.

Although such phrases are used often without a real understanding of what they mean, they do at least indicate the importance and influence of psychological factors within the context of sport. As you read through the next four chapters you will gain a greater insight into the underlying theories and concepts which underpin the behaviour of both individuals and groups at all levels of sport. You will also gain a clearer understanding of the various strategies which sports psychologists have used to help prepare performers individually or in groups (teams) to cope with the increased pressures of modern sport. It is generally recognised that the traditional approach to sport psychology (the pre-competition 'rousing pep-talk', the 'up and at them' approach) is of very little 'real' long-term value and in some cases could even be considered 'counterproductive', perhaps leading to poor performance in the short term.

In the same way that an athlete's physical preparation cannot be developed overnight, psychological preparation needs to be developed over a prolonged period of time in order to be effective and retain long-term value. Developing your knowledge of sports psychology should give you a better understanding of the 'causes' and 'effects' of various psychological phenomena which underpin performance in sport.

After reading this whole section on sport psychology you will gain a better understanding of:

1 Individuals' differences and the resulting influence on sports performance.
2 Social influences and their specific and general effect on both individual, group performers and participants.
3 Management of psychological effects in order to optimise performance.

chapter 24

Individual differences

Similarities and differences between individuals involved in sport are often obvious, eg, size, shape and gender to mention but a few. Similarities and differences in terms of a performer's physiological behaviour can also be easy to recognise, but the reason why a person *behaves* in a certain way is often not so easy to define. Research into the personal and individual factors that can influence sporting behaviour has been widespread. Trying to gain a better understanding of the psychological make-up of performers in a sporting setting, ie, 'what makes them tick?', has traditionally involved research into personality.

Here is a list of the terms to be covered in this chapter. It is important that you understand them.

- Credulous
- Sceptical
- Traits
- Social learning theory
- Interactionist
- Reliability
- Validity
- Iceberg profile
- Mood states
- Attitudes
- Values

- Three components of attitudes
- Attitude scales
- Socialisation
- Social norms
- Persuasive communication
- Cognitions
- Cognitive dissonance
- Dissonance

- Prejudice
- Stereotyping
- Self fulfilling prophecy
- Aggression
- Assertion
- Instinct theory
- Frustration – aggression hypothesis
- Social learning theory
- Observational learning

Personality

The proliferation of research in this area supports the view held by many that personality is a major factor in creating sporting behaviour. The research has traditionally been directed towards the relationship between individual performance and personality variables. Among the questions raised are the following:

- do the personalities of top class performers, moderate performers and non participants differ?
- can sporting success be predicted as a result of a performer's personality type?
- are the personalities of performers in various sports different or similar?

The early research of the 1960s and 70s failed to produce many useful conclusions with regard to the relationship between personality and performance in sport. This was mainly as a result of problems with validity and research methodology.

The fact, however, that people began to predict how their captain, team mate, friend or even opponent was going to behave on the basis of what they believed them to be like (ie, stereotyping), means that personality is a concept that has real meaning in the context of sporting inter-personal behaviour. In presenting this 'credulous' viewpoint (Morgan, 1980) where personality is seen as a significant causal factor of behaviour we must however, be aware that it is questioned by the 'sceptical' viewpoint, which argues that sporting success is *not* related to personality. What we must therefore do is take an overview and accept that we need to be aware of all the major theories of personality and how they relate to performance in sport. The word personality is a term which everybody uses to describe different things. However, psychologists have given a special, precise meaning to it. Personality is seen as a hypothetical construct in that it cannot be directly observed but only inferred from behaviour. It makes no sense therefore, to talk in general terms suggesting that someone has 'lots of personality' which will help them play sport. It is suggested that personality in the context of sport is not a thing that someone has or has not, but is more to do with how a person relates to another whilst taking part in physical activity and how they deal with the demands of a situation.

Consider, for example, the behaviour of people you know well, the captain of your sports team or your closest friend. It would appear that, in the main, their behaviour is hardly ever random or unpredictable. Usually they are consistent in the way they react or approach certain situations, eg, always aggressive and argumentative or stable and reliable. In addition, there are also consistent differences between people we know. Some people are outgoing, easy going, whilst others are quiet, withdrawn and lacking confidence. It is these factors that contribute to both the behavioural differences between people and the behavioural consistency within people that are referred to as their personality.

Definitions of personality

Due to the many different approaches and theories with regard to personality it is almost impossible to present a definition acceptable to all. However, in 1992 Richard Gross put forward a common sense definition which enables us to leave the starting blocks:

'Those relatively stable and enduring aspects of individuals which distinguish them from other people, making them unique but at the same time permit a comparison between individuals.'   *(R. Gross).*

Lazarus and Mowat (1979) gave an earlier definition:

'Personality is the underlying relatively stable psychological structures and processes that organise human experience and shape a person's actions and reactions to the environment.'   *(Lazarus and Mowat).*

Both definitions highlight certain questions that are central to the study of personality and sport.

1 Is personality made up of certain permanent or enduring characteristics?
2 Do these enduring characteristics affect how a person perceives a situation and therefore how they behave towards it?
3 If they are enduring characteristics, can they be identified?
4 Can they be measured?
5 Are they innate?
6 Can these characteristics be influenced or changed?

The trait approach

The trait or dispositional approach dominated the early study of personality but has been criticised for not taking into account how a particular situation might also influence an individual's behaviour in different environments. Thus it emphasises the person as opposed to the situation. Traits can be seen as being **relatively stable** and **enduring** characteristics which could be used to predict an individual's behaviour in a variety of situations.

Trait theorists believed that these personal characteristics or traits could be identified, were consistent and could be generalised across the population as a whole. Thus an extreme trait approach would suggest that if a person was assessed as being aggressive and as competitive then these characteristics would be displayed in all aspects of the person's behaviour (stable) at all times (enduring) and therefore it would be possible to predict this behaviour in all future situations. Two of the better-documented trait/type theories have been associated with Eysenck and Catell. Although both theories have distinct similarities in that they both propose neurological models, their structures of personality were derived quite differently.

Eysenck's type theory

Eysenck regarded personality as largely resulting from inherited (innate) tendencies. He attempted to measure these inherited characteristics through a Personality Inventory (EPI, 1964) and Personality Questionnaire (1975). Those tested were expected to give a yes or no answer to a variety of test questions. Using a statistical technique known as factor analysis to identify general trends in his research evidence Eysenck identified two major personality dimensions which can be viewed more readily as a continuum:

Fig. 24.1 MAJOR PERSONALITY DIMENSIONS VIEWED ON A CONTINUUM

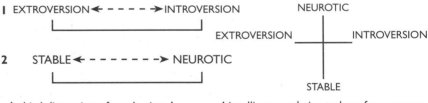

A third dimension of psychotism |_____| intelligence relating to how far a person was prepared to conform to society's rules and conventions was added later, in 1976

Fig. 24.2 EYSENCK'S PERSONALITY DIMENSIONS LINKED TO PERSONALITY CHARACTERISTICS (TRAITS) GENERALLY DISPLAYED. MOST PEOPLE ARE NOT FOUND AT THE EXTREMES OF THE TWO DIMENSIONS BUT TEND TO COME SOMEWHERE IN THE MIDDLE

The better known extroversion/introversion dimension linked to a person's Reticular Activating System (RAS) related to how social or unsocial people appeared to be. The stable neurotic dimension linked to a person's autonomic nervous system referred to the levels of nervousness and anxiety that a person was susceptible to.

The RAS, which Eysenck argued affected the levels of introversion/extroversion, is part of the central cortex of the brain. It acts to either inhibit or excite brain activity in order to maintain optimum levels of alertness or arousal. He suggested that extroverts had an RAS which was biased towards inhibiting or reducing the affects of incoming sensory information therefore creating a severe state of under-arousal. According to Eysenck, extroverts therefore need increased levels of stimulation to maintain optimum levels of attention and brain functioning. They could become bored very easily and would tend to seek out and be happier in new and challenging situations, particularly those involving other people, thus creating higher levels of stimulation to balance their naturally low levels of arousal. Extroverts, for example, were said to achieve optimum performance at higher levels of arousal preferably in team orientated activities or those involving gross motor skills. Activities of a more continuous nature (cross-country and marathon running) could be demotivating to such personalities.

Introverts on the other hand had high levels of excitation naturally occurring within them (highly over-aroused). They therefore tended not to need external or additional stimulation or excitement in order to function at an optimum level. Introverts, for example, were said to achieve optimum performance at lower levels of arousal preferably in individual activities requiring more precision (shooting, archery, etc.). Many spurious claims have been made with regard to extroverts and introverts and tenuous links have been made with sporting performance (see the Evaluation of Trait theory, below). It was claimed that extroverts were more likely to take part in sport and be more successful, that they prefer team games and that:

- extroverts cope better in competitive and highly charged stressful situations
- extroverts cope better in the presence of distracting stimuli (eg, audience/noise)
- extroverts can cope with pain more easily than introverts.

Cattell's theory (1965)

Cattell also adopted a trait approach to personality, but argued that more than just two or three dimensions were needed in order to create a full picture of a person's personality. He proposed that personality could be reduced to and measured in terms of sixteen personality factors, hence his 16 PF Questionnaire. He argued that measuring these factors via his test would give an appropriate personality profile. In identifying certain common traits (possessed by all) and unique traits (possessed by some) he recognised that personality was more dynamic than Eysenck suggested and could fluctuate according to the situation.

By defining a wider personality profile Cattell's model was seen as providing a more accurate description of personality than Eysenck's thus enabling deviations from the norm to be more easily observed and assessed.

Evaluation of trait theory

These two traditional theories received wide criticism and as a result of further research both Eysenck and Cattell continued to update their questionnaires. There has been much discussion as to the validity of the dispositional trait approach but it certainly provided a framework from which future personality research could develop. The trait approach:

- was seen as a rather simplistic or limited view of personality
- failed, according to cognitive theorists, to recognise that individuals are actively involved in subjectively constructing their own personalities
- failed, according to situational theorists, to recognise the specific effects of different environmental situations.

Traits are seen as poor predictors of behaviour or at best predict a limited proportion of behaviour. The view of personality traits as rigid and enduring characteristics is questioned in terms of the validity and long-term reliability of the scales used. It is argued that although people may have certain core tendencies, or are disposed to act in certain ways, these behaviours are not general but specific to certain situations. Thus a more interactionist perspective is suggested. The

Table 24.1   Cattell's 16 point personality traits

STANDARD TEN SCORE (STEN) — AVERAGE ←→

FACTOR	LOW SCORE DESCRIPTION	STEN (1–10)	HIGH SCORE DESCRIPTION
A	RESERVED, DETACHED, CRITICAL, ALOOF (sizothymia)	A	OUTGOING, WARM-HEARTED, EASY-GOING, PARTICIPATING (affectothymia, formerly cyclothymia)
B	LESS INTELLIGENT, CONCRETE-THINKING (lower scholastic mental capacity)	B	MORE INTELLIGENT, ABSTRACT-THINKING, BRIGHT (higher scholastic mental capacity)
C	AFFECTED BY FEELINGS, EMOTIONALLY LESS STABLE, EASILY UPSET (lower ego strength)	C	EMOTIONALLY STABLE, FACES REALITY, CALM, MATURE (higher ego strength)
E	HUMBLE, MILD, ACCOMMODATING CONFORMING (submissiveness)	E	ASSERTIVE, AGGRESSIVE, STUBBORN, COMPETITIVE (dominance)
F	SOBER, PRUDENT, SERIOUS, TACITURN (desurgency)	F	HAPPY-GO-LUCKY, IMPULSIVELY LIVELY, GAY, ENTHUSIASTIC (surgency)
G	EXPEDIENT, DISREGARDS RULES FEELS FEW OBLIGATIONS (weaker superego strength)	G	CONSCIENTIOUS, PERSEVERING, STAID, MORALISTIC (stronger superego strength)
H	SHY, RESTRAINED, TIMID, THREAT-SENSITIVE (threctia)	H	VENTURESOME, SOCIALLY BOLD, UNINHIBITED, SPONTANEOUS (parmia)
I	TOUGH-MINDED, SELF-RELIANT, REALISTIC, NO-NONSENSE (harria)	I	TENDER-MINDED, CLINGING, OVER-PROTECTED, SENSITIVE (premsia)
L	TRUSTING, ADAPTABLE, FREE OF JEALOUSY, EASY TO GET ALONG WITH (alaxia)	L	SUSPICIOUS, SELF-OPINIONATED, HARD TO FOOL (protension)
M	PRACTICAL, CAREFUL, CONVENTIONAL, REGULATED BY EXTERNAL REALITIES, PROPER (praxernia)	M	IMAGINATIVE, WRAPPED UP IN INNER URGENCIES, CARELESS OF PRACTICAL MATTERS, BOHEMIAN (autia)
N	FORTHRIGHT, NATURAL, ARTLESS, UNPRETENTIOUS (artlessness)	N	SHREWD, CALCULATING, WORLDLY, PENETRATING (shrewdness)
O	SELF-ASSURED, CONFIDENT, SERENE (untroubled adequacy)	O	APPREHENSIVE, SELF-REPROACHING, WORRYING, TROUBLED (guilt proneness)
Q₁	CONSERVATIVE, RESPECTING ESTABLISHED IDEAS, TOLERANT OF TRADITIONAL DIFFICULTIES (conservatism)	Q₁	EXPERIMENTING, LIBERAL, ANALYTICAL, FREE-THINKING (radicalism)
Q₂	GROUP-DEPENDENT, A 'JOINER' AND SOUND FOLLOWER (group adherence)	Q₂	SELF-SUFFICIENT, PREFERS OWN DECISIONS, RESOURCEFUL (self-sufficiency)
Q₃	UNDISCIPLINED SELF-CONFLICT, FOLLOWS OWN URGES, CARELESS OF PROTOCOL (low integration)	Q₃	CONTROLLED, SOCIALLY PRECISE, FOLLOWING SELF-IMAGE (high self-concept control)
Q₄	RELAXED, TRANQUIL, UNFRUSTRATED (low ergic tension)	Q₄	TENSE, FRUSTRATED, DRIVEN, OVERWROUGHT (high ergic tension)

a score of	1	2	3	4	5	6	7	8	9	10	is obtained
by about	2.3%	4.4%	9.2%	15.0%	19.1%	19.1%	15.0%	9.2%	4.4%	2.3%	of adults

generalisation of specific traits across the population as a whole in order to predict behaviour is also questioned.

The self report tests themselves have been widely criticised in terms of:

- accuracy
- a participant's honesty
- a participant's desire to create a favourable impression
- a participant's possible lack of objectivity
- the fact that neurotics were seen as possibly over emphasising certain traits.

Answers could also be influenced by:

- the personality of the tester
- time of day
- a participant's previous experience of tests
- a participant's mood swings.

Finally, the concept of personality is seen as far too complex to be measured by a mere yes or no answer.

Personality tests are examples of psychometric testing: a good test should have the following features.

Discriminating power
To be useful a wide distribution of scores should be produced. The 'ceiling' and 'floor' effects should be avoided.

Standardisation
Either norm referencing (Eysenck's EPQ/EPI and Cattell's 16 PF are both examples of normative tests) or criterion referencing can be used. Comparisons using mean/standard deviations are needed and standardised instructions are necessary to avoid possible bias on the part of the tester.

Reliability
All tests should be consistent and be capable of reproduction both **internally** and **externally**: that is, all test items should test something and the test should produce the same results when repeated.

Validity
The test should measure what it claims to measure; in other words, it should have **internal validity**. This is ensured by asking:

- are the questions appropriate?
- does the test content cover the representative sample of behaviour it is intended to cover?

It should also have **external validity**. Is there a high correlation between test scores and the independent variable and can these scores be generalised to the population as a whole? Personality tests therefore, whilst being useful tools to generate impressions of performers, should not be used in isolation or as a means of selecting or assessing performers for teams or events. Care should also be taken in attaching labels to certain individuals or groups (see stereotyping, page 425).

Fig. 24.3 THE FEATURES OF AN EFFECTIVE PERSONALITY TEST

Situational perspective of personality

The situational perspective is based around theories of social learning, discussed in greater detail later in this chapter (see page 431). The situational approach suggests that personality is constructed and shaped as a result of strong environmental influences and indirect reinforcement factors which can override the individual's personality traits. A person learns to behave in specific situations due to what has been observed and reinforced socially. A performer may appear confident in a specific situation, eg, on the pitch or within the context of a game where assertive behaviour is demanded by the coach and the situation. Outside or away from the situation the same assertive performer may behave in a very quiet, unassuming manner. Thus personality is seen as being relatively enduring but only in learned specific situations. Whilst many such as Mischel (1968) supported this perspective, many psychologists viewed the approach with a degree of scepticism. It was felt that in trying to solve the limitations associated with the trait approach the situational perspective had taken up rather too extreme a stance. It was seen as being insufficient to predict behaviour accurately.

Interactionist approach to personality

In deciding between the relative strengths of the person versus situation debate, many psychologists recognised that each, although being limited, represented a degree of 'truth' in explaining the nature of personality. Performers were seen as having certain core elements of personality which pre-disposed them to behave in certain ways, but at the same time were capable of being strongly influenced by changing environmental considerations. This compromise position is one which is taken at present by the great majority of sports psychologists: behaviour is explained as the result of a reciprocal interaction between both the individual's consistent psychological traits (core) and the situational factors present.

This **interactionist approach** suggests therefore that if we wish to try to understand and predict an individual performer's behaviour we need to consider in depth both the individual person and the specific situation. In doing so, a much more complete picture and explanation of a person's behaviour can be developed. An early equation formula suggested by Lewin represents this relationship very simply. B = f(P.E.) where:

B = behaviour
f = function
P = personality traits
E = environment

This is seen as a much more individualistic approach as it recognises that performers in similar sports do not necessarily exhibit the same behaviour. Just because some top class marathon runners appear more introverted in their behaviour does not mean that you have to be the same to get to the top. All rugby players are not extroverts all the time: it is not a pre-requisite for success.

Coaches have to develop an in-depth knowledge of each 'unique' performer.

- **Personality traits**
- **Cognitive variables**
- **Physiological variables**
- **Psychological variables**
- **Sociological variables**

Fig. 24.4 THE VARIABLES CONSIDERED BY SPORTS PSYCHOLOGISTS

Further problems associated with assessment and research into personality

As we have already seen, early research such as Eysenck's EPQ and EPI and Cattell's 16 PF have been criticised for their lack of sophistication and have problems of validity, methodology and interpretation of statistical data. Much of the more up to date research has been dogged by similar problems. The ethics of using personality tests has also been raised. Criticism of such tests as the Athletic Motivation Inventory (AMI) devised by Ogilvie and Tutko (1966) seemed to heighten sensitivity over the use and application of such research.

Most sports psychologists however, still rely heavily on such sport specific objective inventory tests due to their ease of application and analysis. The Sport Competition Anxiety Test (SCAT) (Martens, 1990) is a popular example. Guidelines for the use of such tests have been drawn up to ensure both the validity and the ethical nature of testing.

Fig. 24.5 Guidelines for personality testing — as suggested by the American Psychological Association 1974 in order to ensure tests used are appropriate and ethical

1 Participants should know the purpose and use of the test.
2 Tests should only be carried out and interpreted by qualified/experienced people.
3 Personality test results should not be used in isolation to predict behaviour.
4 Other information taken should include a person's life history, interview, observations, performance assessments.
5 Sport specific tests should be used.
6 Both trait and state measures should be used.
7 Feedback should be given to participants.
8 Personality tests should not be used for selection purposes and/or to discriminate for places on teams.

Returning to the questions posed on page 410, research attempting to clarify these has been found to be very contradictory. However, the general findings of more up to date research indicate that:

1 No obvious sporting personality-type distinguishes those involved in sport and non participants.
2 No obvious consistent personality characteristics have been found to distinguish between different types of sports performers – for instance performers participating in both team or individual sports are not disposed to certain specific types of personality behaviour.
3 Few personality differences have been found between male and female sports performers, particularly at the elite level. There is some evidence to suggest that there is a more marked difference between successful and unsuccessful female performers then in men. However, it has been suggested that this is linked more to socio-cultural effects.
4 To be successful in sport a person needs to demonstrate: positive mental health (iceberg profile); positive self perceptions (self confidence); positive/productive cognitive strategies. The Iceberg Profile (Morgan, 1978) has been related to characteristics associated with elite sports performers; they tend to be more vigorous and have low levels of depression, anger, confusion and fatigue.
5 Mood states have been found to differ in successful and less successful performers. Successful performers generally display more positive mood profiles. Whether this more positive profile of mood state (POMS) helps to create better performance or whether it is itself caused by the success in sport is inconclusive. D. Gill argues that less than desirable mood profiles are negatively associated with success in most achievement situations.

6   Successful performers have been found to be able to internalise – that is use cognitive (mental) strategies such as mental rehearsal, imagery or positive self talk for coping with anxiety more effectively than unsuccessful performers (see strategies for dealing with stress, page 496). However, these cognitive strategies have not been found to change personality traits.

7   The claim that sport can influence or develop certain positive or socially desirable characteristics or attributes has not been supported by research evidence. The philosophical statements often made by physical educationalists and activity centres that certain sports can develop character and socially desirable types of behaviour are therefore quite considerably undermined. There is even some evidence to suggest that taking part in competitive sport can actually have a detrimental effect on social life, by increasing anti-social behaviour and rivalry (see socio-culture section).

8   The effect of taking part in sport and fitness work has been shown to have an immediate effect on mood states in the specific situation, and also help with a performer's concept of 'self'. The long-term or global influence on our individual personality traits is seen however, to be of little effect.

Attitudes

According to some psychologists attitudes are a major foundation stone of social psychology. A great deal of research has been undertaken into people's attitudes; however much of it has been of a descriptive nature and therefore open to similar criticisms to those levelled at personality research. Within the field of physical/health education and sport one of the often stated philosophical objectives is to promote positive attitudes and values, not only in competitive sports performers but also in the population as a whole. It is therefore important to know *how* to promote and maintain positive attitudes towards sport, exercise and health in general. Attitudes are very often linked to the concept of motivation (see motivation, page 436). A performer who is highly motivated usually has a desire to achieve (see achievement motivation, page 437) and thus a positive attitude. They do not look to blame others for any problems associated with performance (see attributions, page 451).

The terms 'attitude' and 'values' are often used synonymously. Both refer to hypothetical constructs similar to personality in that, although they are seen as relatively stable dispositions, they cannot be measured directly, only inferred from behaviour that can be observed and tested, usually via questionnaires.

Although there has been much debate concerning the definition of attitudes, one of the most frequently used is that by Triandis (1971) who defined attitudes as:

'ideas charged with emotion (positive or negative) which pre-disposes a class of actions to a particular social situation.'   *(Triandis).*

DEFINITIONS

***Beliefs* represent the knowledge or information we have about the world.**

***Values* are deep seated feelings or thoughts (emotions) which form the basis for evaluating if something is worthwhile. They are thought to be culturally determined.**

***Attitudes* are therefore a blend of beliefs and values. They are learned via our interaction with the social environment (experience) and provide us with a means to express our values in either a positive or negative way.**

Attitudes and behaviour

As attitudes are one of the key determinants of our behaviour they can heavily influence the way in which we behave towards different types of 'attitude objects':

- people
- objects
- events
- ideas.

In her book *Psychological Dynamics of Sport* Diane Gill argues that our attitudes towards these attitude objects are not necessarily all embracing (global): just because a sports person has a negative attitude towards rugby it does not necessarily mean they have a negative attitude towards all sport. When trying to measure attitudes it is therefore important to be specific.

In order to provide us with a better understanding of attitudes Secord and Backman (1964) proposed a structural approach to analysing the components of attitudes.

Three components of attitudes

1 **Cognitive component:** what a person believes about the attitude object, eg, I believe that jogging is good for me and helps me to keep fit.
2 **Affective component:** what a person feels about the attitude object. This is usually linked to some form of evaluation related to a performer's values and past experience, eg, keeping fit and healthy is important to maintain my lifestyle.
3 **Behavioural component:** reflects how a person actually responds or intends to act towards the attitude object as a result of 1 and 2, eg, I go jogging regularly four times per week and encourage others to go jogging. I watch athletics on TV and purchase fitness and health magazines to supplement my knowledge of jogging and fitness.

This is a simplistic analysis of attitudes, yet it provides a basis from which attitudes can be studied. Although most social psychologists would adhere to the three component analysis of attitudes they would suggest that a flexible approach must be maintained with regard to its application. There is evidence that it is not always possible to accurately predict a person's behaviour so simply. This is due to the fact that a performer's behaviour does not always reflect the inferred correlation to beliefs (cognitive) and feelings (affective). The classic study by La Piere (1934), although criticised by some, is traditionally used to illustrate the inconsistency between stated or observed attitudes and actual behaviour. In travelling over 10,000 miles around the USA with a Chinese couple he visited 251 hotels and restaurants. This period in American history was characterised by racial prejudice and stereotyping (see page 425); however, they only experienced one example of discrimination. When he wrote to the various establishments, six months later, enquiring as to whether they would indeed accept Chinese people as guests 92% of the returns stated no! They would not serve Chinese. Further research in this area to support our earlier view from D. Gill begins to suggest that attitudes can only be used to predict behaviour when we measure and assess attitudes to *specific* aspects of our lives and whether or not there is a *stated intention* of behaving in a particular way. A child or performer is more likely to take part in a specific activity, eg, swimming, if they have stated a 'behavioural intention' to do so: 'I will take part in the swimming gala.' General or apparent positive attitudes towards sport will not be a true determinant of actual sporting behaviour.

Thus in sport we need to ensure that performers, beginners or experienced:

* see the relevance of specific fitness and practice programmes to specific activities
* gain direct experience of the fitness/practice programme thus providing more information about the attitude object;

and that any negative attitudes are dealt with immediately.

Attitude formation

Attitudes are developed by the following:

Learning

Attitudes are almost entirely *learned*, although there is evidence to suggest certain aspects may possibly be genetically instinctive or inherently determined.

Familiarity/availability

If a pupil encounters certain activities or sports on a regular basis they will generally develop a positive attitude towards that activity especially if they have ease of access. Think of the child who is regularly taken by its parents to watch and play a particular sport at the local club. A positive attitude will probably develop and if the child is encouraged to use good facilities they will probably end up (certainly during their early years) playing for the same team or club (see motivation, page 436). Zajonc (1968) supported this notion of frequency helping to develop positive attitudes.

Classical conditioning

Through the association of a certain activity or sport (conditioned stimulus) with a pleasant or unpleasant feeling (unconditioned response) a certain attitude may be formed.

Operant conditioning

Positive reinforcement and rewards have been shown to help positive attitudes or at least strengthen already formed attitudes.

Socialisation

This is seen as a major influencing factor in the formation of attitudes. Attitudes are learned from significant others either explicitly through instruction (see Chapter 21) from teachers, parents or coach or they may develop through social learning via observation, imitation and modelling. We cannot therefore underestimate the power of the media and high profile sports stars particularly in influencing the attitudes of young people. Stereotyping is a major problem created through socialisation, particularly attitudes to issues of gender and different ethnic cultures (see prejudice/stereotyping, page 425).

Peer groups and social groupings

Peer groups have also been found to exert a strong influence on people's attitudes. Inter-group attitudes are often formed as a way of defining, maintaining and possibly protecting the group.

Fig. 24.6 IF A CHILD EXPERIENCES CRICKET FROM AN EARLY AGE THIS FAMILIARITY COULD LEAD TO POSITIVE ATTITUDES LATER IN LIFE

Measuring attitudes

There are several ways in which attitudes can be measured.

- physiological observation, eg, galvanic skin responses (GSR), pupil responses
- observed behaviour – inferences can be made from observing the degree of eye contact, body language or facial responses. Based on the critical assumption that behaviour and attitudes are consistent (not totally reliable)
- opinion polls
- sociometry
- interviews.

The reliability, validity and results of these forms of measurement have again been brought into question. Generally the three main scales used for measuring attitudes have been developed by Thurston, Likert and Osgood.

These attitude scales make certain basic assumptions:

- that attitudes can be expressed by verbal statements
- that statements have the same meaning for all participants
- that attitudes when expressed as verbal statements can be measured and quantified.

Thurston scale (1931)

This is more a method of constructing an attitude scale. A list of statements representing a wide range of views in relation to a specific attitude object are prepared. In order to check any ambiguity and to evaluate the statements in terms of how favourable or not they are towards the attitude object they are given to a group of judges. The judges rate the statements on an 11-point scale (positive to negative). Any statements which produce substantial disagreement are thrown out until a list of 20 statements are left. As a result of the judges 'mean' evaluation each statement is then allocated a rating value. The self report questionnaire is then tested with subjects being asked to state which of the statements they agree with and a mean attitude score is calculated from the value of the selected statements.

Likert scale (1932)

This is the most commonly used form of attitude scale. It generally comprises of a balanced number of statements with regard to a specific attitude object. The subject is asked to indicate how they rate each statement, usually on a 5-point scale:
1 strongly agree; 2 agree; 3 undecided; 4 disagree; 5 strongly disagree. The subject's attitude is measured by totalling the scores for each statement, usually showing a correlation. For example:

Aerobics is an excellent activity for keeping fit : strongly agree ☐ +2
agree ☐ +1
undecided ☐ 0
disagree ☐ −1
strongly disagree ☐ −2

Likert scales have the advantage in that they do not expect a basic yes/no answer but rather they allow for degrees of opinion.

Semantic differential scales (Osgood, Suci and Tannenbaum, 1957)

Usually subjects are asked to rate on a 7-point scale between two bi-polar adjectives which describe best their feelings towards a particular attitude object, eg, aerobics. For example:

Rate how you feel about aerobics for exercise.

good	+3	+2	+1	0	−1	−2	−3	bad
valuable	+3	+2	+1	0	−1	−2	−3	worthless
beneficial	+3	+2	+1	0	−1	−2	−3	harmful

The questionnaires would have at least two bi-polar scales constructed around the three main factors associated with the meaning of words or attitude objects. For example:

- evaluative factor (good/bad)
- potency factor (strong/weak)
- activity factor (active/passive)

The problems associated with attitude measurement are:

- response bias
- people trying to present socially acceptable viewpoints
- people attempting to deliberately distort the results
- people tending always to answer yes or no or preferring certain points on the scale (people tend to agree rather than disagree)
- the way in which the questions are asked can also influence the answer.

Changing attitudes

Up until now we have mainly concentrated on positive attitudes. What happens, however, if a person has a poor or very negative attitude? How easy or difficult is it to change a sports person's attitude?

Although attitudes are thought to be 'deep seated' and therefore resistant to change it is felt that attitudes can be influenced or gradually changed through learning (see Chapter 21), formal or informal social influences or persuasion.

Two of the main ways through which, psychologists have suggested, attitudes may be changed are:

- persuasive communication
- cognitive dissonance theory.

Note: In order to assess any attitude change, a person's or group's attitudes need to be measured prior to the attempt to change and then again afterwards.

Persuasive communication

In their research into how easy it was to persuade a person to adopt a different attitude, Hovland, Janis and Kelly (1953) identified four basic factors (variables) that can affect all persuasion situations:

- who is trying to persuade?
- what is the message?
- whom is the message trying to reach?
- what is the situation context?

If the UK Sports Council are trying to persuade specific groups of the population that participation in sport is good for them, what factors affect the level of success of such a campaign?

- is the fitness/health argument used?
- is the social argument used?

- is a trend/role model argument used?
- is the lifestyle argument used?
- who is going to front the campaign?
- what are the counter arguments?
- who is the target group?

In a sporting context, if we are trying to persuade individuals or groups to change their attitudes towards a particular policy, activity, etc. (attitude object), it is important that the person, teacher or coach presenting the persuasion is an expert and thus perceived as having high status or credibility.

Olympic or professional performers are often used to focus attention on campaigns to promote sport. The high profile and clean image of such sporting role models as Gary Lineker, Kris Akabusi and Sharron Davis mean they are much in demand; all are now respected media personalities.

Teachers and coaches have a vital role to play, using their expertise, likeability and trustworthiness to provide leadership in order to communicate positive attitudes to young people.

You should note that it is important that the person whose attitudes are being influenced does not feel threatened or they may become more defensive (resistant to change).

 **ACTIVITY 1**

Try to set up a campaign, real or bogus, in your school or college, trying to persuade the students and staff to take a positive attitude towards health and fitness. Taking into account the information given in table 24.2 discuss in your group how you will present your campaign. The could also be done in conjunction with attitude measurement. Attitudes could be measured via a group-designed test/scale prior to the campaign and then re-assessed afterwards to judge the level of success.

Table 24.2 SUMMARY OF VARIABLES AFFECTING SUCCESS RATE OF PERSUASION

PEOPLE'S PERCEPTIONS OF

SOURCE (who)	MESSAGE (what)	RECEIVER/OR AUDIENCE (to whom)	CONTEXT (where)
independent variable • status • credibility • expertise • likeability, attractiveness, trustworthiness • intention motives • cultural background	• accurate (easily understood/ makes sense/ unambiguous) • order of argument • presentation: confident/believable • one sided message or two sides • level of emotional appeal/appeals to fear failure • be careful of hardsell (boomerang effect)	• level of education, must be able to understand message • individual differences, gender, intelligence, personality, self esteem • function of original attitude (why they hold present attitude) • persuadability (are they resistant to change)	• formal/informal or sporting/non sporting • level of commitment • real life or experiment • availability of facilities/resources to support message or change

Consonance **is where the cognitions held have a high level of correlation. (Eg, I am being assessed in gymnastics for my A level assessment. I need to train/practise to develop my skills and therefore I train twice a week outside the class.)**

Dissonance **is known as a 'negative-drive state' where the cognitions are at odds or in direct conflict with each other creating a feeling of psychological discomfort or tension. (Eg, I am being assessed in gymnastics for my A level assessment. I need to train/practise to develop my skills. I don't train/practise outside class at all.)**

Cognitive dissonance theory (Festinger, 1957)

There have been several suggested theories associated with the notion of cognitive consistency (Heider, 1958; Osgood and Tannenbaum, 1955). However, based on the human need for cognitive consistency, Festinger's has been the most influential, generating an enormous amount of both research and theorising in relation to attitude change.

According to Festinger an individual knows certain things (cognitions) about their own attitudes, beliefs and thoughts in relation to their own behaviour and surroundings. These cognitions that people know or think about themselves can either be consistent with each other creating a good feeling (feeling of consonance) or they can be inconsistent creating a state of dissonance.

Festinger postulates that if a person experiences feelings of dissonance then they are generally motivated to change their beliefs, attitudes or thoughts in order to return to a feeling of consonance (psychological harmony).

How often have you started a fitness programme, knowing that it is important to keep fit and that at least three sessions per week is desirable, only to lapse after a few sessions or weeks. Not being able to maintain a commitment known to be valuable can create Festinger's feeling of 'psychological discomfort', dissonance. Because of the human need for consonance, you are generally motivated to erase this feeling of dissonance (tension).

In order to rationalise our knowledge, beliefs or thoughts we can reduce dissonance in various ways:

- **change one of the cognitions** eg, training three times per week is only necessary if you don't work and have the time
- **reduce the importance of the cognitions you hold** eg, I'm young, healthy and already reasonably fit therefore it is not as essential for me to train three times per week, as it is for someone who is unfit. You could also begin to associate with other like-minded non-fitness fanatics
- **Suggest more consistent cognitions** eg, either belittle the evidence that fitness is good for you or look for evidence that suggests too much exercise is actually harmful/can cause long-term damage through injuries.

In applying this theory within a sporting context it is suggested that teachers and coaches can try to change beginners' or elite performers' attitudes by highlighting certain cognitions that may create states of dissonance within the performer's mind. Convincing people to change their attitude is not a simple short-term process, however, as individuals/teams are generally resistant to change. They tend to distort the truth or evidence that may prove their thoughts and beliefs wrong in order to maintain their perceptions of the status quo.

There is much anecdotal or 'folk tale' evidence from social psychology with regard to the apparently broad application of dissonance theory to both PE and sport. It is, however, seen as a rather simplistic notion. Counter arguments have suggested that:

- dissonance cannot be measured
- it is difficult to identify states of dissonance
- what creates or is dissonance is not the same for all people
- individuals differ in strategies used to reduce dissonance
- people who experience high levels of anxiety tend to experience greater feelings of dissonance

Fig. 24.7 It has taken a long time for black golfers to be accepted in American golfing society

- issues of no importance do not arouse dissonance
- many alternative experimental explanations have been given for attitude change, eg, incentive/reinforcement theory (Janis et al., 1965); impression management hypothesis (Tedeschi et al., 1971); self perception theory (D. J. Bem, 1965).

Prejudice and stereotyping related to expected behaviour

Prejudice is an extreme or strongly held attitude (resistant to change) held prior to direct experience. Situations or people are pre-judged. In pre-judging a situation or a person we are expecting to see or experience certain types of behaviour in certain situations.

In relation to people, prejudice (extreme attitudes) serves to develop a certain expectancy of behaviour leading to stereotyping.

DEFINITION

prejudice:

'An antipathy either felt or expressed based on faulty or inflexible generalisations directed towards a certain group or an individual who is part of a group.'
(G. W. Allport, 1954)

Stereotyping

This term, first suggested by Lippman (1922), relates to a person having a mental picture (cognitive schema) associating certain behaviour traits with a particular group or type of individual.

Research has tended to focus on the negative aspects of stereotyping in relation to such issues as gender and race. Extremely held attitudes (prejudice) can cause people to expect certain types of behaviour resulting in stereotyping. This can then affect *our* behaviour towards certain individuals or groups of people, eg, if a teacher or coach, as a result of stereotyping, sees boys as having more potential in some sports than girls, this could in turn lead them to having certain expectations of boys and girls. These expectations can influence their behaviour towards both gender groups. They may be more demanding of the boys, perhaps spending more time with them. The boys' skills will probably improve considerably more than those of the girls as a result of this more positive attitude and behaviour thus supporting the teacher's or coach's earlier expectations (a self-fulfilling prophecy).

Discuss in class the reasons why it has taken so long for black Americans to enter golfing society. Why do you think Tiger Woods has been *allowed* in?

Although stereotypes are rarely accurate they are generally extremely resistant to change. Many are derived from indirect contact. The influence of the media has been responsible for portraying many poor images of certain categories of people.

Preconceived views can lead to common held sterotypical views. For example:

- girls are better than boys at aesthetic-type activities
- boys are more competitive than girls
- disabled people cannot play sport
- disabled people do not enjoy competitive sport
- black people are not very good at swimming
- certain sports are better suited to black people than white.

In discussion of the following 'types' of people, think of the behaviour traits you generally associate with or expect from these people in certain situations:

- **male rugby players in your school/college**
- **disabled sports performers**
- **female artists**
- **female athletes**

DEFINITION

stereotyping:

'The general inclination to place a person in categories according to some easily and quickly identifiable characteristics such as age, gender, ethnic group, nationality or occupation and then to attribute certain qualities believed to be typical to members of that category.'
(R. Tagiuri, 1969)

- **male/female hockey players**
- **working class/middle class football/rugby supporters**
- **doctors**
- **politicians**
- **different nationalities: Americans, French, German, Spanish, etc.**

Consider where these perceptions come from. Are they true?

It has been shown that a person's perceptions of self can be affected by exposure to continuous sterotypical attitudes and certain types of behaviour expectancies. This can influence and lead to differences in sporting achievement. Attitudes towards disabled athletes have changed considerably over the past few years due to their success at international level. There is still room for greater improvement!

Social and cultural norms in relation to PE and sport have changed considerably over the last 20 years. In order that they continue to change for the potential good of all in society it is important that teachers and coaches in influential positions (significant others) are very careful not to perpetuate unacceptable/negative stereotypes particularly at the very early stages of development. They must be prepared to challenge any areas of existing or future prejudice in relation to gender, racial or socio-cultural issues.

Aggression and its relationship to sport

In considering modern sport certain types of behaviour within sport are seen as acceptable and certain types of behaviour are unacceptable. So-called aggressive or unacceptable behaviour is witnessed on a regular basis within many sporting situations. It has been argued that the increase in aggressive and unacceptable behaviour on the pitch or court, etc. is merely a reflection of general behaviour within society as a whole.

Discuss, as a group, whether you agree that aggressive and unacceptable sporting behaviour is a reflection of general behaviour trends within society as a whole.

The context in which the term aggression is used sometimes causes confusion. It can be applied in several different ways. Very often coaches demand more aggression from their players to 'win the ball', 'fight for the ball'. Aggressive tactics are often praised, eg, serve/volley in tennis, a full court press in basketball, harder tackling in rugby. These are all examples of where the word aggression is used as an adjective to infer that a performer is being energetic or persistent in their actions.

In discussion can you think of other examples where general types of aggression may be encouraged and certain types may be discouraged?

At the same time, however, many actions or types of behaviour are thought of as being unacceptable forms of aggression, eg, a rugby player stamping on a player in a ruck, brawls amongst players on a pitch, verbal abuse of officials, headbutting of opposition players, etc. None of these can be condoned in any shape or form: the word aggression used in such situations denotes anti-social behaviour intended to harm another.

Opinions of whether an action is acceptable or unacceptable are going to be different for various people, as responses are heavily influenced by value judgements. Two people watching a particular hard tackle in rugby or hockey will very often disagree as to its level of acceptability and level of good or bad aggression. It is important therefore, to note that within sport it is not easy to hang a particular label on actions in order to identify what is meant by aggression.

Finding a definition of aggression

DEFINITIONS

Maslow (1968) distinguished between what he called natural/positive aggression (eg, self defence) and pathological aggression or violence.

Brown (1985) makes a distinction between aggression which does not always involve injury and violence which usually does.

Moyer (1984) introduces the idea of aggression being also verbal or symbolic, whereas violence manifests itself in physical damage to person or property.

Gross (1991) defined aggression as the intentional infliction of some form of harm to others.

It can be seen from the above discussion that finding an acceptable definition of aggression is no simple matter. It is important however, that we do try as problems of misinterpretation by players, administrators and officials could have serious consequences.

Baron's (1977) definition of aggression appears to be a compromise/compilation between the various suggestions given left.

'Aggression is any form of behaviour toward the goal of harming or injuring another living being who is motivated to avoid such treatment.'

(R. A. Baron, 1977).

In relation to sport this definition stresses the idea that aggression is behaviour which is *intentional* and *deliberate* and involves injury to another person. From this, it can be inferred that aggression:

- is a first act of hostility or injury
- involves physical or verbal action/behaviour (thinking is not being aggressive unless it leads to action)
- involves an implied intention (this can be difficult to interpret)
- is ultimately damaging, physically or mentally.

A point worth noting is that anger is not seen as aggression but a state of emotional and physiological arousal – aggression is usually seen as the destructive behavioural expression of anger. The infliction of accidental harm is *not* seen as aggression.

In trying to clarify more clearly what is acceptable and what is not, Buss (1961), Feshback (1964) and Moyer (1976) made the distinction between two types of aggression:

1 **Hostile aggression** – aimed at solely hurting someone, the primary reinforcement is seeing pain or injury inflicted on another person. Moyer also termed this reactive aggression.
2 **Instrumental aggression** – is a means to an end, aggression to achieve a non-aggressive goal. The primary reinforcement being tangible reward (eg, praise–money–victory).

Although instrumental (also known as channelled) aggression appears initially more acceptable and covers most examples within sport, both types involve the *intention* to inflict injury or pain and it is debatable whether either should be encouraged in sport, as they fall outside the accepted rules of most sporting activities.

In trying to end the confusing use of the word aggression to explain acceptable sporting behaviour the term assertive behaviour was suggested by Husman and Silva (1984).

Assertive behaviour

Assertive behaviour is seen as acceptable but forceful behaviour. It is also:

* goal directed behaviour
* the use of legitimate verbal or physical force (involving energy and effort which, outside sport, could be interpreted as aggression)
* behaviour which has no *intention* to harm or injure
* behaviour which does not violate the agreed rules/laws/structures of the sport, eg, strong tackling in hockey, rugby, football; blocking in basketball; smashing in tennis/badminton, etc.

Whilst most sports have specific rule structures to control the degree of assertive behaviour allowed, there are still problems associated with subjective interpretations, both general and specific. When, for instance, does a tackle in rugby become high? What in hockey constitutes a deliberate foul in the 'D'? When should a red card be given in soccer?

You should note that an action is described as aggression when the intention is clearly to harm or injure someone *outside* the laws of the game or activity.

Many sports, by their very nature, involve a high degree of physical contact which can lead either to its misuse or to misinterpretation of actions by an official. Officials often take into account the context of the assertive action, eg, what has gone on prior to the action, state of the game, where the incident happened on the court or pitch. Thus a member of a team winning 1–0 in an important match, who, as the last defender 'takes out' an attacker in the last few minutes, is generally deemed to have committed a conscious aggressive, not assertive, act (intention to harm or injure).

Fig. 24.8 ASSERTION OR AGGRESSION — THE GREY AREA OF AMBIGUITY

Discuss the implications of such activities as boxing.

In discriminating between assertion and aggression sports psychologists accept that there are ambiguities when interpretations are made regarding the 'intention' or degree of force used. Obviously sports such as rugby, hockey, ice hockey or wrestling have a larger grey area than non-contact sports.

Now use what you know of definitions of aggression and compare assertive behaviour with aggressive behaviour in relation to the following scenarios. Tick the appropriate box to show whether you feel they are acts of aggression or assertion.

Assertion	Aggression	
☐	☐	**1 In trying to head a football a player clashes heads with another player causing a serious injury.**
☐	☐	**2 A boxer traps his opponent against the ropes and leads with his head into the chin of the opponent.**
☐	☐	**3 A rugby player studs a player at the bottom of a ruck.**
☐	☐	**4 Having been tackled hard earlier in the game as the attacking hockey**

player approaches the 'D' she lifts her stick to catch the defender's hands and head.

☐   ☐   5 Having been forced off the track the rally car driver runs over to the other driver who caused the crash and punches him in the face.

☐   ☐   6 The bowler in cricket beats the batsman with a fast ball and hits him on the thigh.

☐   ☐   7 A basketball player verbally abuses the referee for giving a personal foul against her.

☐   ☐   8 A basketball coach smashes a chair in protest at a referee's decision.

☐   ☐   9 A racing car driver slows down and cuts across the path of a faster driver coming up behind and stops them getting past.

☐   ☐   10 A bowler in cricket bowls a third successive bouncer in one over, hitting the batsman on the head.

Theories of aggression

Is it nature or nurture? In looking at possible causes of aggression psychologists have considered the following issues:

- are aggressive individuals born with certain innate characteristics or
- are they a product of their learning and environmental influences?

The main theories associated with these questions are:

- instinct theory
- drive theory/frustration aggression hypothesis
- social learning theory.

Instinct theory

Instinct theories view aggression as instinctive within human beings and developed as a result of evolution. In our fight for survival, aggression is seen as inevitable as with any other species. There are, however, two distinct perspectives on this theory: the psychoanalytical approach and the ethological approach.

Psychoanalytical approach

Freud is the name usually associated with this approach to the instinct theory of aggression; aggression being viewed as a destructive drive. Freudian theory argues that our innate aggressive tendencies are expressed in the self destructive or **death instinct** called thanatos. This self directed, inner drive towards self aggression is balanced by our **life instincts** called eros. Freud and Lorenze (see below) saw aggression as building up within a person with eros helping to direct it away from self and into some other form of aggressive behaviour. This could be either acceptable behaviour – sport, expeditions, exploration, etc. or unacceptable behaviour – crime, brutality or eventually back inside a person's mind, leading ultimately to suicide.

Ethological approach

One of the more famous psychologists in this area is Konrad Lorenze who based his views on anthropological studies comparing human behaviour with the 'natural' ritualistic aggressive behaviour of animals. The example of human attempts at territorial control (invasions, etc.) is often cited as justifying the comparison. This perspective sees aggression as building up within humans to create a drive which, if not released in some constructive way achieving catharsis (see below), will inevitably lead to some form of spontaneous destructive or aggressive behaviour. Like Freud, Lorenze argued that in acknowledging our natural aggressive instinct we should be able to control it through socially acceptable competitive sport (eg, invasion games).

Catharsis

For instinct theorists the view that sport and exercise can be used to 'channel' aggressive urges into more socially desirable behaviour (either as a performer or spectator) is very important. This view of purifying the body and reducing drive (catharsis) is not, however, supported by creditable research particularly in sport. Evidence to show psychological differences before and after aggression has proved equivocal. It has even been suggested that rather than having a cathartic effect (drive reducing), watching aggressive behaviour may be drive enhancing, eg, the spectator who, having seen a particularly vicious boxing match, may be driven to reproduce aggressive behaviour (see social learning, page 431).

Criticisms of instinct theory

In evaluating instinct theory psychologists feel that the parallels drawn between humans and animals are over simplified. Furthermore:

- no biological innate aggressive drive has ever been identified
- the measuring of any cathartic effect of aggression has proved difficult
- cross-cultural studies (Sian, 1985) do not support the view that all human beings are naturally aggressive
- cultural influences are seen as being more important determinants of human aggression than biological factors
- human aggression is not seen as being always spontaneous
- human aggression is seen as reactive and modifiable
- Lorenze does not take into account learning and socialising influences which are seen as overriding possible innate aggression
- aggression is seen more as a learned response linked to the human ability to reason.

The frustration–aggression hypothesis

Published as a result of research carried out by Dollard, Doob, Miller, Mowrer and Sears (Dollard et al., 1939) the frustration–aggression hypothesis tried to deal with some of the limitations of instinct theory. Linked to drive theory it proposes that frustration always leads to aggression and aggression is always as a result of frustration.

Players in a major final (eg, rugby) are trying to achieve (drive) a good performance and success (goal orientated behaviour). A player is continually tackled and sees the opposition constantly blocking the ball or encroaching

DEFINITION

Frustration – blocking of goal orientated behaviour.

(blocking of goal orientated behaviour), and becomes frustrated. They are then driven to do something about it (increase drive), possibly playing or working harder. If the frustration continues, this drive may become an aggressive drive and result in transgression of the rules or aggressive behaviour. When held, this player will retaliate with a punch; such aggressive behaviour will reduce frustration, which in turn will have a cathartic effect. However, it may have a negative effect on the game and possibly result in further frustration.

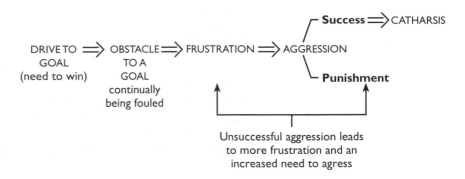

Fig. 24.9 THE FRUSTRATION–AGGRESSION MODEL IS CYCLIC

Criticism of early frustration–aggression hypothesis

This original model (fig 24.9), whilst initially finding support, has been found to have little credence in sport due, in the main, to its insistence that frustration *always* leads to aggression. Critics point out that:

- not all frustration leads to aggression in sport – people have been increasingly shown to be able to deal with frustration in alternative ways, ie, learned helplessness
- aggression can be a learned response and does not always happen as a result of frustration
- individual and situational differences are not taken into account
- the cathartic effect of aggression in sport is not upheld
- some aggressive participants have been shown to become more aggressive through participation in sport.
- frustration leads to a pre-disposition to behave aggressively by increasing anger and arousal. This increased arousal and anger will only lead to aggression if certain socially learned cues or environmental stimuli are present.

A defender in football who is easily beaten by an attacker who could go on to score, may lash out or kick the opponent particularly if the coach or manager has previously accepted such behaviour.

Social learning theory of aggression

Social learning theorists see aggression as being influenced by learning. Bandura (1973) states that aggression is not instinctive but a learned response. In his research Bandura has shown that a performer can learn to be aggressive by either having aggression reinforced (by it being successful or gaining coach approval) or by observation of aggressive behaviour (see social influences, page 461, for a more detailed discussion of this topic).

Table 24.3   REVISED MODEL OF FRUSTRATION—AGGRESSION HYPOTHESIS

FRUSTRATION $\Rightarrow$	INCREASED $\Rightarrow$	SOCIALLY $\Rightarrow$	AGGRESSION
• Failure	AROUSAL	LEARNED	
• Unsuccessful	eg pain/anger	CUES/SIGNALS	
• Goals blocked		ENVIRONMENTAL	
• Lose game or		STIMULI	
play badly		eg overt or	
		covert approval	
		by coach	

The application of this theory to sport is obvious. If sports performers, particularly high status players, are seen to behave aggressively, 'getting away with it' and achieving success, then a young player will be more likely to imitate those actions. This learning through observation of the behaviour of successful 'significant others' is referred to as vicarious learning; this is frequently seen in young players who model their behaviour on the actions of others.

A young player can receive reinforcement of sporting aggression in many ways. Although teachers, coaches, parents, managers, team mates and professional performers will rarely condone blatant aggression these significant others may well inadvertently or covertly support or sanction aggressive behaviour. Young players are often encouraged to 'get their retaliation in first', 'make the opposition know you are there'. Gamesmanship and 'psyching out' the opposition are all condoned. Performers very often verbally abuse the opposition (aggression) in order to goad them into a retaliation which may just be enough to put them off their game or sufficient to warrant their being sent off.

Vicarious or observational learning of aggression usually happens very early in a performer's development: a performer will quickly learn what behaviour is acceptable or unacceptable in various specific situations. When expected rewards (eg, prestige, tactical/psychological advantage or victory) are seen to outweigh the value of the punishment (eg, a foul given away, booking or possible sin-bin) a player will be prepared to transgress the rules.

The situational expectancies of success can be seen as high or low. Social learning theorists believe that reinforcement values/punishment values are major factors in influencing sports performers in the selection of aggressive behaviour (Silva, 1979). Thus performers are being socialised towards deviance. The social learning perspective, however, also sees the process as having possible positive effects. This more optimistic view suggests that if performers can learn aggressive sporting behaviour then they can also learn to be non-aggressive.

Controlling and reducing aggression

When trying to manage or reduce aggression we first need to be aware of which situations are more likely to cause aggression to occur.

Situations that cause aggression

Although activities that have high levels of physical contact are thought to increase the probability of aggression this only happens if aggression increases the team's chances of winning (performance outcome).

Causes specific to individual aggression are:

- facing defeat (particularly when success has a high intrinsic or extrinsic value) (see motivation, page 436)
- when officiating is perceived as unfair
- embarrassment
- physical pain
- playing below expectations.

General causes of aggression are:

- that the effects or demands of the professional game encourage aggressive behaviour
- media intervention and comment
- over emphasis on winning or the achievement of goals
- increased rewards
- linked to situational expectations.

In being aware of what can create or predispose a performer towards aggressive behaviour we can propose the following strategies for trying to limit or control aggression amongst sports performers.

1 If a player is observed as displaying signs which may well lead to possible aggressive behaviour, eg, continual questioning of official's decisions or committing fouls, then a player should be removed from the game or situation in order to 'cool off' (continuous/rolling substitutions in basketball, hockey, allow for this).

2 Stress management techniques such as those discussed in Chapter 27 can be used to teach sports performers to control their emotions and reactions to frustration. Relaxation prior to the game and mental practice focus efforts more effectively on fulfilling their role in the game.

3 Reduce the emphasis on winning (not so easy in professional sport) – aggression should not be the result of losing. Efforts should be made by the teacher or coach (significant other) to minimise any aggression experienced from losing.

4 Increase rewards for sporting or non-aggressive behaviour.

5 Reinforce assertive behaviour not aggressive behaviour.

6 Increase the profile of positive role models.

7 Emphasise the result of unacceptable behaviour by role models, eg, bad publicity; getting sent off.

8 Ensure that players are aware of the 'wider role' they play in society and the possible damaging effects of their behaviour.

9 Make sure that aggression does not pay dividends – check that rules associated with activities deter acts of aggression (increase numbers of red cards). The rules of many sports still present loop holes in control which encourage deviant behaviour.

10 Increase punishments for aggressive behaviour to reduce legitimacy of the action.

11 Players and coaches need to be more sensitive to the differences between assertive and aggressive behaviour in order to reduce the possibilities of retaliation.

12 Educate players and coaches on the appropriateness of certain types of behaviour (ethical/moral development). Emphasise their positive role in the team and discuss how aggressive behaviour may 'let down' their team mates.

Strategies for controlling spectator aggression

Again, observation of aggressive behaviour has been shown to incite violence off the pitch, but only if certain situational factors are also part of the equation, eg, crowd situations and/or large numbers of young males under the influence of alcohol. Controlling strategies include:

- limiting alcohol or banning it altogether
- reducing levels of rivalry
- removing spectators if they display aggressive tendencies
- increasing effectiveness of game officials thus reducing aggressive behaviour within the game
- reducing crowded situations (strict seating control)
- telling coaches that aggressive behaviour or inciting aggressive behaviour by themselves or their teams will not be tolerated
- getting the media to support these views by not positively emphasising aggressive behaviour
- make sporting situations more family orientated.

Summary

Attitudes and stereotypes

1 Attitudes are specific and individual not global.
2 Attitudes can considerably influence behaviour in sport.
3 There is a need for more specific research in this area.
4 Stereotyping is not 'bad' in itself, but it is important for teachers and coaches to be aware of inaccurate stereotypes and challenge them.
5 Once formed, attitudes are very resistant to change and can lead to prejudice.

Aggression

1 Aggression is intentional behaviour outside the rules directed towards the goal of harming or injuring another living being, when they are motivated to avoid such treatment.
2 The main theories associated with the study of aggression are: instinct theory (ethological and psychoanalytical); drive theory; frustration–aggression hypothesis; social learning theory.
3 More up to date research has ensured that instinct theory has little support in relation to sport. There is, however, some recognition of limited innate aggressive tendencies.
4 There is little evidence to support the notion of catharsis.
5 The revised frustration theory of aggression is seen as having some credibility, particularly when it is linked to social learning theory.

Social learning

1 Social learning theory advocates that reinforcement and modelling either of or by significant others are the main influential determinants of aggressive behaviour in sport.
2 Social learning can also be seen as an optimistic approach.
3 Having an understanding of what can cause aggressive behaviour allows teachers, coaches and performers to be more effective in controlling aggressive behaviour.

Revision Questions

1 What do we mean by personality?
2 Explain the credulous and sceptical viewpoints of personality research?
3 What is the trait perspective view of personality?
4 What is the RAS?
5 What are the main criticisms of personality tests?
6 Why is it important that research is valid and reliable?
7 How does the interactionist approach differ from the trait approach?
8 What is the iceberg profile?
9 Do attitudes really help us to predict behaviour?
10 What are the three ways we can analyse attitudes?
11 By giving examples from sport, try to show how attitudes can be formed.
12 What factors are important when trying to persuade someone to change their attitudes? Illustrate your answer with examples from sport.
13 What are the main problems associated with measuring attitudes?
14 What is dissonance?
15 Why are prejudices potentially dangerous?
16 Give a definition of aggression. How does this differ from assertive behaviour? Give examples.
17 Why is instinct theory thought to be a too simplistic approach?
18 By using examples from sport show what you understand by the frustration–aggression hypothesis.
19 Why are significant others so important, related to aggression?
20 How do situational expectancies affect aggressive behaviour?
21 In what ways can we try to limit or control aggression both on and off the field?

chapter 25

Motivation in Physical Education and Sport

Motivation is a key area of sport psychology. It is recognised as an essential feature in both the learning of skills and the development of performance. In addition it plays an important role in a learner's preference for and selection of activities.

In evaluating the research we find that unfortunately there are, once again, no simple answers. What becomes obvious is that in order to gain an understanding of this complex and multi-functional concept we need to consider a wide variety of research. By taking an integrated approach to analysing motivation we will try to bring together the main aspects of various psychological perspectives. Motivation is the global term for a very complex process. Within this chapter we will introduce you to the following questions:

- what do sports psychologists mean by motivation?
- what are the different types of motivation?
- what are the effects of these different types on learning and performance?
- what are the main theories associated with motivation and achievement motivation?
- what different motivational techniques can be used in order to facilitate achievement motivation?
- what are the related and interdependent factors that can influence motivational behaviour?

In considering these areas you should develop a clearer understanding of the underlying processes involved in how and why motivation can differ from person to person.

Here is a list of the terms to be covered in this chapter. It is important that you understand them.

- Intrinsic motivation
- Extrinsic motivation
- Arousal
- Drive theory
- The inverted 'U' hypothesis
- Reticular activating system
- Optimum arousal
- Perceptive narrowing
- Cue utilisation

- Achievement motivation
- n. Ach
- n. Af
- Causal attributions
- Attribution process
- Attribution retraining
- Learned helplessness
- Self efficacy
- Vicarious experience

Defining motivation

Answering the question 'What do we mean by motivation?' has been one of the fundamental difficulties faced by psychologists and explanations differ according to

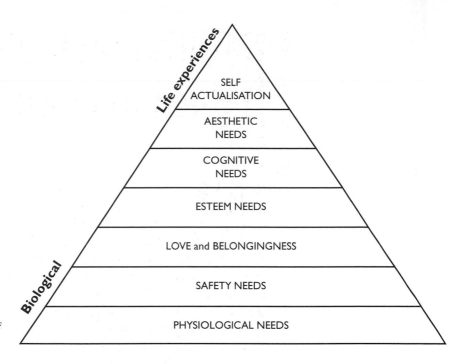

Fig. 25.1 MASLOW'S 1954 HIERARCHY OF NEEDS

the psychological perspective adopted. The term 'motivate' comes from the Latin for move and motives are seen as a special kind of cause of behaviour that **energise**, **direct** and **sustain** a person's behaviour (Ruben and McNeil, 1983).

It has been suggested that human beings have both primary motives (survival and function, etc) and secondary motives which are acquired or learned such as the **need for achievement** and self actualisation which are complex, higher order cognitive behaviours. Maslow highlighted the basic needs of a person as being a mixture of the physiological and psychological. If the body has developed a need then it will eventually strive to meet the need – the body will be driven psychologically to meet its needs. As well as being psychological, the desire to overcome physiological deprivation implies a motivational state.

Maslow (1954) produced a psycho-social model referring to a human being's hierarchy of needs.

Motivation is: 'the internal mechanisms and external stimuli which arouse and direct our behaviour'.   (G.H. Sage, 1974)

Seeing motivation as the direction and intensity of one's effort is regarded by more recent psychologists as too simplistic (M Weiss, 1992) (Weinberg, 1995). However, for the purposes of this book we will accept Sage's definition as a useful starting point.

In analysing the definition we can see that it involves four main aspects:

1 **Internal mechanisms** – integral mechanisms: motivation is linked to and affected by a person's inner drives.
2 **External mechanisms:** motivation is linked to and affected by external factors that we can experience within our learning/performing situations.
3 **Arouse behaviour:** motivation is linked to a person's state of arousal that energises and drives our behaviour. The strength of the energised state will

determine the degree of intensity of effort used to achieve the goal-related behaviour.

4 **Direct behaviour:** motivation in its various forms can affect our goals or selection of activities as well as our maintenance of behaviour in activities (Richard Gross sees motivation as 'goal directed purposeful behaviour').

Motivation refers therefore to a general energised state which prepares a person to act or behave in some way. Motives relate to the direction that the behaviour will take or the goal which is set.

Interactional view of motivation

In recognising that motivation (the intensity and direction of behaviour) is formed as a result of both 'internal and external mechanisms' we are said to be taking an **interactionist perspective** on motivation.

To develop optimum motivation a teacher or coach must not only analyse and respond individually to each of the aspects listed in fig 25.2 but also to how the factors interact together. Very rarely can blame for poor motivation be placed on any one factor alone.

Types of motivation

A person's behaviour is affected by many different kinds of motives coming from both internal and external mechanisms.

Intrinsic motivation

The study of intrinsic motivation has been linked to cognitive theories. Intrinsic motivation is used to explain how learners/performers strive inwardly, being self determined in trying to develop competence or excellence of performance. They are said to have mastery orientation. A person who is intrinsically motivated will want to take part in the activity for its own sake, for pure love of the sport. They will focus on the enjoyment and fun of competition, try to develop their skills to the

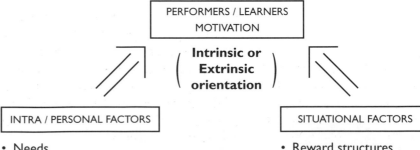

Fig. 25.2 THE INTERACTIONIST VIEW OF
MOTIVATION

highest possible level (pursuit of excellence) and enjoy the action and excitement of seeking out new challenges and affiliations in doing so. A performer pushing themselves hard in difficult circumstances and feeling a sense of control and pride at achieving a high level of personal skill is said to be intrinsically motivated. Intrinsic motivation is greatest when learners/performers feel competent and self determining in dealing with their environment. Sports performers sometimes experience a situation when the timing of movements and actions appears perfect. They seem unable to do wrong. Everything they try works! It's one of those perfect days. They are said to be experiencing the ultimate intrinsic experience. Csikszentmihalyi (1975) describes this as the 'flow experience'; in his research he identified the common characteristics of it as:

- complete absorption in the activity
- action and awareness are merged
- apparent loss of consciousness
- an almost subconscious feeling of self control
- no extrinsic motivation (goals, rewards, etc)
- effortless movement.

Such a peak experience, during which performers are able to lose themselves in the highly skilled performance of their sport, has been likened to Maslow's 'self actualisation' commented upon earlier in this chapter. Although it can not be consciously planned for, the development of 'flow' has been linked to the following factors:

- positive mental attitude (confidence, positive thinking)
- being relaxed, controlling anxiety, and enjoying optimum arousal
- focusing on appropriate specific aspects of performance
- physical readiness (training and preparation at the highest level).

Obviously limitations in any of the above factors can result in 'disrupted flow'.

Extrinsic motivation

Extrinsic motivation is related to Sage's external mechanisms.

If used appropriately extrinsic types of motivation (contingencies) can serve a very useful purpose in effectively developing certain required behaviours (learning) or levels of sporting performance. The behaviouristic view of learning discussed in earlier chapters is founded on the principles of reinforcement (rewards for success) and punishment. The systematic use of rewards, or 'Effective Contingency Management' as it is often referred to, is recognised as playing an important role in modifying and shaping learning and performance (see operant conditioning, page 366). Rewards can expedite learning and achievement, serve to ensure that a good performance is repeated or form an attraction to persuade a person to take part in certain activities (incentive).

While extrinsic motivation is most obviously seen in terms of tangible or materialistic rewards, it can also be intangible.

When using extrinsic rewards and reinforcements to enhance motivation a teacher or coach needs to be aware of how often they are used (frequency). Should reward or reinforcement be used at every good or successful attempt or every so many times (ratio)? How quickly after the event should reinforcement be used (interval)? What is the most effective type of reinforcement to use? (see fig 25.3). The value or quantity of the reward is also important (magnitude). In being aware

TANGIBLE	INTANGIBLE
• Trophies	• Social reinforcers
• Medals	• Praise from teacher
• Badges	/coach/peers
• Certificates	• Smile
• Money	• Pat on the back
	• Publicity/national
	recognition
	• Winning/glory
	• Social status
	• Approval

Fig. 25.3 TANGIBLE AND INTANGIBLE EXTRINSIC MOTIVATION

of the above factors a teacher or coach clearly needs an in-depth knowledge of the likes and dislikes of the people being taught. The use of rewards is therefore closely linked to our earlier discussion in Chapter 21 of reinforcement of learning (page 368).

Research into the use of reinforcement principles has produced the following recommendations when considering extrinsic motivation:

- positive reinforcement is 80 to 90 per cent more effective
- avoid the use of punishment apart from when behaviour is intolerable or unwanted
- in order to be effective, extrinsic feedback and reinforcement must meet the needs of the recipient (they must be important to or desired by the individual)
- continuous reinforcement is desirable in the early stages of learning
- intermittent reinforcement is more effective with more advanced performers
- immediate reinforcement is generally more effective, particularly with beginners
- reward appropriate behaviour (cannot reward all behaviour)
  - (i) reward successful approximations, particularly by beginners (shaping) – performance will not always be perfect (trial and error)
  - (ii) reward performance – do not just focus on the outcome, ie, winning
  - (iii) reward effort
  - (iv) reward emotional and social skills
- provide knowledge of results (information re-accuracy and success of movement (see feedback page 385)
- the use of punishment should be restricted or avoided as although it can be effective in eliminating undesirable behaviour it can also lead to bitterness, resentment, frustration and hostility. It can arouse a performer's fear of failure and thus hinder the learning of skills.

Look at the list of strategies for the use of extrinsic rewards. Try to give practical examples of how a teacher or coach might implement them in real life.

Combining intrinsic and extrinsic rewards

Consider top level sports performers such as Martina Hingis in fig 25.4. In discussion with a partner, try to suggest what motivates them to carry on once they have reached the top.

Both intrinsic and extrinsic motivation obviously play important roles in the development of skilled performance and behavioural change (learning). Extrinsic rewards are used extensively in sporting situations. Most major sports have achievement performance incentives linked to some form of tangible reward system. At first glance it would appear that the 'additive effect' of extrinsic rewards – money, cups and medals – and the high level of intrinsic motivation should result in performers showing a much greater level of overall motivation.

Although early research in this area supported this additive viewpoint, later research, for example by Deci (1971, 1972) and Lepper and Green (1975) began to suggest that under certain conditions (when intrinsic motivation is already high (Orlick and Mosher, 1978)) extrinsic motivation may actually decrease intrinsic motivation. This lead to many practitioners discouraging the use of extrinsic rewards in an educational setting. Further research with regard to the reduction in intrinsic motivation linked this effect more to the person's perception of the original extrinsic reward. To further explain this potential positive or negative effect of extrinsic rewards Deci (1985) developed his cognitive evaluation theory.

What happens when there are no further badges or trophies to obtain? How might a coach try to ensure levels of motivation are maintained?

Fig. 25.4 MARTINA HINGIS COLLECTING HER TROPHY AT WIMBLEDON 1997

Intrinsic motivation can be affected by extrinsic rewards in two ways. The performer may perceive the reward as an attempt to **control** or manipulate their behaviour (the fun aspect becomes work). The performer may also perceive the reward as providing information about their level of performance. A reward could be perceived by a performer as increasing the individual importance of a particular achievement. In receiving the reward that certain level of achievement is perceived as high. If they do achieve and gain the reward (positive information) then this sign of high ability can help intrinsic motivation. If, however, they fail to achieve the reward (negative information) then they may perceive this as being a sign of incompetence or low ability, thus lowering future intrinsic motivation.

If a person perceives extrinsic rewards as controlling their behaviour or providing information that they are competent then intrinsic motivation will be reduced. To increase intrinsic motivation the reward should provide information and positive feedback with regard to the performer's level of competence in performance.

Teachers and coaches should therefore try to involve the performer in decision making and planning with regard to their training programmes and performance goals. By becoming involved the performer will feel a shared responsibility for any success or achievement thus increasing their intrinsic motivation because they feel in control and competent. The now obvious link between competitive success and increased intrinsic motivation was shown by Weinberg (1978).

As success and failure in competitive situations provide high levels of information with regard to a person's level of competence or incompetence it is important that a teacher or coach ensures that intrinsic motivation is not lost by a person who experiences defeat. This is done by emphasising performance or task goals and concentrating on more subjective outcomes, eg, an action performed well. For instance: although you lost the tennis match it was to a better player; your number of successful serves increased and your tactical use of certain ground strokes also improved. By focusing on the subjective evaluation of success or performance outcomes (winning is not everything) teachers, coaches and parents can improve the performer's positive perceptions of themselves (self image, self confidence) and thus dramatically increase intrinsic motivation.

In conclusion then, intrinsic motivation is highly satisfying because it gives the performer a sense of personal control over the situation in which they are performing. Being intrinsically motivated will ensure that an individual will train and practice enthusiastically thus hopefully developing their acquisition of skill (learning) and overall performance.

Extrinsic rewards however, do not inherently undermine intrinsic motivation. It is essential that physical education teachers and coaches use them in addition to other strategies effectively. They must increase a learner's/performer's perceptions of success in order to develop intrinsic motivation within the overall educational and performance environment.

Successful strategies for the use of rewards to help develop intrinsic motivation should include:

1 Manipulation of the environment to provide for successful experience.
2 Ensuring that rewards are contingent on performance.
3 Emphasising praise (verbal – non verbal).
4 Providing variety in learning and practice situations.
5 Allowing learners to participate in decision making.
6 Setting realistic performance goals based on the learner's ability and present skill levels.

Look at the list of reward strategies above. How many more can you think of? Now think of a sport or physical activity that you have taken part in or are still taking part in. Make a list of all the reasons or factors that influenced you to take part in that activity. Consider the following questions:

- **why did you start?**
- **why did you stop?**
- **why are you still taking part?**
- **are the reasons and motives that prompt you to continue taking part the same as the reasons and motives that originally prompted you to start?**
- **was your motivation more to do with intrinsic or extrinsic factors?**
- **did situational factors have an influence on your level of motivation?**

Compare and discuss your findings with the rest of the group.

Arousal

Any discussion of motivation is closely linked to theories of arousal. In the everyday use of the terms it is not always easy to distinguish between motivation and arousal. They are also closely related to the notion of stress and anxiety (see Chapter 27, Optimising Performance). In our earlier consideration of Sage's definition of motivation it was stated that motivation was affected by both intrinsic and extrinsic factors that served to energise and direct behaviour. Arousal is linked therefore to the 'energised' state that drives a person to learn or perform and is therefore associated with the intensity dimension of motivation. Evidence suggests, however, that arousal is not just an internal state.

Definition of arousal

Arousal can be defined as being a general mixture of both the physiological and psychological levels of activity that a performer experiences; these levels vary on a continuum from deep sleep to intense excitement.

Highly energised states can be caused by an individual or team competing in an important competition. Arousal is not to be seen as good or bad, positive or negative, as it appears to represent the level of energy or effort that a learner/performer develops and applies to any sporting or learning situation. A sports performer can be highly aroused as a result of both winning and losing a competition or even looking forward to a competition (apprehension or excitement).

Arousal theories

Arousal theories suggest that our bodies need to be in a state of homeostasis (physiological and psychological balance). If the body is deprived or affected (put under stress – perceived or actual) in any way physiologically or mentally then arousal levels in the body are increased and we are motivated to behave in such a way as to reduce these levels back to the optimum level of arousal. Typical physiological reactions that are associated with increased arousal levels can be measured by heart rate, blood pressure, electronical activity, electromyograph, galvanic skin responses and biomechanical indicators such as adrenaline and epinephrine.

If an athlete is preparing for a big race (highly active) they need to be in a highly alert state (arousal). The body needs to ensure that it can meet all the physiological demands that may be placed on it. Muscles need to be supplied with blood sugars and oxygen, etc. The sympathetic system of the **autonomous nervous system** (ANS), ie, the glands, hormonal and endocrine systems also help to maintain and prepare the body for action. The **parasympathetic system** of the ANS, on the other hand, will work to restore the body's resources for future use.

The **reticular activating system** (RAS), which is part of the ascending structure of the spinal cord's link to the fore brain, is responsible for maintaining the general level of arousal or alertness within the body. It plays a part in our selective attention processes and serves either to inhibit or excite incoming sensory information to help our attention processes (see Chapter 24 for a discussion of Eysenck's work on personality and arousal levels linked to the effect of the RAS). The psychologists' interest in arousal has tended to focus on the links between the physiological aroused state and the experience of associated emotions. Just as periods of high intense exercise (eg, playing football or netball) are associated with all the symptoms of a highly aroused state, eg, high levels of adrenaline, increased HR, breathing rates, etc, aroused states can be equally associated with the emotional states of fear, anger, apprehension, tension, worry and anxiety. Some evidence suggests that these emotional states are reciprocal with one affecting the other and vice versa. They are closely linked to the physiological state (see Chapter 27). Within this chapter we are mainly interested in the psychological effects of arousal.

The various emotional states mentioned above are easily developed and often experienced particularly when exploring the unfamiliar (meeting something new or being asked to do something important or perform at a new high level of competition) and in the learning or acquiring of motor skills as well as the ultimate performance.

As a learner's/performer's levels of arousal are important it must be equally important that they have the **appropriate** levels of arousal in order to promote effective concentration, attention and decision making levels to produce optimum performance. Teachers and coaches have been aware for a long time of the need for performers to be mentally prepared and alert; this is commonly referred to as a sports performer being 'psyched up' (readiness to respond). The intensity of

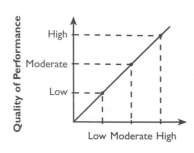

Fig. 25.5 ORIGINAL DRIVE THEORIES'
VIEW OF THE AROUSAL/PERFORMANCE
RELATIONSHIP

arousal levels is often a crucial factor in both competitive sport and learning situations. If arousal gets too high a learner/performer can become anxious and equally if it is too low then they may become bored and demotivated, both states resulting in a negative effect on learning and performance.

Drive theory

Early research carried out by Hull in 1943 and later modified by J Spence and K Spence in 1966 suggests that the relationship between arousal and performance is a linear one. All performance was originally thought to improve directly in proportion to increases in arousal (see fig 25.5).

In other words, the more a sports performer was aroused the better they would perform. Further research by Spence and Spence adapted this view slightly. This relationship has been expressed in the equation

$$P = H \times D$$
Performance = habit strength × drive

Hull saw drive as being synonymous with arousal. Habit strength was seen as the learned response or performance behaviour; essentially, it is a theory related to learning – Hull saw the likelihood of learned behaviour (dominant response) occurring as being greater as drive (arousal) levels increased. This theory has very close links with Zajonc's theory of social facilitation (see page 467). However, learned habitual behaviour may not always be the correct behaviour. The theory goes on to suggest that if the performer is a beginner trying to carry out newly acquired skills then increased drive (arousal) for whatever reason may cause the performer to rely on previously learned skills, thus the dominant response may be an incorrect response. A good example would be a beginner learning to serve in tennis. They have just been taught correctly how to serve, practised several times, appear to understand and carry out a reasonable serve. However, in a following competitive match their first serve hits the net and because of the increased pressure (drive/arousal) to get the second serve in they subconsciously revert back to their previously error-ridden learned serve, a little tap over the net in order to get the ball in play. Thus in the early stages of learning the effects of increased arousal on skill acquisition could lead to the dominant response being an incorrect one. In the latter stages of learning (autonomous) increased drive (arousal) levels would have a positive effect, as the dominant response would be the well learnt (habitual) and generally correct one. This is often called a 'grooved skill'. The many criticisms of this theory as a result of further research, together with observations of 'real life' situations in which even top class performers with highly developed habitual skill levels have been seen to fail in high arousal situations, has meant that this approach has generally lost credibility.

The inverted 'U' hypothesis

This explanation of the relationship between arousal and performance originated as a result of work carried out as early as 1908 when the Yerkes and Dodson Law first suggested that complex tasks are performed better when one's level of drive (arousal) is low, while simple tasks are performed better when drive/arousal is high. It recognises that there are different degrees of arousal, over or under arousal, and that different people can be affected in different ways depending on the type of tasks they are faced with. This view contends that the relationship between

Fig. 25.6 EVEN HIGHLY TALENTED SPORTS
PERFORMERS HAVE 'CHOKED' IN HIGHLY
CHARGED SITUATIONS

Fig. 25.7 THE INVERTED 'U' PRINCIPLE STATES THAT INCREASED AROUSAL IMPROVES PERFORMANCE ONLY TO A CERTAIN POINT AFTER WHICH FURTHER INCREASED LEVELS OF AROUSAL WILL HAVE AN ADVERSE EFFECT

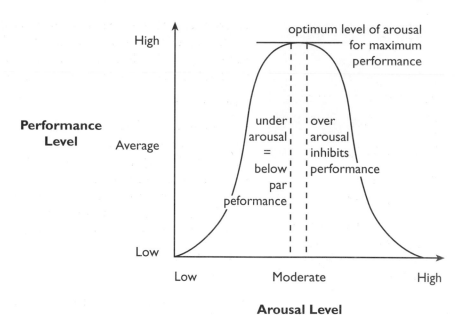

optimum level of arousal for maximum performance

Performance Level

High

Average

Low

under arousal = below par peformance

over arousal inhibits performance

Low   Moderate   High

Arousal Level

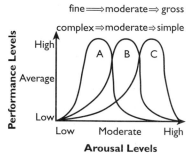

fine ⟹ moderate ⟹ gross
complex ⟹ moderate ⟹ simple

Fig. 25.8 THE INVERTED 'U' PRINCIPLE FOR DIFFERENT TASKS: OPTIMUM AROUSAL IS HIGHER FOR MORE SIMPLE TASKS WITH MORE GROSS-MOTOR CONTROL

arousal and performance is curvilinear, hence the inverted 'U' shape of the graph (see fig 25.7 above). Performance is said to improve up to a certain point of arousal; if arousal continues to increase beyond the optimal state then the performance will begin to decline.

It has been argued, however, that as a general principle, optimum levels of arousal are not the same for all activities or for all performers. The idea that optimum levels of arousal are variable according to the type and complexity of the task in relation to the individual performer has meant that the basic principles can be generalised and used by teachers and coaches to explain and predict behaviour in a whole host of situations. Teachers and coaches began to realise that the usual all-rousing pre-event pep talk was not necessarily the answer for all performers.

Using fig 25.8, try to place the following list of activities to one of the three curves A, B or C in relation to the level of arousal you would think might be appropriate to carry out the skill effectively:

- **free throw in basketball**
- **rugby prop**
- **a gymnastic routine**
- **boxing**
- **putting in golf**
- **tennis**
- **archery**
- **rifle shooting**

- **figure skating**
- **shot put**
- **power lifting**
- **swimming 100 m sprint**
- **running a marathon**
- **taking a penalty kick in football**
- **slip fielder in cricket.**

Consider a game or activity that you take part in regularly. In conjunction with a partner think of the levels of appropriate arousal you might need at various stages in the game and with certain types of skills.

It has been found that motor skills generally need an above average level of arousal. If the skills or activity involve mainly gross movements and relatively simple skills using strength, endurance and speed, requiring little decision making, then highe

Fig. 25.9 ARCHERY/RIFLE SHOOTING REQUIRES FINE MUSCULAR CONTROL AND HIGH LEVELS OF CONCENTRATION AND AS SUCH OPTIMUM LEVELS OF AROUSAL WOULD BE LOWER THAN THOSE OF THE POWER LIFTER

levels of arousal will be found more effective. Activities involving very fine, accurate muscle actions or complex tasks requiring higher levels of perception, decision making, concentration and attention will be carried out more effectively if the point of optimum arousal is slightly lower.

It is therefore very important that a teacher or coach assesses the appropriate levels of arousal for each task in order to ensure that the optimum level is achieved. Even within teams the different requirements of each particular role or position may require different levels of arousal at various times, eg, batting and bowling in cricket, where loss of concentration and co-ordination could be disastrous, require different levels of arousal to those of a general fielder. Adjusting arousal levels to suit both task and situation could involve the coach in trying to increase or decrease a performer's arousal levels. Levels of excitement and anxiety caused by high arousal may need to be controlled by various stress management techniques (see Chapter 27). As you can appreciate, many sports or tasks involve combinations of both fine and gross skills along with varying levels of information processing linked to complexity. Even within the context of a game different players will need different levels of arousal and at different times. Past experience, amount of practice and stage of learning will also have an effect on the choice of appropriate level of arousal.

Beginners need different levels of arousal to those of a professional sports person. In addition the level of complexity is relative to the stage of learning and/or experience. What for an experienced performer is a relatively easy task may be very difficult and involve a great deal of information processing for a beginner (see Chapter 22, page 371). Even at moderate levels of arousal a beginner may 'go to pieces' and be unable to cope with what is required of them; an even lower level of arousal may be more appropriate.

The inability of a performer, particularly a beginner, to process the relevant information effectively has been linked to what has been called **perceptual narrowing** and **cue-utilisation theory**. These concepts help us to understand that as arousal levels increase a performer tries to pay more attention to those stimuli, cues and signals that are more likely and relevant in order to help them carry out the task (cue-utilisation). They focus their attention (perceptual narrowing). However, a performer's ability to focus their attention is severely hampered if arousal levels continue to increase. Perceptual narrowing continues which may cause a performer to miss important cues and signals (ineffective cue-utilisation) which could have a detrimental effect on performance.

This effect is even more noticeable if the cues and signals are not what was expected. Extreme levels of arousal can cause such acute levels of perceptual narrowing that a person is not able to concentrate or make decisions effectively, and can even hinder the smooth control of physical movements. This state of 'hyper vigilance' is commonly known as 'blind panic'. Perceptual narrowing is therefore an important aspect of both learning and performance where, in a state of high arousal, reactions to expected stimuli can be enhanced and reactions to inappropriate or unexpected cues and signals can be inhibited.

In discussion with your group try to recount a specific situation in which you have experienced 'panic' and been unable to concentrate on making the correct decisions. What sort of things 'triggered' these feelings? How did perceptual narrowing affect your cue-utilisation?

It would be more appropriate, therefore, when dealing with inexperienced performers or beginners in a learning situation to ensure that levels of arousal are initially very low. Audiences, evaluation and competitive situations are best avoided.

Teachers and coaches need to get to know the learner/performer and be aware of the effects that the situation can have on them.

Catastrophe theory

Several modifications to the inverted 'U' hypothesis have been put forward. One of the more interesting is that suggested by Hardy and Frazey (1987). The catastrophe theory is similar to the inverted 'U' hypothesis in that both argue that if arousal increases it will have a positive effect on performance up to a certain optimal level. Hardy and Frazey then argue that in highly competitive and important matches, where both high physiological arousal combines with high cognitive anxiety, if a squash player for example becomes upset enough (over aroused) for it to have a detrimental effect on their game, the deterioration is much more extreme and cannot be arrested merely by calming the player down a little. 'Going over the top' in this situation will have a dramatic effect on their ability to concentrate, make decisions and play shots effectively. In other words a catastrophe. Recovery from this catastrophe can be very difficult; extreme 'mental toughness' will be required if they are to work their way gradually back to optimum arousal and peak performance.

Figure 25.10 illustrates the different shape and effect (catastrophe predictions) of arousal on performance:

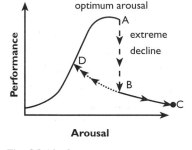

Fig. 25.10 CATASTROPHE THEORY
Source: adapted from 'A catastrophe for sport psychology', by L. Hardy and J. Frazey, in Bass Monograph No. 1 (p 21), (British Association of Sports Science N.C.F., Leeds, 1988)

- at point A cognitive anxiety (worrying) and physiological arousal (somatic) are high – reaching this threshold creates a catastrophic effect
- at point B the performer either continues with their extreme over arousal causing performance to decline further to C or
- they get to grips with their problem, taking serious steps to calm down and re-focus – performance will gradually improve to point D when arousal levels can return to the optimum levels: performance may once again reach the maximum effective level.

Achievement motivation

Achievement motivation is related to the often-asked questions:

- why is it that some learners/performers achieve and some don't?
- why is it that certain performers are driven to be more competitive than others?

'The need to achieve is a relatively stable disposition to strive for success.'
(A.A.H.P.H.E.R.D. 1981)

The term achievement motivation was first put forward by Murray (1938) who, in describing 20 different human motives or needs, identified a human being's need for achievement as being linked to the personality of the performer. Whether it is in competition or not, the fact that certain types of people are prepared (more motivated) to place themselves regularly in situations where their achievement is being compared or evaluated in some way generally labels them as being more competitive or 'achievement orientated' than others.

Gill (1986) gives the following definition:

'A person who has high levels of achievement motivation would have a tendency to strive for success, persist in the face of failure and experience pride in accomplishments.'

(D. Gill)

The level of a person's need to achieve (drive for success) is seen as a relatively stable disposition. A person who has a high need to achieve has a tendency to display a positive approach in relation to their achievement orientation as well as a positive success tendency. They will strive to achieve a high level of performance (mastery accomplishment). Thus having high levels of achievement motivation can make all the difference to how successful a performer is in both learning and high level performance situations.

Most of the research associated with achievement motivation in sport has revolved around the early classical theories put forward by Atkinson (1964 and 1974) and McCelland (1961). In trying to explain how a person's need to achieve (n. Ach) developed, thus enabling predictions of their future behaviour to be made, Atkinson took an interactionist stance, proposing that both personality factors and situational factors have to be considered.

Atkinson's personality components of achievement motivation

Atkinson suggested that all a performer's behaviour is greatly affected (eg, achievement motivation, competitiveness) by their ability to balance two underlying motives that we all possess within ourselves;

- **the need to achieve success (n. Ach)** – a person is motivated to achieve success for the feelings of pride and satisfaction they will experience
- **the need to avoid failure (n. Af)** – a person is motivated to avoid failure in order not to experience the feelings of shame or humiliation that will result if failure occurs.

You can probably appreciate from your own experience that sporting situations provide us with regular opportunities to experience success or failure. All sports performers are motivated by a combination of both, a need to be successful and the good positive feelings that are associating with winning, together with a wish to avoid the feelings of shame, embarrassment and possible humiliation associated with losing.

 **ACTIVITY 8**

You must have experienced pride at gaining some form of success. You may also have experienced the occasional dent to your pride.
    Discuss in your group the different feelings that you have experienced, as a result of success or failure. How did they affect your future attitude and levels of motivation?

Atkinson's research suggested that high achievers in sport tended to have high levels of n. Ach and low levels of n. Af whereas low achievers in sport tended to have low n. Ach levels and high n. Af levels. Low achievers do not fear failure but they fear the negative evaluation associated with failure.

The situational component of achievement motivation

Atkinson supports his predictions of behaviour and performance by cross referencing a performer's personality factors with situational factors. He claims that a performer will assess the situation they are faced with and evaluate:

- the probability of success along with
- the incentive value of that success.

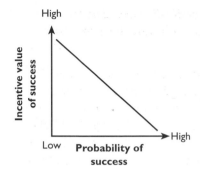

High

Incentive value of success

Low   **Probability of success**   → High

Fig. 25.11 Atkinson's suggested relationship between the probability of success and the incentive value

The probability of success will obviously depend on who you are competing against and/or the difficulty of the task. Thus if you are an average club golfer playing against Nick Faldo, the probability of success is not very high. Your chances would be higher against a complete novice. The incentive value, however, of playing against Nick Faldo and the satisfaction gained if you beat him, would be far greater. The satisfaction gained from you beating the novice would not be as high, as you would have expected to win (high probability).

Thus Atkinson's view of what factors contribute to levels of achievement motivation in people can be expressed by the following equation:

Tendency of a person's achievement motivation or competitiveness $=$ $(\mathbf{Ms} - \mathbf{Maf}) \times (\mathbf{Ps} \times [\mathbf{I} - \mathbf{Ps}])$

$$\underset{\text{motive to succeed}}{\uparrow} - \underset{\text{motive to avoid failure}}{\uparrow} \times \left(\underset{\text{of success}}{\text{probability}} \times \underset{\text{of success}}{\text{incentive value}} \right)$$

Current research and thinking on achievement motivation

Although Atkinson's work has been used as a platform more up to date research in this area of motivation has tended to take a wider perspective. Achievement motivation is considered not merely as a single construct but from a more multi-dimensional perspective.

It has been argued by Maehr and Nicholls (1980) and Dweck that levels of achievement motivation will vary between performers according both to the reasons they are taking part in the activity (achievement goals) and the different meanings that success or failure has for the performer. Achievement goal theories suggest that a performer's different 'achievement goals' can be either

- outcome orientated or
- task orientated.

Outcome goal orientation

A performer who is motivated by winning and beating the opposition because they enjoy the feelings they get from competing and comparing themselves with others is said to be 'outcome orientated'. When this type of performer wins they are said to have high perceived ability. Their 'ego' is boosted as they see their success as a result of their own ability and develop high expectations of future success. When they lose, however, the opposite occurs. They see failure or lack of success as a result of their own limited ability (perceived low competence). This perceived low ability serves to increase their feelings of shame and humiliation as their 'ego' is deflated. It will probably have a negative effect on future expectations of success and thus achievement motivation. These feelings will be heightened if they have been unsuccessful in what they perceive as relatively easy tasks. They will tend to avoid challenging situations; reduce effort and possibly select activities or tasks that are either easy or ridiculously difficult.

Task goal orientation

Performers who are task orientated also want to win but are not so interested in demonstrating their own ability in comparison to others. They are motivated by developing their own technical standards or personal performance levels in relation to their own previous levels of success. This more intrinsic type of motivation where performers are trying to master the inherent demands of the task are said to be more effective in the long run. Because task orientated performers judge their success against their own standards they generally have high levels of perceived competence. They do not fear failure. It is not an affront to their own perceived ability nor is it internalised as a permanent personal characteristic. They see it as part of the challenge to improve. A performer will persist, effort will be increased or strategies changed in order to accomplish new goals or targets; very often this leads to improvements in their personal performance. This alternative task orientated view means that a performer focusing more on effort and personal standards will generally be protected from the feelings of frustration and disappointment associated with losing and be able to maintain motivation for longer. In reality most performers are motivated by both outcome and task mastery of performance goals. It is important, however, to know whether a performer is more task or outcome orientated. Teachers and coaches should try to stress task or mastery goals rather than outcome goals (see intrinsic motivation, page 438).

Stages of achievement motivation

Achievement motivation is thought to develop through three sequential stages (Veroff, 1969) beginning in early childhood and continuing into adulthood. Being aware of these stages will help you understand why certain types of people are always competitive, develop rivalries and try to win everything in order to boost their own egos.

Veroff's three sequential stages of achievement motivation

A child must achieve success in each stage before they move on to the next stage. Many people may never reach the final stage in the sequence.

1 **Autonomous competence stage** – very early stage in a child's development, usually the first three to four years of life. Children focus on mastering skills in the environment and testing themselves. Autonomous evaluation builds up perceptions of personal competence.
2 **Social comparison stage** – at approximately the age of five years, children begin to compare themselves with others, focusing on competition. They want to be seen as being better than others within their peer groups. Some people are continually making normative comparisons (focusing on winning), whereas others focus on the informative value of comparisons (evaluating their own mastery of skills).
3 **Integrated stage** – there is no particular age level for entering this most desirable stage of achievement motivation. This involves a person in both autonomous competence and social comparison stages. A person who has reached this stage is able to mix and move from one stage to the other depending on the appropriateness of the situation.

It is important that children are taught when it is appropriate or inappropriate to compete and compare themselves socially.

Developing achievement motivation

It is not easy in today's society to downplay or easily avoid outcome goals. It is important therefore that teachers and coaches are careful in the way they emphasise certain kinds of behaviour and goals. They can greatly influence a performer's perceptions of success or failure, and thus future motivation.

Whilst an integrated achievement orientation is said to be the ideal several factors are thought to influence achievement motivation orientation:

- childhood experiences
- social environment (social learning)
- cultural differences
- significant others
- emphasis (direct or indirect) on task or outcome goals
- expectations
- attributions – those conveyed by the teacher or coach and those expressed by the performer.

Attribution theory

Definition of attribution

Attributions are seen as being what an individual or team interprets or perceives as being the causes of theirs or others' particular behaviour, particular outcomes or events. The reasons/causes or attributions that an individual or team gives for their success or failure can affect:

- immediate emotional reactions
- actual behaviour.

In addition it can have serious effects on a performer's aspirations, expectations, achievement, motivation and future participation.

1 **Imagine a winning team and a losing team. Discuss what reasons the different performers may give to explain their success or defeat.**
2 **Will they be the same reasons?**
3 **How do you think the reasons they give will affect future efforts and possible participation?**
4 **Attributions that we give for other people's behaviour can also affect our future attitudes towards them. What reasons do you think the coaches of the different performers might give for success or failure?**
5 **Do you think these might have any effect on their future relationships with the performers?**

Now think of the last time you personally were successful in a physical activity and compare it to a time when you have been unsuccessful.

1 **What reasons did *you* give for both performances?**
2 **Can you suggest reasons why you may have attributed the reasons you did?**
3 **Was it possibly to make you feel better about winning or losing?**

In your discussions you will probably have come to realise that the different 'attributions' a person gives to explain success or failure are important. In referring back to our earlier discussion of what motivation is, attributions can affect the *intensity* and *direction* of our behaviour. If a performer taking part in a new activity, eg, basketball, is not getting on very well the reasons they perceive as being the cause for their apparent lack of success can have quite serious consequences for their future behaviour on court.

Since Fritz Heider first carried out his classic study on attributions in 1958 there have been several theories and models of attribution put forward. Although Weiner's model is not sport specific, it serves as a useful starting point in helping us understand the attribution process and its effects. In his research Weiner suggested that all the many thousands of reasons and explanations we might give for what has caused our success or failure can be grouped into certain common categories. These categories could then be related, compared and initially placed across two dimensions. After further research he later added a third dimension.

The four categories of **causal attributions** given by people for their level of success or failure were:

- ability
- effort
- task difficulty
- luck.

In fig 25.13 you can see how Weiner placed these on his model.

Using Weiner's two dimensional model of attribution, place the following attributions for success or failure into the model, taking care to consider the various categories.

- **'I'm not very good at badminton'**
- **'our swimming team is the best in the region'**
- **'our team is not really good enough to win the cup'**
- **'the referee was biased'**
- **'the coach made us play to an unusual pattern'**
- **'I couldn't be bothered to try'**
- **'the opposition employed better strategies and tactics than us'**
- **'they were better organised'**
- **'the goalkeeper dropping the ball enabled Shearer to score'**
- **'everybody tried their best'**
- **'the rain caused the match to be abandoned and saved us'**

Fig. 25.12 SOMETIMES SPORTS PERFORMERS WHO DO NOT SUCCEED EXTERNALISE ATTRIBUTIONS IN ORDER TO REDUCE THE EMOTIONAL EFFECT OF 'SHAME' AND THUS PROTECT THEIR 'SELF ESTEEM' AND SAFE FACE

The stability dimension is referring to whether the reasons/causes were relatively permanent (stable) or changeable (unstable) in relation to time. **Ability** and **task** difficulty are seen as being stable factors in relation to time. **Effort** and **luck** are factors that can change from time to time. The stability dimension is related to our expectancies of future outcomes, for instance if you attribute success to your ability then as this is a relatively stable factor (at the time of the activity) you will probably expect to gain success at similar activities or tasks in the future. The opposite effect will occur if you attribute failure to the stable factor of ability.

The locus of causality dimension is mainly linked to whether the attributions are internal (within performers) or external factors to the performer, eg, environmental. Ability and effort are therefore internal or personal to the performer. Task difficulty and luck are seen as being external to the performer.

Following criticisms of his work and further additional research (1985) Weiner reformulated his model, adding a further causal dimension, that of **locus of control**. This helped to explain the effective consequences of attributions that appear to be in or out of a person's control. The locus of control dimension has been shown to relate to the intensity of a performer's personal feelings of pride and

(a)

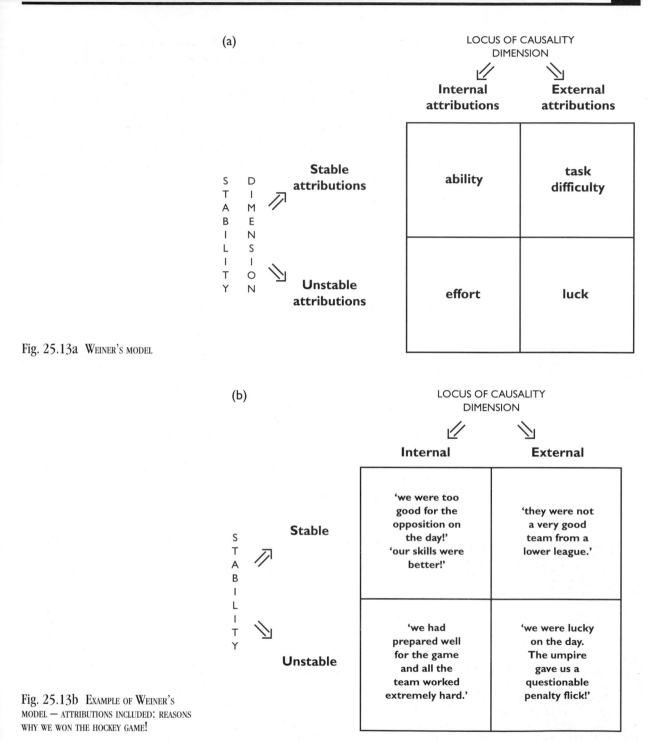

Fig. 25.13a WEINER'S MODEL

(b)

Fig. 25.13b EXAMPLE OF WEINER'S
MODEL — ATTRIBUTIONS INCLUDED: REASONS
WHY WE WON THE HOCKEY GAME!

satisfaction, shame and guilt. If a performer relates their success to internal causes
and factors within their control, eg, ability (I was better) and effort (I tried hard)
rather than external and uncontrollable factors, eg, I was lucky, and the task was
simple, then feelings of self satisfaction and pride will be maximised. As a result
motivation will probably continue and possibly increase. The opposite effect will
generally occur if failure is also attributed to internal and controllable factors. The
emotional effect will be one of increased shame and dissatisfaction leading to
possible decreased levels of motivation.

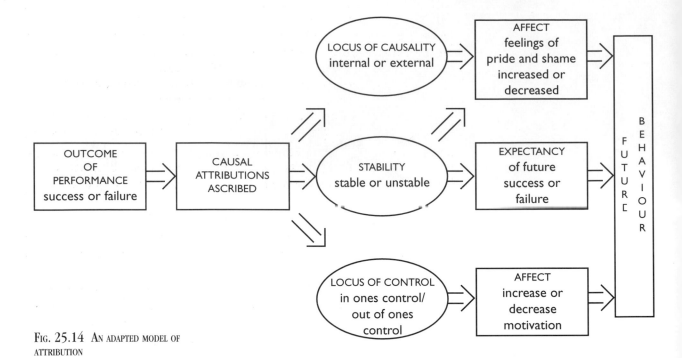

Fig. 25.14 An adapted model of attribution

The application of attribution theory in sport

Self-serving bias

When making attributions performers very often have biases in common, tending to take credit for success and disassociating themselves from failures, blaming external factors. It has been shown that successful performers *do* tend to attribute their success to internal factors (ability/effort) (a self-serving bias) to make them feel better about themselves, their group or team (self esteem is protected or enhanced). More up to date research, however, has suggested that contrary to original research and popular belief (see your answers to activities nine and ten) unsuccessful performers (losers), particularly individuals, do not try to protect their self esteem by *always* attributing failure to external factors (task difficulty or luck) in order to reduce feelings of shame. The performer's *perception* of the causes in relation to perceived success/failure are seen as being more important.

A performer's attributions will of course be affected by whether they view success or failure in terms of winning or losing (outcome goals) or whether they view it in terms of individual 'task' or 'mastery goals'. If a performer who has lost a tennis match judges their performance against previously set personal performance targets (mastery goals), eg, they achieved more first serves and their consistency of ground strokes improved, then their feelings of pride/shame will be different to those of the performer who judges themselves on outcome goals alone (I lost).

Learned helplessness

It was Carol Dweck who first categorised performers as 'helpless' or 'mastery orientated'. Helpless performers attribute failure to themselves and see the task (stable factor) as insurmountable. 'Learned helplessness' is an acquired state or

	HIGH ACHIEVER	LOW ACHIEVER
motivational orientation	high motivation to achieve success low motivation to achieve failure focuses on the pride of success	low motivation to achieve success high motivation to achieve failure focuses on shame and worry that may result from failure
attributions	ascribes success to stable factors and internal factors in one's control ascribes failure to unstable factors and external factors out of one's control	ascribes success to unstable factors and external factors out of one's control ascribes failure to stable factors and internal factors in one's control
goals adopted	usually adopts task goals	usually adopts outcome goals
task choice	seeks out challenges and able competitors/tasks	avoids challenges; seeks out very difficult or very easy tasks/competitors
performance	performs well in evaluative conditions	performs poorly in evaluative conditions

Fig. 25.15 SUMMARY OF BEHAVIOUR ASSOCIATED WITH ACHIEVEMENT MOTIVATION

condition related to the performer's perceptions that they do not have any control over the situational demands being placed on them and that failure is therefore inevitable (ie, they are 'doomed to failure'). After experiencing initial failure as a result of their perceived lack of ability (internal factor) in relation to the very hard task (stable external factor) they inevitably give up trying.

Characteristics of self helplessness

- it can be **specific** to one activity or **general** to all sports
- performer is outcome orientated
- it usually results from previous bad experiences
- attributions to uncontrollable stable factors
- perceptions of low ability (feels incompetent)
- rarely tries new skills
- experiencing initial failure in new skills supports perceptions of limited ability
- feelings of embarrassment
- future effort is limited (why bother? I'm no good).

Interestingly it has been noted that often both teacher or coach and performer attribute success or failure to different reasons. Research has shown that when attributing reasons for our own behaviour we tend to relate it to external factors and when attributing reasons for others' behaviour we tend to relate it to internal factors, such as lack of effort or poor ability. These differences in the application of attributions between an observer and performer are known as fundamental attribution errors. It is important that teachers and coaches are aware that this can happen.

The teacher or coach has a very important role to play in preventing the formation of, or changing, inappropriate attributions in order to develop achievement motivation. It is important that when giving feedback to performers the teacher or coach does not negatively influence the performer's interpretation of success or failure by emphasising their lack of ability in relation to the task. If the teacher or coach implies that whatever the performer does they will never achieve the task then this could lead to the performer experiencing even greater levels of 'learned helplessness'.

A performer's lack of success should be attributed to problems with lack of consistency in technique, limited understanding, bad tactical decisions, lack of experience or insufficient effort. By attributing failure to things that are within their control, ie, things they can do something about, motivation can be maintained through the development and setting of realistic mastery goals in relation to the task. The performer will not become frustrated, behave badly or aggressively and become de-motivated.

Getting performers to realise that failure is not inevitable and teaching them how to make appropriate attributions with regard to their performance, especially when they are possibly already experiencing 'learned self helplessness' is called 'attribution retraining' and is an important responsibility of the teacher or coach. In her research Dweck reported that 'attribution retraining' was even more effective than initial performance success in ensuring that performers deal more effectively with failure.

Strategies for attribution re-training

- individual attention
- emphasise task goals
- monitor performer's attributions
- ensure teacher or coach's attributions do not make negative inferences.

One interesting factor to emerge from Dweck's work (and also emphasised by Gill) is that in heavily influencing the appropriateness of attributions for success or failure in children teachers and coaches have to be careful not to subconsciously infer gender inequalities; via their expectations of success teachers can considerably influence young children's perceptions of their ability to achieve in and deal with situations.

It is also important that teachers and coaches are relatively honest in their approach to performers. There is no point in being unrealistic in the attributions given for success or failure. Young children in particular are relatively astute in perceiving their own levels of competence in relation to what is being asked of them. They need to know that they have the necessary skills to achieve the task even if their initial failure is attributed to a lack of effort. They must be confident in their own ability. If failure is as a result of a performer's limited ability then it is important that the teacher or coach re-defines the goals/targets in relation to personal achievement, fitness, etc, rather than set goals which rely on comparisons (performance goals).

Self efficacy

It was Albert Bandura (1977) who put forward the concept of self efficacy claiming the concept to be one of the more important explanations of success or failure. In his research he considered how a performer's self confidence can affect their motivation and ultimate performance. Bandura stated that whilst self confidence can be viewed as a global disposition it is not always general but often specific to certain situations. Self efficacy is seen as the belief in one's ability in relation to a specific task in a specific situation. In its simplest form self efficacy = situation specific confidence.

Picture the team captain who is very confident during the match, coping with every demand. Yet the same person is lacking confidence and feels intimidated when asked to speak to TV reporters after the game or speak at the after-match dinner. Generally in this context 'self efficacy' relates to the number of similar activities in which the performer feels efficacious.

Imagine again a young swimmer. She may have high levels of self efficacy when swimming in the shallow end of the pool, when she knows she can touch the bottom if needed. She may not experience high levels of self efficacy when she first performs in the deep end. It is therefore important that when we try to assess a person's levels of self efficacy we are aware that, although a performer may feel confident in some aspects of a skill, they may not feel confident in others due to the variations in perceived demand and perceived ability. A gymnast may feel confident at floor work but experience low levels of self efficacy when faced with the vault.

Bandura suggests that a performer makes judgements with regard to their capabilities to perform a specific task or deal with a certain situation. A performer's perceptions of the situation related to their expected level of self efficacy will affect their:

- choice of activity (direct)
- degree of effort (energise)
- level of persistence (sustain).

A performer therefore experiences high or low levels of self efficacy in a variety of situations. Although Bandura's earlier research provided a clear conceptual model of self efficacy, claiming it to be the critical variable, later research has shown that high self efficacy alone is not enough. A performer must also want to succeed and have the capability (ie, necessary skill levels/techniques) to succeed. In addition the other cognitive processes underpinnning causal attributions will also affect the performer.

According to Bandura the expected levels of self efficacy experienced by our example swimmer would have been developed from four main sources of information. These are shown in fig 25.16 below and explained on page 458.

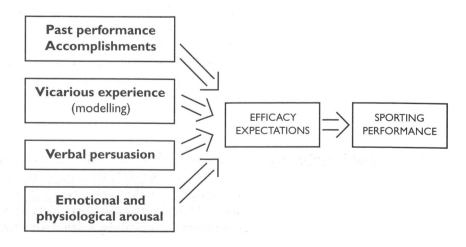

Fig. 25.16 ADAPTED MODEL SHOWING
INFORMATION THAT AFFECTS SELF EFFICACY

Past performance accomplishments

Previous successful experience or mastery of specific or similar skills involved in the particular task faced is seen as the major and most reliable predictor of self efficacy. If you have practised hockey penalty flicks or basketball free throws regularly and have taken them at critical points in previous matches then you will feel confident of scoring if a similar situation arises again. The effect would be enhanced further if your previous success was attributed to controllable factors. Practising a specific skill successfully has more effect than being told you will be able to do it by the teacher or coach. This has obvious repercussions for teaching and coaching methodologies where building up a skill and gaining early success, eg, lowering the net in netball or making games simpler, eg, short tennis, have a much greater effect on a beginner's future specific confidence and thus effort and participation levels than just telling them they can do it in the main sport. Obviously previous failure could result in low levels of expected self efficacy.

Vicarious experience

Sometimes referred to as modelling, vicarious experiences although less effective than previous success has been found to be a reliable source of self efficacy. When a performer observes a successful demonstration, particularly by someone of similar ability, they are more likely to feel confident that they too can accomplish the same task. They are less anxious and are encouraged to 'have a go' themselves.

Verbal persuasion

Teachers and coaches often try to persuade performers that they are capable of carrying out certain tasks. I have spent a considerable amount of time in gymnastics lessons encouraging students to attempt a certain vault, explaining that it will be perfectly safe, etc, in order to try and boost their confidence. In the majority of situations this type of social persuasion (see social learning theory, page 463) can work, although its effectiveness very much depends on who is doing the persuading (see attitudes, page 418).

Occasionally teachers or coaches may distort results or levels of truth (KR) in order to persuade performers that they are better than they are. They must be careful not to undermine their credibility. The learner/performer must have trust in them (significant other) and value their opinion.

Emotional arousal

Very often performers perceive their 'natural' physiological arousal effects as being something negative. 'Why am I sweating?' 'Why is my heart beating faster?' 'Why am I breathing quickly?' Rather than interpreting these naturally occurring effects as signs of being ready and prepared physiologically for the activity performers often view these as being signs of physiological stress. They think they are not prepared. Bandura saw this as having a negative effect on their self efficacy. They feel ill-equipped to carry out the activity.

ACTIVITY 12

Think of an activity/game that you or your group/team have taken part in and consider all the things that caused you initially to lack confidence. It may be that you still do. Make a list of all the causes of your lack of confidence. Now, for a different activity, make a list of why you felt very confident when taking part. Then, in relation to Bandura's model, try to

suggest as many methods as possible by which your low self efficacy could have been increased.

Consider the statement below in relation to elite sports performers such as the British Lions team in South Africa in 1997.

'Teams exhibit group or collective self efficacy. They have a group belief that they can win and perform well in the forced adversity.'

Summary

Motivation

1 Motivation is seen as energised, goal-directed purposeful behaviour.
2 Motivation is closely linked to inner drives and arousal.
3 Motivation can affect the direction and intensity of behaviour.

Arousal

1 The concept of arousal is very closely linked to motivation.
2 Drive theory states that there is a linear relationship between arousal and performance (the more the better!).
3 Inverted 'U' hypothesis suggests that the relationship is curvi-linear. Increased arousal improves performance up to a certain point. Increases in arousal beyond this optimum level will have a detrimental effect on performance.
4 Levels of optimum arousal will be different according to the complexity and nature of the specific task in relation to the individual's characteristics and the specific situation.
5 Extrinsic motivation is behaviour motivated by external rewards, tangible and intangible, or punishment.
6 Intrinsic motivation develops as a result of internal drives to achieve feelings of personal satisfaction and fulfilment (the flow experience).
7 Rewards should be monitored carefully and linked to giving information regarding a performer's level of competence.
8 Performers and coaches should have a shared responsibility in the planning and setting of achievable targets.
9 Current thinking supports the interactionist view.

Achievement motivation

1 Achievement motivation is a pre-disposition to strive for success, to persist and to experience pride in one's success.
2 Two types of motives which are likely to exist in evaluative situations have been identified: need to achieve (n. Ach); need to avoid failure (n. Af).
3 Whether a person is a high achiever or low achiever has been found to affect task selection, effort and persistence.
4 Goal setting is seen as an important tool in developing achievement motivation.
5 The adoption of task orientated goals (mastery goals) which emphasise comparisons with one's own performance rather than outcome or ego orientated goals has been found to be more effective in developing achievement motivation.

Attributions

1 The reasons performers give to explain success or failure (causal attributions) have been found to be very influential on their expectations of future success or failure, level of emotional reactions (feelings of pride or shame) and thus future achievement motivation (high or low).
2 Weiner's attribution model originally identified *two* dimensions: locus of

causality (internal or external factors); stability (stable or unstable). A third dimension of locus of control was added later. This related to whether attributions given were under the performer's control or not.

3   High and low achievers have been found to differ in the attributions they give (self-serving bias).

Learned helplessness

1   A performer who focuses on outcome goals and attributes failure to perceived low ability (internal stable factor), or success to external unstable factors (luck), all of which are out of their control, is likely to experience learned helplessness.

2   Attribution re-training, if used effectively, can help performers reduce feelings of being inevitably 'doomed to failure'.

Self efficacy

1   Self efficacy theory has provided a model for social psychologists to study the effects of self confidence on behaviour.

2   Self confidence in specific situations (self efficacy) has been closely linked to motivation and can affect choice, effort and persistence.

3   Performance success is seen as the most important factor in developing a performer's expectations of self efficacy.

R e v i s i o n   Q u e s t i o n s

1   What is meant by the term motivation?

2   How is arousal linked to motivation?

3   Outline the differences between drive theory and the inverted 'U' hypothesis in relation to arousal and performance.

4   What does a curvi-linear shaped graph infer?

5   In what ways can arousal levels affect learning and performance?

6   Explain the different types of extrinsic and intrinsic motivation and give examples.

7   Why is intrinsic motivation thought to be more effective than extrinsic?

8   What factors should a teacher or coach be aware of when using extrinsic rewards?

9   If a performer is intrinsically motivated will the introduction of extrinsic reward enhance motivation? Discuss whether you agree or disagree.

10 Explain three ways to develop intrinsic motivation.

11 What is meant by an interactionist view of motivation?

12 Give a definition of achievement motivation.

13 Explain the differences between a performer who has a high need to achieve and one who has a low need to achieve.

14 What did Atkinson mean by his formula:
n. Ach
motivation $= (Ms = Maf) \times (Ps \times [I - Ps])$?

15 How does achievement motivation affect sports behaviour?

16 What is meant by mastery/task goals and outcome goals?

17 What are the effects of emphasising one or the other on achievement motivation?

18 What are the three suggested stages of achievement motivation? Why are they important?

19 What is meant by the term causal attributions?

20 Why do sport psychologists think that attribution theory is important?

21 Explain the three dimensions identified in Weiner's model of attributions.

22 Using an example from sport explain how attributions can affect a performer's future behaviour.

23 What type of attributions might a high achiever give for their success or failure? (Give examples.)

24 What is meant by learned helplessness? And why is it important?

25 How can teachers or coaches try to alleviate the problem of learned helplessness?

26 How does self efficacy affect a performer's behaviour? Give specific sporting examples.

27 According to Bandura, what are the four sources of self efficacy? Explain their effectiveness using examples.

chapter 26

Social influences and performance

In accepting the interactionist viewpoint you should have become aware that a performer's behaviour is rarely as a result of individual factors, but usually as a result of many interrelated factors.

Every teacher or coach knows that they are not dealing with 'cocooned individuals': most sporting situations involve some form of social interaction. They have to be aware not only of the previous influences (sporting and non-sporting) of groups and teams on performance, but also that present performance is being either directly or indirectly linked to or influenced by the behaviour of others (reciprocal interaction).

This does not mean to say that we ignore all the individual factors discussed earlier in the book; rather the whole situation becomes more complicated. All the variable factors are impinging on the individual and each individual is affecting the others.

Psychologists have carried out a great deal of research into the many different ways in which sports performers interact with one another and how other people's behaviour, or the social situation in which the performance is taking place, can influence performance.

Within this chapter we will explore these direct or indirect effects and you will become aware of what is meant by the following terms and how they can influence sporting performance:

- socialisation/social effect
- social learning
- social facilitation
- group dynamics/cohesion
- leadership.

Here is a list of the terms to be covered in this chapter. It is important that you understand them.

- Socialisation
- Socialising agents
- Norms
- Values
- Roles
- Social learning
- Vicarious experience
- Observational learning
- Modelling
- Group dynamics

- The six Is
- Group structure
- Ringlemann effect
- Social loafing
- Cohesion
- Social facilitation
- Arousal
- Coactors
- Evaluation apprehension
- The 'Great man' theory

- Nature/nurture
- Emergent leader
- Prescribed leader
- Task orientated
- Person/relationship orientated
- Situation favourableness
- Contingency
- Autocratic
- Democratic

Socialisation

In global terms socialisation is seen as the life-long process of transmitting a culture by teaching and learning behaviours appropriate to the accepted norms, values and expectations of a society.

Socialisation, particularly within a sporting setting, is a dynamic process linked to the way in which people are influenced to conform to expected appropriate behaviour. Socialisation plays an important role in social integration.

General socialisation is heavily influenced by **prime socialising agents**. These are seen as:

- parents/family
- teacher/school
- peers/friendships
- coach/club
- media
- role models.

Although the parents and family are seen as the most important agents of socialisation all the others can exert a great influence in helping to create role models, real or imagined, that can be imitated. While socialisation can be considered in the global or national context of learning the **norms**, **values** and **expectations** of society, it can also be view in the more specific context of how:

- sport can act as an agent of socialisation for society in general
- performers are socialised into specific sports/teams or groups norms, values and expectations.

Sport as an agent of socialisation

Sport in its widest sense is seen by many as an important aspect of life in most societies, and therefore a fundamental component of the socialisation process experienced by the vast majority of young people. Research in this area, although often criticised, argues that performers, particularly young children, who take part in sport are being taught skills both physical (motor) and cognitive that will enable them to participate fully and effectively within society as a whole (social learning).

The focus of this research has been on personality, moral behaviour, leadership roles, character building, co-operation, social roles and so on. It has been claimed that games teach young performers to develop appropriate attitudes and values by providing specific learning experiences. It has been shown, however, that not all learning in these situations is positive. The specific type of experience is important and has to be taken into account. The increasing 'professionalisation' of sport can serve to promote the 'win at all costs' attitude, thus leading young performers possibly to imitate deviant behaviour, e.g. cheating and aggression. It has also been suggested that the traditional values and roles portrayed by sport and performers have heavily influenced gender stereotyping both in sport (e.g. female activities, weaker, less suited to sport) and outside sport. This influence is coming under increasing criticism from within society at present. It is felt that sport and physical education should be doing much more to influence the image of women positively, together with that of other equally under-represented groups in both sport and society in general.

Social learning

In the previous section we discussed the concept of socialisation through sport; the social learning perspective has been the traditional theme behind this notion. Learning is seen as taking place within a social setting in the presence of others with the learner and the socialising agent being involved in a two way (reciprocal) interaction. A person, therefore, observes other people's behaviour in various ways not necessarily through direct interaction. The behaviour is taken in, the consequences assimilated and then copied in the appropriate situation at the appropriate time.

Observational learning

In identifying observational learning, social learning theorists have emphasised a type of learning distinct from conditioning. New behaviour and attitudes are acquired by a performer in a sporting situation through watching and imitating the behaviour of others. The person who is being observed is referred to as the model and 'modelling' is a term used synonomously with observational learning. Within physical education and sport, demonstrations are often used by teachers and coaches to give beginners a good technical model to work to. Very often this also serves to help a learner's specific confidence (see self efficacy). The degree of this effect will be enhanced if the person doing the demonstration is of similar ability (team mate) (similarity) and/or is of a high status (professional performer). In addition to showing a current technical model observational learning or 'modelling' can also influence a performer's attitudes and moral behaviour by inhibiting or encouraging certain behaviour/performance (see Chapter 24, persuasive communication/attitudes, p 422).

Fig. 26.1 TOP SPORTS PERFORMERS CAN ACT AS POSITIVE ROLE MODELS FOR BEGINNERS

Teachers and coaches often hope that the consequences of disciplining a certain team member for unacceptable behaviour, e.g. substituting a player for fighting or arguing, will not only have an effect on the specific player substituted but will also affect the behaviour of other team members who are watching. The other players will **internalise** the consequences of the team mate's behaviour and are thus warned against copying it. Modelling is not always carried out either by the observer or the model at a conscious or intentional level.

Very often the model does not intend their behaviour to be copied and is usually unaware that their behaviour is acting as a model for others. The behaviour of top professional sports performers can therefore, have either positive or negative repercussions for the behaviour of beginners. Although role models are an important factor within observational learning they do not always have to be real or in direct contact. Remote sports stars, cartoon characters or fictional media related models can prove equally influential. By identifying with the model the performer will not only replicate existing behaviour but may also reproduce certain behaviour in novel situations.

People of influence in physical education and sport have to be aware that unacceptable models of behaviour or attitudes are often being presented and possibly influencing the behaviour of others eg gender stereotyping and aggression.

Although for most learners and beginners the model is known directly by the observer and is usually a significant other, eg parent, teacher, coach, team mate or professional sports person, the degree of the effect or endurance of observational behaviour will depend on several factors (see social learning and aggression, Chapter 24, p 431).

Bandura's often quoted 'Bobo doll' experiments in relation to children learning aggressive behaviour through the observation of others, led him to suggest that imitation is more than just copying a model's behaviour and depends very much on how **appropriate**, **relevant**, **similar**, **nurturant**, **reinforced**, **powerful** and **consistent** the behaviour is. Further research has also shown that the learner not only has to imitate the behaviour but also identify with the role model.

Important characteristics of models

Appropriateness

If the behaviour of the model being observed is perceived by the observer as being appropriate in relation to accepted norms and values then it will increase the probability of it being imitated. For instance in our society male aggressive behaviour appears more acceptable than female aggressive behaviour (accepted norm) and therefore young beginners/learners are more likely to copy male aggressive behaviour than female.

Relevance

Again, in relation to the young performer's perceptions of the model is how relevant is the behaviour? Young males are more likely to imitate male models of aggression than are girls as they have in general been socialised into seeing this as part of the accepted male role in society.

Similarity

By as young as three years of age youngsters are beginning to identify with their 'gender roles' and will identify more readily with similar models.

Nurturant

Whether the model is warm and friendly will have an effect on the likelihood of their behaviour, attitudes and morals being imitated. A teacher presenting an activity in a friendly unthreatening way is more likely to be taken notice of and is thus nurturing the appropriate behaviour (see styles of leadership, p 480).

Reinforced

If a model's behaviour is reinforced or rewarded in any way then it is more likely to be imitated. Again this has repercussions for the media who very often directly or indirectly draw attention to certain behaviour thus reinforcing it in the eyes of the beginner. The imitation of gender appropriate behaviour is often reinforced by parents (significant others).

Powerful

The more powerful model is seen to have a more significant effect than a less powerful one.

Consistency

The more consistent the model's behaviour is the more likely it is to be imitated. Research has shown, however, that sometimes a role model's inconsistent behaviour can inadvertently have an effect on young performers' behaviour.

A performer will take into account the above factors and evaluate them in relation to the consequences of the behaviour. These consequences can be viewed in two ways, the second more crucial than the first.

1 What were the consequences of the model's behaviour?
2 What are the perceived consequences of modelling the same behaviour for the observer (learner/beginner)?

The consequences may either be immediate or appear at a later stage.

If observers can imitate a certain behaviour at a later appropriate stage, then they are said to have socially learned it. In physical education and sport more long term learning can also occur when young performers begin to 'think', 'feel' and 'act' as if they *were* the role model rather than consciously copying technical motor skills. Over a longer period young performers can assimilate the attitudes, values, views, philosophy and levels of motivation demonstrated by significant others (teacher or coach) to ensure that they become a 'model' professional themselves.

Bandura's four stage process model of observational

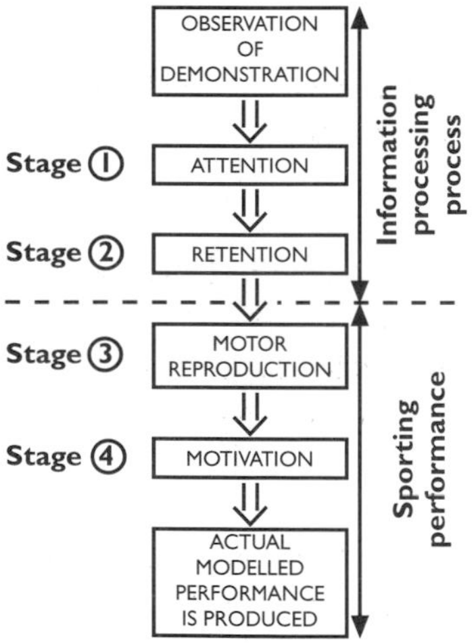

While social learning theory (and others) takes into account the effect of reinforcement, Bandura's original model referred to learning without any direct rewards or reinforcement. He argued that beginners/performers learn and behave by observing other performers or events (vicarious experience), not merely from the direct consequences of their own behaviour.

The practical application of Bandura's research into observational learning can be related to the four stages of the modelling process identified in fig 26.2. This will help teachers and coaches to ensure that learners are focused and maintain their attention in order to produce a learned competent performance.

Fig. 26.2 ADAPTED MODEL OF BANDURA'S OBSERVATIONAL LEARNING PROCESS

Stage 1 – Attention

In order to ensure that a performer learns through observing it is very important that they give careful and specific attention to the model. The level of attention paid to a model will depend on the level of respect that the learner has for the perceived status and attractiveness of the model.

Attention is gained by models that are:

- attractive
- successful
- powerful

or those whose behaviour is

- functional.

Teachers and coaches must also be aware of the beginners/learners stage of learner in order to ensure that they don't overload them with too much information. A good coach will ensure that a beginner focuses on the main points and that their attention is not distracted in any way from the task. It is important that the demonstration:

- can be seen and heard
- is accurate
- focuses attention on specific details and cues
- maintains the level of motivation.

Stage 2 – Retention

In order that modelling is effective the beginner must be able to retain the skill in their memory and recall it when appropriate. One way of achieving this is to use mental rehearsal. Another way is to ensure that the demonstration/practice is meaningful, relevant or realistic.

Stage 3 – Motor production

While a performer can pay attention and retain a clear picture of what is required of them they will in general need time to practise the modelled technique if they are to be able to carry out the skill themselves. It is important therefore, that the 'model' is appropriate to the capability level of the learner/observer: the observer must be able to act out the task.

Stage 4 – Motivation

Without motivation a learner will not carry out the previous three stages, i.e. pay attention, remember and practise the task.

According to Bandura, the level of motivation is dependent on:

- the level of external reinforcement (praise, appropriate feedback)
- the level of vicarious reinforcement
- the level of self reinforcement (sense of pride or achievement)
- the perceived status of the model
- the perceived importance of the task.

Practical application of Bandura's model

In order to make demonstrations more effective a teacher or coach should:

- make sure the learner is aware of the importance and relevance of the skill to the final performance
- refer to a high status model
- get someone of similar ability to demonstrate to help self efficacy
- make sure the performer can see and hear well
- show complex skills from various angles and at different speeds
- highlight the main aspects of technique
- focus attention on a few points particularly for beginners and children
- not have too long a delay between instruction and demonstration
- allow time for mental rehearsal
- not allow too long a delay between demonstration and mental rehearsal
- repeat the demonstration if necessary
- reinforce successful performance.

Social facilitation

As already stated in the introduction to this chapter, sporting performance is rarely carried out in total isolation. Usually our presence has an effect on another's sporting performance and the presence of others is seen as having an influence on our own behaviour and performance. Very often we are entirely unaware of these effects – thus the behaviour of a person either taking part in a physical education learning environment or performing at the very highest level is said to be influenced socially either directly or indirectly. The study of this effect is the study of social facilitation. In a sporting context the presence of others is usually thought of as the 'audience'; however, in social psychology 'presence of others' takes several different forms. The 'audience' can be **primary spectators**: those present at the event; or **secondary spectators**: those watching at home on TV or possibly reading about the event in the media. The audience can be also **passive** or **supportive**.

In addition to those watching, 'others present' can be fellow competitors, both opposition and team mates, teacher or coach. They could also be other people performing the same task or skill but not in direct competition, called **coactors**. When you practise at a golf driving range, for instance, although you are not in direct competition you are made aware of the presence and calibre of other players by your observation of the direction and length of their shots. This may influence your own efforts as though you were in competition. It has even been suggested that a performer actually training alone may have thoughts that will be enough to influence behaviour at the present time, e.g. spur them on to greater effort as they imagine someone, somewhere, checking training schedules or observing the results of training made evident in a future performance. In other words, they are performing for a hidden audience.

Although the great majority of research in this area relates to work carried out by Zajonc, the earliest recorded research was by Norman Triplett in 1898. He established that the motor performance of cyclists differed according to whether they rode alone, in pairs or groups. To further his understanding of the effect of competition on performance he supported his earlier findings by conducting laboratory testing of children performing a fishing reel winding experiment. Triplett originally interpreted his findings in relation to the competitive element involved. The children were seen as unconsciously competing with one another showing a competitive 'instinct' or 'drive' which served to increase performance speed.

However, later research e.g. Allport (1924), Dashiells (1930) suggested that it was actually the 'mere presence' of others working alongside a person performing (coaction) that was the important factor, not necessarily the competition. Allport suggested that 'coaction' may increase quantity at the expense of quality. Inconsistencies within this early research were evident with both positive and negative effects being found.

DEFINITIONS

Coaction is the presence of other people currently performing the same task but not directly in competition.

Audience means the other people present but not competing or doing what the performer is doing.

Zajonc and social facilitation

Zajonc proposed that whether social facilitation occurred, and the level to which it occurred, depended very much on the nature of the activity or task being carried out. His theory was based around the notion of drive theory. He contended that the presence of an audience in any shape or form raised a performer's level of arousal. This level of arousal would increase a performer's drive. Thus the presence of others can serve to enhance the performance of well-learned or simple tasks, but have a negative effect on poorly-learned skills, or reduce the accuracy when complex skills are involved.

A high drive state caused by the presence of an audience is likely to increase the number of mistakes made, particularly by the inexperienced or beginners, thus increasing anxiety and further increasing arousal. This will have a 'snowball' effect further increasing the chances that irrelevant or incorrect motor performance will be carried out.

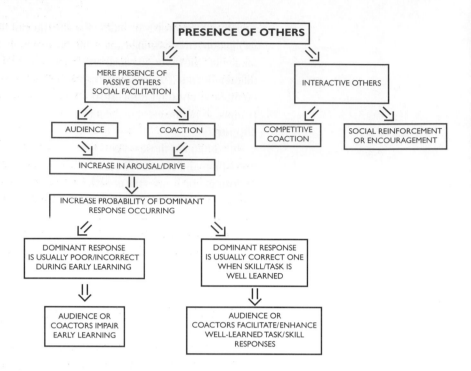

Fig. 26.3 ZAJONC'S VIEW OF THE
RELATIONSHIP BETWEEN DRIVE THEORY AND
SOCIAL FACILITATION

There are, however, several other views on the origins and effects of social facilitation. Cottrell (1968) argued that it wasn't just the mere presence of others that created higher arousal; there were different types of presence and each could have different effects on arousal (increasing or decreasing). Cottrell went on to suggest that it was more to do with a person's perceptions that they were being 'evaluated' or assessed in some way by the 'others' present that created the higher arousal.

Thus the effects of social facilitation are enhanced by a performer's feelings of **evaluation apprehension**.

Other psychologists have questioned Zajonc's model which views the audience in a passive role, arguing that there is no such thing as a passive audience (Gahagan, 1975). Research has looked at the effect of 'home' and 'away' venues and supporters on performance. While we may intuitively imagine home advantage as a bonus it has in fact been shown to have possible negative effects with players feeling increasingly under pressure due to the greater expectations of the home crowd. The effect has also been shown to vary in relation to different sports.

In relating the effects of social facilitation to cognitive factors Baron (1986, Distraction conflict theory) suggested that audience effects occur because the performer is distracted from the task. This distraction creates tension and conflict within their mind which increases arousal, leading to a greater number of errors.

In his 'self presentation theory' Bond (1982) has suggested that a performer's main aim when performing in the presence of others is to present and maintain a favourable image to the audience. With easy tasks this is not a problem, but as tasks get progressively difficult they have two problems to face. One is the complexity of the task and the other their awareness that errors made are being seen by the audience. They then become embarrassed, increasingly self conscious and possibly over anxious as a defence against social ridicule; thus concentration and attention to the task is again divided and in general even more errors occur. This effect has also been linked to the 'home and away' phenomenon mentioned earlier. Although in physical education and sport we tend to draw intuitive conclusions regarding social facilitation, several researchers have in fact advised that the effects of social facilitation are so small that this possibly negates the drive effect of arousal. The inverted U hypothesis has also resulted in many studies related to the causes and effects of arousal.

Due to the inconclusive and equivocal nature of past and current research the main conclusions that can be drawn are that well-learned skills are generally affected in a positive way by the presence of an audience. However, performance can also be inhibited. If we could make more specific predictions then we would be able to explain why even highly experienced and very often 'extrovert' players who are supposed to be able to deal with audience expectations, pressure and evaluation sometimes 'choke' in the final rounds of an important competition.

Note: for further discussion of the effects and management of stress, arousal and anxiety see Chapter 27.

Group dynamics related to sport performance

Within physical education and sport the study of groups comes under the umbrella of 'social psychology'. Research has generally shown that people tend to behave differently within the context of a group than they do as individuals. As most physical education and sporting situations, including most individual activities, tend to involve the interaction of performers the study of group dynamics is seen as an important topic. Research into small group processes in sport has generally revolved around the idea of 'teams' and how teachers and coaches can encourage them to work together to produce effective performance. It has also been related to such specific areas as group cohesion, leadership, structure, size, motivation, conformity and so on.

What is a group?

What do we mean by the term group?

At first glance it may appear relatively simple: several people who come together? A meeting of more than one person? However, does that include people waiting at a bus stop? Or all the people actually swimming at the local pool?

The main feature that helps to define a group is that the members of the group must be **interacting** in some way over a period of time.

This inter-relationship within 'the group' will involve mutual interdependence, communication and conformity to the same shared goals, norms and values. The members of the 'group' need to perceive the group's existence, be aware of its effect and that they are all members. They will therefore, have a group identity which differentiates them from other groups.

'Groups are those social aggregates that involve mutual awareness and potential interaction.' (J.E. MacGrath, 1984)

A group is '... two or more people who are interacting with one another in such a manner that each person influences and is influenced by each other person.' (M.E. Shaw, 1976)

Fig. 26.4 ALTHOUGH A CROWD OF SUPPORTERS INVOLVES MORE THAN ONE PERSON IT WOULD BE THOUGHT TOO LARGE FOR MUTUAL AWARENESS AND CLOSE INTERACTION — IT WOULD PROBABLY CONSTITUTE MANY DIFFERENT GROUPS

The six Is

Groups are seen as continually changing and developing units of people; hence the term **group dynamics**, but however they are changing dynamically groups will exhibit and can be identified by the 'six Is'. *When you think of groups think of the six Is.*

Groups have:

- Interaction (communication over a period of time)
- Interdependence (person and task)
- Interpersonal relationships (mutual attraction)
- Identical goals/norms/values
- Identity (perception of groups' existence)
- Independence.

How groups become teams

Although we have stated that groups in sporting terms would generally develop and exhibit the six Is, this process is not a short one. A coach bringing together several individuals would have to work extremely hard over a considerable period of time to develop the six Is in order to maximise performance.

In order for groups of individuals to become a 'real team' Tuckman (1965) suggested that although the time scale may differ from situation to situation they all go through four key stages of development: forming, storming, norming and performing.

Stage 1 – Forming

The individuals come together and try to find out about each other. They try to get to know and understand what theirs and others' roles are within the group. Do they belong? Can they identify with or accept the expected and perceived roles, more formal structures and relationships within the group?

Stage 2 – Storming

In this stage individual members or cliques within the group may begin openly to question certain formal group power structures and very often also challenge the status of the leader. Open hostility and stress may result as the members compete for power. The coach/teacher/leader has to work hard to reduce the effects of this situation.

Stage 3 – Norming

The group instability begins to disappear. The members begin to work together, displaying group cohesion. The members recognise the need for common goals and gain personal satisfaction from achieving tasks collectively and effectively.

Stage 4 – Performing

The members of the group now primarily identify with the team. They all have and are aware of their and others' roles within the team structure. All feel that they contribute individually and collectively to the productivity and success of the team. Each individual is said to experience psychological security within the context of the team.

Imagine you are a coach of a newly-formed team. What strategies might you employ to try to reduce the effects encountered in the storming stage? Discuss with the rest of the group. (You may find it useful to return to this activity after you have read the section on leadership, p 476.)

Structures and roles within groups and teams

All aspects of group structure are important to the effectiveness of the group or team. The structure will develop as a result of group interaction. During the 'forming stage' the group's structure will begin to develop; because of their perceptions of their own and others' expectations the individuals within the group will begin to adopt certain roles, both formally and informally. A role is the specific behaviour expected of a person occupying a certain position in the group's structure.

1 **Formal roles** – teacher; coach; team captain.
2 **Formal task or performance roles** – striker in football/hockey; goalkeeper football/netball/hockey, etc.; penalty taker (hockey/football); goal kicker (rugby); goal shooter (netball).
3 **Informal roles** – team diplomat/social roles; team comedian/joker; team 'hardman' or 'stopper'.

Roles within a team or group structure:

• only have meaning within the context of the group/team
• can be expected, perceived and acted out
• are assessed or evaluated against expected behaviour (normative)
• have a certain level of status attached to them
• can lead to 'role conflict' (a person having more than one role).

It is important that players within a team or members of a group are aware of their role (role clarity) and are prepared to accept it and function in that role (role acceptability).

The effectiveness of the team can be seriously affected if a player is unaware of, doesn't understand or is unwilling to fulfil the role expected of them by the rest of the team. This area has obvious links to intrinsic motivation and the setting of clear and specific goals by the teacher, coach or leader (see goal setting and leadership p 477).

In addition to accepting and taking on certain specific roles within the group/team, members will also adopt certain general and specific patterns of behaviour or beliefs. These are known as the **group norms**. All groups/teams will develop established norms of behaviour and performance, e.g. degrees of effort in training, codes of dress, ways of celebrating or certain aggressive styles of play. Performers and coaches will have different ways of ensuring that team members conform to these norms. These could involve either formal sanctions, e.g. fines for being late, substitutions or suspensions, or informal sanctions, e.g. the social pressure of being made fun of, etc. It is very important, therefore, that the teacher or coach establishes clear expectations of behaviour (norms) in order to ensure the highest standards of performance possible within a positive and supportive climate. It is, however, the team members' perceptions of these norms and roles which will be the main influence on whether a positive team climate is established.

Adherence to specific group roles and norms in relation to the task can have a possible negative effect by inhibiting individual flair and development. Groups can also begin to be over comfortable with the situation and limit their effort.

Having looked at how groups are formed discuss in your groups the types of problems, both positive and negative, that managers or coaches may encounter by bringing into their teams big 'named stars' from different teams.

Establishing effective group performance

In modern day performance-orientated sport it is essential that the teacher or coach can develop the highest standards of performance possible. The **process** of bringing together talented individuals that interact effectively to produce successful teams is central to the role of a teacher or coach.

We often hear generalised statements from coaches and the media, such as:
- **'They are a team of individuals!'**
- **'They were all playing for themselves.'**
- **'They were the most talented team on paper.'**
- **'The best individuals don't always make the best team and win leagues.'**

Look at the above quotes and discuss what you think they mean. What are the implications for the potential success levels of the teams involved?

Although most sports coaches would support the notion that bringing together the most talented players or performers would increase their chances of team success, they are also aware that this does not guarantee success. Following your discussions in the activities above, you will appreciate some of the pitfalls involved. In trying to account for this problem theoretically, Ivan Steiner (1972) suggested the following theory and model of group productivity.

Steiner's model

As a result of his research Steiner suggested that a successful team is often more than the sum of its parts (individual talents). Equally so an unsuccessful team is often less than the sum of its parts. The team's **actual productivity** (best level of performance) is equal to its potential productivity minus process losses due to poor team co-ordination, use of resources (talent) or limited motivation.

Actual productivity = potential productivity − losses due to faulty group processes
Potential productivity = quantity and quality of the group's resources relevant to the task

Resources relevant to the task include:

- an individual player's motor, physical and perceptual abilities
- an individual player's skills level
- group skill levels
- individual/group knowledge/experience
- individual/group physical/psychological resources – size, weight, fitness
- individual/group mental (cognitive) resources.

Socially identified resources relevant to the task include:

- age
- education
- religion
- occupation
- race
- gender
- socialisation.

In assessing a group's potential a coach can either average out or total up the attributes of the individuals concerned. However, the notion that the team possessing 'more' will perform better (whilst being a 'gut reaction' and one that usually rings true) is not always correct. According to Steiner's model, individual ability and skill level is probably the major influence on potential success thus the team with the best individuals has the greater **potential** for success. This very much depends however, on the type of activity, specific skill and the level of expected play (recreational/fun) or performance. The coach's job is, therefore, to ensure that the talent resource available is used effectively and that potential process losses are minimised. Only when this happens will **actual productivity = potential productivity**.

Problems with the group process

Very often the underdogs can outshine the top team due to problems with co-ordination of the relevant resources available (process faults).

Process faults can be of two types, either:

1 **Co-ordination losses:** team work/strategies break down or are not understood or are ineffective. Coaches of very complex team games, e.g. basketball or netball, very often blame a team's inability to maintain their 'shape' as a reason for losing a game.
2 **Motivational losses:** individual or group loss of confidence, perhaps all team members may not be giving 100 percent effort or individuals are relying on other 'star' players.

Different sports require different resources and levels of interaction. Consider the following sports and answer the questions.

rugby   bowls   synchronised swimming   cricket   athletics volleyball   tennis (doubles)

(a) What do you think would be the valuable physical and mental resources needed to help develop potential success?
(b) What would be the potential problems (process faults) that a coach may have to deal with?

Group co-ordination and co-operation

When working together as a pair (e.g. a tennis double) or as a group, research has shown that the most effective teams include not only talented players but players that complement each other. In activities that require complex levels of interaction such as basketball, rugby, **co-operation** between team members is essential in order that intricate tactical manoeuvres can be carried out effectively. It is also essential that team members can rely on each other to do their own job and not interfere with someone else's efforts. Very often in hockey and soccer, skilful forwards will feel isolated and possibly starved of chances because the midfield are not doing their job in getting the ball 'up front' quickly enough. They therefore decide to go back and 'help' to do the job of the midfield players. The midfield players may well now win the ball but are unable to release it forward as there are no forwards in position to give the ball to.

Group size

The size of the group is also thought to be a problem affecting 'productivity' that has to be addressed in terms of both co-ordination and motivation. In developing a successful team the teacher or coach needs to harness the talents of many individuals, but how many is always a problem. There comes a point in a team's development when all the resources for potential success are in place and adding further so-called talented players may actually be unproductive. Duplication of roles and effort is not necessary as it very often leads to confusion and lack of effort. An interesting aspect of research has shown that group size has a direct correlation with group effectiveness. As group size increases there is a decline in individual effort and eventual productivity. This phenomenon was first noted over 100 years ago by a Frenchman called Ringlemann.

The Ringlemann effect

Research has generally shown that in larger groups each individual does not always give their best effort. In observing a 'tug-of-war' competition during the nineteenth century, Ringlemann noted in various events two, three, and up to eight competitors. As the groups got bigger, the individual effort within the group deteriorated. Instead of the eight-man team pulling eight times as hard as one man, they actually only pulled approximately four times as hard, thus showing a positive decline. Ringlemann showed this decline as follows: One person 100%, two persons 93%, three persons 85%, four persons 77%, five persons 70%, six persons 65%, seven persons 58% and eight persons 49% of potential.

In following up this very early and potentially worrying research Ingham and colleagues (1974) concluded that this effect first noted by Ringlemann and originally attributed to poor co-ordination (e.g. a lack of simultaneous maximal tension) was actually more related to decreased motivation.

Social loafing

The conclusions of Ingham et al. that differences or losses in actual group productivity (performance) were more likely as a result of reduced motivation has been termed social loafing.

Research directed towards explaining social loafing has grown. Latane, Harkins and Williams (1979) proposed that performers demonstrated both **allocation strategies** and **minimising strategies**. This suggests that performers *are* motivated to work hard in groups, but save their best performances for when they are performing alone or under close scrutiny, when it personally benefits them more (allocation strategies). The minimising strategy proposes that performers are motivated to give as much or as little (minimum) effort in order to 'get by' and achieve the task.

Group activities and team games provide plenty of opportunity for performers to 'loaf' and take it easy, as their individual performance is not necessarily being scrutinised or assessed. They may also feel that their performance is not bringing them the recognition it deserves, e.g. they feel 'lost' in the crowd or anonymous. Their individual performance/role is not easily identifiable. Performers within a team situation have also been shown to reduce effort as they don't wish to make it easy for less accomplished or less productive individuals to get a 'free ride'. They themselves don't wish to be seen as the 'sucker' doing other people's jobs.

Strategies for reducing social loafing

1 Identify situations that allow social loafing to occur.
2 Identify individual contributions and not just group outcomes.
3 Ensure that individuals understand the importance of their contribution and role within the team.
4 All players' contributions should be identified and evaluated individually and sometimes publicly (statistics should be kept).
5 Regular feedback on individual's contributions and effort should be given.
6 Although extrinsic rewards/reinforcements can be used to motivate individuals, eg players of the week, tackle of the week, most assists of the season, intrinsic motivation should mainly be used.
7 Ensure that players know what others' roles and contributions should be.
8 Games can be videoed to carry out observation checklists.
9 Ensure that fitness is at a high level thus ensuring that players don't feel the need to take strategic rests (loaf) at crucial times.
10 Develop variety in practice and training to ensure that players stay interested and maintain levels of attention.
11 Develop a good knowledge of each player to ensure that personal or non-game issues are not having a detrimental effect on the performance.
12 Develop team cohesion.

Cohesion

Cohesion is now generally defined as a continuously changing (dynamic) process which is shown by the tendency of a group to stay together in order to achieve certain objectives, targets or goals. An earlier and even more general definition by Festinger, Shacter and Back (1950) defined cohesion as 'the total field of forces which act on members to remain in a group'. Thus individuals are seen as being motivated to stay together as a group by *either*:

1 the attractiveness of the group, i.e. the person wants to be involved in the group and values membership; or
2 the benefits they can gain from it.

In this early research the effects of cohesion were also assessed in terms of both interactive and coactive groups. In 'interactive' teams such as basketball, soccer, netball and hockey (where there is a high division of labour and specialised skills are brought together for the good of the whole) perceived cohesion was thought to be important for success. In contrast, team cohesion was seen as less vital for coactive teams such as rowing, swimming and relay, where members rely less on each other and just have to complete their own task successfully.

Later research during the 1970s and 80s developed these two basic assessments of cohesion into two further categories, referred to as task cohesion and social cohesion.

Task cohesion relates to how well the team works together to achieve common targets or goals, i.e. win the league. The level of a team's 'desire to win' and be the best is directly linked to their level of group effort and teamwork.

Social cohesion relates to how much the members of the team like each other and integrate socially (interpersonal attractions among members).

Research in this area has raised many questions along the following lines.

1 In order to be successful do teams need to have both task and social cohesion?
2 Is one more effective than the other in developing success?

Albert Carron (1982) proposed a conceptual model in order to highlight the many pre-existing variables (antecedents) that could influence the development of group cohesion. Carron's framework highlighted four major categories of antecedents that contribute to group cohesion:

* **situational/environmental elements** (usually consistent), e.g. group size; age; contracts; geography
* **personal elements**, e.g. similar/dissimilar; gender; motivational reasons, i.e. task, affiliation, self
* **team elements**, e.g. desire for success; shared team experiences (winning and losing can both create cohesion)
* **leadership elements**, e.g. decision-making style adopted; participative style helps create cohesion (see leadership, p 480).

These four categories of antecedents were seen as affecting both 'task' and 'social' cohesion in relation to either the group or the individual. Thus whilst the team's objectives may be the same for all, the individual motives for joining and maintaining the group may well be different.

Taking this view, later research by Carron (1988), Widmeyer et al. (1985, 1990) began to look in more detail at this apparent circular relationship between

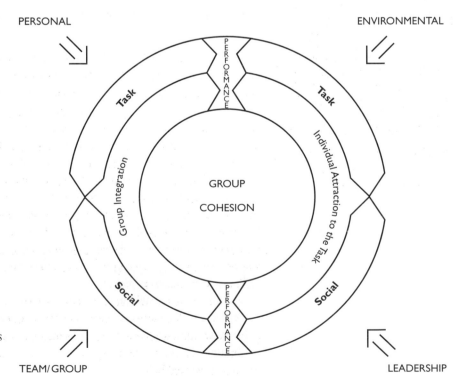

Fig. 26.5 An illustration of both the reciprocal and circular relationship between group and individual perceptions on group cohesion and the influencing variables

success and cohesion, suggesting that both group members' perceptions of the total group (group integration) and the individual's attractions to the group needed to be looked at in detail. Thus both individual and group attributions could be measured and analysed in relation to whether they were either task or socially orientated.

What this research has shown is that there appears to be a more positive relationship between task cohesion and performance than between social cohesion and performance. Thus, groups performing at the highest professional levels are very often able to put aside their negative personal feelings for one another (poor social cohesion) and work incredibly hard to promote the team effort and performance in order to win (high task cohesion). Questions have been raised, however, as to whether this is because individuals perceive co-ordination and interdependence on one another as being essential for success and thus work hard to ensure it happens, particularly in interactive team sports rather than coactive sports.

Leadership

Before you read on, what specific and general qualities do you think a leader needs to possess to make them a good leader? Compare your list with the rest of your group. Are they similar? Choose a leader to write them up!

The study of leaders and leadership has always been based on the assumption that the leadership of a group, e.g. team captain, teacher or coach, is a crucial element affecting overall group performance. Thus leadership is seen as any behaviour that moves a group closer to attaining its goals.

Leadership is: 'the behavioural process of influencing individuals and groups towards set goals.' (J.L. Barrow, 1977)

This view probably includes all or most people's ideas of what constitutes the role of leadership in all areas of society, not just sport. We all feel that a leader is good at making decisions and has good interpersonal qualities such as a high level of communication skills. They can motivate by giving appropriate feedback and are generally tactful and diplomatic. They are confident, show initiative in being able to organise and direct the group, giving good instructions and advice.

The leader must know what the goals and objectives of the group are (have vision) and be able to organise and structure the situation in order to achieve them. In order to achieve targets a leader should be seen as part of the group. The leader should have all the qualities, skills and beliefs of the group but to a greater degree; they will, therefore, tend to serve as a model for the group in some way. It is important however, that a leader does not appear too remote or excessively advanced compared to the group, as its other members may feel that they can never achieve the standards being set.

Very often the role of leader becomes entwined with that of manager. Martens (1987) warns that these two roles, whilst very often being carried out by the same person, are actively different. He views leaders in a sporting situation as having a significant impact on both the sports performers' actual performance and their psychological well being.

Fig. 26.6 A GOOD LEADER IS ABLE TO ARTICULATE AND EXEMPLIFY THE GOALS AND VALUES OF THE GROUP

Theories related to leadership: Nature or nurture?

Three general groups of theories have emerged relating to the effectiveness of a leader. As in most of the topics we have discussed, the traditional early research into what makes an effective leader was carried out from either a trait or behaviouristic perspective.

Effective leadership was believed to be as a result of specific innate personality characteristics. Thus the theory of the 'great man' emerged (Carlyle, 1841) which fostered a belief that great leaders, more often than not men, were born not made. Trait theory suggested that certain personality and physical attributes such as height, weight, physical attractiveness, self confidence, intelligence and sensitivity might be associated with leader success. If this view were true, then we would assume that the same leaders would be effective in all situations. Do you think this is true for all sport?

In discussion with your group, try to think of examples of sports which have individuals strongly associated with them, possibly from your own personal experience. Is the leader on the field necessarily the leader off the field? Do different types of situations require different types of leader? If so, why?

It may be true that the particular traits identified are all useful or necessary, to some degree, for leadership to be effective. Penman, Hastad and Cords (1974) identified a positive correlation between successful coaches and behaviour tending towards an authoritarian style of leadership. However, a person possessing these particular skills or abilities is not necessarily guaranteed to be a good leader. Research has generally proved inconclusive in identifying consistent personality characteristics, ie leaders are not consistently found to be particular kinds of people who differ in predictable ways from non-leaders.

Disillusioned with the shortcomings of the trait approach psychologists began to adopt a more situational approach to their research. The situational approach recognises that the leaders and group members are involved in a variety of roles according to the demands of the situation. Different kinds of leader may be needed for dangerous and technically demanding situations, particularly if large numbers are involved. Developing out of this view the interactional approach proposed that the effectiveness of leadership is as a result of both situational and individual factors.

While not ignoring the leader's personal characteristics, the interactional approach stresses their appropriateness to the group in a given situation. Thus what the group's goal or task is will be highly influential in the selection of the right type of leader – someone who can fulfil the specific demands of the situation. It also acknowledges that there is more than one way of becoming a leader. Two ways in which leaders develop or are validated have been suggested.

1 **Prescribed leaders** – in a more formal situation the leader is assigned by a higher authority and imposed on a team or a group. The captain of the English cricket team is appointed by the T.C.C.B.
2 **Emergent leaders** – a leader who achieves their status or authority by having the support of the group usually emerges from the group as a result of having the appropriate skills, knowledge or expertise that the group members need or value.

(a) What do you think might be the problems you would encounter by being either a prescribed or emergent leader?

(b) Do you think there may be possible advantages to being either a prescribed or emergent leader?

(c) Do you think either may be more appropriate for specific situations or types of group?

(d) Do you think there could be times when a group would withdraw their support for a previously emerged leader?

(e) Do you think there may be times when individuals become leaders for the wrong reasons?

Discuss your ideas with the rest of the group.

Whether a leader emerges from the 'pack' or is prescribed from above they will still exert their influence among the team or group by virtue of their personal qualities which we highlighted earlier. Leadership is generally seen as very complex social interaction.

Fiedler's contingency theory of leadership

Tentatively linked to the original trait theory, Fiedler's contingency model (1967) tried to analyse and explain the apparent link between a leader's personal qualities or leadership style and the situational requirements of the task. He emphasised that the effectiveness of a leadership style is contingent (dependent) on the overall situation and can't just be determined by assessing the leader's traits or behaviour. He identified and used two types of leadership style to highlight his findings.

1 **Task centred leader** – a leader who focuses on setting goals; getting the task done; meeting the objectives; performance and productivity.

2 **Relationship centred leader** – a leader who focuses on developing and maintaining good interpersonal relationships, is considerate and permissive.

According to Fiedler, how effective each of these styles of leadership was depended on the 'favourableness' of the situation, i.e. certain situations suit certain styles of leadership. The 'favourableness' of the situation depends on three factors.

1 The quality of the leader's relationship with the rest of the team or group.

2 The leader's position of power and authority and resources available for them to use to carry out the task.

3 The structure of the task itself.

Although Fiedler's contingency theory was not directly a sport specific model, the variety of situations in which it was tested included a basketball team. What the theory demonstrated was that in order to be effective teachers and coaches must be able to adapt their style of leadership according to the favourableness of the situation.

For a teacher or coach a highly favourable situation would be one in which:

• the teacher or coach has good/positive/warm relationships with their students or community

Fig. 26.7 A TEACHER WHO IS NOT TRUSTED, LIKED OR BELIEVED WILL NOT BE EFFECTIVE

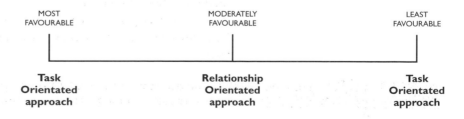

Fig. 26.8 CONTINUUM TO SHOW THE RELATIONSHIP BETWEEN SITUATION AND LEADERSHIP APPROACH

MOST FAVOURABLE	MODERATELY FAVOURABLE	LEAST FAVOURABLE
Task Orientated approach	**Relationship Orientated approach**	**Task Orientated approach**

- there are clear discipline structures
- the teacher is highly respected and has power and authority
- the parents/community are very supportive
- the institution has excellent all round facilities
- the calibre of the students is high
- the students have good levels of motivation to achieve the task/skills
- the task is clear/unambiguous.

A moderately favourable situation would be one in which:

- the teacher or coach has friendly relationships with students
- the venue is an urban school or club
- limited facilities are available
- good parental support is offered.

The least favourable situation would be one in which:

- there are poor relationships with group or community
- the task is unstructured
- the leader's position is weak
- there is no community support
- there is a poor discipline structure
- there are only poor facilities.

As can be seen in fig 26.8 above a task orientated approach adopted by a teacher or coach will be more effective in either highly favourable or least favourable situations, i.e. the extremes of the continuum. A relationship orientated style is thought to be more effective in a moderately favourable situation. By adopting or emphasising a certain style of leadership, a teacher or coach does not necessarily exclude any other ways of dealing with the players or group members.

What teachers and coaches must keep in mind is that leadership, particularly in a sporting environment, is a highly dynamic process. More recent research has suggested that there are many more variable factors to consider when deciding on which style to adopt, e.g. gender, motives, abilities, previous experience, level of learning of both individuals and the group as a whole, as well as the demands of the situation.

Styles of leadership

We have already identified several leadership styles. Two of the more popular styles being task orientated (focus on task production) and personal relationship orientated (concern for people). Also refer back to the section on teaching styles in Chapter 23.

Different styles of leadership were identified as early as 1939 by Lewin et al. In their investigations of adult leadership styles on 10-year-old boys attending after-school clubs Lewin used three basic styles. Different groups of boys experienced different styles of leadership.

Autocratic leaders

This type of leader adopts a very authoritarian style generally based on strong rule structures. They tend to be very inflexible, make all the decisions and rarely get involved on a personal level with the group or team members (remote). They are usually very task orientated.

Democratic leaders

This type of leader only makes decisions after consulting the group. They are usually more informal, relaxed and active within the group than the autocratic leader. In addition, they show a keen interest in the various people within the group. They are prepared to help and explain appropriate feedback and encouragement.

Laissez-faire

This type of leader leaves the group to 'get on' by themselves and generally plays a passive role. They do not interfere, either by directing or co-ordinating. Being generally unsure of the task they tend not to make or give any positive or negative evaluations.

The results put forward by Lewin et al. were specifically related to patterns of aggression and co-operation. Those boys in the group with the autocratic leader tended to become aggressive with each other, working independently and in competition with each other. They also worked hard when the leader was present and were generally submissive to the leader.

Those boys with the democratic leader were more consistent in their approach to work – although less work was completed it was of a similar quality. They related better to one another. They were generally more interested, cheerful and co-operative, altogether more amenable and continued to work when left alone.

The boys in the *laissez-faire*-led group were also generally aggressive towards each other, being restless and easily discouraged. They also produced very little work.

Lewin et al.'s study indicates that leadership style is a more important factor than personality, i.e. that democratic leaders are apparently more effective. Further research and critics (e.g. Smith and Peterson, 1988) have argued that the 'effectiveness' of leadership style depends on what the targets or set criteria are. If measured in terms of productivity then the autocratic leader would have been the more effective as that group produced the most work, but only when directly supervised. The implications of this may be that performers used to an autocratic style of leadership/coaching/teaching do not take responsibility for themselves when the leader is not present. In addition an authoritarian leadership style may lead to hostility. Alternatively, if the effectiveness of a leadership style was judged on developing good group mood, co-operative behaviour and steady work then the democratic style was best. The fact that the third group hardly did any work at all indicates however, that leadership of some sort is important. This is definitely the case in sport where the *laissez-faire* approach is generally not recommended.

Chelladurai's multi-dimensional model of leadership related to sport

There has been a great deal of research to try to apply the many non-sporting contingency models and theories to the sporting setting. The so-called 'unique' characteristics of sporting teams/groups, however, together with a lack of specific support and application success, suggested that a more sports-specific model of leadership was required. By bringing together the many positive aspects of different research and contingency models Chelladurai put forward his sport specific multi-dimensional model in 1980. Through this model he argued that the style adopted by a leader in sport, and its relative effectiveness, depended not only on the demands and constraints of the situation together with the characteristics of the leader, but also on the characteristics and demands of the group. Thus more detail was added to the effectiveness 'melting pot'. His model suggests therefore, that in order to achieve

- high performance levels and
- good group team satisfaction

(both Chelladurai's measures of effective leadership), a leader has to be even more dynamic and changeable in relation to the characteristics of the situation, leader and group. These types of interdependent behaviour will help to produce the required outcomes.

1 **Required behaviour** – the type of behaviour appropriate to or required by the situation or task, eg teachers are expected to conform to certain norms and express certain accepted values.
2 **Preferred behaviour** – the type of behaviour preferred by the group or performer. Different groups will demand different things from the leader, ie achievement of performance levels (task orientated) by some or fun and enjoyment for others, eg professional sports team and an over 60s keep fit class.
3 **Actual leader behaviour** – the behaviour shown by the teacher or coach in a specific situation. This is usually as a result of group preferences and situational demands.

The more that the actual behaviour of the teacher or coach matches that of the behaviour preferred by the group and is demanded by the situation (high congruence) then the greater the probability that the desired outcomes will be achieved, ie the performance will be of a high quality and the group will experience enhanced levels of satisfaction and enjoyment. Thus leadership will have been effective, but only in that specific situation.

The many and various factors (antecedents) which can influence the three dimensions of effective leadership can be seen in fig 26.10, which highlights the main finding of leadership research that there is no ideal or perfect type of style that is guaranteed effective in all situations. A leader must adopt and adapt the style according to the group and the situation.

Research into performers' preferred styles of leadership have been rather inconclusive and open to cross interpretations and criticism. The research has however helped to give the sports profession and sports psychologists in particular certain insights into preferred notional styles.

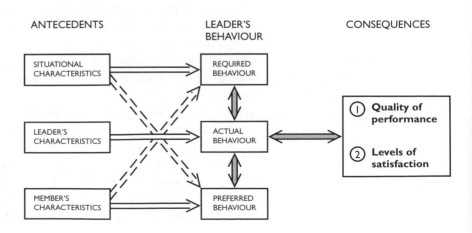

Fig. 26.9 An adaptation of Chelladurai's multi-dimensional model (1980)

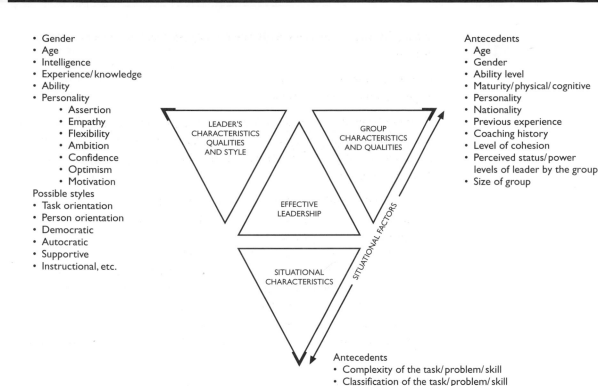

- Gender
- Age
- Intelligence
- Experience/knowledge
- Ability
- Personality
  - Assertion
  - Empathy
  - Flexibility
  - Ambition
  - Confidence
  - Optimism
  - Motivation
- Possible styles
- Task orientation
- Person orientation
- Democratic
- Autocratic
- Supportive
- Instructional, etc.

LEADER'S CHARACTERISTICS QUALITIES AND STYLE

GROUP CHARACTERISTICS AND QUALITIES

EFFECTIVE LEADERSHIP

SITUATIONAL CHARACTERISTICS

SITUATIONAL FACTORS

Antecedents
- Age
- Gender
- Ability level
- Maturity/physical/cognitive
- Personality
- Nationality
- Previous experience
- Coaching history
- Level of cohesion
- Perceived status/power levels of leader by the group
- Size of group

Antecedents
- Complexity of the task/problem/skill
- Classification of the task/problem/skill
- Type of team/group/individual/sport
- Interactive or coactive sport
- Goals: organisational/management/performance
- Socio cultural environment
- Size of group
- Time demands/restrictions
- Resources/facilities
- Coaching/results history

Fig. 26.10 AN INTERACTIONIST MODEL SHOWING THE MANY COMPONENTS OF EFFECTIVE LEADERSHIP

1 **Slightly older performers** with well developed (mature) physical skills tend to prefer a more autocratic style of coaching. Equally, as performers get older, they tend to prefer or require a more socially supportive coach.

2 **Elite athletes** tend to prefer a coach to take over control and responsibility for their training. They feel this helps them to achieve their goals more effectively (high task motivation). They have also been shown to prefer high levels of social support in a more democratic atmosphere.

3 **Beginner/novice performers** generally prefer a low level of heavy instruction and training.

4 **Male sports performers** prefer coaches or teachers to demonstrate high levels of autocratic behaviour together with high levels of instructional and training behaviour. They also prefer their coach to be more socially supportive than do female performers.

5 **Female sports performers** tend to prefer teachers or coaches to be more democratic enabling the performers to participate more in the decision making process.

6 **Team sports performers**, particularly those who take part in interactive activities like basketball, football, netball rather than coactive activities like rowing, prefer a more autocratic style with high levels of demanding training and instruction, but they also require regular rewards and praise.

7 **Coactive sports performers** have been shown to prefer a more democratic style of leadership with higher levels of social support. These findings are similar to those suggested by the path-goal contingency model.

You will have now realised that choosing the correct style of leadership according to the demands and constraints of the situation, type of group and the leaders personal characteristics is crucial for leadership to be effective. Look at the following scenarios and try to assess and explain which style of leadership you would adopt in each situation as the teacher or coach.

(a) One of your better players is having a bad game and you need to substitute them.

(b) You have been appointed as the new team manager of a top football team who have previously had the same manager for ten years. You are meeting them for the first time.

(c) You are the coach of a top international athlete.

(d) One of your team members is not playing well and is obviously distracted from the task.

(e) Your team are top of the league but keep letting in silly goals.

Summary

Socialisation

1 Most behaviour in sport takes place within a social setting.

2 Socialisation is the general continuous process of transmitting a culture to people and teaching them behaviour appropriate to the accepted norms, values and expectations of society.

3 As a member of a sports group/team a performer can be socialised into the 'modelled' norms of that sub-culture. These can be carried over and influence behaviour outside the sporting situation.

4 The family is the most important 'prime' socialising agent. However, teachers, coaches and high status models and peers can also heavily influence a performer's behaviour.

Social learning and observational learning

1 Social learning theory advocates that we learn and acquire new behaviours and attitudes, both acceptable and unacceptable, as a result of vicarious reinforcement through observation and imitation.

2 Observational learning can take place without intention.

3 The effect and level of social learning through observation is increased if the model is of a high status and their behaviour is reinforced.

4 Demonstrations are an important aspect of observational learning.

5 The process of observational learning involves attention, retention, motor production and motivation.

Social facilitation

1 Social facilitation is the arousal effects that the presence of others, either audience or coactors, has on a person's level of performance.

2 The presence of others will increase the probability that the dominant response occurs by increasing levels of arousal – this observation is based on the drive theory. For beginners or those with poorly learned skills the dominant response will generally serve to inhibit performance. For experts or those performing well-learned tasks the effect will generally be to enhance the quality of the performance level.

Group dynamics

1 Group dynamics are inter-group processes such as cohesion, communication, power roles, leadership and social facilitation.
2 A group in sport has a collective identity and a sense of shared purpose and objectives. It involves interpersonal attraction, person and task interdependence and very often structured levels and modes of communication.
3 Groups are characterised by the Six Is.
4 Effective groups/teams are formed in four stages: forming, storming, norming and performing.
5 Teachers and coaches are continually striving to enhance the performance of groups/teams by bringing together the best individuals.
6 Group productivity = potential productivity − losses due to faulty group processes. Therefore, although the best individuals do usually make good teams, good performance is not always guaranteed.
7 The Ringlemann and social loafing effects have been used to explain the effects of increase of group size and reduced motivation on group effectiveness.
8 Social loafing often occurs when within a team, a player loses their sense of identity and individuality. Social loafing can be reduced by *increasing* personal responsibility, identifiability and social incentives.

Cohesion

1 Debate over the effects and results of cohesion is still going on but generally success is more likely to result in cohesion than derive from it.
2 Team cohesion is a dynamic process whereby the members of the team are motivated to stay together as a group.
3 Groups are motivated to stay together and work together for either task and/or social orientated reasons.
4 Cohesion can therefore take the form of task cohesion or social cohesion.

Leadership

1 Leadership is any behaviour that enables a group to attain its goals.
2 Emergent or prescribed leaders possess a variety of characteristics which are both innate and learned, but there are no specific traits that guarantee a good leader.
3 Effective leaders learn to be both task orientated and person orientated according to their own characteristics/qualities and the demands of the situation, together with the demands and expectations of the group.
4 There are several models and theories of leadership including Fiedler's contingency model, which links the choice of effective styles to the favourableness of specific situations.
5 Chelladurai's multi-dimensional model is specific to sporting situations and states that optimum performance and enhanced satisfaction are more likely to occur when a leader's required, preferred and actual behaviours are consistent.

Revision Questions

1 What do social psychologists mean by socialisation?
2 What part can sport play in this process?
3 What are socialising agents?
4 Why is observational learning important to social learning theory?
5 According to Bandura what are the main characteristics of a model that influence the likelihood of imitation taking place?
6 Explain Bandura's four stages of observational learning.
7 What is the phenomenon known as social facilitation?
8 Explain the six Is related to groups.
9 Explain how groups develop through various stages.
10 What factors influence a group's productivity?
11 Why is role clarity and acceptance important?
12 How might a performer experience role conflict?
13 Explain by using a sporting example what the Ringlemann effect is.

14 What is social loafing?
15 Using an example from sport, show how a teacher or coach could try to limit the effects of social loafing.
16 Explain the trait approach to leadership.
17 Explain the behavioural approach to leadership.
18 Within a sporting context, how can a person become a leader? Give examples.
19 What advantages does the interactionist approach to leadership have?
20 Explain the three types of 'leader behaviour' suggested by Chelladurai's model.
21 What did Fiedler mean by favourableness?
22 How did Fiedler see favourableness affecting the style of leadership?
23 Using examples from sport explain the positive and negative effects of autocratic style of leadership.
24 What is a person orientated leader?

chapter 27

Optimising Performance

Within competitive sport and physical education in general performers are continually in situations which affect their emotional state. Certain emotional states can strengthen a person's motivation and enhance their performance. However, being in an energised state, creating drive and experiencing increased arousal as a result of stress can lead to anxiety, which may in turn have a negative effect on performance.

Before you read this chapter it may be beneficial to remind yourself of what is meant by arousal and its associated effects (see Chapter 25). For the past 20 years or so the inverted 'U' hypothesis has been found a more convincing explanation for predicting the relationship between arousal and performance. Below par performance is seen as a result of either too high or too low levels of arousal. However, don't forget that not all performers or sports have or need the same levels of optimum arousal.

We also considered some of the newer research in this area, for instance catastrophe theory, which suggests that the relationship between anxiety and performance does not follow the symmetrical shaped inverted 'U'.

Due to the multi-dimensional nature of arousal and anxiety many people within sport use the terms arousal, stress and anxiety synonomously and continually interchange the terms. It is important however, that we have clear definitions of these three terms in order to appreciate that although they are very closely related they are also distinct concepts. Within this chapter we will consider the nature of the relationship between stress and arousal and anxiety together with the causes and effects. In addition we will consider what effective measures can be taken to control a performer's levels of stress, arousal and anxiety.

Once you have read this chapter you should have a better understanding of:

- anxiety
- stress
- stress management
- goal setting.

Here is a list of the terms to be covered in this chapter. It is important that you understand them.

- Anxiety
- Cognitive anxiety
- Somatic anxiety
- State anxiety
- Trait anxiety
- Competitive anxiety
- A-trait
- A-state
- Competitive A-trait
- SCAT
- Stress

- Control
- Coping strategies
- Imagery
- Visualisation
- Self directed relaxation
- Progressive relaxation techniques
- Biofeedback
- Self talk
- De-sensitising procedures
- Outcome goals
- Performance goals

DEFINITIONS

Arousal is seen as a general internal state of physiological and psychological activity and alertness varying from deep sleep to intense excitement (highly energised) and is linked to the intensity dimension of motivation (see Chapter 25).

Anxiety is seen as being a negative emotional state usually associated with feelings of apprehension and worry, caused by over arousal due to a person being stressed.

Stress **is seen as being the result of the performer perceiving an imbalance between what is being demanded of them (stressors can be physiological or psychological) and whether they think they are capable of meeting that demand, particularly if failure has serious consequences.**

- Eustress
- Stressors
- General adaptation syndrome
- Stress process

- Long term goals
- Short term goals
- Goal specificity
- Realistic goals

Anxiety

The concept of anxiety is linked to the negative emotional feelings a person experiences as a result of the cognitive and physiological effects of arousal and stress (see stress, p 491). Anxiety is usually therefore associated with feelings such as nervousness, worry and apprehension. These feelings are particularly prevalent in sporting situations when winning or not losing are very important for various reasons. Related to sports psychology anxiety is usually seen as having two different components, cognitive anxiety and somatic anxiety.

Cognitive anxiety

The vague unpleasant thoughts a sports person may develop which are usually associated with concerns about under achieving are said to be the results of cognitive anxiety brought on by stress. A sports person experiencing cognitive anxiety would have problems with concentration as levels of attention are interfered with.

Somatic anxiety

This type of anxiety is usually as a result of a performer's negative perception of the body's physiological reactions to stress. A performer worries more because they perceive that a queasy stomach, increased sweating, clammy hands and so on – all the body's naturally occurring responses to increased arousal – are going to have a negative effect on performance.

For some performers the prospect of facing an 'extreme' climb, playing in their first big final or facing their first vault in a gymnastic lesson holds no real threat and creates only a slightly increased level of nervousness. They are rarely seriously unnerved by the prospect of new experiences and accept the slight apprehension as natural.

For others, however, the mere thought of being asked to demonstrate in front of a class or audience always triggers extreme arousal and serious levels of anxiety. In their research psychologists have therefore differentiated between anxiety that results from a changing 'mood state' and is usually short lived and anxiety that is more associated with a person's general characteristics or personality traits (see Speilberger's 1966 self report test: State, trait anxiety inventory – STAI).

State anxiety

In certain situations sports performers do not feel anxious at all yet in others they feel highly anxious. State anxiety refers to subjective but consciously perceived feelings of nervousness and worry as a result of increased arousal when faced with certain situations. A player's levels of state anxiety can vary in intensity from situation to situation and also at various times within the situation. For instance defending a corner in the last minute of a game you are winning 1–0 will obviously increase your level of state anxiety. State anxiety can be either cognitive or somatic and research has shown it can even be a learned response, i.e. certain situations create or cause it more than others. More up to date research has suggested that:

- somatic state anxiety is related to the performer's *perceptions* of their level of physiological arousal not arousal *per se*
- cognitive state anxiety is related to the mental appraisal of arousal – it can be both negative (telic) or positive (paratelic).

Trait anxiety

The general acquired behavioural tendency of a person to become worried or anxious, i.e. a stable characteristic, is referred to as 'trait anxiety'. A person with a high level of trait anxiety is generally predisposed to develop high levels of arousal quickly and easily. They generally react to situations with a very high and often disproportionate level of state anxiety. They have a tendency to over react in situations that the vast majority of people would view objectively as non threatening. This has been referred to by some as a possible innate response.

TRAIT

Trait anxiety
A motive or acquired behavioural disposition that predisposes a person to perceive a wide range of objectively non dangerous circumstances as threatening and to respond to these with state anxiety levels disproportionate in intensity and magnitude to the objective threat.

STATES

Arousal
A general physiological and psychological activation of the organism that varies on a continuum from deep sleep to intense excitement.

State anxiety
Moment-to-moment changes in feelings of nervousness, worry, and apprehension associated with arousal of the body.

Cognitive state anxiety	Somatic state anxiety
Moment-to-moment changes in worries and negative thoughts.	Moment-to-moment changes in perceived physiological arousal.

Fig. 27.1 TRAIT ANXIETY AND STATE ANXIETY
Source: Weinberg and Gould, 1995

Anxiety within sport (competitive anxiety)

Research in this area has shown that both state and trait anxiety can usually be measured through self report tests (eg Speilberger's STAI). State anxiety can be measured in relation to specific situations and circumstances. The general predisposition of a person to worry more, ie trait anxiety, can also be measured. The application of these general research measures to sport has shown that people in sport who are measured as having high levels of trait anxiety (high A-trait) will perceive certain situations particularly competitive situations as highly threatening (stressful). Their response will be a disproportionate one, resulting in severe state anxiety (high A-state) together with a possible inhibited performance.

 ACTIVITY 1

1 **What might sports performers find threatening in general sporting situations?**
2 **Why do you find situations in sport threatening?**
3 **Discuss your findings with the rest of the group.**

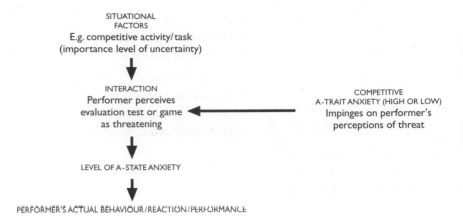

Fig. 27.2 INTERACTIONIST RELATIONSHIP
BETWEEN SITUATION AND PERSONALITY
FACTORS

Martens: sport competition anxiety test (SCAT)

It is a generally accepted view that competitive situations in sport create anxiety at varying levels in the vast majority of performers. Martens identified that certain performers suffered from this global competitive trait anxiety: a performer's tendency specifically to perceive competitive sporting situations as potentially threatening and to respond to these situations with heightened feelings of apprehension and/or tension. The SCAT test developed over five years was a simple, straightforward 15 item scale self report test (don't forget that self report tests in general have been questioned because of bias). However, it proved generally very reliable in measuring levels of trait anxiety in competitive situations and thus in helping coaches to predict a performer's probable specific anxiety state.

Martens went on to develop his SCAT further in recognition of the more up to date multi-dimensional view of the nature of anxiety: The competitive state anxiety inventory (CSAI2) had separate measures for both cognitive and somatic anxiety and has been the most commonly used within sports psychology.

As research into this area of anxiety developed, the reliability of basic pre-competitive tests as predictors of actual state anxiety and ultimately behaviour and performance is being called into question. Anxiety states, as we have already said, are changing mood states, and these have been shown to alter considerably in relation to arousal once games or competitions have started. Although many performers measure high levels of competitive A-trait this may not directly affect

		HARDLY EVER		SOMETIMES		OFTEN
1	Before I compete I worry about not performing well.	a ☐	b ☐		c ☐
2	When I compete I worry about making mistakes.	a ☐	b ☐		c ☐
3	Before I compete I am calm.	a ☐	b ☐		c ☐
4	I get nervous waiting to start a game.	a ☐	b ☐		c ☐

Fig. 27.3 EXAMPLES OF SPORT
COMPETITION ANXIETY TEST (SCAT)
QUESTIONS — A PERFORMER IS ASKED TO
COMPLETE A NUMBER OF QUESTIONS OF WHICH
THE FOLLOWING ARE SELECTED EXAMPLES.
DUMMY QUESTIONS ARE ALSO INCLUDED TO
DISGUISE WHAT IS BEING ASKED

		NOT AT ALL	A LITTLE BIT	MODERATELY SO	VERY HIGHLY SO
1	I am nervous about the competition.	1	2	3	4
2	My body feels tense.	1	2	3	4
3	I feel uncomfortable.	1	2	3	4
4	I don't feel relaxed.	1	2	3	4
5	I am confident.	1	2	3	4
6	I don't think I will perform as well as I can.	1	2	3	4

Fig. 27.4 EXAMPLES OF QUESTIONS TO MEASURE STATE ANXIETY (CSAI2) – THESE ARE RELATED TO FEELINGS EXPRESSED BY SPORTING PERFORMERS PRIOR TO A SPECIFIC COMPETITION (UP TO ONE HOUR BEFORE). PERFORMERS ARE ADVISED THAT THESE FEELINGS ARE NATURAL AND TO FILL IN THE QUESTIONS QUICKLY, NOT WORRYING OVER THE QUESTIONS THEMSELVES

Fig. 27.5 MANY INDIVIDUALS SEEK OUT POTENTIALLY STRESSFUL SITUATIONS

their anxiety state and thus actual performance. They may have learnt through experience to cope with it, or through specific psychological coaching how to reduce their own levels of anxiety.

Stress

As we have already stated, the term stress is very often used in conjunction with or instead of anxiety and vice versa. It is generally seen as a state of psychological tension produced by certain perceived physiological and/or psychological pressures or forces acting on a performer within a certain environment or situation.

Research in this area has suggested that in analysing stress as a sequential process it is important to differentiate between the performer's perceptions of stress and actual potential environmental stressors. The effects of these two aspects have been shown to be different. Additional research (Selye, 1974) has also shown, if the performer's perceptions of the situation are taken into account, that although stress is usually viewed as having a negative or damaging effect on performance and behaviour, it can also have positive effects.

Eustress (good stress)

Many sports performers such as rock climbers, hang gliders, etc. positively seek out so-called stressful situations in order to test their capabilities to the limit. Others claim that being in a relatively stressful situation helps them focus, pay attention and generally develop skills and enjoyment within the context of sport. The positive benefits in terms of self satisfaction and enhanced intrinsic motivation gained from having coped with a stressful situation are seen as being greater than the negative effects of the stress. It is, however, the potentially harmful distress or bad stress that has generally generated most of the research.

ACTIVITY 2

1 **Make a list of all the activities in sport that you feel may create eustress.**
2 **Compare your list with the rest of the group.**
3 **Is your list the same? If not, why not?**

4 Try to explain the sorts of feelings that are developed when taking part in these activities.

5 Do you think these experiences happen more during or after the activity (retrospectively)? Why?

The stress process

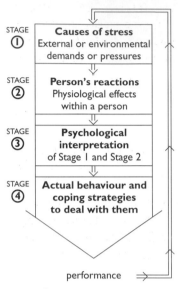

STAGE ①	**Causes of stress** External or environmental demands or pressures
STAGE ②	**Person's reactions** Physiological effects within a person
STAGE ③	**Psychological interpretation** of Stage 1 and Stage 2
STAGE ④	**Actual behaviour and coping strategies to deal with them**

performance →

Fig. 27.6 THE FOUR STAGES OF STRESS

Various sequential models (eg McGrath, 1970; Cox, 1975) have been put forward to illustrate the multivariate nature and the stages involved in the stress process. In general *four* basic stages of stress have been identified (fig 27.6).

A performer is said to experience stress when they perceive that they are not capable of carrying out a particular task. Faced with a particular situation, game or task that may have been set by the teacher or coach, a performer will make a quick cognitive evaluation of what is required, comparing this with what they think are their own abilities, skill levels and experience. The demands of the situation/task are then perceived as threatening or not depending on whether an imbalance between task and capabilities is detected.

Research has shown that problems occur because the performer's subjective perceptions of the situational demands and their own capabilities are used to evaluate the situation, not the objective or actual demands and capabilities. Different performers and athletes will not perceive demands always in the same way and, obviously, they will therefore respond and ultimately perform in different ways. Viewing stress as a sequential process has certain advantages. It has been suggested that it is a cyclic process: the performer's actual behaviour feeds back and affects their future evaluations and perceptions.

In discussion with your group make a list of all the things that you find stressful. Do you all find the same things stressful or are there differences of opinion? Why do you think this is the case?

Causes of stress

Events, constant irritations or demanding situations that confront us in daily life that lead to stress are called **stressors**. However, people's perceptions of what constitutes a stressor are different. In a tennis competition a performer who is there for the first time may perceive the experience as highly stressful. A well-established performer may not.

Within life in general there are said to be three basic categories of stressors:

- environmental
- occupational
- life events.

The general stressors a performer may have to face up to in sport are said to fall into two categories: intrinsic within the performer themselves or to do with the situation. Examples of more sports specific stressors are given below.

Competition

Competitive situations have been shown to be potentially very stressful particularly if the event is important. A cup final or a last game of the season with relegation looming are obviously potentially more stress producing than a mid season game.

Even within the context of a game there are certain periods which are more critical than others and thus potentially more stressful (see anxiety, p 488). Uncertainty within players/performers with regard to the outcome or over evaluation by others has also proved to be a serious source of stress.

Frustration

Frustration occurs when a performer is prevented from reaching their goal and can be a common source of stress (see aggression, p 429). It may be that a performer feels generally inadequate or specifically inadequate, for instance they want to be a good basketball player but are too small or they keep continually losing out to an opposition attacking player. A performer can become frustrated by external factors over which they have no control (see attributions, p 451). Frustration can lead to possible aggression and potentially even more stress.

Conflict

The very nature of physically demanding sport can lead to stress through physical contact. However, conflict in this sense usually refers to a performer experiencing two or more contradictory motives or goals. A player may have to make a decision between playing for their club or playing for a representative team or within the context of a particular game between playing safe or taking a chance and possibly risk losing the game. External influences or domestic difficulties, e.g. family social pressures, may also conflict with a demanding training schedule.

Personal

Many performers will put undue pressure on themselves thus heightening state anxiety and therefore stress. As already discussed, performers with high levels of trait anxiety (high A-trait) are predisposed to seeing sporting situations as more threatening than people with a low A-trait.

Physiological and climatic

Placing the body under severe physical, physiological or climatic strain has also been shown to create stress. Intense or unusual levels of training or playing in very hot, humid conditions can create enormous amounts of physiological stress on a performer. The perceived pressure and necessity to train at extreme levels can also lead to stress. Over using injuries can develop stress both physically and psychologically.

Audience

While some may find performing in front of an audience an exhilarating experience, others may find it extremely stressful.

Further examples of sporting stressors

- Rewards/incentives/prizes
- Prestigious events
- Representative honours/games
- Social evaluation
- 'Win at all costs' attitude
- Pre-match pep talks
- Parental pressure
- Inconsistent coaching/training
- Excessive time demands
- Repetitive practices
- Excessive expectations
- Emotional blackmail
- Concerns about self image, eg overweight.

Fig. 27.7 LONG TERM STRESS, PARTICULARLY AT AN EARLY STAGE, CAN LEAD TO BURN OUT!

Responding to stress

Having perceived an imbalance between the general or specific demands of the task and their own capabilities a performer's stress response can either be psychological (cognitive) or physiological (somatic). Their response will vary according to the degree of perceived threat. Anger, apathy and anxiety are the most common psychological (cognitive) responses to stress. When faced with an immediately threatening situation the body reacts in the short term by increasing psychological arousal.

In describing the general adaptation syndrome (GAS) Selye (1956) explained his generally accepted view of how a person's body responds to prolonged stress. Selye identified three stages of the GAS.

Alarm reaction stage

This involves physiological changes associated with the emotions of 'fight or flight' reactions. The sympathetic systems of the ANS (autonomic nervous system) are therefore activated. Levels of adrenaline, blood sugar, heart rate, blood pressure all increase. Sympathetic arousal can continue for some time after the level of stress or perceived threat has reduced or disappeared.

Resistance stage

If the stress continues the body will try to revert to normal levels of functioning thus coping with the increased adrenaline levels. Usually the level of sympathetic nervous activity decreases.

Exhaustion/collapse stage

In trying to deal with the continued stress and coping with the various hormonal changes the body has gradually depleted its own resource. The adrenal cortex fails to function correctly resulting in physiological problems like ulcers, heart disease, high blood pressure. The body is unable to fight infection and in extreme cases death can occur.

Reducing stress

Stress to a certain degree can be good for a performer or even actively sought (eustress). It is important though that the negative aspects of stress and anxiety states, e.g. worrying about not performing to our capabilities, etc. are not allowed to inhibit performance – very often performers get caught up in a downward stress cycle. Therefore, in order to optimise performance they need to be able to manage or cope with stress in order that the optimal combination of arousal related to emotions is achieved.

1 As the effects of stress and anxiety are almost unique to each sports performer it is important that the coach has an in-depth knowledge of the performer's psychological and physiological makeup.
2 In addition, the coach/performer must be aware of all the various effects and responses associated with stress and heightened state anxiety, e.g. both somatic and cognitive anxiety, before they can learn to control them.
3 The coach/performer also needs to be aware of the sources of stress.
4 Both coaches and performers need to be able to *recognise* the various signs and realise that some of these are the body's natural ways of preparing. Being aware of these effects can help to reduce cognitive anxiety at experiencing them.

SYMPTOMS OF HEIGHTENED STATE ANXIETY		
Physiological	**Psychological**	**Behavioural**
• Increased heart rate • Increased blood pressure • Increased sweating • Increased pupil dilation • Increased respiration • Increased muscle tension • Increased blood sugar • Increased adrenaline • Cold, clammy hands • Constant need to urinate • Butterflies in stomach • Constantly feeling sick • Cotton mouth • Headaches	• Worry • Apprehension • Inability to make decisions • Narrowing of attention • Limited direction of attention • Feeling of lack of control • Feeling overwhelmed • Negative self talk	• Nail biting • Rapid talking • Muscle twitching • Scowling • Pacing • Yawning • Trembling • Broken voice • Dazed look in eyes • Sleeping difficulties • Perform better in non evaluative situations

Fig. 27.8 SYMPTOMS OF STRESS, AROUSAL AND HEIGHTENED STATE ANXIETY

Measuring and recognising stress

The following are aids to assessing stress levels in performers.

1 Self report tests.
2 Observation.
3 Measuring physiological responses.

A teacher or coach must be able to differentiate between long and short term stress.

Often stress is inadvertently placed on a performer particularly young performers see further examples of sporting stressors, p 493. It is most important that teaching and coaching should be appropriate to the individual or team.

Choose a practical activity and, working through the four-stage model, write down the practical situation demands, cognitive appraisal, perceived level of threat, somatic and physiological reactions and actual behavioural performance responses under the headings Stage 1 through to Stage 4 (fig 27.6 p 492).

Managing stress

A simplistic way of viewing the management of stress is that teachers and coaches should try to:

• reduce the problem
• reduce the stress.

Reducing the problem

Direct action can be taken to alleviate the stress, for instance:

• don't enter competitions
• don't ask novices or people with high A-trait to demonstrate in front of a class
• don't set targets too high
• reduce stressors to match the appropriate levels of the performer's perceived ability, e.g. lower box/vault height
• reduce teacher/coach/parental unrealistic expectations and pressure
• don't ask performers to do dangerous activities or activities they may perceive as frightening
• de-value the importance of the competition.

Control is a key issue here. If a performer feels in control of a situation then stress can be reduced considerably, in particular cognitive anxiety. This will also help to alleviate learned helplessness.

Cognitive re-appraisal

Possible redefinition or modification are also important, that is encouraging a performer to reduce the effects of irrational beliefs, e.g. that they always have to play well. Cognitive redefinition/modification of the situation can help a performer (noting that things could be worse), e.g. the performance was worse in training. Or it could be getting them to accept that even if they lose it does not make them a bad person or a poor, incompetent performer.

Attribution retraining already mentioned can also be helpful in these situations by encouraging a performer to attribute control internally. Being in control of the situation will help a performer develop both general confidence and self efficacy. By persuading a performer to take responsibility for themselves and cope with the situation a teacher/coach can help a performer deal with any problems they may have to face. A performer can be helped to take responsibility by getting them involved in setting their own goals. Realistic short term, long term and performance goals should be negotiated. Again this should help a performer's self efficacy together with their ability to cope. Giving a performer as much information as possible about the competitive situation (their progress, goals, etc.) can help to reduce a performer's level of uncertainty.

Reducing or coping with stress

Imagery

The intervention technique of imagery has become very popular with sports psychologists. However, imagery has been used for many different purposes. As well as the control or regulation of arousal and stress management, it has been used for:

- skill and strategy acquisition (mental rehearsal)
- skill maintenance
- self imagery manipulation
- attention/pain control.

Although imagery and mental rehearsal are often closely associated some psychologists argue that there is a distinction between them.

Imagery is a basic cognitive function and is associated with long term changes in a performer's behaviour. By recalling appropriate stored information from the memory a player is able to generate images of movement experiences. In many cases this has been shown to be almost as good and effective as actual movement experience.

Imagery can be used to:

- create a mental picture of new experiences in the mind; or
- recreate a mental picture of a previous experience.

Although it is usually associated with visualisation imagery can be:

- **visual** – picture yourself being successful, e.g. hitting winning smash at Wimbledon
- **auditory** – you hear the sound of the ball hitting the racket
- **kinesthetic** – tactile, e.g. feel the power and muscular control associated with the smash

- **emotional** – imagine feelings of success, self satisfaction from the victory, confidence, etc.

Close your eyes and try to concentrate on a good previous sporting experience and a previous bad sporting experience. Try to think of the visual, auditory, kinesthetic and emotional aspects of the image.

1 Make a list of the images you can think of.
2 Compare your list with a partner's.

Did anything interfere with your ability to picture and think about your sporting experiences?

Ideally, imagery should involve as many of the senses as possible in order to develop or recreate a more distinct image. Achieving a relaxed state of attention will facilitate the use of all the senses during imagery.

By attaching emotions and feelings to the image performers can help themselves recall situations or behavioural responses more effectively. This can help in the control of current emotions and anxieties and by developing self confidence in the control of potential emotions and anxieties. Research to support the fact that imagery works explains that it is only really effective when a performer can link psychological and symbolic coding of movement patterns to psycho/neuro muscular actions.

The use of imagery to control arousal

Imagery can be used either to decrease or increase arousal. Research has suggested that imagery can help to:

- improve concentration
- reduce anxiety
- develop confidence
- control emotions.

In order to reduce arousal, images of previous situations when certain responses have had a negative effect on performance are imagined by the performer. They then try to imagine themselves dealing with and controlling the stress in different circumstances, for instance dealing with the bad call in tennis in a more positive manner, possibly linking an appropriate phrase to remind them to take a deep breath and 'stay cool' in the future. They then imagine themselves carrying out this more positive behaviour. In a more relaxed state they are then able to concentrate more on the task and not allow their overall arousal levels to get the better of them in the actual situation when and if it arises. Arousal, and thus state anxiety, can also be reduced by a performer picturing a place where they feel emotionally at ease with themselves and totally unstressed, perhaps on a beach in the sunshine or by the pool. This process has obvious links with relaxation techniques. The cognitive coping strategy of focusing on emotional images particularly related and relevant to the impending activity has been shown to be very effective in creating positive attitudes, developing confidence and achieving objectives. This has been termed **preparatory arousal**, and is commonly known as 'psyching up'.

There are two basic types of imagery: internal and external.

Internal imagery

You only see what you would see if you were actually executing the skill yourself. As a hockey player taking a penalty flick you would see the goal, goalkeeper, the ball going in the net and the kinesthetic feelings associated with your grip on the stick and stance and so on.

External imagery

You see yourself as others would see you, as though you were watching yourself perform on video. Although techniques in relation to others would be seen, as it is external there would be little kinesthesis attached to the image.

There is evidence to suggest that internal imagery is slightly more effective than external due to the fact that it helps to develop kinesthetic awareness. The general view, however, is that most performers tend to choose a style which suits them and often continually interchange between both types in order to develop the necessary clear and effective image.

Effective imagery

In order to develop effective imagery a performer and coach should ensure that:

- performers' present image skills levels are evaluated
- imagery is practised regularly and built into the daily routine of the performer
- the performer tries to use as many senses as possible to develop a vivid image
- image is controllable by the performer
- imagery is carried out in an appropriate setting (initially this may mean no distractions)
- the performer believes it can work
- the performer does not have unrealistic expectations
- the performer builds up the levels and use of imagery over a period of time
- the performer imagines both carrying out the movement and the end result
- images should not be overly long; usually the same length of time as the actual movement
- the performer practises using the image in realistic situations.

After practising and developing imagery skills an experienced performer will be able to use imagery even under potentially distracting circumstances.

Relaxation

Psychologists have suggested and researched many forms of relaxation to reduce stress. Meditation, breathing control, self hypnosis, biofeedback techniques are all ways that have been used to reduce arousal, and thus reduce stress and anxiety. What has been realised is that just telling someone to relax before or during a game is not enough. The performer needs to know *how* to relax in order that they can have self control and be able to direct relaxation when and where necessary. Relaxation skills involve both somatic relaxation learned through various progressive muscle relaxation training and cognitive relaxation through Benson's (1975) meditation techniques. Many sports performers actively use and extol the virtues of self-induced relaxation to reduce arousal levels to the optimum. Relaxation helps to inhibit panic and self doubt enabling the performer to stay calm. By helping people to sleep it also helps reduce the effects of fatigue.

Progressive relaxation technique

This technique has been regularly developed and modified by sports psychologists, although the central theme of it was first developed by Edmund Jacobson in 1938. This is generally a lengthy process whose main purpose is to reduce somatic stress by teaching performers to recognise and feel tension and then to be able to progressively reduce it by 'letting go'. Performers are asked to tense specific muscles. By learning what tension feels like they are then taught to experience relaxing specific muscles. By progressively relaxing and tensing a performer is able to develop an awareness of what tension feels like, as the two feelings are mutually exclusive. Thus, when in a performance situation, they can recognise tension and carry out the relevant relaxation of not only specific muscles but general groups of muscles in order that total relaxation can be experienced. Eventually with practice this can be a relatively quick process which can be carried out before, after or during time breaks within games. It is felt that learning to reduce body tension will serve to decrease mental pressure (stress) by allowing the player to worry less. In a relaxed state they can maintain sufficient levels of attention on the necessary techniques of the game and not on muscle tension. Ideally conditions should be appropriate to allowing relaxation to happen, e.g. quiet, subdued surroundings, lying down, loose clothing, etc. More experienced athletes, however, are able to focus and, by using 'trigger' controls, can relax almost at will.

Mental relaxation (cognitive control)

The technique of relaxation response was developed by Herbert Benson (1975). It is a form of meditation, but linked directly to sport. Again this is a lengthy process. Performers are asked to find a quiet place conducive to relaxing. Although it is difficult, in practising to try to focus the mind on one key point, very often breathing, a performer eventually learns to induce a feeling of calm and can reduce and control the attentional wandering of the mind. Eventually a person will be able to relax and concentrate or focus on one particular thing. A performer must be aware though that for many events total relaxation immediately prior to an event is not necessarily a good thing.

Breathing control

There are many general techniques for controlling breathing. Offering a means of controlling breathing has been shown to be an effective method of helping a performer to reduce muscle tension and relax. This again initially reduces the somatic effects of stress and anxiety. However, breathing control can be practised before, after or during the event in order to produce relaxation which can help with imagery, thus helping to enhance technique and performance. Practice is again necessary in order to develop the correct techniques. By consciously controlling the depth and rate of breathing immediately prior, for instance, to an important shot performers can reduce distractions. It will help to maintain their level of control and composure and thus reduce the effects of both somatic and cognitive anxiety.

Biofeedback

This technique is again linked to controlling muscular tension and helps a performer deal with long term stress. Performers are taught to control muscle tension by being attached to a machine which measures and amplifies specific internal muscular nervous action. Through practice the performer learns to relax the specific muscles that the machine is attached to by using a method that suits them; the performer is able to assess the level of tension in the muscles by the noise levels of the machine and learns to reduce it by relaxing. The machine provides objective biological feedback with regard to their success rate at reducing tension, thus helping motivation. The main point of developing this awareness is so that eventually the performer can transfer this relaxation technique to the competitive or game situation. They no longer have to rely on the machine to inform them of muscle tension, but can recognise the tension via natural physiological changes occurring. Relaxation techniques can then be applied. Biofeedback has also been developed further by some to include the voluntary control of other bodily functions such as heart rate and blood pressure.

Self talk

Self talk is linked to controlling cognitive anxiety. Interpretations and perceptions of performance during and after an activity can also have a considerable effect on either the present performance or future performance. Different interpretations and reactions can also affect our emotions and feelings. How a performer interprets their actual performance can therefore lead to stress, anxiety, frustration and anger. A performer can interpret both their good and bad performance in either a negative or positive way: this can lead to what is known as **positive** or **negative self talk**.

Positive self talk

This is used to maintain attention levels and focus positively on the task. Remaining optimistic helps a performer's level of motivation and self esteem; it can also reduce cognitive state anxiety. They are able to focus on the task and what to do better and not on worrying. Positive self talk is therefore crucial for concentration. A performer should always try to avoid the negatives can't, never and not.

Negative self talk

In using negative self talk the performer is usually self critical and undermines confidence. It serves to increase worry and doubt about future performance, e.g. the next serve. It can lead to frustration, anger and increased muscle tension. For instance, having just double-faulted in tennis the resulting negative self talk would be:

- 'What a totally stupid shot that was'
- 'What a time to double fault'
- 'I've no chance of getting back into the game now!'

This could result in smashing the racket into the ground. This performer is not concentrating on what can be done or what should be done to improve the situation. In this situation the positive self talk would be:

- 'I need to watch the ball more when I throw up the ball higher'
- 'This next one goes in'
- 'There's still plenty of time left to turn this match around.'

Thus, whilst being aware of the difficulties, this positive performer is motivated to carry on and persists. Positive self talk therefore emphasises the importance of developing and maintaining both a constructive mood and approach. It is important that a performer does not allow negative thoughts to become the focus of attention even though, because of stress, they are usually the ones that come into a player's head or mouth first, because self-fulfilling prophecy may be the result.

 **ACTIVITY 6**

For the following situations suggest two positive and two negative comments to go with them in relation to both technique and emotions.

1 A missed tennis forehand.
2 A missed penalty in football, hockey, or free shot in netball or basketball.
3 A missed putt in golf.
4 A player returning from injury has a setback in training.

In future practical situations, try to substitute a positive thought or comment for a negative one!

Very often experienced performers use cue words to trigger off positive thoughts either to reduce anxiety or increase levels of attention and concentration on specific details. Examples are as follows.

1 A basketball player when learning a new skill such as a set shot may use simple cue words like: 'flex' (knees), 'sight' (basket), 'extend' (knees), 'push' (ball forwards basket), 'flick' (wrist).
2 Tennis players or cricketers who repeatedly fail to watch the ball on the racket or bat may use self instructional cues of 'watch!' or 'ball' in order to try and break the habit.
3 A skier hitting a mogul may shout 'bend!', 'extend!' or 'down!' and 'up!' in order to remind themselves of the technique.
4 A performer can also motivate themselves, e.g. a 400 m runner coming off the last bend can shout to themselves, 'fast! fast! fast!' or 'attack! attack!' in order to help them kick for the line and keep pushing hard!

Systematic de-sensitising procedures (SD)

SD is generally seen as a procedure for learning and practising relaxation as an active coping skill for self control of anxiety. Although there has been some debate, this technique has been shown to be effective in a wide range of situations including sport. As a form of 'counter conditioning' it was mainly developed by Joseph Wolpe (1958). The main principles of the procedures are that a sports person highlights specific situations (10 to 15) that they either fear or that produce levels of anxiety associated with a specific problem. These scenarios are then placed in a hierarchical list with the least intensity of anxiety at the bottom and the greatest intensity of anxiety at the top. Relaxation techniques such as those already described are then used to deal with the least threatening but still anxiety-producing situation. When in a totally relaxed state the performer is clearly able to visualise themselves, through internal imagery, dealing successfully with this anxiety-producing situation. They then move on to dealing with the next level of threatening situation. With help and by pairing potentially stress-provoking situations with relaxation they are gradually able to work through the hierarchical list of anxiety-producing situations in their mind.

Ultimately they are able to deal confidently with situations that they previously found very stressful. Once they can do this visually without feeling anxious, the chances are they will be able to cope with the real life situations. The SD technique has been shown to work very quickly in as few as eight one-hour sessions. However, the technique does require the performer to be able to carry out relaxation and interrelated visualisation techniques which obviously require more long term psychological training.

In order for these various stress controlling or anxiety reducing techniques to be effective the performer needs to be trained to use them. This psychological skills training needs to be carried out over a prolonged period and is not just something that can be quickly taught or developed. It needs to be practised regularly as an integrated part of training and development. Mental preparation and control is now seen by many as the essential difference between successful top level performers and those who 'can't cope' and are generally unsuccessful. Many coaches have been quoted as saying that sport at the very top levels is up to 80 percent mental! It is now clearly realised that just getting a performer to practise and practise their movement skills in order to correct poor performance is often not the answer. There can be many underlying root causes of a performer's inability to carry out skills under pressure.

Goal setting

Goal setting is generally seen as an extremely powerful technique for enhancing performance. However, it must be carried out correctly. When used effectively, goal setting can help focus a performer's attention, help self confidence, enhance both the intensity and persistence dimensions of motivation and ultimately have a positive effect on performance. As can be understood from the previous section, goal setting can be used to help performers feel in control of relatively stress provoking situations and thus help them to cope with their anxieties. However, if you refer back to intrinsic and extrinsic motivation, you will understand that when used improperly the setting of goals, particularly the wrong or unrealistic goals, not only has a negative effect on motivation but can also be a significant source of stress and anxiety in the immediate performance situation. This can lead in turn to impairment, not enhancement, of performance in the long term. Goal setting should be used with caution by coaches and teachers.

According to research based around the findings of industrial research carried out by Lock et al. (1985) goals are seen as direct motivational strategies setting standards a performer is psychologically motivated to try to achieve, usually within a specific time.

In these discrete terms goal setting is generally thought to affect performance in the following way.

1 **Attention** – goal setting helps to direct a performer's attention (focus) to the important aspects of the task.
2 **Effort** – goal setting helps to mobilise or increase the appropriate degree of effort a performer needs to make in relation to specific task.
3 **Persistence** – goal setting helps a performer maintain their efforts over time.
4 **New strategies** – goal setting helps a performer to develop new and various strategies in order to achieve their goals, e.g. learning (problem solving).

Most coaches and performers in sport, and people throughout their lives in general, set goals for themselves: the secret is to set the right goals and use them in the right context. Generally, in order to be effective, goals need to provide direction and enhance motivation. Goals are also seen as playing an important role in stress management. They are the standards against which perceived success or failure are measured and thus link to present attributions of success or failure.

Types of goals

The types of goals a performer either adopts or is set by the coach (goal orientation) can have a significant effect on both the performer and ultimately the performance. In addition to subjective goals, e.g. having fun and enjoyment, and objective goals, e.g. reaching a particular standard, two further goals have been identified: outcome goals and performance goals.

Outcome goals

Outcome goals generally focus on the end product. Successful competitive results, that is winning a match or gaining some tangible reward, are usually the standard or goal set. Performers who continually make social comparisons of themselves against other performers are said to be outcome goal orientated. Winning and being successful enables this type of performer to maintain a positive self image as they perceive themselves as having high personal ability (see intrinsic and extrinsic motivation and attribution, pp 438, 451).

Performance or process goals

These generally focus on a performer's present standard of performance compared with their own previous performance, that is they are self referent. Levels of success are judged in terms of mastering new skills or beating a personal best. Developing a performance goal orientation has been shown to reduce anxiety in competitive situations as the performers are not worrying about social comparisons and demonstrating their competence. They can concentrate on the process of developing their performance further.

Sports psychologists have suggested that performers who adopt different goal setting styles (outcome or performance) set different types of practice and competitive goals that will affect future cognitions and ultimately performance.

Although it is difficult for performers in modern sport not to consider winning and losing, by continually emphasising and focusing on performance goals the coach should ensure that ultimately outcome goals are achieved.

Fig. 27.9 TELLING A PERFORMER THEY NEED TO IMPROVE IS TOO GENERAL

Goal specificity

Very often when teachers or coaches set goals for performers they are far too general. Telling a performer to 'try hard' or 'do your best' have been shown to be less effective than more specific objective goals. It is important that goals are specific, clear and unambiguous. This helps when evaluating goals as improvements can be assessed more easily.

Imagine you are the coach of the swimmer in fig 27.9 above. Rather than just saying 'You need to improve', make a list of what specific goals you think would be effective to develop their performance.

Goal difficulty

In general psychological research supports the view that difficult but realistic goals are the most effective type of goals to set. Setting easy goals has been shown to be of little value as this can result in lack of real effort and therefore motivation. Goals that are very difficult have not been shown to significantly impair performance in the long run, particularly for performance orientated athletes. However, unrealistic goals have been shown to be stressful leading to heightened arousal, high A-state anxiety, possibly frustration, reduced future confidence and ultimately poor performance. It is obviously important therefore, that teachers and coaches have a good understanding of the performer's or group's level of experience, ability and skill in order that appropriate goals can be set.

Additional factors affecting goals

Long and short term goals

Individual research into whether short or long term goals are best is somewhat equivocal. It has generally supported the view that both need to be set. A performer needs to have an overview of where they are heading. At the same time they need to have sub-goals to enhance and reinforce development towards the main long term goal. Short term goals can be used to give the performer levels of progress and achievement. Interim success can serve to develop confidence, reduce anxiety, and maintain levels of motivation. Developing psychological training goals in order to reduce aspects of anxiety such as learning relaxation techniques can be seen as short term goals within the context of overall performance.

Goal acceptance and commitment

It is important that the performer is involved in the goal setting process rather than having them set from some external source. The performer is more able to perceive the targets as fair and achievable and therefore more likely to accept them. They are also far more likely to be prepared to work towards them if they have been responsible for setting the goals in the first place. By understanding the needs and personality of the performer a coach is more aware of how much time is available for training, etc. and through negotiation they can endeavour to foster goal acceptance and commitment.

Goal evaluation

In setting short and long term goals in order to chart progression, it is important that the goals can be measured in order that evaluation can take place. Setting goals without evaluation is generally a waste of time – evaluation should be accurate and happen on a regular basis. However, if evaluation becomes excessive it could possibly lead to an outcome orientated approach rather than a performance process approach.

It may be that, in the light of progress, new short term goals can be negotiated and set. A performer may be finding the training too easy or may have achieved certain levels of success earlier than expected. New variables not thought of at first may also need to be taken into account. However, goals should not be continually changed as this may lead to a performer's uncertainty. It may also prove difficult to lower goals as performers may perceive this as some form of failure. It is important to emphasise their temporary nature and inform the performer of possible setbacks.

This point links closely with the fact that a coach must take on the following responsibilities.

1 **Develop goal achievement strategies** – there is no point in goals being set if a performer is not given strategies for reaching those goals. These strategies can actually also be the short term goals. This is where the teachers or coaches sporting specific knowledge comes into play. Running, training or skills schedules can be put into operation, e.g. a performer may have to cover so many miles per week or train for longer than 20 minutes, three times per week, etc.

2 **Log the goals** – by committing the goals to paper there is no chance of their being forgotten or misinterpreted. It can be seen as a kind of unofficial contract between performer and coach/teacher.

3 **Provide goal support** – in order to achieve certain goals the performer will need to make a certain commitment in terms of time and possibly even

financially. This may need the regular support and understanding of their families. Facilities will be needed along with possible physiotherapy and rehabilitation support. Financial backing, motivation or an occasional shoulder to cry on may be needed.

Simple principles of goal setting

1 Set specific goals	6 Develop goal achievement strategies
2 Set difficult but realistic goals	7 Consider participant personality
3 Set long and short term goals	8 Foster individual goal commitment
4 Set performance goals	9 Provide goal support
5 Write down goals	10 Provide for goal evaluation

Summary

Anxiety

1 The concepts of stress, arousal and anxiety are closely associated terms and are often used interchangeably.
2 Anxiety is a negative emotional state associated with feelings of apprehension and worry caused by over arousal as a result of being stressed.
3 There are two distinguishable types of anxiety. Trait anxiety is a predisposition to perceive situations as potentially more threatening than they are. State anxiety is the changing emotional state experienced in specific situations.
4 A person with high levels of A-trait anxiety is likely to respond with potentially higher levels of A-state anxiety.
5 State anxiety responses can be somatic or cognitive.

Anxiety within sport

1 Competitive A-trait has been found to be a general characteristic to perceive competitive situations as highly threatening and to respond disproportionately with higher levels of state anxiety.
2 Competitive A-trait can be measured via SCATs.

Stress

1 Stress can be either positive (eustress) or negative.
2 The causes of stress are referred to as stressors.
3 Stressors can be very specific or general. The level of their effect depends on a person's perceptions of them in relation to their own perceived capabilities (cognitive appraisal).
4 Specific examples of sporting stressors are competition, frustration, conflict, environmental factors.
5 The general adaptation syndrome has been used as a way of explaining the body's actual stress response.
6 The GAS is seen as developing through three stages: alarm/reaction, resistance and exhaustion.
7 The overall psychological and physiological stress process is seen as being a cyclic one.

Managing stress

1 Stress management helps reduce both somatic and cognitive anxiety.
2 Personal control is seen as a key issue in reducing stressful situations. Cognitive

modification, attribution retraining and coping strategies have all been developed to help.

3 Somatic techniques deal with mainly the physiological aspects of stress and involve various types of 'relaxation' such as progressive relaxation.

4 Imagery, goal setting and cognitive modification techniques can help to improve concentration; improve attention; control emotional states. This is generally known as cognitive stress management.

5 Imagery can be internal or external.

6 All psychological skills training techniques require regular practice and integration into the normal preparation routines of performers.

Revision questions

1 Give a definition of arousal.

2 Using examples from sport explain the differences between **trait anxiety** and **state anxiety**.

3 Using examples from sport distinguish between somatic and cognitive anxiety.

4 What do sports psychologists mean by competitive trait anxiety?

5 Explain how psychologists have tried to measure competitive trait anxiety.

6 Explain and give sporting examples of the effect a high competitive A-trait can potentially have on performance.

7 Give a definition of stress and eustress.

8 What are the four stages of stress development?

9 What are stressors?

10 Give two specific sporting examples for each of the following types of stressors: competition; frustration; conflict; physiological; climatic; personal.

11 How can parental pressure cause stress?

12 Explain the three stages of the GAS.

13 Why is stress management in sport so important?

14 What are the main ways we can measure and recognise stress?

15 Describe the main physiological signs associated with increased levels of stress.

16 Describe the main psychological/cognitive and behavioural signs associated with increased levels of stress.

17 Choose an example from sport other than the one in the chapter and work through the stress process model (fig 27.6, p 492) giving practical examples all the way through from environmental demands to behaviour/performance and feedback.

18 Explain what the technique of imagery involves and how it can help stress management.

19 What are the two types of imagery? Explain the difference.

20 How can a coach and performer ensure that imagery is effective?

21 How does relaxation help to reduce somatic stress?

22 What is the intervention technique of progressive relaxation?

23 What is the biofeedback technique?

24 Give examples of positive self talk and explain why it is important.

25 What is the systematic de-sensitising procedure?

26 What are the main effects of goal setting?

27 Explain **outcome goals** and **performance goals**.

28 Why are social comparisons important for outcome goal orientated athletes?

29 Explain the many important factors that have to be taken into account when setting goals.

30 What are goal achievement strategies?

31 Is goal support important?

Further reading and references

A.A.H.P.H.E.R.D., *Psychological Aspects of PE* (1981)

J A Adams, 'A Closed-loop theory of motor learning', *Journal of Motor Behaviour*, 3, pp 111–50

G W Allport, *Attitudes* (Clark University Press, 1935)

——*The Nature of Prejudice* (Addison-Wesley, 1954)

R Arnot & C Gaines, *Sports Talent* (Penguin, 1986)

R Atkinson & R Shiffrin, 'Human Memory: A proposed system of its control processes', in K Spence & J Spence (eds), *The psychology of learning and motivation* vol 2 (London Academic Press, 1968)

——'The Control of Short Term Memory', *Scientific American*, 224, pp 82–90 (1971)

A Bandura, *Aggression – Social Learning Analysis* (Prentice-Hall, 1973)

R A Baron, *Human Aggression* (Plenum, 1977)

H Benson, *The Relaxation Response* (Morrow, 1975)

J Billing, 'An Overview of Task Complexity – Motor Skills', *Theory into Practice*, 1980, 4, pp 18–23

E Bilodeau & I Bilodeau, 'Motor Skills and Learning' in P Farnsworth (ed) *Annual Reviews of Psychology* (CA Annual Review, 1961)

——'Variable frequency of knowledge of results and the learning of a simple skill', *Journal of Experimental Psychology*, 55, pp 379–83

D Broadbent, *Perception and Communication* (Pergamon, 1958)

J Bruner, 'The nature and uses of immaturity', *American Psychologist*, 27, pp 687–708

R B Cattell, *The Scientific Analysis of Personality* (Penguin, 1965)

P Chelladurai, 'Leadership in Sport Organisations', *Canadian Journal of Sport Psychology*, 5, p 226

B J Cratty, *Teaching Motor Skills* (Prentice-Hall, 1973)

D Coon, *Introduction to Psychology* (West Publishing Co, 1983)

M Czikszentmitialyi, *Beyond Boredom and Anxiety* (Jossey-Bass, 1975)

E Deci, *Intrinsic Motivation and Self Determination in Human Behaviour* (Plenum, 1985)

H Eysenck, 'Biological Basis of Personality' *Nature*, 199, pp 1031–4 (1963)

L Festinger, *A Theory of Cognitive Dissonance* (Harper Row, 1957)

P Fitts, 'Perpetual Motor Skills Learning', in A W Melton (ed), *Categories of human learning* (New York Academic Press, 1964)

P Fitts & M Posner, *Human Performance* (Brooks Cove, 1967)

E Fleishmann, *The Structure and Measurement of Physical Fitness* (Prentice-Hall, 1964)

R Gagne, *The Conditions of Learning* (Holt, Rinehart & Winston, 1977)

A M Gentile, *A Working Model of Skill Acquisition with application to teaching* (Quest, 1972)

D Gill, *Psychological Dynamics of Sport* (Human Kinetics, 1986)

R Gross, *Psychology: The Science of Mind and Behaviour* (Hodder & Stoughton, 1996)

E R Guthrie, *The Psychology of Learning* (Harper & Row, 1952)

C L Hull, *Principles of Behaviour* (Appleton-Century Crofts, 1943)

E Jacobson, *Progressive Relaxation* (University of Chicago Press, 1938)

F S Keller, 'The Phantom Plateau', *Journal of Experimental Analysis of Behaviour*, 1, pp 1–13

J Kelso, *Human Motor Behaviour and Introduction* (Hillsdale, 1982)

B Knapp, *Skill in Sport* (Routledge, 1972)

R Lazarus & A Monat, *Personality* (Prentice-Hall, 1979)

E Lock & G Latham, 'The Application of Goal Setting to Sport', *Journal of Sport Psychology*, 7, pp 205–22 (1985)

R A Magill, *Motor Learning: Concepts and Applications* (Wm C Brown, 1989)

A Maslow, *Towards a Psychology of Being* (Van Nostrand-Reinhold 1968)

R Martens, *Competitive Anxiety in Sport* (Human Kinetics, 1990)

E McBride & A Rothstein, 'Mental and physical practice and the learning and retention of open and closed skills,' *Perceptual and Motor Skills*, 49 (1979)

J McGrath (ed) *Social and Psychological factors in stress* (Holt, Rinehart & Winston, 1970)

E D McKinney, *Motor Learning: Concepts and Applications* (Wm C Brown, 1989)

G P Meredith, *Information and Skill* (BBC, 1958)

W Mischel, *Personality and Assessment* (Wiley, 1968)

M Moston & S Ashworth, *Teaching Physical Education* (Merril, 1986)

B Ogilvy & T Tutko, *Problem Athletes and How to Handle them* (Palham Books, 1966)

C Osgood & Tannenbaum 'The principle of congruity in the prediction of attitude change', *Psychology Review*, 62, pp 42–55 (1955)

Y D Oxendine, *Psychology of Motor Learning* (Prentice Hall, 1984)

M Robb, *The Dynamics of Motor Skill Association* (Prentice-Hall, 1972)

Z Ruben & E McNeil, *The Psychology of Being* (Harper & Row, 1983)

G H Sage, *Sport and American Society* (Addison Wesley, 1974)

R A Schmidt, *Motor Learning and Performance* (Human Kinetics, 1991)

R A Schmidt, *Motor Control and Learning. A Behavioural Emphasis* (Human Kinetics, 1988)

——*Instructor's Guide* (Human Kinetics, 1991)

——*Motor Learning and Performance* (Human Kinetics, 1991)

P Secord & C Backman, *Social Psychology* (McGraw-Hill, 1964)

H Selye, *Stress without Distress* (New American Library, 1974)

R Singer, *The Learning of Motor Skills* (Macmillan, 1982)

B F Skinner, *Science and Human Behaviour* (Macmillan, 1953)

L Stallings, *Motor Learning from Theory to Practice* (C V Cosby Co, 1982)

E L Thorndike, *Human Learning* (Appleton-Century Crofts, 1931)

N Triplett, 'The dynamogenic factors in pace making and competition, *American Journal of Psychology*, 9, pp 507–33 (1989)

R Weinberg & D Gould, *Foundations of Sport and Exercise Psychology* (Human Kinetics, 1995)

B Weiner, *Theories of Motivation from mechanism to cognition* (Rand McNally, 1972)

——*Achievement Motivation and Attribution Theory* (General Learning Press, 1974)

——*An Attribution Theory of Motivation and Emotion* (Springer-Verlag, 1986)

A T Welford, *Fundamentals of Skill* (Methuen, 1968)

——*Skilled Performance: Perceptual and Motor Skills* (Glenview, Scott Foresman & Co, 1976)

H T A Whiting, *Acquiring Ball Skill* (Bell & Sons, 1969)

W Widmeyer, L Brawley, A Carron, 'The effects of group size in sport', *Journal of Sport and Exercise Psychology*, 12, pp 177–90 (1990)

J Wolpe, *Psychotherapy by Reciprocal Inhibition* (Stanford University Press, 1958)

R Zajonc, 'Attitudinal Effects of Mere Exposure', *Journal of Personality and Social Psychology – Monograph Supplement*, 9, part 2, pp 1–27

chapter 28

Requirements and Assessment of the Individual Project

The following chapters give details about the optional project component of the Associated Examining Board (AEB) physical education/sport studies course. Although this section is specifically aimed at the AEB examination, the principles applied could be adopted for a variety of extended pieces of work where similar criteria are required.

This chapter gives a brief overview of the requirements for the project and information about the method of assessment. The remaining chapters deal in more general terms with aspects of good practice regarding development of an extended piece of research. Guidance is also given for addressing the assessment criteria effectively.

An empirical study involves the collection of data. This data could arise naturally, for example by recording the quantity of newspaper coverage of women's sport in the popular press. Data can also be obtained from an experiment that you have set up, for example, the times achieved by middle distance runners in front of and then without an audience.

The individual project – a general overview

If you choose this course work option from the AEB syllabus, you will be given the opportunity to complete a sport related project investigation linked to any area of the physical education/sport studies syllabus. In so doing you will complete 30% of your course. This means that despite the inevitable pressures that course work brings, it does provide an opportunity to go into the final examination having gained over half the marks required to pass, provided you are motivated and work within the guidelines given. This should go a long way to helping you achieve a good overall grade, and giving you some confidence before taking the final two papers. It is not therefore, something which you should attempt to 'rush off' in a week (especially as your staff will be marking your planning!).

Project requirements

The project should be an empirical study. It should be approximately 3,000 words in length (18–20 sides of A4). The AEB have specified a format which should be

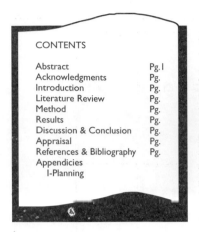

CONTENTS

Abstract   Pg. I
Acknowledgments   Pg.
Introduction   Pg.
Literature Review   Pg.
Method   Pg.
Results   Pg.
Discussion & Conclusion   Pg.
Appraisal   Pg.
References & Bibliography   Pg.
Appendicies
    I-Planning

Fig. 28.1 Specified format for the project

adopted. This is dealt with in detail in subsequent chapters, but the headings are given in fig 28.1.

Your completed work is assessed by your teachers. A representative sample of the work carried out in your school or college is then sent to an external moderator, who compares this work from other centres and hopefully confirms the marks awarded by your teachers.

Your teachers will base their assessment on specific criteria laid down by the AEB. You should ask them for an up-to-date version of these criteria. At the time of writing (1997), there are 50 criteria, arranged into nine groups, and the marks available for each group will depend on the number of criteria within it. It would be a good idea to become familiar with these groupings before starting work, so that you gain an overall impression of the requirements. It will also be necessary to refer back to these pages as you progress.

The nine groups are:

1   Planning
2   Support from relevant literature
3   Reporting of method
4   Results
5   Discussion/Conclusion
6   Appraisal
7   Abstract
8   References
9   Communication

Planning

You will be awarded marks for evidence of your planning throughout the development of your project, so this needs to be demonstrated. This may be achieved in part through discussion with your tutor, but something more tangible will probably be required in the form of project briefs, initial hypothesis/ses, estimated timetable for development of each stage of the project development (see table 28.1) etc. The planning stage of the project development will greatly affect the outcome. In addition to outlining what you hope to achieve, and how you intend to achieve it, you should also show that you are prepared to modify your initial plans in the light of subsequent developments.

Project brief

A project brief is a summary of your intended project, giving information on the title, anticipated outline, hypothesis/ses, means of collecting data etc.

Hypothesis/ses

A statement/prediction about the outcome of the experiment you have devised; ie, what you expect to happen. For example, if looking at the effects of different types of feedback on a beginners performance of a series of basic trampoline skills you might predict that: Visual feedback, will significantly improve a beginner's performance of a series of basic trampolining skills. This would be your experimental hypothesis.

Table 28.1 PROJECT DEVELOPMENT PLAN

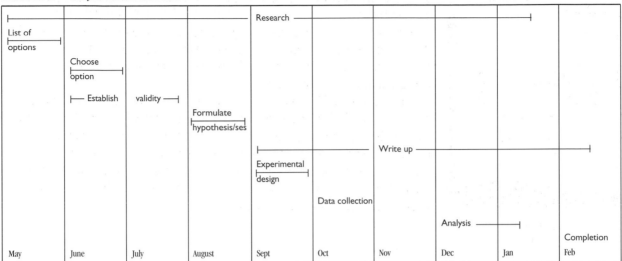

List of options				Research						
	Choose option									
	├— Establish	validity —┤								
			Formulate hypothesis/ses							
						Write up				
				Experimental design						
					Data collection					
								Analysis —┤		
										Completion
May	June	July	August	Sept	Oct	Nov	Dec	Jan		Feb

NB Choice of research area may determine point at which data collection is carried out. If data needs to be collected early ensure sufficient data is gathered to allow for modifications to design if required.

Support from relevant literature

Here you must demonstrate that you can access information relevant to your topic from a variety of sources. Having gathered this information, you must demonstrate understanding of it, by using it to develop your ideas and to establish a clear link between the review material and the resultant hypothesis/ses. As with the planning criteria, you could be assessed by your teachers on your ability to communicate your knowledge orally.

Reporting of method

This part of the assessment is concerned with writing up the experimental design: you need to explain in detail how the data was gathered. You should take care to give a precise account of the method employed, so that someone else could replicate the procedure if they wished.

Results

The results section should be a presentation of the data gained from the experimental design.

Discussion/ Conclusion

The discussion should explain what the results mean. This is your opportunity to show your understanding by analysing the findings and comparing them with previous studies. At this point the research hypothesis can be accepted or rejected. You should then state a conclusion based on this, which links in with your initial hypothesis/ses and review section.

Appraisal

An appraisal is a critical summary of the experimental method and outcomes. It should be in two parts:

1 The first should outline appropriate modifications to the methodology in the

light of experience so that the reliability and/or validity of the design can be improved; ie, you should highlight errors or pitfalls to be avoided if the experiment were to be repeated.

2 The second part should include appropriate suggestions for further research, ie, suitable follow-ups to the work completed.

Reliability

The **reliability** of a test means that the test will give repeatable results; ie, if you were to follow the same procedure again, using the same subjects, or subjects with similar qualities, the results would match those initially obtained. For example if you were measuring VO_2 max using the step test, it would be considered a reliable test if you gained similar results for the same person on a number of occasions (provided the person had not been training). If you obtained significantly different results each time (due to the test and not the athlete), the test would not be reliable.

Validity

The **validity** of a test ensures that it measures what it is supposed to measure; ie, in retrospect you might decide that the design you set up for your experiment did not really test what you had wanted to test, or at least could be improved to make it more valid. For example, you might be measuring the effects of verbal feedback versus visual feedback in terms of performance of a basketball lay-up shot. It would therefore be important that the groups only received the 'correct' type of feedback. To address this problem you could hold separate training sessions for both groups. However, the verbal group would still receive visual feedback, in the form of the rest of the group's attempts. Thus the test would not be totally valid.

Abstract

An abstract is a summary. It is included so that individuals looking for specific information (possibly to complete a project of their own) can read the abstract and establish whether it is worth considering further; ie, does it cover the area that they are researching? As such, an abstract should include information on the problem you are addressing, the subjects you used, the measurements used and your findings. It should be fairly short – no more than 200 words.

References/ Bibliography

This section should contain a record of the publications used. There are several recognised ways in which to record sources used:

For a text book:
Author/s (Year) *Title*, where published: publisher.
Coolican, H. (1990) *Research Methods and Statistics in Psychology*, London: Hodder & Stoughton.

For a journal:
Author/s (Year) Title of article. *Journal*, Volume No, Pages.
Biddle, S. Mitchell, J. Armstrong, N. (1991) The assessment of physical activity in children. *British Journal of Physical Education, Research Supplement*, 10, 4–8.

Before adopting an approach check with your tutor in case a specific method is required.

The important point about this section is that:

- it should be accurate, ie, you have actually used the articles/books that you list;
- it should reflect all aspects of your research title. For example, if conducting an investigation into the effects of fatigue on reaction time in tennis, you should have referenced articles/books on tennis, exercise physiology and sports psychology.

Communication

To score highly on this section you will need to ensure that your project:

- is well written
- is clearly presented – neatly written or word processed

If word processed, the text should:

- be well spaced (1.5 line spacing)
- have a reasonable sized font (point 12, Times New Roman)
- be spell checked.

In addition the report will need to be well organised. If you follow the guidelines contained in this section, including the headings given this should satisfy the criteria. Examiners/moderators also normally appreciate inclusion of *appropriate* diagrams, sketches, graphs, charts, tables, etc; but they must enhance and support the report, rather than merely adding bulk.

In addition you will be expected to demonstrate orally your understanding of the work you have undertaken. At various points through the completion of your project, you will probably be involved in individual interviews with your tutor. During these sessions, it is important that you convince your tutor that you are knowledgeable about the work you are undertaking, have been actively researching information and understand the concepts involved.

Further detail on each of the groupings may be found in the following chapters.

chapter 29

Planning

This chapter discusses the planning aspects of developing a research project. Planning is obviously vital at the start of any activity, but it should be remembered that the whole of the project development should be considered, and plans modified when necessary.

There are many approved methods of carrying out empirical research, and while they are not all identical, there appears to be a common consensus about the overall stages that should be employed. Before planning can really begin, an understanding of the task ahead is essential so that it can be broken down into manageable stages. The basic steps that should be followed are outlined in fig 29.1.

Identifying the research problem

The first stage as indicated in fig 29.1 is to identify the research problem. In other words you know that you have to carry out some research, but on what? What do you want to do the project on? One of the most difficult aspects regarding the project is deciding what to study; what at first seems to be a straightforward task, becomes complex. Faced with the problem of becoming committed to a specific idea, it is easy to put off the inevitable in the hope that inspiration will come, but unfortunately you could have a long wait! While it is good that you are not restricted in your choice of study (other than to the syllabus), this does present you with a vast choice and makes your decision harder.

In an attempt to get started, it is often helpful to break this first stage down into smaller tasks as shown in fig 29.2. A good starting point is to identify the areas of the course that are of specific interest to you. In order to do this:

- read through the syllabus and your course work notes to date and 'grade' each of the sections and sub-sections (don't forget the areas of the syllabus still to be covered);
- continue and complete table 29.1, listing in rank order, your 'top ten' in terms of areas of interest from the syllabus.

The area of study is obviously important, as you should be working on your project over a nine month period (see table 28.1 for a suggested timetable). You should choose something that *you* will be interested in, and not something that someone else thinks will be a good idea.

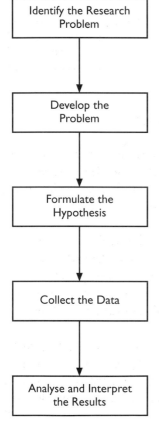

Fig. 29.1 TASKS ASSOCIATED WITH IDENTIFYING THE RESEARCH PROBLEM

Table 29.1   SYLLABUS 'TOP TEN'

SYLLABUS AREA	TOPIC	RANK ORDER	TAUGHT BY
eg, section B – social aspects	sport, sex and gender	I	JS

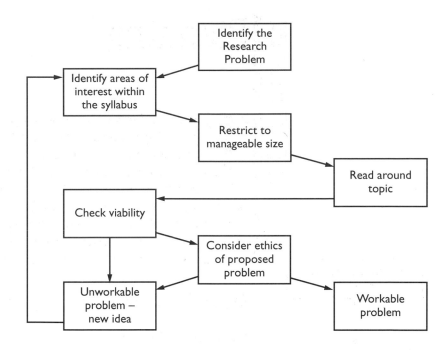

Fig. 29.2 REFINING THE TOPIC

Developing the research problem

Having established some areas of the syllabus of interest, you need to consider each in turn in order to determine whether there is a question you wish to pursue; in other words, what would you be investigating? Continue and complete table 29.2 by turning your area of interest into a potential area of research.

Don't be afraid to start – write down your general ideas as they arise: however vague or confused these are, they can be refined or discarded later on. If you try to create the perfect sentence to describe your ideas, you are unlikely to write anything at all. Once you have something written down, it can be shown to staff or discussed with other students. In this way your initial ideas can be sorted and refined.

When you have established the area of the syllabus to work within, it will now need refinement. Although the project must ultimately be your own work, the more discussion you have with others at this stage the better. Therefore try to address the following questions with someone else as you will benefit from hearing their ideas and points of view.

Is the scale of the project appropriate? (If the scale or scope is too broad the study will be too large to research in depth.) Look at table 29.3. Which research areas are appropriate or inappropriate in terms of scale?

Table 29.2   DEVELOPMENT OF SYLLABUS AREA OF INTEREST

RANK ORDER FROM TABLE 29.1	RESEARCH AREA
1 (sport, sex and gender)	women in sport
2	
3	

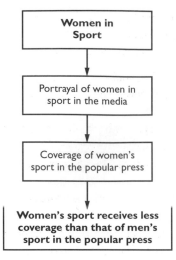

Fig. 29.3 REFINING THE TOPIC

Table 29.3   SCALE OF TOPICS

• women in sport	[appropriate/inappropriate]
• reaction time in sport	[appropriate/inappropriate]
• factors affecting performance in a gymnastic routine	[appropriate/inappropriate]
• a comparison of the effects of two different teaching methods on the performance of a trampolining skill	[appropriate/inappropriate]
• sponsorship and sport	[appropriate/inappropriate]
• a comparison of sport performance between the USA and England	[appropriate/inappropriate]

Although all of the examples given in table 29.3 could be used as the basis of a study, none could be used as they stand at the moment; some obviously need more work than others in order to arrive at a manageable area to research.

Refining the initial topic can be difficult; you could try to create levels and increase the focus of the topic at each level for the topics shown in table 29.3 (the first is done for you in fig 29.3). Apply this method to refine the topic you ranked at number 1 in table 29.2 so that the final level focuses on a particular question or issue that reflects what you would like to investigate.

Formulating the hypothesis

Experimental design is the method you devise to test your hypothesis; ie, the situation you set up so that you can collect data to support your initial prediction.

Your next step is to establish whether your idea is viable. To help you check this you need to form a draft hypothesis (see page 510) and experimental design. These are dealt with in more detail in the following chapter; all you need at present is an *idea* of the question you want to ask (the research problem), your predicted outcome to the question (hypothesis) and the experimental design you will use to test your prediction. Complete table 29.4 with this information.

Although you will probably alter your hypothesis and design in the light of further research, this is an important part of the process. Failure to establish that your idea asks a valid question and is measurable at this stage could result in a waste of your time. For example, at first glance the following idea – *Examination of the provision for badminton within two local areas* – would seem appropriate, but in fact the researcher has failed to ask a question.

This would normally be picked up at this stage of development, allowing the candidate to develop the title or choose a different area. The next example does ask a question – *An investigation into the effects on performance of male squash*

Table 29.4   RESEARCH QUESTION, HYPOTHESIS & DESIGN

RESEARCH PROBLEM	PREDICTED OUTCOME (DRAFT HYPOTHESIS)	DESIGN OUTLINE
the effects of an audience on club swimmers swimming times over 50 m	swimming times will improve in the presence of an audience	identify club swimmers; time them over 50 m during training time trials; times over 50 m in a Gala

players when playing 'quality' female opposition. Although potentially very interesting, this would prove difficult to measure in an empirical fashion.

You should therefore consider the following before progressing further:

- Is there available literature on the topic? Your staff, school/college or local library staff might know where to look. You could browse through references and recommended reading books.
- Are there likely to be any organisations you could approach for information? You will need to be careful here though as many organisations (especially the Football Association) receive so many requests for information that they are usually unable to respond.
- Can you get the information you need from media sources (eg, newspapers, radio, television)?
- Who do you know who can help? If you are involved with a good standard sports club, are there people with the expertise you require (especially in terms of 'volunteers' for any experiment you may wish to conduct)?

To summarise:

1 What data/information do you need to collect?
2 Can it be collected?
3 How will you collect it?

If your response to these questions relies solely on someone else, or you cannot answer some of the questions, you should probably reconsider your topic and select another option from table 29.2. If however you feel your idea is still viable, the final task relating to this first stage is to ensure your project does not pose an ethical problem.

Ethical considerations

When conducting research, you need to be aware of a variety of ethical issues. The most relevant ethical areas for you to avoid are:

- plagiarism
- fabrication and falsification of data and information
- selective use of data
- inappropriate use of subjects.

The first three areas will be dealt with in turn at a later stage. At this point of the development process however, the fourth area should be considered in more detail. Most projects will involve the use of volunteers, who will place a large amount of trust in you to treat them fairly, psychologically as well as physically. The following titles are all related to the syllabus, but would be rejected on the grounds that they are potentially unethical. Why do you think they are considered unethical?

- The effect of alcohol on reaction time.
- Attitude surveys of junior county football and hockey squads in relation to parental pressure.
- Effects of leg strength training programmes on sprinting performance of 11-year-old males.
- Optimum length of practice times on a trampoline.
- Affects of reversibility of training in county standard rugby players.
- Sprint times over 30 m before and after ingestion of caffeine tablets.

- Comparison of sprint times with and without a warm up.
- Women in football – what's the point?
- Maximal heart rate values in the under 19s, under 35s and over 50s.

See table 29.5 for reasons for rejection. In addition to the points emphasised from the above examples, you should also ensure:

- that you comply with any guidelines given by your school/college;
- that where a physical session is taking place, there is a properly qualified coach taking the session or close at hand;
- that any practice is safe, especially when in a potentially dangerous situation or if using potentially dangerous equipment: eg, diving or martial arts sessions, cycling road races, use of gymnastic apparatus, use of trampolines, use of javelin, etc.;
- that the title does not imply racial discrimination.

Once satisfied that your project is ethical you should be in a position to begin your work on developing the research problem (stage 2, fig 29.1). If you are still experiencing difficulty in choosing a project, some suggested titles from the syllabus areas are given in Appendix 2.

Table 29.5   ETHICAL PROBLEMS POSED BY TITLES

the effect of alcohol on reaction time	involves administration of drugs
attitude surveys of junior county football and hockey squads in relation to parental pressure	this is a potentially very sensitive area and is really an invasion of privacy
effects of leg strength training programmes on sprinting performance of 11-year-old males.	most 11-year-olds will still be developing physically. Strength training programmes should therefore be avoided as this could lead to physical damage/injury
optimum length of practice times on a trampoline.	this implies the need to go beyond the optimum in order to establish the optimum, ∴ this is potentially dangerous to the performer
affects of reversibility of training in county standard rugby players	to measure reversibility the performer would need to stop training. Projects should not interfere with the normal training programme of an athlete
sprint times over 30 m before and after ingestion of caffeine tablets	involves administration of drugs
comparison of sprint times with and without a warm up	this could lead to injury of the athletes taking part without a warm up
women in football – what's the point	there is implied sexual discrimination in this title. A project on women's football would be acceptable given an appropriate context
maximal heart rate values in the U19, U35 and O50s	it is not appropriate to inflict high intensity exercise on elderly groups, from a safety point of view

chapter 30

Developing the Research Problem and using Relevant Literature

This chapter discusses ways to complete the second and third phases of the project as shown in fig 29.1 – how to develop the research problem and formulate the experimental hypothesis. In order to develop the research problem, you will need to gain a greater understanding of it. This is achieved by completing a **review** of the available literature on the topic. This chapter gives a general overview of the requirements of a review section, and then gives a more detailed account of how to construct the review.

The purposes of a review

The general purpose of the review is:

- to give an introduction to the research area related to your draft hypothesis;
- to give you an opportunity to demonstrate your knowledge and understanding of the research relating to your hypothesis;
- to give you sufficient knowledge to make informed decisions about the content and format of your hypothesis and design.

To complete a good review you will need to access the appropriate (and hopefully recent) research and literature available for your topic; analyse and evaluate it; and include conflicting research where it exists. It should be your evaluation of the available research, not just a repeat of it. Great care must be taken while writing the review not to plagiarise other people's work. Note-taking rather than copying from the text should help you avoid this potential pitfall.

Plagiarism means the copying of other people's work and reporting it as your own. There is no problem with using other people's work, provided that you acknowledge whose work it is.

During the first phase of development (planning), you established that there was available literature related to your topic. You should now locate this literature, carrying out an intensive library search to gather as much information as possible. Reference to the school or college set text book will not be considered extensive! You need to provide evidence of your research by referencing a number and variety of sources of information. Some towns and counties have specialist libraries which you could visit or contact to ask for specific information. It is worth asking your school/college librarians if they know of any such specialist centres that you could access. There is no short cut to this part of the process; it will be time consuming, but it lays the foundations for the rest of your project.

Figure 30.1 summarises the process of developing the literature review. Firstly it shows the work conducted during the planning stage as necessary input in order to determine an appropriate problem for investigation. Once this is established you need to identify all related topics within the area of investigation, and find

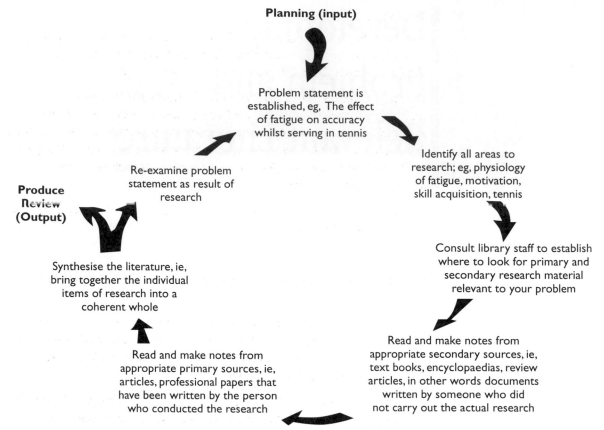

Fig. 30.1 Constructing a review

information relating to these areas. (Libraries will have a variety of indexes to different bodies of knowledge. You should use these indexes to establish what publications will be of use to you, and where they can be found). Having located relevant sources of information you will need to read and make notes from them (remember to record the sources used for the bibliography).

Secondary sources of information may also provide references to primary sources, which you could obtain if you needed more detail on a particular study. Next follows the processing of this information which will hopefully lead to the output of the components of the review. If you are unable to construct a suitable review at this stage it might be necessary to re-examine your problem statement and modify it in some way, starting the 'cycle' again.

The structure of the review

The final review should cover three distinct areas (*although presented under one heading*):

1 an introduction to the project;
2 evidence of research relating to your title;
3 hypothesis/ses relating to your title.

Introduction   Although it is probable that the reader of your project will be knowledgeable about the topic you are investigating, you still need to 'set the scene' for them.

First part

Firstly you should give a general introduction to the topic; ie, rather than simply stating that your project is investigating the effects of anxiety on performance, you should try to place the investigation into context. For example:

Coaches are always striving to find ways to enhance the performance of their athletes. As the gap between first and second place becomes even smaller, it is essential that the coach examines all possible areas for improvement. In recent years this has lead to an increase in studies concerned with the psychology of sports performance, and in particular the relationship between arousal, anxiety and performance.

The reader should be given a clear idea of your choice of topic and its relevance to the course you are studying.

Second part

Secondly you should give some *brief* background information to the topic; for example:

Theories relating to the relationship originated with the Drive Theory and have continued to be developed as greater knowledge and understanding has been acquired. In more recent years Hanin presented his theory called Zones of Optimal Functioning. He established that . . .

In this way the reader is being provided with the necessary background information so that they may understand the direction of your project and its connection to existing theory.

Third part

Thirdly you should give a brief introduction to the nature of the problem you will be researching; for example:

It would appear therefore that athletes have an optimal state anxiety which will vary from individual to individual. Knowledge of the athlete's own specific optimal zone of state anxiety would presumably be of great interest to the coach. This study attempts to examine whether it is possible to identify an individual's optimal zone of state anxiety.

(Can you identify the problem statement?)

By the end of the introduction the reader should have a clear idea about the area of theory being dealt with and the purpose of the project. It should lead them gently into the remainder of the review section which examines existing theory in more depth.

The introduction should not be lengthy – a side of A4 (or less) is normally sufficient.

Evidence of research

Depending on the research problem you may need to give operational definitions at this point; ie, explain the terms or concepts you are using. For example, if discussing the effects of fatigue, an explanation of the types and causes of fatigue may be given in the review section (although a clear explanation of your working definition of the subjects fatigued state must also be given in the method section). It might be appropriate to give more than one definition where different

An operational definition is an explanation of the meaning of a specific term in the context of your experiment. For example your study might be investigating the effects of different motivational techniques on delaying fatigue. Although we all have an idea of the meaning of the term fatigue, this isn't concrete enough. We need to know how you will establish at what point the performer becomes fatigued. You might decide that for this experiment a subject is fatigued once they are unable to stay with the 'bleep' in the Bleep Test, or when the performers maximum heart rate has been achieved. Either explanation would be your operational definition of fatigue.

interpretations of the term exist; for example, if discussing fitness you might give examples of the different types before establishing which particular aspect you were concerned with.

Once these terms have been explained the main analysis and synthesis of the research material should be recorded. The process of gathering and recording the research material is dealt with in fig 30.1, but the processing of this information and final output needs further explanation:

Analysis

As mentioned above, repeating other people's work will not meet the review requirements. Once you have gathered and made notes on all sources of information you require, you need to analyse it so that you understand the concepts involved. Armed with a greater understanding of the topic, you then synthesise the information; ie, you bring together the individual items of research into a coherent whole, looking for similarities and differences amongst the information you have gathered. This is not an easy task; you need to find a way to break the research up into manageable chunks, and group the information you have found.

Synthesis

One approach is to look for concepts within your investigation. For example, if looking into the effects of massed versus distributed practice, it would be simpler to deal with one type of practice first; begin with a definition of its meaning, based on the ideas of the majority of the research references, but comment where there appears to be disagreement or inconsistencies. Next you could establish the situations where its use appears to be most and least successful, looking for consensus and differences of opinion among researchers.

Once you have pursued all aspects of that form of practice, repeat the process for the other type of practice. You could also look out for any overlap between the types of practice. In this way you can bring together the work of different people rather than keeping it separate, and demonstrate your understanding. You must however remember to make specific references to the original authors when making a point, so that the reader knows that your comments are substantiated by acknowledged experts in the field, and are not simply your thoughts and feelings on the subject.

It is unlikely that you will be conducting an experiment identical to that which you are evaluating. Therefore you need to ensure that you can relate the theory to your intended work so that a link develops between the review and your resultant hypothesis and design. If you are studying the effects of massed versus distributed practice in the lay-up shot in basketball, although there may not be studies on basketball there will be studies on other skills which bear reasonable similarities. You must be able to identify and make reference to this. Hence the value of becoming knowledgeable about *all* aspects of your topic.

Conclusions

If the synthesis is thorough, an overall picture of the available research should emerge, making conclusions a fairly straight forward process. Once this is completed you should be in a position to write a structured and logical review (output).

Hypothesis/ses

A variable in an experiment is something which can be changed or altered whilst other aspects of the experiment remain constant. For example, the method of providing feedback to a performer could be varied during an experiment, as could their level of performance, whilst the task they were completing (a specific move) remained the same.

At the end of the review section you should specify the research problem in a concise manner. This is achieved through formulating and then recording hypotheses, which are statements about the relationship between at least two variables.

For example, if the problem being investigated was:

'an investigation into the effects of fatigue on accuracy of service scores of club tennis players'

then the hypotheses associated with this problem might be as follows:

A – Club tennis players would gain greater service scores in a non-fatigued state, compared to that achieved when fatigued.

B – There will be no significant difference between the service scores achieved by club tennis players when in a fatigued or non-fatigued state.

The variables in these statements are service scores and level of fatigue.

Both of these hypotheses should be included, although apparently conflicting. They represent two of the types that can be used in project work, a summary of which is given below:

Research hypothesis

All hypotheses are research hypotheses, thus any statement about the predicted outcome of an investigation could be called the research hypothesis. For example, a study looking into sports participation by school children and school leavers might have the following hypothesis:

Year 12 pupils will spend a greater amount of time participating in sporting activities than their 16 year old counterparts who have left school.

The variables here are: amount of time spent participating in physical activity, and age.

Experimental hypothesis

This is the name given to hypotheses when they refer to the predicted outcome of an experiment. Therefore projects containing an experiment will have experimental hypotheses. (Projects without an experimental design, for example those using surveys or interviews as a means to collect data, are not classified as experimental, thus they have research hypotheses rather than experimental.)

Directional/one-tailed hypothesis

These predict the direction of the outcome of the investigation, for example:

The use of verbal feedback in the learning of a basic netball skill will result in an increase in performance.

Two-tailed hypothesis

The direction of the outcome of the investigation is not predicted. The hypothesis simply states that there will be an effect, thus the example above would now read:

The use of verbal feedback in the learning of a basic netball skill will have an effect on the subject's performance.

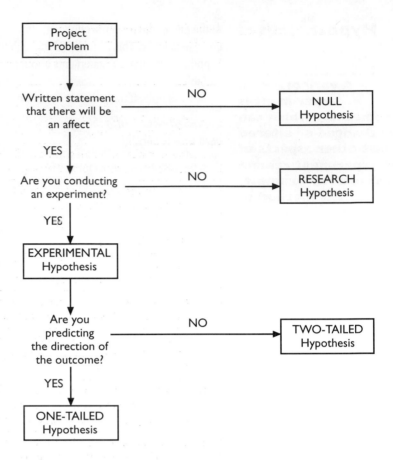

Fig. 30.2 CLASSIFYING HYPOTHESES

Null hypothesis

This is the prediction that the variables will have no effect, ie, that any changes in results are due to chance. Using the above example, this would become:

The use of verbal feedback in the learning of a basic netball skill will have no effect on performance.

See table 30.1: to test your understanding categorise hypotheses A and B on p 523 and the following examples by using fig 30.2. (You will need to decide from the statement, the way the data is likely to be collected in order to answer the second question on fig 30.2. Answers are given in table 30.2.)

When recording your hypotheses, you need only state whether they are research, experimental or null. You need to know whether they are one-tailed or two-tailed if you are going to carry out statistical tests, but this information is not recorded at this stage.

As mentioned above, a hypothesis is a statement about the relationship between at least two different variables: the **dependent** variable or **independent** variable. See table 30.3.

When drawing up your research hypothesis ensure that it:

- leads naturally from your review
- is concise
- contains an independent and dependent variable
- is testable.

The review is complete once the hypothesis/ses has been stated.

The dependent variable is the reason for the project: it is what we are trying to find out. For example, trying to establish the best method of providing feedback.

The independent variable is used to see if it is related to the dependent variable eg, a specific method of providing feedback. You can control this variable.

Table 30.1   CLASSIFYING HYPOTHESES

	HYPOTHESIS	TYPE
A		
B		
1	women's sports events receive a different amount of newspaper coverage to men's;	
2	the number of women's football clubs in my area is unaffected by the local development plan;	
3	reaction time of 100 m sprinters will improve as a result of sound stimuli training;	
4	fatigue will affect the quality of a backhand drop shot in the game of squash;	
5	economic factors have lead to the majority of first division rugby clubs using shared grounds;	
6	the use of verbal feedback in the learning of a basic basketball skill will affect performance;	
7	more fouls will be committed by Premiership standard football players during tournament matches than league games;	
8	a greater number of year 7 pupils (age 11) will participate in extra-curricular sport sessions than those in years 9 and 11 (age 13 and 15);	
9	there will be no significant difference in the VO_2 max of race walkers and middle distance runners;	
10	socio-economic grouping will have an affect on the types of sports participated in	

Table 30.2   CLASSIFYING HYPOTHESES — ANSWERS

A	EXPERIMENTAL hypothesis (one-tailed)
B	NULL hypothesis
1	RESEARCH hypothesis (two-tailed)
2	NULL hypothesis
3	EXPERIMENTAL hypothesis (one-tailed)
4	EXPERIMENTAL hypothesis (two-tailed)
5	RESEARCH hypothesis (one-tailed)
6	EXPERIMENTAL hypothesis (two-tailed)
7	RESEARCH hypothesis (one-tailed)
8	RESEARCH hypothesis (one-tailed)
9	NULL hypothesis
10	RESEARCH hypothesis (two-tailed)

Table 30.3   DEPENDENT AND INDEPENDENT VARIABLES

	HYPOTHESIS	DEPENDENT VARIABLE	INDEPENDENT VARIABLE
1	the number of women's football clubs in my area is unaffected by the local development plan;	no of women's football clubs	local development plan
2	reaction time of 100 m sprinters will improve as a result of sound stimuli training;	reaction time	sound stimuli training
3	fatigue will affect the quality of a backhand drop shot in the game of squash;	quality of backhand drop	level of fatigue
4	economic factors have lead to the majority of first division rugby clubs using shared grounds;	no of clubs using shared grounds	economic factors
5	the use of verbal feedback in the learning of a basic basketball skill will affect performance;	performance level	verbal feedback
6	more fouls will be committed by Premiership standard football players during tournament matches than league games;	no of fouls committed	type of match
7	a greater number of year 7 pupils (age 11) will participate in extra-curricular sport sessions than those in years 9 and 11 (age 13 and 15);	no of pupils participating	age
8	there will be no significant difference in the VO_2 max of race walkers and middle distance runners;	VO_2 levels	type of athlete
9	socio-economic grouping will have an affect on the types of sports participated in;	types of sports participated in	socio-economic group
10	women's sports events receive a different amount of newspaper coverage to men's	amount of newspaper coverage	gender of sports event

1 You decide to research the effects of social facilitation on performance. Your initial belief is that the presence of an audience will enhance the performance of novice players.

- **State your likely hypothesis.**
- **State the corresponding null hypothesis.**
- **What would the dependent variable be?**
- **What would the independent variable be?**
- **Is the hypothesis likely to be an experimental hypothesis or research?**

2 Check your progress in this chapter, by filling in table 30.4.

Table 30.4   PROGRESS REPORT

TASK	COMPLETED ✓	STILL TO DO ✗
completed project brief		
extensive and relevant notes from secondary sources		
extensive and relevant notes from primary sources		
record of resources for reference/bibliography section		
research hypothesis/ses arising from research		
null hypothesis/ses arising from research		

chapter 31

Reporting of Method

T his chapter looks at some of the common experimental designs that you could use, depending on your research problem. It also looks at the style that should be employed when writing the method section and its content; thus it covers the fourth phase of the project development in fig 29.1 – collecting the data.

Before discussing the necessary content for the method section, a selection of some of the experimental designs you could use are shown below. Not all methods are included here, and you would be well advised to refer to the additional reading list given on page 541 before deciding on the design for your research.

Experimental designs

These may be categorised into related or unrelated designs, which refer to the subjects used:

- **Related designs** – when the same subjects are used for the whole of the experiment (repeated measures); when this isn't appropriate, 'doubles' are used. Subjects are matched with another using relevant criteria – one completing one part of the experiment while their double completes the other (matched pairs).
- **Unrelated designs** – when no attempt is made to match subjects. They might involve just one subject (single subject design), or groups who have not been matched (independent samples).

Each design type has its own advantages and disadvantages. You need to select the most appropriate for your experiment to ensure you obtain data relevant to your hypothesis.

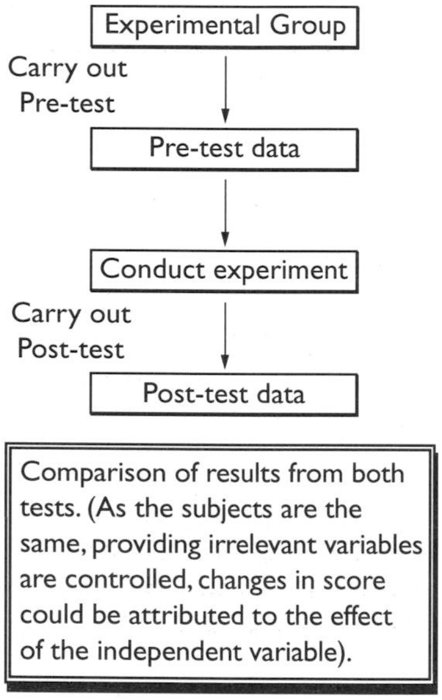

Experimental Group

Carry out
Pre-test

Pre-test data

Conduct experiment

Carry out
Post-test

Post-test data

Comparison of results from both tests. (As the subjects are the same, providing irrelevant variables are controlled, changes in score could be attributed to the effect of the independent variable).

Fig. 31.1 Repeated measures design

Repeated measures

In this type of design the experimental group are tested before and after the experimental treatment (see fig 31.1). For example, if investigating the possible effect of an audience on performance, performance will be tested before the audience are introduced and then again when the audience is present. Therefore data is collected from the same group twice in the form of a pre- and post-test.

The main disadvantage of this test is that the subjects may improve their performance due to practice. This is potentially overcome by counterbalancing: one of the possible ways of achieving this is shown in fig 31.2.

Matched pairs

This method has the advantage that different subjects are used in each condition, therefore the data obtained will not be affected by practice. It does present other problems though: you must ensure that each member of group A is matched with a subject in group B. Careful selection of subjects is therefore required, plus an understanding of the important variables for the experiment.

An example of the design is shown in fig 31.3. A possible experimental

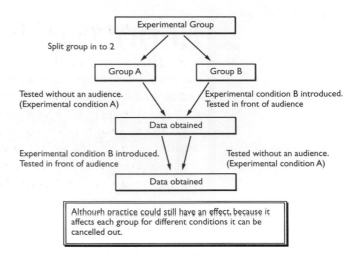

Fig. 31.2 REPEATED MEASURES DESIGN USING COUNTERBALANCING. ALTHOUGH PRACTICE COULD STILL HAVE AN EFFECT, IT CAN BE CANCELLED OUT BECAUSE IT AFFECTS EACH GROUP FOR DIFFERENT CONDITIONS

hypothesis for this type of design would be that distributive practice will be more effective than massed practice in improving the success rate of basketball lay-ups. In other words, it provides the opportunity to measure the effects of more than one condition.

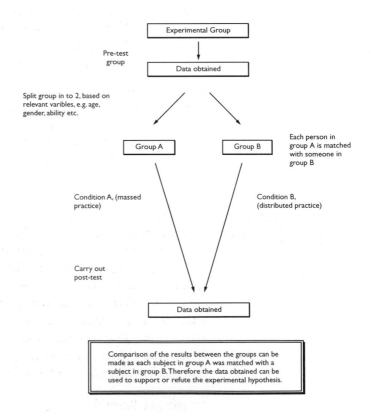

Fig. 31.3 MATCHED PAIRS. COMPARISON OF THE RESULTS BETWEEN THE GROUPS CAN BE MADE AS EACH SUBJECT IN GROUP A WAS MATCHED WITH A SUBJECT IN GROUP B. THEREFORE THE DATA OBTAINED CAN BE USED TO SUPPORT OR REFUTE THE EXPERIMENTAL HYPOTHESIS

Independent samples

This design involves the use of two different groups of subjects who have not been specifically matched. The advantages here are that it saves time trying to find 'like pairs' of subjects, and means there will be no practice or order effect. The obvious disadvantage is that the data obtained may be due to the independent variable or due to the differences in the individuals between the groups. One way of attempting to overcome this problem would be to allocate subjects at random to each of the groups, although this might still be ineffective.

Writing up the method section

At first this might appear to be a less significant part of the project, and consequently one which does not require as much attention. This is not the case! Writing up your method provides the reader with information about your design and an explanation of the design decisions that you have made. Thus not only will you be gathering marks for your write up in this section, but also for your choice of method, ie, the means by which you attempted to gain the necessary data to support your hypothesis.

The method section can be presented in continuous format, or broken down into separate sub-headings. Whichever format you prefer you should ensure that it contains the following information:

Operational definitions

(See page 522.) These are not always necessary, but it is a good idea to look at the dependent variable in your research/experiment hypothesis and decide if it requires defining in this way. Which of the dependent variables listed in table 30.3 would you give operational definitions? For example, do you know exactly what is meant in the following hypotheses:

- number 1: What is meant by 'my area'?
- number 4: What exactly is a quality shot?
- number 5: How is performance being measured?
- number 6: What constitutes a foul?

The independent variable does not normally require an operational definition as a greater explanation of it is automatically given when writing up the method section. For example the independent variable for hypothesis number 4 is level of fatigue. During the course of the write up, you would probably explain how to induce the different levels of fatigue required, thus giving a working definition.

An outline of the design adopted

You need to state whether you are conducting an experiment or using another method to collect data. If you are following an experimental design, then which one? Why did you select this particular research method and what were the conditions that the research was carried out under? What are the independent and dependent variables? What irrelevant variables have you managed to control? (If you want to measure the effect of the independent variable, remove the potential irrelevant variables; you need therefore to identify them and then control their effects by keeping them out of the project where possible.) What irrelevant variables could not be controlled? (There will be some beyond your control. If you are aware of them, their possible effects can be examined in the discussion section of the project.)

Irrelevant Variable

These are variables which are irrelevant to the experiment, but which might have an effect. For example the weather would be irrelevant to a study concerned with the effectiveness of types of practice and distance thrown in the discus. However although irrelevant it could affect the results of the study if after the practice sessions one group were tested on a calm day, and the other were tested on a very windy day. This irrelevant variable would need to be controlled, possibly by carrying out the tests at the same time, or by moving the tests inside.

Try to remember that this section should not give details about *how* the data was collected, but *why* it was collected in the manner it was. It should outline the design decisions that you made so that you could collect data appropriate to your hypothesis.

An explanation of how and why subjects were

You should give details regarding the number of subjects and the requirements they needed to satisfy (if any), to be included in your research (eg, did they need to be a specific age, gender, skill level, from a specific geographical location etc?). If using more than one group of subjects, you should explain how they were allocated to a specific group (although this could be equally well covered in your design).

Outlining equipment, materials and resources

You need to include sufficient detail so that the investigation could be replicated; leave out unnecessary detail which states the obvious. For example, detail regarding the number of basketballs required would be useful, but information about the pencil the researcher uses to record the scores would not! Specifications of specific equipment should be given and if commercial items are used the source of such items should be listed (eg, Multi-Stage Fitness Test, Loughborough University). If conducting an experiment, a diagram or photograph of the lay-out might also be useful. If you have designed a data collection sheet or questionnaire a copy of this should also be included.

A precise and full account of the procedure adopted

The procedure should be described with sufficient clarity that the experiment could be duplicated accurately by the reader. Try to describe exactly what happened from the start of the experiment to the finish. The most common problem here is lack of relevant detail. Include any standardised instructions, ie, any instructions given to each participant, or those participants within a specific group. For example, if teaching a lay-up shot in basketball using massed and distributed practice, what were the common coaching points given to the performers? Exactly what format did the practice sessions take? Were all performers present at the same time? If not, where were they? You must ensure the reader is left in no doubt about the procedure that was adopted.

The bulk of the information for this part of the project should already be available to you from the planning stages. It might be necessary however, to alter some of your initial plans in the light of research you carried out whilst compiling the literature review. For example you might have decided to investigate the effects of an audience on an accuracy task, believing that all subjects would perform better when an audience was present. As a result you may have chosen a variety of subjects assuming this would have no effect on the results as each performer would respond to the audience in a similar way. Further research as a result of compiling the review may have thrown some doubts on your original beliefs. As a consequence you may decide to alter your design, selecting a particular group of 'like' individuals in terms of age, skill level and so on, now that you have a greater awareness of the variables that can influence your results. This is to be expected so don't worry if your design has changed since the planning stage.

The experimental design and procedure should be written in standard academic prose – in the third person and past tense. For example, rather than writing:

I instructed the group to hit the twenty golf balls to get the ball to stop as close to the marker as possible. Then I measured the distance of each ball from the marker.

a more acceptable format would be:

Subjects were instructed to hit 20 golf balls using their normal swing, so that the ball came to rest as close to the marker as possible. The distance of each ball from the marker was then measured.

Once you are satisfied that you have recorded all the necessary information you should move on to analyse your results. This is dealt with in the next chapter.

Check your progress, by filling in table 31.1.

Table 31.1   PROGRESS REPORT

TASK	COMPLETED ✓	STILL TO DO ✗
operational definitions stated if necessary		
written up an outline of the design adopted		
controlled irrelevant variables listed (and how)		
variables listed that you can't control		
explanation given of how and why subjects were selected		
details of main items of equipment, materials and resources required		
procedure recorded IN DETAIL		

chapter 32

The Results

This chapter discusses ways to address the final phase of the project (see fig 29.1) – how to analyse the results. The chapter begins by giving a general overview of some of the methods that could be employed to analyse your data, and then discuss ways in which your data could be organised and presented. Examples are also given of students' work to illustrate some of the points made.

Data analysis

Once you have gathered your data, it needs to be analysed in order to support or refute your hypotheses. In other words it is not sufficient to leave it in its 'raw' form. The purpose of data analysis is to organise your data in such a way that it can be summarised and easily interpreted by the reader. Analysis can be through the use of descriptive or inferential statistics.

Raw data

This means data collected from the research experiment which has not undergone any refinement. For example, if you use a written questionnaire to collect data from a group of 30 people, each person's written response would form part of the raw data. If conducting a match analysis of several badminton matches, the data sheets from each match would be the raw data. Raw data is all the data that you collect.

Descriptive statistics

These allow you to organise your raw data into a more easily readable and understandable form. For example, rather than merely listing 20 subjects raw scores the scores could be presented in graphical form or frequency distribution tables. Descriptive statistics also allow you to summarise your data, commonly using the mean, median and the mode depending on the type of data you have acquired.

Inferential statistics

These are used to infer or imply that the results gained from an experiment using a relatively small sample of subjects would be the same even if a larger group were used. For example if you found that distributive practice resulted in greater improvements in performance of say, the forehand drive in squash, and this was supported by the use of inferential statistics then you could assume that this would be the case for all groups with the same characteristics as the subjects in your sample.

Unfortunately you cannot choose any statistical method for your results. The nature of your research question and the data you collect will affect your choice. For example, someone researching a possible relationship between ethnic grouping and sports participated in would be unlikely to use the same method to analyse their results as someone measuring the effects of a training schedule on performance. The reason for this is that the data, although numerical in both cases,

Table 32.1   DIFFERENT TYPES OF DATA

1	write 1 if you play every day, 2 for every other day, 3 for once a week
2	45% of the audience agreed that this was a better match than last week
3	the home team won 28–15
4	50 people said that whilst they preferred hockey to football they still liked badminton the best
5	there was a total of 12 cm² of women's sports coverage in local papers that week
6	the fastest time was 10.25 seconds
7	the furthest distance was 15.50 metres

is actually of different types; so that there are different mathematical rules governing what can be done to it. Table 32.1 contains different types of data that might be recorded whilst carrying out a research project:

Whilst the data gained from table 32.1 is written as numbers, the numbers cannot all be mathematically manipulated in the same way. For example, it is possible to subtract the losing team's score shown in '3' from the winning team's score to establish their winning margin. The resulting figure would make sense in the context of the statement, ie, the winning team won by a margin of 13 points. This makes sense, but the same mathematical manipulation of the figures shown in '1' would not: if you subtracted the '1' representing playing every day from the '3' representing once a week, the answer would be '2'. This number would be meaningless in terms of the initial question asked. Thus different types of numbers have different allowable manipulations, that can be performed on them if a meaningful result is to be obtained. The allowable types of manipulation are based on whether the numbers are categorised as **nominal**, **ordinal** or **interval**. These categories are explained below. You must ensure that you know the type or level of data you are collecting so that you choose an appropriate statistical method to summarise your data.

Nominal data

These are numbers which are used as a convenient means of categorising data. Nominal data often occurs in questionnaires. For example:

Question 1
State the number that represents the type of school you attended:

1. Comprehensive	*2. Grammar*	*3. Technical*
4. Church	*5. Private*	*6. Boarding*
7. Other		

Question 2
State the number/s that represent the different types of sport you have participated in during school physical education lessons:

1. Netball	*2. Football*	*3. Rugby*
4. Hockey	*5. Basketball*	*6. Badminton*
7. Squash	*8. Tennis*	*9. Swimming*
10. Athletics	*11. Other*	

The responses to the questions are really only short-hand labels, used to represent the different categories. Nominal scales do not therefore have size or order. Results using this scale cannot be mathematically manipulated (ie, use of addition, division etc.). For example, the '9' representing swimming above cannot be compared to the '7' representing squash in the way we would normally compare numbers – the '9' does not mean that swimming is bigger, better, or worth more than squash! Despite this, nominal data is still useful in those projects where categories of answers need to be recorded. If your data is nominal, the following tables show some of the allowable types of manipulation on this data.

Table 32.2   EXAMPLE OF DESCRIPTIVE STATISTICS ALLOWABLE ON THIS TYPE OF DATA

TYPE	COMMENTS
mode	allowable as it does not change the categories, but simply states the most frequently occurring one

Table 32.3   EXAMPLE OF INFERENTIAL STATISTICAL TEST ALLOWABLE ON THIS TYPE OF DATA

TYPE	COMMENTS
sign test	experiment must have a related design so that pairs of scores may be used
chi-squared	the data must be unrelated

(*Note:* see page 541 for some appropriate statistics texts, if you are unsure about how to carry out any of these tests.)

Ordinal

Unlike nominal data, ordinal data *does* have an implied order. For example, the numbers assigned to athletes to represent their placing after a race are ordinal, as it is possible to tell from the data the order that the athletes crossed the line. Data obtained from the following question would also be ordinal:

Question 3
Place the following sports in order of preference:
> *Badminton*
> *Squash*
> *Cricket*
> *Volleyball*

Ordinal data still does not contain size: although we know which activity subjects prefer, we cannot tell from the data how much they prefer one activity over another.

Ordinal data can result from questionnaires; eg, where subjects are asked to rank activities, their attitudes and so on; or in more traditional experimental projects where the researcher 'invents' a scale to measure a subject's performance. For example, a researcher might divide a football goal into sections as in fig 32.1. The subject would be allocated points depending in which section they managed to strike the ball. In this way the scores of one subject could be compared to that of another, or the scores of the same subject could be compared under different conditions, such as in a non-fatigued and fatigued state, with and without an audience etc.

This type of data is still classified as ordinal as it is not possible to measure the exact difference between scores. Look at fig 32.2: three subjects' shots at goal are recorded, in which subject X scores 59, subject Z scores 58 and subject Y scores 70. From these scores we can place the players in order:

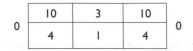

Fig. 32.1 POINTS ALLOCATION BASED ON RESEARCHERS' DIVISIONS OF FOOTBALL GOAL AREA

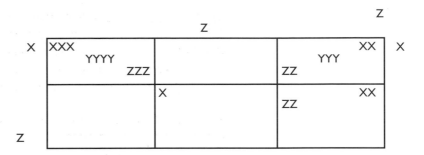

Fig. 32.1 AREAS HIT BY SUBJECTS

1 Subject Y: 70 points
2 Subject X: 59 points
3 Subject Z: 58 points

We cannot however say exactly how much better one player was than another, as the scale used is not precise enough. It could be argued from the raw data shown in fig 31.2 that subject X and subject Y were much closer in terms of performance (the discrepancy between scores was 11), than they were to subject Z, despite the apparent closeness of X's and Z's scores. As a result of this, the statistics that can be applied to this type of data are still restricted.

Table 32.4   EXAMPLE OF DESCRIPTIVE STATISTICS ALLOWABLE ON THIS TYPE OF DATA

TYPE	COMMENTS
mode	allowable as it does not change the categories, but simply states the most frequently occurring one
median	states the middle number of the resultant ordered list (in the above example the median would have been 59)

Table 32.5   EXAMPLE OF INFERENTIAL STATISTICAL TEST ALLOWABLE ON THIS TYPE OF DATA, IN ADDITION TO THAT STATED ABOVE FOR NOMINAL DATA

TYPE	COMMENTS
Wilcoxon (T) signed ranks test	experiment must have related design
Mann-Whitney (U) Test	experiment must have an unrelated design
Wilcoxon rank sum test	experiment must have an unrelated design
Spearman's p correlation coefficient	used to establish a correlation between variables. data is in the form of related pairs

(*Note:* see page 541 for useful statistics texts which explain in detail the required procedure to conduct these tests.)

Interval   This type of data allows an additional level of measurement to be carried out. It is allowable because this type of data not only gives an implied order to results obtained, but also uses a scale where the intervals between each value along the scale are identical in size. For example, suppose a researcher is measuring the

Table 32.6   Example of descriptive statistics allowable on this type of data

TYPE	COMMENTS
mode	allowable as it does not change the categories, but simply states the most frequently occurring one
median	states the middle of the resultant ordered list (in the above example the median would have been 59)
mean	states the mathematical average of a set of scores
standard deviation	gives an estimate of the difference of the scores of a particular group from the mean

Table 32.7   Example of inferential statistical tests allowable on this type of data, in addition to those given for nominal and ordinal data

TYPE	COMMENTS
t-test for related sample	experiment must have related design
t-test for unrelated designs	experiment must have an unrelated design
Pearson's r correlation coefficient	used to establish a correlation between variables data is in the form of related pairs

(*Note:* see page 541 for useful statistics texts which explain in detail the required procedure to conduct these tests).

effects of different types of feedback on accuracy of a golf putt. If the researcher measures the exact distance the ball rests from the pin (rather than banding as in the football example above) under different experimental conditions, any arithmetic operation can be carried out because the data recorded is *interval* – the scale used when measuring distance uses equal intervals (the distance between 1.4 m and 2.4 m will be the same as the distance between 4.4 m and 5.4 m).

To check your understanding of the different categories of data, complete the activity below.

Classify the following types of data:
  1 **Answer to a questionnaire about preferred sports:**
      7 badminton
      12 soccer
      3 squash
      10 hockey
  2 **1st, 2nd and 3rd place in an athletics event.**
  3 **Number of points scored in a basketball match.**
  4 **Numbers used to represent playing positions in a rugby team.**
  5 **Time taken to complete a task.**
  6 **Rank order of players in terms of ability.**
  7 **Actual distance thrown in an athletic competition.**
  8 **Measures of 'quality': Marks out of 5 for the 'nearness' to the basket – 5 points if the basket is scored, 3 if it hits the rim, 1 if it hits the backboard.**

9 **Survey of local newspapers to establish media coverage of 6 different sports activities, using the following classification:**
   1 men's football   2 women's football   3 men's hockey
   4 women's hockey   5 men's tennis   6 women's tennis

10 **Lane numbers used to represent lanes on an athletics track.**

Table 32.8a and b   NUMBER OF POINTS SCORED BY EACH SUBJECT (IN SUBJECT ORDER), EXPERIMENTAL CONDITION: (A) REACTION TEST SCORES WHEN SINGLE RESPONSE WAS REQUIRED (B) REACTION TEST SCORES WHEN A CHOICE OF RESPONSES WAS REQUIRED

28	15	28
25	23	28
40	34	40
19	18	28
40	45	25

(a)

14	10	15
13	13	13
28	15	13
8	10	15
26	26	13

(b)

Organisation and presentation of data

Once you have established the type of data you have collected and analysed it, you need to consider how to organise and present it so that it is easy to understand. There are many ways of doing this, and part of your task will be to select an appropriate method.

Raw data   This can be included in the results section if it is not too bulky. (For example, you would not include all 100 of your questionnaire returns, or 50 match analysis sheets! But you should not discard this material; keep it in case it needs to be viewed by the person assessing your project.)

Non-bulky raw data can be represented in the results section in tabular form; tables 32.8a and 32.8b show scores gained by subjects during an experiment.

Whilst 'complete', data presented in this manner is not easy to interpret at a glance. The following are not immediately obvious: the range of scores, the most common scores or which experimental condition resulted in lower scores. Therefore organisation of data does not stop here. Data could be rearranged in one of several more meaningful forms, depending on what the experimenter is using it for. For example frequency tables could be used.

Table 32.9   FREQUENCY DISTRIBUTION OF DATA — NUMBER OF TIMES OF OCCURRENCE INDICATED IN BRACKET

SINGLE RESPONSE	CHOICE OF RESPONSE
15 (1)	8 (1)
18 (1)	10 (2)
19 (1)	13 (5)
23 (1)	14 (1)
25 (2)	15 (3)
28 (4)	26 (2)
31 (1)	28 (1)
40 (3)	
45 (1)	
n = 15	n = 15

Frequency distribution of data

The presentation of data in table 32.9 has shown some progression. In other words it is easier for the reader to make sense of the results. This is because the data has been rearranged into numerical order and the number of times a particular score has been recorded is indicated in brackets. Therefore the reader can see at a glance the range of scores, the most frequently occurring one and the condition when the lowest scores were achieved.

If there was a large range of scores it is also possible to produce grouped frequency distribution tables; for example, see tables 32.10 and 32.11.

Obviously you need not restrict yourself to the use of tables, a variety of graphs may be used equally effectively to organise your data, or a mixture of the two.

Project example 1 (see p 543) was produced by a student investigating whether 14 strides was the optimum run up length (in terms of distance achieved) for 14-year-old novice long jumpers. Notice how they have displayed the raw data (Table A1.1) and then developed this (Tables A1.2 and A1.3) to highlight the critical aspect of the results in relation to their experimental hypothesis, ie, the length of run up which produced the furthest distance jumped and then a comparison with the distance achieved when using 14 strides. The table containing the raw data includes this information, but it is much easier to see in the subsequent tables. The student has then represented this data graphically (fig A.1) to reinforce the

Table 32.10   SINGLE RESPONSE SCORES

number of points	1⇨10	11⇨20	21⇨30	31⇨40	41⇨5
number of subjects	0	3	7	1	4

Table 32.11   CHOICE RESPONSE SCORES

number of points	1→10	11→20	21→30	31→40	41→5
number of subjects	3	9	3	0	0

information. In project example 2, the student was investigating the aerobic fitness of race walkers compared to runners. Again they have included their raw data (the levels achieved by each subject for the multi stage fitness test – Tables A1.4 and A1.5) and from this they have used standard tables to predict the subjects VO_2 max. This information is also represented in table form – Tables A1.6 and A1.7. They then condense this information by establishing the average VO_2 max of each group of athletes (Table A1.8), again supporting this table graphically (fig A.2). They have then placed the subjects performances in rank order and conducted an inferential statistical test on this data to see if there is a significant difference in the values achieved (Table A1.9).

Whether you use descriptive or inferential statistics to analyse your data, it is important to complete each of the following steps:

1 Organise data into a form which is easy to read (remember to show progression).
2 Use descriptive statistics to summarise the important features of the data (by using an appropriate method for the type of data you have collected, as outlined above).
3 If necessary or desirable, carry out an appropriate statistical test using inferential statistics (as outlined above), to establish whether the results gained support your initial experimental hypothesis.
4 Make a simple statement of results at the end of the results section. The data collected from the experiment should have related to the project hypothesis/ses. If the results are inconsistent with your initial hypothesis, then that hypothesis should be refuted. If however the results *are* consistent, then the hypothesis should be accepted and the initial theory which you were examining, supported.

chapter 33

The Final Stages

Τhis chapter covers the remaining items you need to complete in order to finish your project. The discussion, conclusion and appraisal are all important aspects of the project and you will need time in order to complete them thoroughly. They provide you with the opportunity to demonstrate to the reader that you have understood the work you have undertaken and the implications of your results. To illustrate the points made, examples of students' work have been included.

Discussion

At the end of the results section, you should have clearly stated the outcome of your experiment in relation to your original hypotheses. The discussion section should be used to justify to the reader why you rejected or accepted the hypotheses; you need to *interpret* your results. This means that you will have to examine and critically evaluate the findings of your study. You can achieve this by:

- explaining in words what your results mean (to supplement the graphical representation of data used in the results section)
- stating how the results relate to your original hypothesis
- commenting on the similarities/differences of your findings to accepted theories or results from similar experiments
- mentioning any inconsistencies or contradictions in the results and possible reasons for these. Remember, this should be a discussion; if possible try to present more than one potential explanation.

Try not to forget that the purpose of conducting the investigation was to establish the effect of one variable on another, eg, the effect of the independent variable on the dependent variable, such as the effect of fatigue (independent variable) on reaction time (dependent variable). Your discussion should therefore reflect this, and you should comment on whether your results have shown a relationship between the variables under investigation, or whether some other variable is responsible for the results you obtained.

Conclusion

This follows on from the discussion. It should be a brief summary of the outcome of the study confirming the findings stated at the end of the results section. It should be used to reiterate the relationship of the outcome to the hypotheses. See Project examples 3 and 4 on pages 548–550.

Appraisal

This should be split into two sections:

1 evaluation
2 modifications/extensions.

The first part should be used to evaluate your method, while the second gives you the opportunity to make suggestions regarding possible modifications to your design.

Evaluation

Even if you obtained the result you expected, you should still look carefully at your design in case you found any built-in bias which *might* account for the results rather than the independent variable. Similarly, if the results were not as expected, you should try to establish whether this was due to flaws in your design.

Although the appraisal should be critical, try to make sure you only mention factors which might have had an effect on your experiment; don't list variables which although not controlled, did not actually affect the outcome, eg, weather conditions. Depending on the nature of the experiment, these will sometimes be important, and other times not. If measuring dribbling skill in hockey, all subjects will be subjected to the same weather conditions if tested at the same time, thus negating any effects. If, however, you were measuring accuracy when serving in tennis over a number of different days, weather conditions would become extremely important.

Modification/ extensions

The second part of the appraisal should be based on the flaws that you mentioned in the first part. You should be able to suggest some appropriate modifications to your experimental design in an attempt to address the problems you observed; if your experiment was reproduced by someone else, they should be able to follow these recommendations to improve the original design.

Finally you should make suggestions as to how your experiment might be extended. Project examples 5 and 6 (pages 551–553) show the appraisals for the VO_2 max and long jump projects already mentioned.

Further reading

H Coolican, *Research Methods and Statistics in Psychology* (Hodder & Stoughton, 1990)

MD Gall, WR Borg, JP Gall, *Educational Research, An Introduction* 6th edition (Longman, 1996)

J Green, M D'Oliveira, *Learning to Use Statistical Tests in Psychology* (Open University Press, 1982)

S Heyes, M Hardy, P Humphreys, P Rookes, *Starting Statistics in Psychology and Education a Student Handbook* (Weidenfeld & Nicolson, 1986)

JR Morrow Jr, AW Jackson, JG Disch, DP Mood, *Measurement and Evaluation in Human Performance* (Human Kinetics, 1995)

JR Thomas, JC Nelson, *Research Methods in Physical Activity* 3rd edition (Human Kinetics, 1996)

WJ Vincent, *Statistics in Kinesiology* (Human Kinetics, 1995)

Project examples

Contributions from Kevin Middleton and Stuart Monk.

Project example 1

Table A1.1 RAW DATA

SUBJECT NO.	SEX	AGE	HEIGHT	WEIGHT	TAKE OFF FOOT	LENGTH OF INSIDE LEG (CM)	LENGTH OF STRIDE (CM)	6 STRIDES	10 STRIDES	14 STRIDES	18 STRIDES	22 STRIDES
1	m	14	1.60 m	44 kg	right	81	90	4.50 m	4.90 m	5.05 m	5.08 m	4.72 m
2	m	14	1.67 m	44 kg	left	78	85	3.20 m	4.00 m	4.40 m	4.45 m	3.95 m
3	m	14	1.60 m	51 kg	left	84	95	3.30 m	3.53 m	3.60 m	3.90 m	3.70 m
4	f	14	1.49 m	51 kg	left	71	109	3.56 m	3.61 m	3.80 m	3.94 m	3.45 m
5	f	14	1.47 m	38 kg	left	67	90	3.03 m	3.70 m	3.95 m	3.96 m	3.20 m
6	f	14	1.52 m	57.5 kg	left	68	102	3.35 m	3.75 m	3.80 m	3.80 m	3.70 m

Table A1.2 FURTHER DISTANCE JUMPED

SUBJECT NO.	BEST DISTANCE JUMPED	STRIDE LENGTH
1	5.08 m	18
2	4.45 m	18
3	3.90 m	18
4	3.94 m	18
5	3.96 m	18
6	3.80 m	18

Table A1.3 DISTANCE ACHIEVED AT 14 STRIDES COMPARED WITH FURTHEST DISTANCE ACHIEVED

SUBJECT NO.	14 STRIDES	FURTHEST DISTANCE ACHIEVED AT	BEST DISTANCE JUMPED	DIFFERENCE
1	5.05 m	18 strides	5.08 m	+.03 cm
2	4.40 m	18 strides	4.45 m	+.05 cm
3	3.60 cm	18 strides	3.90 m	+30 cm
4	3.80 cm	18 strides	3.94 m	+14 cm
5	3.95 cm	18 strides	3.96 cm	+.01 cm
6	3.80 m	18 strides	3.80 m	—

The data clearly shows that for these novices, 18 strides would appear to be the optimum with an overall average improvement of 8.8 cm (44.09 cm/6).

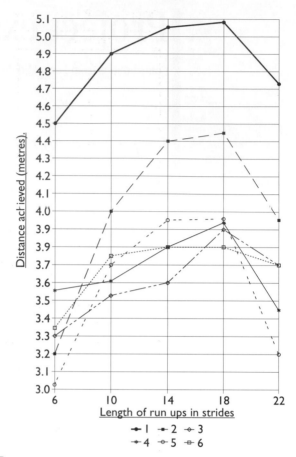

Figure A1.1   Raw data outcomes on the lengths of run ups

Project example 2

Investigation results

The following two tables display the results obtained by all of the athletes taking part in the MSFT on both days, in terms of levels achieved alongside resting pulse rates.

Table A1.4   Walkers' MSFT levels

SUBJECT NO.	RESTING PULSE	MSFT LEVEL
1	72 bpm	9.8
2	72 bpm	14.3
3	80 bpm	10.7
4	70 bpm	14.4
5	76 bpm	9.0
6	76 bpm	10.7
7	72 bpm	12.6
8	68 bpm	15.1
9	76 bpm	11.0

The above results are given, where bpm is equivalent to beats per minute, and the MSFT score is shown with the level first followed by the shuttle; ie, 10.7 where 10 is the level and 7 is the shuttle.

Table A1.5 RUNNERS' MSFT LEVELS

SUBJECT NO.	RESTING PULSE	MSFT LEVEL
1	68 bpm	15.3
2	76 bpm	13.2
3	78 bpm	12.0
4	76 bpm	12.0
5	80 bpm	13.3
6	80 bpm	12.0
7	72 bpm	10.8
8	72 bpm	10.8
9	70 bpm	11.6

The same conditions apply for this table for the runners as for the previous table with the walkers.

These results now require **transformation**, from the level/shuttle format that

Table A1.6 WALKERS' $\dot{V}O_2$ MAX LEVELS

SUBJECT NO.	PREDICTED $\dot{V}O_2$ MAX
1	45.8
2	61.1
3	48.7
4	61.7
5	43.3
6	48.7
7	55.4
8	64.0
9	50.2

they are currently in to show the true level of $\dot{V}O_2$ max achieved by each athlete, to see if the experimental hypothesis stays true.

The transformation from the current form to the $\dot{V}O_2$ max format, is achieved using a booklet included with the MSFT package, which shows all the level/shuttles with the appropriate level of $\dot{V}O_2$ max. This can be shown by two similar tables.

Table A1.7 RUNNERS' $\dot{V}O_2$ MAX LEVELS

SUBJECT NO.	PREDICTED $\dot{V}O_2$ MAX
1	64.6
2	57.6
3	53.7
4	53.7
5	57.6
6	53.7
7	49.3
8	62.7
9	51.9

Note: the above results for the corresponding $\dot{V}O_2$ max levels to the MSFT levels, are in this instance given as $\dot{V}O_2$ max in: Millilitres of oxygen per kilogram of body weight per minute, and are as calculated by Loughborough University.

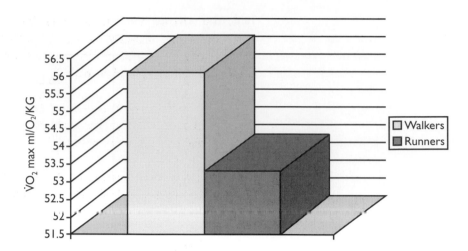

Figure A1.2 AVERAGE $\dot{V}O_2$ MAX VALUES
FOR RACE WALKERS AND RUNNERS

Again, $\dot{V}O_2$ max is measured as millilitres of oxygen per kilogram of body weight per minute. A statement of results can be expressed thus:
The runners scored higher in the MSFT than the walkers. Therefore the experimental hypothesis:

'An endurance runner will reach a higher level on the MSFT than an endurance race-walker on the same level of competition',

is highlighted as being accepted prior to statistical analysis and average working, the next step to strengthen the validity of the experimental hypothesis.

Table A1.8   AVERAGE $\dot{V}O_2$ MAX VALUES FOR RACE WALKERS AND RUNNERS, MEASURED IN ML/O^2/KG BODY WEIGHT

TYPE OF ATHLETE	AVE. $\dot{V}O_2$
walkers	53.22
runners	56.09
difference	−2.87 ml/O2/kg

Statistical analysis of results

The validity of the results *may* become a lot clearer following the undergoing of some sort of statistical analysis. It must be remembered that inferential statistical tests do not 'prove' anything; they only indicate which of the two hypotheses is preferable on the basis of the given data and are not the 'be-all and end-all' of the investigation conclusion. The hypotheses being analysed are:

Null (Ho): There will be no difference between the $\dot{V}O_2$ max of a runner and race-walker, as tested by the MSFT.

Experimental (H1): An endurance runner will reach a higher level of the MSFT than an endurance race-walker, thus having a higher $\dot{V}O_2$ max level.

There are various statistical tests that are to mathematicians and biologists alike, which are suitable for this type of data analysis.

The test used in this instance will be the Mann Whitney U-Test, a test for comparing two sets of data with null and experimental hypotheses linking them. The method used in the Mann Whitney U-Test is set out using ranks and set formulae to link the sums of the ranks:

$Ua = Ra - \frac{1}{2}na(n + 1)$, & $Ub = Rb - \frac{1}{2}nb(n + 1)$, where 'a' and 'b' are the two sets of data, 'n' is the number of athletes in each group and 'R' is the sum of the ranks for that particular set of athletes.

The given answers or 'U' a and b, will then be compared and the smallest taken to be compared with a critical value from the Mann Whitney U-Test table of critical values.

The test will commence thus:
Treating *all* of the data as a whole, rank the data from 1–18:
(*Note:* A signifies the walkers data, B the runners.)

The results are given in the transformed $\dot{V}O_2$ max forms, where:
  Res = result
  Ran = rank
  Gro = group (walker or runner)

The ranks for A and B will now be summed thus:

$$R(a) = 2 + 4 + 5 + 8 + 13 + 15.5 + 15.5 + 17 + 18\{ql\}$$

{text} $R(a) = 98$

$$R(b) = 1 + 3 + 6.5 + 6.5 + 10 + 10 + 10 + 12 + 14\{ql\}$$
$$R(b) = 73\{ql\}$$

Now the values of Ua and Ub will be calculated using the formulae already given previously:

$Ua = Ra - \frac{1}{2}n(n + 1)$, where n is the number of terms
$Ua = 98 - \frac{1}{2} \times 9(9 + 1)$
$Ua = 98 - \frac{1}{2} \times 90$
$Ua = 98 - 45$
$Ua = 53$

$Ub = Rb - \frac{1}{2}n(n + 1)$, where n is the number of terms
$Ub = 73 - \frac{1}{2} \times 9(9 + 1)$
$Ub = 73 - \frac{1}{2} \times 90$
$Ub = 73 - 45$
$Ub = 28$

TABLE A1.9   MANN WHITNEY U-TEST

res	64.6	64	62.7	61.7	61.1	57.6	57.6	55.4	53.7	53.7	51.9	50.2	49.3	48.7	48.7	45.8	43.3	
ran	1	2	3	4	5	6.5	6.5	8	10	10	10	12	13	14	15.5	15.5	17	18
gro	B	A	B	A	A	B	B	A	B	B	B	B	B	A	A	A	A	A

The smallest value out of Ua and Ub is now selected from the two. This value (in this case it equals 28) is now compared to the **critical value** for the appropriate values of 'n' for both sets of athletes, in this instance 9.

From the Mann Whitney Table of critical values, this value for 9 sets of data in both groups is equivalent to **17** degrees of freedom.

Mann Whitney says that:

'When the smallest value of U (28) is compared to the critical value for N a and b, if the U value is less than or equal to this critical value then the Null Hypothesis is rejected.'

So:

17 < 28, so in this case the null hypothesis:

'There will be no difference between the $\dot{V}O_2$ max of a runner and a race-walker as tested by the MSFT,'

is rejected, throwing further backing behind the experimental hypothesis to be true.

Project example 3

Investigation discussions

The general results collected from the investigation and the resulting transformation of raw data to a more applicable format of straight format, make for interesting and clear reading. Both the tables and resultant average graph show an obvious trend, which has been firmly backed up by the use of the Mann Whitney U-Test statistical analysis. Firstly, one obvious conclusion needs to be drawn direct from the available data in its various forms:

'These results show that runners featured in this investigation do in fact seem to have scored better on the MSFT, in general, than the race-walkers.'

There are of course one or two exceptions to this theory, but it must be said that in virtually all of the runner/walker pairings, the runner will have scored the superior result on the MSFT.

The runners scores simply at a glance do appear to be uniformly higher than the walkers, with a higher, smaller range of scores than the walkers.

- runners range of results = 49.3–64.6
- walkers range of results = 43.3–64.0.

These further conclude that:

'The results further show that runners levels of $\dot{V}O_2$ max are comparatively higher than those of the race-walkers, as shown by this particular MSFT.'

This last statement is the key to the whole of the investigation intent. The initial aim of the investigation was to compare the maximum oxygen uptake of long distance runners and race-walkers (or $\dot{V}O_2$ max), and this has been clearly defined by the results.

Whether or not the trends shown in this instance are uniform for *every* race-walker and runner comparison the world over, is obviously a matter for alternative investigation.

Indeed one major fault with this experiment, is that the size of the samples were small, but were the best that could be utilised (see appraisal).

However, even with this said and done, the results show a clear superiority with the runners and therefore the experimental hypothesis:

'An endurance runner will reach a higher level on the Multi Stage Fitness Test than an endurance race-walker on the same level of competition,'

is *accepted* as being proved to be correct.

Therefore, the null hypothesis:

'There will be no difference between the $\dot{V}O_2$ max levels of a runner or a race walker as tested by the MSFT,'

is *rejected* as being proved to be incorrect.

Note: the above conclusions are made following strict statistical analysis, as-well as simple observation of the raw data and data transformation.

The next question to be answered is, 'Why has this difference occurred?'

From a physiological point of view the results *should* concern any endurance athlete with regards to maximum oxygen uptake, as it is a vital component of general aerobic fitness.

- The walkers scored inferior $\dot{V}O_2$ max levels compared to the runners. This may have been down to the fact that a 'running test' was used as the measure, instead of an alternative, such as the Rockport walk protocol (see experimental design). This does of course place the walkers at an immediate disadvantage and has a strong case to be the main reason for the differences in result.
- Another possible avenue to look down, is that of training methods used by both the walkers and the runners. Whilst the basic principles of training will remain the same for walkers and runners, there are obviously differences in components such as:

  1 time spent on training by each individual involved
  2 types of training used by each athlete
  3 frequency of each training genre undertaken by each athlete.

- Consequently, certain athletes undertaking the MSFT in this instance will appear to be 'fitter' (in terms of performing the MSFT), than others and score superior levels of $\dot{V}O_2$ max.

Runners may evolve different physiological features directly from being runners, with the same rule applying to walkers. For example, walkers hip and ankle flexibility has to be apt enough to deal with the walking technique, very much different to runners whose power comes from their quadriceps and hamstrings.

This type of physiological difference between the two types of athlete *may* lead to better suitability in carrying out the MSFT, and it is a view that makes sense.

Note: it must once again be said that most walkers in their time as athletes will have undergone some sort of running-type training so it is not completely alien to them.

Whatever the reason for the runners' apparent superior $\dot{V}O_2$ max levels, it should be reminded that this *does not* make the runners any 'fitter' generally than the walkers. Any athlete is only as fit as they need to be in order to perform their necessary tasks in their given sport.

The investigation here has highlighted $\dot{V}O_2$ max as an aerobic fitness component, and has shown that with the athletes tested in this instance, the runners have come up trumps. The walkers can perhaps gear their training schedules to improve their personal $\dot{V}O_2$ max levels, and a subsequent *improvement in performance levels* may result.

The conclusions have been drawn; the feedback will be given to all of the athletes who participated, in the hope that they will take notice and keep training hard, striving to reach the best performance levels possible.

Project example 4

Discussion   The graphs clearly show an increase in the distance jumped as the length of the run up increased up to 18 strides. They also show a decrease in distance as the run up is increased further. The reason for the decrease after 18 strides could be that the run up may have been too long. This idea was put forward by Geoffrey Dyson, ie, that the length of run up is determined by the athletes ability to accelerate at top speed at the board, without being tried out before take-off.

There were no anomalies in the raw data apart from subject 6 who achieved the same distance for both 14 and 18 strides. The reason for this could be that the subject had a long running stride which meant they would have a longer run up, in terms of metres covered compared to the other subjects. This may have had the run up too long for them.

Although the average improvement is shown as 8.8 cm, this could be misleading as this is due mainly to subjects 3 and 4; ie, their improvements were 30 cm and 14 cm. The other subjects improvements were only marginal. Subjects 3 and 4 may have made such drastic improvements because they needed a longer run-up in order to reach their optimum speed off the board.

Closer inspection shows that subjects 1, 2 and 5 have very similar distances achieved and that they have only improved by a few centimetres unlike subjects 3 and 4. Thus although they did improve they must have had around their optimum run-up length.

Referring to table A4 to review the theory that Roy Hawkey stated, ie, that a greater speed can be achieved through increasing the length of the run-up, this would appear to be the case for subjects 1, 2, 3, 4 and 5 up to the 18 strides.

In conclusion these results clearly show that distance achieved is affected by run up length. In all but one case the subjects showed improvement (although small in some instances competitions could be won or lost on these types of differences). Therefore the experimental hypothesis:

H_1 = *The Long jump distance achieved by 14-year-olds will be reduced, when using a run-up, less than 14 strides,*

is accepted and N_1 rejected.

H_2 = *The Long jump distance achieved by 14-year-olds will be reduced, when using a run-up, greater than 14 strides,*

is rejected and therefore N_2 accepted.

Appraisal of the investigation

Project example 5

Before entering the mainstream appraisal of the investigation, it is important to note that the experiment as a whole ran very smoothly and was an enjoyable task to have to carry out.

- The pattern that it followed was as easy to perform as the results were to interpret. Luck was obtained in that the weather conditions were near enough the same (give or take a slight change in the wind speed on one occasion), and that all of the athletes taking part were *fit* and *enthusiastic*, a vital factor in the successful running of an experiment of this particular nature.
- The investigation in general gave the required results that could undergo worthwhile comparison, possible because of the factors mentioned above.
- The pre-test (basic 'training sessions' that both sets of athletes were put through before the start of the MSFT) were well organised and ran smoothly on both occasions, whilst the MSFT was staged at the same time of day in both instances to avoid any correctable differences between the running of the two tests.
- The equipment used for the investigation is naturally very simplistic in design, and so was easy to set up and administer. The tape recording of the MSFT was heard amicably at *all* points of the shuttle in both directions by *all* of the athletes on *both* occasions that the test was run.
- The width of the track meant that competitors had to settle for *less* than one lane (6 lanes, 9 competitors), a small problem in design and procedure, but one that was easily dealt with by allocating each athlete their own 'space'.
- Of course it must be remembered that as each athlete dropped out more room was available so it was not that a significant design flaw.

As the investigation developed, the major design flaw encountered was in the way that the athletes **final** MSFT level was collected. Athletes were requested to remember exactly what shuttle they were on, whilst the recording would indicate what level they had reached.

Fatigue as the test progressed may have meant that the athletes in both instances almost forgot what shuttle they were up to, until the recording indicated that a new level had begun.

None of the competitors indicated that this was an actual flaw in the investigation, but if the investigation were to be modified, a person would be assigned the job of counting every competitors shuttles using a sheet like this running example (using numbers on each competitors' t-shirt).

Table A1.10 is shown as a worked example, where the athletes are numbered 1–9 as with the experiment in this instance.

The top row displays the levels of the MSFT, while the left-handside column shows the shuttles completed of that particular level. Thus, whilst the MSFT is running the grid reads downwards from the top left hand corner. The / symbol indicates that no athletes dropped out on that particular shuttle, whilst the numbers in the boxes show the numbered athletes that *did* drop out on that shuttle: eg, athletes 4 and 6 dropped out on level 9, shuttle 7.

This would make the whole administration of the MSFT easier for both the invigilators and the athletes themselves, giving even less opportunity for experimental error in the results.

Other modifications to the general experimental design could include:

- holding the test *indoors* instead of outdoors to eliminate weather conditions appearing as a variable.
- Holding the test along a slightly wider shuttle to give each athlete more room in which to run.
- Selecting up to 20 athletes *in each group*, in order to give a better comparison of results, therefore giving a better, more reliable, mean/average result and firmer conclusions.
- Having athletes of exactly the same age, sex and ability in each group thus giving the best possible comparison of results.

One other possible 'modification' would be to hold the two sets of athletes' MSFT tests *simultaneously*. This would create a sense of competition between race-walkers and runners which may have a positive or negative effect on the results validity. It is either way, a change in procedure.

A lot of these modifications are, most of the time, simply not possible so while they exist it must be said that the investigation carried out in this instance, *met and achieved* all of the goals that it set out to meet. The hypotheses were answered to a satisfactory standard and the MSFT carry-out was an excellent experience in organisational skills.

To sum up, a worthwhile investigation on an interesting topic, that could have been better but could also have been worse.

Table A1.10   WORKED EXAMPLE

6	7	8	9	10	11	12	13	14	15	16
1	/	/	/	/	/	/	1			
2	/	/	3	7	/	/	/			
3	/	/	/	2	/	/	/			
4	/	/	/	/	/	/	/			
5	/	/	/	/	/	/	/	8		
6	/	/	5	/	/	/	/	/		
7	/	/	/	4 6	/	/	9	/		
8	/	/	/	/	/	/	/	/		
9	/	/	/	/	/	/	/	/		
10	/	/	/	/	/	/	/	/		

Project example 6

Appraisal of the work

Although the project went well, if it were to be repeated some changes could be made, for example,

- the subjects could have been filmed when they were doing their run ups and jumps. With this source of information I could then look at the film and do an observation and see if the subjects were actually picking up speed as they got closer to the board, or slowing down. I could also use the film to see if all subjects were using the same method of take off and landing phase.
- As speed was a factor of affecting how far the subject jumped, I could run an experiment to see if these subjects were naturally fast, ie, by timing them over a 40 m spring. From this, I could then tell if they were capable of picking up

speed quickly. I could compare these times, ie, to how long it took the subjects to run each different length of run-up.

- The subjects I chose were not all the same height, weight, did not have the same length of stride, or take-off foot. Although I felt this did not affect the results, if subjects were selected with the same characteristics, this would ensure that there was no effect.
- This project could be extended by the following: selecting a second group, who were equivalent to the first apart from long jump experience. It should then be possible to see how ability affects the length of run up.

The project established 18 strides as the optimum for most subjects. However, while 18 strides may have been better than 14 it is not possible to say what the exact run-up would be:

- Subject 1 could have an optimum of 15 strides and not 18
- Subject 2 could have an optimum of 16 strides and not 18
- Subject 3 could have an optimum of 17 strides and not 18
- Subject 4 could have an optimum of 19 strides and not 18.

It would be interesting to repeat the experiment, but this time concentrating on run-ups of 14, 15, 16, 17, and 18 strides to find the true optimum run-up length.

Suggested Project Titles

Anatomy and physiology

- The effects of plyometric training on the performance of a line out in rugby.
- A comparison of the relative efficiency of power weight training circuit and a plyometric circuit in improving jumping ability of volley ball players.
- The effect of fitness levels on the amount of unforced errors in the game of badminton.
- The effects of fatigue on the performance of a 5-a-side association football penalty shot.
- The effectiveness of a variety of training methods to increase VO_2 max in cyclists.

Historical, social and cultural

- Sporting activity amongst post school 16–19-year-olds.
- Coverage of men's and women's sport in the popular press.
- Law breaking within amateur and professional football.
- A survey of sporting opportunity within two different locations.
- An investigation into the different use of language when reporting on male and female athletes sporting achievements.

Psychology

- Transfer of learning between the volleyball overhead serve and the tennis overhead serve.
- The effects of exercise at different heart rate intensities on a persons choice reaction time.
- The effectiveness of different types of feedback influencing a simple skill.
- The speed of learning using a variety of guidance techniques.
- The effects of mental and physical practice on the performance of a cricket 'off drive'.
- Massed versus distributed practice on the teaching of the badminton high serve to a group of novice players.
- Whole versus part learning practices in the coaching of the basketball lay-up shot to a group of novice players.
- The effects of using short tennis to improve tennis skills with a group of beginners.
- Audience effects on the accuracy of a tennis service.
- The effect of extrinsic motivation on the performance of a hand–eye co-ordination task.
- The effects of goal setting on performance in a range of sporting activities.

Fitness Test Ratings

The following tables gives test ratings for fitness tests described in Chapter 7.

Table A3.1 GRIP STRENGTH NORMS

CLASSIFICATION	NON-DOMINANT (KG)	DOMINANT (KG)
Women		
Excellent	>37	>41
Good	34–36	38–40
Average	22–33	25–37
Poor	18–21	22–24
Very poor	<18	<22
Men		
Excellent	>68	>70
Good	56–67	62–69
Average	43–55	48–61
Poor	39–42	41–47
Very Poor	<39	<41

For persons over 50yrs of age, reduce scores by 10%

Source: Data from Corbin, Lindsay and Tolson (1978) Concepts in Physical Education

Table A3.2 30M SPRINT TEST

TIME (SECS) MALE	TIME (SECS) FEMALE	RATING
<4.0	<4.5	excellent
4.2–4.0	4.6–4.5	good
4.4–4.3	4.8–4.7	average
4.6–4.5	5.0–4.9	fair
>4.6	>5.0	poor

Table A3.3   Classification of aerobic fitness ($\dot{V}O_2$ max in ml kg^1 mcn^1)

AGE YRS	LOW	FAIR	AVERAGE	GOOD	HIGH
Women					
20–29	<24	24–30	31–37	38–48	49+
30–39	<20	20–27	28–33	34–44	45+
40–49	<17	17–23	24–30	31–41	42+
50–59	<15	15–20	21–27	28–37	38+
60–69	<13	13–17	18–23	24–34	35+
Men					
20–29	<25	25–33	34–42	43–52	53+
30–39	<23	23–30	31–38	39–48	49+
40–49	<20	20–26	27–35	36–44	45 ı
50–59	<18	18–24	25–33	34–42	43+
60–69	<16	16–22	23–30	31–40	41+

Source: Data from American Heart Association (1972)

Table A3.4   Normative scores for the abdominal curl conditioning test

STAGE	NUMBER OF SIT UPS	STANDARD	
	CUMULATIVE	MALE	FEMALE
1	20	poor	poor
2	42	poor	fair
3	64	fair	fair
4	89	fair	good
5	116	good	good
6	146	good	very good
7	180	excellent	excellent
8	217	excellent	excellent

Table A3.5   Sit and reach test ratings

MALE	FEMALE	RATING
>35	>39	excellent
31–34	33–38	good
27–30	29–32	fair
<27	<29	poor

Table A3.6   Illinois agility run test

TIME IN SECONDS		RATING
MALE	FEMALE	
<15.2	<17.0	excellent
16.1–15.2	17.9–17.0	good
18.1–16.2	21.7–18.0	average
18.3–18.2	23.0–21.8	fair
>18.3	>23	poor

Table A3.7   STICK DROP TEST

REACTION TIME	RATING
>42.5	excellent
37.1–42.5	good
29.6–37.0	average
22.0–29.5	fair
<22	poor

Table A3.8   VERTICAL JUMP TEST SCORES

DISTANCE (CMS) MALE	DISTANCE (CMS) FEMALE	RATING
>60	>47	excellent
51–59	36–46	good
41–50	29–35	average
27–40	25–34	poor
<26	<24	very poor

Index

ability 343–6
Aborigines 332–3
acceleration 136–9
achievement motivation 447–51
administration of sport 226
adventure sports 200
   see also outdoor education
AEB (Associated Examining Board)
   course 509
aerobic system 69–70
aerobic training 111–12
affective learning 356–7
age and sports participation 219–20, 313
ageing 130–2, 381
aggression 253–4, 426–34
agility 87, 91
air resistance 141
alactacid debt 78
alactic system 65, 66
alertness 381
all or none law 30
amateur sport 205, 243, 245, 270–1, 335
American football 310
AMI (Athletic Motivation Inventory) 417
amphetamines 258
anabolic steroids 259
anaerobic capacity test 92
anaerobic threshold 94–6, 112
'anatomical position' 2
Ancient Greece 240–1
Ancient Rome 241
angling 287
angular motion 149, 150–3, 154
anticipation 380
anxiety 487, 488–91
apartheid 232
appendicular skeleton 7
appraisal section of projects 511–12,
   540–1
aquatic activities 290–2
archery 284
Arnold, Thomas 272, 274–5
arousal 381, 442–7, 487
arteries 34, 41–2, 45
arterioles 41–2
Asian groups 212
assertive behaviour 428
Associated Examining Board (AEB)
   course 509
atherosclerosis 126–7
Athletic Motivation Inventory (AMI) 417
athletics 206, 243–4, 273, 297

Atkinson, R. 448
ATP-PC system 65, 66
atrioventricular node (A.V. node) 36–7
attention 381
attitudes 418–26
attribution re-training 456
attribution theory 451–8
audience stress 493
'Aussie Sport' initiative 328–9
Australia 324–33
   Aborigines 332–3
   'Aussie Sport' initiative 328–9
   disabled people 333
   education system 324
   government sports policy 331–2
   major sports 330–1
   physical education 326–8
   politics 324
   talent identification 329–30
Australian football 330–1
autocratic leaders 480
autonomic nervous system 37, 443
autonomous organisations 168–71
A.V. node (atrioventricular node) 36–7
axial skeleton 7

Bandura, A. 456–7, 464–6
Barr Sex Test 213
baseball 309–10
basketball 310
bear baiting 289
behaviourism 365
Bernouilli effect 143–5
bibliographies 512–13
biofeedback 499–500
biomechanics 134
blood
   circulatory system 43–50
   composition 41
   doping 259
   function 40–1
   lactacid debt 79
   oxygen transportation 57–8
   pressure 45–6, 113
   production 5, 13
   redistribution during exercise 47–8
   vascular network 41–2
   viscosity 41
blood sports 288–9
body composition 86, 90
body planes 3
Bohr shift 58

bones
   growth and development 13–14
   joints 14–15
   and mineral storage 6
   surface features 11
   tissue 12–13
   types of 10
boxing 284–5
bradycardia 39, 113
breathing *see* respiration
breathing control 499
Brighton Declaration on Women and
   Sport 215–16
British Academy for Sport 176
British Empire 269–70
British Olympic Association 170–1
bronchioles 54–5
bull baiting 289
Butler Education Act (1944) 280

Callois, R. 181–2
capillaries 42
'CAPS' (Challenge, Achievement and
   Pathways in Sport) 329
carbohydrates 74–5, 119
carbon dioxide transportation 58–9
cardiac cycle 35–6
cardiac muscle 19
cardiac output 39
cardio-respiratory endurance 86
cardiovascular system 33–40, 89
   diseases 126–9
   and exercise 38, 40, 111, 113–15
cartilage 12
catastrophe theory 447
Cattell's personality theory 413
Central Council of Physical Recreation
   (CCPR) 164–5
central government *see* government
   policy; politics
centralised political systems 229
centre of gravity 146–7
CGF (Commonwealth Games Federation)
   172
Challenge, Achievement and Pathways in
   Sport (CAPS) 329
character-building 227–8
Charles II, King 264
Chelladurai multi-dimensional model
   481–2
children 220–1, 312–13
choice reaction time 379

cholesterol 127
circuit training 104, 282
circulatory system 43–50
Cities of Sport Programme 176
Clarendon Report 272
classical conditioning 365–6, 420
climatic strain 493
coaching 222–3, 311
    see also teaching
Coca-Cola 247
coccyx 9
cock fighting 289
cognitive anxiety 488
cognitive control 499
cognitive dissonance theory 424–5
cognitive learning 356–7
    theories 370
cognitive re-appraisal 496
cognitive skills 341
cohesion 475–7
command teaching style 405
commentators 249
commercialism of sport 242–8, 335
commitment 504
Commonwealth Games Federation (CGF)
    172
community sports centres 173
competition stressors 492–3
competitive anxiety 489–91
competitive societies 236, 239
complex skills 342
complex tasks 392–3
Compulsory Competitive Tendering 230
conditioning activities 205
conditioning learning theories 365–9
conflict 493
consonance 424
contingency theory of leadership 479–80
continuous training methods 101–2
continuum 348–9
contraction of muscles 27, 28–31
control of movement 382–3
cool downs 101
cooperation in teams 473–4
cooperative cultures 236, 239
Cotswold Olympian games 264
Council for Europe 172
Counter culture 304
Countryside Commission 165
cricket 272, 296–7
Cromwell, Oliver 264
cue-utilisation theory 446
cultural traditions 212, 236–41
cycling 294

data
    analysis 532–6
    organisation and presentation 536–9
decentralised political systems 229

decision making 377
deer stalking 287–8
democratic leaders 481
Department of National Heritage 160–1
descriptive statistics 532
developing countries 240
developing research problems 515–16
deviant behaviour 251–3
diet 121–3
disabled people 216–19, 307, 333
discovery learning 406
discrete, serial, continuous continuum
    348
discrimination 210–11, 213
discussion section of projects 540
dissonance 424
distributed practice 398–400
dog fighting 289
doping 259
double circulatory system 43–50
drag 142
drive reduction theory 369
drive theory 444
drug abuse 257–60

eating 74–6, 121–3
eccentric force 149–50
education see schools
effective learning 356–7
electron transport system 70
Elizabeth I, Queen 263
Ellis, M. 182
emotional arousal 458
endorsements 245
endurance training 111–14
energy systems 65–76
English Tourist Board 171
EPOC (Excess Post-exercise Oxygen
    Consumption) 77–8
ethical issues of projects 517–18
ethnic minorities 211–12, 312, 322–3
    Aborigines 332–3
    Maoris 237–8
eustress 491–2
excellence 222–5, 320–2
Excess Post-exercise Oxygen
    Consumption (EPOC) 77–8
exercise
    and ageing 130–3
    body adaptations
        cardiovascular 38, 40, 111, 113–15
        muscular 111–12
    and health 129
    programme design 132–3
    recovery process 77
    redistribution of blood 47–8
    and respiration 53–6, 62, 111, 114
    and the skeletal system 18
    see also training

exhaustion 494
expectations 462
experimental design 516, 527–31
expiration 55–6
extrinsic motivation 439–42
Eysenck, H.J. 412–13

F.I.I.T. regime 98–100
facilities 172–6, 219
Fartlek training 101–2
fat 75, 120
fatigue 77–81
feedback 374, 385–9
females see women
fencing 285–6
Fiedler's contingency model 479–80
field sports 286–8
50+ sports participation 219–20
'fight or flight' reactions 494
finance for sport 176–8, 218
fitness
    and health 126–9
    health-related components 84–7
    measurement and assessment 88–94
    and physical activity 83
    skill-related components 84, 87–8
fives 293
Fleishman, E. 343–5
fluid forces 140–6
food 74–6, 121–3
football 272–3, 295–6
    American football 310
    Australian football 330–1
force 134
    eccentric force 149–50
    fluid forces 140–6
Forestry Commission 165
Foundation for Sport and the Arts 178
fox hunting 286–7
France 315–24
    ethnic communities 322–3
    and excellence in sport 320–2
    physical education 315–18
    politics 315
    school sports associations 319
    'Sport Pour Tous' 319–20
frequency distributions 537–9
friction 138–9, 140
frustration 493
frustration-aggression hypothesis 430–1

gambling 177
games 206–8
gaseous exchange 56–60
gender 212–16
globalisation 242, 335
glucose 67
glycogen 67, 81
glycogen loading 124

glycolysis 68, 112
goal setting 502–5
golf 297–9
Golgi tendon organs 31
governing bodies 168–70, 177, 243
government policy
    in Australia 331–2
    in the UK 157–61, 176, 227, 229–31
    in the USA 303–4
    see also politics
gravity 146–7
Greece 240–1
Gross-Fine classification 347–8
group dynamics 469–77
guidance 396–8
guided discovery 406
gymnastic movements 208

haematocrit 93
haematology 93
haemoglobin 41, 57–8, 113
Hanoverian era 264–5
hare coursing 284
health 126–33
heart
    cardiac cycle 35–6
    cardiac muscle 19
    cardiac output 39
    pacemaker impulses 36–7
    regulation 37–8
    structure and function 33–5
    see also cardiovascular system
Henley regatta 291
Henry VIII, King 263
Hering-Breur reflex 63
Hick's Law 379
hierarchy of needs 437
hooliganism 254–7
horse racing 288
Howell Report (1983) 247–8
Huizinga, J. 181
Hull, C.L. 369
hypertension 126
hypotheses 510, 516–18, 523–6

ice hockey 310–11
identifying research problems 514
imagery 496–8
impacts 139–40
impulse 140
independent sampling 528
individual differences 392
inferential statistics 532–3
information processing 371–7, 381
inns 267
inspiration 55
instinct theory 429–30
Institute of Sports Sponsorship (ISS) 245
intellectual skills 341

interactionist approach to personality 416
intermittent training 102
International Olympic Committee 171
international organisations 171–2
International Sports Federation (ISF) 172
interval data 535–6
interval training 102–4
intrinsic motivation 438–9, 440–2
inverted 'U' hypothesis 444–7, 469
ISF (International Sports Federation) 172
ISS (Institute of Sports Sponsorship) 245

James I, King of England 264
joints 14–15
    flexibility 86, 90
jousting 284

Karnoven principle 98
kinesiology 27–8
knowledge of results (KR) 387–9
krebs cycle 70

lactic acid 67–9, 79–80, 112
laissez-faire leaders 481
laminar flow 142
larynx 53
law and order 230–1
lawn tennis 293–4
laws of learning 367–9
leadership 477–83
learned helplessness 454–5
learning
    cognitive theories 370
    conditioning theories 365–9
    definitions 354–5
    drive reduction theory 369
    feedback 385–7
    information processing 371–7, 381
    knowledge of results (KR) 387–9
    motor programmes 382–5
    observational learning 463–4
    and performance 359–61, 391–2
    phases of motor skill learning 357–9
    reaction time 377–81
    social learning 431–2, 463–6
    transfer concept 393–6
    types of 355–7
    variables 361–2
leisure 165–8, 186–9
    facilities 172–6, 219
levers 147–50
Likert scale 421
linear motion 135–9, 154
lipoproteins 127–8
local authorities 159, 165–8, 172–3,
    218, 230
locus of control 452–3
Lombardian ethic 304
lungs 61–4

lymphatic system 50–1

magnus effect 143–5
manual guidance 398
Maori culture 237–8
marathon runs 83
Maslow, A. 437
massed practice 398–400
matched pair design 527–8
maximum oxygen uptake 92–3, 94–6
mechanical guidance 398
media 248–51
medieval England 262
memory 374–7
mental practice 400–1
mental relaxation 499
metabolic rate 130
Middle Ages 262
minerals 6, 121, 123
Minister for Sport 159–60
mobility training 109
Modern Educational Dance 280
moment of force 149
moment of inertia 151–2
momentum 139
mood states 417
motivation 436–51, 466
    achievement motivation 447–51
    and arousal 442–7
    defining 436–8
    types of 438–42
motor abilities 344
motor learning 356, 357–9, 361–2
motor neurones 29
motor programmes 382–3
motor skills 341, 445–6
motor units 30–1
Much Wenlock Olympic Games 270
multi-dimensional model of leadership
    481–2
muscles 19–32
    adaptations during training 111–12
    connective tissues 25
    contraction 27, 28–31
    coordinated movement 25–6
    fibre types 23–4
    and gaseous exchange 59–60
    measuring muscle power 94
    muscular endurance 86, 90
    shapes and sizes 20–3
    skeletal muscle 28–31
Muscular Christianity 267–8
myoglobin 60

narcotic analgesics 258–9
nasal passages 53
National Cities of Sport 176
National Coaching Foundation 163
National Curriculum 194, 195, 200, 231

National Lottery 177–8
national parks 202–3
National Playing Fields Association 171
National Rivers Authorities (NRA) 171
national sports centres 174–5
national stadiums 176
nervous system
    and arousal theory 443
    and heart regulation 37–8
    and muscle contraction 29–31
    and ventilation 62–3
newspapers 248
Newton's laws of motion 134, 136–8, 152–4
nominal data 533–4
Norman conquest 261
norms 462
NRA (National Rivers Authorities) 171
null hypothesis 524
nutrition 119–25

obesity 129–30
OBLA (Onset Blood Lactate Accumulation) 80, 92
observation 355
observational learning 463–4
obstacle training 279
Olympic Accreditation Scheme 176
Olympic Games 232–6, 245
Onset Blood Lactate Accumulation (OBLA) 80, 92
open/closed continuum 349
operant conditioning 366, 420
operational definitions 522, 529
ordinal data 534–5
ossification 13–14
outcome goal orientation 449
outcome goals 503
outdoor education 199–203, 282, 313–14, 322
outdoor pursuit centres 173
Outward Bound Trust 203
oxy-myoglobin link 81
oxygen
    debt 77–8
    maximum oxygen uptake 92–3, 94–6
    transportation 57–8, 114

pacing continuum 349
Paralympics 218–19
parasympathetic nervous system 37–8, 443
parks 202–3
part method of learning 401, 402
Pavlov, I.P. 365–6
peer groups 420
perception 373
perceptive skills 341
perceptual narrowing 446

performance
    curves 359–61
    goal setting 503
    group performance 472
    and learning 391–2
    and self efficacy 458
periodisation 116
personal stress 493
personality 410–18
personality tests 415, 417–18
persuasive communication 422–3
physical education 190–9, 279
    in Australia 326–8
    in France 315–18
    preparation of teachers 334
    in the USA 305–9
physiological strain 493
physiology 1
Piaget, J. 181
plagiarism 519
planes of movement 3
planning research projects 510–11, 514–18
plasma 40, 41, 113
play 180–3, 189
plyometrics 107–8
politics
    and administration of sport 226
    in Australia 324
    in France 315
    and international events 232–6
    political uses of sport 227–8
    relationships between states 226–7
    types of political systems 228–9
    in the USA 302–3
    see also government policy
power 88, 91–2
practice 379, 396–404
prefixes of anatomical terms 3–4
primary schools 196
private schools 195
problem solving 406
professional sport 205, 213, 243–4, 270–1
proficiency abilities 344–5
progressive overload 97
progressive part method of learning 402–3
progressive relaxation technique 498–9
project requirements 509–13
proprioceptors 31, 373
protein 76, 120
psychological refractory period (PRP) 380
psychology 408–9
psychometric testing 415, 417–18
pub games 267
public schools 270, 271–6
pulmonary circulation 43

pulmonary diffusion 56–60, 114
pulse 49
punishment 368
Puritans 262, 264

quangos 161–5
quintain 283–4

racism 210–12, 244, 312
racket sports 292–4
rackets 292–3
Radical ethic 304
radio coverage 248
RAS (reticular activating system) 443
raw data 532, 537
reaction time 88, 91, 377–81
real tennis 292
reciprocal teaching style 405–6
recovery process 77–81
recreation 183–6, 189
references 512–13
reinforcement techniques 366–8
relaxation 498–9
religion 267–8
research problems 514–16
respiration
    and exercise 53–6, 62, 111, 114
    lungs 61–4
    pulmonary diffusion 56–60, 114
retention tests 355
reticular activating system (RAS) 443
retrieval of information 377
reversibility 97–8
reviews 519–26
rib cage 9
Ringlemann effect 474
roles 462, 471–2
Romantic Movement 268–9
Rome 241
rowing 290–1
rugby 273
rule changes 243

S.A. node (sino-atrial node) 36
Samoa 237
SCAT (Sport Competition Anxiety Test) 417, 490–1
schema theory 383–5
School Community Sports Initiative 178
schools
    Australian education system 324
    developments in sport 197
    educational reform 280
    female education 276–7
    National Curriculum 194, 195, 200, 231
    outdoor education 199–203, 282, 313–14, 322
    private schools 195

public schools 270, 271–6
sports schools 223
Sportsmark scheme 197–8
state education 196, 277–9
SD (systematic de-sensitising
    procedures) 501–2
sea bathing 291–2
secondary schools 196
selective attention 374–5
self efficacy 456–8
self talk 500–1
self-helplessness 455–6
self-serving bias 454
semantic differential scales 421–2
sesamoid bones 10
Sex Discrimination Act (1975) 213
sexism 213, 306
Sharpey's fibres 25
shooting 287
simple skills 342
simple tasks 392–3
sino-atrial node (S.A. node) 36
situational perspective of personality
    416–18
size of groups 474
skeletal muscle 28–31
skeletal system 5–9
    see also bones
skills 339–43, 393
    classification systems 347–50
Skinner, B.F. 366, 367
sliding filament theory 28–9
smoking 127
social cohesion 476
social facilitation 466–9
social learning 431–2, 463–6
social loafing 474–5
socialisation 420, 462
socio-economic groups 221, 420
    upper class sports 266–7
    working class sports 265–9
somatic anxiety 488
somatotyping 86
South Africa 232
Soviet Union 239
spa towns 290
specificity 97
spectator violence 254–7, 434
speed 86, 89, 135–6
speedplay 101–2
sponsorship 178, 244–8
sport
    amateur 205, 243, 245, 270–1, 335
    benefits 205
    classification of activities 205–8
    definition 203–4
    facilities 172–6, 219
    problem areas 205
    professional 205, 213, 243–4, 270–1

Sport Competition Anxiety Test (SCAT)
    417, 490–1
'Sport Pour Tous' 319–20
'Sport-Everyone's Game' programme
    328–9
'Sportif' programme 328
Sports Aid Foundation 177
sports centres 173, 174–5
Sports Council 157, 162–4
    development continuum model 209
    projects for disabled people 217–18
sports physiology 1
sports schools 223
Sportsmark scheme 197–8
Sportsmatch 245–6
Sportstart programme 328
sprinting 83
stadiums 176
Starling's Law 39
state anxiety 488–9
state education 196, 277–9
statistics 532–3
status 462
Steiner, R. 472–3
stereotyping 425–6
stimulants 258
stimulus identification 372–3
stimulus-response compatibility 379
stimulus-response theories 365
stratification of society 210
streamlining 142, 143
strength 85, 89
    testing 94
    training 104–8
stress 488, 491–502
    causes 492–3
    managing 495–502
    reducing 494–5, 496–7
    responding to 494
Stuarts 264, 298
suffixes of anatomical terms 3–4
Sunday sports 268
supercompensation 124
swimming 145–6
systematic de-sensitising procedures
    (SD) 501–2
systemic circulation 43, 45

talent identification 329–30, 346
    see also excellence
task cohesion 475–6
task considerations 392–6
task goal orientation 449–50
tax 178
Taylor Report 256
teaching
    and ability identification 346
    coaching 222–3, 311
    preparation of teachers 334

styles 404–6
teams 470–2
television coverage 248–51
tendons 25
tennis 293–4
terms of direction 2
theories of association 365
Thorndike, E.L. 367–9
Thring, Edward 272, 275–6
throat 53
Thurston scale 421
Title IX 306
torque 149
tourism 201–2
Tourist Board 171
tournaments 284
trachea 54
training
    aerobic training 111–12
    and body development 1
    cool downs 101
    and energy systems 71–4
    methods 101–9
    principles 97–100
    programme design 116–17
    responses and adaptations to 109–15
    warm ups 100
    see also exercise
trait anxiety 489
trait approach 411–12
trait theory 413–15
transfer of learning 393–6
transfer tests 355
transport revolution 269
Trust Funds 245
Tudors 262–3
turning effects 149–50
type theory 412–13

Uniform Business Rate 178
United States of America 238–9, 300–15
    children's programmes 312–13
    coaching 311
    concepts of sport 304
    government
    sports policies 303–4
    structure 302–3
    inter-collegiate sport 308–9
    inter-school competitions 307–8
    outdoor education 313–14
    physical education 305–9
    popular sports 309–11
    racism 312
    sexism 306
upper class sports 266–7
USSR 239

vascular system 40–3
    see also cardiovascular system

vasomotor control 47
veins 42
velocity 135–6
ventilation 62–3
venules 42
verbal guidance 397–8
verbal persuasion 458
Veroff's stages of achievement motivation
    450
vertebral column 8–9
vicarious experience 458
Victoria 327–8
Victorian Britain 265–79

Victorian Institute of Sport (VIS) 332
violence 254–7
visual guidance 396–7
vitamins 120, 122

warm ups 100
water 121
weight control 129–30
whole method of learning 401
William the Conqueror 261
windpipe 54
women
    female education 276–7

participation in sport 213–16, 306
    reaction times 381
Womens Sports Foundation (WSF) 213
working class sports 265–6
wrestling 285
writing up projects 513

Yerkes and Dodson Law 444
YMCA 268
young people 220–1, 312–13

Zajonc, R. 467–8